Good Writing Guide

Good Writing Guide

THE ESSENTIAL GUIDE TO GOOD WRITING

Graham King

HarperCollins*Publishers*

HarperCollins*Publishers*
Westerhill Road, Bishopbriggs, Glasgow G64

www.collins.co.uk

First published 2001 as *The Times Writer's Guide*
This revised and updated edition published as *The Collins Good Writing Guide* 2003

Reprint 10 9 8 7 6 5 4 3 2 1 0

© 2001, 2003 Estate of Graham King

Cartoons on pages 29, 32, 42, 51, 60, 74, 85, 95, 180, 192, 201, 218, 249, 254, 264, 280, 296, 305, 315, 317, 459, 473–77, 479–486 and 509 by Hunt Emerson (Hunt Emerson's website is at www.largecow.demon.co.uk). Cartoons on pages 342, 361, 385, 398, 410, 432 by Bill Tidy (Bill Tidy's website is at www.broadband.co.uk/billtidy). Cartoons on pages 615, 631, 642, 648, 651, 656, 663, 668, 678, 681 and 690 by Chris Tyler (Chris Tyler's website is at www.chriscartoons.co. uk). Cartoons on pages 703, 721, 736, 747, 749, 764, 779, 798, 815 and 818 by Cinders McLeod (Cinders McLeod's website is at http://freespace.virgin. net/cinders.mcleod; see also www.broomielaw.com).

The Collins Good Writing Guide includes revised and updated texts from the following Collins *Wordpower* titles, first published in 2000: *Punctuation, Good Grammar, Super Speller, Good Writing, Vocabulary Expander, Abbreviations, Foreign Phrases* and *Word Check*.

HarperCollins Publishers would like to thank Bob Coole for reading and commenting on the original *Wordpower* texts, Mike Munro for recommending amendments for *The Times Writer's Guide* and Clare Crawford for implementing them.

ISBN 0 00 716539 0

A catalogue record for this book is available from the British Library

Printed and bound in Great Britain by Clays Ltd, St Ives plc.

Foreword

by

Philip Howard

You cannot learn to drive from a motoring manual. Nobody becomes computerwise merely from the instructions, which in any case are written in an alien language by nerds from another planet. To acquire these skills, you also need instructors, skill, practice and the flexibility to learn from your own mistakes.

Similarly, you cannot learn language just from a book. Language is a far more complex skill than automobiles and computers. It is the quality that differentiates humans from the other animals. We pick up the deep structures of language with our mothers' milk. As we learn to speak, we build on these deep structures by talking, reading, writing, school, college, the social intercourse of languages, and learning from our own mistakes. Language is a kind of human reason, which has its own internal logic of which man knows nothing.

A grammar cannot teach you to write or talk well. To do that, you also need talent, perseverance, humility and practice. A grammar can teach you only how to avoid obvious mistakes and point you in the right directions for homework. Most grammars are written by professional grammarians and pedagogues. So they are as impenetrable by 'ordinary people' (have you ever met an ordinary person?) as the computer guides. And grammar, once the queen of the sciences, is now generally regarded as boring, difficult, elitist, pedantic and useless.

Wrong, of course. But if you were looking for somebody to write an English grammar that was both useful and fun, your first candidate for the task might not be an Australian who worked in newspapers for News International and was not even a journo but a marketing man. Wrong again, as it happens. Australians are less hidebound by correctitude, fear of looking foolish and snobbery than Brits. A newspaper executive works in a word factory, but he is far enough removed from the inkface to avoid the professional deformities, vices and prejudices of the journalists. And Graham King was more than the marketing man who transformed the *Sun* and *The Sunday Times*. He was also a poet, painter and author. And he developed the *One-Hour Wordpower* series of guides to English usage and grammar for those 'ordinary people'.

This is a compilation and distillation of the eight little books written by Graham King for the *Collins Wordpower* series. It covers the nuts, bolts and exhaust, but also the accessories and upholstery of language. There are chapters on grammar and spelling. But there are also chapters on improving your writing and expanding your vocabulary. With deplorable lack of didactic solemnity, this book also includes jokes and games to play with language. It demonstrates that grammar is not just the necessary cement of language but also the queen of the sciences, and fascinating.

You might assert that English spelling is an insanely illogical system that has in any case been automated by computer spellcheckers. Read here the perils of spelling by computer, that translates 'How pleased older collectors are to get an Ericsson' into 'How pleased older collectors are to get an erection'. A letter from Ms Hilary Abbot Wimbush appeared in *The Times* attributed to Ms Hairy Abbot Wombat. This book's list of the 2,000 most misspelt words in the English language (unsurprisingly) does not include 'eschschol(t)zia', the California poppy. This is not a word that I often have to use. But I offer sixth formers a prize if they can spell the hellhound word. For it illustrates the wonderful linguistic archaeology of our mongrel language. It is the eponym in honour of J. F. von Eschscholtz (1743–1831), a German member of the expedition that discovered the yellow poppy in 1821. This was a Russian expedition. So the Russians spelt his Prussian name wrongly, and we mistransliterated it into English. Spell it Escoltsia, and you lose something of value: the crazy paving poetry of spelling.

Of course, it was an advantage for Graham to be working in the same plant as *The Times*, the oldest and most authoritative English daily newspaper. Though not always the advantage that its journalists assumed. The Fowler brothers, who compiled entertaining and brilliant guides to English usage early in the last century, used for the examples of how not to write well their daily newspaper. This was, of course, *The Times*. The notion that *The Times* is an infallible authority of 'good' English is, alas, not the whole truth. We are fallible. How could we be otherwise, when we research, write and publish every day as many words as are in five novels of average length, not starting until after lunch? And we all know what journalists' lunches are, or rather, used to be, by reputation.

But Graham King had at his disposal more than two centuries of *Times*' style guides. Every publishing house needs its stylebook to ensure that its writers all sing from the same hymn sheet, when, for example, spelling the tricky name of a tricky man such as Colonel G/Qaddafi. Some of *The Times*' rules used to be High Victorian Pomposo. For example, we had the instruction to spell connexion sic, with an x (in order to show that the English noun is derived from a Latin noun, connexio, not from a past participle, *connectus*). Until recently *Times*' style was to spell the Monna Lisa thus, with a double *n*. This was meant to imply to the reader that *Times* writers were polyglot men of the world, who had done the Grand Tour and knew that Monna was derived from the Italian Madonna. Our rule was a work of supererogation, since the Italians call the lady La Gioconda, the rest of the world refers to her as Mona Lisa with a single *n*. So our 'correct' rule has been dropped.

Graham King was a humane grammarian who recognised that all 'rules' of grammar are not moral absolutes. They are provisional, problematic and continually changing. Language is the only true democracy. It belongs to all of us. If enough of us carry on saying 'try and . . .' rather than the logical 'try to . . .', 'try and . . .' will become idiomatic. At present Graham allows us to say 'try to . . .' without sounding stuck-up or pedantic. It is magnificent to have a management man excoriating the ghastly pretentiousness and pseudo-caringness of the Management-Speak 'human resources'. Thank you, Graham, for being the small boy seeing through the McKinsey Emperor's new clothes. We already guessed that the phrase from the Mahogany Floor, 'remuneration package', means nothing more than 'salary and other benefits'. According to Graham, 'Pleasant working manner essential' in advertisements for human resources means, 'Must be subservient'. He is very funny and subversive about the ghastliness of political correctness that would change knights in chess to horseriders, and kings and queens into sovereigns and deputy sovereigns. He is humorous about the dangers of humour in writing. (The stylebook of *The Daily Another Newspaper* legislates simply: 'Irony is strictly forbidden'.)

What a waste for such a man to go into management rather than the News Room. But our loss has also been our gain, in his wise observations of our inky trade from the touchline. This wise Aussie, naturally, has no time for the taboo against splitting infinitives, apart from the caution that a split infinitive excites rage and letters to the Editor from British readers. 'Thou shalt never split' is the one 'rule' of grammar that some of them remember. It was beaten into them at boarding school. The example I use of a 'correctly' split infinitive (in which the adverb is so closely attached to the stem of the verb that it should not be separated even by 'to') is of a teacher addressing a class: 'Now, children, I want you to try this time. I want you to really try.' Any other order of words is either unintelligibly stuffy or gibberish.

And I wish that Graham were still with us so that I could give him my favourite example against the mad fewer/less fetishists. Their 'rule' is that few/fewer/a few goes with objects that you can count, such as few books, fewer typos, a few mistakes. And less goes with uncountables, such as less sugar, less clarity, less arrogant pomposity. OK, Mr Fetishist. You insist that 'few' must go with countables. Accordingly, you must say: 'My house is fewer than five miles from the station. So it takes a taxi fewer than 15 minutes to take me there, and costs fewer than £5.' In my idiolect, I prefer to say 'less than five miles . . .', 'less than 15 minutes' and 'less than £5'. How many miles to Babylon? Less than a thousand. How many wise men in Babylon? Fewer than five.

Graham would have explained this apparent paradox in terms that we could all understand. His book is a valuable 'reference resource' to keep on your desk for the little accidents and uncertainties of writing. It will not turn you into a Matthew Parris or a Margaret Atwood, a Penelope Fitzgerald or a Bron Waugh. But it will certainly make you a better writer, who drops fewer clangers. This is one of the very rare grammars (Sam Johnson, Fowler Bros, Mencken and Burchfield are others) that can be read for pleasure as well as correctitude. It will make you laugh.

CONTENTS

Graham King   12

Introduction   13
The Thirteen Gremlins of Grammar   14

1 Grammar   15
What is Grammar? Why Use it?   15
Let's Look at Sentences   17
The Building Blocks of Sentences: Parts of Speech   31
Naming Things: Nouns   42
You, Me and other Pronouns   49
It's a plane! It's a bird! No! It's SUPERVERB!   60
Describing Things: Adjectives and Adverbs   74
Grammatical Glue: Determiners, Conjunctions and
  Prepositions   85

2 Punctuation   95
What's the Point   95
Devices for Separating and Joining   97
Symbols of Meaning   118

3 Spelling   137
The 2,000 Most Misspelt Words in the English Language   137
❏ *Computer Spellcheckers*   141
❏ *To Double or not to Double – Focussed or Focused?*   143
❏ *Enquire or Inquire: Enquiry or Inquiry?*   144
❏ *Words that Always End in 'ise'*   147
The Famous Broken Rule of Spelling: I before E except
  after C   159
Problem Proper Nouns and Commonly Misspelt Names   160
❏ *Grass Roots of Spelling*   163
❏ *Kingsley Amis on Spelling*   170
Ways to Improve Your Spelling   171
American Spellings   174

4 A Guide to Difficult and Confusable Words   175
A-Z Listing, with definitions of easily confused words   175
❏ *Britain*   198
❏ *Condone, Approve, Allow*   208

❏ *Who's Coming to Dinner, Supper, Lunch or Tea?* 220
❏ *Draught, Draughts, Draughtsman, Draftsman* 224
❏ *Extract the Extract, and Other Lookalikes* 235
❏ *It, Its, It's* 261
❏ *Law and Lawyers* 266
❏ *Lend and Loan* 268
❏ *Petrol and Other Hydrocarbons* 293
❏ *Prostates and Proctors* 302
❏ *Sex and Gender* 318
❏ *Situation, Position – It's a Problem Situation* 319
❏ *Sweater, Jersey, Jumper, Pullover, etc* 327

5 Expanding Your Vocabulary 340
A-Z Series of Tests to widen your word use, plus
clues to meaning, recognising word elements 340
❏ *Neologisms, or New Words* 392
❏ *Numbers, Sizes and Amounts from Word Roots* 393
❏ *The 'Ology Department* 397
❏ *Qantas, Qintar and Other U-less Q-words* 407
How to Buy a Dictionary 431
Searching for Synonyms: The Thesaurus 435
Answers, Definitions and Meanings 436

6 How to Improve Your Writing 445
From Here to Obscurity 445
The No-Good, the Bad and the Ugly: Obstacles to
Clear Communication 450
The Long, Long Trail A-winding: Circumlocution 450
An Utterly Unique Added Extra: Tautology 454
Witter + Waffle = Gobbledegook 458
Smart Talk, but Tiresome: Jargon 461
Saying it Nicely: Euphemism 469
A Word to the Wise about Clichés 472
Clarity Begins at Home: How to Improve Your Powers
of Expression 489
Circumambulate the Non-representational: Avoid the
Abstract 489
Overloading can Sink Your Sentence 491
Avoiding the Minefield of Muddle 495
Writing Elegant, Expressive English: The Elements of Style 500
Add Colour to Your Word Palette 504
How to Write a Better Letter: Say What You Mean, Get
What You Want 509
Communicate Better with a Well-Written Letter 509

Relationships by Post: Strictly Personal 513
Announcements and Invitations 527
Protecting Your Interests: Complaining with Effect 530
Staying Alive: Employer and Employee 554
Selling Yourself: Creating a Persuasive CV 564
Getting It and Keeping It: Money Matters 569
Writing in the New Millennium: Word Processing
and E-mail 581
Forms of Address 584

7 Foreign Words and Phrases 589
A Note on Pronunciation 589
Guide to Abbreviations 590
A-Z Listing of Common Foreign Terms 590
❏ Accents Make a Difference 590
❏ The Language of Ballet 597
❏ Countries, Cities and Place-names 606
❏ False Friends 614
❏ German 619
❏ Italian 625
❏ Latin 630
❏ Pidgin 643
❏ A Saucière of Sauces 651
❏ Winespeak 662
❏ Yiddish 664

8 Abbreviations and Acronyms 665
A-Z Listing with Full Explanations 665
❏ Acronyms 667
❏ American States and Territories 669
❏ Canadian Provinces and Territories 677
❏ The Chemical Elements 679
❏ Doctors' Abbreviations 685
❏ East, West and Other Points of the Compass 687
❏ E Numbers 690
❏ Ibid, Idem, Inf and Other Footnotes 704
❏ Portmanteau Words 737
❏ European Car Registration Letters 743
❏ Text Messages 768
❏ UK Postcodes 798

Index 820

GRAHAM KING (1930-99)

Graham King was born in Adelaide on 16 October 1930. He trained as a cartographer and draughtsman before joining Rupert Murdoch's burgeoning media empire in the 1960s, where he became one of Murdoch's leading marketing figures during the hard-fought Australian newspaper circulation wars of that decade. Graham King moved to London in 1969, where his marketing strategy transformed the *Sun* newspaper into the United Kingdom's bestselling tabloid; subsequently, after 1986, he successfully promoted the reconstruction of *The Sunday Times* as a large multi-section newspaper.

A poet, watercolourist, landscape gardener and book collector, Graham King also wrote a biography of Zola, *Garden of Zola* (1978) and several thrillers such as *Killtest* (1978). Other works include the novel *The Pandora Valley* (1973), a semi-autobiographical account of the hardships endured by the Australian unemployed and their families in the 1930s.

In the early 1990s, inspired by the unreadability and impracticality of many of the guides to English usage in bookshops, Graham King developed the concept of a series of reference guides called *The One-Hour Wordpower* series: accessible, friendly guides designed to help the reader through the maze of English usage. He later expanded and revised the texts to create an innovative series of English usage guides that would break new ground in their accessibility and usefulness. The new range of reference books became the Collins Wordpower series. The first four titles were published in March 2000, the second four in May 2000. Graham King died in May 1999, shortly after completing the *Collins Wordpower* series.

Introduction

This book represents a distillation of eight volumes written by Graham King in the *Collins Wordpower* series. In these guides to various aspects of current English usage the author's blend of a wide-ranging knowledge of the language with the practical advice of a highly experienced writer, leavened by humour, proved extremely popular with readers. Now the best of their content has been combined in one handy and compendious text.

Those who seek to improve their use of English will find accessible and comprehensive guidance on a wide range of topics, comprising:

- **Grammar** – a clear exposition of the rules and workings of the language, aimed at improving your communication skills;

- **Punctuation** – how to present written English clearly using the vital 'nuts and bolts' of the language;

- **Spelling** – a comprehensive listing (correctly spelt!) of the most difficult-to-spell words, proper nouns, and names;

- **Confusable Words** – how to be sure about using words that are easily confused with others, whether through similar spelling or pronunciation;

- **Expanding Your Vocabulary** – a series of entertaining mini-vocabulary tests to help you make fuller use of the riches of the language in expressing yourself and understanding the many forms of communication we are met with daily. There are also features on clues to meaning, recognising word elements, and a guide to buying a dictionary;

- **Improving Your Writing** – how to achieve clarity, how to improve your powers of expression, better letter-writing, and how to write an effective CV;

- **Foreign Words and Phrases** – translates the most commonly used foreign terms and encourages confident use of them;

- **Abbreviations** – explains the host of abbreviations and acronyms likely to be encountered in everyday life.

The Collins Good Writing Guide maintains Graham King's aims of offering user-friendly practical advice rather than expounding a complex set of rules that are difficult to grasp and remember. The wit and wisdom with which all its topics are treated (along with illustrations by some of Britain's most popular cartoonists) ensure that this concise one-volume guide, while authoritative, is never a dull read. It will entertain and instruct all readers, and those who truly aspire to better their use and understanding of the English language will find it an invaluable resource.

The Thirteen Gremlins of Grammar

1   Correct speling is essential.

2   Don't use no double negatives.

3   Verbs has got to agree with their subjects.

4   Don't write run-on sentences they are hard to read.

5   About them sentence fragments.

6   Don't use commas, that aren't necessary.

7   A preposition is not a good word to end a sentence with.

8   Remember to not ever split infinitives.

9   Writing carefully, dangling participles must be avoided.

10 Alway's use apostrophe's correctly.

11 Make each singular pronoun agree with their antecedents.

12 Join clauses good, like a conjunction should.

13 Proofread your writing to make sure you don't words out.

And, above all, avoid clichés like the plague.

1

GRAMMAR

What Is Grammar? Why Use It?

This won't take long.

A language requires two elements to fulfil man's need to communicate effectively: a vocabulary and a grammar.

The vocabulary is the language's stock of words: combinations of symbols, signs or letters that have evolved to identify things and ideas. But words by themselves can never constitute a language. Imagine someone possessing all the words required to express the message in the first three sentences, but no method of putting them together to make sense. An attempt might look like this:

> *Grammar about what duration of the clock will not take much duration not take small duration reasons to tell.*

It would be like trying to build a solid wall with tennis balls. What's needed is some cement or glue to stick them together, to create a structure that others will recognise. In the case of a language this glue is a system of rules called grammar.

Languages aren't created in a day; some have evolved over hundreds, even thousands of years, and are still evolving. The users of any language must constantly invent to adapt to fresh circumstances, and when invention flags they must borrow.

Not only words, but rules, too. English grammar contains rules that can be traced back to the Greeks and Romans: rules that helped the early users of our language to string their words together to create increasingly clearer and more complex messages. They enabled that meaningless jumble of words to take shape as a recognisable sentence:

> *To tell what grammar is and that grammar should be used will need not little time not long time but some little long time.*

A big improvement, but still clumsy and vague. Obviously the language still required some more words and rules. The speaker needed a word more precise than *tell*, such as *explain*. Also needed was a system for building phrases with their own meanings, and another system for adding inflections to basic words to indicate time and sequence: *explain*, *explaining*, *explained*. With such improvements the sentence not only becomes shorter but also expresses the speaker's intentions with greater accuracy:

Explaining what grammar is and why you should use grammar will not take a long time.

Then users began to get clever by inventing idioms such as not too long to say in three words what it took nearly a dozen to say in an earlier version. They also learned about ellipsis. To avoid repetition they created pronouns to substitute for nouns, phrases and whole sentences. Here, this stands for the two questions:

What is Grammar? Why use it? This will not take long.

And then, finally, in the quest for even greater economy, the newly invented apostrophe was brought into play, saving yet one more word:

What is Grammar? Why use it? This won't take long.

And, having recognised that the promise following the original question is now history – in the past – our grasp of grammar's immense potential allows us to write:

It hasn't taken long, has it?

None of this should really surprise you, because if you are a native user of English you are also an intuitive user of its grammar. Although you may have either never known or have forgotten the difference between a common noun and a proper noun; are a little uncertain about using semicolons and possessive apostrophes; are sublimely unconscious of piling on clichés and couldn't recognise a split infinitive even if you were offered a fortune, you have always managed to be understood, to get your point across, to enjoy reading newspapers and magazines, to write letters and cards to your family and friends, to deal adequately with the demands of the workplace.

But ask yourself: am I cringing along in the slow lane, grammatically speaking, aware of the ever increasing traffic in the faster lanes?

More than at any time in history, you are judged on your communication skills, whether in speech or in writing. The successful development of your personal life, your relationships and your career is now more and more dependent upon the way in which you express your thoughts, your insights, knowledge and desires into language. How well you accomplish this is just as dependent upon your understanding of grammar. In so many ways you are only as good as your grammar.

Few would dispute that this is the Age of Communication. Its message is that the media are expanding exponentially. You can respond to the challenges and demands, or you can allow it to pass you by.

By reading this far, you appear to have chosen the former course. That's courageous, and you should feel encouraged.

And that will be a great start to mastering this essential and exciting skill.

Let's Look at Sentences

Every time we speak we use sentences. They are the easiest of all grammatical units to recognise, so it seems sensible to begin with them.

Easy to recognise, yes, but hard to define. In his *Dictionary of Modern English Usage*, H. W. Fowler gives ten definitions by various grammarians, including:

- A group of words which makes sense.

- A word or set of words followed by a pause and revealing an intelligible purpose.

- A combination of words that contains at least one subject and one predicate.

- A combination of words that completes a thought.

None of these, however, exactly fills the bill, although it is difficult not to agree with the *Collins English Dictionary's* definition: 'A sequence of words capable of standing alone to make an assertion, ask a question, or give a command, usually consisting of a subject and predicate containing a finite verb.'

More important is what sentences are for:

- To make statements

- To ask questions

- To request or demand action

- To express emotion.

From a practical standpoint, a sentence should express a single idea, or thoughts related to that idea. It should say something. A popular rule of thumb is that a sentence should be complete in thought and complete in construction. And, from a practical point of view, you will soon find that certain rules must be observed if your sentences are to be clear, unambiguous, logical and interesting to the listener or reader.

That said, you still have plenty of scope to fashion sentences of almost any size and shape.

Here is a sentence: the opening sentence of Daniel Defoe's *The Life and Strange and Surprising Adventures of Robinson Crusoe* (1719).

I was born in the year 1632, in the city of York, of a good family, though not of that country, my father being a foreigner of Bremen, who settled first at Hull: he got a good estate by merchandise, and leaving off his trade, lived afterward at York, from whence he married my mother, whose relations were named Robinson, a very good family in that country, and from whom I was called Robinson Kreutznoer; but, by the usual corruption of words in England, we are now called, nay, we call ourselves, and write our name Crusoe, and so my companions always call me.

Very few novelists today would have the nerve or the skill to begin a novel with a long sentence like that; for apart from its length it is also a skilfully wrought passage: clear, supple, flowing and ultimately riveting. If it were written today it would most likely appear as a paragraph of several sentences:

> *I was born in York in 1632, of a good family. My father came from Bremen and first settled at Hull, acquired his estate by trading merchandise, and then moved to York. There he met and married my mother, from a well established family in that county named Robinson. I was consequently named Robinson Kreutznoer, but in time my own name and that of our family was anglicised to Crusoe. That's what we're now called, that's how we write our name, and that's what my friends have always called me.*

Defoe's original is a fairly long sentence by any standards. Now try this sentence for size:

> *'But —— !'*

This one appears to defy everything we think we know about sentences, but it is a valid sentence just the same, as you will see when it is placed in its correct context:

> *Jane turned abruptly from the window and faced him with blazing eyes.*
> *'Well, you've finally done it! You realise we're all ruined, don't you? Don't you!'*
> *'But ——!' Harry was squirming. Speechless. He stepped back in an attempt to evade the next onslaught.*
> *It never came. Instead, weeping uncontrollably, Jane collapsed on to the settee.*

You can see that *'But —— !'*, short though it is, quite adequately expresses a response and an action in the context of the middle paragraph (a paragraph can consist of one or more sentences with a common theme). Despite its seeming incompleteness, it is nevertheless a sentence of a kind, although some grammarians would label it a sentence fragment. Here are some more:

> *Her expression conveyed everything. Disaster. Ruin. Utter ruin.*

Three of the four sentences here are sentence fragments. They're perfectly legitimate, but use them for emphasis only, and with care.

The Long-winded Sentence

Another kind of sentence, and one to avoid, is seen rather too often. Typically, it is rambling and unclear, usually the result of having too many ideas and unrelated thoughts jammed into it, like this one:

He said that the agreement would galvanise a new sense of opportunity and partnership between the countries and enable them to articulate the targets with regard to inflation, set by economically enlightened governments, which was always of great concern to every family in the European Union.

Would you really bother to try to unravel that sentence? No, life is too short, and that sentence is most likely destined to remain unread, its author's voice deservedly unheard. That's the price you pay for writing bad sentences. To demonstrate how the inclusion of irrelevant matter can cloud the intent and meaning of a sentence, consider this example:

Jonathan Yeats, whose family moved to the United States from Ireland in the late 1950s, and who later married a Mormon girl from Wisconsin, wrote the novel in less than three months.

We are bound to ask, what has the novelist's family to do with his writing a book in record time? Did the Mormon girl help him? Did his marriage inspire him to write like a demon? If not, why mention these facts? By the time we've reached the important part of the sentence – the fact that he wrote the book in less than three months – our attention has been ambushed by two extraneous thoughts.

American presidents are notorious for irrelevant rambling. The tradition began, apparently, with President Harding, of whom, when he died in 1923, a wit observed, 'The only man, woman or child who wrote a simple declarative sentence with seven grammatical errors is dead.' A sample:

I have the good intention to write you a letter ever since you left, but the pressure of things has prevented, speeches to prepare and deliver, and seeing people, make a very exacting penalty of trying to be in politics.

But we must not grieve over Harding when we have former US president George Bush Snr gamely carrying the national flag of gobbledegook:

I mean a child that doesn't have a parent to read to that child or that doesn't see that when the child is hurting to have a parent and help out or neither parent there enough to pick the kid up and dust him off and send him back into the game at school or whatever, that kid has a disadvantage.

Well, enough of warnings. The point to remember is that although a sentence may be as long as a piece of string, long sentences may land you in trouble. A good sentence will be no longer than necessary, but this doesn't mean that you should chop all your sentences to a few words. That would be boring. To keep the reader alert and interested you need variety. If you examine this paragraph, for example, you'll find a sentence sequence that goes short/long/long/short/medium/long/medium. It's not meant to be a model, but it aims in the right direction.

When a Sentence isn't a Sentence

Here are some constructions that aren't regarded as 'proper' sentences:

> *Are unable to fill any order within 21 days.*

> *Date for the closing of.*

> *Thinking it an excellent opportunity.*

Clearly, there's something wrong with these. What is wrong is that these examples do not make sense. Nor are they in any context that would help them to make sense. They are incomplete because they are ungrammatical and do not express a thought or an action or carry any recognisable information. It has nothing to do with length, either; the following examples are extremely short but are grammatical and convey the intended information in such a way as to be unambiguous:

> *'Taxi!'   ONE WAY   Stop!   Amount Due   'Damn!'*

> *'Leaving already?'*

Sentences are so versatile that they can be confusing, so this might be a good time to take a closer look at the inner workings of the sentence. Despite the demonstration that even single-word 'sentences' can make sense, let's concentrate on what we might call a 'classic' sentence.

The Inner Workings of the Classic Sentence

Try to think of a sentence as a combination of two units:

The **subject** – what it is

The **predicate** – what we're saying about it

Here are some simple examples:

SUBJECT	PREDICATE
My	*word!*
Your book	*is over there.*
Dr Smith	*will see you tomorrow.*

The subject of a sentence does not have to precede the predicate. Every day we'll read hundreds of sentences in which the predicate precedes the subject:

PREDICATE	SUBJECT
It gradually became apparent that it was	*the odour of death.*
Over the horizon appeared	*an immense armada.*

Sometimes the subject of a sentence can be buried, or at least disguised. What are the subjects in these sentences?

A   *How many more times must we do this long journey?*

B   *Brusque is my friend Jeremy's response to pushy salesmen.*

C   *Take this load of rubbish to the shop for a refund.*

A is what is called an interrogative sentence, which often transposes subject and predicate. If you think carefully about this example you'll probably conclude that the only possible candidate for the subject is *we* (*We must do this journey how many more times?*).

If you flushed out the subject in **A**, you should have little trouble with example **B**, which is a similar construction. The subject here is *my friend Jeremy's response to pushy salesmen*.

Example **C** has what you could call a 'ghost' subject. It is an imperative sentence in which the subject is implied. What the sentence is really doing is commanding someone to undertake a task:

(Will you please) Take this load of rubbish to the shop for a refund.

or   *(You) Take this load of rubbish to the shop for a refund.*

If you follow the logic of this, you'll see that the subject here is *You*; the sentence itself is the predicate.

Quite often both the subject and predicate of a sentence can consist of two or more parts, or compounds:

SUBJECT		**SUBJECT**	**PREDICATE**
French	*and*	*English literature*	*were not Amy's favourite subjects.*

SUBJECT	**PREDICATE**		**PREDICATE**
The three lads	*partied at night*	*and*	*recovered by day.*

If you can digest all this you can put it at the back of your mind but you will find it a helpful guide in sentence construction. It will help you to know, for instance, that in a long sentence such as **James, my close friend and the grandson of the French artist Bernard Agate**, *is moving to New York,* that the portion in bold is the subject and *is moving to New York* is the predicate, while in **James** *is moving next month to the place he's always wanted to be – New York*, the single word *James* is the subject and the rest is the predicate.

The predicate can be a bit of a puzzle, mainly because it can consist of just a single verb or a number of elements that describe, modify or supply extra information. We make sense of this by recognising a **direct** and **indirect object**. In the sentence:

James is moving to New York.

James is the subject and the rest is the predicate. The direct object of the predicate is *New York*. It isn't actually doing anything but is having something done to it. If, however, the sentence expands a little:

James told me he was moving to New York.

we now have not only a direct object (*New York*) but an indirect object – *me*.

Simple, Compound and Complex Sentences

Apart from the subject/predicate concept of sentences, there is another way of classifying these constructions. Single-word expressions such as 'Hey!', signs, catchphrases, greetings, and so on, are called **irregular**, **fragmentary** or **minor sentences**. Sentences that are constructed to express a complete, independent thought are called **regular sentences**, and these are divided into **simple**, **compound** and **complex sentences**. These are worth exploring because in writing and speaking we use them all the time. Knowing about them should help us use them to better advantage.

A **simple sentence** consists of a single main clause:

We went to Bournemouth last week.

The storm brought down all the power lines.

A **compound sentence** consists of two or more main clauses, indicated in bold:

The storm brought down all the power lines *and* **caused havoc throughout Montreal.**

Sam finally agreed to buy the car *but still* **had doubts about the steering.**

Both simple and compound sentences have one thing in common: neither has subordinate clauses (you'll find more on clauses on page 38). When you add one or more subordinate clauses to the sentence mix, you create a **complex sentence**. In these examples the main clauses are in bold and the subordinate clauses are in parentheses.

The spacecraft *(that caused the emergency)* **was considered obsolete.**

She bolted through the door *(which slammed behind her)*.

My grandfather has now retired, *but* **the family business** *(that he started in 1928)* **is still going strong.**

The last example, consisting of two main clauses and a subordinate clause, is really a **compound-complex sentence**, one of the most common sentence constructions.

From these examples you'll see that, unlike simple sentences, compound and complex sentences express two or more thoughts. Let's take two simple sentences:

> *The money was spent on urban regeneration. The money provided hundreds of families with excellent houses.*

Most of us, seeing this pair of sentences, would find it difficult to resist the urge to combine them:

> *The money was spent on urban regeneration and it provided hundreds of families with excellent houses.*

Compound and complex sentences link connected thoughts in an economical way. Indeed, a third thought could safely be added:

> *The money was spent on urban regeneration and provided hundreds of families with excellent houses, but it did not take funds away from existing public housing schemes.*

Beyond this you have to be careful, or risk confusing or overloading the reader. By the way, did you notice the two words used to link the three thoughts or sentences into one? They are *and* and *but*, conjunctions that are commonly used to build compound and complex sentences. (See discussion under *Grammatical Glue*, page 85.)

Types of Regular Sentences

Earlier, we defined four uses for sentences. Each of these calls for a different type of sentence, and it's worth knowing what they are:

- **A DECLARATIVE SENTENCE** makes a statement:
  A rose bush grew in the garden.
  Ben has just thrown a ball through the window.

- An **INTERROGATIVE SENTENCE** asks a question:
  Is that a rose bush in the garden?
  Did Ben just throw a ball through the window?

- An **IMPERATIVE SENTENCE** directs or commands:
  Look at that rose bush in the garden.
  See if Ben's thrown a ball through the window.

- An **EXCLAMATORY SENTENCE** expresses emotion:

I wouldn't dream of touching that rose bush!
I'll scream if Ben's thrown a ball through the window!

Another aspect of a sentence is that it can express thoughts or actions positively or negatively:

- *I like eating in restaurants* is a **positive sentence**.

- *I don't like eating in restaurants* is a **negative sentence**.

The difference may seem obvious in these two examples but a sentence can damage itself with the inclusion – sometimes unconsciously – of double negatives and near or quasi-negatives:

- **I don't** *know* **nothing**. (non-standard double negative)

- *It was a* **not unusual** *sight to see the heron flying away.* (acceptable double negative)

- *I* **hardly** *saw* **nobody** *at the sale.* (negative and quasi-negative)

- *There's* **no question** *that Robert will pay the debt.* (negative, but the *no question* is intended to positively express 'no doubt whatsoever')

- *I* **can't help but** *applaud her generosity.* (intended to be positive but grammatically the sentence expresses a negative sense)

The second example is an instance of what is called **litotes** (pronounced *LY-to-tees*), which is an elegant form of understatement expressed by denying something negative:

She's not a bad cook means *She's quite a good cook.*

The effect is by no means negligible means *The effect is quite noticeable.*

The negative/positive aspect of sentences is worth noting because a diet of too much negativism in your speech and writing can have an overall negative or depressing effect, and can be confusing, too. Sometimes it is better to express negative thoughts in a positive way. *She is not beautiful* or *She's by no means beautiful* are not only negative but vague – she could be statuesque or handsome. A more positive and precise description might be: *She is rather homely.*

The 'Voice' of a Sentence

All sentences are either **active** or **passive**, and it is up to the user to decide which 'voice' to use. This voice is not something you hear, by the way; it is rather a point of view. The voice of a sentence is the kind of verbal inflection used to express whether the subject *acts* (active voice) or is *acted upon* (passive voice). Here are a few examples of both:

- **ACTIVE**   *The favourite won the 3.30 hurdle event.*
                  Her boyfriend bought the ring.
                  Very few can appreciate his paintings.

- **PASSIVE**   *The 3.30 hurdle event was won by the favourite.*
                  The ring was bought by her boyfriend.
                  His paintings can be appreciated by very few.

Even a cursory glance at these sentences tells you that active sentences are more direct, lively and interesting than passive sentences, which tend to be detached and impersonal – ancient history, as some would have it. Generally, we use the active voice almost exclusively in our everyday speech and writing, while the passive voice is reserved mostly for technical, scientific and academic writing.

Being aware of the roles of active and passive voice in sentences helps to avoid mixing them – a topic discussed a little later (see *Harmony in the Sentence*, page 27).

The Mood of a Sentence

Another quality of a sentence is its 'mood', or more accurately the mood of its verb – another kind of verbal inflection used to express the speaker's intention in a sentence, such as making a statement (**indicative**), giving a command (**imperative**), or posing a hypothetical situation (**subjunctive**). Here are some examples:

- **INDICATIVE MOOD**   *She's tired and exhausted.*
                           Summer is just around the corner.
                           Is that all we're having for dinner tonight?

- **IMPERATIVE MOOD**   *Call me tomorrow.*
                           Don't call me, I'll call you.
                           Tell me about it tomorrow.

- **SUBJUNCTIVE MOOD**   *If I were you, I'd tell them about it.*
                           The judge ordered that he be tried for theft.
                           The poor girl wished she were dead.

Although we often use the subjunctive mood without being aware of it (*I wish you were here; God save the Queen; So be it; If I were you I'd . . .*) perhaps because such utterances are idiomatic, it is nevertheless the mood that gives us the most trouble.

Here is a sentence from *The Guardian* which, if it were grammatically correct (note the subjunctive *were*, indicating an imagined or possible situation), would have been expressed in the subjunctive mood:

Incorrect   *No wonder the Tory Party turned him down as a possible candidate, suggesting he **went away** and **came back** with a better public image.*

Correct   *No wonder the Tory Party turned him down as a possible candidate, suggesting he **go away** and **come back** with a better public image.*

Let's face it – most of us would avoid such a construction where the correct use of the subjunctive mood requires grammatical know-how of a very high order. On the other hand we might have the wit to insert *should* before the verb *go away*, rendering the sentence both grammatically correct and more readable:

No wonder the Tory Party turned him down as a possible candidate, suggesting that he should go away and come back with a better public image.

The correct use of the subjunctive can undoubtedly look strange, as in this example quoted by Eric Partridge in his *Usage and Abusage: Although he die now, his name will live*. Not surprisingly, most writers tend to avoid or ignore the subjunctive, so that sentences such as *I insist that he is sacked (I insist that he **be** sacked)* and *It is to be hoped that she stops her bad behaviour (It is to be hoped that she **stop** her bad behaviour)* are now considered acceptable. This may be so, but careful and elegant writers will always fall back on the subjunctive mood to express hypothetical situations in sentences usually containing *if* and *that (If she were here, I would tell her about Tom; I suggest that she be told immediately.)*

Ellipsis: Trimming Away 'Sentence Fat'

Nobody these days wants to write more words than necessary, or to be forced to read fifty words when the information could have been conveyed with half that number. We have already seen that by combining simple sentences into compound and complex sentences we can economise on words and even enhance clarity; but there is another grammatical convention that allows us to trim away words we don't need. It's called **ellipsis** and it works like this:

WITHOUT ELLIPSIS   *When the children were called to the dinner table they came to the dinner table immediately.*
Harry Green had more coins in his collection than Thomas had coins in his collection.

WITH ELLIPSIS   *When the children were called to the dinner table they came immediately.*
Harry Green had more coins in his collection than Thomas had in his.

The reason we can get away with omitting part of the structure of sentences is that, if the listener or reader is paying attention, he or she will automatically supply the missing words from the context of what is being said or written. There is no loss of clarity, either; on the contrary, repetitive words can lead to boredom.

We resort to ellipsis constantly in our everyday communicating:

Leaving already?	means	*(Are you) leaving already?*
See you!	means	*(I will) see you (later, tomorrow, etc)*
Coming?	means	*(Are you) coming (with me)?*

Sometimes our economising extends to dropping what were once considered essential words:

He was unceremoniously kicked out the door.

The hat Rita bought is a total disaster.

If we heard these sentences spoken in an informal context we would hardly regard them as ungrammatical as, nowadays, even the strictly grammatical versions look a little odd to our eyes:

He was unceremoniously kicked out of the door.

The hat that Rita bought is a total disaster.

Such sentences are considered informal, although their meanings are perfectly clear. If a hostess greets a guest with, 'I am delighted that you could come', isn't she being a trifle formal? More likely, the greeting would be, 'I'm delighted you could come!'.

Although omitting *that* in sentences may now be acceptable, remember that it can sometimes lead to ambiguity. At the other extreme is the multiple *that*: *He pointed out that that that in the sentence was superfluous.* What can you do about *that*?

Harmony in the Sentence

What if Shakespeare had written in *Hamlet: To be, or not being – that is the question?* Well, of course he didn't, and wouldn't. From time to time scholars have pointed out examples of the Bard's bad grammar but sentences with faulty harmony in his plays would be hard to find.

Perhaps the most important principle in the construction of sentences is what is called **harmony** – or concord, consistency or parallelism – meaning that all the units in a sentence must agree and harmonise with each other. We can spot most inharmonious constructions because they usually jar:

February is usually a succession of rain, hail and snowing.

That sentence mixes two nouns and a participle, and it screams out at you, doesn't it? An harmonious construction would prefer to group three nouns:

February is usually a succession of rain, hail and snow.

Alternatively, we could use a trio of participles to achieve harmony:

In February, it is usually either raining, hailing or snowing.

Phrases in a sentence should match, too. In this example the second phrase is out of harmony with the first:

Bad grammar *is like* **having bad breath** *– even your best friends won't tell you.*

There are two easy ways to remove the discord here. One is to match the phrase *bad grammar* with a similar adjective/noun phrase; the other is to add a parallel participle to *bad grammar* to match *having bad breath*:

Bad grammar *is like* **bad breath** *– even your best friends won't tell you.*

Using bad grammar *is like* **having bad breath** *– even your best friends won't tell you.*

Misplaced conjunctions (joiners) are another source of discord in sentences. Perhaps the two most common offenders are *either/or* and *not only/but also*:

CONFUSING   *They had to agree* **either** *to visit the museum* **or** *the gallery.*
The house was **not only** *affected with woodworm* **but also** *by years of neglect.*

CORRECT   *They had to agree to visit* **either** *the museum* **or** *the gallery.*
The house was affected **not only** *by woodworm* **but also** *by years of neglect.*

Another form of discord is the shift from active to passive voice in a sentence, or vice versa:

My father painted those pictures, which he left to me.

That sentence switches from **active** (*My father painted those pictures*) to **passive** voice (*which he left to me*). To achieve harmony, keep to the same voice:

ACTIVE   *My father painted those pictures, and left them to me.*

PASSIVE   *Those pictures, which were left to me, were painted by my father.*

Clearly, the sentence that uses the active voice is the easier to read.

A similar sort of discord is created when a sentence mixes personal and impersonal points of view:

The **student** *should always exercise care and judgement because* **you** *will never succeed with slipshod thinking.*

One should always exercise care and judgement because **you** will never succeed with slipshod thinking.

In the first example, consistency in person can be achieved by replacing *you* with *he or she*; in the second, the writer should either stick to the generic pronoun *one* throughout the sentence or change the opening *One* to *You*.

Although perhaps not causing discord, faulty word order or misplaced modifiers in sentences can create confusion and chaos in otherwise simple sentences:

I saw you in my underwear!

could mean either *I saw you when I was wearing only my underwear* or, more ominously, *I saw you, wearing my underwear!* Such a sentence could create not only confusion but a most alarming scene. The misplaced modifier has been responsible for some hilariously ambiguous sentences:

Last night Helen went to see Elton John in a new dress.

We have a parrot in a cage that talks.

We can fit you in a new swimsuit that flatters – right over the phone!

You see very few signposts rambling around Wales.

The bomb was discovered by a security man in a plastic bag.

Send us your ideas on growing dwarf roses on a postcard.

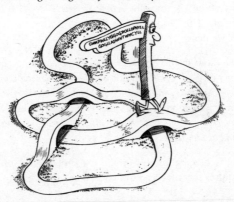

SENTENCES – *You see very few signposts wandering around Wales . . .*

However, of all the factors that can result in inharmonious sentences, the most prevalent is probably disagreement between the verb with its subject. In other words, a singular subject requires the singular form of a verb, and a plural subject requires the plural form of a verb: *this book, these books; that book, those books; she sings, they sing.* The following sentences ignore this:

> **We was** furious at the umpire's crazy decision.
> Fifteen **paintings was** sold at auction last week.

They should, of course, read:

> **We were** furious at the umpire's crazy decision.
> Fifteen **paintings were** sold at auction last week.

But look what happens when we 'collectivise' the subjects:

> The **team was** furious at the umpire's crazy decision.
> A **collection** of paintings **was** sold at auction last week.

Because we've gathered the players together into a team, and combined the paintings into a collection – that is, into single groups – we're back to using singular verbs. The important thing is to keep subjects and verbs in agreement in a sentence. While most of us would regard these examples as obviously faulty, many of us might stumble when confronted by nouns and noun phrases that can take either singular or plural forms. Nouns such as *team, family* and *committee* can be treated as singular or plural depending upon the context in which they are used. This is discussed at some length in *Singular* and *Plural Nouns*, page 45, but meanwhile here is an example of how carelessness with verb and subject agreement can cause bewilderment and ambiguity.

The noun, in this case, is a name: the Human Fertilisation and Embryology Authority. What follows is from an article in *The Times* (22/11/96 – 'Widow Barred From Taking Husband's Sperm Abroad'), which is an extraordinary cocktail of inconsistencies:

> *She was told by the Human Fertilisation and Embryology Authority that* **they** *would review her case . . . Diane Blood is outraged at the way the Authority has behaved . . . The Authority* **have** *not even given any of* **their** *reasons . . . the Authority said* **it** *would review the issue . . . and* **it** *would not use* **its** *discretionary powers . . . but said* **they** *wanted to 'leave no stone unturned' in* **their** *review and would give* **its** *reasons . . .*

That passage is a sobering lesson on the importance of, first, deciding whether your noun is singular or plural, and then sticking with the decision!

Starting a Sentence with 'And' and 'But'

One of the more persistent grammatical superstitions is that you can't begin a sentence with conjunctions such as *and* and *but*. This is curious, because many of the finest writers in the English language – Shakespeare, Blake, Tennyson,

Kipling, to name just four – have kicked off sentences with *And*, and so has the Bible: read the opening chapter. Probably the most popular rebel was Blake, who chose to begin his poem (better known as *Jerusalem*) with 'And did those feet in ancient time . . . '

Much the same applies to *But*. This time Thomas Macaulay, in his *The History of England*, is the hero of the rebel cause:

> *There were gentlemen and there were seamen in the navy of Charles the Second.*
> *But the seamen were not gentlemen; and the gentlemen were not seamen.*

There is no rule to say that you can't begin a sentence or a paragraph with the conjunction *But*. When you want to express a doubt or outright disagreement, beginning a sentence with *But* can emphasise and dramatise your point. *But* don't let it become a sloppy habit!

The Daily Express some years ago carried a memorable sentence in its sporting pages that not only began with *But*, but ended with *but*. And the sentence that followed it began with *And*:

> *Northumberland and Humberside will each hold the trophy for six months after*
> *fighting out an exciting 1–1 draw. But if the result was indecisive, then the soccer*
> *was anything but. And when all the medals have been engraved . . .*

The sentence, as you will have seen, is all at once a simple, complex and beautiful construction. As Winston Churchill, one of the most expert users of the language, once wrote: ' . . . I got into my bones the essential structure of the ordinary British sentence – which is a noble thing'. Before we pass on to how a sentence is actually assembled with different kinds of words, it's worth remembering the hierarchy in which it exists:

A **word** consists of one or more morphemes (speech elements).

A **phrase** consists of one or more words.

A **clause** consists of one or more phrases.

A **sentence** consists of one or more clauses.

A **paragraph** consists of one or more sentences.

The Building Blocks of Sentences:
Parts of Speech

In Victorian times, when life was simpler, so, apparently, was grammar. Here is a little verse widely used to teach young children the parts of speech during the latter part of the 19th century:

Three little words we often see,
Determiners, like *a*, *an* and *the*.

A *Noun's* the name of anything,
A *school* or *garden*, *hoop* or *string*.

An *Adjective* tells the kind of noun,
Like *great*, *small*, *pretty*, *white* or *brown*.

Instead of nouns the *Pronouns* stand –
John's head, *his* face, *my* arm, *your* hand.

Verbs tell of something being done,
To *read*, *write*, *count*, *sing*, *jump* or *run*.

How things are done, the *Adverbs* tell,
Like *slowly*, *quickly*, *ill* or *well*.

A *Preposition* stands before
A noun, as *in* a room, or *through* a door.

Conjunctions join the nouns together,
Like boy *or* girl, wind *and* weather.

The *Interjection* shows surprise,
Like *Oh!* How charming. *Ah!* How wise!

The whole are called 'Nine Parts of Speech',
Which reading, writing and speaking teach.

For millions of Victorian children this rhyme served as a gentle introduction to
the terrors of **parsing** – the art of analysing the various roles played by words in
a sentence. Whether the terror was real or imagined no doubt depended upon
how the subject was taught. For the majority of children it was probably never
an easy business to grasp, and this went for the teachers, too, to the extent that
for a quarter of a century from the 1960s it was the misguided fashion in many
quarters not to teach it at all. As a result many millions of today's adults in the

English-speaking world have a big black hole in their grammatical education.

The fact that many words defy a single classification doesn't make things easier. The word *round*, for example, can play five different roles depending upon how it is used in a sentence. Many other words are similarly versatile: *love* can act as a noun, verb and adjective, and so can *light*; *fast* can play the roles of noun, verb, adjective and adverb, and so on. *That* can be used as an adjective and as a pronoun:

> **That** *jacket belongs to me.* (adjective)
> **That** *is my jacket.* (pronoun)

Words – especially **neologisms**, or newly coined words – also have the confusing habit of migrating from one class to another:

> *The doctor observed the patient's* **knee jerk**. (noun/verb)
> *His speech produced the inevitable* **knee-jerk** *reaction.* (adjective)
> *The President was a master of the art of the* **knee-jerk**. (noun)

Not all words have this chameleon quality, however. All words can be divided into two broad classes: **open classes** (which freely admit new words) and **closed classes** (which rarely do). For example:

OPEN CLASSES

Nouns	*software, gazumper, Fergy, tummytuck, spin doctor*
Adjectives	*neural, digital, cellular, quaffable, hands-on*
Verbs	*outed, overdosed, stargaze, deselect, nuke*
Adverbs	*breezily, chaotically, totally, tackily*
Interjections	*Phew! aahhh, ouch! Phooorrh!*

CLOSED CLASSES

Determiners	*the, which, my, that, your, these*
Pronouns	*I, me, we, hers, someone, whom*
Conjunctions	*and, or, but, when, since, as*
Prepositions	*at, with, in, by, to, from*
Auxiliaries	*be, may, can, will, were, must*

You can see from these examples that the closed classes of words are more or less static; it is very difficult to create new determiners or substitutes for *the*, *my* and *your*. The open classes, however, are expanding all the time.

At this point a pause may be useful, because you are being confronted with grammatical terms that may mean little or nothing to you. But to make sense of grammar it is impossible to avoid familiarity with at least a handful of basic terms. These will, however, be kept to a workable and untaxing minimum.

Let's begin with the 'parts of speech' – the components or building blocks of human communication. While you may not recognise the terms nor fully appreciate the roles they play, you are using them almost every minute of the day in your speech and writing. A simple analysis of a sentence might look like this:

An	acting	spokesperson	for	the	Navy
determiner	*adjective*	*noun*	*preposition*	*determiner*	*proper noun*

has	predictably	outlined	the	various	options.
auxiliary verb	*adverb*	*verb*	*determiner*	*adjective*	*plural noun*

If you're ever in doubt about the grammatical status of any word, a good dictionary will tell you. Apart from defining a word's meaning the entry will also identify its use as a noun (*n*), adjective (*adj*), adverb (*adv*), etc, and often give examples of usage.

What follows now is a brief outline of each of the nine classes into which all words are grouped according to their function. This is designed to help you find your feet on the nursery slopes of the grammatical piste. A more detailed discussion on each word class follows.

Nouns

A **noun** is a name – of a place, an object, a person, an animal, a concept, of anything:

PLACES	*street, home, Germany, Paris, heaven*
OBJECTS	*plate, chair, tree, chamber pot, air*
PERSONS	*Einstein, Michael Jackson, Caroline*
ANIMALS	*pony, pig, wolfhound, chimpanzee*
CONCEPTS	*option, bad temper, ability, direction*

We also recognise types of nouns. All nouns are either **proper nouns** – that is, names that are specific or unique:

Marilyn Monroe, Saturday, The Rake's Progress, Mercedes, Brooklyn Bridge, Easter

or **common nouns**, which describe groups or members of groups, rather than individuals, or which broadly identify something:

boy, motor cars, tea, hair, darkness, opinions, anger, idea

You'll notice that proper nouns start with capital letters, and that common nouns don't. Common nouns are also divided into **concrete** and **abstract** nouns, **count** and **non-count** nouns, **singular**, **plural** and **collective** nouns, and these are all discussed in *Naming Things: Nouns*, on page 42.

Verbs

Verbs are all about doing and being. They're action words. They're the engines that drive sentences to make them do something. Imagine trying to get through a day without these workhorses:

> *wake, woke, eat, drink, walked, drove, go, talked, do, keep, appear, exist, become, sleeps, dream*

You can see, even from these few examples, that verbs take several forms, some ending in *-s*, *-ed*, and so on, and in fact most verbs have four or more forms to help us grasp when an action is taking place:

> *eat, eats, eating, eaten, ate*
> *write, writes, writing, wrote, written*

If you look up the words *eats, eating, eaten* or *ate* in a dictionary you may have difficulty finding them. However you will find them in the entry following the basic verb *eat*, which is called the **headword**, along with derivatives such as *eatable, eater, eating house, eatables, eat out, eat up, eat one's heart out*, etc.

Apart from their multiplicity of forms, verbs are notoriously variable: they can be **regular** (where they follow certain rules) and **irregular** (where they don't); they can be **main** verbs or **auxiliary** verbs, **transitive** and **intransitive**, **finite** and **infinite**. But don't let these grammatical gremlins scare you because they will be exposed for the poor, simple workaholics they are in the section on verbs on page 60.

Adjectives

Life without adjectives would be difficult, frustrating and extremely dull, because adjectives describe and modify things:

> *hot, freezing, beautiful, hairy, user-friendly, brainless, distasteful, pathogenic, pliable*

Some adjectives give themselves away by their endings: *-ing, -y, -less, -ful, -ic,* and so on. They can also end with *-ly*, which can cause us to confuse them with adverbs, which often end with the same suffix.

Simply put, adjectives add something to nouns and pronouns by modifying –

> *It was a **dreary** match.*
> *We made a **late** start.*

or by extending or reinforcing a noun's descriptive power –

> *It was an **obvious** mistake.*
> *The lady possessed **hypnotic** charm.*

You'll see that all the adjectives in the examples so far have come before the noun, but this need not always be the case:

*The lady's charm was **hypnotic**.*

There is a fuller discussion of adjectives and their usage on page 74.

Adverbs

Because they add information, **adverbs** are close relations to adjectives, as you can see:

Adjectives	Adverbs
essential	*essentially*
hypnotic	*hypnotically*
interesting	*interestingly*
dark	*darkly*

Don't be tricked, however, by believing that all adverbs end in *-ly*. They're very common, but the adverb family includes several other forms: *afterwards, enough, always, nevertheless, otherwise.*

The difference between adjectives and adverbs is that **adjectives** modify **nouns** and **pronouns**, while **adverbs** describe or modify **verbs**, **adjectives** and even other **adverbs**:

MODIFYING A VERB	*He **trudged wearily** along the road.*
	(How did he walk along the road?)
MODIFYING AN ADJECTIVE	*She's an **exceedingly lucky** girl.*
	(To what extent is she lucky?)
MODIFYING ANOTHER ADVERB	*The engine turned over **very smoothly**.*
	(How smoothly did it turn over?)

Adverbs are often required where adjectives are incorrectly used, and vice versa. A guide to their usage will be found on page 81.

Pronouns

Pronouns are stand-ins for nouns and noun phrases, and are especially useful for avoiding repetition:

WITHOUT A PRONOUN	*He saw James in the bar, and went over to meet James.*
	Was I aware that Marcia was married?
	Of course I knew Marcia was married.

WITH A PRONOUN   He saw James in the bar, and went over to meet **him**.
Was I aware that Marcia was married.
Of course I knew **she** was.

You can readily see that pronouns are indispensable, and *they* (pronoun) form a major part of *our* (pronoun) everyday speech.

We divide pronouns into **personal pronouns** (*I, me, you, she, it*), **possessive pronouns** (*mine, ours, his, theirs*), **reflexive pronouns** (*myself, themselves*), **demonstrative pronouns** (*this, these, those*), **interrogative pronouns** (*who? what? which?*), **relative pronouns** (*who, whom, which, that*), **indefinite pronouns** (*all, any, many, everyone, few, most*) and **reciprocal pronouns** (*one another, each other*).

If you experienced a slight prickly sensation when glancing through those definitions, the reason is most likely that pronouns can create more grammatical havoc than any other class of words. But when you've studied the detailed section on pronouns on page 49, you'll feel much more at home with these useful surrogate nouns.

Determiners

Determiners precede nouns and noun phrases, and the best known and most common of them are:

* *the* – known as the **definite article**, and

* *a* and *an* – known as **indefinite articles**

It's easy to see why they are described so; *the* is always specific, referring to a definite thing, person or entity, while *a* and *an* are used to refer to singular count nouns:

* **the** *house over there;* **the** *woman in the red dress;* **the** *Hippodrome*

* **a** *large house;* **an** *angry young man;* **a** *good party;* **an** *eel pie*

Words functioning as determiners – adjectives and pronouns, for example – exist in great variety, and help us to indicate quantity (***some*** *wine*); ask questions (***whose*** *wine?*); denote possession (***my*** *wine*), and express emotion (***what*** *wine!*). Numbers can function as determiners, too: *a **thousand** thanks!* ***first*** *race,* ***half*** *a minute.* Get the full story on determiners on page 86.

Conjunctions

Think of **conjunctions** as link-words that join two nouns, phrases, clauses or parts of a sentence:

*She asked Bernard if he intended going out **and** he told her to mind her own business.*

*She told him he could stay **if** he promised to be more polite.*

There are three types of conjunctions: **coordinating conjunctions**, which link words, phrases and clauses of equal importance; **subordinating conjunctions**, which link less important units to one or more of greater importance; and **correlative conjunctions**, which are used in pairs. They are all described on page 88.

Prepositions

While conjunctions link in a fairly straightforward way, **prepositions** link by relating **verbs** to **nouns**, **pronouns** and **noun phrases**. In particular, they unite two sentence elements in such a way as to provide extra information about space, time and reason:

*Judith travelled to New York **in** a 747 and flew **through** a storm.*

*Lawrence went down to the beach **at** noon.*

*Lizzie went to the arcade **for** a new swimsuit.*

We use prepositions constantly (try getting through a day without using *as, by, in, on, to* and *up*, to name just a few!) and misuse them occasionally. Should you, for example, end a sentence with a preposition? The answer, and more about this interesting member of the grammatical glue family, will be found on page 90.

Interjections

Interjections and **exclamations** are self-explanatory:

Wow! Hey! Shhhh! Blimey! Oh! Cheers!

Although these examples, expressing surprise, excitement or some other emotion, are followed by exclamation marks, these are not always necessary:

Okay, *let's get it over with.* ***Ah-ha***, *that's better.* ***Mmmm*** . . .

For further insight into interjections, see page 94.

Phrases and Clauses

We've now surveyed the different classes of words we use to construct sentences. However we should, at this point, also familiarise ourselves with two units or groups of words that are usually found in sentences: **phrases** and **clauses**.

A **phrase** is a group of words working as a unit but unable to stand alone or to make sense, but the definition can also include single words. The logic of this is demonstrated when we shrink a conventional phrase:

> I love **that dry white wine from Australia**.
> I love **that dry white wine**.
> I love **that white wine**.
> I love **that wine**.
> I love **wine**.

The sets of words in bold are all phrases. The key word *wine* is called the headword, and because it is a noun, all five phrases are called **noun phrases**.

There are five kinds of phrases, each named after the class of the headword:

NOUN PHRASE	*They loved **their first home**.* (*home* is a noun)
VERB PHRASE	*We **have been burgled**.* (*burgled* is a verb)
ADVERB PHRASE	*Come **through the doorway**.* (*through* is an adverb)
ADJECTIVE PHRASE	*It's too **difficult to do**.* (*difficult* is an adjective)
PREPOSITIONAL PHRASE	*They walked **along the path**.* (*along* is the introducing preposition; *the path* is a noun phrase)

In the previous section we described three kinds of sentence: the **simple sentence**, consisting of a single main clause; the **compound sentence**, consisting of two or more main clauses, and the **complex sentence**, consisting of a main clause and one or more subordinate clauses. Fine – but what, exactly, are clauses?

A **clause**, quite simply, is a unit of related words that contains a subject and other words, always including a verb, which give us information about the subject:

> *The patient stopped breathing, so I shouted for the nurse.*

In this example, *The patient stopped breathing* is a main clause of the sentence, because it can stand alone. In fact, if you put a full stop after *breathing* it becomes a legitimate sentence. But *I shouted for the nurse* is also a main clause because it can stand alone, too. What we have is a **compound sentence** consisting of two main clauses coordinated by the adverb *so* – here used as a conjunction:

main clause	*coordinator*	*main clause*
The patient stopped breathing	*so*	I shouted for the nurse.

Now let's construct a sentence in a different way – this time with a main clause and a subordinate clause:

> *This is the patient who stopped breathing.*

You can pick the main clause because it can stand on its own: *This is the patient*. The rest of the sentence consists of *who stopped breathing*, which is the **subordinate clause** because it can't stand on its own:

main clause	**subordinate clause**
This is the patient	*who stopped breathing.*

You can add more information to a subordinate clause, but regardless of how much extra information you pile on, it remains a subordinate clause because it is always subordinate to the main clause, serving only to influence the word *patient*:

main clause	**subordinate clause**
This is the patient	*who, when I visited the hospital yesterday, stopped breathing for several minutes.*

It's worth spending a little more time with subordinate clauses because no matter how long they are they have the ability to function as nouns, adjectives and adverbs. Understanding this should help you construct more precise and efficient sentences.

We recognise three kinds of subordinate clauses:

NOUN CLAUSE – where the clause acts as a noun.
*She told him **what she thought**.*
***What's right** and **what's wrong** are the questions at the heart of true civilisation.*
*I told him **that Judy was coming**.*

ADJECTIVAL CLAUSE – where the clause acts as an adjective.
*This is the door **that won't close properly**.*
*The parcel **that's just arrived** is for you.*
*London is the place **which offers the greatest opportunities**.*

ADVERBIAL CLAUSE – where the clause acts as an adverb.
*You should go there **before the shops open**.*
***Because it began to rain** I had to buy an umbrella.*
*We were quite upset **when John came in**.*

Look at the **noun clauses** closely and you will see that they really do function as nouns. Try mentally rewriting the sentence *She told him what she thought* as *She told him [thoughts]* and – Presto! – the clause becomes a noun.

Do the same for the **adjectival clauses**. What the sentence *This is the door that won't close properly* is saying is, *This is the [jammed] door*. The adjectival clause *that won't close properly* is merely substituting for the adjective *jammed*. Incidentally, you may have noticed that the adjectival clauses are introduced by the **relative pronouns** *that* and *which*. These and *who, where, whose, what* and *as* are typically used for this purpose, which is why you may sometimes see adjectival clauses referred to as **relative clauses**.

Functioning as adverbs, the **adverbial clauses** give us information about time, place and purpose. The sentence *You should go there before the shops open* could be saying *You should go there [now, soon, quickly]* – all of which are adverbs. In this case, however, the adverbial clause *before the shops open* may have been chosen over a simple adverb as being more informative. This is the real point of adverbial, adjectival and noun clauses – they enable us to add unlimited shades of information and meaning to our sentences.

Misplaced Clauses

There is also another important point in knowing about clauses and how to use them – and that is how not to misuse them. Unfortunately clauses that are placed incorrectly in sentences are not uncommon, and can cause great confusion, not to mention embarrassment and hilarity. The BBC once carried a breathless report about a Russian demonstration, where protesters

> *who lay down outside the Kremlin . . . were carried away bodily singing hymns by the police.*

However, hymn-composing Russian policemen appear to have more class than their British counterparts who were recently called out to subdue a young lady, the result of which was that 'She was arrested by police wearing no knickers' (also BBC).

A similar state of undress was promised in another case of a misplaced clause when *The Times* reported that 25 women were planning to compete in the London Marathon 'wearing nothing but a Wonderbra above the waist'. A hurried consultation with the organisers eventually sorted it out: rather less outrageously the women planned to run 'wearing nothing above the waist but a Wonderbra'.

Perhaps one of the most notorious misplaced clauses occurred in a report, also in *The Times*, in which a young woman was fined by magistrates for falsely accusing a man of rape. The report went on to state that she 'claimed he had raped her twice to avoid getting into trouble for arriving home late'.

How this got through the serried ranks of subeditors is anyone's guess, but it certainly provided readers with a baffling mental picture of the alleged rapist apologising to his parents for being late home and offering the excuse that he had had to rape someone twice. Perhaps what was really meant was that 'to avoid getting into trouble for arriving home late, she claimed that a man had raped her twice'.

Don't let a clause be the cause of confusion!

Naming Things: Nouns

Nouns make up by far the biggest family of words in the English language. This is because nouns name things: everything, everyone, almost every place in the world has a name. The common and scientific names of all the plants and creatures in the natural world – from moss to mighty oaks, from insects to elephants, from mites to molluscs – add a few more million to the pile. There are nearly four billion people living in the world and all of them have one or more names. Not all human names are unique, of course; Korea is dominated by just four surnames, and in China combinations of surnames and given names are often shared by several hundred thousand individuals, but it still adds up to a mind-boggling total. The names or titles of every book written, every song composed, every movie made and every product marketed help to expand this colossal lexicon by tens of thousands of new names every day of our lives.

So although our everyday working vocabulary of pronouns, verbs, adjectives, and so on, remains more or less static year after year, new nouns continue to cascade into our memories, so that someone with a working vocabulary of several thousand non-noun words might have memory access to a hundred thousand common and proper nouns.

All names are nouns, but not all nouns are names. We have a habit of grabbing all sorts of words and turning them into nouns. They're sometimes well disguised, so beware:

*She was always on the side of the **dispossessed**.*

*He ordered the **destruction** of the French Fleet.*

*Give me your **tired**, your **poor**, your huddled masses . . .*

*You can have any colour providing it's **black**.*

*He promised to show me the **way** to happiness.*

Common and Proper Nouns

Perhaps the most important distinction we make among nouns is that some are **common nouns** and some are **proper nouns**:

COMMON NOUN	PROPER NOUN
car	*Jaguar*
aircraft	*Boeing 747*
vacuum cleaner	*Hoover*
country	*Britain*
mushroom	*Garicus campestris*
singer	*Madonna*

It's a basic distinction that separates the general from the particular. **Common nouns** describe groups or members of groups while **proper nouns** identify a unique example. There are many *countries*, but only one *Britain*. There are many makes of *aircraft*, but only one called the *Boeing 747*.

Proper nouns are invariably capitalised and common nouns are not, but there are exceptions. Curiously, we capitalise words like *Saturday* and *September*, but not the seasons: *summer, autumn, winter* and *spring*.

Having established that other word classes can disguise themselves as nouns, and that nouns can often change themselves into adjectives and verbs, how can we tell when a word is really a noun? One way is to place a determiner in front of the word, such as *the, a* or *an*:

NOUNS	NON-NOUNS
a **racehorse**	*a* **racing**
the **park**	*the* **parked**
an **assembly**	*an* **assemble**
some **cash**	*some* **cashable**

Other tests include a noun's ability to take on singular and plural form (try to pluralise the non-nouns above: you can't); to be replaced by pronouns (*he, she, it*, etc); and to accept add-ons to form new nouns:

book / booking / booklet / bookman / bookmark / bookshop

More strikingly, nouns have the ability to 'possess', to indicate ownership:

My **assistant's** *desk*
The **president's** *concern*
His **uncle's** *death*
It's **yesterday's** *news*

Nouns can also be **concrete nouns**, the names of things we can see and touch, or **abstract nouns**, which describe concepts, ideas and qualities:

CONCRETE NOUNS   *earth, sky, vapour, girl, window, concrete*

ABSTRACT NOUNS   *instinct, strength, coincidence, existence, Christianity*

Both common and proper nouns have **gender**, too, which we learn to distinguish from a very early age:

	MASCULINE	**FEMININE**	**NEUTER**
Common nouns	*boy, bull, cock, stallion, grandpa*	*woman, cow, hen, mare, actress*	*letter, box, gun, house, sky*
Proper nouns	*Frank Sinatra, Peeping Tom*	*Joan of Arc, Cleopatra*	*Xerox, Aida, China, Ford*

There are a few nouns that defy this three-way gender classification for which we might invent a fourth type: **dual gender**: *parent, cousin, teacher, student, horse,* etc.

Another class of noun familiar to everyone is the **compound noun** – again demonstrating a noun's potential to grow:

> *gin and tonic, scotch on the rocks, grass-roots, Eggs McMuffin, mother-in-law, attorney general, Coca-Cola, swindle sheet.*

Still another fascinating quality of the noun is its capacity to be countable or uncountable.

Countable and Uncountable Nouns

A **countable noun** is usually preceded by a determiner such as *a, an* or *the*, and can be counted. It can also assume singular or plural form:

*a **hamburger***	*five **hamburgers***	*several **hamburgers***
*an **egg***	*a dozen **eggs***	*a nest of **eggs***
*the **mountain***	*the two **mountains***	*the range of **mountains***
*a **salesperson***	*three **salespersons***	*a group of **salespersons***

Uncountable nouns, as the name suggests, cannot be counted; nor do they have a plural form:

> *music, poetry, cement, light, luck, greed, geography*

But be careful here, because nouns, including uncountable nouns, are slippery. Take the uncountable noun *light*, as in the sentences *There was **light** at the end of the tunnel,* or, *Eventually he saw the **light***. But in a different context, *light* becomes a countable noun: *The ship was lit by many bright **lights***.

Other seemingly uncountable nouns can be counted, too. Take *bread*. It is not unusual to read these days that some bakeries carry 'up to 50 varieties of breads'.

We can also quantify non-count nouns such as *bread*; we can have *slices, pieces, bits, chunks, lumps, ounces* and even *crumbs* of bread. Or take music. We can get around its uncountability to some extent by using such terms as a *piece / fragment / snippet /* etc *of music*.

Singular and Plural Nouns

Of all the chameleon qualities of the countable noun, its capacity to exist in singular and plural forms is perhaps the most interesting and certainly – for most of us – the most perplexing.

Singulars and plurals have for a century or two provided wordsmiths and gamesters with a playground for puzzles like these:

- Name words ending in *-s* that are spelt the same in singular and plural forms. (Answer: *shambles, congeries*)

- Name the plural of a noun in which none of the letters are common with the singular. (Answer: *cow = kine*)

- Name any plural words with no singular. (Answer: *scissors, jeans, trousers, knickers, binoculars, spectacles, marginalia,* etc)

In the last category you could include the uncountable nouns known as 'mass nouns' (*police, poultry, timber, grass, cattle, vermin, manners, clothes,* etc) which are, in a sense, plurals without singulars. If it's beginning to dawn on you that the singular/plural double act is littered with inconsistencies, you would be right.

But there *is* a sort of system. Most nouns change from singular to plural by the simple addition of an *-s*:

shop, shops	*boat, boats*	*girl, girls*	*cloud, clouds*

This is by far the largest group. Notice, by the way, that there are no apostrophes before the *-s*. Then there is another, smaller group that requires an added *-es* to become a plural:

circus, circuses	*bush, bushes*	*tomato, tomatoes*	*bus, buses*

So far, so good. But now we come to other – fortunately smaller – groups that pluralise in quaint and random ways:

mouse, mice	*loaf, loaves*	*tooth, teeth*	*foot, feet*
child, children	*ox, oxen*	*lady, ladies*	*wife, wives*
oasis, oases	*man, men*	*wharf, wharves*	*index, indices*

Foreign-derived words – mostly Greek, Latin and French – have their own rules concerning plurals:

phenomenon, phenomena	*medium, media*	*tempo, tempi*
alumnus, alumni	*formula, formulae*	*bureau, bureaux*
automaton, automata	*datum, data*	*criterion, criteria*
paparazzo, paparazzi	*kibbutz, kibbutzim*	*graffito, graffiti*

One small group that plays tricks consists of words that are plural in form but singular in meaning: *news, economics, acoustics, premises, thanks, savings.* What's confusing about these is that some take a singular verb (*the news that night **was** bad; acoustics **is** a much misunderstood science*) while others require a plural verb (*the premises **were** empty; her entire savings **have been** stolen*).

Another bunch that lays trip-wires are the compound nouns:

Is it *two gins and tonic, please, two gin and tonics* or *two gins and tonics*?
Is it *poet laureates* or *poets laureate*?
Is it *mother-in-laws* or *mothers-in-law*?
Is it *scotches on the rocks* or *scotch on the rocks's*?
Is it *Egg McMuffins* or *Eggs McMuffin*?

These are conundrums that have tortured us for ages. There is, however, a view, which sounds reasonable, that hyphenated compounds should be pluralised by adding an *-s* at the end (*forget-me-nots, stick-in-the-muds, 15-year-olds*) with, strangely, the exception of *mothers-in-law*; and that unhyphenated compounds should have the *-s* added to the central or most important noun. If we follow this advice, we get *gins and tonic, poets laureate, scotches on the rocks* and *Egg McMuffins* (it is the McMuffin bit that creates the difference, not the eggs).

But inconsistencies will still pursue us. Some people (including newspaper and book publishers) will hyphenate compounds such as *gin-and-tonic* and some won't. You will also see *right-of-way, right of way, rights-of-way, right-of-ways* and even *rights-of-ways* – so who's right? Similar arguments surround *spoon full* and *mouth full*, and *spoonful* and *mouthful*. The plurals of the first pair are straight-forwardly *spoons full* and *mouths full*. But the meanings of the second pair are different; here the attention is on the fullness of a single spoon or mouth, so *-ful* is the central or important part of the compound and should have the *-s* added to it: *spoonfuls* and *mouthfuls*. But remember that these recommendations are not bound by strict rules; many grammarians will opt for *spoonsful* and *mouthsful* and *mother-in-laws*, and will expect to be served like anyone else when they ask the barman for two *gin-and-tonics*.

Collective Nouns

Collective nouns identify groups of things, people, animals and ideas:

audience, council, staff, team, enemy, collection, herd, quantity

The effect of a collective noun is to create a singular entity that, although many creatures (bees in a *swarm*), people (members of a *jury*) or objects (a *number* of entries) are involved, should be treated as a singular noun:

*The **army** is outside the city gates.*
*Will **this** class please behave **itself**?*
*The **management has** refused to meet us.*

Sometimes, however, a collective noun is a bit equivocal, taking singular or plural form according to context. Unsurprisingly, this can lead to confusion:

*A vast **number** of crimes **is/are** never reported at all.*
*The **majority is/are** in favour of the merger.*

Such collective nouns sometimes lead to grammatically correct but odd-sounding emissions such as ***none** of us **is** going to work today*, and *a **lot** of things **is** wrong with the world*, and this has led to the relaxation of the old rule of always following a collective noun with a singular verb. This makes sense when the context refers to individuals within the group rather than the group as a whole. Look at this sentence in which *family* is the collective noun:

*The **family was** given just one week to find a new home.*

Here the family is treated as a single entity and the noun is therefore followed by a singular verb – *was*. But there are occasions when a family can be viewed more as a number of individual members:

*The **family were** informed that if **their** aggressive behaviour continued, **they** would be evicted.*

In this case the writer assumes two things – first, that the family did not act aggressively as a unit, as an army would, but that aggressive acts were carried out by members of the family, and not necessarily all of them; and, second, that the members of the family were not necessarily consulted or warned *en masse*, but individually – not an unreasonable assumption. In this context, therefore, *family* has a very strong case for requiring a plural verb and pronouns.

Too often, however, collective nouns are followed by plural verbs willy-nilly, regardless of context. *The Times* recently carried this front-page report: 'Diplomats like to stress the BBC *are* seen in Riyadh as the voice of the British establishment . . .' And again: 'Michael Howard, the Home Secretary, said: "*The Daily Mail haven't* done anything against the law . . ."' In these contexts it is very difficult to see how the BBC and *The Daily Mail* can be anything but singular entities.

Many caring users of English are beginning to complain about this creeping plurality of collective nouns. Here are some more examples, all from national newspapers:

A team were forming, the captain was in command, a spinning pitch had been prepared . . . (The Sunday Times)

Your committee of ten are about to take a trip . . . (Daily Telegraph)

. . . the family who own the site charge admission . . . (Daily Telegraph)

. . . the leadership have decided . . . (Daily Telegraph)

The Government are absolutely clear that the right . . . (The Times)

And this quite baffling sentence: 'Railway are dying' (*The Times*). Of course individual writers and publications will continue to differ on how to treat collective nouns, but this liberalisation inevitably leads to sentence discord and confusion. An example of this was given in the section on *Sentences* (page 17) but here is another.

In an article on the 'Americanisation of Europe' *The Observer* could not make up its mind whether MacDonald's was corporately collective or not:

*. . . MacDonald's **are** well used to the accusation . . . the trouble with MacDonald's is that everybody has an opinion about **it** . . . yet MacDonald's, with its training 'universities' . . . MacDonald's **has** become a symbol . . . yet MacDonald's stress that **they** go out of their way . . .*

A real mess, isn't it?

Regardless of your views on the merits or otherwise of the 'institutional plural', it is important that, once you are committed to a singular or plural verb, you don't change in midstream:

NOT *The Tilner Committee **has** a week in which to announce **their** findings.*

BUT *The Tilner Committee **has** a week in which to announce **its** findings.*

OR *The Tilner Committee **have** a week in which to announce **their** findings.*

It's also worth mentioning a quite minor category of nouns that can cause bewilderment – noun phrases in which two nouns, including plural nouns, combine to form a single entity, and which usually take singular verbs:

*Bacon and eggs **is** always served at the Sportsman's Cafe.*

*Tripe and onions **seems** to be disappearing from British menus.*

*Two months **is** too long for the school holidays.*

*Whisky and soda **was** his favourite tipple.*

Collective nouns aren't always so mind-bending. Knowing the correct collective labels for groups of birds, animals and humans can score you points at quiz nights. There are hundreds of them; here are a few:

*A **murder** of crows*	*A **convocation** of eagles*
*An **exaltation** of larks*	*A **chattering** of starlings*

A **dray** of squirrels   A **knot** of toads
A **business** of ferrets   A **charm** of finches
A **gaggle** of geese (on water)   A **skein** of geese (when flying)
A **colony** of penguins   An **ostentation** of peacocks
A **clamour** of rooks   A **parliament** of owls

How Nouns Become Possessive

We have seen that when we pluralise most nouns, we add an -s (*ghost, ghosts*). Note, no apostrophe. But when a noun changes to its possessive form, we indicate this by adding an -*'s*. Note the apostrophe:

a ghost   *a ghost's shroud*
the team   *the team's triumph*

Where common singular nouns end with -s (*bus, atlas, iris*) we add an apostrophe after the -s:

the bus's route   *the atlas's value*   *the iris's colour*

For common plural nouns ending with -s (*girls, paintings*) or nouns plural in form but singular in meaning (*ashes, bagpipes, works*) we simply add an apostrophe – in effect an apostrophe inserted between the end of the word and an invisible second -s:

*The invitation went out for the **girls'** party.*
*The **paintings'** ownership was being contested in court.*
*She objected to the **bagpipes'** capacity to disturb her sleep.*

With proper nouns ending in -s (Jesus, James, Jones) we have the option of adding the -*'s*, or simply adding an apostrophe after the final -s of the name:

*They decided to go to **James's** party after all. (or James')*
*The **Jones's** house was always kept spick and span. (or Jones')*

As many of us find that apostrophe spells catastrophe there is a more detailed session on the contentious 'upstairs comma' in *Punctuation*, page 121.

You, Me and Other Pronouns

As we saw in the section on *The Building Blocks of Sentences*, pronouns are versatile stand-ins or substitutes for nouns and noun phrases. We also noted how they spread like a rash through our speech yet at the same time can cause us no end of problems. But before we worry ourselves too much about problematical pronouns, let's find out what they are.

Pronouns work like this:

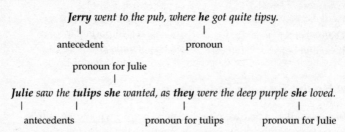

That demonstrates the basic way in which pronouns function, even when there appears to be no antecedent in a sentence:

Who would have imagined it would come to this?

Help! Where are the antecedents for *Who, it* and *this*? What is happening is that the three pronouns are standing in for three 'ghost' antecedents. Let's try to construct a sentence that might have preceded the above sentence, with all antecedents present:

The coach, the team and all the supporters would never have imagined that kicking an umpire would result in the captain being banned for a year.

That sentence spells out all the facts without any pronouns. Now identify the antecedents and their matching pronouns:

The coach, the team and all the supporters – antecedent for the pronoun *Who*.
kicking an umpire – antecedent for the pronoun *it*.
the captain being banned for a year – antecedent for the pronoun *this*.

You should now clearly see that if the first sentence had been preceded by a sentence similar to the information-packed second sentence, it would have made perfect sense with just its three pronouns.

We recognise and constantly use eight types of pronouns:

- **PERSONAL PRONOUNS** – *I, me, you, she*

- **POSSESSIVE PRONOUNS** – *her, their, our*

- **REFLEXIVE PRONOUNS** – *myself, yourselves*

- **DEMONSTRATIVE PRONOUNS** – *these, that*

- **INTERROGATIVE PRONOUNS** – *who?, which?*

- **RELATIVE PRONOUNS** – *that, whose, what*

- **INDEFINITE PRONOUNS** – *all, any, someone*

- **RECIPROCAL PRONOUNS** – *one another, each other*

Personal Pronouns

We use these to identify ourselves and others, and they are probably the most commonly used of all pronouns. Nevertheless it is important to know how to use them. Fortunately we learn what personal pronouns are for in early childhood, but imagine how someone with only a basic knowledge of English might use them:

I look at she,
Her look at me;
Her see much not,
Me see quite lot.

Personal pronouns are used in three ways:

- In the **first person**, the most intimate, which includes the person or persons doing the speaking or writing: *I, me, we, us.*

- In the **second person**, which embraces those who are being addressed or spoken to: *you.*

- In the **third person**, or 'all the others'– those who are being spoken about: *he, him, she, her, it, they, them.*

With the exception of *it*, which refers to things (although sometimes to babies and animals), all personal pronouns refer to people, while *them* can refer to people or things. There are some exceptions: a ship is customarily not an *it*, but a *she* or a *her*.

Problems with Personal Pronouns

Using personal pronouns is usually a straightforward business – except when used in certain combinations, when all hell breaks loose. Despite reams having

Problems with personal pronouns

been written about *you and me, you and I, he/she and me, he/she and I, us and we,* a good many of us remain determinedly confused.

To understand and avoid problems with these pronouns it may help to refer back to the section on *Let's Look at Sentences.* There we recognised that a sentence has two major components: a subject and a predicate (page 20) or, looked at in another way, a subject and an object or objects. Both subjects and objects, whether direct or indirect, can include pronouns, and here it helps to know that some pronouns are used in subject positions in a sentence, and some in object positions:

PRONOUNS SERVING AS SUBJECTS: *I, you, he, she, it, we, they, who, whoever*

PRONOUNS SERVING AS OBJECTS: *me, you, him, her, it, us, them, whom, whomever*

It is when the subjective form of a pronoun is used in an objective position that trouble starts. Take the phrase *between you and I.* Shakespeare famously used it ('All debts are settled between you and I' – *The Merchant of Venice*) and today it is commonly accepted. Grammatically, however, it is incorrect. *Just between you and I, Lucy has a secret* is wrong because Lucy is the subject and the preposition *between* should be followed by the objective forms of the pronouns, *you* and *me.*

But *you and I* can be grammatically correct when used in a different construction. *You and I are having the day off,* for example, is correct because *you* and *I* are the subjects of the sentence.

Here's another sentence that your ear will tell you is wrong:

Ask Tony and I for any further information you need.

To correct this you need to recognise that *Ask* is the subject and the phrase *Tony and I* is the direct object, because *Tony and I* are receiving the action as the result of the verb *ask.* As *I* can only be used in a subjective position, it is therefore wrong and should be the objective pronoun *me*: *Ask Tony and **me** for any further information you need.* There's a simple 'ear' test for such sentences – omit mention of any other names and you get *Ask I for any further information you need,* which is patently wrong.

Another quick test is to think of *you and I* as **we**, and *you and me* as **us**:

WRONG   *You and me are going to be late. (**us** are going to be late)*

RIGHT   *You and I are going to be late. (**we** are going to be late)*

WRONG   *They're calling you and I liars. (they're calling **we** liars)*

RIGHT   *They're calling you and me liars. (they're calling **us** liars)*

In other words, you can mix and match pronouns that serve as subjects (*we and they, she and I, he and she, he and I,* etc) and those that serve as objects (*me and him, me and her, us and them,* etc) but not subject pronouns with object pronouns (*she and him, we and them, he and her, they and us,* etc).

A similar test can be applied to the troublesome duo *we* and *us*:

> *Us vintage car enthusiasts are going to be hit hard by the new tax.*
> [Drop *vintage car enthusiasts* and you get *Us are going . . . !*]

> *It's no good telling we poor farmers about export prices.*
> [Drop *poor farmers* and you get *It's no good telling we about . . .*]

The Generic Personal Pronoun 'One'

The indefinite pronoun *one* is used as a personal pronoun in two ways:

- As a pronoun standing for an average or generic person, as in *One can be the victim of aggressive neighbours without any reason.*

- As a pronoun substituting for the personal pronoun *I*, as in *One is always being invited to openings but one simply can't attend them all.*

Most speakers and writers in English tend to regard either use as affected. Still, there is no valid reason for discouraging its use as in certain circumstances it can render a certain elegance to expression.

If you do use *one*, however, make sure you maintain sentence harmony by following through with *one's* (for *my, our*), *oneself* (*myself*) and *oneselves* (*ourselves*) and not mixing in clashing pronouns such as *my, you, our,* etc.

The Versatile Personal Pronoun 'It'

In our list of pronouns that serve as subjects and objects you may have noted that, like *you*, the pronoun *it* can perform both as a subject pronoun and as an object pronoun. And for a personal pronoun *it* seems to be used in 1,001 different impersonal ways! *It* is truly a multipurpose pronoun.

We use *it* to refer to all or parts of a sentence, where *it* anticipates the antecedent (*It is a pity she is not going to sing tonight*); to refer to a previous statement, which becomes the antecedent (*Are you coming tonight? I'm thinking about it*); to fill in a space with no particular meaning (*Jenny hated it here; It is pointless to travel further; I think it is going to rain*). We also habitually use it in a ghostly form – by dropping it altogether:

Looks like rain.	*(It) Looks like rain.*
Do you like it? Yes, tastes good.	*Yes, (it) tastes good.*

Possessive Pronouns

These indicate possession or ownership and are sometimes called **possessive adjectives**. Some are used as determiners and are dependent on nouns:

my groceries, *her* hairdresser, *his* anger, *our* house, *your* car, *their* washing machine

while other possessive pronouns are used on their own:

it is *ours*, it is *mine*, *theirs* is out of date, *his* is that one, *hers* is over there

Notice that possessive pronouns do not need apostrophes to indicate possession. Do not fall for the unfortunately too common errors: *it's our's*, *have you seen their's*, etc.

Reflexive Pronouns

This tribe, so called because they 'reflect' the action back to the self, or subject, insinuates its members into our lives in various ways:

Look after *yourself*, they keep to *themselves*, *myself* included.

Other reflexive pronouns are *herself, himself, itself, yourselves, ourselves*. And if you have a good biblical ear, you'll recognise the archaic *thou, thee, thy, thine* and *ye* as reflexive pronouns.

Some grammarians recognise a subgroup called **intensifying pronouns**, which are used to emphasise, or sometimes clarify, a meaning:

*The programme, consisting of tunes **he himself** selected, was too long.*

*Although the aircraft was declared faulty, the **engine itself** never missed a beat.*

*The **various committees** wouldn't **themselves** promise a more democratic style of government.*

Demonstrative Pronouns

These help us to demonstrate something, or to point out things:

*I'll take **this**.   Look at **that**!   **These** will do.   **Those** are stale.*

You'll note that these statements make sense only when the reader (or listener) has been made aware of the pronouns' antecedents. For example, if those sentences were uttered in a bakery, with the speaker pointing to various items, there would be little doubt about the meaning of the statements:

SPEAKER   (choosing a loaf): *I'll take **this**.* (Pointing to a large iced birthday cake): *Look at **that**!* (Picking up some buns): ***These** will do.* (Gesturing to some tarts as she leaves the shop): ***Those** are stale.*

In writing, however, the reader should not be left in doubt as to the identity of what it is the pronoun is supposed to be possessive about.

Interrogative Pronouns

We use these to ask questions: *who, what, which, whose, whom*:

> **Who** *is she, anyway?*   **Which** *one?*   **Whose** *are these?*   **What** *is it?*

You'll notice that all these are direct questions, which require question marks. However we can also use interrogative pronouns to introduce indirect questions, which are not followed by question marks:

> *The reporter wanted to know* **who** *saw the accident.*
> *He wondered* **what** *they were going to do with the body.*

You will often see *what* used in a way that's hardly interrogative: **What** *a load of nonsense! Oh,* **what** *a lovely war.* **What** *beautiful eyes you have.* In these examples, *what* jumps out of the pronoun class and becomes an **exclamative determiner**.

Who or Whom: That is the Question!

Who is a subject pronoun; *whom* is an object pronoun – and if you make them stay in their proper places you'll have no trouble with this troublesome pair. They must also match similar subject and object pronouns: *who / he / she / we / they* and *whom / him / her / us / them*. Your ear should immediately tell you if you have applied this logical rule correctly or not:

WRONG   **Who** *shall it be? (Should it be* **he***? Should it be* **she***?)*

CORRECT   **Whom** *shall it be? (Should it be* **him***? Should it be* **her***?)*

WRONG   **Whom** *do you think is cheating? (Do you think* **him** *is cheating? Do you think* **her** *is cheating? (Do you think* **them** *are cheating?)*

CORRECT   **Who** *do you think is cheating? (Do you think* **he** *is cheating? Do you think* **she** *is cheating? (Do you think* **they** *are cheating?)*

In practice, however, *who* invariably doubles for *whom* and few people seem to mind or even notice. There are some constructions, though, where substitution is difficult (*From* **whom** *did you catch your cold? She was pleased with her pupils,* **whom** *she thought had tried really hard*) and where reconstruction can be clumsy: **Who** *did you catch your cold from? She was pleased with her pupils* **who** *had tried really hard, she thought.*

The rules for *who* and *whom* also apply to *whoever* and *whomever*.

Relative Pronouns

These are *that, which, who, whom, whose, whatever, whoever* and *whomever*, and we use them to introduce relative clauses, as in *It was Clarissa* **who** *told me first.*

We use relative pronouns indiscriminately and, with some exceptions, with confidence:

> The suit **that** he was supposed to mend is ruined.
> I wish I knew **whose** parcels were delivered by mistake.
> I'd like those shoes **which** I saw yesterday.
> She's the lady to **whom** I gave the keys.

Can you see any traps hidden here? Taking the last example, most of us would try to avoid the formal-sounding *whom* and say something like, *She's the lady I gave the keys to*. And we're increasingly dropping *that* and *which* from sentences, so that the first and third examples would customarily be spoken as:

> The suit he was supposed to mend is ruined.
> I'd like those shoes I saw yesterday.

The relative clauses in the examples above are adjectival in use: they qualify the nouns *suit*, *parcels*, *shoes* and *lady*. But relative pronouns can also work without antecedents when they introduce relative clauses that act as nouns:

> She thinks she can do **whatever** she likes.
> I think I know **whose** mistake it was.
> They couldn't care less about **what** I think.

Indefinite Pronouns

This is a very large and mixed bunch of words that can be called upon to function as pronouns, taking the place of undefined persons or objects. They also have a common bond, which you should spot fairly quickly:

> all, any, every, everything, each, some, one, both, either, neither, few, little, less, least, many, everyone, someone, no one, something, anybody, nobody, more, most, nothing, enough, plenty, several.

The bond? They all have to do with number or quantity: nothing at all, a little, some, enough, or plenty. Here are a few pointers on using them:

- Note that pronouns such as *little, less, some, none* and *more* indicate portions and should be applied only to uncountable nouns (a **little** sugar, but not a **little** cakes; **much** trouble, but not **much** problems; **less** fat but not **less** calories).

- Always decide whether your antecedent is singular or plural, and then choose a pronoun to agree with it. Note that *each, one, either, neither, someone, anyone, no one, nobody* and *something* are all singular.

- If an indefinite pronoun is used with a verb or a personal pronoun in a sentence, make sure it agrees in number: *Each* one of us *has* problems; *Neither* of the actors could remember *his/her* lines; *Few* of the players *are* likely to turn up today.

- Note that *no one* is the only two-word indefinite pronoun.

Reciprocal Pronouns

This is the smallest group of pronouns – just two, in fact: *each other* and *one another*. They are called reciprocal because they express a mutual, give-and-take relationship. *Each other* refers to two people or things; *one another* is usually meant to refer to more than two:

*The two children were constantly talking to **each other**.*
*The women of the district earned extra cash by taking in **one another's** washing.*

When using the possessive form of these pronouns remember that the apostrophe comes before the *-s*, not after: *each other's, one another's*.

Number Pronouns

Although not strictly a class – numbers are perhaps more properly defined as determiners – numerals often function as pronouns. They exist in three forms: **cardinal numbers** (*5, five, 99, ninety-nine, two hundred, zero, dozen, million*); **ordinal numbers** (*first, tenth, twenty-fifth*) and **fractions** (*half, halves, a quarter, two-fifths*). Here are some in use as pronouns and, for comparison, as determiners:

CARDINAL PRONOUN	*I get up at **seven** every morning.*
CARDINAL DETERMINER	*The kitchen was **seven** yards in length.*
ORDINAL PRONOUN	*He was **one** of the first to visit there.*
ORDINAL DETERMINER	*It was the **first** occasion I'd met the PM.*
FRACTION PRONOUN	*In our class, **half** haven't got a clue about spelling.*
FRACTION DETERMINER	*Half the class simply can't spell.*

Avoid Perplexing Pronouns

A common piece of advice is to avoid using a pronoun without first introducing its antecedent, although in practice it's done all the time:

*It's very difficult, **this job**. Here **it** comes! (**the bus**)*

Try also to avoid using a pronoun when it results in confusion and ambiguity. It is difficult to resist trotting out the old chestnut, *She wore a flower in her hair which was yellow speckled with mauve*. The pronoun *which* probably referred to the flower, but hair comes in some amazing colours these days, so that possibility can't be ruled out. A rewrite is called for: *In her hair she wore a flower which was yellow speckled with mauve*. Here are a few more 'pronoun howlers'; try rewriting them so that the intended meaning is instantly clear:

> *Young William told his granddad he was too old to play with Lego.*
> *When Alan patted the guard dog, his tail wagged.*
> *Joyce's mother was remarried when she was sixteen.*
> *My father told his brother that he'd had too much to drink.*
> *The vet said that the rabbit's foot was healed, and we could take it home.*
> *If your baby has trouble digesting cow's milk, boil it.*
> *He loved browsing through his doctor father's old medical books so much that he eventually decided to become one.*

That and Which

The relative pronouns *that* and *which* are becoming more interchangeable despite long-standing rules about their usage. Careful writers will use *that* to define the meaning or intention of the preceding phrase or clause: *The hotel **that** Helen stayed at has burnt down*. *That* defines or identifies the hotel for us. Use *which* when the identifying information is already supplied in the sentence: *The Imperial Hotel in Brighton, **which** Helen stayed at last year, has burnt down*. Here, *which* introduces a relative clause that merely adds extra, possibly non-essential, information and is cordoned off by commas. If you have developed a grammatical 'ear', you will readily detect the essential difference between the two.

That and Who

Whether to use *who* or *that* for persons can sometimes present a problem but, generally, *that* is used to refer to *any* persons, and *who* to a particular person: *The mechanics **that** fixed my car ought to be shot*; but – *My mate Jim, **who** was supposed to fix my car, ought to be shot*. However, using *that* for persons can sometimes look and sound odd: *To all **that** protest that this is quick-fix politics . . .* Most writers would in this instance use *who*.

Drop 'that' with Care

The common practice of omitting *that* from many sentence constructions is considered acceptable if the meaning remains clear:

Are you pleased [that] I bought it?
I know [that] Claire will be here tomorrow.
Don't you think [that] it's a beautiful car?

All these statements are unambiguous with *that* omitted. But proceed carefully. *Mr Benton said yesterday some shares dropped as much as 20 per cent* could mean two things: that Mr Benton made the statement yesterday (*Mr Benton said yesterday [that] some shares dropped as much as 20 per cent*) or that Mr Benton said some shares dropped 20 per cent yesterday (*Mr Benton said [that] yesterday some shares dropped as much as 20 per cent*). If you were the owner of those shares you'd be mighty interested in what Mr Benton actually meant. The appropriate insertion of *that* would make either sentence crystal clear – so when in doubt, retain *that*.

The Search for the Uni-gender Third Person Pronoun

For centuries we've used *man* and *men* generically to embrace *woman* and *women*, and this practice has extended to the use of *he, his* and *him* to include both sexes:

Any runner who does not finish will have his application for next year's race reconsidered by the committee.

In an age when the number of female runners is at least equal to the number of their male counterparts, the use of the masculine pronoun in contexts like this, although for so long accepted, is no longer appropriate. The problem is that the English language has no gender-neutral singular pronoun that includes both men and women, an omission that hasn't gone unnoticed by the feminist movement. Feminists argue that current usage is not only biased against women but is also illogical. Here's an example from *The Times* in which, despite the subject being a woman (Mrs Thatcher, in fact), she is referred to by the masculine pronoun *his*:

*The Prime Minister and the Opposition Leader each received a huge cheer from **his** own side as they entered the chamber yesterday.*

So what can we do in this age of gender equality? One suggestion is to use the *his* or *her* or *his/her* formula: *Any runner who does not finish will have **his or her** application* . . . but many writers consider this to be a clumsy solution which can be intensely irritating if repeated throughout a passage.

The most accepted course today is to either reconstruct sentences to avoid the offending pronouns or to pluralise them: *Runners who do not finish will have **their** applications* . . . This works when the subject can be pluralised, but when it can't we're forced to use plurals like *their, they, them* and *themselves* as generic singulars:

*Judgements are made about a **person's** competence on the basis of **their** ability to spell correctly.*

Here the plural *their* agrees in person with *person's* but not in number – because *a person's competence* is singular, referring to a single person's competence. Despite continuing complaints from purists, most grammarians now accept the compromise as the only practical way out of the problem. Nevertheless, some cute paradoxes will persist. Which is correct, or 'more correct'?

> *Everyone was blowing their trumpets.*
> *Everyone were blowing their trumpets.*
> *Everyone was blowing their trumpet.*

The answer is that none is grammatically correct, but that the first example is considered to be acceptable. Here are some more well-known examples of pronoun disagreement. Try to rewrite them elegantly, but grammatically correctly, while avoiding sexism. Remember that *anyone, everyone* and *someone* are singular subjects.

> *Everyone immediately returned to their cars.*
> *Someone called but they didn't leave a message.*
> *James saw everyone before Sue noticed them.*
> *Anyone who feels that the slimfast regime has reduced their weight, please raise your hand.*

Or could you do better than the American author J. D. Salinger who, in his novel *Catcher in the Rye*, has his character Holden Caulfield say, 'He's one of those guys who's always patting themselves on the back.'

It's a Plane! It's a Bird! No!
It's SUPERVERB!

The verb is usually the most important element in a sentence. It is the engine that makes the sentence go. Its business, its *raison d'être*, is to express action, or to indicate a condition or a state:

| **ACTION** | *He is **running** away.* | *She **intended** to **live** here.* |
| **STATE** | *She **loathes** rap music.* | *Gordon **looks** quite ill.* |

Action verbs express what someone or something is, was or will be doing. In other words, verbs possess **tense** to help us express **time**: Although there are 12 tenses (which we'll discuss later), here is the basic trio:

PRESENT TIME	*He **listens** to her.*	*She **is** home today.*
PAST TIME	*He's **been sacked**.*	*He **was** very ill.*
FUTURE TIME	*I **will come** if I can.*	*Jeanne **will be** here.*

Verbs are among the most versatile of all our words. You can see how clever they are in these two paragraphs. The first is a fairly matter-of-fact descriptive passage:

> *The helicopter banked and almost stalled. The engines raced and the craft tilted and a body fell out of the hatch. The machine rapidly lost height and the engines failed. Only the sound of wind could be heard. Then the machine began to revolve, out of control, throwing the pilot off and finally plunging into the sea.*

That could have been a report of a helicopter accident at sea written by an aviation safety officer with just the facts in mind. Here, though, is essentially the same passage but brought graphically to life by selective verbs:

> *Suddenly the helicopter banked, shuddered, and seemed to stall, its arms rotating wildly, scrabbling and clawing the black sky for a grip. The engines whined and screamed, the craft lurched and a body shot out of the hatch and hurtled into the void below. The machine was now losing height, dropping at a breathcatching rate until the engines abruptly died, their howling replaced by the eerie whistling of the wind. Then, slowly at first, the fuselage itself began to spin around the stilled rotors, gyrating faster and faster, whirling and spinning out of control, spiralling down through the tunnel of rushing air until, a few seconds after the pilot was hurled out of the cabin, the rotors disintegrated into shards of rocketing metal and the grey coffin plummeted into the heaving black water.*

You can easily see how certain verbs – *shuddered, rotating, scrabbling, clawing, whined, screamed, shot, hurtled, dropping, spin, gyrating, spiralling, hurled, disintegrated, rocketing, plummeted* – contribute to this vivid, action-packed word picture. To heighten the effect even further, some writers might move the verbs into the present tense, to give the reader a 'you are here now' sensation:

> *. . . then, slowly at first, the fuselage itself **begins** to spin . . . the rotors **disintegrate** . . . and the grey coffin **plummets** . . .*

We like using verbs so much that when we don't have one to describe an action or a condition we simply create one. Notice the verb *rocketing* in the passage above; it was once created from the noun *rocket*. In fact about 20 per cent of English verbs were once nouns, and we're still at it. Here are a few recent coinages from our verbing activities:

> *to host, to progress, to showcase, to doorstep, to hoover, to trash, to shoehorn, to video, to rubber stamp, to input, to impact, to access, to bankroll.*

Because verbs are so useful, so versatile, it's well worth finding out what they can do, and how we can put their potential to work in our speech and writing.

Regular and Irregular Verbs

Verbs are divided into two groups: **regular**, or **weak**, verbs, of which there are tens of thousands, and slightly fewer than 300 **irregular**, or **strong**, verbs. Regular verbs stick to certain rules, while irregular verbs live up to their name and are real wild cards, as you will see.

REGULAR VERBS	*laugh, look, play, advises, loved*
IRREGULAR VERBS	*begin, chosen, speak, freeze, shrink*

The difference between these two groups is in their behaviour when they change shape to express tense or time: present and past time. **Regular verbs** follow a pattern: the basic form of the verb simply adds an *-s*, *-ing*, or *-ed* to express a different time or mood:

BASIC FORM	*laugh, look, play, advise, push*
PRESENT	*laughs, looks, plays, advises, pushes*
PRESENT PARTICIPLE	*laughing, looking, playing, advising, pushing*
PAST/PAST PARTICIPLE	*laughed, looked, played, advised, pushed*

Irregular verbs, however, can behave quite erratically:

BASIC FORM	*begin, choose, speak, freeze, shrink*
PRESENT	*begins, chooses, speaks, freezes, shrinks*
PRESENT PARTICIPLE	*beginning, choosing, speaking, freezing, shrinking*
PAST	*began, chose, spoke, froze, shrank*
PAST PARTICIPLE	*begun, chosen, spoken, frozen, shrunk*

Irregular verbs trouble writers because they change in such unexpected ways:

> *The verse we **write** we say is **written**,*
> *All rules **despite**, but not **despitten**,*
> *And the gas we **light** is never **litten**.*
> *The things we **drank** were doubtless **drunk**,*
> *The boy that's **spanked** is never **spunk**,*
> *The friend we **thank** is never **thunk**.*
> *Suppose we **speak**, then we have **spoken**,*
> *But if we **sneak**, we have not **snoken**,*
> *And shoes that **squeak** are never **squoken**.*
> *The dog that **bites** has surely **bitten**,*
> *But after it **fights** it has not **fitten**.*

That doggerel highlights the daffy illogicality of irregular verbs. While regular verbs have only four forms, the irregular variety can have up to five – the verb *to be* has no fewer than ten – and there is no easy way of learning them. With a little patience and practice, however, they can be memorised. Here are some irregular verbs you'll come across in everyday speech and writing:

Some Disorderly, Disobedient, Deviating Irregular Verbs

BASIC FORM	PRESENT	PAST	PRESENT PARTICIPLE	PAST PARTICIPLE
arise	*arises*	*arose*	*arising*	*arisen*
awake	*awakes*	*awoke*	*awaking*	*awoken*
bear	*bears*	*bore*	*bearing*	*borne*
bid	*bids*	*bad(e)*	*bidding*	*bidden*
bite	*bites*	*bit*	*biting*	*bitten*
blow	*blows*	*blew*	*blowing*	*blown*
bring	*brings*	*brought*	*bringing*	*brought*
choose	*chooses*	*chose*	*choosing*	*chosen*
dive	*dives*	*dived*	*diving*	*dived*
do	*does*	*did*	*doing*	*done*
drive	*drives*	*drove*	*driving*	*driven*
fly	*flies*	*flew*	*flying*	*flown*
forgive	*forgives*	*forgave*	*forgiving*	*forgiven*
freeze	*freezes*	*froze*	*freezing*	*frozen*
go	*goes*	*went*	*going*	*gone*
hang	*hangs*	*hung/hanged*	*hanging*	*hung/hanged*
kneel	*kneels*	*kneeled/knelt*	*kneeling*	*knelt/kneeled*
lay	*lays*	*laid*	*laying*	*laid*
lie (recline)	*lies*	*lay*	*lying*	*lain*
lie (untruth)	*lies*	*lied*	*lying*	*lied*
mistake	*mistakes*	*mistook*	*mistaking*	*mistaken*

BASIC FORM	PRESENT	PAST	PRESENT PARTICIPLE	PAST PARTICIPLE
quit	*quits*	*quit/quitted*	*quitting*	*quit/quitted*
sew	*sews*	*sewed*	*sewing*	*sewn*
shear	*shears*	*sheared*	*shearing*	*shorn/sheared*
shoe	*shoes*	*shoed/shod*	*shoeing*	*shod*
slay	*slays*	*slew*	*slaying*	*slain*
speed	*speeds*	*speeded/sped*	*speeding*	*sped/speeded*
spell	*spells*	*spelled/spelt*	*spelling*	*spelt/spelled*
steal	*steals*	*stole*	*stealing*	*stolen*
stink	*stinks*	*stank*	*stinking*	*stunk*
strew	*strews*	*strewed*	*strewing*	*strewn*
stride	*strides*	*strode*	*striding*	*stridden*
strike	*strikes*	*struck*	*striking*	*struck*
strive	*strives*	*strove*	*striving*	*striven*
tear	*tears*	*tore*	*tearing*	*torn*
thrive	*thrives*	*thrived*	*thriving*	*thrived*
tread	*treads*	*trod*	*treading*	*trodden/trod*
undergo	*undergoes*	*underwent*	*undergoing*	*undergone*
undo	*undoes*	*undid*	*undoing*	*undone*
wake	*wakes*	*waked/woke*	*waking*	*woken*
wet	*wets*	*wet/wetted*	*wetting*	*wet/wetted*
wring	*wrings*	*wrung*	*wringing*	*wrung*
write	*writes*	*wrote*	*writing*	*written*

Auxiliary Verbs

These are a group of words that, added to a main verb to form a verb phrase, enables us to express an amazing range of meanings. They are 'helping' verbs, an army of waiting assistants. Apart from much else, they help us to express the relationship between the information given in a sentence and the time it was uttered or enacted – in other words, a sense of time.

At the start of this section we saw how verbs can change to express present, past and future time: *she listens; she listened; she will listen.* Those are the three basic tenses. But there are nine more, and these enable us to express a wide and subtle range of behavioural chronology:

The Twelve Tenses

PRESENT   I **go** to the city once a week.

PAST   I **went** to the city last week.

FUTURE   I **will go** to the city next week.

As you can see, these are straightforward expressions indicating present action, past action and future intention. Sometimes, however, we need to express continuing action in these three tenses. We achieve this by using what are called **progressive forms**:

PRESENT PROGRESSIVE   *I **am going** to the city to see Simon.*

PAST PROGRESSIVE   *I **was going** to the city but Simon cancelled.*

FUTURE PROGRESSIVE   *I **will be going** to the city again next week.*

The next set of tenses allows us to qualify the basic past and future tenses. If, for example, we use the past tense to say *I went to the city*, we are referring to an action that took place some time before the present; perhaps I went to the city last week, yesterday, or an hour ago, but since then I have returned. The action is over. But what if we need to convey the impression that I've gone to the city but haven't returned? What we need here is a tense that indicates not only past action, but past action that continues or could continue right up to the present moment:

PRESENT PERFECT   *I **have gone** to the city and will be back tonight.*

PAST PERFECT   *I **had gone** to the city without my briefcase.*

FUTURE PERFECT   *I **will have gone** to the city by the time you get to my flat.*

You will see that the **present perfect** tense indicates that while I have gone to the city I am still there – in other words, the action that began in the past is extended to the present moment. The **past perfect** tense indicates that a past action had taken place (my going to the city) at an earlier time than another action (discovering that I'd forgotten my briefcase). The **future perfect** tense indicates that a future action (my going to the city) is likely to take place at an earlier time than another future action (your getting to my flat).

Just as the simple present, past and future tenses require auxiliary tenses to indicate action that is or may be continuing, so do the perfect tenses:

PRESENT PERFECT PROGRESSIVE   *I **have been going** to the city for years.*

PAST PERFECT PROGRESSIVE   *I **had been going** to the city regularly until last month.*

FUTURE PERFECT PROGRESSIVE   *If I make three more trips I **will have been going** to the city every week for the past fifteen years.*

The Expressive Power of Auxiliary Verbs

Although auxiliary verbs can't stand on their own, they help to extend the expressive range of other verbs to an extraordinary degree. We've seen how preceding the main verb *go* with such auxiliary verbs as *will, was, am, will be, have, will have, have been* and *will have been* helps us understand when an action is, was or will be taking place. But auxiliary verbs can do much more than that.

There are two kinds of auxiliary verbs: the three **primary auxiliaries** (*be, do, has*), which often double as main verbs; and what are known as **modal auxiliaries** (*can/could, may/might, must, shall/should, will/would*), which form verb phrases that enable us to express a truly amazing range of meanings: whether or not something is possible; making demands; giving permission; deducing or predicting some event, and so forth. And, by following such verb phrases by negatives (*not, never*), we can express an equal range of opposite meanings. So, to the sequential variations of the verb *go* that were illustrated in the table of tenses, we can add:

I must/must not go.	*I should/should not go.*
I could/could not go.	*I can/cannot go.*
I might/might not go.	*I may/may not go.*

Further, there are such things as 'fringe modals', so called because they are used rarely, that we can trot out to contribute other possibilities: *I ought/ought not to go. Dare I go? I used to go. I had better/better not go. I would rather/rather not go. Need I go?* . . . and so on. Thus you can see that auxiliary verbs allow us to give each of the main verbs in the English language the power to express an additional fifty meanings at least. And with an admirable economy, too.

Will and Shall

Using *will* and *shall* frequently confuses writers. The traditional rule is: *shall* and *should* are used with the first person, singular and plural, *will* and *would* with all the other persons: *I shall, we shall, he will, she will, they will, you will, it will; I should, we should, he would, she would, they would, you would, it would*:

*We **shall** go there first thing tomorrow.*
*They **will** be arriving here this afternoon.*

There are, however, the usual exceptions. We often switch *shall* and *will* around for emphasis: *I will! You shall!* In legal and government circles *shall* is used willy-nilly in the belief that it carries more force and compulsion: *You shall complete all forms before applying; Claimants are warned that false statements shall be subject to severe penalties.*

Because of these inconsistencies – not to mention the tortuous grammatical logic behind the rule – the traditional distinctions are now rarely observed in ordinary speech (odd exceptions being *Shall we dance? You shall die!*) and increasingly ignored in writing (in American English *shall* is hardly ever heard or seen; *will* is standard) to the extent that there is a danger of *shall* disappearing altogether, helped on its way by the use of contractions (*I'll, she'll, he'll, they'll, it'll*), which conveniently can mean either.

May and Might

Of these two auxiliary verbs, always remember that *might* is the past tense form. *May* is correct when an outcome is still unknown. *Might* is right when an *if* is lurking in the background – when we discuss something that was likely or possible on some past occasion:

WRONG	*If it had not been for the paramedics, I **may** have died.* (Did I or not?)
CORRECT	*If it had not been for the paramedics, I **might** have died.* (But we know that I obviously didn't!)
WRONG	*Mr Perlman **might** leave for New York tonight.*
CORRECT	*Mr Perlman **may** leave for New York tonight.*
WRONG	*Mr Perlman **may** have left last night.*
CORRECT	*Mr Perlman **might** have left last night.*

Transitive and Intransitive Verbs

The distinction between the two is that an **intransitive verb** can stand alone (*she **speaks**; I **smile**; the clock **strikes***) while nearly all **transitive verbs** won't work unless they have some sort of relationship (*he **raised** his fist; she **laid** the book on the bed.*) You can readily see that you can't just *raise* – you have to raise *something* – a glass, a shovel, a laugh – *something*. In other words, a transitive verb transfers action from the subject to the object that follows to complete the thought; an intransitive verb doesn't require an object to complete its meaning.

The test is simple. In a sentence such as *They were told the money had vanished without trace*, the verb *had vanished* is intransitive because it can stand alone: *The money had vanished*. End of story. But if we take another sentence: *The disappearance of the money caused big problems*, the verb *caused* is transitive because it transfers the action from the subject (*disappearance of the money*), which makes no sense by itself, to the object (*big problems*). Then it all makes sense.

Some verbs can be both transitive and intransitive. A person can *breathe*, as in *That smoke was awful – at last I can **breathe***! In that sentence, *breathe* is an intransitive verb. But here it is in a dependent, transitive role: *I wish I could **breathe** some confidence into that pupil*.

The way in which intransitive and transitive verbs work isn't merely academic. It isn't unusual for even professional writers to fall into the transitive trap. In fact it's quite usual to read sentences like this one: *The Olympic hope*

tested *positive for drugs.* If this means anything, it means that the athlete tested himself; what it presumably meant was *The Olympic hope **was tested** positive for drugs.* A small lapse, perhaps, but such sloppiness can lead to silliness, as in a newspaper report about a fire in a shop that resulted in 'customers having to evacuate on to the pavement'.

It is worth noting that in the USA the verb *write* can be used transitively, as in *You should write your Congressman* or *I have written my mother several times without a reply.*

This is a carry-over from the English used by early British settlers, when it was standard usage; now it is standard in the USA while British English insists on *You should **write to** your MP.*

Phrasal Verbs

We have seen how auxiliary verbs can form verb phrases. But verb phrases can also incorporate prepositions or adverbs, resulting in a single, and sometimes new, meaning. We call these **phrasal verbs**: *look up, look out, look after, look for, give up, take off, look forward to, fall out, fall down.*

Do you notice an idiomatic feel about these examples? We toss them off all the time and quickly become familiar with their often confounding meanings. If we hear someone say, 'She loves to *run down* her in-laws', we don't jump to the conclusion that she's trying to kill them with her car. The same applies to such expressions as 'Do you think Mrs McDonald will *run up* a pair of curtains for me?'

Thousands of such verb phrases have acquired precise idiomatic meanings that have little or no relationship with the words that comprise them. If a lorry driver is requested to *back up*, we know what is meant because we're looking at the verb *back* followed by the preposition *up*: it means *reverse this way.* But if you were advised not to get a certain person's *back up*, or asked to *back up* a friend in an argument, you have to know or be told the different meanings because you simply can't work them out by any existing system of logic.

Although many phrasal verb constructions add nothing but paradox to the original verbs (*shout down, settle up, go back on, ring up*) and although we are somehow expected to know the difference between *checking the speedometer* and *checking up on your husband,* not even gelignite will stop us from using phrasal verbs.

Verbals and Verb Phrases

By now you should know the difference between **phrasal verbs** and **verb phrases** (which we discussed under *auxiliary verbs*, page 64), but you should also be aware of the difference between **verb phrases** and **verbal phrases**, or **verbals**.

Although derived from verbs, and often looking like verbs, **verbals** (a better name than the old *verbids*) are never used as verbs in a sentence but as nouns, adjectives or adverbs. This probably sounds confusing – but don't give up!

Understanding what verbals are and how they work in a sentence will help you avoid some of the most common mistakes in the whole of grammar.

There are three kinds of verbals: **participles**, **infinitives** and **gerunds**, and you're probably more familiar with them than you realise.

Participles

We have seen, in the discussions of regular and irregular verbs (page 62) and the various tenses (page 64), that two important parts of a verb are the present participle and past participle, as in *go* (basic verb), *going* (present participle) and *gone* (past participle). Both participle forms are used freely as verbs:

*Hilda **was going** away.   William **had gone** to the beach.*

You'll notice that both participles need auxiliary verbs to work as verbs. They can't do their work as verbs on their own (*Hilda **going** away? William **gone** to the beach?*).

But although participles can't work on their own as verbs, they *can* as verbals – functioning as adjectives:

*The company paid us at the **going** rate. (*adjectivally modifies *rate)*

*The herb farm was a **going** concern. (*adjectivally modifies *concern)*

Note that when a participle is used as an adjective it sits next to its noun: ***kneeling** figure, **driving** rain, **forgiven** sinner*. The same applies even when, as a participial phrase, it roves around a sentence:

*The book, **stolen only yesterday from the library**, was on the table. (*adjectivally modifies *book)*

*We gazed at the book, **torn to shreds**. (*adjectivally modifies *book)*

The Dangling or Misplaced Participle

Almost the whole point of acquiring an understanding of participle usage is to learn how to avoid committing that very common grammatical gaffe – the **dangling** or **misplaced participle**. Here are a few examples:

The exhibition features works by fashion photographers executed between 1940 and 1990.

After descending through the clouds, London lay beneath us.

Rolf is found murdered, spurring on his friends to hunt down the drug barons responsible.

We wandered around the markets for several pleasant hours, followed by the 400-odd steps leading to the castle.

These are all examples of dangling, disconnected or missing participial phrases, participles that have lost their way or lost their noun. The result, as you can see, is ambiguity and even hilarity.

Were the photographers actually executed? Did London really descend from the clouds? If Rolf is dead, it's hard to imagine him spurring on anyone, including his friends. Finally, would you care to be followed around on your holiday by 400-odd steps?

All these sentences require rewriting, either to restore the link between noun and modifying participle, or to arrive at a reconstruction in which the meaning is clear:

> *The exhibition features fashion photographers' works executed between 1940 and 1990.*

> *After we descended through the clouds, London lay beneath us.*

> *When Rolf is found murdered, his friends are spurred on to hunt down the drug barons responsible.*

A number of participles are capable of laying well-disguised traps for writers – particularly *including, providing, provided, depending on, following* and *followed*. In our example, the past participle *followed* is not attached to any noun or pronoun in the sentence so it attempts to link itself with the 400-odd steps. The sentence should be reconstructed either by introducing a noun:

> *We spent several pleasant hours wandering around the markets, followed by **the climb** up the 400-odd steps leading to the castle.*

or by replacing the participle with a verb to explain our relationship with the steps:

> *We wandered around the markets for several pleasant hours, then **climbed** the 400-odd steps leading to the castle.*

Use participles by all means, but don't let danglers do you in.

Infinitives

An infinitive is the preposition *to* followed by a verb. Or, put another way, one of the forms of a verb preceded by *to*. Infinitives can function as nouns, adjectives or adverbs:

AS NOUNS   ***To err** is human, **to forgive**, divine.*
           *He admitted that **to go** there made him ill.*
           *Merely **to be watched** made the bird fly away.*

AS ADJECTIVES   *Her desire to confess was welcomed.* (modifies *desire*)
                     It's time to go. (modifies *time*)

AS ADVERBS   *He wrote the article to attract attention to the scandal.* (tells
                     why he wrote the article)
                     *More players are using Japanese pianos to achieve a more
                     rounded tone.* (tells how they are using pianos)

Infinitives can be sly creatures because they sometimes omit the *to: Help John [to]
move that heavy wardrobe; The new legislation should help [to] resolve the problems.*

Misuse of infinitives is not uncommon and occurs in much the same way as
misuse of participles: they become detached from the words they are supposed
to modify:

*Limpets, barnacles and winkles all have devices to survive prolonged periods of
immersion.*

Here the infinitive to survive has attached itself to *devices* instead of the intended
limpets, barnacles and winkles. A grammatically correct construction would be:

*Limpets, barnacles and winkles all have devices enabling them to survive
prolonged periods of immersion.*

Another common mistake is to insert an infinitive inappropriately in a
sentence: *The Green Hills Building Society offers its PEP as an efficient financial
instrument to pursue long-term gains.* On analysis this makes no sense; it suggests
that the PEP will be doing the pursuing, rather than the purchaser of the PEP.
What it should be saying is . . . *an efficient financial instrument with which to pursue
long-term gains.* Or . . . *an efficient financial instrument intended to help you pursue
long-term gains.*

Of all the abuse that the infinitive suffers, however, it is the so-called **split
infinitive** that is the most prevalent and most contentious form.

To boldly go . . . the Split Infinitive

A century or so ago it became a solecism to split an infinitive – that is, to place a
word (usually an adverb) or words between the to and the verb that creates the
infinitive: *to boldly go, to madly love, to properly understand.* The reason for this is
said to stem from the fact that Latin infinitives were one word, not two
(e.g. *amare*, to love) and therefore impossible to split.

Gallons of metaphorical blood have been shed over this legendary
grammatical no-no, most of it on the arid sands of indifference. The position
today is a little clearer, but not much. While many grammarians and writers
recommend allowing splitting where appropriate, others still advise against it,
not merely to conform to the old rule but because they believe an unsplit
infinitive to be more elegant in a well-written sentence and 'unlikely to offend'.

The trouble with many unsplit infinitive constructions is that they can look and sound decidedly inelegant and formal.

Certain Shadow Cabinet members have secured agreement from Mr Hague that they will not have publicly to renounce their views.

Elegant? Surely to most ears to *publicly renounce* would be more euphonic. Or place *publicly* at the end: *to renounce their views publicly*.

Unsplit infinitives can also lead to ambiguity. When Sherlock Holmes told Dr Watson about a blow he received, he took the trouble to say that he 'failed to entirely avoid' it rather than that he 'entirely failed to avoid' it – a rather more painful experience.

On the other hand, some split infinitive constructions are unnecessarily tortuous. While *She was ashamed **to so much as mention** it to her husband* might be considered acceptable to most, *You should begin **to, when you can find the time, re-read** some of the classics* is screaming for a rewrite: *When you can find the time you should begin **to re-read** some of the classics*.

When you find yourself straining to keep your infinitives unsplit, or detect a tendency towards ambiguity, either split the thing or, if this is unacceptable, rewrite the sentence. *The Government is attempting dramatically to increase the number of students in higher education*. What is meant, presumably, is that the proposed increase will be dramatic, but here it looks as though it is the attempt itself that is full of drama. A split infinitive – *to dramatically increase* – in this case would convey the required meaning with precision. And – *ahem!* – with no loss of elegance, either.

To split or to not split, that is the question all writers face. The decision is yours.

Gerunds

Although the gerund is really the most straightforward of the three verbals its usage is for some reason probably the most misunderstood.

We have seen how the present and past participles of verbs are used like adjectives. Similarly, present participles of verbs (ending with *-ing*) can be used as nouns. When they function as nouns we call them **gerunds**. Let's take the verb *go* and its present participle form *going*. It looks a bit unlikely that *going* can ever make it as a noun, but it can:

*We made good **going** on the outward journey.*

*At the President's **going** the whole panoply of state was on display.*

*The **going** at the racetrack is good today.*

***Going** isn't the fun part – it's the **arriving**.*

As with these examples a gerund can stand alone as a noun, functioning as the subject of a sentence (***Running*** *is her favourite sport*) or as an object (*Her favourite sport is* ***running***). But, equally, a gerund can help form a phrase that acts as a noun:

She enjoys ***running through the woods***.

Our neighbour objects to our ***holding parties all night***.

So far, so good. So why do many people have problems with gerunds? The problem arises because many forget that nouns or pronouns that modify gerunds must be possessive. *Mr Phillips did not like Joe smoking in the storeroom* may look about right, but it's not. Mr Phillips does not dislike Joe, but he objects to his smoking in the storeroom. To make this clear we must treat the gerund phrase (the gerund *smoking,* modified by *in the storeroom*) as a noun. That noun (*smoking in the storeroom*) is Joe's problem; it *belongs* to Joe, and therefore we must indicate that Joe possesses it: *Mr Phillips did not like Joe's smoking in the storeroom*.

A good many writers (some of whom should know better) either don't give a damn about this possessive quality of gerunds or simply don't understand what a gerund is.

But writers such as Jane Austen never had a problem with them; *Pride and Prejudice* is in fact an excellent object lesson in their correct use:

> *His* ***accompanying*** *them was a double advantage . . . it was not to be supposed that their absence from Netherfield would prevent Mr Bingley's* ***being*** *there . . . but at last, on Mrs Bennet's* ***leaving*** *them together . . . she caught a glimpse of a gentleman . . . and fearful of its* ***being*** *Mr Darcy, she was directly retreating . . .*

Although many might find Jane Austen's writing style quaintly mannered, few would contest its elegance, nor would they challenge her grammatical skill. She certainly knew how to use the gerund – in every case the synthesised noun phrases are treated as requiring possessives: *His, Mr Bingley's, Mrs Bennet's, its.*

There's a line from George Bernard Shaw's play *Pygmalion* that could help you remember this principle, one that's more often misquoted than not. It is not 'It is impossible for an Englishman to open his mouth without another Englishman despising him'. It is, with the gerund *despising* treated with respect:

> *It is impossible for an Englishman to open his mouth without another Englishman's despising him.*

There will be occasions when the proper use of gerunds will result in awkwardness, and these often lead to their omission:

'. . . one of the book's concerns is the importance of the press bearing witness to apartheid's horrors' (*The Times*). Here, *bearing* is a gerund and should therefore be preceded by a possessive noun – *the press's*. A careful writer would probably find this clumsy; but rather than falling into the genitive trap would reconstruct thus:

'. . . one of the book's concerns is to emphasise how important it is for the press to bear witness to apartheid's horrors'.

The other common error with gerunds is to allow them to become orphans, screaming 'Where's my subject?'

The new kit costs £6.50 and allows the fanbelt to be easily installed without getting covered in grease.

Here the gerund *getting* and its modifier *covered in grease* is an orphan phrase looking for a subject. In its present form the sentence is telling us that the fanbelt will get the benefit of not being covered by grease, not the missing motorist. To make things clear it needs to be rewritten, either with the gerund being attached to a noun (*without the motorist's getting covered in grease*); or, better, a pronoun (*without you getting covered in grease*); or, better still:

The new kit costs £6.50 and allows you to install the fanbelt without getting covered in grease.

Describing Things:
Adjectives and Adverbs

Adjectives define and modify nouns and pronouns while **adverbs** do the same for verbs, adjectives and other adverbs. They are two big families of words, interrelated and often difficult to tell apart, which is why we sometimes misuse or abuse them. Nor are they always amicable; as with the Martins and McCoys or the Montagues and Capulets, a bit of inter-family feuding goes on. It's therefore useful to learn all we can about adjectives and adverbs and how we can use them to better effect.

Adjectives and adverbs: inter-family feuding

Here's a sentence in which the meaning depends almost entirely on adjectives and adverbs:

You're buying the **best**	*adjective*
most	*adverb*
expensive	*adjective*
exciting	*participle used adjectivally*
and **arguably**	*adverb*
highest performance	*adjective/noun*
saloon	*noun used adjectivally*
car	*noun*

There are four kinds of modifier in that vertical sentence: three adjectives, two adverbs, a participle (a verb turned into an *-ing* adjective) and two nouns (*performance, saloon*) that are used in an adjectival way.

Writing a sentence like that is a bit like juggling four balls in the air, but most of us manage to do it tolerably well without too many mishaps.

In the section on *Parts of Speech* we found that adverbs could be identified by their *-ly* endings. That's fine for adverbs with *-ly* endings, but there are many without, and there are also some adjectives with *-ly* endings. It is these that cause confusion:

ADJECTIVES	ADVERBS
*He is a **slow** driver.*	*He drives **slowly**.*
*She is an **early** riser.*	*She always rises **early**.*
*That's very **loud** music.*	*John's playing **loudly**.*

Further confusion is caused by the same word doubling as adjective and adverb:

ADJECTIVE	ADVERB
*It was a **straight** road.*	*Anne drove **straight** home.*
*She took the **late** train.*	*Brian was always **late**.*
*He read a **daily** newspaper.*	*He reads a paper **daily**.*

Obviously we must be wary of adjectives and adverbs that don't play by the rules.

We've all seen road signs that say *GO SLOW!* and perhaps wonder, on reflection, if it ought to say *GO SLOWLY!* It may be that we have a subconscious awareness that *slow* in *SLOW LANE* is an adjective, and that *slowly*, because of its *-ly* suffix, is an adverb, and therefore the sign should warn us to *GO SLOWLY*. That would be grammatically correct but the road engineer would argue the safety benefits of brevity, and few today would dispute the usage. The following adverbial examples, however, are not regarded as good usage:

*She put her lips to his ear and spoke **soft**.*   (**softly**)

*I'm afraid I've let him down **bad**.*   (**badly**)

*That feels **real** great!*   (**really**)

Now that we've been introduced to the two families (with the usual bewilderment following such meetings: who's who, who does what, who gets on with whom), let's subject them to some closer scrutiny.

Adjectives

Here are some adjectives in use to demonstrate how free-ranging they are:

DESCRIBING SIZE   *It was a **huge** marquee.*

DESCRIBING COLOUR   *The carpet was **burgundy**.*

DESCRIBING A QUALITY   *I loved the **plush** armchairs.*

DEFINING QUANTITY   *There were **five** windows.*

DEFINING SPECIFICITY   *Did you see her **Persian** rug?*

. . . and so on.

Adjectives can precede a noun (***huge** marquee*) or follow one (*the man, **wrinkled** with age; he requested that all the journalists **present** should leave*). They can follow a number of verbs: the *be* family – *is, are, was, were, am, being, been, look, seem, become, stay,* etc (*the carpet is **red**, William was **angry***). They can follow pronouns (*did you find anything **useful**? Is she **unhappy**?*). They can 'top and tail' a sentence (***Welsh** choir singing is justly **famous***). A few rare adjectives can stand alone after nouns (*whisky **galore**, apples **aplenty***). Adjectives can also introduce extensive adjectival phrases (*The **highly criticised** 1994 **Jefferson Agricultural Economics** Report came in for another battering*), and of course they can be sprinkled liberally throughout a sentence:

*What impressed her most of all were the **three big ancient green-tinged metallic Burmese religious** statues, the **size of tree trunks**.*

A bit over the top, perhaps, but here we have no fewer than eight adjectives (the adjectival phrase *size of tree trunks* counts as one), each adding something to the description of the statues. It's worth noting that, although no strict rules exist to tell us in which order our adjectives should be, it should follow a common-sense sequence.

For example, you sense immediately that something's wrong here:

*What impressed her most of all were the **Burmese religious three big green-tinged ancient metallic** statues . . .*

An acceptable rule-of-thumb for arranging your adjectives is:

1	**QUANTITY**	*five, a hundred, three-quarters*
2	**EMOTIVE**	*lovely, ugly, rare, formidable*
3	**SIZE**	*large, tiny, immense*
4	**AGE**	*old, brand new, recent*
5	**COLOUR, TEXTURE**	*ochreous, blue, smooth, waxy*
6	**SPECIFICITY**	*Jewish, Japanese, Xeroxed*
7	**PURPOSE**	*dining table, wine glass*

which, followed to the letter, might result in a sentence such as this:

> *The catalogue listed* **two exquisite 23-inch-high 18th-century silver Peruzzi candle** *sticks.*

The sentence packs in a lot of information but because the adjectives follow a sort of logical sequence we can efficiently absorb the facts and probably remember them better, too.

Recognising Adjectives

What makes an adjective? Some are original descriptive words such as good, dark, hot and rough, many of which have their adjectival opposites: bad, fair, cold and smooth. But tens of thousands more began life as nouns and verbs and were changed into adjectives by having various endings tacked on to them. Most are fairly easy to recognise as adjectives:

-able	*notable, fashionable, detestable, desirable*
-al	*natural, mortal, skeletal, oriental*
-ar	*jocular, circular, spectacular, singular*
-ed	*excited, crooked, married, cracked*
-ent	*excellent, indulgent, emergent, persistent*
-esque	*picturesque, Romanesque, statuesque*
-ful	*wonderful, hopeful, forgetful, thoughtful*
-ible	*sensible, comprehensible, horrible, responsible*
-ic	*heroic, psychic, angelic, romantic*
-ical	*periodical, magical, farcical, psychological*
-ish	*liverish, childish, quirkish, British*
-ive	*reflective, massive, defensive, offensive*
-less	*endless, cloudless, hopeless, legless*
-like	*lifelike, ladylike, childlike, warlike*

-ous	*nervous, herbaceous, piteous, officious*
-some	*meddlesome, awesome, loathsome, fearsome*
-worthy	*newsworthy, praiseworthy, seaworthy*

and two adjectival endings to watch for:

| -ly | *lonely, crinkly, sickly, prickly* |
| -y | *earthy, shaky, funny, tacky, kinky* |

These two endings provide a *wildly* (adverb) *bubbly* (adjective) brew of pitfalls and booby traps. Try to separate the adjectives from the adverbs among these examples:

> *truly   idly   gravelly   loyally   woolly   yearly*
> *thankfully   gentlemanly   brazenly   properly   holy*

If you try placing each of the words before a noun (**truly** car, **idly** book, **gravelly** *voice*) you should easily score 100 per cent. The adjectives are *gravelly, woolly, yearly, gentlemanly* and *holy*. The rest are adverbs. It's simple if you remember that adjectives alone qualify nouns and pronouns.

Kinds of Adjective

You must be aware by now that adjectives cover a lot of ground. Nouns are always eager to spring into adjectival roles: *book shop, lawn seed, mineral rights, orange drink*. Adjectives breed fast. While one group of logophiles is enthusiastically creating perfectly serviceable adjectives to describe animal qualities by adding *-like* to nouns (*cat-like, ape-like, bear-like, cattle-like, thrush-like*), another bunch doubles up with Latin-derived versions: *feline, simian, ursine, bovine* and *turdine*. Even pronouns enter the fray to serve as adjectives:

POSSESSIVE ADJECTIVES	*our home, **your** responsibility, **his** car*
DEMONSTRATIVE ADJECTIVES	*this movie, **those** strangers, **that** dog*
RELATIVE ADJECTIVES	*I know **what** matters most. She is the woman **whose** bag was stolen.*
INTERROGATIVE ADJECTIVES	***Whose** idea? **Which** jacket? **What** smell?*
INDEFINITE ADJECTIVES	***any** person, **each** tree, **another** problem*

The adjectival ambitions of pronouns, especially demonstrative pronouns, can cause understandable confusion. 'When is a pronoun a pronoun? When is a pronoun an adjective?' you may ask. Perhaps you should remind yourself of the role of pronouns – they stand in for other nouns:

	This is my diary.	Is **that** the car you bought?
i.e.	This [diary] is my diary.	Is that [car] the car you bought?

But these statements can be expressed differently, by using pronouns as adjectives to modify the nouns:

> **This** diary is mine.   Did you buy **that** car?

You can see here that the diary is described as *mine*, and that the car I'm asking about is described as *that* car. Clearly in these two sentences the pronouns are playing their adjectival roles.

We have already witnessed the dexterity with which verbs, via their participles, can serve as adjectives – how, for example, the basic verb *go* can, through its present participle *going*, spurn its auxiliary verb (*is*, *was*, *will be*, etc) and turn into a verbal participle, an *-ing* adjective: *We were paid at the **going** rate*. Here are some more examples:

VERB PARTICIPLE	**ADJECTIVAL PARTICIPLE**
The kangaroo went **springing** away.	They chased the **springing** kangaroo.
He hated **waking** up in the mornings.	He spent all his **waking** hours eating.
The fire was **roaring** through the woods.	She enjoyed the **roaring** fire.

There are adjectives that can roam around a sentence with considerable freedom, and others that are locked into certain positions. The former are called **central adjectives** and the latter are **peripheral adjectives**:

CENTRAL ADJECTIVE	This is a **new** car.
	This car is **new**.
	New the car may be, but it is too expensive.
PERIPHERAL ADJECTIVE	The man spoke **utter** nonsense.

Here you can see that *utter* cannot be moved to any other position (*The man spoke nonsense that was **utter**?*); its function here as an adjective is specifically to modify the noun *nonsense* (or nouns such as *amazement*, *fool*, *limit*, *bliss* to create well-known clichés).

Another way to look at adjectival positioning is to consider their use as **attributive** (*dark night*, *rank odour*) or **predicative** (*the night is dark, the odour was rank*). Adjectives that can function both attributively and predicatively are usually central adjectives, which can move about. But a few adjectives can be used only in a predicative way. We can write *They were filled with **sheer** terror* but not *They were filled with terror that was **sheer***.

In an earlier example we saw *Welsh* used as an adjective and noted also that *British* could act as an adjective. You could call these **proper adjectives** because they define particular things: ***Chippendale*** *furniture,* ***Shrewsbury*** *cake,* ***Scotch*** *whisky*. Adjectives that describe classes of things (***leafy*** *tree,* ***white*** *house,* ***angry*** *bull*) are of course **common adjectives**.

The E-x-p-a-n-d-i-n-g Adjective

One of the most valuable services that adjectives provide is a range of comparisons. Imagine trying to describe the comparative sizes of several people or things without *small* / *smaller* / *smallest* and *big* / *bigger* / *biggest*. Most adjectives work like that; they can express several comparative qualities: the same, less, least, more, most. With many adjectives we simply add *-er* (*taller, weaker, angrier*) or *-est* (*tallest, weakest, angriest*), but there are some that resist this convenient treatment. Even though Lewis Carroll got away with *curiouser* and *curiouser* we don't try to imitate *prettiest* with *beautifulest* or *brightest* with *colourfulest*. Instead we attach intensifiers such as *more, most, less* and *least*: *the **most** beautiful, the **least** colourful*. An exception is *unkind*; although we don't have *unkinder* as a word, *unkindest* survives from the 16th century in the phrase ***unkindest*** *cut of all*.

There are, as you can see, three comparative forms of adjectives: the basic **descriptive adjective**, the **comparative adjective** (where two entities are compared), and the **superlative adjective** (where three or more entities are compared):

DESCRIPTIVE	COMPARATIVE	SUPERLATIVE
big	*bigger*	*biggest*
loud	*louder*	*loudest*
many	*more*	*most*
few	*fewer*	*fewest*
endearing	*more endearing*	*most endearing*

Using this fairly limited range of comparisons, supplemented by intensifiers such as *quite, incredibly, somewhat* and *very*, we are able to convey mental pictures of almost anything with startling verisimilitude:

> *It was a **big** celebration. It was a **very big** celebration. It was the **biggest** celebration **ever**. It was bigger than any other celebration I've seen. It was **fairly big**. It was **quite big**. It was **incredibly big**. Well, it was a **biggish** celebration . . .*

Watch for **absolute adjectives**, however, such as *dead, square, circular, equal, total, unique, absolute, infinite* and *impossible*. These cannot usually be modified by adverbs; after all if you've expired you can't be *more dead* or *less dead* or *deader*! If something is impossible, that's it. And *unique* means exactly that: one of a kind. So you cannot have something that's *more unique* or *uniquer* than anything else.

Tips on Using Adjectives

- **Be aware of cliché adjectives**. These are what are known as 'limpet adjectives' – they always seem to stick to certain host nouns:

absolute *certainty*	**actual** *facts*	**arid** *desert*
audible *click*	**free** *gift*	**general** *consensus*
drastic *steps*	**full** *inquiry*	**lonely** *isolation*
mutual *cooperation*	**new** *creation*	**long-felt** *want*
past *history*	**personal** *friend*	**safe** *haven*
unexpected *surprise*	**widespread** *concern*	**utmost** *urgency*

- **Practice adjectival economy – 1**. Adjectives allow us to reduce verb phrases to single words without sacrificing meaning:

  BEFORE   *Patricia came to the party wearing a frock **that was embroidered by hand**.*

  AFTER   *Patricia came to the party wearing a **hand-embroidered** frock.*

  BEFORE   *I apologised to Margaret for my behaviour, **which I regretted**.*

  AFTER   *I apologised to Margaret for my **regrettable** behaviour.*

- **Practice adjectival economy – 2**. On the other hand, avoid adjectival tailbacks. Descriptive traffic jams can be self-defeating; by the time the reader has reached the last adjective, the first is probably forgotten. If you find you've written a sentence in which half the words are adjectives, try another construction.

- **Make sure your adjectives are working**. Make sure every adjective you use adds something essential to the sentence: *Her skis sliced through the **powdery white** snow on her **downward** trajectory.* Most of us know that snow is white and believe it is quite difficult to ski uphill, so the adjectives *white* and *downward* are superfluous and can be returned to the dictionary.

Adverbs

As with adjectives, we use adverbs to add information and extra layers of meaning to a statement. Adverbs, however, are far more versatile; while adjectives can modify nouns and pronouns, adverbs are regular Houdinis, qualifying a verb here, boosting an adjective there, appearing in disguise to support another adverb – even bossing phrases and whole sentences about!

MODIFYING A VERB	*The choir sang **sweetly**.*
MODIFYING AN ADJECTIVE	*The choir sang for **almost** three hours.*

MODIFYING ANOTHER ADVERB   *The choir sang **very** sweetly.*

Because of their chameleon-like quality, adverbs, as we've already seen, can easily be confused with adjectives, which leads to incorrect usage. At the risk of being repetitious, it's worth looking again at how adverbs and adjectives disguise themselves:

ADVERBS   *The train arrived **early**.*
                     *Ellen hadn't **long** left home.*

ADJECTIVES   *They caught the **early** train.*
                     *There was a **long** queue at the ticket office.*

You should satisfy yourself now that you know why *early* and *long* are adverbs in the first two sentences (they modify the verbs *arrived* and *left*, telling *when* the train arrived, and *when* Ellen left home) and adjectives in the second two (they modify the nouns *train* and *queue*).

How Adverbs Work

Adverbs are used to supply additional information and meaning to otherwise bald statements. They do this by:

DEFINING MANNER   *They played **happily** together.*

DENOTING PLACE   *They can play over **there**.*

FIXING TIME   *We can all go there **afterwards**.*

CONVEYING EXTENT   *We never seem to get **enough**.*

EXPRESSING FREQUENCY   *We **hardly ever** go there.*

INDICATING VIEWPOINT   *I would never go there, **personally**.*

INDICATING ATTITUDE   ***Curiously**, she has never been there.*

LINKING A PREVIOUS THOUGHT   ***Nevertheless**, I feel we should go.*

MODIFYING A STATEMENT   *It is **possibly** the best solution.*

You'll notice that while some adverbs are stand-alone words such as *there, enough, up, now, here* and *very*, others appear to have been created from existing words. The most common of these are created by adding *-ly* to adjectives (*usually, kindly, romantically, roughly, sincerely, cheaply, quickly*, etc) or by using existing adjectives (*friendly, early, hard, fast*) in an adverbial way. Still other adverbs are created by the suffixes *-wise* (*clockwise, otherwise*); *-wards* (*backwards, homewards*) and *-ways* (*endways, always*).

Positioning Your Adverbs

Another aspect of an adverb's versatility is its mobility in a sentence. While adjectives are fairly restricted in their movement, most adverbs can wriggle in anywhere. The linguist David Crystal has demonstrated this all-purpose quality with devastating effect, using a seven-way sentence:

1.   *Originally, the book must have been bought in the shop.*
2.   *The book originally must have been bought in the shop.*
3.   *The book must originally have been bought in the shop.*
4.   *The book must have originally been bought in the shop.*
5.   *The book must have been originally bought in the shop.*
6.   *The book must have been bought originally in the shop.*
7.   *The book must have been bought in the shop, originally.*

Not all adverbs are so flexible, however. Many feel uncomfortable in certain positions while others, wrongly placed, can convey a different meaning altogether or, at the very least, result in ambiguity. Here's a brief guide to help you position your adverbs for the intended effect:

DEFINING MANNER (adverb usually at the end of sentence)
Not advised – *He rather **erratically** walked.*
Much better – *He walked rather **erratically**.*

DENOTING PLACE (adverb typically at the end of sentence)
Not advised – *Over **there** he threw the stone.*
Much better – *He threw the stone over **there**.*

FIXING TIME (adverb best towards the end of the sentence)
Not advised – *I **recently** saw that movie.*
Much better – *I saw that movie **recently**.*

CONVEYING EXTENT (adverb works best in the middle)
Not advised – *The jar is full, **almost**.*
Much better – *The jar is **almost** full.*

EXPRESSING FREQUENCY (adverb usually not at the beginning)
Not advised – ***Always** he is going to the pub.*
Much better – *He is **always** going to the pub.*

INDICATING VIEWPOINT (adverb best placed at the front of the sentence)
Not advised – *I shouldn't comment, **strictly speaking**.*
Much better – ***Strictly speaking**, I shouldn't comment.*

INDICATING ATTITUDE (adverb most effective at the beginning)
Not advised – *They both decided to **wisely** stay away.*
Much better – ***Wisely**, they both decided to stay away.*

A guide like this is not a rule book, for there are many exceptions. For example, *enough* is an adverb of extent or degree and it is commonly placed in the middle of a sentence: *I've done **enough** work for the day*. But see what happens when *enough* is placed at the beginning and end of sentences: *Do you think we've had **enough**? **Enough** has been said on the subject already*. What has happened is that in both these sentences *enough* has turned into a pronoun! Look at the sentences again and you will see that this is so.

Tips on Using Adverbs

- **Beware of misplaced adverbs**. Always keep adverbs such as *nearly, only, even, quite, just*, etc, as near as possible to the words they're meant to modify. *She **just** went to the store to buy some jeans* appears to mean that, only a short while ago, she went to the store to buy jeans. But what the statement was intended to convey was *She went to the store **just** to buy some jeans*.

- **In particular, be careful about misplacing the adverb 'only'**. This adverb is the cause of many mistakes – and misunderstandings. *Professor Hawking **only** published his book after years of deep thought*. Does this mean that all Professor Hawking ever did, after years of deep thought, was to publish this book? It seems so, but it isn't true. What the sentence intended to convey was *Professor Hawking published his book **only** after years of deep thought*. When using *only*, make sure it is placed next to the word or phrase it modifies – in this case *after years of deep thought* and not *published his book*.

- **Avoid the 'squinting' adverbial modifier**. Ingeniously named 'squinting modifiers' by American grammarians, these are adverbs that can ambiguously attach themselves to different parts of a sentence to give two meanings: *They keep their TV going **often** without a glance all day*. Do they often have their TV on without paying attention to it, or is it on all day during which they often pay no attention to it? *Women who sunbathe **frequently** run the risk of skin disease*. Are we talking here about women running the risk of skin disease because they sunbathe too frequently, or saying that *every* woman who sunbathes runs the risk of skin disease frequently? Make sure your adverb placement conveys *exactly* what you mean.

- **Be wary of starting sentences with adverbs**. *Interestingly*, this advice is given by *The Times* to its journalists (this sentence is an example). 'Such constructions,' advises *The Times*, 'are not forbidden, but sentences starting with adverbs are normally built on sand.'

- **All is not well and good**. Many writers misuse *good* (adjective) and *well* (adverb). When we use *well* to describe the state of someone's health we use it as an adjective (*Do you feel **well**? Judith is quite **well**. Did you hear about that **well**-woman programme?*) but at all other times it is an adverb that describes how something is done: *That horse runs **well**. Your tie goes **well** with that shirt*.

*The medicine is working **well***. Don't use *good* as an adverb (*Elizabeth can cook quite **good***) but always as an adjective (*Elizabeth's cooking can taste **good***).

- **Use accumulated adverbs only for effect**. There are a number of adverbial clichés that should normally be avoided but can sometimes be used for effect and emphasis: *I've told you **over** and **over** again . . . **never**, **never**, go there . . . you go **on** and **on** and* on *. . . **rightly** or **wrongly** . . . I was **madly**, **crazily**, **hopelessly**, **desperately** in love.*

- **'Hopefully' is respectable**. Many writers frown over the adverb *hopefully* when it's used to mean 'let's hope' or 'it is hoped', as in *Hopefully, the team will play better next time*. Purists insist that its traditional meaning is 'full of hope'. However the respectability of the 'new' meaning can be readily defended. It originated from the German *hoffentlich*, meaning 'I hope so', which travelled with German migrants to the USA in the 19th century, there to be translated as – *hopefully*. After a hundred years of standard usage in the USA it re-crossed the Atlantic to Britain where it now firmly resides, although it's still a much misunderstood orphan.

- **Avoid 'neutralising' adverbs**. Such phrases as *faintly repulsive, rather appalling, somewhat threatening* and *slightly lethal* cancel out the intended effect. Such an oxymoronic habit should be *gently stamped out*.

Grammatical Glue:
Determiners, Conjunctions and Prepositions

We have our nouns and pronouns, verbs, adjectives and adjectives – but what now? However much we arrange them they don't seem to make sense, or form proper sentences. Something's missing.

What's missing is the 'grammatical glue' that helps us unite the main action, idea and descriptive words to form clear, cohesive, meaningful statements. This glue consists of relatively small, insignificant words, but don't be fooled. Here are a few of them:

DETERMINERS   *a, the, this, my, which, all*

CONJUNCTIONS   *and, but, or, if, because, like, whereas*

PREPOSITIONS   *with, at, to, for, on, in, around*

INTERJECTIONS   *Ah! Oh! Whew! Wow! Shhh!*

These words and their companions form a mass of grammatical glue with which we construct all our writing and speech. It is simply impossible to communicate without this glue, except perhaps by grunts. If anyone should attempt even a short passage of English without it, the result might look like this:

> *Windows room were wide open, Paris unfolded immense level abyss hollowed itself foot house, built perpendicularly hill. Helene, stretched out long chair, was reading windows.*

It's a bit like listening to particularly bad reception on a radio, or looking at one of those model kits in which all the pieces are present but nothing makes sense until you stick them all together. Here's the paragraph assembled and glued:

> *Both windows of the room were wide open, and Paris unfolded its immense level in the abyss that hollowed itself at the foot of the house, built perpendicularly on the hill. Helene, stretched out on her long chair, was reading at one of the windows.*

Obviously, we should know more about this useful glue.

Determiners

Although they are usually words of fewer than a handful of letters and mean little or nothing by themselves, **determiners** can help add a lot of information when they precede nouns and noun phrases. They can tell us which particular one or which ones, whose, or how many.

Does that description make determiners sound a bit like adjectives? Well, yes. That's why it's important to know at the outset that while both determiners and adjectives modify nouns and pronouns:

- **Determiners** have very little or no meaning in themselves. What is *the*? Or *my*? Or *which*?

- **Adjectives**, even when they stand alone, convey some meaning. We have a fairly good idea of what the words *black, hot, crazy, lovely* and *clever* mean even when they're not modifying nouns or pronouns.

The two most important determiners are *the*, which is known as the **definite article**, and *a* (or *an* when the attached noun begins with a vowel: *an apple, an orchard*), which is called the **indefinite article**. The terms are logical: the definite article *the* is used exclusively to indicate specificity and uniqueness, one of a kind: *the* Prime Minister, *the* Archbishop of Canterbury, *the* criminal class, *the* River Thames. The indefinite article *a* and *an* indicates the general, the non-specific, the collective.

Determiners group themselves under these two headings:

Definite Determiners

DEFINITE ARTICLE   *I will buy **the** car. She will see **the** car.*

POSSESSIVE   *It is now **my** car. He says it's **his** car.*

POSSESSIVE PROPER   *It is **Fred's** car. I say it's **Lynn's** car.*

DEMONSTRATIVE   *I'd like **that** car. He bought **this** car.*

NUMBER   *You have **two** cars? No, just **one** car.*

All these definitive determiners refer to something specific; we are left in no doubt about the identity of the subjects the speaker is referring to. Indefinite determiners, as their name suggests, refer to unspecified, abstract and impersonal entities: *a car* could be one of a million cars.

Indefinite Determiners

INDEFINITE ARTICLE   *I saw **a** great movie. She ate **an** ice cream.*

QUANTIFIER   *She saw **every** movie. I saw **most** movies.*

EXCLAMATORY   ***What** a great movie! It was **such** a good movie!*

INTERROGATIVE   ***Which** movie? **Whose** ticket did you use?*

Using determiners correctly comes easily during childhood and they rarely give us trouble. We know not to use two determiners together: *I will buy **the a** car. Did you see **some several** movies?* We also learn to drop following nouns: *I saw them **all*** [movies]. *I bought **both*** [cars].

The only source of confusion that arises from using determiners is that many look like pronouns:

DETERMINER   *I find **that** word very confusing.*

PRONOUN   *Do you find **that** confusing?*

Not confusing, really, when you remember that pronouns stand for nouns and stand alone. Determiners always precede the noun they modify.

Conjunctions

Conjunctions are very strong glue because their exclusive purpose in life is to join words and groups of words together:

*Gayle plays the piano **and** the harpsichord.*

In that example, *and* is the conjunction that links two parts of the sentence. It is the simplest kind of conjunction in that it is a link or joiner and nothing more; it adds no new information to the sentence. You could turn it right around without altering the meaning one iota:

*Gayle plays the harpsichord **and** the piano.*

But there are other conjunctions that, while gluing a sentence together, can also impart some extra meaning:

*Gayle likes the piano **but** prefers to play the harpsichord.*

You'll note here that now we have not two, but three items of information: Gayle plays the piano, Gayle plays the harpsichord, Gayle prefers the harpsichord to the piano. The conjunction *but* not only links all this information but supplies an element of exception and contrast.

Here are some other conjunctions, grouped according to the meaning they add to the join:

Expressing	Some examples	Typical usage
TIME	*before, after, until, till, since, as soon as, while*	*She'll be here **after** dinner.*
PLACE	*where, wherever*	*I'll find out **where** he comes from.*
CAUSE	*because, as, for*	*I feel ill **because** I ate too much.*
CONDITION	*if, although, unless, or, as long as*	*I'll feel better **if** I lie down.*
COMPARISON	*as, than, like, as if, as though*	*It looks **like** it will rain.*
CONTRAST	*although, while, whereas*	*I'm good at English **while** she's best at maths.*
PURPOSE	*so that, so as to, lest, in order that*	*I must stop **so as to** allow others to speak.*
RESULT	*so, so that, such, that*	*He shouted **so that** they could hear.*

Expressing	Some examples	Typical usage
PREFERENCE	*sooner than, rather than*	*I'd eat worms **rather than** go hungry.*
EXCEPTION	*except, except that, excepting that, but*	*He'd play today, **except that** he's torn a muscle.*

It's quite important to know how conjunctions work because they play such a vital part in the construction of well-made sentences. (Note the conjunction *because* in that sentence. Would *as* or *for* have worked as well?) So let's analyse the three groups of conjunctions and see how they operate in sentences.

Coordinating Conjunctions. These are so called because they coordinate units of equal importance, usually units of the same grammatical class:

NOUNS WITH NOUNS	*Daisy planted roses **and** clematis.* *Will you have tea **or** coffee?*
VERBS WITH VERBS	*The engine coughed **and** slowed to a stop.*
ADJECTIVES WITH ADJECTIVES	*The painting was dark **yet** uplifting.*
ADVERBS WITH ADVERBS	*Slowly **but** surely the tension rose.*
PREPOSITIONAL PHRASES	*Hemingway's* Across the River **and** into the Trees *is a stirring novel.*
TWO EQUAL IDEAS	*It's my rule never to drink by daylight **and** never to refuse a drink after dark.*

The coordinating conjunctions are *for, and, nor, but, or, yet, so* (there's a mnemonic to help you remember them: *FANBOYS*). Sometimes, for effect, they can start a sentence – but still functioning as conjunctions coordinating two thoughts or ideas:

*Victoria told me she'd divorce him. **And** she did.*
*He promised he'd pay the money back. **But** he didn't.*

At the risk of stating the obvious, conjunctions are usually dropped when there are more than two repeated units to be joined:

*Neither wind, rain, hail **nor** snow will stop him.*
*They searched for him everywhere: on the continent, in the Caribbean **and** throughout South America without success.*

Subordinating Conjunctions. As the term implies, a subordinating conjunction joins a subordinate unit to the main part of a sentence:

*They were late **because** of the train derailment.*
*He'll have indigestion **if** he eats all that pie.*
***When** the food arrives, watch Jim dive in.*

You'll notice that even when you turn these sentences about, the role of the subordinating conjunction remains the same:

> **Because** of the train derailment, they were late.
> **If** he eats all that pie he'll have indigestion.
> Watch Jim dive in **when** the food arrives.

You will also see that, unlike coordinating conjunctions, which join equal units or thoughts, subordinating conjunctions link unequal units and thoughts. The key point in the first sentence is that they were late; that is a fact. The reason why they were late, in this context, is of secondary importance.

There are quite a few subordinating conjunctions, including *after, although, as, as if, as long as, as soon as, because, before, how, if, inasmuch as, in order that, since, so that, than, unless, until, till, when, whereas, whether, while, why.*

Correlative Conjunctions. These are used in pairs to join units or thoughts that have a mutual relationship. And, as with coordinating conjunctions, the units they join are of the same grammatical class: nouns and nouns, adverbs and adverbs, and so on:

> **Either** you go **or** I go.
> **Neither** Rick **nor** I is prepared to put up with this.
> He said that the pair were driving **not only** recklessly **but also** without a proper licence.
> **Both** Liberals **and** Tories are likely to protest.

Other common correlatives are *either / or, whether / or* and *whether / if*.

Conjunctions are fairly straightforward although some double as prepositions and can cause confusion. A couple of words in particular need treating with kid gloves: *since* and *like*. Primarily a preposition, *since* expresses an aspect of elapsed time: *Since the storm it's rained only once*. It does much the same as an adverb (*She was here last week but we haven't seen her since*) and as a conjunction: *Since Joe met Sally he hasn't been the same*. The trouble starts when we try to use *since* as a conjunction in place of *because, as* or *for*: *Since they knew their MP quite well, they soon got the council's attention*. This usage plainly leads to ambiguity, as we're not sure that they got the council's attention because they were friendly with their MP, or only since they got to know him quite well.

The word *like* functions legally as a verb, an adjective, an adverb and as a preposition in various usages. But when it overstretches its versatility to try to be a conjunction it falls flat on its face: *You look **like** you've just seen a ghost. **Like** I was saying, we'll win tomorrow*. Use genuine conjunctions (*as if* and *as* in those sentences) and you'll stay out of trouble.

Prepositions

About the only thing many of us know about prepositions is that they should never be used to end a sentence *with*! This old rule is mostly ignored these days;

instead we are encouraged to use our own judgement on how we should close our sentences. Of greater importance is mastering the subtleties of this energetic, enterprising and indispensable group of words.

A **preposition** usually acts as a joining word, like a conjunction, but it also always adds extra information to the words or sentence elements it links:

We went	**to**	the beach.
He rose	**at**	dawn.
She shopped	**for**	some shoes.

From just these three examples you will have noticed that the prepositions have a particular ability to unite two elements in terms of space (*to*), time (*at*) and reason (*for*). To clarify this important point, here are some of the more common prepositions:

SPACE   *above, between, over, into, near, beside, along, amid*

TIME   *after, at, before, during, since, until, past*

OTHERS   *as, for, in, to, but, by, with, without*

COMPLEX   *instead of, other than, in front of, up to, owing to*

We're familiar with all these common words, even though we may not recognise them as prepositions. Here are a few more that we certainly don't think of as prepositions, but they are: *apropos, bar, circa, cum, minus, notwithstanding, per, plus, pro, qua, re, via* and *vis-à-vis*. Let them be a reminder that prepositions pop up just about everywhere!

Prepositions are especially adept at creating phrases that can function adverbially or adjectivally:

ADVERBIAL PHRASE   *The farmer drove **through the gate**.*
                          *She was sitting **in the alcove**.*
                          *Eric vanished **with the cash**.*

ADJECTIVAL PHRASE   *He drove along the road **to the farm**.*
                          *She sat on the seat **in the alcove**.*
                          *Eric was one **of the crooks**.*

In the first three sentences the adverbial phrases are telling us *where* the farmer drove, *where* she sat, and *how* Eric vanished. In each of the other sentences the phrases modify the nouns *road* and *seat* and the pronoun *one*. And to emphasise just how adept prepositions are at creating phrases here's a sentence containing three of them, all functioning as adverbs:

adjective	prep phrase	noun	verb	prep phrase	prep phrase
|	|	|	|	|	|
According	*to the movie*	*the hero*	*fell*	*from the cliffs*	*into the sea.*

Another interesting thing about prepositions is that when you use one in a sentence, it can be replaced only by another preposition:

*She found a mouse **in** the house.*
*She found a mouse **under** the house.*
*She found a mouse **near** the house.*

. . . and so on. You could substitute any number of prepositions – *beside, inside, behind, beneath* – but only with some difficulty could you substitute any other class of words. It could be said that a preposition is like the keystone of an arch: take it away and . . . you're in trouble!

As with other short versatile words that duck and dive among the grammatical classes, some prepositions can be confused with conjunctions and adverbs:

PREPOSITION   *We had a few drinks **before** dinner.*

CONJUNCTION   *I saw that movie **before** Sarah told me about it.*

ADVERB   *I've seen this movie **before**!*

So, to recap: a **preposition** is followed by its linked noun or noun phrase; a **conjunction** links two elements of a sentence, usually clauses; an **adverb** modifies verbs, adjectives and other adverbs. In the examples above, they all tell us that some event took place previously, but in different ways. As with most of grammar, it's horses for courses.

Another common problem with prepositions is that we tend to create long-winded ones when short ones are freely available. In his *The Complete Plain Words*, Sir Ernest Gowers refers to these as **verbose prepositions** and gives a list of them together with simpler variants. Here are a few worth avoiding:

Sir Ernest's Verbose Prepositions

*as a consequence of (**because of**)*
*in the course of (**during**)*
*for the purpose of (**to**)*
*in the neighbourhood of (**about**)*
*in addition to (**besides**)*
*in case of (**if**)*
*subsequent to (**after**)*
*on the grounds that (**because**)*

*in the event of (**if**)*
*in excess of (**more than**)*
*for the reason that (**because**)*
*in the nature of (**like**)*
*with a view to (**to**)*
*prior to (**before**)*
*in order to (**to**)*

Sometimes we're faced with a choice of prepositions and can't decide between them. For example,

Do you	*aim **for***	or	*aim **at**?*
Is it	*disgust **over***	or	*disgust **for**?*
Is it	*superior **than***	or	*superior **to**?*
Are you	*oblivious **to***	or	*oblivious **of**?*

According to the great grammarian Eric Partridge the latter choice in each case represents the correct usage. But this could be disputed, for in many cases the choice can depend on the grammatical construction or the context of the statement. You may *have a dislike for curry dishes* (*dislike* here is a verb) or you may *take a dislike to curry dishes* (*dislike* here is a noun). You may be *possessed of* a sound mind but *possessed with* an uncontrollable desire to scream frequently. Here the choice is an idiomatic one because *possessed* is a verb in both cases. An even greater choice challenge is between *admit to* [a crime] and *admit of* [no human failings], both verbs. Fortunately the latter usage, meaning 'leave room for', is now quite rare. There is, however, general agreement about the following choices:

RECOMMENDED	NOT ADVISED
identical to	*identical with*
affinity between/with	*affinity for/to*
inferior to	*inferior than*
brood over	*brood about*
consequent on	*consequent to*
to die of [something]	*to die from* [something]
different from	*different than*

Idiomatic Prepositions. To those you can add a small collection of common sayings in which the choice of preposition is mostly idiomatic: *an ear for music, they'll stop at nothing, he's a bit off colour, it's all above board, it's beyond our means, go with the flow, go against the grain, you'll be on call, straight from the horse's mouth.*

Using 'onto' and 'on to'. The word *onto* became a preposition by combining *on* and *to*. Once condemned by purists, it is now well established, but that doesn't mean that it is always interchangeable with *on*. *Harry was fined when he drove onto the traffic island*, and *Harry was fined when he drove on the traffic island* convey two different actions. The first sentence suggests that, accidentally or deliberately, Harry's car mounted the traffic island and then presumably stopped or drove off again, whereas the second implies that Harry was having a merry time driving around and around on the traffic island. Nor is *onto* interchangeable with *on to*. *When he'd repaired the puncture he drove on to his destination. Bill immediately passed the information on to the police. Although injured, Zapotek kept right on to the finishing line.* In all three cases *on to* is used adverbially and to use the preposition *onto* would be wrong.

The double preposition 'off of'. This double preposition is fairly common, especially in American English. But the *of* is redundant because any sentence written without it loses none of its intended meaning. Thus *He told the boys to get off of the grass* should be rewritten as *He told the boys to get off the grass*.

Using 'among' and 'between'. Use *between* to connect two persons, objects or ideas: *There is little difference between the two of them. She couldn't tell the difference between either of them. Among* is used in connection with several entities: *There is little difference among all five candidates. He shared the reward among his friends.* Where several things are considered individually, however, *between* might be a better choice: *He divided the reward equally **between** the five of us.* It's also worth remembering that when describing a choice, *between* is followed by *and*, not *or*: *It's a matter of choosing **between** Jane **and** George* (not *Jane **or** George*). And although *amongst* is still widely used, discriminating writers prefer *among*.

Using 'round' for the preposition 'around'. *The lady looked **round**,* or, *The lady looked **around**?* In the unintentionally comic first example there is a temptation to substitute *around*, but that would be a departure from standard British usage; in British English *round* used prepositionally is a linguistic fixture, while *around* is standard in American English. It is now accepted that they are interchangeable, the choice depending on euphony, but the use of *around* to mean 'approximately' is still frowned upon: *They collected **around** £60 for the fund.* Use *about*.

Ending sentences with prepositions. Once the biggest prepositional bogey of them all, today the argument about ending sentences with prepositions hardly merits serious comment. The reason for the objection can be traced back to the influence of Latin grammar on English; in Latin, ending a sentence with a preposition was a non-starter. Generations of scholars upheld the rule, although when such masters of the language as Shakespeare (in *Hamlet*: 'No traveller returns, puzzles the will, / And makes us rather bear those ills we have / Than fly to others that we know not of?') used them unapologetically, a rethink on the positioning of prepositions began. The view today is that unless a prepositional ending sends jarring notes to the ear (*I think we'll find that sour wine is what that barrel is probably full of*), let it stay. A sentence such as *That's the restaurant we ate in* is perfectly acceptable to all but a few pedants. Quite often, extremely clumsy sentences will result from straining to avoid finishing with a preposition – a practice famously lampooned by Winston Churchill when, criticising a civil servant's prose, he commented: 'This is the sort of English *up* with which I shall not put'.

One final but growing problem with prepositions is that the lazier among us tend to drop them altogether: *Defenestration means throwing someone out the window* should of course read *out **of** the window*. It is a habit to be discouraged.

Interjections!

These are exclamatory expressions used to add force and meaning to our speech and writing. Some have been converted from existing words (*Look out! Oh dear! Cheers!*); some have been converted to verbs (to *pooh-pooh*, to *shoo*, to *boo*) or nouns (*boos*, a *boo-boo*). As a family of words – if they are a family – they resist being governed by any rules, except perhaps those of taste. A few examples:

Ah! Aaaah. . . . Aha! Oh! Ooh! Eh? Shhh! Ouch! Pwawh!

Gee! Ha-ha! Ha-ha-ha Te-he-he Hey! Oops! mmm . . .

Phew! Wow! Yuk! Whoops! uh-uh tsk tut-tut psst . . .

Gosh! Blimey! Cheers! Damn! Ugh! Gordon Bennett!

2

PUNCTUATION:

What's the Point?

The dots, strokes and squiggles may appear physically insignificant on a page of print and evanescent in our speech, but without them all would be chaos. Not knowing how to use them correctly can result in even greater chaos. If you were to say to someone:

I hate habitual liars; like you, I find them detestable.

that person would very likely agree. But imagine the reaction should you monkey slightly with the punctuation:

I hate habitual liars like you; I find them detestable.

Old-time teachers were fond of quoting this chestnut: CHARLES I WALKED AND TALKED HALF AN HOUR AFTER HIS HEAD WAS CUT OFF. A stop in the right place (between TALKED and HALF) returns the statement to history as we know it. Another well-known illustration recounts the fate of a warrior in ancient Greece who, on the eve of leaving for a war, consulted the Oracle at Delphi. *Thou shalt go thou shalt return never by war shalt thou perish,* he was told. The overworked Oracle spoke without pause, so the warrior naturally assumed that he meant *Thou shalt go, thou shalt return, never by war shalt thou perish* and departed with great confidence. Unfortunately he was killed in the first battle, never realising that what the Oracle really meant was, *Thou shalt go, thou shalt return never, by war shalt thou perish.*

Less morbid are those grammatical gags and puzzles based on the omission of commas and other marks: *The farmer raised sheep dogs and pigs (The farmer raised sheep, dogs and pigs*); *What is is what is not is not is it not* (*What is, is; what is not, is not; is it not?*). You can clearly see that we need punctuation to help us express and make clear on paper what is intuitively easy with speech.

Two centuries ago, most punctuation took its cues from speech. This was a period when the predominant practice of reading aloud, with its pauses and dramatic stresses, was translated into written punctuation – rhetorical punctuation.

A hundred years on, with increased literacy, the spoken word gave way to the written. The emphasis now was on meaning rather than dramatic effect, and rhetorical (or oratorical) punctuation bowed to a more logical system. Today we have a blend of both: a system capable of conveying force, intonation, urgency, tension, doubt, rhythm and passion while never abandoning its duty to consistency and clarity of meaning.

Punctuation probably reached its zenith in the late 19th century, helping to make sense of the then fashionably interminable sentences. Sentences held together by a dozen or more commas, semicolons, brackets and other marks were commonplace. Nowadays sentences, influenced by the brevity of newspaper style, are shorter, and the need for the complicated division within long sentences has all but disappeared. Commas are freely dropped where the meaning remains unaffected. Stops after abbreviations are disappearing in a general quest for typographic tidiness. The majority of the English-speaking population probably goes through life without ever using, on paper, any punctuation marks other than the comma, dash and full stop.

Don't, however, be led astray by this tolerance. While parsimony in punctuation may be adequate for the majority, it will be of little use to you if you wish to raise your standards of communication. The role of punctuation in writing good English cannot be underestimated.

And take heart! Somerset Maugham couldn't handle commas. Jane Austen got her quotation marks in a twist. George Orwell feared semicolons so much he wrote a novel without any at all. The competition isn't so awesome after all.

The marks that help us punctuate our writing can be divided into three groups:

- **UNITS OF SPACE**: Sentences and paragraphs.

- **DEVICES FOR SEPARATING AND JOINING**: Full stops, commas, semicolons, colons, brackets, dashes and hyphens.

- **SYMBOLS OF MEANING**: Question and exclamation marks, quotation marks, apostrophes, strokes, asterisks, bullets, italics and underlining.

Units of Space are a basic form of punctuation. They separate words, sentences and paragraphs and have already been discussed in the section *Let's Look at Sentences* (page 17). Now let us look at the remaining two groups.

Devices for Separating and Joining

Sentences begin with a Capital letter / To help you make your writing better / Use full stops to mark the end / Of every sentence you have penned. So runs the old schoolteachers' rhyme, and although it seems absurdly basic you'd be surprised by the number of people who either use full stops where they shouldn't or neglect to use them where they should.

The Full Stop

'Punctuation,' *The Times* advises its journalists, 'is . . . not a fireworks display to show off your dashes and gaspers. Remember the first rule: the best punctuation is the full stop.'

The **full stop** (or **stop**, **point** or **period**) is the most emphatic, abrupt and unambiguous of all the punctuation marks. It is used like a knife to cut off a sentence at the required length. The rule is *that* simple: where you place your stop is up to you, but generally it is at the point where a thought is complete. When you are about to embark on another thought, that's the time to think about a full stop. Master this principle and you can then move on to using full stops stylistically, for emphasis:

> *You couldn't get near Harry all day because he was constantly on the prowl, hunched in his greasy pants and dirty sweater, looking mean and taciturn and with his mind no doubt churning with murderous thoughts, for he had announced to too many people in too many places and in too loud a voice that he would kill Evans the instant he clapped eyes on him. And he did.*

That delayed full stop, preceded by mounting tension and followed by the shock conclusion delivered in just three words, helps to convey an almost casual callousness. The two stops serve their purpose perfectly; they make the reader stop and reflect. Here's another passage, this time displaying a variety of punctuation marks. The full stop, however, is easily the most predominant:

> *With intense frustration, Giles grabbed the man, surprising him. 'No you don't!' he yelled hoarsely.*
> *The man recovered, fighting back. Fiercely. Savagely. Hard breathing. Curses. Grunts. The wincing thud of fists. An alarming stream of crimson from Giles's left eye. Pulses racing, they glared at one another, each daring the other to make a move. A car horn in the distance. Shouts.*

That's highly stylised prose, and could be criticised for its over-use of sentence fragments rather than complete sentences. But here the heavy-handed application of the full stop is deliberate, for we can see what the writer is getting at – capturing the harsh punch-punch-punch of a ferocious fist fight.

At the other extreme many writers try to project a stream-of-consciousness effect by chucking out all punctuation, including full stops. One famous example is a passage in James Joyce's *Ulysses* that goes on and on for over a thousand words without so much as a pause. But the author did need a full stop at the end!

Full stops control the length of your sentences, so remember:

- Try to keep sentences variable in length, but generally short.

- Using long sentences doesn't necessarily make you a better writer.

- To use only full stops is as unnatural as walking without using your knee and ankle joints. Consider the use of other punctuation marks.

Full Stops and Abbreviations

Full stops have also been used traditionally to shorten words, names and phrases. The convention was to use full stops for chopped-off words, or abbreviations:

doz. Sat. Oct. Prof. Staffs. lab. Inst. Fahr.

but not for shortenings consisting of the first and last letters of the word, or contractions:

Mr Dr gdn mfr St yd Revd wmk

Thus, by the rules, *per cent.* was considered to be an abbreviation because it chopped off the '*um*' from *per centum*. And while the *Rev. Golightly* required a full stop, the *Revd Golightly* didn't.

All this, however, has gone by the board because, increasingly and remorselessly, the stops are being abandoned in favour of speed, economy and cleaner typography. You will still see stops used for both abbreviations and contractions (for not everyone knows the difference) and sometimes to avoid ambiguity. Here is a sampling of the new order:

Formerly	**Now** (mostly)
6 a.m.	*6am*
e.g.	*eg*
1472 A.D.	*1472 AD*
16 Jan.	*16 Jan*
Wm. Shakespeare	*Wm Shakespeare*
viz.	*viz*
R.S.V.P.	*RSVP*
Capt. Johns, D.F.C.	*Capt Johns, DFC*
U.K.	*UK*

Full stops are still required for certain other functional expressions:

- For money units: *£6.99, $99.89*

- For decimals: *20.86, 33.33%*

- For time (hours and minutes): *11.45am, 23.45 hrs*

The Comma

The **comma** is the most flexible and most versatile of all the punctuation marks. And because it is also the least emphatic mark it is also the most complex and subtle. Not surprisingly, many writers feel a nagging uncertainty about using commas.

A lot of the trouble with commas arises because many people seem to think of them as indicating 'breath pauses'. That may have been the case when the language was more orally inclined, and in much early prose it is common to find commas following speech patterns. Today, however, the placement of commas invariably follows grammatical logic rather than indicating rhetorical pauses:

Every year over the British Isles, half a million meteorites enter the atmosphere.

You can hear the lecturer intoning that, can't you – with a dramatic pause before announcing 'half a million meteorites enter the atmosphere.' Try it. But when you write it as a sentence you'll find that the comma is redundant:

Every year over the British Isles half a million meteorites enter the atmosphere.

Even so, wrong comma placement is exceedingly common. Here's a typical offender in *The Economist*: 'But the ferry's high cost and steadily declining number of passengers, cannot be cured by government subsidy.' Such a sentence needs no commas at all.

Most writing today requires commas that serve a logical purpose, usually to separate different thoughts or nuances of thought within sentences:

The snapshot with its naively honest images revolutionised our way of seeing the world.

Because this sentence would make essentially the same statement if it were written as *The snapshot revolutionised our way of seeing the world*, the incidental clause *with its naively honest images* is a relevant but separate thought and should be separated from the main thrust of the statement by commas:

The snapshot, with its naively honest images, revolutionised our way of seeing the world.

You'll notice that two commas are required for this job; a common mistake is to omit the second enclosing comma.

Functions of the Comma

SETTING APART NAMES AND PERSONS

Are you meeting him tomorrow, John?
Listen, Joyce, I've had enough.
And that, ladies and gentlemen, is that.

ITEMISING WORDS

Please place all towels, costumes, clothing and valuables in the lockers provided.

ITEMISING WORD GROUPS

Please place any articles of clothing, swimming and sporting equipment, personal belongings, but not money and jewellery, in the lockers.

ENCLOSING ADDITIONAL THOUGHTS OR QUALIFICATIONS

The occasion was, on the whole, conducted with considerable dignity.
The judges thought it was, arguably, one of his finest novels.

SETTING APART INTERJECTIONS

Look, I've had enough!
Blimey, isn't the beach crowded!

BEFORE DIRECT SPEECH

Jill turned abruptly and said, 'If that's the way you feel, then go home!'

INTRODUCING QUESTIONS

You'll be going soon, won't you?
She's marrying James tomorrow, isn't she?

EMPHASISING POINTS OF VIEW

Naturally, I'll look after the car.
Of course, she fully deserves it.

SETTING OFF COMPARATIVE OR CONTRASTING STATEMENTS

The taller they are, the farther they fall.
The more he said he adored Maisie, the less she cared.

REINFORCING STATEMENTS

She's ill because she won't eat, that's why!
It'll come right in the end, I'm sure.

AFTER INTRODUCTORY WORDS

Sausages, which are far from fat-free, pose a problem for dieters

Omitting the opening comma required to separate a subordinate clause (*which are far from fat-free*) from the main clause (*Sausages . . . pose a problem for dieters*) is a common mistake and one that usually leads to ambiguity. With the commas correctly in place, as in our example, we are in no doubt that the description 'far from fat-free' applies to all sausages. But omit that opening comma and a different meaning can be conveyed: *Sausages which are far from fat-free, pose a problem for dieters.*

Now the statement is saying that only those sausages that are 'far from fat-free' are a problem. But if that is what is actually meant, the remaining comma is redundant.

Here's another example, from *The Times*:

> *Overnight fans had painted messages on the road outside his home . . . 'We love you Frank'.*

Overnight fans? Are these a different breed from ordinary fans? Obviously a comma after the separate thought 'Overnight' is required to make things clear.

Using commas appropriately also includes not over-using them:

> *It is, curiously, surprising when, say, you hear your name announced in a foreign language, or even in a strange accent.*

Although grammatically correct that sentence seems to be hedged with *ifs*, *buts*, *maybes* and pontifications. Can it be rewritten in a more direct style, while still conveying the several shades of meaning?

> *Curiously, it is surprising when, for example, you hear your name announced in a foreign language or even in a strange accent.*

The sentence, less two commas, is now a little more direct. Here's another example of 'comma bloat' which can be rewritten without using any commas at all.

> *Mr Burkitt had not, previously, met the plaintiff, except when, in 1974, he had, unexpectedly, found himself in Paris.*

It's worth looking a little closer at comma-reduction. Take this simple sentence:

A   *My hobby, trainspotting, is, to many, a bit of a joke.*
B   *My hobby, trainspotting, is to many, a bit of a joke.*
C   *My hobby, trainspotting, is to many a bit of a joke.*
D   *My hobby trainspotting, is to many a bit of a joke.*
E   *My hobby trainspotting is to many a bit of a joke.*

Pedants might claim that all these sentences differ in nuances of meaning, but to the average reader they all mean the same thing. So we are left with choosing which one we would use to express our thought clearly, economically and elegantly. Which version would you choose? (Our choice would be C, but it is our personal preference and not one we would wish to impose on others).

To some extent the apt use of commas is an acquired skill – but certainly one worth pursuing. Merely scanning a sentence for sense and clarity will usually tell you. The writer of the following sentence was either afraid of commas or intent on speed of delivery:

> *The land is I believe owned by the City Council.*

Most of us would place commas after *is* and *believe*, because the phrase 'I believe' is an important qualifier and needs to be highlighted from the main statement, *The land is . . . owned by the City Council* which, by itself, may or may not be true.

Using Commas with Adjectives

See if you can work out, in these two sentences, why one has the adjectives separated by commas, and the other does not:

The night resounded with a loud, chilling, persistent ringing.
It was a large brick Victorian mansion.

The reasons are embodied in two seemingly simple rules worth remembering:

- Where the adjectives (or other modifiers) define *separate* attributes (*loud, chilling, persistent*), they are best separated by commas.

- Where the adjectives work together to create a *single* image (*large, brick, Victorian*), the commas are best omitted.

Two seemingly simple rules, but they can be tricky to apply. Sometimes you may be led into ambiguity and have to resort to common sense:

Myra was a pretty smart young woman.
Myra was a pretty, smart young woman.

Well, does the writer mean that Myra was pretty and smart, or just very smart?

Using Commas with Adverbs and Adverbial Phrases

It is customary to use commas to enclose modifying adverbs and adverbial phrases such as *however, indeed, nevertheless, in fact, needless to say, no doubt, incidentally, anyway, for example, on the contrary, of course* and *as we have seen*:

*You are, **nevertheless**, guilty of the first charge.*

Increasingly, however, [notice the enclosing commas!] such commas are dropped when the meaning remains clear without them:

You are nevertheless guilty of the first charge.

But be alert for ambiguity: *The hospital informed us that both victims were, happily, recovering.* Remove the enclosing commas either side of *happily* and you'd give the impression that the victims were not only recovering but having the time of their lives! And see, in the next example, reporting on a parliamentary debate about field sports, how vital a pair of enclosing commas can be:

Mr Douglas Hogg said that he had shot, himself, as a small boy.

Commas are also needed for sentences beginning with adverbs:

Curiously, *the two cousins had never met.*
Ironically, *they discovered they were sisters.*
Looking scared, *Peter peered out of the window.*

and also for sentences containing adverbial clauses:

Peter, **not usually given to heroics,** *smartly lowered his head.*

The Oxford, or Final Comma

The Times advises its journalists to 'avoid the so-called Oxford comma: *x, y and z* and not *x, y, and z'*. What this means is that:

Martin spoke to Edith, Lesley, Bunty and Samantha.

is preferred to

Martin spoke to Edith, Lesley, Bunty, and Samantha.

Sound advice; a final comma before *and* in a list is now outmoded – except in the USA – unless there is the possibility of ambiguity:

The colours of the flag are red, green and gold in stripes.

What does this mean? Red and green, with gold stripes? Red, green and gold stripes? Red, with green and gold stripes? What the sentence needs is a comma for clarity. If, as intended, the statement was meant to describe a flag consisting of just three bold stripes, it should say so: *The colours of the flag are red, green, and gold, in stripes.*

Using Commas to Parenthesise

One of the most interesting, but also perhaps the most contentious, uses of commas is to parenthesise (or bracket) relevant but not essential matter from the main part of the sentence:

The wild hyacinths (which are now at the height of their season) tint the woods with a pale blue mist.

The essential message here is *The wild hyacinths tint the woods with a pale blue mist.* But then we've had a further thought – *which are now at the height of their season* – which we'd like to include in the same sentence. Sometimes we enclose such additions in parentheses (brackets) as above, but mostly we use a pair of far more convenient and less disruptive commas:

The wild hyacinths, which are now at the height of their season, tint the woods with a pale blue mist.

Now that we've seen how commas are used to isolate subordinate statements, what are these two commas doing in this sentence?

The two lead actors, who appear in 'Grease', won their respective roles after many gruelling years in musicals.

The two enclosing commas here are telling us that *who appear in 'Grease'* is non-essential information. But if you rewrite the sentence without that phrase it doesn't make sense: we don't know who the lead actors are or what they are doing.

In fact *who appear in 'Grease'* is a defining or restrictive phrase – one that identifies, modifies or qualifies its subject. It is essential, not non-essential, information. So the sentence should read:

The two lead actors who appear in 'Grease' won their respective roles after many gruelling years in musicals.

To summarise:

- Where a phrase or clause does not define or qualify the subject, indicate that it is non-essential matter by isolating it with a pair of commas.

- Where a phrase or clause defines or qualifies the subject, weld it to the subject by omitting the commas.

The Semicolon

There is something about semicolons that can raise the blood pressure. The writer George Orwell was so against them that he wrote one of his novels, *Coming Up For Air* (1939), without a single semicolon in it. Actually, three crept in, only to be removed in later editions. George Bernard Shaw complained of T. E. Lawrence that while he threw colons about like a madman he hardly used semicolons at all. More recently, Martin Amis, in his novel *Money*, reportedly used just one. Indeed, the heat provoked by the anti-semicolonists some years ago led to fears that the mark would become an endangered species, and a Society for the Preservation of the Semicolon was formed.

A **semicolon** is a pause somewhere between a strong comma and a weak full stop. And despite its dismissal by many writers and teachers it has a number of practical grammatical and stylistic functions:

- **To join words, word groups and sentences**. Occasionally we find ourselves writing a long sentence with too many connecting words such as *and*, *but* and *also*, with the danger of getting into an impossible tangle:

The history of the semicolon and colon is one of confusion because there are no precise rules governing their use and, furthermore, many writers would argue that both marks are really stylistic rather than parenthetical devices, and can in any case be easily replaced by commas, stops and dashes, and there the argument rests.

There's nothing grammatically wrong with that, but it is unwieldy and unappealing to both eye and mind. Many writers would, without hesitation, recast it as two or more separate sentences:

The history of the semicolon and colon is one of confusion. There are no precise rules governing their use. Many writers argue that both marks are really stylistic rather than parenthetical devices which can easily be replaced by commas, stops and dashes. And there the argument rests.

We have previously seen how the judicious use of full stops to achieve shorter sentences can aid understanding, and that is certainly the case here. But some writers, feeling that the original long sentence is, after all, about a single subject and should therefore be kept as a whole and not split apart, would turn to the semicolon to achieve unity of thought without making things hard for the reader:

The history of the semicolon and colon is one of confusion; there are no precise rules governing their use; many writers argue that both marks are really stylistic rather than parenthetical devices and that they can easily be replaced by commas, stops and dashes; and there the argument rests.

- **To separate word groups already containing commas**. Any sentence that is essentially a list should be crystal clear and easily read. Most 'sentence lists' adequately separate the items with commas, but sometimes the items themselves are groups containing commas and require semicolons for clarity. These two examples illustrate just how handy semicolons can be:

Those present included Mr and Mrs Allison, their daughters Sarah, Megan and Sue; the Smith twins; Reg and Paul Watson; Joyce, Helen and Bill Hobson; etc.

The line-up consisted of Bix Beiderbecke, cornet; Al Grande, trombone; George Johnson, tenor sax; Bob Gillette, banjo; Dick Voynow, piano, and Vic Moore on drums.

- **To restore order to sentences suffering from 'comma riot'**. Here's a longish but reasonably accomplished sentence spoiled by 'comma riot':

His main aims in life, according to Wilma, were to achieve financial independence, to be powerfully attractive, not only to women but in particular to rich ladies, to eat and drink freely without putting on weight, to remain fit, vital and young-looking beyond his eightieth birthday and, last but not least, to not only read, but fully understand, Professor Stephen Hawking's 'A Brief History of Time'.

Many professional writers would defend this sentence, despite its eleven commas. But others, perhaps more concerned with clarity than rhythm, would suggest that some of the thoughts at least should be separated by the longer pauses provided by semicolons:

His main aims in life, according to Wilma, were to achieve financial independence; to be powerfully attractive, not only to women but in particular to rich ladies; to eat and drink freely without putting on weight; to remain fit, vital and young-looking beyond his eightieth birthday and, last but not least, to not only read but fully understand Professor Stephen Hawking's 'A Brief History of Time'.

- **To provide pauses before certain adverbs**. There are certain adverbs and conjunctions that require a preceding pause, but one longer and stronger than that provided by a comma. Look at this example:

WITH A COMMA   *It was a beautiful car, moreover it was economical to run.*

WITH A SEMICOLON   *It was a beautiful car; moreover it was economical to run.*

You can see and *hear* that need for a substantial pause before *moreover*, can't you?

A comma is wrong on both grammatical and rhetorical counts. Here's another example; read it and note your instinctive pause before *nevertheless*:

Joe claimed he'd beaten the bookies on every race; nevertheless he was broke as usual when he left the track.

Watch out for *therefore, however, besides, also, moreover, furthermore, hence, consequently* and *subsequently*; in many constructions they will require a preceding semicolon.

- **To induce a mild shock or make a joke**. Semicolons can help the writer emphasise contrast and incongruity. For a woman to remark,

I thought his wife was lovely but that her dress was in poor taste.

would be fairly pedestrian and certainly lacking in feminine acuity. Here's what she might wish she'd said with the tart use of a mental semicolon:

I loved his wife; pity about the frock.

A semicolon is adroitly used by Henry Thoreau in *Walden*, although in a more self-deprecating vein:

I had more visitors while I lived in the woods than at any other period in my life; I mean that I had some.

The Colon

The legendary grammarian Henry Fowler defined the function of the **colon** as 'delivering the goods that have been invoiced in the preceding words'. More matter-of-factly, the colon acts as a pointing finger, as if to warn the reader about a statement ahead: 'Wait for it . . . here it comes!'

Although under threat from the dash, the colon is a versatile workhorse, and many colon-scoffers are silenced when confronted with the range of its functions:

- **To introduce a list**. This is probably how colons are most commonly used:

  Detective Stevens entered and took it all in: the body, the still smouldering mattress, the cigarette butts on the floor . . .

- **To present a conclusion**.

  There was one very obvious reason for Ernest's failure to keep the job: his right hand never knew what his left was doing.

- **To present an explanation or example**.

  There are three reasons why Lainston House near Winchester is an outstanding restaurant: excellent cuisine, beautifully restored interiors, and super-attentive staff.

- **To introduce a quotation or indirect speech**.

  Gradually, one by one, the words came back to me: 'And we forget because we must and not because we will.'

  The Mayor strode to the platform, opened his notes and glared at the assembly: 'You have not come here for nothing,' he growled.

- **As a substitute for a conjunction**. In this example, the writer preferred the punchier colon to a choice of conjunctions such as *and* or *but*:

  Rodriguez felled him with a dazzling left hook that came out of nowhere: Hayman did not get up.

- **To introduce questions**.

  The essential issue is simply this: did she or did she not seduce Sir Timothy in the stable block?

- **To introduce subtitles**.

  Gilbert White: Observer in God's Little Acre.
  Men at War: An Introduction to Chess.

- **To link contrasting statements**. In this role the colon shares with the semicolon the ability to administer surprise and shock. The choice is a matter of taste:

  Her love affair with her son's school, its history, its achievements, its famous alumni and its crumbling charm would have endured for ever but for one minor consideration: the £12,000 yearly fees.

- **Other sundry uses**.
  If you ever read a stageplay, you'll often find it laid out something like this:

  GEORGE: *You've said enough –*
  ANNA: *I haven't even started!*
  GEORGE: *Enough! D'you hear me!*

  Then there is the 'biblical' colon, separating chapter and verse (*Ecclesiastes 3:12*); the mathematical colon used to express ratios (*Male athletes outnumber females by 3:2*); and the time colon (*The train departs at 12:45*). In the USA it is customary to use colons to open a letter: *Dear Anna: I do look forward to seeing you soon . . .*

  It's worth remembering that:

  —The difference between a colon and a semicolon is not a difference in weight or force; the two marks are mostly used for quite different purposes.

  —Except in the case of introducing subtitles (*see* above), a colon is not followed by a capital letter unless the word is a proper noun: *Emma, Ford Motor Co*, etc.

  —Don't use colons where they are not needed, as in: *The man was amazing and was able to play: the piano, violin, double bass, trombone, clarinet, harp and drums.* The colon is clearly redundant.

Brackets and Parentheses

In our discussion of commas we saw how material could be set apart or parenthesised (the term *parenthesis*, via Latin and Greek, means 'an insertion besides') by enclosing it between two commas.

The sentence above is just such an example, except that instead of using a pair of commas we have used a pair of **brackets** or, more correctly, **parentheses** or **round ( ) brackets**. The function of square brackets is discussed later.

If you look at that first sentence again, you will see that the brackets serve to set apart relevant matter which could, if you wished to be ruthless, be dropped altogether.

The bracket's embrace is seductive and extremely adaptable, as the following catalogue of examples of usage will demonstrate:

ADDING INFORMATION	*One of the earliest dictionaries is that of Elisha Coles (London, 1685).*
OFFERING EXPLANATION	*Unable to follow the instructions in French and after nothing but trouble she returned the car (a Renault saloon) to the garage.*
AFTERTHOUGHT	*Travel by car, choose the cross-channel route that offers best value for money, and look out for bargains (like newspaper tokens. Last summer we scored a free hotel in France).*
CLARIFICATION	*The directive stated quite clearly (page 396, second paragraph) that the department would be closed from March 1.*
COMMENT	*Cruelty to animals (I noted a scene in which a donkey's tail was tied to a post, and another where a tin can with a lit firecracker in it was attached to a dog's tail) was a fairly common sight in children's comic papers in the 1920s.*
ILLUSTRATION	*The candidate spent far too long discussing irrelevancies (20 minutes on the price of footwear; another ten on tax havens) with the inevitable result that most of us walked out.*
TO EXPRESS AN ASIDE	*She claims to be 35 (and pigs can fly).*
TO INDICATE OPTIONS	*Your document(s) will be returned in due course.*

There is an important grammatical difference between parenthesising material within commas and within brackets. Generally, material enclosed by commas is still very much part of the sentence and should observe the grammatical conventions of that sentence. Bracketed material, on the other hand, is rather more distanced from the sentence into which it is inserted, and can assume its own punctuation.

The Square Bracket

The square bracket has an entirely different function from that of parentheses: words enclosed within them are not intended to be part of a sentence, but as an editorial or authorial interjection:

It was a matter of opinion that if offered the position, he [Professor Brandmeyer] would most likely refuse it on moral grounds.

That sentence came at the end of a very long paragraph; the professor's name had been mentioned at the beginning, but other names and much discussion followed so that the late reference to he was in danger of being misunderstood. The editor therefore inserted the name [*Professor Brandmeyer*] in square brackets as a reminder and also to indicate that the intervention was the editor's and not the author's.

One of the most common uses of square brackets is to enclose the adverb *sic* (from the Latin *sicut*, meaning 'just as') to indicate that incorrect or doubtful matter is quoted exactly from the original:

> *Pink and yellow concubines [sic] climbed in great profusion up the trellis.*
> *Miss Patricia Wall Wall [sic] with her fiance Mr Gerald Kleeman.*

The second example was a caption under a photograph of the newly engaged couple; *The Times* wanted to make sure that readers understood that 'Wall Wall' really was the young lady's surname and not a misprint.

The Dash

Although the dash is a much maligned mark – especially by punctuation purists who decry its substitution for the colon – it has in recent times attracted a growing band of defenders. 'It's the most exciting and dramatic punctuation mark of them all!' claim some.

Primarily used to interrupt or extend a sentence, the dash is an extraordinarily versatile mark when used creatively. It is a bit of a larrikin with a disdain for rules and thus can be a lot of fun in the often po-faced world of punctuation. But here are some of the more respectable ways in which the dash will be found useful:

LINKING DEVICE	*Mrs Sims had four daughters – Poppy, Iris, Pansy and Petal.*
AS A PAUSE	*Everyone expected the poet to be controversial – but not to the extent of swearing at the chairwoman and falling off the stage.*
CUEING A SURPRISE	*The adhesive gave way, the beard came adrift and Santa Claus was revealed as – Aunt Clara!*
NOTING AN EXCEPTION	*A straight line is the shortest distance between two points – when you're sober.*
INDICATING HESITATION	*'There will be, of course, er– a small charge, because – well, er – '*
SEPARATING LISTS	*She assembled all the ingredients – flour, sugar, eggs, salt, lard and raisins – and started on the pudding.*

AFTERTHOUGHTS   *They babbled on, delighted at sighting the rare*
                                     parakeet – I didn't see so much as a feather.

Where the dash is used parenthetically – to enclose matter in much the same way as with brackets or commas – don't forget the second dash. It's an omission that trips many people – even the grammar authority G. V. Carey in his *Mind The Stop* (1939):

> *No wonder that in some matters the dash has fallen into disrepute; but I still maintain that, if kept in its place – and I make one here for luck, it is a very useful stop.*

The sentence calls for a dash, not a comma, after luck. It's a lesson to us all – not to be slapdash with the dash!

The Hyphen

Although both are little horizontal lines – albeit one a shade shorter than the other – hyphens and dashes are not related. A hyphen joins two or more words together, while a dash keeps them apart. What they do have in common is that they are inclined to be overused and abused.

The rules governing the use of hyphens, such as they are, are about the most contradictory and volatile in grammar. And yet their purpose is simple: to help us construct words to clarify meaning and avoid ambiguity. Take these two similar newspaper headlines:

MAN EATING TIGER SEEN NEAR MOTORWAY.

MAN-EATING TIGER SEEN NEAR MOTORWAY.

The first headline suggests that a hungry gourmet has decided to barbecue some choice jungle beast near a motorway, while the second could prove fatal should you be carelessly wandering along the hard shoulder. A hyphen has made all the difference.

Hyphens enable us to create useful compounds by uniting two or more associated words. Sometimes the marriage is permanent. A *book seller* became a *book-seller* and is now a *bookseller*. *Life* got engaged to *like* to become *life-like*; they are now commonly married as *lifelike*. Many other common words began their careers as two separate words before being temporarily linked by hyphens: *earring, lampshade, postgraduate, prehistoric, seaside, today, washbowl*.

Many hyphenated couplings exist primarily to obviate confusion. Have you ever seen a stick walking? Or shuddered at an ear splitting, or witnessed a room changing? Obviously not, but just in case of a misunderstanding we hyphenate: *walking-stick, ear-splitting, changing-room*.

Then there are hyphenated couples never destined to become permanent partners because of 'letter collision', which is visually disconcerting: *shell-like* (not *shelllike*); *semi-illiterate* (not *semiilliterate*); *de-ice* (not *deice*); *co-wrote* (not *cowrote*) – although we accept such unhyphenated words as *cooperative* and *coordination*.

Generally, hyphens are used after the prefixes *ex-* (*ex-cop*); *non-* (*non-starter*) and *self-* (*self-employed*). They are not usually required after *anti-* (*antifreeze*); *counter-* (*counterweight*); *co-* (*coreligionist*); *neo-* (*neoclassicism*); *pre-* (*prehensile*); and *un-* (*unconditional*). But there are some exceptions: *co-respondent* (to distinguish it from a somewhat misspelt *correspondent*!) and *re-creation* (not *recreation*).

Wordbreaks and Linebreaks

Aside from helping to construct compound words, hyphens enable us to split words at the end of lines. Normally, words are split according to **syllabication** (or syl-lab-i-ca-tion) which follows the logic of word construction. But it is apparent that a lot of modern typesetting follows no such rules and words are likely to be split on rather more *laissez-faire* principles, giving rise to such unlikely compounds as *fig-urine*, *the-ories*, *should-er*, *condom-inium*, *physiothe-rapists*, *hor-semen*, and *mans-laughter*.

Hassle-free Hyphenating

Unfortunately the business of hyphenating is never likely to be completely hassle-free. The reason is that hyphenated and unhyphenated compound words are being created all the time and it can take a decade before there is anything like universal agreement on the final fixed form of a word. Most professional writers, while conscientious about hyphen correctness, take the advice of Sir Ernest Gowers who, in his *The Complete Plain Words*, wrote, 'If you take hyphens seriously you will surely go mad'.

Meanwhile here is a guide to many hyphenated words and names likely to crop up in everyday usage:

accident-prone	bird-brain
acid-free	black-eyed
age-old	bleary-eyed
air-conditioning	blood-alcohol
air-cooled	blood-red
air-dried	bloody-nosed
all-American	blue-pencil
all-clear	bone-shaking
ankle-deep	break-even
anti-abortion	break-in
armour-piercing	breast-fed
attorney-at-law	brick-built
awe-inspiring	bright-eyed
bandy-legged	broad-beamed
billet-doux	broken-down

brother-in-law
bull's-eye
burnt-out
by-and-by
call-up
cane-backed
card-index
carpet-sweeping
catch-as-catch-can
cat-o'-nine-tails
cat's-eye
cattle-raising
check-in
child-proof
city-bred
clear-cut
clean-shaven
clear-eyed
clip-clop
close-knit
closed-circuit
Coca-Cola
cold-shoulder
come-on
co-op
copper-bottomed
court-martial
co-worker
cross-channel
cross-country
cross-dressing
cross-examine
cross-purposes
crow's-foot
custom-tailored
cut-throat
daddy-longlegs
daughter-in-law
deaf-and-dumb
deep-freeze
deep-sea fishing
dew-laden
die-cut
dog-eared
do-it-yourself

door-to-door
double-barrel
double-cross
double-dealing
double-decker
double-entendre
double-park
double-quick
double-up
Dow-Jones
drip-dry
drive-in
drug-addicted
duck-billed
dust-laden
ear-splitting
earth-shaking
east-northeast, etc
even-numbered
even-tempered
ever-present
ever-ready
ex-husband
ex-serviceman
extra-large
face-saving
fact-finding
fair-skinned
far-distant
fat-free
father-in-law
feeble-bodied
fever-stricken
fill-in
fine-drawn
fire-resistant
five-ply
flag-raising
flat-bottomed
flea-bitten
fleet-footed
flip-flop
fly-by-night
follow-on
foot-and-mouth disease

fore-edge
forget-me-not
four-letter word
four-o'clock (five-o'clock, etc)
four-part (five-part, etc)
free-spoken
front-end
full-grown
full-strength
fur-lined
get-at-able
get-together
give-and-take
go-ahead
go-between
go-getter
God-fearing
gold-plated
good-for-nothing
good-looking
grass-roots
grey-haired
gun-shy
habit-forming
half-and-half
half-alive
half-baked
half-breed
half-hourly
half-mast
hard-of-hearing
hard-on
half-true
half-yearly
hand-built
hand-in-hand
hand-knit
hand-me-down
hand-out
hand-picked
hands-off
hard-and-fast
hard-hat
hard-hit
hard-won

head-on
heart-throb
heart-to-heart
heaven-sent
helter-skelter
high-class
high-minded
higgledy-piggledy
high-spirited
high-tech
hit-and-miss
hit-and-run
hog-tie
hollow-eyed
home-baked
horse-racing
hot-blooded
how-do-you-do
ice-cold
ice-cooled
ice-cream cone / soda (*but* ice cream)
ill-advised
ill-fated
ill-timed
ill-treat
ill-use
in-flight
infra-red
Irish-born (British-born, American-
   born, etc)
ivy-covered
jack-of-all-trades
jack-o'-lantern
jerry-built
jet-propelled
jewel-studded
jiggery-pokery
Johnny-come-lately
jump-start
jury-rigged
kiln-dry
king-size
kiss-and-tell
knee-brace
knee-deep

knee-high
knock-for-knock
knock-kneed
know-all
know-how
know-it-all
lace-edged
lady-in-waiting
land-based
Land-Rover
large-scale
late-lamented
Latter-day Saint
lay-by
lean-to
left-bank
left-handed
life-size
light-footed
light-headed
light-year
like-minded
lily-white
little-known
little-used
long-awaited
long-distance
long-handled
long-legged
long-lived
loose-limbed
love-lies-bleeding
low-key
low-lying
mail-order
make-believe
man-hours
man-of-war
many-coloured
mare's-nest
mass-produced
May-day
mean-spirited
micro-organism
middle-aged

middle-of-the-road
mid-Victorian (mid-forties, etc)
mile-long
mother-in-law
mother-of-pearl
motor-driven
mouth-filling
mud-splashed
muu-muu
name-dropping
near-miss
near-sighted
needle-sharp
ne'er-do-well
never-ending
never-never
new-mown
nickel-plated
night-flying
noble-minded
non-starter,
oak-beamed
odd-job man
odd-numbered
off-season
off-licence
off-peak
off-putting
off-the-record
old-fashioned
old-maidish
O-level
on-and-off
one-night stand
one-sided
once-over
open-air
out-and-out
out-of-date
out-of-doors
out-of-the-way
over-the-counter
pace-setting
pale-faced
paper-thin

part-time

passers-by

penny-pinching

pest-ridden

photo-offset

pick-me-up

pigeon-toed

pile-driving

pitch-black

place-name

plain-spoken

pleasure-bent

pleasure-seeking

pocket-sized

point-to-point

pole-vault

post-natal

pre-natal

price-cutting

price-fixing

pro-Arab (pro-German, etc)

public-spirited

punch-drunk

put-on

quasi-legal

quick-change

quick-tempered

quick-witted

rat-infested

razor-keen

razor-sharp

re-cover (e.g. a sofa)

ready-built

ready-mix

red-faced

red-hot

right-angle

right-handed

right-minded

right-of-way

ring-fence

ring-in

road-test

rock-climbing

roll-on roll-off

Rolls-Royce

rose-scented

rough-and-ready

rough-and-tumble

rough-coat

rubber-stamped

run-in

run-on

rye-grass

St Martin-in-the-Fields

Saint-Saens

sabre-toothed

saddle-backed

sawn-off

say-so

scar-faced

second-class

second-guess

second-rate

set-aside

set-to

sharp-witted

shell-like

shilly-shally

shop-soiled

short-changed

short-circuited

short-handed

short-lived

shut-in

sign-on

silver-haired

silver-tongued

simple-minded

single-breasted

single-seater

Sino-Japanese, etc

sister-in-law

six-cylinder

six-shooter

skin-graft

sky-high

slap-up

slow-motion

small-scale

snail-paced
so-and-so
so-called
soft-boiled
soft-pedal
soft-shelled
son-in-law
spoon-fed
spot-check
spread-eagle
stage-struck
stand-in
steel-framed
stick-in-the-mud
stick-up
stiff-backed
stock-still
stone-cold
stone-dead
storm-tossed
straight-backed
straight-faced
strong-arm
sub-lieutenant
sugar-coated
sun-baked
sun-dried
sure-fire
sure-footed
swollen-headed
T-shirt
tail-ender
take-home
tax-exempt
tax-free
test-tube baby
thought-provoking
three-cornered
three-piece
three-ply
three-ring circus
tie-break
tight-fitting
time-consuming
time-honoured

tip-off
tom-tom
tone-deaf
top-hatted
trade-in
trans-Siberian (trans-Canadian, etc,
   but transatlantic – no hyphen)
trap-door spider,
trouble-free
true-blue
try-on
twenty-first (twenty-third, forty-sixth,
   etc)
tutti-frutti
tut-tut
twice-told
two-faced
two-sided
two-step
two-up
U-boat
un-American, etc
uncalled-for
unheard-of
unthought-of
up-and-coming
U-turn
value-added tax
velvet-pile
vice-chairman (*but* vice admiral, vice
   president, etc, no hyphens)
V-neck
voice-over
waist-high
walkie-talkie
walk-in
walk-on
warm-hearted
washed-out
washed-up
water-cooled
water-soaked
water-soluble
wave-worn
weak-kneed

weak-willed
weather-beaten
weather-bound
weather-wise
web-footed
week-ending
week-old
weigh-in
well-being
well-bred
well-deserving
well-informed
well-known
well-read
well-spoken
well-thought-of
well-thought-out
well-to-do
well-wisher
well-worn
wet-nurse
wide-angle
wide-awake

wide-open
will-o'-the-wisp
window-cleaning
window-dressing
window-shopping
wire-haired
wood-panelled
word-perfect
work-and-turn
world-beater
worm-eaten
would-be
wrong-thinking
wych-elm
x-ray or X-ray
Y-chromosome
year-old
year-round
yellow-bellied
Y-fronts
young-womanhood
Z-chromosome
zero-rated.

The way out of hyphenation hassles is to curb your logical and investigative urges. That way you won't have to wonder why it is *mother-of-pearl* and *government-in-exile* (hyphenated) but *next of kin* and *officer in charge* (unhyphenated). And why is it *razzle-dazzle* but *razzmatazz*, *nitty-gritty* but *riffraff*, *willy-nilly* but *dilly dally*, *nick-knack* but *nickname*?

Don't even ask.

Symbols of Meaning

Apart from enabling us to join, separate and manipulate words and word units, punctuation also allows us to add extra meaning to bald statements:

You're going.	is not the same as	*You're going?*
Not again.	is not the same as	*Not again!*
Lucy and Joe's parents.	is not the same as	*Lucy's and Joe's parents.*
He said I'm mad.	is not the same as	*He said, 'I'm mad'.*

You can see that these marks possess the power to alter dramatically the meaning of statements – as it were with a single stroke. So learning how to use them, and how to use them correctly, is just as important as learning the functions of nouns and pronouns, adjectives and adverbs.

The Question Mark

The exclamation mark and question mark share a common ancestry. The exclamation mark consists of a hanging stroke pointing emphatically to the stop to make the reader screech to a halt. The **question mark** has a squiggle atop the stop, not unlike a 'q' (for query?), and its purpose is to warn the reader that the preceding word or statement is interrogative, or of doubtful validity.

A sentence that asks a question *directly* requires a question mark, but a sentence that poses an *indirect question* does not:

DIRECT QUESTION   *Are you going to the match?*

INDIRECT QUESTION   *I asked him if he was going to the match.*

This looks fairly simple but sometimes an indirect question can be disguised:

Why should allegations that go unchallenged in America be the subject of legal action in Britain, asks Roy Greenslade.

Not a question mark in sight. Now look at this similar example:

I wonder how many people will be homeless this Christmas?

The first example seems to be shouting for a question mark after *Britain*, but if you study the sentence carefully you will see that it is just a novel form of an indirect question. We could rewrite it more clearly as an indirect question:

Roy Greenslade asks why should allegations that go unchallenged in America be the subject of legal action in Britain.

Or, in the form of a *reported direct question*:

Roy Greenslade asks, 'Why should allegations that go unchallenged in America be the subject of legal action in Britain?'

The second example is also an indirect question, so why is it followed by a question mark? This is because many writers fall into this error; the sentence should end with a full stop. Either that, or rewrite the sentence to include a direct question:

I wondered, 'How many people will be homeless this Christmas?'

Generally question marks come at the end of sentences but sometimes can be inserted within them:

Perhaps – who knows? – there may in the future be some belated recognition for his services to mankind.

Don't forget that, no matter how long your sentence is, if there is a direct question contained in it, the question mark is still required:

Is it not curious that 'Lourdes', which within a year of publication sold over 200,000 copies, had critical acclaim poured over it like champagne and which provoked such a furore that it was instantly placed on the Vatican's Index of prohibited books, is not still widely read today?

The 'Semi'-question

One very common use of the direct question is in the form of a polite request:

Would you let me know if either Monday or Tuesday next week will be suitable?

There is little doubt that the question mark is required; it is after all a straightforward question directed at someone. But here's a similar request-question:

Would you be good enough to ensure that in future cars and other vehicles belonging to non-staff are parked outside the gates.

Well, what is it – a request or a question? It is in fact both: part question, part demand, and writer and reader both sense that a question mark would weaken its authority. Many writers are troubled by this weasel-like quality. Look at these examples – all questions but all reasonably comfortable without a question mark:

You're not going to give in yet, I trust.
I hope you're not calling me a liar.
I wonder if I might borrow the car tomorrow.

In these cases, the expressions of personal feeling – *I trust, I hope* and *I wonder* – tend to undermine the question content of the statements. If you wrote *You're not going to give in yet?* or *May I borrow the car tomorrow?* you'd unhesitatingly finish with question marks. But there are some questions that look quite strange with a question mark:

How dare you?   *How dare you!*

Here the expression is more an angry exclamation than a query, and a question mark would, in most similar cases, seem inappropriate.

The Exclamation Mark

Discouraged, if not banned, by modern newspapers (where it is referred to as a 'startler', 'gasper', 'screamer', and by tabloid subeditors as a 'dog's dick'), and with a reputation for over-use, the **exclamation mark** nevertheless earns its keep with a surprisingly wide range of legitimate uses.

It's hard to imagine the following examples conveying anything like the same force and feeling without the screamers:

Shut up!   You bitch!   What a mess!   Damn!

Literature would undoubtedly be the poorer without them. Good writers aren't afraid of exclamation marks and use them judiciously for a number of functions:

CONVEYING ANGER, SCORN, DISGUST	*You're out of your mind!* *You must be joking!*
INDICATING SARCASM AND REVERSE MEANING	*Thanks a lot!* *That's bloody lovely, that is!*
UNDERLINING INSULTS AND EXPLETIVES	*You bastard!* *Shit!*
CONVEYING IRONIC TONE	*You're not so smart!* *And you said we wouldn't win!*
COMMANDING	*Come here! Right now!* *Get lost! And don't come back!*

All very well, but remember H. W. Fowler's warning: 'Excessive use of exclamation marks in expository prose is a certain indication of an unpractised writer or of one who wants to add a spurious dash of sensation to something unsensational.' Let this piece of gush provide a cautionary reminder:

Patricia went to Venice – again! That's the second time in a year!! And you'll never guess who she met there!!!

The Apostrophe

Most of us have seen and chortled over everyday apostrophic clangers like these:

Lilie's, Anemone's and Mum's (London florist's shop)
Fresh Asparagu's (Edinburgh greengrocer)
Her's is a warm, informal home. (newspaper interview)
Bargain Mens Shirt's (street market sign)
This school and it's playground will be closed over Easter (sign on gate of a Croydon primary school)

If we're honest many of us have to admit that there are times when we're forced to think quite hard about the use – or non-use – of apostrophes. So what's the problem?

The problem lies simply in an ability to recognise that there are two – and only two – kinds of apostrophes. One kind indicates the possession of something; the other kind indicates a contraction or abbreviation – a letter or letters left out of a word:

POSSESSIVE APOSTROPHE   *Did you know Jack's car is a write-off? I heard*
                                   that Jack's kids have the flu.

CONTRACTION APOSTROPHE   *Did you know that Jack's had a bad accident?*
                                   I heard that Jack'll be out tomorrow.

In the first two examples the apostrophes tell us that the car and the kids belong to Jack; they are **possessive apostrophes**. In the second pair of examples the apostrophes tell us that something is left out: that *Jack's* is a shortened version of *Jack is*, and that *Jack'll* is a shortened version of *Jack will*; they are **contraction apostrophes**. We're (*We are*) expected to work out what these mean, and with a little experience we soon learn to fill in the gaps:

> *My God! Did you hear? London's burning!* (contraction: *London **is** burning*)
> *I hope London's fire services can cope!* (possessive: *the fire services that belong to or are situated in London*).

Possessive Apostrophes

If we wish to indicate that something belongs to somebody we use the possessive apostrophe: *Joyce's house, Michael's mountain bike, the girl's tunic, his uncle's car, her grandfather's clock.*

Possession, ownership or association can also apply to things: *a good day's work, the company's policy, the tree's branches, the door's hinges.*

And the same goes for certain plural nouns: *men's trousers, children's toys, mice's tails, people's charter.*

No problems there. But all the above examples have something in common: none of the possessor words or names ends with an 's' – *Joyce, Michael, girl, uncle, grandfather, day, company, tree, door, men, children, mice, people,* etc. So what's the problem with words ending with an 's'?

The problem is that adding possessive apostrophes to words and names, such as *boss, surplus, Thomas,* and to plurals, such as *cats, hours* and *friends,* is not such a straightforward business. Let's look at some examples:

WORDS AND NAMES ENDING WITH 'S'	**POSSESSIVE FORM**
the boss	*the **boss's** temper*
Thomas	***Thomas's** recent illness*
mistress	*a **mistress's** secrets*
Charles Dickens	***Dickens's** novels*

Now see what happens when *plural nouns* that end with '*s*' become possessive:

PLURAL WORDS ENDING WITH 'S'	**POSSESSIVE FORM**
Penny's parents	*Penny's parents' caravan*
her friends	*her friends' parties*
the members	*the members' privileges*
our employees	*our employees' bonuses*
the girls	*the girls' classroom*

Get the picture? For singular ownership we simply add '*s*, but for plural or shared ownership we add the apostrophe *after* the *s – s'*. The system enables us to distinguish the different meanings. When we read:

The opera star heard the girl's singing

we are being told that the star listened to only one girl singing, whereas

The opera star heard the girls' singing

tells us (if we've learned the rules!) that the diva is listening to many girls singing.

In some cases, especially with names, we have choices, according to taste. We can add the final '*s* (*Tom Jones's songs, Prince Charles's opinions*) or drop it (*Wales' ruggedness, Dickens' characters, Jesus' teachings*), or observe tradition (*Queens' College, Cambridge; Queen's College, Oxford*). Here are a few more oddities:

WITH A POSSESSIVE APOSTROPHE	*Lord's Cricket Ground, St John's Wood, St John's (Newfoundland), St Michael's Mount, Regent's Park, St Katharine's Dock, Court of St James's, King's Cross, Land's End, St Giles' Cathedral, Christie's and Sotheby's, King's College, London.*
WITHOUT A POSSESSIVE APOSTROPHE	*Earls Court, St Kitts, Golders Green, Shepherds Bush, St Andrews University, St Helens (Lancashire), Missing Persons Bureau, Pears soap, Gas Consumers Council.*

However, beware of adjectives that look like possessives, such as **games** *mistress*, that require no apostrophe. And watch out for units of time, such as *a* **day's** *work, a* **minute's** *delay* and *six* **months'** *salary* in complex sentences such as these:

I'm taking a three weeks holiday in three weeks' time.

An hour's delay or two hours' delay – I wish the airline would tell us the facts.

In the first example, the first *a three weeks* is an adjective phrase modifying the noun *holiday*. The second *three weeks'* has a possessive apostrophe to indicate that they are attached to the time that will elapse before the holiday is taken. In the second sentence both apostrophes are possessive: the first attached to the singular *hour = hour's*, and the second to the plural *hours = hours'*. Strictly according to the rules!

Pronouns can also be perplexing. Some have possessive apostrophes and some do not:

PRONOUNS WITH   *one's problems, anyone's idea, someone's shoes,*
APOSTROPHES   *one another's responsibilities, nobody's fault,*
                             anybody's luggage, each other's possessions

PRONOUNS WITHOUT
APOSTROPHES   *his, hers, its, ours, yours, theirs*

The most difficult apostrophe placements of all are probably those that serve to indicate a missing possession:

Sotheby's	stands for	*Sotheby's Auctions*
Lord's	stands for	*Lord's Cricket Ground*
Cruft's	stands for	*Cruft's Dog Show*

Confusion arises when such organisations drop the apostrophe: *Harrods, Ladbrokes, Womens Institute, Pears Soap*. *Lloyds Bank plc* carries no possessive apostrophe, but *Lloyd's* (standing for Lloyd's coffee house, the place where the famous London insurance house began business in the 17th century) does. In this context you may care to ponder over this unusual example of apostrophe usage, from an article in *The Times*:

> Sally Knowles, a name, said: 'When is Lloyd's going to accept that their's has been a society of overpaid incompetents and cunning, greedy people who make double-glazing and time-share salesmen look like amateurs?'

These are unusually strong words but the most unusual word is *their's*. We have noted that *theirs* is a pronoun that never carries an apostrophe, so can this usage be correct? There is a fallacious notion that as the pronoun stands for *Lloyd's [Society of Underwriters]*, a 'double' possessive pronoun is required: *their's*. This is wrong, although similar forms of possessives are legitimate (*that story of Fred's* = Fred's story; *a friend of my father's* = my father's friend). If you find yourself not fully understanding the role of your apostrophe, reconstruct the sentence.

Contraction Apostrophes

One of the most frequent errors is the use of *it's* for the possessive form of *it*. This is wrong, of course: *it's* is the accepted contraction for *it is* or *it has*. For the record:

POSSESSION   *The newspaper claimed **its** punctuation record was unmatched by any of its rivals.*

CONTRACTION   ***It's** (It is) a fact that the punctuation record of the newspaper **isn't** (is not) so clever after all.*

Also for the record is this list of most of the accepted contractions:

aren't	*are not*	**she'll**	*she will, she shall*
can't	*cannot, can not*	**she's**	*she is, she has*
couldn't	*could not*	**there's**	*there is*
hasn't	*has not*	**they'll**	*they will, they shall*
haven't	*have not*	**they're**	*they are*
he'll	*he will, he shall*	**they've**	*they have*
he's	*he is, he has*	**we'll**	*we will, we shall*
I'd	*I would, I had*	**weren't**	*were not*
I'm	*I am*	**who's**	*who is, who has*
it's	*it is, it has*	**won't**	*will not*
I've	*I have*	**wouldn't**	*would not*
let's	*let us*	**you'll**	*you will, you shall*
ma'am	*madam*	**you're**	*you are*
mustn't	*must not*	**you've**	*you have*

There are many more idiomatic contractions: *sweet'n'lo*, *'alf a mo'*, *finger lickin'*, *Ah'm talkin' to yuh*, *rock'n'roll*, and so forth. Some antique contractions survive: *o'er* (over), *ne'er* (never) and *e'en* (even). But quite a few common words formerly carrying contraction apostrophes (*'cello*, *'flu*, *'phone*, *'til*, standing for *violoncello*, *influenza*, *telephone* and *until*) are now accepted without them.

One final apostrophic tip: *who's* is short for *who is* or *who has*; *whose* indicates possession: *whose wallet is this?*

Quotation Marks

Although **quotation marks** are often called 'inverted commas', if you look closely you will find they are not. You'll see that only the opening mark is inverted – that is, with the 'tail of the tadpole' pointing up; the closing mark is a normal raised or hanging comma or pair of commas. So we should use the term *quotation marks* (or *quotes* for short) exclusively.

Another thing about quotes that bothers some people is whether to use single ('single') marks or double ("double") marks:

Heather said flatly, 'I never want to see him again.'
Heather said flatly, "I never want to see him again."

Newspaper and book publishers are divided on this; while most use double quotes, many have switched to single quotes perhaps because they are less typographically fussy – it's a matter of taste. But whether you use double or single marks you need to be aware of the convention for enclosing a quoted passage within another. If you are a single-quote writer, an additional direct speech quote within your first quote must be enclosed within double marks (or vice versa):

> The sales assistant said, 'We have them only in grey and blue but yesterday my boss told me, "I don't know why they don't make them in other colours".'

On the rare occasions where it is found necessary to have a third quote within a second quote in the same sentence, the formula is single/double/single, or double/single/double.

Quoting Direct Speech

When we read a newspaper report or story we want to know when we're reading reported or paraphrased speech and when we're reading words actually spoken. Quotation marks allow us to differentiate between the two forms:

> Mr Murphy said that in his view the value of the pound would drop towards the end of the year. 'I also believe most European currencies will follow suit,' he added.

This tells us that the writer has summarised the first part of the statement in his own words, and we have to accept that his summary is a correct interpretation of what Mr Murphy said. But we should have no doubts about the accuracy of the second part of the statement because the quote marks have signalled that the words are those actually spoken by Mr Murphy.

When you are quoting direct speech you must ensure that the words enclosed by your quotation marks are *exactly* those spoken. Not approximately, but *exactly*. Important – and costly – legal actions have been won and lost on this point.

It is also vital to make sure your reader knows who is responsible for the quoted statement. This is usually accomplished by what is called a reporting clause, which can introduce the statement or follow it or even interrupt it:

* **Jones stated**, 'I am innocent and I can easily prove it.'

* 'I am innocent and I can easily prove it,' **Jones stated**.

* 'I am innocent,' **Jones stated**, 'and I can easily prove it.'

Another point to remember is that when quoted speech is interrupted by a reporting clause, two rules apply. If the quoted statement is interrupted at the end of a sentence it should be finished with a comma and resumed with a capital letter:

'I knew I'd seen that bird before,' said Gavin. 'It was a cormorant, wasn't it?'

But if the speech is interrupted mid-sentence, it should be resumed in lower-case:

'Don't you agree,' asked Gavin, 'that the bird over there is a cormorant?'

How to Close Quotations

It is easy to remind writers not to forget to close their quotation; like enclosing brackets, the marks always operate in pairs. What is a little more difficult is . . . *how*?

Look at this example:

Louis then asked her, 'Do you think I'm drunk'?

Do you place the question mark outside the quotation mark that closes the direct speech, or inside?

Louis then asked her, 'Do you think I'm drunk?'

The answer is that it depends on the relationship between the quotation and the sentence that contains it. The rule is worth engraving on the memory:

PUNCTUATION MARKS (full stops, commas, question and exclamation marks, etc.) GO **INSIDE** THE FINAL QUOTATION MARK IF THEY RELATE TO THE QUOTED WORDS, BUT **OUTSIDE** IF THEY RELATE TO THE WHOLE SENTENCE.

In our example, the question mark relates only to the quoted statement, *'Do you think I'm drunk?'* and so it rightly belongs inside the final quote mark, not outside.

But let's change the sentence slightly:

Should Louis have asked her, 'Do you think I'm drunk'?

Here, if you remember the rule, you can see that the question is an essential part of the whole sentence, and so the question mark *outside* the final quote mark is correct. To be pedantic, the sentence should properly be written like this:

Should Louis have asked her, 'Do you think I'm drunk?'?

Here you see that the quotation has its own question mark inside the final quote mark (quite correctly), and the overall sentence has its mark outside (again correctly). But the two piggybacked question marks look a bit silly and everyone accepts that in a case like this the inside question mark can be dropped without causing confusion.

With full stops, however, a different principle applies. If the quotation is a complete sentence that would normally end with a full stop, the stop outside the final quote marks is omitted and the whole sentence ended with a stop inside the final quote mark:

WRONG   *Louis tried to tell her, 'I think I'm drunk.'.*

CORRECT   *Louis tried to tell her, 'I think I'm drunk.'*

British and American Punctuation

With an increasing number of American-published and printed books circulating in Britain it is understandable that the aforegoing rules could cause confusion. They are, in fact, rules peculiar to British English. American English (and that of some Commonwealth countries) adopts a significantly different rule about quotation marks.

Generally, quotation marks in British English are logical in that they are placed according to sense and context. Their placement in American English may lack logic but does have the virtue of simplicity: *all punctuation* (stops, commas, colons and semicolons, exclamation and question marks, etc) *precedes all final quotation marks*.

Compare the following examples:

BRITISH QUOTE MARKS

Dr Johnson described a lexicographer as 'a harmless drudge'.

Dr Johnson said that a lexicographer was 'a harmless drudge', yet was himself one.

AMERICAN QUOTE MARKS

Dr Johnson described a lexicographer as 'a harmless drudge.'

Dr Johnson said that a lexicographer was 'a harmless drudge,' yet was himself one.

BRITISH QUOTE MARKS

The lecturer said that 'Dr Johnson described a lexicographer as "a harmless drudge".'

AMERICAN QUOTE MARKS

The lecturer said that 'Dr Johnson described a lexicographer as "a harmless drudge." '

Most punctuation marks are multi-functional and quotation marks are no exception. They can be used to indicate titles (*His favourite film was the Marx Brothers' classic, 'Duck Soup'*); to identify nicknames (*Henry 'Rabbit Punch' Watson; Al 'Scarface' Capone*); to indicate doubt, cynicism or disbelief (*the hamburgers contained a mixture of liver, chicken parts and 'organic' beef*); and to indicate that a word or phrase should not be taken literally (*We are 'giving away' this nationally advertised Pyramid X100 Fresh Air Ioniser for only £19.99*).

The Three-dot Ellipsis

The science fiction pioneer H. G. Wells is credited with the invention of this mark
. . . the **three-dot ellipsis**. But Mrs Henry Wood's immortal line, 'Dead! and . . .
never called me mother', from the stage version of *East Lynne* (1874) antedates
Wells' claim by at least a couple of decades. What this line of dots does is to
indicate missing matter, which may consist of a single word:

> *Get the . . . out of here!*

or matter considered to be non-essential:

> *Yesterday the shares stood at just over £4.65, which if you believe last night's
> closing statement . . . at that price the company is valued at almost £1.6 billion.*

or an implied quotation or phrase that the reader is expected to know:

> *So then she bought contact lenses: you know, men don't make passes . . . And she
> really believes that, too!*

or indicating an unfinished thought:

> *The troubling question was, would Mrs Benedict sue, or . . .*

or indicating a time lapse:

> *Kimball crashed to the floor with eye-wincing force . . . only later, much later, in
> the darkness, did he realise he was a marked man.*

or indicating disjointed speech:

> *She paced the room. 'I don't know . . . every way I look at it . . . what would you
> do?' She drew deeply on the cigarette. 'I mean, surely he wouldn't do this to me
> . . . or would he?'*

The Asterisk

This complaining letter to *The Times* adequately explains the function of the
asterisk:

> *In your paper last week I noticed a f***, a b***** and a f***ing and this made me
> wonder just who you think comprises your readership. If you feel that you have to
> censor any word that could possibly upset anybody, why do we not have M******
> H****tine, the M********t Treaty and the C****n Ag********l P****y?**

The final asterisk is in its customary role of guiding the reader to a footnote or
explanation elsewhere in the text, thus:

* *Michael Heseltine, Maastricht Treaty, Common Agricultural Policy.*

Bullets

In our busy age the bullet point (• in this text) has found increasing favour, perhaps because:

- It enables us to summarise clearly a series of facts or conclusions.

- It sends a signal to the eye that 'here are the essentials'.

- It encourages writers to be brief: to use words and phrases rather than long sentences.

- It captures readers who are too lazy or too harassed to read solid texts.

The Stroke

Fancily called the **virgule**, **solidus**, **shilling mark**, **slash** and **diagonal**, this oblique **stroke /** (also called **oblique**) has a few limited uses in texts:

TO INDICATE OPTIONS	*It depends upon how he/she behaves. The situation calls for guile and/or force.*
TO SEPARATE LINES OF VERSE	*The mist as it rises / touched with gold of the morning / Veils over the sadness / and lifts, soaring . . .*
TO ABBREVIATE	*A/c = account; C/o = care of; km/hr = kilometres per hour.*

With the advent of the Internet, however, along with the *at* symbol (@), it has gained importance as an integral part of Internet addresses. In this context it is called the **forward slash**, to differentiate it from the backslash, which is used in some computers' operating systems.

Italics, Bold and Underlining

As tools for separating, highlighting and clarifying text, these devices are on the margins of punctuation. Although they can hardly apply to hand-written prose, in this word-processing age the *italic*, **bold** and <u>underline</u> keys make possible a range of typographic effects. They have all been used in this book:

FOR EMPHASIS	Do **not** use a capital letter after a colon.
TO DISTINGUISH A WORD OR WORD GROUP	Less than a century ago, <u>tomorrow</u> was hyphenated as <u>to-morrow</u>.

TO IDENTIFY EXTRACTS AND QUOTATIONS	The *Collins English Dictionary* describes an adjective as **a word imputing a characteristic to a word or pronoun**.
TO INDICATE TITLES	Several errors involving quotation marks will be found in Jane Austen's *Pride and Prejudice*.
TO INDICATE A FOREIGN WORD OR PHRASE	The movement's meetings were always heavy with *Sturm und Drang*, shouting and argument.

Capitalisation

Capital letters are a form of punctuation in that they help guide the eye and mind through a text. Try reading this:

on sunday, april 7, easter day, after having been at st paul's cathedral, i came to dr johnson, according to my usual custom. johnson and i supt at the crown and anchor tavern, in company with sir joshua reynolds, mr langton, mr [william] nairne, now one of the scotch judges, with the title of lord dunsinan, and my very worthy friend, sir william forbes, of pitsligo.

That's a paragraph shorn of capital letters. It's readable, with some effort, but how much easier would the eye glide through it were it guide-posted with capitals at the start of each sentence, proper name and the abbreviation *Mr*!

Capitals are used at the beginning of sentences, after full stops, and for the first word in direct speech:

CORRECT	*Sentences begin with capitals. And they follow full stops.*
WRONG	*They do not follow commas, Nor do they follow semicolons or colons; But they do follow exclamation and question marks.*
CORRECT	*He told us, 'Always use a capital when quoting direct speech.'*
WRONG	*He told us, 'always use a capital when quoting direct speech.'*

Using capital letters to start sentences and surnames is clear enough, but a good deal of mystery surrounds the use of capitals in some other areas of writing. Here is a brief **Guide to Capitalisation**:

Aircraft	*Concorde, Airbus, Boeing 747*, etc.
Armed forces	*British Army, Italian Navy, Brazilian Air Force*, but *navy, air force*. Ranks are capitalised: *Sergeant, Admiral, Lieutenant*, etc.
The calendar	*Monday, March, Good Friday, the Millennium Dome* but *the new millennium*.

Compass points	*northwest, south-southwest* but *mysterious East, deep South, frozen North.*
Days	*Christmas Day, New Year's Day, Derby Day.*
The Deity	*God, Father, Almighty, Holy Ghost, Jesus Christ*; also *Bible, New Testament, Book of Common Prayer, Koran, Talmud*, etc; and religions (*Judaism, Baptists, B'nai B'rith*). *Hades*, but *heaven and hell.*
Diplomatic	*Nicaraguan embassy* (*embassy* is lower case).
Dog breeds	*Labrador, Afghan hound, Scotch terrier*, etc, but *rottweiler, lurcher, bulldog*, etc, lower-case (check the dictionary as capitalisation is inconsistent).
Exclamations	*Oh! Ahrrgh! Wow!*
First person pronoun	*I told them that I was leaving.*
Flora and fauna	*Arab horse, Shetland pony, Montague's harrier* but *hen harrier* (capitals where a proper name is involved). Plants are lower-case, but with scientific names, orders, classes, families and genuses are capitalised; species and varieties are lower-case: *Agaricus bisporus.*
Geographical	*The West, the East, the Orient, Northern Hemisphere, Third World, British Commonwealth, the Gulf, the Midlands, South-East Asia.*
Headlines	With capital and lower-case headlines, capitalise nouns, pronouns, verbs and words of four or more letters. Generally, capitalise *No, Not, Off, Out, So, Up* but not *a, and, as, at, but, by, for, if, in, of, on, the, to* except when they begin headlines. Capitalise both parts of hyphenated compounds: *Sit-In, Cease-Fire, Post-War.*
Heavenly bodies	*Mars, Venus, Uranus, Ursa Major, Halley's Comet.*
History	*Cambrian Era, Middle Ages, Elizabethan, the Depression, Renaissance, Year of the Rat.*
Law and lords	*Lord Chancellor, Black Rod, Master of the Rolls, Lord Privy Seal, Queen's Counsel.*
Local government	*council*, but *Kent County Council, Enfield Borough Council, Lord Mayor of Manchester.*

Member of Parliament	lower case, except when abbreviated: *MP*.
Nations, Nationalities	*Venezuela, Alaska, Brits, Estonians, Sudanese. Indian ink, Indian file, Indian clubs,* but *indian summer; French polish, French stick, French kiss, French letter* but *french window; Chinese,* but *chinaware; Turkish bath, Turkish delight.*
Personification	*The family gods were* **Hope** *and* **Charity**.
Political parties and terms	*Tory, Conservative Party, Labour Party, Liberal Democrats, Communist Party,* but *communist, Thatcherism, Leninist, Luddites, Marxist, Gaullist,* etc.
Popes	*The Pope,* but *popes, Pope Paul, Pope John,* etc.
Proper names	Names of people (*Tony Blair, Spice Girls*); places (*Europe, Mt Everest*); titles (*Pride and Prejudice, Ten O'Clock News*); epithets (*Iron Duke, Iron Lady*); nicknames (*Tubby Isaacs, 'Leadfoot' Evans*).
Races	*Aztecs, Shawnees, Aboriginals, Asiatics.*
Religion	*Rev Adam Black, Fr O'Brien, Sister Wendy, Mother Teresa, Archbishop of Canterbury, Catholics, Jew, Jewish, Semitic, anti-Semitism, Protestants.*
Royalty	*The Queen, Duke of Edinburgh, Prince of Wales, Queen Mother, Princess Anne, the Crown.*
Rulers	*Her Majesty's Government, House of Commons, Secretary of State, Chancellor of the Exchequer; Prime Minister* (*PM* when abbreviated).
Satirised references	*In Crowd, Heavy Brigade, She Who Must Be Obeyed, Bright Young Things, Her Indoors.*
Scouts	*Scouts, Guides, Cubs.*
Seasons	*spring, summer, autumn, winter* (all lower-case).
Street names	*road, avenue, crescent, square,* etc, but *Highfield Road, Spring Avenue, Eagle Crescent, Sloane Square,* etc.
Titles	*Sir Thomas More, Lord Asquith, Mr and Mrs, Dr,* etc.
Trade names, marks	*Hoover, Peugeot, Kentucky Fried Chicken, Gillette, Durex, Xerox,* etc.

Van	When writing Dutch names *van* is lower-case when part of the full name (*Hans van Meegeren, Vincent van Gogh*) but capitalised when used only with the surname (*Van Gogh, Van Dyke*).
von	In Germanic names, von is always lower-case.
World War	Capitalise, as in *World War II, World War II.* The usage *First World War* or *Second World War* is sometimes preferred.

Punctuation: Numbers and Figures

Writing and communicating aren't confined to letters and words. Numbers figure largely in our lives, too: money, time, dates, measurements, locations. The principle behind the punctuation of numbers is simply this: seek clarity; eliminate ambiguity.

Numbers from one to ten are generally spelled out; thereafter *11, 23, 785*, etc. Round numbers and approximate amounts can be expressed in words or figures, according to taste:

Nearly six hundred feet high; she was in her early eighties; the population was well over two million; three or four feet long.

Nearly 600 ft high; she was in her early 80s; the population was well over 2,000,000 (or 2m); 3–4 ft long.

Avoid beginning sentences with numerals; they look better spelt out:

UGLY	*160 deer were culled on the estate last week.*
BETTER	*A hundred and sixty deer were culled on the estate last week.*

Alternatively, rewrite the sentence to avoid starting with a numeral:

UGLY	*35 employees are expected to leave the firm this year.*
BETTER	*This year, 35 employees are expected to leave the firm.*

Use figures to express specific amounts and large numbers:

The authority stated that 21,456 firms were actively operating in the City during December. The hotel was finally sold for £620,000.

Try to be consistent within a sentence:

WRONG	*During the survey the team counted forty-two thrushes, 12 magpies and 15 pied wagtails.*

CORRECT   *During the survey the team counted 42 thrushes, 12 magpies and*
                    15 pied wagtails.

Where two numbers adjoin, remove the visual confusion by spelling out one
and expressing the other in numerals:

CONFUSING   *In 1991 37 people were executed in Djakarta.*

CLEARER   *In 1991, thirty-seven people were executed in Djakarta.*

- In expressing **time**, except where the 24-hour clock is required for technical
  reasons, use the 12-hour clock, indicating morning or afternoon:

  8.30 am   5.15 pm   11.00 pm   12.00 midnight

  8:30 am   5:15 pm   11:00 pm   12:00 midnight

Of the two styles, the single stop separating hours and minutes seems to be
preferred, with *am* and *pm* expressed without stops. When the time is spelled
out, also spell out whether it is morning or afternoon:

They arranged to meet at ten in the morning.
We arrived at half-past four in the afternoon.

- For **dates**, the following styles are generally accepted:

  Friday, October 29, 1999. However, many individuals and publishers write
  the day before the month: *Monday, 5 January, 1999* or *12 March 2001*, or *12th
  March, 2001.*

  September 26, 1998

  September 1998 (no separating comma)

  December 17 (preferred); *December 17th; 17 December; 17th December*

  March 6–23, 1998; March 6th-23rd, 1998

  1975–6; 1975–79; 1914–18 but *1975–1985; 1939–1945*

  1980s; 70s; but *swinging sixties; gay nineties, roaring twenties*

  20th century; twentieth century

  160BC; AD225

- As a general rule, numerals convey **ages** with greater clarity than when
  spelled out, but either form is acceptable:

  The wanted man is aged between 50 and 55.

Among the missing is a 7-year-old girl.

They left an 18-month-old child.

Mr Morgan was believed to be in his late eighties (preferred to 80s).

- Use these guidelines for **ordinal numbers**:

first, third, eighth, nineteenth, sixty-fourth (up to *a hundredth*), then use numerals: *101st, 112th, 143rd*, etc.

but a thousandth, millionth.

5th Avenue, 42nd Street, 38th parallel.

- **Fractions** sometimes involve a hyphen:

three-quarters, half-dozen, half-hour, two-thirds (hyphenated).

half a dozen, quarter of an hour, two thirds of the country (unhyphenated).

Keep numerical expressions consistent; don't mix fractions and percentages in the same sentence:

WRONG *While almost two out of three were for the recommendations, a worrying 28% voted against them.*

CORRECT *While just under 65% voted for the recommendations, a worrying 28% voted against them.*

- Figures are generally clearer and preferable for **dimensions and measurements**: *7ft 3in by 5ft 4in; 2.4 by 3.3 metres; 3lbs 12oz; 6.55kg; 6 parts gin, 1 part vermouth; 35ft yacht; 6-inch blade.*

- Numerals are preferred for **money**, except for very large amounts (*four billion pounds' worth of shares*) and when treated idiomatically (*she looked like a million dollars*):

£8.99; 49p; £1,000; $5,500; £3.4m; a £6.5bn loan (often spelled out: *'a six-and-a-half billion pound loan'* or *'a £6.5 billion loan'* because large amounts are difficult to grasp – figuratively and literally).

3

SPELLING

The 2,000 Most Misspelt Words in the English Language

Including anglicised foreign words and a few dozen real stinkers

abacus, abacuses
abate, abatable
abattoir
abbreviate
abdominal
aberration
abhorrent
abrogate
abscess, abscesses
absorption
abstemious
abyss, abysmal
accelerate, accelerator, acceleration
accessory
acclimatise
accolade
accommodate, accommodation
accompanist
accordion, accordionist
accrue, accruing, accrued
acetic (*acid*); ascetic (*austere*)
acetylene
achievable, achievement
aching, achingly
acidophilus
acknowledgment *or*
    acknowledgement
acolyte
acoustic, acoustical
acquaintance
acquiescence, acquiescent
acquire

acquittal, acquitted
acumen
acupuncture
address, addressee
adenoid, adenoidal
adieu [*in Spanish,* adios]
adjourn, adjournment
adjunct
admissible, admissibility
adolescence, adolescent
ad nauseum
adulatory, adulate
advantageous, advantageously,
    advantageousness
adventitious
adze {adz *in USA*]
aegis
aeolian
aeon
aerial
aesthete, aesthetic, aestheticism
    [*in the USA the 'a' is dropped*]
affidavit
aficionado
a fortiori
ageing *or* aging, ageless, ageism
agent provocateur
agglomeration
aggrandise *or* aggrandize;
    aggrandisement *or*
    aggrandizement
aggrieve

agribusiness
aide-de-camp
aide memoire
à la carte
alienate, alienation
alimentary
allege, alleging
alter ego
aluminium [aluminum *in the USA*]
alumnus, alumnae [*plural*]; alumna
   [*feminine*]
amanuensis, amanuenses [*plural*]
ambidextrous, ambidexterity,
   ambidextrousness
amoeba
amok
amortisation *or* amortization
amphibious
anachronism, anachronistic
anaemia, anaemic
anaesthetic, anaesthesia, anaesthetise
   or anaesthetize
analytical
anathema
ancillary
androgynous, androgyne
anemone
aneurism
aniline
animadvert, animadversion
ankh
anneal
annihilate, annihilation
annotate, annotator
annulment
anodyne
anoint, anointment
anomalous, anomaly
anomie
anonymous, anonymously,
   anonymity
antediluvian
antenna, antennae [*plural*]
antihistamine
antimacassar

antipodes, antipodean
aphrodisiac
apiary, apiarian, apiarist
apocalypse, apocalyptic
apogee
apophthegm
apoplectic, apoplexy
apostasy
apostrophe, apostrophise *or*
   apostrophize
apothecary, apothecaries [*plural*]
appal, appalled, appalling
apparel
apparently
appellant, appellate
appendicitis, appendicectomy *or*
   appendectomy
appliqué
apposite
approbate
appurtenance
aqueous
aqua vitae
arbitrage, arbitrageur
arbitrary, arbitrarily
arboretum
archetypal
archipelago, archipelagos *or*
   archipelagoes (*plural*)
areola [*human tissue*], aureola [*halo*]
armadillo, armadillos
armature
armoire
arpeggio
arraign, arraignment
arriviste
arrondissement
artefact *or* artifact
ascendancy
ascetic [*austere*]; acetic [*acid*]
asinine, asininely, asininity
asphyxiate, asphyxiation
asphalt
assassin, assassinate, assassination
assessable

assuage

asthma, asthmatic

astrakhan

atelier

attenuate, attenuation

aubergine

auxiliary

avocado

awesome, awesomely

awe-stricken, awe-struck

baccalaureate

bacchanalia, bacchanal

bachelor, bachelorhood

bacillus, bacilli [*plural*]

baguette

bailiff

balalaika

balletomane

ballot, balloted, balloting

balsam, balsamic

balustrade, baluster

banisters *or* bannisters

banns

banquette

barbiturate, barbital

barcarole *or* barcarolle

baroque

barre

barrel, barrelled, barrelling

barrette

barroom

bas-relief

bassinet

bathyscaph *or* bathyscaphe *or* bathyscape

battalion

bayonet, bayoneting *or* bayonetting, bayoneted *or* bayonetted

beatific, beatify, beatitude

beaujolais

béchamel sauce

behemoth

beige

belles-lettres, belletrist

belligerent

bellwether

benefice, beneficence, beneficent

biannual [*twice yearly*], biennial [*every two years*]

bias, biased *or* biassed, biases *or* biasses

bijou

bilingual

bilious, biliousness

billet-doux, billets-doux [*plural*]

bimetallism

biopsy, biopsies

bisque

bituminous

bivouac, bivouacking

blancmange

bluer, bluest, blueing, blued

bogie [*under-carriage*]; bogey [*golf*]; bogie *or* bogy [*ghostly*]

bookkeeper

bonhomie

bon vivant

bougainvillea *or* bougainvillaea

bouillabaisse

bouillon

boules [*the game*]

bourgeois, bourgeosie

boutonniere

bouzouki

braggadocio

braille

bric-a-brac

briquette *or* briquet

broccoli

bronchopneumonia

bronco

brooch

brougham

brusque, brusquely, brusqueness

buccaneer, buccaneering

bucolic

budgerigar

bulimia

bulrush

bulwark

bureaucracy, bureaucrat

caballero
cabriolet
cachet
cacophony
caesarean *or* caesarian. [*cesarian in
    the USA*]. *Sometimes capitalised:*
    Caesarean
caffeine
caique
caisson
calendar [*of days, weeks, months*];
    calender [*paper manufacture*].
    See colander
calibre
callisthenics
calypso
camaraderie
camellia
camomile *or* chamomile
camouflage, camouflaging
candelabra
cannibal, cannibalism, cannibalise *or*
    cannibalize
cantaloupe
cappuccino
carat *or* karat
carburettor *or* carburetter [*carburetor
    in the USA*]
carcass *or* carcase, carcasses [*plural*]
caress, caresses, caressing
carpeted, carpeting
carte blanche
caster [*sugar*]; castor [*roller*]
casualty
casuistry
cataclysm, cataclysmic
catalogue, cataloguing, catalogued
catarrh, catarrhal
catastrophe, catastrophic
catechism
cauliflower
cause célèbre
caveat
cemetery
centenary, centennial

cerebellum
cerebral, cerebrum
cerebral palsy
chaise longue, chaises longues *or*
    chaise longues [*plural*]
chamois
champignon
chandelier
changeable, changeability,
    changeling, changeover
chaparral
chaperone
chargé d'affaires
charisma, charismatic
chauffeur
chauvinism
chiaroscuro
chicanery
chiffonier
chihuahua
chinoiserie
chlorophyll
cholesterol
chromosome
chrysalis
chrysanthemum
cicada
cicatrix
cinnamon
cirrhosis
clairvoyant, clairvoyance
clandestine, clandestinely
clangour [*loud noise, uproar*]; clanger
    [*mistake*]
claque
clarinet, clarinettist
cliché
climacteric [*critical period*]; climactic
    [*causing a climax*]; climatic [*of weather*]
clique, cliquey *or* cliquy, cliquish
cloisonné
coalesce, coalescing
cockieleekie [*Scottish soup*] *or* cock-a-
    leekie
coconut *or* cocoanut

cocoon
codicil, codicillary
cognisance *or* cognizance
cognoscente, cognoscenti [*plural*]
colander [*perforated pan*] *or* cullender.
   See calendar
coleslaw
colitis
collapsible
colloquial, colloquialism, colloquy,
   colloquium
colonnade
coloratura
colossal, colossus, colossi *or*
   colossuses [*plural*]
colosseum *or* coliseum
combated, combating, combative
comedienne
comeuppance
commemorate, commemoration,
   commemorative

commensurate
commiserate, commiseration
commissary, commissariat
commissionaire
committed, committal
commodore
communiqué
complaisance, complaisant
complement [*complete amount*];
   compliment [*remark*]
concomitant
concours d'élégance
concupiscence, concupiscent
condominium
confrère
conjunctivitis
connoisseur, connoisseurship
connubial
consanguinity
conscience
conscientious

Computer Spellcheckers

Computer spellcheckers should not be given the final word: it will always be
extremely useful to have a basic knowledge of spelling. One journalist who
writes technical articles for broadcasting journals is well aware of this. In the
course of an article he was writing,

HE WROTE . . .	AND THE SPELLCHECKER CORRECTED
How to deal with a battery-driven Philips super heterodyne	How to deal with a battery-driven Phallus superheater
how pleased older collectors are to get an Ericsson . . .	how pleased older collectors are to get an erection . . .
a good review of the book Syntony and Spark, a real encouragement to Hugh Aitken.	a good review of the book Synonmy and Spark, a real encouragement to hug airmen.

Although many first names and surnames are now incorporated into most
spellcheckers, bizarre results are not uncommon. A letter addressed to
Ms Hilary Abbot Wimbush managed to arrive at the intended destination
although unfortunately addressed to Ms Hairy Abbot Wombat.

consensus

consommé

consummate

contemporaneous, contemporaneity

continuum

contractual, contractually

contretemps

coolie

coquetry, coquette, coquettish

cordon bleu

cornucopia

coronary

corpuscle, corpuscular

correlate, correlation

corrigendum, corrigenda [*plural*]
   [*error in printing*]

corroborate, corroboration

coup [*takeover*]; coupe (*dessert*) coupé
   [*car*]

coup de grâce, coups de grâce [*plural*]

coup d'état, coups d'état [*plural*]

couscous

couturier, couturière [*feminine*]

crèche

crepe de Chine

crêpe suzette, crêpes suzettes [*plural*]

cretonne

crochet [*knitting*]; crotchet [*music*]

croupier

cueing

cuisine

cul-de-sac, culs-de-sac *or* cul-de-sacs
   [*plural*]

culottes

cuneiform

curriculum vitae, curricula vitae
   [*plural*]

cutaneous

cutthroat

cynosure

cyst, cystic fibrosis, cystitis [*bladder
   inflammation*]

cytotoxic, cytotoxin

czar *or* tsar, czarina *or* tsarina

dachshund

daguerreotype

dahlia

daiquiri

debonair *or* debonnaire

debut, debutante

deceased [*dead*, often the consequence
   of *disease*]

deciduous

decolletage

decor

defendant

defibrillation, defibrillator

deign

deleterious

delicatessen

deliquescence, deliquescent

delirium, delirium tremens

demagogue, demagoguery,
   demagogy

demesne

demonstrable

demurrer

demythologise *or* demythologize

denouement

deodorise *or* deodorize, deodoriser *or*
   deodorizer

de rigueur

desert [*dry sandy expanse*]; deserts
   [*as in 'he got his just deserts'*] *see*
   dessert

desiccate, desiccation, desiccated

dessert [*sweet or pudding course of a
   meal*] *see* desert, deserts

desuetude

detente

deter, deterring, deterrent

develop

dhow

diabetes. diabetic

dialysis, dialyser *or* dialyzer

diaphragm

diaeresis *or* dieresis, diaeretic *or*
   dieretic
diarrhoea
dichotomy, dichotomous
diesel
dilemma
dilettante, dilettantish
dinghy, dinghies
diocesan, diocese
diphtheria
diphthong
dirndl
disagreeable
discernible
discombobulate
dismissible
dissimilar, dissimilarity
dissociate, dissociation
dissolution
dissonance, dissonant
dissuade
divertissement
doctrinaire
doggerel
doily

domino, dominoes [*plural*]
double entendre
doyen, doyenne [feminine]
drachma
dumbbell
duodenum
dyeing [*colouring*]; dying [*facing death*]
dysentery
dyspepsia, dyspeptic
ecumenical
eczema
efflorescence, efflorescent
eleemosynary
elegiac
embarrass, embarrassing,
   embarrassment
embouchure
embryo, embryos, embryology
emolument
empyrean, empyreal
enamel, enamelled, enamelling
enchilada
encumbrance *or* incumbrance
encyclopaedia *or* encyclopedia,
     encyclopaedic *or* encyclopedic

To Double or not to Double – Focussed or Focused?

Here is a practical rule which, in the case of certain words, will help you to decide whether to double letters or not.

1. If the last syllable of the word is stressed and ends with a consonant, double the last letter:

forbid	*forbidding, forbidden*
commit	*committing, committed*
remit	*remitting, remittance*
inter	*interring, interred*
sublet	*subletting, etc*

2. If the last syllable is not stressed, do not double the last letter:

market	*marketing, marketed*
target	*targeting, targeted*
gallop	*galloping, galloped*
focus	*focusing, focused*
pivot	*pivoting, pivoted, etc*

endeavour, endeavouring
enfant terrible
enforceable, enforcement
en passant
en masse
enrol or enroll [USA]; enrolment or
    enrollment [USA]
ensconce
ensuing
enthral, enthralling, enthralled
entrée
entrepreneur, entrepreneurial
envelop [to wrap around]; envelope
    [for letters]
epiglottis
epitome
equivocal, equivocation
erogenous, erogenic
erratum, errata [plural]
erroneous
escritoire
espadrille
estrangement
eucalyptus
eulogy, eulogise or eulogize
eunuch
euthanasia
evanescence, evanescent
exaggerate, exaggeration
excerpt
excrescence, excrescent
exculpate, exculpation
exegesis

exhilarate, exhilaration
exhort, exhortation
exhumation
exorbitant
expatiate, expatiation
expatriate
extirpate
extrasensory
extrovert
eyrie
facade
facetious, facetiousness
fascia
faeces, faecal [feces and fecal in the
    USA]
Fahrenheit
faience
fait accompli, faits accomplis [plural]
falafel
fallacy, fallacious
fallible, fallibility
faux pas (singular and plural)
feasible, feasibility
fiasco, fiascos
filmmaker, filmmaking
finagle
fjord
flamboyant, flamboyance
fledgeling or fledgling
flibbertigibbet
fluorescence, fluorescent
focus, focused, focusing, focuses
foetid or fetid

Enquire or Inquire: Enquiry or Inquiry?

Although, by a fine margin, the *Collins English Dictionary* and the *Oxford* prefer *INquire* to *ENquire*, it still remains a free choice. *ENquire* is the Old French and Middle English form, while *INquire* is the Latinised version. Caxton (inquyred), Spenser (inquere), Bacon and Tennyson plumped for the *IN* prefix, while Chaucer (enquyrid), Shakespeare and Milton preferred the *EN* style. Some draw the fine distinction between *enquire* (to ask a question) and *inquire* (to investigate). In the USA, *inquire* is standard, as it always is in *The Sunday Times* and several other newspapers.

foetus [fetus *in the USA*]
forbade forbad [*past tense of* forbid]
forbear, forbearance
forebode, foreboding, forebodingly
forego [*to precede*], foregone *see* forgo
foreman
foresee, foreseeing, foreseeable
forewarn
forfeit, forfeited, forfeiting
forge, forged, forging
forgo [*to go without, relinquish*],
    forgone *see* forego
formatted
fortieth
fortissimo
fortuitous, fortuity
forward [*ahead*]; foreword [*preface*]
frangipani
fricassee, fricasseeing, fricasseed
fuchsia
fugue
fulfil, fulfilling, fulfilled, fulfilment
fullness
fulsome
funereal
furore
fuselage
fusilier, fusillade
gaiety, gaily
gallimaufry
gallivant, gallivanting
gallop, galloping, galloped
galoshes
gargantuan
garnishee
garrulous
gaseous,
gasoline
gastroenteritis, gastroenterostomy
gauge
gazetteer
gazpacho
gelatinous, gelatin *or* gelatine
gelignite

gemology, gemological, gemologist *or*
    gemmology, *etc*
generalissimo
genius, geniuses [genii *is not the*
    plural except in the sense of 'spirit or
    demon']
geriatric, geriatrician
germane
gerrymander
gesundheit
geyser
ghetto, ghettos
ghoul, ghoulish, ghoulishness
gigolo
gladiolus, gladioli [*plural*]
glassful, glassfuls [*plural*]
glaucoma
glazier
glutinous [*resembling glue*]; glutenous
    [*containing the protein gluten*]
glycerine *or* glycerin
gnocchi
gnome, gnomic
gobbledegook
gonorrhea, gonorrheal
gouache
goulash
gourmet, gourmand, gourmandise *or*
    gormandize
grammar
grandeur
grandiloquence, grandiloquent
gratuitous, gratuity
grievance [*causing resentment*];
    grievous [*severe or painful*]
grippe
groin [*lower abdomen*]; groyne [*sea wall*]
guacamole *or* guachamole
guarantee, guaranteeing, guarantor
guesstimate
gubernatorial
guerrilla [*warfare*]; gorilla [*ape*]
guillotine
gumption
guttural, gutturally

gymkhana

gymnasium, gymnast, gymnastics

gynaecology [gynecology *in the USA*]

habeas corpus

habitué

haematology [hematology *in USA*]

haemoglobin [hemoglobin *in USA*]

haemophilia [hemophilia *in USA*];
   haemophiliac [hemophiliac *in
   USA*]

haemorrhage [hemorrhage *in USA*]

haemorrhoids [hemorrhoids *in USA*]

hairsbreadth

halcyon

hallelujah

handful, handfuls

hangar

hara-kiri

harangue, haranguing, harangued

harass, harassing, harassed,
   harassment

harebrained [not hairbrained!]

hashish

hausfrau

haute cuisine

hauteur

headdress

hegemony

heinous

herbaceous

heredity [*noun*]; hereditary [*adj*]

hermaphrodite, hermaphroditic

herpes

heterogeneous, heterogeneity

heterosexual, heterosexuality

hiatus

hibachi

hiccup [hiccough *is now outdated*]

hierarchy, hierarchical

hieroglyphic

hijack, hijacking

hippopotamus, hippopotamuses *or*
   hippopotami [*plural*]

hirsute

histrionic

hoeing, hoed, hoes

holocaust

homage

hombre

homeopath, homeopathy *or*
   homoeopath, homoeopathy

homogeneous [*composed of the same
   kind*]; homogenous [*of common
   descent*]

homogenise *or* homogenize

homo sapiens

homunculus

honorarium, honorary, honorific

hors-d'oeuvre, hors-d'oeuvres [*plural*]

hullabaloo *or* hullaballoo

humanitarianism

humerus [*arm bone*]; humorous
   [*funny*]

hummus *or* hoummos *or* houmous
   [*Middle Eastern food*]; humus
   [*decomposing organic matter*]

hundredth

hyacinth

hydrangea

hymn, hymnal

hyperbole [*exaggeration*]; hyperbola
   [*geometry*]

hypnosis, hypnotise *or* hypnotize,
   hypnotist, hypnotism

hypochondria, hypochondriac

hypocrite, hypocrisy, hypocritical

hypotenuse

hypothesis, hypotheses [*plural*]

hyssop

hysterectomy

hysteria, hysterical, hysterics

ichthyosaurus *or* ichthyosaur

idiosyncrasy

idyll, idyllic, idyllically

iguana

imminent [*pending*]; immanent
   [*inherent, permanent*]; eminent
   [*important*]

immeasurable

immense, immensely

immobile, immobility
immovable *or* immoveable
immunodeficiency
impassable, impasse
impeccable
impecunious
imperturbable, imperturbability
impostor *or* imposter
impresario
impressionism
imprimatur
impromptu
incandescence, incandescent
inchoate
incisor
incognito
incommunicado
incumbent, incumbency
indefatigable, indefatigability
indefensible
independence, independent
indict, indictment
indigenous
indigent

indigestible
indispensable, indispensability
indivisible, indivisibility
inexhaustible
inexpressible
infinitesimal
inflammable
inflammation, inflammatory
inflatable
ingenious [*inventive*]; ingenuous
　　[*naive*]
inherit, inheritance, inheritor
inimical
innocuous, innocuously
innuendo
inoculate, inoculation
inopportune
inquire *or* enquire
insistence
insolvent, insolvency
insomniac
insouciance, insouciant
instal *or* install, installing, installed,
　　installation

Words that Always End in 'ise'

Many people are confused by words that end with the suffixes -*ise* and -*ize*.
In hundreds of cases the use of either is optional (usually -*ize* in the USA and
increasingly so in Britain) as with oxidise/oxidize, sanitise/sanitize,
tyrannise/tyrannize.

But for some words there is no such option: they are always spelt with an
-*ise* ending. It's well worth parking these in the back of your memory to
avoid future confusion:

advertise	*demise*	*excise*	*premise*
advise	*despise*	*exercise*	*reprise*
apprise	*devise*	*exorcise*	*revise*
arise	*disenfranchise*	*franchise*	*rise*
chastise	*disguise*	*improvise*	*supervise*
circumcise	*enfranchise*	*incise*	*surmise*
comprise	*enterprise*	*merchandise*	*surprise*
compromise		*mortise*	*televise*

But watch out for *prise* (to force open) and *prize* (reward, or to value).

instalment [installment in USA]
instil [instill *in USA*], instilling,
    instilled
insure [*to guarantee or protect against
    loss*]; ensure [*to make certain*]
insurrection
intercede
interment [*burial*]; internment [*prison*]
intermezzo
internecine
interrogate, interrogation,
    interrogator
interrupt, interruption
intransigence, intransigent
inveigh
inveigle, inveigling
ipecacuanha
irascible, irascibility
iridescence, iridescent
irreconcilable
irrelevance, irrelevant
irreparable
irresistible
irrevocable
irretrievable
isosceles
isotype
isthmus
itinerant, itinerary
jalapeno
jalopy
jalousie
jamb *or* jambe
jambalaya
jardinière
jejune
jeopardy, jeopardise *or* jeopardize
jeremiad
jeweller, jewellery [jeweler, jewelry *in
    the USA*]
jihad *or* jehad
jocose, jocular, jocund
jodhpurs
joie de vivre
jonquil

judgement *or* judgment, judgemental
    or judgmental
juggernaut
juicy, juiciness, juciest
jujitsu *or* jujutsu *or* jiujitsu *or* jiujitsu
jurisprudence
juvenescence, juvenescent
juvenilia, juvenility
juxtapose, juxtaposition
kaleidoscope
keenness
kerosene *or* kerosine
khaki
kibbutz, kibbutzim [*plural*]
kibitzer
kidnap, kidnapped, kidnapper,
    kidnapping [kidnaped, kidnaper,
    kidnaping *in the USA*]
kitsch
kleptomania, kleptomaniac
kohlrabi [the cabbage]
kowtow
label, labelled, labelling
laboratory
laborious
labyrinth, labyrinthine
lachrymose
lackadaisical, lackadaisically
lacquer, lacquering, lacquered
laissez faire
laity, laic, laical
lama [*Buddhist priest*]; llama [*South
    American animal*]
lamppost
landau, landaulet
langoustine
languor, languorous
lapis lazuli
largess *or* largesse
larrikin
laryngitis, larynx
lascivious, lasciviously, lasciviousness
lassitude
lasso, lassoing, lassoed
laudable, laudatory

laundrette *or* launderette, laundromat
legerdemain
legionnaire, legionnaire's disease *or*
  legionnaires' disease
legitimatise *or* legitimatize, legitimise
  or legitimize
leitmotiv *or* leitmotif
leopard
leprechaun
lese-majesty *or* lese-majeste
leukaemia [leukemia *in the USA*]
level, levelling, levelled
liaise, liaison
libelled, libelling [*in USA*, libeled,
  libeling]
libido, libidinous
licence [*a permit or authorisation*]
  [license *in the USA*]
license [*to permit, allow*], licensing,
  licencer *or* licensor
licentious, licentiousness
lieutenant
likeable *or* likable
likely, likeliest
likelihood *or* likeliness
lilliputian *or* Lilliputian
limousine
lineage [*ancestry*]; linage [*number of
  lines*]
lingua franca
liquefy, liquefaction
liquidambar
liquorice [licorice in the USA]
lissom *or* lissome
litterateur
littoral
loath *or* loth [*unwilling*]; loathe [*to feel
  hatred*]; loathsome
locum tenens, locum tenentes [*plural*]
lodge, lodging, lodger
longevity
longueur
loquacious, loquacity, loquaciousness
loquat
lorgnette

louche
loupe *or* loup
louvre [louver *in the US*]; louvred
loveable *or* lovable
lumpenproletariat
luscious, lusciously, lusciousness
lustre [luster *in the USA*]; lustreless;
  lustrous
luxuriant [*abundant*]; luxuriate [*to take
  pleasure*]; luxurious [*characterised
  by luxury*]
lymph, lymphoma, lymphatic
lynx
macabre, macabrely
macadam, macadamise *or*
  macadamize
macaroni
machete
mackintosh *or* macintosh
macramé
maelstrom
maestro
maharajah *or* maharaja; maharani
  [*the wife of a maharajah*]
maharishi
mahjong *or* mah-jongg
mahogany
maillot
maisonette
maître d'hôtel, mâitres d'hôtel (*plural*)
majolica
mal de mer
manacle
manageable, management
manikin *or* mannikin
mannequin
manoeuvre, manoeuvred,
  manoeuvrable [maneuver, *etc*,
  in the USA]
manqué
maraschino
mariage de convenance
marijuana *or* marihuana
marquee
marriageable

marvelled, marvellous
masochism, masochistic
masquerade
massacre, massacred
masseur, masseuse
matriarch, matriarchal
mattress
mayonnaise
meagre [meager *in the USA*];
    meagrely, meagreness
meanness
medieval *or* mediaeval, medievalism
    or mediaevalism
mediocre, mediocrity
megalomania, megalomaniac
mellifluous, mellifluence, mellifluent
ménage, *ménage à trois*
menagerie
menstruation [*female period*];
    mensuration [*geometry*]
meretricious
meringue
metamorphosis, metamorphoses
    [*plural*], metamorphosise *or*
    metamorphosize
meteorology, meteorological,
    meteorologist
mezzanine
mien
migraine
mileage *or* milage
milieu
millennium, millennial
millipede
mimic, mimicking, mimicked,
    mimicry
minuscule
misanthrope, misanthropy,
    misanthropic
miscegenation
mischievous, mischievously
misfeasance
misogyny, misogynist, misogynous
misshapen

misspell, misspelt *or* misspelled,
    misspelling
mistakable *or* mistakeable
mnemonic
moccasin
modelling, modelled, modeller
    [modeling, modeled, *etc, in the*
    USA]
modus operandi
moiety
moiré
monastery, monasterial, monastic
monocoque
moratorium
mortice *or* mortise
mousse
moustache [mustache *in the USA*]
mozzarella
mucilage
mulligatawny
murmuring, murmured, murmurer
muu-muu
myalgic encephalomyelitis
myrrh
myxomatosis
nadir
naiad
naive, naïve *or* naïf, naivety, naiveté
    or naïveté
naphtha
narcissus, narcissi *or* narcissuses
    [*plural*]; narcissism *or* narcism,
    narcissistic
nascent, nascence
nasturtium
nauseous, nauseousness, nauseate,
    nauseating
necessary, necessity, necessitate
neophyte
nephritis
neuralgia, neuralgic
neurasthenia
newsstand
nickelodeon
niece

noblesse oblige
noisette
noisome
nomenclature
nonagenarian
non sequitur
nougat
nous
nouveau riche
nuptial
nymph, nymphet, nymphomania
oasis, oases [*plural*]
obbligato *or* obligato, obbligatos *or*
    obbligati [*plural*]
obdurate, obduracy
obeisance, obeisant
obfuscate, obfuscation
oblique, obliquely
obloquy, obloquies
obnoxious, obnoxiousness
obsequious, obsequiously,
    obsequiousness, obsequies
obsolescence, obsolescent
obstetrics, obstetrician
obstreperous
occur, occurring, occurred,
    occurrence
octogenarian
octopus, octopuses [*plural*]
octoroon *or* octaroon
odyssey *or* Odyssey, odyssean *or*
    Odyssean
oesophagus [esophagus *in the USA*]
oestrogen [estrogen *in the USA*]
oeuvre
offence [offense *in USA*], offensive
ombudsman, ombudswoman
omniscience, omniscient
omnivorous
onerous, onerously
onomatopoeia
onyx
opaque, opaquely, opacity
openness

ophthalmia, ophthalmic,
    ophthalmologist
opportunity, opportunistically,
    opportunely
opprobrium
optometrist, optometry
orang-utan *or* orangutan
ordinance [*regulation*]; ordnance
    [*military supplies*]
organdie [organdy *in the USA*]
orientate, orientation, orienteering
ormolu
orthopaedics, orthopaedist
    [orthopedics, orthopedist *in USA*]
oscillate, oscillating, oscillation,
    oscillatory, oscilloscope
osmosis
osteopathy
otiose, otiosity
outmanoeuvre [outmaneuver *in the*
    USA]
outré
outspokenness
overall
overrate; overreach; override;
    overrule; overrun
oxidise *or* oxidize, oxidisation *or*
    oxidization
oxyacetylene
ozonosphere
paean
pachouli *or* patchouli
paedophile [pedophile *in USA*]
page, paging, pagination
paleontology
palate, palatable
palette
palimpsest
palliasse [*often* paillasse *in USA*]
pamphleteer, pamphleteering
panacea
pancreas, pancreatic
pandemonium
paparazzo, paparazzi [*plural*]
papier-maché

papyrus, papyruses *or* papyri [*plural*]
paradigm
paradisiacal *or* paradisaical
paraffin
parallel, paralleled, parallelogram,
    parallax
paralyse [paralyze *in USA*],
    paralysis, paralytic
paranoia, paranoiac *or* paranoic,
    paranoid
paraphernalia
parenthesis, parentheses [*plural*],
    parenthesise *or* parenthesize,
parenthetical
pari-mutuel
paroxysm
parquet, parquetry
parthenogenesis, parthenogenetic
pas de deux [*singular and plural*]
passable
passé
pasteurise *or* pasteurize,
    pasteurisation *or* pasteurization
pastiche
pastille
pastime
pâté de foie gras
pavilion
peccadillo, peccadilloes
pedal, pedalling, pedalled, pedaller
pedlar [peddler *or* pedler *in USA*]
pejorative, pejoratively
pelargonium
pencil, pencilling, pencilled
penicillin
peninsula [*noun*] peninsular [*adjective,*
    e.g. Peninsular War *and* P&O
    (Peninsular and Orient Steamship
    Co)]
penitentiary
penniless
perceive, perceiving, perceived,
    perceivable
peremptory, peremptorily
perennial

periphery
periphrasis
perorate, peroration
perquisite
personnel
perspicacious, perspicacity,
    perspecuity
pétanque
petit bourgeois
petit four, petits fours [*plural*]
petits pois
phaeton
phantasmagoria
pharmacopoeia [*often* pharmacopeia
    in USA], pharmaceutical
phenomenon, phenomena [*plural*]
phlebitis
phlegm, phlegmatic
phlox
phoenix [phenix *in the USA*]
phosphorescence, phosphorescent
phosphorus [*element*]; phosphorous
    [*containing phosphorus*]
photosynthesise *or* photosynthesize
phrasal
phrenitis
phylloxera
physique
pibroch
piccalilli
picketing, picketed
picnic, picnicking, picnicked,
    picnicker
pièce de résistance
pied-à-terre, pieds-à-terre [*plural*]
pietà
pilau *or* pilaf *or* pilaff [*flavoured rice*]
pineapple
piranha *or* pirana
pituitary
pity, pitied, pitiful, pitiable, pitiless,
    pitiful
placebo
plagiarise *or* plagiarize
plankton

playwright
plebeian
plebiscite
pneumatic
pneumonia
poignant, poignancy, poignantly
poinsettia
poliomyelitis
politicking
polyp
polythene, polyurethane, polystyrene
pomegranate
pompon *or* pompom
poof *or* poove [*effeminate man*]; pouf
    or pouffe [*cushion*]
porphyry, porphoritic
poseur
posthumous
potato, potatoes
practice [*noun*]; practise [*verb*];
    practised *or in the USA* practiced
    [*adjective*]
preciosity
predecessor
predilection
prefer, preferring, preferred,
    preference
premier [*head of state*]; premiere [*first
    performance*]
presbytery
prescience, prescient, presciently
presentient, presentiment
prestidigitation, prestidigitator
preventive *or sometimes* preventative
prima facie
primordial
principal [*the chief*]; principle [*code of
    conduct*]
privilege
profit, profiting, profited, profiteer
progesterone
proletariat, proletarian
promiscuous, promiscuity
promissory note

pronounce, pronounceable,
    pronouncement, pronunciation
propeller, propelling, propelled
prophecy [*the forecast*]; prophesy
    [*to forecast*]
prophylactic, prophylaxis
proprietary [*ownership*]; propriety
    [*appropriate, conforming*]
pros and cons
prosciutto
proselyte, proselytise *or* proselytize
prostate gland
prosthesis, prosthetic
protégé, protégée [*feminine*]
protuberance, protuberant
psalm, psalmist
pseudonym, pseudonymous
psittacosis
psoriasis
psychedelic, psychedelia
psychology, psychoanalysis,
    psychiatry, psychotherapy,
    psychotic, psychosomatic
ptarmigan
pterodactyl
ptomaine poisoning
pubescence, pubescent
puerile
puerperal fever
puisne
puissance, puissant
pulchritude
punctilious, punctiliousness
purée, puréeing, puréed
puritanical
purlieu
pursuivant
pusillanimous, pusillanimity,
    pusillanimously
putsch
pygmy *or* pigmy [*or as proper nouns,*
    Pygmy *or* Pigmy]
pyjamas [pajamas *in the USA*]
pyorrhoea [pyorrhea *in the USA*]
pyrrhic

quadruped
quadruplets
quagmire
quango, quangos [*plural*]
quarrel, quarrelling, quarrelled
    [quarreling, *etc, in the USA*],
    quarrelsome
quatrefoil
quay, quayside
questionnaire
queue, queueing, queued
quiescence, quiescent
quieten, quietude, quietus
qui vive
quoin *or* coign *or* coigne
quoits
quotient
rabbi, rabbis
raccoon
raconteur
racquet *or* racket [*for tennis*]
radius, radii [*plural*]
raison d'être
rancour, rancorous [rancor *in USA*]
ranunculus
rapprochement
rarefy, rarefaction
ratatouille
rateable *or* ratable
ratiocinate, ratiocination
recalcitrance, recalcitrant
reconnaissance, reconnoitre
    [reconnoiter *in the USA*]
receivable
recherché
recognise *or* recognize, recognising,
    recognised, recognition,
    recognisance
recommend, recommendable,
    recommendation
recondite
recrudesce, recrudescence,
    recrudescent
recur, recurring, recurred, recurrence
recumbent

redundant, redundancy
refer, referring, referred, referral,
    reference
reggae
regime *or* régime
rehabilitate, rehabilitation
reindeer
reiterate
rejuvenate, rejuvenescence,
    rejuvenescent, rejuvenation
reminiscence, reminiscent,
    reminiscing
remuneration
renaissance *or* renascence [*also the
    proper noun* Renaissance],
    renascent
repellent *but a* repellant *or* repellent
repertoire
replace, replacing, replaced,
    replaceable, replacement
reprieve
repudiate, repudiation
requiescat
reredos
rescue, rescuing, rescued, rescuable
resplendent, resplendence
restaurateur
resurrection [*also proper noun*
    Resurrection]
resuscitate, resuscitation
retrieve, retrieval, retrievable
retrousse
reveille
rhapsody, rhapsodise *or* rhapsodize
rheostat
rheumatism, rheumatoid arthritis,
    rheumatology
rhinoceros
rhizome
rhododendron
rhubarb
rhythm, rhythmic *or* rhythmical
ricochet, ricochetting *or* ricocheting,
    ricochetted *or* richocheted
riposte *or* ripost

risqué
rivet, riveting, riveted
rodomontade
roommate
rotisserie
roughage
rumbustious, rumbustiously,
    rumbustiousness
rutabaga
sabbatical
saccharin [*the substance*]; saccharine
    [*over-sweet*]
sacrilege, sacrilegious
sacrosanct
sagacious, sagacity
samurai
sanatorium [sanitarium *in USA*],
    sanatoria *or* sanatoriums [*plural*]
sanctimonious, sanctimoniously,
    sanctimony
sanguine, sanguinary, sanguinely,
    sanguinity
sapphire
sarsaparilla
sassafras
satellite
satyr
sauerkraut
sauté
savoir-faire
schadenfreude *or* Schadenfreude
schematic
scherzo
schism
schizophrenia, schizophrenic,
    schizoid
schlemiel
schlep
schlock
schmaltz
schmuck
schnapps
schooner
schottische
sciatica

scimitar
scintilla, scintillate, scintillating,
    scintillation
sclerosis, sclerotic
scourge
scurrilous
scythe, scything
seance *or* séance
secateurs
secretaire
secretary, secretarial, secretariat
segue, segueing, segued
seismic, seismograph, seismoscope
seize, seizing, seized, seizure
senescent
septicaemia [septicemia *in the USA*]
septuagenarian
sepulchre, sepulchral [sepulcher *in
    the USA*]
sequestrate, sequestration
sequoia
serendipity, serendipitous
sewage [*waste*]; sewerage [*waste
    system*]
sexagenarian
shellac, shellacking
shenanigans
shibboleth
shillelagh
shrapnel
siege
sieve
silhouette, silhouetted
simulacrum
sinus, sinusitis
sirocco
skilful, skilfully [skillful *and* skillfully
    in the USA]
skulduggery [skullduggery *in the
    USA*]
slough [*pronounced slow, as in cow,
    a bog*]; slough [*pronounced sluff,
    to cast off*]
smorgasbord
sobriquet *or* soubriquet

soi-disant
soigné, soignée [*feminine*]
soiree
soliloquy, soliloquise *or* soliloquize
somersault, somersaulting,
    somersaulted [*sometimes*
    summersault]
sommelier
somnambulism, somnambulist,
    somnambulation
sophomore
soufflé, souffléed
soupçon
spaghetti
spalpeen
sphagnum
spina bifida
spinnaker
spontaneity
squeegee
staccato
stalactite [*hanging*]; stalagmite [*rising*]
staphylococcus
stationary [*still, fixed*]; stationery
    [*writing materials*]
steatopygia
stevedore
stiletto, stilettos [*plural*]
stoic, stoical, stoicism
storey [*floor of building*]; story [*tale*]
straight [*line*]; strait [*sea channel*];
    strait-laced, strait-jacket
stratagem
strychnine
stupefy, stupefying, stupefied
styptic
suave, suavely, suavity, suaveness
subpoena, subpoenaed
subterranean
subtle, subtlety
succinct, succinctly
succour [succor *in the USA*]
succubus [succubi, *plural*]
suddenness
suede

suffrage, suffragette, suffragist
sulphanilamide
sumptuous, sumptuously,
    sumptuousness
superannuation, superannuated
supercilious
superintendent
supersede
suppository
suppress, suppressing, suppressed,
    suppression, suppressor
surreal, surrealism, surrealistic
surreptitious, surreptitiously
surrogate
surveillance
susceptible, susceptibility
suzerainty
sycophant, sycophantic, sycophancy
syllable, syllabic, syllabus
syllabub
sylphlike
symbiosis
symmetry
symptomatic
synagogue
synchronise *or* synchronize,
    synchronous, synchronicity
synonymous, synonymously
synopsis, synopses [*plural*]
synthesis, synthetic
syphilis, syphilitic
syringe, syringing
syrup, syrupy
tableau, tableaux *or* tableaus [*plural*]
table d'hôte
tagliatelle
tacit, tacitly
taciturn
tactician
taillight
taipan
tamale
tambourine
tam-o'-shanter
tarantula

target, targeting, targeted
tassel, tasselled [tasseled *in USA*]
tattoo, tattooing, tattooed
teammate
teetotal, teetotaller
telecommunications
temperance
tendentious, tendentiousness
tepee *or* teepee
tergiversate, tergiversation
teriyaki
terracotta *or* terra-cotta
terrazzo
testosterone
tête-à-tête
therapeutic
thesaurus
thief, thieves, thieving, thievery
thyme
thyroid, thyroidectomy
timpani
tinnitus
tintinnabulation
titillate, titillating, titillated, titillation
toboggan, tobogganing
toccata
tocsin [*alarm bell*]; toxin [*poison*]
tollbooth, tollgate
tomato, tomatoes [*plural*]
tonneau, tonneaus [*plural*]
tonsillitis, tonsillectomy
toque [*woman's headwear*]; torque
     [*rotational force*]
tornado, tornados *or* tornadoes
     [*storm*]; tournedos [*beef steak*]
torpedo, torpedoes [*plural*]
totalisator *or* totalizator
toucan
touché
toupee, toupees [*plural*]
tourniquet
toxin [*poison*], tocsin [*alarm bell*]
trachoma, tracheostomy, tracheotomy
traffic, trafficking, trafficker

tranquil, tranquillise *or* tranquillize,
     tranquillity *or* tranquility
transatlantic
transcendent, transcendental,
     transcendentalism
transcontinental
transmissible
transsexual, transvestite
trauma, traumatic, traumatise *or*
     traumatize
triptych
triumvirate
trompe l'oeil, trompe l'oeils [*plural*]
troop [*army*]; troupe [*actors*]
trousseau, trousseaux *or* trousseaus
     [*plural*]
tsar *or* czar, tsarina *or* czarina
tsetse fly
tuberculosis, tubercular
tunnel, tunnelling, tunnelled
     [tunneling, tunneled *in the USA*]
turmeric
twelfth
tyranny, tyrannical, tyrannise *or*
     tyrannize
tyrannosaurus
ubiquitous, ubiquity
ukulele *or* ukelele
ululate, ululation
umbrella
unaffected
unanimous, unanimously
unapproachable
unappropriated
unassailable
unbiased *or* unbiassed
unconscionable, unconscionably
unctuous, unctuously
unguent
unmistakeable *or* unmistakable
urethra
useable *or* usable
usury, usurer
utilitarianism

vaccine, vaccination

vacillate, vacillating, vacillated, vacillation

vacuous

vacuum, vacuuming, vacuumed

variegated, variegation

vassal

vehicle, vehicular

veldt *or* veld

vendetta

ventriloquism, ventriloquist

veranda *or* verandah

verbatim

verisimilitude

vermilion *or* vermillion

verruca

veterinary, veterinarian

vicarious

vichyssoise

vicissitude

victuals, victualling, victualled, victualler

vilify, vilification

vinaigrette, vinegar

vin ordinaire

violoncello

virulence, virulent

vis-à-vis

viscose [*rayon*], viscous [*thick and sticky*], viscosity

vituperate, vituperation

vocabulary

volcano, volcanoes *or* volcanos [*plural*]

volte-face [*singular and plural*]

voluptuous, voluptuary

vouchsafe

voyeur, voyeuristic, voyeurism

vulcanise *or* vulcanize

wagon [*increasingly preferred to* waggon]

wainscot, wainscoting *or* wainscotting

weather (*climate*); wether (*sheep*); whether (*question*)

werewolf

whereabouts

whereas

wherein

wherewithal

whinge, whingeing, whinged

whisky [*Scotch*]; whiskey [*Irish and American*]

whitlow

whole, wholly

wilful [willful *in the USA*], wilfully, wilfulness

will-o'-the-wisp

withhold, withholding

witticism

wizen, wizened

woebegone, woeful, woefully

wolfsbane *or* wolf's-bane

woollen, woolly [woolen, wooly *in the USA*]

worshipping, worshipped, worshipper [worshiping, *etc, in the USA*]

wrath, wrathful

wreath [*flowers*]; wreathe [*intertwining*]

wunderkind

xerography

xylophone, xylophonist

yacht, yachting, yachtsman

yashmak

yodel, yodelling, yodeller [yodeling, yodeler *in the USA*]

yoghurt *or* yogurt *or* yoghourt

zabaglione

zeppelin

zucchini

zwieback

The Famous Broken Rule of Spelling:
I before E except after C

Of all the rules of spelling none is more capricious than the 'i' before 'e' except after 'c' rule, or, as the ancient jingle has it:

> I before E
> Except after C,
> Or when sounded like A
> As in *neighbour* or *weigh*.

As it happens, most words in the English language do follow this rule:

* *achieve, brief, fierce, relieve, shield, shriek, thief, yield*

* *conceivable, deceive, perceive, receive*

and those words sounding like 'ay':

* *reign, veil, beige, feint, freight, skein, rein*

But what about *either*? And *heifer, weird, sovereign* and *foreign*? These are all 'ei' words in which there is no 'c'. Nor is the 'ei' in these words sounded like 'ay'.

To deal with these rule-breakers, some grammarian invented another rule: 'i' before 'e' except after 'c' and before 'g'. This effectively takes care of such words as *sovereign* and *foreign* and also of words like *height* and *sleight*, especially if you can remember this extension to the original rhyme:

> I before E,
> Except after C,
> Or when sounded like A
> As in *neighbour* or *weigh*,
> Or when sounded like 'ite'
> As in *height* and *sleight*.

For a while, everyone was happy. But eventually it dawned on people that still lurking in the dictionary were such outlaws as *either, seize, seizure, weird* and *heifer*. To our knowledge they are still there, still untamed by any rule or guideline except perhaps that of the renowned schoolmistress Miss Hall, who insisted that her pupils learned the following:

> 'Neither leisured foreign neighbour seized the weird heights
> during the reign of the sovereign king who forfeited the reins of
> government. The heir feigned that the neigh of either reindeer was due to
> the weight, which was eighty skeins of yarn in the sleigh.'

Now, has Miss Hall apprehended all the renegades?

Problem Proper Nouns and Commonly Misspelt Names

Abergavenny, Wales
Aberystwyth, Wales
Abu Dhabi, United Arab Emirates
Abyssinia
Aldeburgh, Suffolk
Appelation Controlée
Archimedes
Achilles tendon
Acquired Immunodeficiency
    Syndrome (Aids)
Addis Ababa, Ethiopia
Aer Lingus
Afghanistan
Afrikaans
Agamemnon
Aladdin
Albuquerque
Aldwych, London
Allegheny mountains
Algonquin Hotel, NY (*but*
    Algonquian Indians of North
    America)
Alsace-Lorraine
Alzheimer's disease
Amontillado sherry
Andorra
Annunciation
Anorexia nervosa
Apache
Aphrodite
Apocalypse
Apollinaris mineral water
Appalachian Mountains,
    Appalachians
Arbroath, Scotland, Arbroath smokies
Arc de Triomphe
Archimedes
Aristotle, Aristotelian
Armageddon
Art nouveau

Ascension Day
Ashby-de-la-Zouch, Leicestershire
Ashkenazi
Athanaeum Club, London
Aubusson carpets
Auchtermuchty, Scotland
Audubon Society
Augean stables
'Auld Lang Syne'
Auld Reekie (*Edinburgh*)
Aurora Borealis
Auschwitz
Axminster carpets
Azerbaijan
Babylon
Baccalauréat (*more often anglicised as*
    baccalaureate)
Bacchus, Bacchic
Baedeker (*travel guidebooks*)
Baghdad
Baha'i, Baha'ism (*religion*)
Bahrain
Balthazar
Bannockburn, Scotland
Barabbas
Bar Mitzvah
Bas Mitzvah
Bathsheba
Baudelaire
Bayeaux Tapestry
Bayreuth Festival
Béarnaise sauce
Beau Brummell
Beaufort scale
Beau Geste
Beaujolais
Beaulieu Castle, Hampshire
Beaune
Bechuanaland
Beelzebub

Beijing, China
Belshazzar's feast
Berchtesgaden
Betws-y-Coed, Wales
Bhutan
Blenheim Palace, Oxfordshire
Bletchley Park
Bloemfontein, South Africa
Boadicea (*popular spelling of the more correct* Boudicca)
Boccaccio
Bohème, La (*opera*)
Bohemia, Bohemian
Bokhara rugs
Bophuthatswana, South Africa
Bordeaux
Boris Godunov (*opera*)
Bosnia-Herzegovina
Botticelli
Boughton Monchelsea, Kent
Bourgogne, France
Bovey Tracey, Devon
Bovine Spongiform Encephalopathy (BSE)
Braille
Brecht, Brechtian
Britannia, Britannica (as in *Encyclopaedia Britannica*)
Brobdingnag (*Gulliver's Travels*)
Brueghel *or* Bruegel *or* Breughel (*Flemish painters*)
Buccleuch
Buchenwald
Buddha
Buddleia (*popular spelling of the more botanically correct* buddleja)
Bundestag
Burkina Faso
Byelorussia
Cadillac
Caedmon
Caernarfon (*not* Carnarvon), Wales
Caerphilly, Wales
Caius College, Cambridge
Camembert

Canaan
Cape Canaveral
Capodimonte porcelain
Caractacus
Caribbean
Carrara marble
Casablanca
Cerberus
Cerne Abbas, Dorset
Chapel-en-le-Frith, Derbyshire
Charlemagne
Chartreuse
Chateaubriand
Chateauneuf-du-pape
Chateau d'Yquem
Cheyenne
Cincinnati
Cinque ports
Cirencester, Gloucestershire
Coq au vin
Coquilles St Jacques
Coliseum (*London theatre*)
Colosseum (*Rome ampitheatre*)
Comanche (*North American Indian tribe*)
Comédie-Française
Comédie humaine
Compton Wyngates, Warwickshire
Concertgebouw Orchestra, Amsterdam
Connecticut
Correggio
Cosa Nostra
Cosí fan tutte (*opera*)
Côte d'Ivoire (*former* Ivory Coast)
Courtauld Institute
Creutzfeldt-Jakob disease (CJD)
Criccieth, Wales
Curaçao (*Caribbean island and liqueur*)
Cyrillic
Czech Republic
Dadaism, Dadaist
Daguerrotype
Dáil Éireann (*Republic of Ireland parliament*)

Daiquiri (*Cuban rum, thence the cocktail*)

Dalai Lama

Daphnis and Chloe

Darby and Joan

Dardanelles

Darjeeling

Debrett (*short for* Debrett's Peerage, *the aristocrats' bible*)

Deity, the

Déjeuner sur l'herbe (*Manet's famous painting*)

Demoiselles d'Avignon (*Picasso's famous painting*)

Demosthenes

Des Moines, Iowa, USA

Deuteronomy

Deutschmark

Dien Bien Phu, Vietnam

Dionysus

Disraeli, Benjamin

Djibouti (*East African republic*)

Dobermann pinscher

Dolgellau, Wales

Domesday Book

Don Juan

Don Quixote

Doppelgänger

D'Oyly Carte Opera Company

Dungeness, Kent

Dun Laoghaire, Ireland

Dunsinane (*Shakespeare's Macbeth*)

Ebbw Vale, Wales

Ecclesiastes (*Old Testament*)

Ecumenical Council

Edgbaston (*Birmingham cricket ground*)

Edinburgh

Eichmann Trial

Eiffel Tower

Eisteddfod

Elysée Palace, France

Emmentaler cheese

Encyclopaedia Britannica

Endymion (*the lover of Selene in Greek mythology; Keats's poem; Disraeli's novel*)

Entre-Deux-Mers

Epaminondas

Epernay

Epiphany

Epithalamion (*Spenser's poem*)

Epithalamium *or* Epithalamion (*song or poem celebrating a marriage*)

Erewhon (*Samuel Butler's novel*)

Eritrea

Eroica Symphony

Euripides

Eurydice (and Orpheus)

Eustachian tube

Excalibur

Existentialism

Ezekiel

Exocet (missile)

Fabergé (*jewelled eggs*)

Faerie Queene, The (*Spenser's great poetic work*)

Faeroes (*North Atlantic island group*)

Fair Isle (knitwear)

Fauves, Les

Feock, Cornwall

Fernet Branca

Filipino

Finisterre, France

Fledermaus, Die (*J. Strauss opera*)

Folies-Bergère

Fontainebleau

Forsyte Saga

Fraulein, Frau

Führer, Der

Fujiyama *or* Mt Fuji (*not* Mt Fujiyama)

Fu Manchu, Dr (*Chinese movie detective*)

Fyffes (*banana-exporting company*)

Galapagos Islands

Gallipoli

Gandhi, Mohandas Karamchand

Gauguin, Paul

Geffrye Museum, London

Genghis Khan

Gethsemane

Gewürztraminer

Gioconda, La (*Mona Lisa*)

Givenchy

Glyndebourne Festival

Gnostic

Gobelins Tapestry

Godalming, Surrey

Goethe

Gomorrah

Gondoliers, The (Gilbert and Sullivan
opera)

Gonzalez, Byass sherry

Goonhilly Downs

Gorgonzola

Götterdämmerung

Graf Zeppelin

Grand Guignol

Gruyère cheese

Guadeloupe, Caribbean

Guangdong (*formerly Kwangtung*)

Guatemala

Guggenheim Museum, New York

Guinevere

Guinness

Gujarati (*the people and language of the*
Indian state of Gujarat)

Gulbenkian Foundation

Gurkha

Guyana

Gypsy or gipsy

Haarlem, Holland; *but* Harlem,
New York.

Habakkuk

Habeas Corpus

Hallelujah Chorus

Hallowe'en

Hannukah (*Jewish festival sometimes*
called and spelt Chanukkah)

Hare Krishna

Hawaii, Hawaiian

Heraklion, Crete

Herodias

Herstmonceux, Sussex

Hippocratic Oath

Hiroshima

Ho Chi Minh

Hogmanay

Holofernes

Holyroodhouse, Scotland

Houdini

Houyhnhnms (*talking horses in*
Gulliver's Travels)

Huguenot

Iago

Ightham, Kent

Ile de la Cité, Paris

Illinois

Immelmann turn (*aerobatics*)

Indianapolis

Innisfail, Ireland

Internationale, the (*Socialist hymn*)

Grass Roots of Spelling

Names of plants, flowers and trees are a real trap for anyone who writes
about gardening. Here are some of the tricky ones:

Agapanthus, Amaranthus, Amaryllis, Anemone, Antirrhinum, Aquilegia,
Aspidistra, Aubrieta, Bignonia, Bougainvillea, Buddleia, Calycanthus, Camellia,
Ceonothus, Chrysanthemum, Convolvulus, Cotoneaster, Cyananthus, Cymbidium,
Cytisus, Dahlia, Deutzia, Dryopteris, Eucalyptus, Freesia, Fuchsia, Gypsophila,
Hyacinth, Impatiens, Liquidambar, Narcissus, Nymphaea, Pelargonium,
Philodendron, Phlox, Pieris, Pyracantha, Rhododendron, Strelitzia, Stephanotis,
Tradescantia, Weigela, Yucca

Inuit (*North American Eskimos*)
Inveraray Castle
Iolanthe (*Gilbert and Sullivan opera*)
Iroquois
Ishmael
Istanbul
Jacuzzi
Jaipur, India
Jakarta, *also often spelt* Djakarta
Jehoshaphat
Jekyll and Hyde
Jeroboam
Jervaulx Abbey, North Yorkshire
Jodrell Bank
Judaism
Juilliard School of Music, New York
Juneau, Alaska
Jungian psychology
Juventus
Kafka, Franz, Kafkaesque
Kalahari Desert
Kalashnikov
Kama Sutra
Katmandu, Nepal
Kazakhstan
Kewpie doll
Keynesian, Keynesianism
Khartoum
Khmer Rouge
Kircudbright, Scotland
Kirkintilloch, Scotland
Kirriemuir, Scotland
Kiwanis (*American men's clubs*)
Knaresborough
Koskiusko, Mt (Australia)
Krakatoa volcano
'Kubla Khan' (*Coleridge's poem*);
    Kublai Khan (*Mogul emperor*)
Kuomintang
Kyrie eleison
La donna e mobile (*aria from*
    Rigoletto)
Laertes (*in* Hamlet)
La Guardia Airport, New York
Lalique glass

Languedoc, France
Laphroaig (*Scotch whisky*)
Lascaux Caves, France
Lausanne, Switzerland
Legionnaire's disease (*sometimes*
    Legionnaires' disease)
Leicestershire
Leighton Buzzard, Bedfordshire
Leipzig, Germany
Liebfraumilch
Liechtenstein
Liege
Lilliput, Lilliputian
Lindbergh (*famous solo pilot whose*
    baby was kidnapped)
Lindisfarne, Holy Island (*off*
    Northumberland coast)
Linguaphone
Linlithgow, Scotland
Linnaeus, Linnaean, Linnaean Society
Lipizzaner (*Austrian performing*
    horses)
Ljubljana, Slovenia
Llandaff, Wales
Llandrindod Wells, Wales
Llandudno, Wales
Llanelli, Wales
Llangollen, Wales
Llareggub (*the 'spelt backwards' town*
    in Dylan Thomas's Under Milk
    Wood)
Lohengrin (*in German legend*)
Looe, Cornwall
Louis Quinze
Lourdes, France
Louvre, Paris
Lucia di Lammermoor (*Donizetti's opera*)
Lufthansa
Luxembourg
Lyme Regis, Dorset
Lyonnaise
Lysistrata (*Aristophanes' comedy*)
Maastricht, Holland
Mabinogion (*ancient Welsh tales*)
Maccabees

McCarthyism
Machiavelli, Machiavellian
Machu Picchu, Peru
Maeterlinck, Maurice
Mackintoshes Toffee
Macintosh (*waterproof coat*)
Madame Tussaud's
Maecenas
Magdelen College, Oxford
Magdalene College, Cambridge
Mahabharata (*Sanskrit epic poem*)
Mahdi (*Muslim messiah*)
Mahé, Seychelles
Maigret, Inspector
Majolica (*opaque glazed pottery*)
Malacca
Malagasy (*former* Republic of
    Madagascar)
Malawi (*formerly* Nyasaland)
Malmesbury, Wiltshire
Malthus, Thomas; Malthusian,
    Malthusianism
Mancunian
Manon Lescaut (*Abbé Prevost's novel
    and Puccini's opera*)
Manzanilla dry sherry
Mao Tse-tung *or* Mao Zedong (*former
    Chinese leader*)
Mappa Mundi
Maraschino cherries
Mardi Gras
Margaux, Chateau
Marrakech *or* Marrakesh, Morocco
Marseillaise, the
Marseille, France
Marylebone, London
Massachusetts
Mato Grosso
Mau Mau (*former Kenyan nationalist
    movement*)
Maupassant, Guy de
Mauritania
Meccano
Mediterranean
Mehitabel

Meissen porcelain
Menai Strait
Mennonite religion
Mephistopheles
Mesopotamia
Messerschmitt
Methuselah
Meursault white wine
Michaelmas
Michelangelo
Middlesborough
Milwaukee, Wisconsin, USA
Minneapolis, Minnesota, USA
Minnehaha
Minotaur
Misérables, Les (*Victor Hugo's novel*)
Mississippi
Missolonghi, Greece
Missouri
Mistinguette (*Paris music hall star*)
Mitsubishi
Mnemosyne (*goddess of memory*)
Mobius loop
Moby-Dick, *not* Moby Dick
Mogadishu, Somalia
Mohammed *or* Muhammad
Mohave Desert
Mohican Indians
Moholy-Nagy, Laszlo (*Hungarian-US
    photographer*)
Mohorovicic discontinuity
Molière
Monegasque (*citizen of Monaco*)
Montaigne (*French essayist*)
Montessori teaching system
Montezuma, Montezuma's revenge
Montmarte, Paris
Montparnasse, Paris
Montreaux Festival
Mont-Saint-Michel, France
Montserrat, West Indies (*but* Nicholas
    Monsarrat, *author of* The Cruel
    Sea)
Morocco

'Morte D'Arthur' (*Tennyson's poem*);
    Le Morte d'Arthur (*Malory's*
    Arthurian legends)
Moulin Rouge, Paris
Munchhausen, Baron;
    Munchhausen's syndrome
Mussorgsky, Modest Petrovich
    (*Russian composer*)
Mustapha Kemal (*Turkish leader*)
Mycenae, Mycenaean civilisation
My Lai massacre
Narcissus
Nassau, Bermuda
Navaho Indian tribe
Navratilova, Martina (*tennis star*)
Neanderthal Man
Nebuchadnezzar
Nefertiti
Nehru, Jawaharlal (*Indian statesman*)
Nestlé
Neuilly, Paris
Nietzsche, Friedrich; Nietzschean
Nihilism, Nihilist
Nijinski, Vaslav (*Russian dancer and*
    choreographer)
Nkrumah, Kwame (*former president of*
    Ghana)
Nostradamus
Novaya Zemlya (*Arctic island group*)
Nuits-Saint-Georges, France
Nuneham Courtenay, Oxfordshire
Nürburgring (*grand prix motor racing*
    circuit, Germany)
Nyerere, Julius (*first president of*
    Tanzania)
Obadiah
Oberammergau, Bavaria
Odysseus
Odyssey, The (*Homer's epic poem*)
Oedipus, Oedipus complex
Oerlikon gun
Oistrakh, David (*Russian violinist*)
Olympian, Olympiad
Omar Khayyam
Omdurman, Battle of

Oradour massacre, France
Orpheus and Eurydice
Orrefors glass
Oswestry, Shropshire
Oundle, Northamptonshire
Ouagadougou, Burkina Faso
Ouija board
'Ozymandias' (*Shelley's sonnet*)
Paganini, Niccolò (*Italian violinist and*
    composer)
Palatinate
Paleolithic Age
Paleozoic Era
Palladian architecture
Panmunjom, Korea
Papeete, Tahiti
Paraclete
Paraguay, Paraguayan
Paraquat
Parisienne
Passchendaele (*Belgian World War I*
    battlefield)
'Pathétique, The' (*Beethoven piano*
    sonata)
Pavarotti, Luciano
Pavlovian
Peloponnesian War
Penmaenmawr, Wales
Pennsylvania
Pentateuch (*first five books of the*
    Old Testament)
Pepys's Diary
Petulengro (*popular Gypsy name*)
Pevsner, Nikolaus (*art historian*)
Phaedra (*Greek mythology*); Phaedrus
    (*Roman writer*); Phaethon (*Greek*
    mythology)
Pharaoh
Pharisee
Pheidippides (*Greek athlete*)
Philadelphia
Philippines
Piccadilly, Piccadilly Circus, London
Piemonte (*English form* Piedmont),
    Italian region

Pierrot
Pinocchio
Piraeus, Greece
Pitlochry, Scotland
Pittsburgh, USA
Plaid Cymru (*Welsh nationalist party*)
Pleiades (*star cluster*)
Pleistocene
Pocahontas
Poitiers, France
Pollyanna
Pompeii
Pompidou Centre, Paris
Pont-l'Evêque cheese
Pontypridd, Wales
Popocatepetl (*Mexican volcano*)
Portuguese
Poseidon
Poughkeepsie, New York
Pre-Raphaelite, Pre-Raphaelitism
Presbyterian
Prestatyn, Wales
Prix Goncourt
Psalter
Ptolemy, Ptolemaic
Puerto Rico
Punt e Mes (*Italian apertif*)
Puvis de Chavannes (*French painter*)
Pygmalion
Pyongyang, North Korea
Pyramus and Thisbe
Pyrrhic victory
Pythagoras, Pythagoras's theorem
Qaddafi, Muammar el-, *often* Gadhafi
    (*ruler of Libya*)
Qantas
Qatar
Quai d'Orsay, Paris
Quasimodo
Quattrocento
Quebecois
Quirinale, Rome
Quonset hut
Rachmaninov, Sergei
Rabelais, Rabelaisian

Ramadan (*ninth month of the Islamic
    year during which Muslims fast*)
Rashomon (*classic 1951 Japanese movie*)
Rastafarian
Rauschenberg, Robert (*US pop
    painter*)
Rechabites (*friendly society*)
Reichstag, Berlin
Rembrandt, Rembrandtesque
Renaissance
Reykjavik, Iceland
Rhesus (Rh) factor
Richelieu, Cardinal
Richthofen, 'Red Baron' (*World War I
    German flying ace*)
Riefenstahl, Leni (*German filmmaker*)
Rievaulx Abbey, Yorkshire (*see*
    Jervaulx Abbey)
Rijksmuseum, Amsterdam
Riyadh, Saudi Arabia
Robespierre (*French revolutionary
    leader*)
Rockefeller Center, New York
Roget's Thesaurus
Rolleiflex
Rolls-Royce (*not* Rolls Royce)
Romania, Romanian, *sometimes*
    Roumania, Roumanian
Röntgen, Wilhelm
Roosevelt, Franklin Delano
Roquefort cheese and dressing
Rorschach test
Rosencrantz and Guildenstern
Rosenkavalier, Der (*R. Strauss opera*)
Rosh Hashanah (*Jewish New Year*)
Rosicrucian
Rotherhithe, London
Rothschild
Rousseau, Jean-Jacques (*French
    philosopher*); Henri (*painter*)
Roussillon, France
Rubaiyat of Omar Khayyam, The
    (*12-century Persian poem*)
Rumpelstiltskin
Runnymede, Surrey

Ruysdael, Jacob (*Dutch painter*)
Rwanda
Ryukyu Islands, Japan
Sacco-Vanzetti trial
Sacre-Coeur, Paris
Sagittarius
Saint-Saens
St-Germain, Paris
Salmonella
Salzburg Festival
Samson Agonistes (*Milton's poem*)
Santayana, George (*philosopher*)
Sarajevo, Bosnia-Herzegovina
Sartor Resartus (*Carlyle's satire*)
Saskatchewan, Canada
Sassenach
Savile Club, London
Saxe-Coburg-Gotha
Saxmundham, Suffolk
Scheherazade
Schiaparelli, Elsa (*couturière*)
Schleswig-Holstein
Schoenberg, Arnold (*composer*)
Schopenhauer
Schumann, Robert (*composer*)
Schwarzenegger, Arnold
Schwarzkopf, Elizabeth (*German soprano*); 'Stormin' Norman' (*US Army general*)
Schweppes
Scorsese, Martin (*film director*)
Scylla and Charybdis
Sennacherib
Sequoia
Sevastopol, Ukraine
Sèvres porcelain
Shakespearean *or* Shakespearian
Shangri-la
Shenandoah
Shepheard's Hotel, Cairo
Shi'ite *or* Shiah (*Muslim sect*)
Shoeburyness, Essex
Siegfried
Sierra Leone
Sikh

Sinai, Mt
Sinn Fein
Sioux (*North American Indian tribe*)
Sisyphus, Sisyphean
Skopje, Macedonia
Slivovitz (*plum brandy*)
Sodom and Gomorrah
'Sohrab and Rustum' (*Matthew Arnold's epic*)
Solihull, near Birmingham
Solzhenitsyn, Alexander (*Russian novelist*)
Sophocles, Sophoclean
Sorbonne, Paris
Spandau (*Berlin jail where Nazis were held*)
Sri Lanka (*formerly* Ceylon)
Stanislavsky, Konstantin (*teacher of acting*)
Stockhausen, Karlheinze (*German composer*)
Stoke Poges, Buckinghamshire
Stornoway, Outer Hebrides
Stradivarius
Struwwelpeter (*children's storybook character*)
Sturm und Drang
Subbuteo
Sudetenland
'Sumer is icumen in' (*13th-century English poem*)
Svengali
Swahili
Sylphides, Les (*ballet*)
Syracuse, Sicily; *also* New York
Taj Mahal
Tammany Hall, New York
Tanganyika
Tannhäuser (*Wagner opera*)
Taoiseach (*Irish prime minister*)
Tauchnitz editions
Tchaikovsky, Pyotr Il'yich (*Russian composer*)
Tecumseh (*Shawnee North American Indian chief*)

Teesside
Tegucigalpa, Honduras
Tehran, Iran
Telemachus
Tennessee
Terpsichore, Terpsichorean
Thermopylae, Greece
Thessaloniki, Greece; *sometimes*
    Salonika
Thyssens (*German industrial family*)
Tiananmen Square, Beijing
Tierra del Fuego
Tiffany
Timbuktu, Mali; *also* Tombouctou
    and, popularly, Timbuctoo
Timotei shampoo
Tipperary, Ireland
Titicaca, Lake
Tocqueville, Alexis (*French political
    scientist*)
Tokugawa (*Japanese shoguns*)
Tolpuddle Martyrs
Tonton Macoute (*Haiti death squads*)
Torquemada, Tomas (*Spanish
    Inquisitor*)
Toulouse-Lautrec, Henri
Tourette's syndrome
Toynbee Hall, London
Trawsfynydd, Wales
Triboro' Bridge, New York
Tristan da Cunha
Troilus and Cressida
Trossachs, Scotland
Trovatore, Il (*Verdi opera*)
Tschiffeley's Ride
Tuareg
Tutankhamen
Tuvalu
Tynwald (*Isle of Man parliament*)
Tyrolean
Uccello, Paolo (*Italian painter*)
Ulaanbaatar, Mongolia; *more
    popularly,* Ulan Bator
Ulysses
Unter den Linden, Berlin

Uriah Heep (*Dickens' character*)
Ursprache (*hypothetical language*)
Uruguay, Uruguayan
Uttar Pradesh, India
Uttoxeter
Uzbekistan
Valkyries
Valenciennes, France
Valhalla
Valletta, Malta
Valparaiso, Chile
Van Heusen shirts
Vanuatu (*formerly* New Hebrides)
Vargas Llosa, Mario (*Peruvian
    novelist*)
Velasquez, Diego (*Spanish painter*)
Venezuela
Versailles
Veuve Clicquot champagne
Vientiane, Laos
Vietcong, Vietminh
Vieux Carré, New Orleans
Vinho verde
Vladivostok, Russian Siberia
Vlaminck, Maurice (*French painter*)
Vonnegut, Kurt (*American novelist*)
Vouvray
Vuillard, Edouard (*French painter*)
Waikiki Beach, Hawaii
Walpurgis Night
Watteau, Jean-Antoine (*French
    painter*)
Wedgwood pottery
Wehrmacht
Weimaraner (*dog breed*)
Welwyn Garden City, Hertfordshire
Wensleydale
Wickhambreaux, Kent
Widnes, Lancashire
Wienerschnitzel
Wilhelmstrasse, Berlin
Windhoek, Namibia
Winnie-the-Pooh
Witwatersrand, South Africa
Wodehouse, P. G.

Woden *or* Wodan (*Anglo-Saxon god*)
Wolfenden Report
Wolsey, Thomas (*English cardinal and statesman*)
Wollstonecraft, Mary (*British feminist*)
Woolf, Virginia
Wooloomooloo, Sydney
Wootten Bassett, Wiltshire
Worcestershire, Worcestershire sauce
Wroxeter, Shrewsbury
Wykehamist
Wynken, Blynken and Nod
Xanadu (*fabled city of Coleridge's poem, 'Kubla Khan'*)
Xanthippe (*Socrates' shrill wife*)
Xerxes
Xhosa
Yangtze Kiang, *or* Yangtze River, China

Yaoundé, Cameroon
Yom Kippur
Yosemite National Park, USA
Ypres, Belgium
Yves Saint Laurent
Zaire
Zeebrugge, Belgium
Zeitgeist
Zeppelin
Zeus
Ziegfeld Girls
Zimbabwe
Zimmer frame
Zinoviev letter
Zoroaster, Zoroastrianism
Zouave
Zuider Zee, Holland

Kingsley Amis on Spelling

The late novelist Sir Kingsley Amis had firm views on correct grammar and spelling (expressed in The King's English).

On spelling, he had two arguments for avoiding incorrect spelling. One was that 'the neglect of this precaution goes down badly with people, including some who may be thought generally unworthy but whose disapproval may be worth avoiding'.

The second argument, he wrote, was more in the nature of an appeal. 'If writing is worth doing it should be done as well as possible. Waiting at table is also worth doing, and simple pride should prevent a waiter from serving from dirty plates and with dirty hands.' And so it goes with spelling.

Ways to Improve Your Spelling

This book offers a number of ways to help you improve your spelling. These are listed here, along with a few other ideas you might like to try.

1. Learn the basic rules of spelling (*see* below)

2. Use mnemonics, which are jingles or patterns that jog your memory to help you to remember words that you find difficult to spell. You will find them in many entries in this book. If you don't know or can't find one that exists for a particular word you want to remember, try making up your own. Examples of mnemonics are:

   There's **a rat** in sep**arat**e

   It is ne**c**es**s**ary to have one collar (**c**) and two socks (**ss**)

3. Break the word down into smaller parts and learn each small part separately. This is recommended for a number of words in this book.

4. Visualize a difficult word. Try to remember its letters and the shape they make. This will give you a feel for whether a word looks right or wrong when you write it down.

5. Exaggerate the pronunciation of the word in your head. Sound out all the letters, including any silent letters.

6. Look at the word, cover it up, attempt to write it down, then check to see if you are correct. Keep doing this until you spell the word correctly.

7. Write out the word many times in your own handwriting until you feel it flows without you hesitating.

8. If you spell a word wrongly, make a note of the error. You can learn to recognise the mistakes you tend to make and so prevent yourself from repeating them.

9. Make a habit of looking up any word that you are not absolutely sure about in a good dictionary.

Some Spelling Rules

Here are some basic spelling rules. If you recognize and remember these rules, it will help you to spell a difficult or unfamiliar word.

1. **a.** A final silent *e* is dropped when an ending that begins with a vowel is added. For example:

    abbreviate+ion > abbreviat+ion = abbreviation
    argue+able > argu+able = arguable
    fascinate+ing > fascinat+ing = fascinating

    b. This *e* is retained for the endings *-ce* or *-ge* when these letters keep a soft sound. For example:

    change+able = changeable
    courage+ous = courageous
    outrage+ous = outrageous

2. When the adverb suffix *-ly* is added to an adjective that ends in a consonant followed by *-le*, the *-le* is usually dropped. For example:

    gentle+ly > gent+ly = gently
    idle+ly > id+ly = idly
    subtle+ly > subt+ly = subtly

3. When an ending that begins with a vowel is added to a word that ends in a single vowel plus a consonant, the consonant is doubled if the *stress* is on the end of the word or if the word has only one part. For example:

    admit+ance > admitt+ance = admittance
    begin+ing > beginn+ing = beginning
    equip+ed > equipp+ed = equipped

4. When an ending that begins with a vowel is added to a word that ends in a single vowel plus *l*, the *l* is doubled. For example:

    cancel+ation > cancell+ation = cancellation
    excel+ent > excell+ent = excellent
    fulfil+ing > fulfill+ing = fulfilling

5. When an ending that begins with *e*, *i*, or *y* is added to a word that ends in *c*, a *k* is also added to the *c* to keep its hard sound. For example:

    panic+ing > panick+ing = panicking
    An exception is *arc, arced, arcing*.

6. When the adjective suffix *-ous* or *-ary* is added to a word that ends in *-our*, the *u* of the *-our* is dropped. For example:

    glamour+ous > glamor+ous = glamorous
    honour+ary > honor+ary = honorary
    humour+ous > humor+ous = humorous

7. When an ending is added to a word that ends in a consonant plus *y*, the *y* changes to *i* (unless the ending added already begins with *i*). For example:

> *beauty+ful > beauti+ful = beautiful*
> *carry+age > carri+age = carriage*
> *woolly+er > woolli+er = woollier*

8. **a.** The plural of a word that ends in a consonant plus *y* is made by changing the *y* to *i* and adding *-es*, for example:

> *accessory > accessori+es = accessories*
> *diary > diari+es = diaries*
> *whisky > whiski+es = whiskies*

b. The plural of a word that ends in a vowel plus *y* is made by adding *s*. For example:

> *jersey+s = jerseys*
> *journey+s = journeys*
> *whiskey+s = whiskeys*

c. The plural of a word that ends in *-s*, *-x*, *-z*, *-sh* or *-ch* is made by adding *-es*. For example:

> *bus+es = buses*
> *focus+es = focuses*

d. The plural of a word that ends in *-eau* is made by adding *s* or *x*. For example:

> *bureau+s = bureaus* or
> *bureau+x = bureaux*
> *gateau+s = gateaus* or
> *gateau+x = gateaux*

9. When *al-* is added as a prefix at the beginning of a word to make a new word, it is spelt with one *l*. For example:

> *al+ready = already*
> *al+though = although*
> *al+together = altogether*

10. The suffix *-ful* is always spelt with one l. For example:

> *faithful, grateful, hopeful*

11. The 'uss' sound at the end of an adjective is almost always spelt *-ous*. For example:

> *courageous, courteous, luscious*

12. *i* before *e* except after *c*, when they make the sound 'ee'. For example:

> *fierce, niece, relieve*
> but   *ceiling, deceive, receive*

For a fuller discussion of this rule, *see* page 159.

13. a. The name or names of areas on the map begin with a capital letter:

> *Britain, Mediterranean*

b. The name of a religious group or its teachings begins with a capital letter:

> *Buddhism*

American Spellings

The main differences in US spellings from the British spellings are

1. British words that end in *-our* are usually spelt *-or* in the USA:

> *favor, glamor, humor, rumor*

2. British words that end in *-re* are usually spelt *-er* in the USA:

> *center, liter, meter, theater*

3. a. British words that end in *-ize* or *-ise* are always spelt *-ize* in the USA:

> *apologize, emphasize, recognize*

b. Those that end in *-yse* are spelt *-yze*:

> *analyze, breathalyze*

4. Some words containing *ae* or *oe* in Britain always have *e* on its own in the USA:

> *anesthetic, diarrhea, fetus, maneuver*

5. A final *l* is not doubled when an ending that begins with a vowel is added:

> *canceled, jeweler, traveled*

4

A GUIDE TO DIFFICULT AND CONFUSABLE WORDS

A-Z Listing

With definitions of easily confused words

a, an
Use *a* before words beginning with consonants (*a book, a cup, a video*) and *an* before words beginning with vowels: *an apple, an ice cream, an omelette, an undertaker*. There are some exceptions: the word *one*, because of the way it is pronounced (wun), demands an *a* (*a one-horse town*), as do certain words beginning with the long *u* (pronounced yew): *a ukelele, a uniform, a used car*. Words beginning with a soft *h* need *an* (*an heiress, an honest man*), but words that sound the *h* don't: *a horse, a hat, a hooter*. For cooks and gardeners, in British English it's *a herb*, whereas in the USA it's *an herb*.

abet *see* **aid, abet; aid and abet.**

abjure, adjure
While not words you use every day, they are useful to know. You often see them in newspapers: *Elsewhere governments under threat of sanctions merely adjured their subjects to tighten their belts*. **Abjure** means formally and solemnly to renounce something, usually on oath. **Adjure** is (equally solemnly) to charge someone with a serious responsibility: *He abjured his former way of life and adjured his family to protect him from further temptations*.

abnegate, abrogate, arrogate
To **abnegate** is to deny oneself; **abnegation** is self-denial. To **abrogate** is to repeal or abolish something: *The abrogation of the despised emergency laws was a cause for national celebration*. **Arrogate** means to claim or seize without right; note the close tie with *arrogant*.

abnormal, subnormal
Note the significant difference: **abnormal** means 'not normal, departing from the norm or average'; an **abnormality** is an irregularity. **Subnormal** means 'below normal' and is often applied to individuals to indicate low intelligence.

about *see* **just, about, just about**

above *see* **beneath, below, under, over**

abrogate *see* **abnegate, abrogate, arrogate.**

abstruse, obtuse
A concept that's **abstruse** is one that's hard to understand – fairly similar to *obscure*, meaning 'unclear'. **Obtuse** derives from *dull* and means 'slow, stupid and insensitive': *The obtuseness of her pupils kept Miss Hayworth in a constant state of dismay.*

abuse, misuse, disabuse
Abuse and **misuse** have roughly the same range of meanings: 'to maltreat, insult, or damage someone or something'. **Misuse** is the milder expression (*he misused his talents*) while **abuse** continues to become more condemnatory, as with *child abuse* and *drug abuse* with their moral and legal overtones. But **disabuse** has just one specific meaning, which is 'to rid a person of a mistaken idea': *She lost no time disabusing the girls of the notion that life at St Agatha's was going to be one big party.*

accede, agree
Accede, meaning 'to agree or give consent to', has become a pompous word now mostly confined to legal and regal circles. Use plain **agree to**, consent to, or allow. *See also* **agree with, agree to, agree about, agree on** also **concede, accede**.

accent, ascent, assent
The word **accent** (pronounced *AX-sent*) has to do with emphasis, usually with some aspect of speech and its pronunciation; **ascent** (pronounced *a-SENT*) is the act of moving or climbing upwards. **Assent** (also pronounced *a-SENT*) means 'to express agreement' or, as a noun, 'an agreeing'. A *royal assent* is the Crown's formal agreeing to an Act already passed through the Houses of Parliament.

accent, dialect
An **accent** is a variation of pronunciation from the standard language; a **dialect** also strays from standard pronunciation but in addition can use different vocabulary and grammar.

accept, except
To **accept** is to receive something or to agree with something; **except** means 'to exclude, omit, leave out, reject'.

accidental, incidental
An **accidental** happening occurs unexpectedly and unintentionally. Something **incidental** happens in relation to something else of greater importance *One incidental result of the calamitous floods was a renewed friendliness among neighbours.*

account: on account of *see* **because, since, on account of, owing to, due to**

accountable, responsible
There seems to be no good reason to regard these words other than as synonyms, although **accountable** sounds more serious. *See also* **cause**, **responsible**.

acetic *see* **aesthetic, ascetic, acetic**

acoustics
Acoustics is plural: *He thought the acoustics of the new opera house were wonderful.* But there is a singular exception: *Acoustics is his favourite subject.*

acquire *see* **get, acquire, obtain, secure**

activate, motivate
Activate is sometimes wrongly used to mean 'motivate'. You **activate** things (*He activated the fuse*) but **motivate** people. However, motivate is an overused vogue word for *encourage*.

actor, actress, authoress, poetess, sculptress, etc
Actor was used for both sexes before the introduction of **actress**, but today there is a general return to **actor**. There is, for example, no Actress's Equity in the UK, nor a Screen Actress's Guild in the USA. The move to non-feminine labels is happening to **authoress** (author), **poetess** (poet) and **sculptress** (sculptor). An *aviatrix* is now, simply, a pilot. The reason for all this is that feminists felt that the old labels perpetuated the notion that the male form is the norm and the female a secondary or inferior exception. However, to insist that *hero* should replace *heroine*, *heir* replace *heiress*, *waiter* replace *waitress* and for *god* to replace *goddess* is perhaps going too far.

actually, virtually, really
Actually scored a high place in the *Sunday Telegraph*'s 1995 Collection of Irritating Words and is certainly grossly overused. **Actually** and **really** mean 'in fact': *Did he actually call me that?* is legitimate usage; *Well, actually, I wouldn't mind a drink* is not. If **actually** doesn't change or add to the meaning of a sentence, then forget it! **Virtually** means 'in effect, mostly, for all practical purposes'.

acute *see* **chronic, acute**

AD *see* **BC, AD**

adapt, adopt
To **adapt** means 'to change or adjust something to suit different conditions'; to **adopt** is to take over something or someone as one's own: *In time they adapted their eating habits to the tropical climate; Once he understood what it was all about he adopted the idea with enthusiasm.*

adapter, adaptor
An **adapter** (and, interchangeably, **adaptor**) is someone who adapts something

for another purpose: *As an adapter of plays for children she is undoubtedly the best.* But the electrical fitting that you plug into a socket is always an **adaptor**.

adduce *see* **deduce, deduct, adduce**

adjacent, adjoining, contiguous
If two things are **adjacent**, they are close to each other. If they are **adjoining**, they are joined or touching: *My room adjoins hers; Marie's house is adjacent.* **Contiguous** means sharing a common boundary.

adjudge, adjudicate
To **adjudge** is to decide, but more usually to decide judicially in a court of law. To **adjudicate** is a serious although less formal process of giving a decision.

adjure *see* **abjure, adjure**

administer, minister
In the sense of treating and tending to, both words have similar meanings but are used differently: *The nurse **administered** what emergency first aid she could; Over the course of the next few months she patiently **ministered** to their medical needs.* Note that in this context **minister** is always followed by *to*.

admit
There is nothing wrong with *Thief admits committing four burglaries in West London.* But what we increasingly see is *Customs Officer admits to filing false claims.* If you substitute *acknowledges* for *admits*, would you write *acknowledges to*? In this sense the *to* after *admits* is redundant.

adopt *see* **adapt, adopt**

adopted, adoptive
A child is **adopted**; those who adopt the child are the **adoptive** parents.

advantage, benefit
An **advantage** is a situation that favours success; a **benefit** is a form of help that is earned, paid for, or given.

adventitious, adventurous
Adventitious is seen less nowadays than *fortuitous* or *serendipitous*; they all mean 'happening by chance'. **Adventurous** means 'daring, enterprising, bold and audacious'.

adversary, opponent
Both are interchangeable, a fine difference being that **adversary** has a hostile and antagonistic ring to it, while **opponent** has sportier, friendlier connotations.

adverse, averse
They look and sound similar but are used in very different ways. **Adverse** means 'hostile and damaging': *The adverse conditions wrecked their holiday*. **Averse** indicates disinclination and reluctance: *She is averse to handing out favours*. Note that **averse** is followed by *to*. *See also* **averse to, averse from**.

advice, advise, advisedly
The first two are easy. If you give counsel to or **advise** someone, you are giving them helpful information or **advice**. **Advisedly** is the tricky word: it has nothing to do with being advised or receiving advice. It means to take your own counsel. In a looser sense, it can mean 'prudently and cautiously': *The king made the decision, advisedly, no doubt with the intention of dividing the troublesome clans*.

adviser, advisor
Both mean 'someone who advises' (*Brett hired a financial adviser*) and both spellings are acceptable. But remember that the adjective is **advisory**.

aeroplane, airplane, aircraft
British English has it as **aeroplane**; American English as **airplane**, with **plane** common to both. However, the industry on both sides of the Atlantic usually calls them **aircraft**, which has the advantage of being singular *and* plural.

aesthetic, ascetic, acetic
Aesthetic (usually **esthetic** in American English) relates to the appreciation of beauty in art and nature above material considerations; an **aesthete/esthete** is one who has a highly developed appreciation of artistic beauty. An **ascetic** is a person who rejects worldly comforts in favour of self-denial, often for religious reasons. **Acetic**, from acetic acid, the main component of vinegar, is sometimes used as an adjective for sour and bitter. Pronounce them as *es-THET-ik, ah-SET-ik, ah-SEE-tik*.

affect, effect
These two words are super-confusables! To **affect** is to cause or influence something to happen: *Smoking can adversely affect your health*. An **effect** is a result: *One effect of smoking can be lung cancer*. Other meanings are close but not quite the same: *The burglar effected entry by the bathroom window; The third movement of the symphony always affected him greatly*. Remember that:
- **affect** – cause – usually a verb
- **effect** – result – usually a noun.

affecting, affection, affectation
A troublesome trio. An **affecting** play is one that touches the deeper emotions; **affection** describes the act or state of fondness and attachment; while an **affectation** is a pretence.

affinity with, affinity for
If you respect the definition of **affinity** as a relationship involving a natural

inclination towards someone or something, you will use **affinity with**. But recently **affinity** has become a loose synonym for 'liking', in which case users will logically opt for **affinity for**.

affront, effrontery

These are easily confused but are used in different ways. An **affront** is a deliberate, contemptuous insult. **Effrontery** means 'barefaced insolence, audacious impudence': *The effrontery of the performers was an affront to every decent family present.*

afraid *see* frightened, scared, alarmed, afraid

Afrikaans, Afrikaners

The language of South Africa is **Afrikaans**; the people are **Afrikaners**.

after, afterwards, afterward

He ran after the thief is used here to mean to pursue or seek. But **after**, like **afterwards** (**afterward** in the USA), can also mean merely following, or later in time: *After the escape the detective resumed his investigations . . .* or: *Afterwards/Afterward the detective resumed his investigations.*

afternoon tea *see* dinner, supper, lunch, tea

aggravate, exasperate

Aggravate means to make a condition worse. It does not mean to annoy – except in everyday speech where its use annoys the purists! If you want to **exasperate** someone, try teasing, irritating or provoking him or her, which could *aggravate* his or her ill-temper. *See also* **exacerbate, exasperate, aggravate**.

agnostic *see* atheist

ago, before, back, past

Most dictionaries define **ago** as 'in the past', so it is correct to write: *The O'Briens left these shores over a century ago.* In such a context, **ago** is preferable to the other

Aggravate, exasperate

choices; *a century before* and *a century past* beg the question, 'Before or past what?' while *a century back* is idiomatic. A common mistake is to couple **ago** with *since*: *It was over a century ago since the O'Briens left*, where *since* is clearly redundant. The correct version would be: *It was over a century ago that the O'Briens left*. Or, without **ago**: *It was over a century since the O'Briens left*.

agree with, agree to, agree about, agree on

One usually **agrees with** a person but **agrees to** a proposition or an idea: *I agreed with him about using the car but couldn't agree to his taking it for a whole week.* Other combinations include: *We eventually agreed on a deal*, and *This is the deal we've agreed upon*. Sometimes the preposition is omitted altogether: *We agreed the deal on Thursday. See also* **accede, agree**.

aid, abet; aid and abet

Aid and **abet** have a common meaning: 'to assist, help or encourage'. **Abet** is now virtually confined to 'encouraging a criminal act', while **aid and abet** is little more than legal tautology.

Aids, HIV

Aids or **AIDS** is the acronym for Acquired Immune Deficiency Syndrome and is a medical condition, not a disease. **HIV** is Human Immunodeficiency Virus and, again, is not a disease. People who are *HIV-positive* may suffer and die from *Aids-related* diseases.

aircraft, airplane *see* aeroplane, airplane, aircraft

akimbo

Akimbo describes a position of a person's arms: hands on hips with the elbows pointing outwards. To describe a man 'standing at ease, legs akimbo', as a well-known novelist recently did, is to describe an osteopathic impossibility.

alarmed *see* frightened, scared, alarmed, afraid

Aleut *see* Inuit, Aleut, Eskimo

alibi, excuse

Increasingly, **alibi** is being used as a synonym for **excuse**, to the extent that many grammarians worry that we shall be left with no word for the true meaning of **alibi**. *The Government is using French intransigence as an alibi for its own slow progress on free trade agreements* is wrong. An **alibi** is the defence that an accused person could not have committed a crime because he or she was elsewhere at the time. Ignore dictionaries that suggest **excuse** as an informal meaning of alibi; **excuses** are explanations to cover some fault or shortcoming; they can be true or false and come in a thousand guises.

alimentary *see* elemental, elementary, alimentary

allege, allegedly
Both are useful warning qualifiers to make it clear that something is not yet proved: *The alleged bribe was in the form of an envelope full of banknotes stuffed into his pocket. See also* **claim, allege, assert, maintain**.

allegory, fable, myth, parable, legend
An **allegory** is a play, poem or picture in which the characters symbolise a deeper moral message. A **fable** is a short story, usually improbable, usually with a moral, and usually with animals as characters. A **parable** is a short and simple story that illustrates some religious or moral principle. The original **myths** used gods and superhuman characters to explain natural phenomena and social customs; today the word is used mostly to describe a baseless popular belief. A **legend** is a traditional story, popularly thought to be true or based on fact: the Arthurian legends are an example. But **legend** is now extensively and incorrectly used to describe an enduring feat, or someone whose notoriety has spread and persisted – *the legendary baseballer Babe Ruth* – even though Ruth did exist in fact. The cliché *He was a legend in his own lifetime* is incorrect.

allergy, aversion
An **allergy** is an oversensitive reaction by the body to some substance; hay fever is an **allergic** reaction to pollen. But **allergy** is not a synonym for **aversion**. We sometimes read, *The man is allergic to any form of hard work*, whereas what is meant is, *The man has an aversion (i.e. dislike) for hard work*.

allow *see* **condone, approve, allow**

all ready, already
All ready, meaning 'prepared and ready for some proposed action', is clear enough, but **already** can present problems. **Already** means 'by a certain time' or 'before some specified time', but other shades of meaning abound. Sentences like: *You want me to leave already?* have a certain Jewish flavour, meaning, *Are you telling me to leave?* Other expressions include: *We're already in plenty of trouble; I've already done the work; The deliveries are already running ten minutes late.* You can see that *already* is a sort of all-purpose word that vaguely expresses or emphasises a time relationship.

all right, alright
If we accept *already, altogether* and *almost*, why not **alright**? Although it carries with it the whiff of grammatical illegitimacy it is and has been in common use for a century, as in: *I got the exam questions all right and overall I think I did alright.*

all together, altogether
All together is a grouping phrase meaning 'gathered in the same place at the same time'. **Altogether** means 'completely, entirely, totally': *When you put the facts all together you will realise that you are altogether wrong.*

allude, elude, elide
Allude means 'to refer to something indirectly'; **elude** (think of *elusive*) means 'to escape by cunning and skill'. **Elide** means 'to omit or ignore'.

allusion *see* **illusion, allusion, delusion**

almost *see* **most, almost**

alright *see* **all right, alright**

Alsatian, German Shepherd
Both are correct when referring to the dog, the latter being used more commonly in the USA.

altar, alter
Discussing the refurbishment of the church, the builder said to the bishop: *I'm sorry, but I can't alter the altar*.

alternate, alternative
Alternate means 'one after the other', 'to take turns', or 'to substitute' An **alternative** is a choice between two or more options. The same applies to **alternately** and **alternatively**: *You can work alternately, that is on alternate days, or alternatively you might prefer to work one week on and one week off*. **Alternative** cannot be used without relating it to a prior option. *The non-alcoholic beer is to be marketed as a party alternative* is nonsense: alternative to what? *The non-alcoholic beer is to be marketed as an alternative to the range of alcoholic drinks consumed at parties* is sobering but clear.

although, though
Both are generally interchangeable but **though** is considered to be more colloquial. **Though** means 'despite the fact that . . . ; **although** means 'even though'. It's largely a matter of which looks and sounds right. *Although it was a mongrel I bought the dog anyway; I bought the dog even though it was a mongrel*. **Though** can also be used to end a sentence as an afterthought: *I happen to like mongrels, though*. Avoid *tho* and *altho*.

altogether *see* **all together, altogether**

alumnus, alumna, alumnae, alumni
An **alumnus** is a male graduate of a college or university (plural **alumni**) while an **alumna** is a female graduate (plural **alumnae**). Collectively they are *alumni*.

always *see* **invariably, always**

amateur, novice, tyro
An **amateur**, as opposed to a professional, indulges in an activity as a pastime. A **novice** is a beginner, while a **tyro**, a word used less frequently, is an awkward, raw beginner.

ambiguous, ambivalent
The two are not synonyms. **Ambiguous** is used to refer to a confusing situation that has two or more meanings or interpretations. To be **ambivalent** is to be confused by two contradictory or conflicting thoughts or emotions.

ameliorate *see* improve, ameliorate

amend, emend
In relation to a text, **amend** means 'to correct, improve, change or revise it', while **emend** means 'to correct it by removing errors'. **Amend** is nowadays acceptable to describe both tasks.

amiable, amicable
Both words imply friendliness but with this difference: **amiable** generally applies to people and living things (*I always remembered him as an amiable sort of fellow*) while **amicable** can also be used to describe inanimate relationships: *They quickly reached an amicable agreement.*

amid, amidst
Use **amid**; **amidst** is considered rather flowery.

amoral, immoral
Amoral means 'unconcerned with morals', 'an unmoral person', 'someone without a moral code'. To be **immoral** is to offend against an established moral code.

amuse, bemuse
To **amuse** someone is to divert and entertain them and to make them smile or laugh: *The baby's antics never failed to amuse the family.* **Bemuse**, however, is to confuse and bewilder: *She could see that the guests were totally bemused the moment they walked into the gallery.*

analysis, synthesis
Analysis means 'to take apart, to examine, to reduce something to its elements'. **Synthesis** means the opposite: 'to combine, to build something from various elements'.

anemone, anenome
Perhaps because it is easier to pronounce this way, the latter is often used as the spelling, but it is incorrect.

anaesthetic, analgesic
An **anaesthetic** (American English = **anesthetic**) produces a loss of physical feeling and an **analgesic** reduces sensitivity to pain: *He was given a general anaesthetic for the operation; Paracetamol is a widely used analgesic.*

angry *see* mad, angry

annex, annexe
Two common confusables worth separating by their different spelling. To **annex** is to attach or to take possession of something: *The lawyer said she would annex the extra paragraphs to the will; The government lost no time announcing the annexation of the adjoining territory.* An **annexe** (but often **annex** in the USA) is an addition or extension: *The new annexe will provide accommodation for another sixty students.*

anniversary, birthday, jubilee
A small point, perhaps, but humans and animals celebrate their birth with **birthdays**, while everything else has **anniversaries**. A **jubilee** used to be a 25th or 50th anniversary but is now used to describe any important periodical celebration.

anorexia *see* **bulimia, anorexia**

answer *see* **react, respond**

antagonist *see* **protagonist, antagonist**

ante-, anti
When using words beginning with these prefixes it may help to remember that **ante** = before; **anti** = against.
Before – *antebellum, antecedent, antedate, antediluvian, antenatal*
Against – *antibody, antifreeze, antimacassar, antinuclear*

anticipate, expect, hope
The traditional meaning of **anticipate** is to foresee, or to think of beforehand, or forestall: *The captain anticipated the cyclone and put into the nearest harbour.* It is now general usage to use **anticipate** for **expect**, which really means 'to look forward to something that is certain or fairly likely to happen': *I now expect you to arrive early every Monday; We can expect some rain over the next day or two.* Admiral Nelson exhorted his men with *England expects every, man will do his duty*, rather than England hopes . . . ; **hope** is an altogether more wish-oriented word implying no certain outcome: *I hope the neighbour's party won't be too noisy.*

anxious, eager
She was anxious to get home is probably a shortening of *She was anxious (about the dangers of walking alone in the dark) and eager to get home.* **Anxious** implies a degree of worry, fear or apprehension, while to be **eager** is to be impatient, keen, enthusiastic.

any *see* **either, any**

anybody, anyone, any one
The first two are interchangeable and, strictly speaking, singular: *If anybody/anyone is there, will he please answer the doorbell?* is correct. However, with objections to *he*, and with the questioner not knowing the gender of the person

on the other side of the door, it is now acceptable to use the plural forms *they* or *their*: *Will they please answer the doorbell?* The same principles apply to **somebody/someone**. **Any one** is used when single persons or objects are being described: *'Is there anyone there,' asked the traveller, knocking at the moonlit door; The first prize could go to any one of the entries.*

anymore, any more
Anymore is preferred in the USA, **any more** in the UK, but both mean 'not now': *Marilyn doesn't work here anymore/any more.* **Any more** is correct when referring to quantity: *I don't want any more porridge.*

anyplace, anywhere
Anywhere means any unspecified place. **Anyplace** is the American English version.

apartment *see* flat, condominium, apartment

apparent, evident
Apparent means 'seeming to appear, or appearing to exist', but dictionaries also define the word as meaning 'readily seen or understood', which creates a mighty confusable! **Evident** means 'conclusive, obvious, clear to one's understanding'. We often hear something like *It's fairly evident that the home team will lose*, which is confusing until you delete the 'fairly'. Good alternatives are **clear** and **unclear**: *It was clear that the home team would lose; At halftime it was still unclear whether the home team would lose, as expected.*

apposite, apt
Both mean 'appropriate', or 'ideal for the occasion or purpose'. **Apposite** perhaps carries a little more literary weight.

appraise, apprise, assess, evaluate
To **appraise** is to estimate the worth of somebody or something; to **assess** is to estimate the value of something, for example, property for tax purposes; to **evaluate** is to determine the numerical or monetary value of something. **Apprise** is the odd man out; it means 'to inform': *After the desserts were served the waiter quietly apprised him of the size of the bill.*

appreciate *see* understand, appreciate, comprehend

approve *see* condone, approve, allow

a priori, prima facie
The Latin term *a priori*, which is sometimes misapplied, defines reasoning deductively, from cause to effect, which, without supportive observation, leads to a conclusion. *A priori* reasoning can, of course, lead to a wrong conclusion. *A priori* is sometimes confused with *prima facie*, which means using available but not necessarily complete or tested evidence to arrive at a conclusion: *His a*

priori *view was that there was sufficient evidence to convict the man; The fact that the notes were found in the student's locker was* prima facie *evidence of his cheating.* Note that both should normally appear in italics.

apt *see* **apposite, apt** and **likely, liable, apt, prone**

arbitrate, mediate
These words represent quite distinct methods of settling a dispute. An **arbitrator** hears evidence from both sides before handing down a decision, which is binding; an **arbitrary decision** is one over which the disputants have little or no say. A **mediator** is much more involved in negotiating (or 'arm-twisting') with the parties in dispute and aims more for a compromise solution.

Argentina, Argentine
Argentina is the country although old hands may still refer to it as **The Argentine**; more to the point, **argentine** refers to silver or something with silvery qualities. There's a lot of argy-bargy (which is from Scots, incidentally) about whether its citizens should be called **Argentinians** or **Argentines**. Purists prefer the latter although the former is perfectly acceptable. As one wit has pointed out: 'Would Evita have been so successful if the composer had scored "Don't whine for me, Argentine"?'

arouse *see* **rouse, arouse**

arrogate *see* **abnegate, abrogate, arrogate**

arthritis, rheumatism, lumbago, sciatica
Arthritis is painful inflammation of the joints; **rheumatism** is a similarly painful joint disorder but can extend to muscle and connective tissue; **rheumatoid arthritis** is a chronic condition often characterised by swollen joints. **Lumbago** is backache, usually in the lower lumbar region, while **sciatica** is neuralgic pain in the thigh and leg caused by inflammation of the sciatic nerve.

artist, artiste
A painter or public performer is an **artist**; although the inflated term for an entertainer, **artiste**, still survives, it is best avoided.

Art Nouveau, Art Deco
Both define styles of decorative art and architecture. **Art Nouveau** is a highly stylised form based on natural vegetation, especially leaves and flowers; it arose in the 1890s and extended well into the 20th century. **Art Deco** evolved in the 1920s and is a style primarily based on geometric and symmetrical forms.

as *see* **like, as, as if, such as, just as**

ascent *see* **accent, ascent, assent**

ascertain, find out
Jim, find out how many people are waiting out there, will you? Jim, ascertain how many people are waiting out there, will you? Which would you prefer to use? If you can substitute **ascertain** for **find out** without appearing pompous, feel free to do so.

ascetic *see* **aesthetic, ascetic, acetic**

ascribe *see* **prescribe, proscribe, ascribe**

as if *see* **like, as, as if, such as, just as**

ass *see* **donkey, ass, burro, mule**

assent *see* **accent, ascent, assent**

assert *see* **claim, allege, assert, maintain**

assess *see* **appraise, apprise, assess, evaluate**

assume, presume
One meaning of **assume** is quite unambiguous: 'to undertake something', as in: *He rather arrogantly assumed the role of team leader.* The other meaning – 'to suppose, to take for granted, to conclude on the basis of existing evidence', is often confused with **presume**, which means 'to take for granted without any proof or reasoning': *Knowing Jennifer was a close friend of Margaret's, she naturally assumed she'd be going to the party; He presumed for some reason that Fred was an insurance salesman, but he was wrong.*

assurance, insurance
Assurance is life insurance in the form of a policy that ensures an eventual financial benefit. **Insurance** is a guarantee of payment only if there is damage to person, property or financial expectation through some unexpected event.

assure, ensure, insure, promise
To **assure** somebody is to give him or her confidence or reason to be sure about something: *James assured Helen that everything would be fine.* To **ensure** is to make sure or certain: *He went around the house to ensure that all the doors were locked.* To **insure** is to protect against risk or loss. To **promise** is to undertake or pledge something in the future, but is increasingly and wrongly being used as a synonym for **assure**: *Mark promised his mother that he had done his homework.* Mark might correctly promise his mother that he would *do* his homework, but could not possibly promise that he had *done* it!

astonishing *see* **incredible, incredulous**

as well as, besides
As well as means 'and not only', and links two things: *As well as the funfair they went to the theatre.* **Besides** means 'in addition to': *Besides gardening, they love classical music.* See also **beside, besides**.

atheist, agnostic

An **atheist** believes that there is no God or gods; an **agnostic** insists that it is impossible to know whether God exists or not. *'I'm still an atheist, thank God'*, *said the film director Luis Buñuel.*

auger, augur

American author Bill Bryson quotes *The Guardian*: *'The results do not auger well for the President in the forthcoming mid-term elections'*. What *The Guardian* is saying is that *results do not drill well for the President* . . . an **auger** is a tool for boring holes in wood or earth. **Augur** means to foresee or presage: *the results do not augur well for the President,* or a suitable substitute: *the results do not bode well for the President.*

aural *see* oral, aural, verbal

auspicious *see* propitious, auspicious

authentic, genuine

Authentic is usually applied to something that is produced by someone, about which there is no doubt; it is the opposite of *counterfeit*: *The expert agreed that the painting was an authentic Titian.* **Genuine** has a wider range of meanings and is generally used to imply some innate or original quality: *The handbag was made of genuine Italian leather; She seemed genuinely apologetic.*

authoress *see* actor, actress, authoress, poetess, sculptress, etc

authoritarian, authoritative

An **authoritarian** dominates or rules by fear, demanding obedience and submission. An **authoritative** person (or text) commands respect through being accepted as true and reliable: *Her work is regarded as the authoritative text on Hardy's poetry.*

autobiography

If you should ever commit your life story to print, don't refer to it as *my autobiography*: it's tautological. Anyone else can say *It's Bill's autobiography*, but if you need to refer to your masterpiece you say or write, *It's an autobiography.*

avenge *see* revenge, avenge, vengeance

average, ordinary

To say that someone lives in an *average* home is fairly meaningless; the person probably lives in an **ordinary** home. Perfectionists insist that **average** should only be used in its mathematical sense. If five individuals for example, the average age of 5, 11, 14, 20 and 25, 18, 15, their average age is calculated as the total of all the ages (75) divided by the number of individuals in the group. Generally, however, **average** is used to mean 'usual' or 'typical': *As far as' till takings went it was an average day; On average the business takes about £800 a week.*

averse to, averse from

Etymologically, **averse from** has a sound case, but usage now favours **averse to**: *She was not averse to his offer; She had an unreasonable aversion to open windows.* *See also* **adverse, averse**.

aversion *see* allergy, aversion

avocation *see* vocation, avocation

avoid *see* evade, elude, avoid

await, wait

The two forms are used differently although in the end they amount to much the same thing. *We await the judge's decision; We await news of the survivors.* In other words, one *awaits* something. But, *We wait for the judge's decision; We wait to hear about the survivors; We wait until early morning for the news.* **Await** sounds a bit formal for everyday use.

a while, awhile *see* while, a while, awhile, whilst

axiom, axiomatic

An **axiom** is not an absolute or self-evident truth but a generally accepted statement, law or principle. Likewise, **axiomatic** does not refer to an absolute or self-evident truth but to something resembling an axiom, a self-evident statement or some universally accepted principle that is not necessarily absolutely true. *See also* **maxim, axiom**.

back *see* ago, before, back, past

back, behind, backward, backwards

Back is a true all-purpose word describing a position at the rear, away from you, reversed or returning, and, with its other meanings, is used in an amazing number of ways (**quarterback, backchat, backslider, back off, back down, back up**). American English relates **back** and **front** in a logical way: *He hid in back of the house; he appeared in front of the house;* whereas British English insists on *He hid behind (or at the back of) the house.* **Backward** is an adjective: *He was a backward child; It was a backward step;* but it can also be used adverbially, like **backwards**: *They all fell over backward/backwards.*

bacteria, virus, bug

Bacteria is the plural of **bacterium** but is now generally used as the singular form. They are single-celled micro-organisms (also called *germs* or *microbes*) and can be observed through an optical microscope. A **virus** is a sub-microscopic nucleic acid entity, with a protein coating, that replicates only within plant and animal cells. Most people give up and call them all **bugs**.

bail, bale
Today's liberal acceptance of interchangeable spellings has added to the confusion that these two words have always caused. The money paid into a court to release a person charged with an offence and forfeited if that person absconds is always spelled **bail**. A bundle of hay, wool, paper or other material is always spelled **bale**. But do you **bale out** or **bail out** the water in a swamped dinghy? If you respect the Old French origin of bucket (*baille*), you will use **bail**; otherwise either will do. More perplexing is whether you **bale out** or **bail out** of a doomed aircraft; or usually you **bail** someone out of trouble, following the idea of releasing someone from trouble, while you **bale out** of a doomed aircraft, following the figurative idea of dropping a **bale** from the plane. Either spelling is now acceptable. The two wooden spindles placed on top of cricket stumps are spelt **bails**; the mystery is, why?

baited, bated
Bated means restrained or diminished; **bait** is a lure to catch something: *He stood by the stream with bated breath while his wife baited the hook.*

balcony, circle, dress circle, gallery, stalls
In most theatres, the **stalls** are at floor level, with the **circle**, usually divided into **dress circle** and **upper circle**, on the next level. Above the circle is the **balcony**, with the **gallery** at the very top.

bale *see* **bail, bale**

baleful, baneful
Baleful is sometimes used incorrectly to mean 'miserable or gloomy': '*As one who has never denied his youthful homosexual encounters, what did he think the age [of consent] should be? He looks baleful. "I think I'm in favour of 18, I'm rather ashamed to say."*' (Interview with poet Sir Stephen Spender in *The Times*). The modern meaning of **baleful** is 'menacing, malign or destructive'. **Baneful** is little used today, but means 'poisonous or harmful'.

balk, baulk
The former spelling is the modern version and predominant in American English; either is acceptable to mean 'to suddenly refuse or be reluctant to do something': *The horse baulked at the first hurdle.*

balmy *see* **barmy, balmy**

ballot *see* **plebiscite, referendum, poll, ballot, election**

bankruptcy *see* **insolvency, bankruptcy**

barbaric, barbarous
Both adjectives mean 'primitive, uncivilised, brutal and cruel' and are synonymous.

Barbecue, barbeque

barbecue, barbeque

Barbecue derives directly from the Spanish-Caribbean *barbacoa*, a fire surmounted by a grid of sticks on which to cook, and is the correct spelling. **Barbeque** may have originated from the common American abbreviation, *BBQ*.

baring, barring, bearing

These three derive from *bare, bar* and *bear*, meaning respectively: 'to uncover', 'to obstruct', and 'to carry'.

barmy, balmy

Occasionally confused. **Balmy**, usually applied to describing weather, means 'mild, pleasant and soothing'. **Barmy** is a British slang word meaning 'mentally not quite all there': *Everyone thought the boss was a bit barmy*.

base, basis

Base has a wide range of meanings, defining a foundation, a support or a fundamental element in a structure. Both **base** and **basis** can mean the same but are used differently. **Base** is usually applied to literal description (**base** of a pyramid, a skull, a compound) while **basis** finds more figurative or abstract uses (**basis** of an agreement; **basis** of a solution to the problem).

base, bass

Whatever confusion there is between these two probably derives from the fact that the musical **bass** (voice range, musical instrument) is pronounced *bas* or *bayss*.

bated *see* baited, bated

bath, bathe

Bath can be used as a verb (*She baths twice a day*) but nowadays is usually used as a noun (*She takes a bath twice a day*). **Bathe**, meaning 'to wash', is used as the verb: *She bathes twice a day*.

bathos, pathos, bathetic, pathetic

Apart from its precise meaning of 'an undignified descent from the sublime to the commonplace', **bathos** is also loosely used to convey pompous insincerity, excessive sentimentality and a really low point – the pits. **Pathos** is the quality of drama capable of arousing deep feelings of pity and compassion. The adjectives **pathetic** and **bathetic**, however, are today often contemptuously used to indicate utter worthlessness, so be careful.

bathroom see **lavatory, toilet, loo, bathroom**

baulk see **balk, baulk**

BC, AD

AD comes before the date, and **BC** after: *Emperor Augustus died in AD 14; The archaeological discoveries were dated between 400 and 250 BC.* **BC** and **AD** can appear with points, i.e., **B.C.** and **A.D.**, and are usually printed in small capitals, AD, BC.

bearing *see* **baring, barring, bearing**

bears *see* **bulls and bears**

because, since, on account of, owing to, due to

Some delicate decision-making here! **Because** means 'for the reason'; **because of** roughly translates as 'by reason of': *He had to buy a new car because his other one packed up; He had to return his new car because of a faulty gear box.* **On account of** is used to qualify a phrase: *He can't drive the car on account of the faulty gear box.* The correct use of **since** is to imply a time lapse: *He's been cycling to work since his car broke down.* **Owing to, on account of** and **because of** are for all practical purposes synonymous. **Due to** invites grammatical error; it means 'caused by' and should logically link the result with the cause: *His lack of success with girls was due to his not having a car.* Grammarians warn against using **due to** as a substitute for **because**, but long usage has now established them as synonymous.

begging the question, beg the question

The term is commonly misused to mean 'evading the question' or 'avoiding the point of the argument'. It really means 'assuming as true some point has not yet been proved': *That God exists, because there are stars, begs the question.*

before *see* **ago, before, back, past**

begin, commence, inaugurate, initiate, start

Although all have much the same meaning, they are used differently. **Initiate** and **inaugurate** are rather formal and are mostly used to describe the origination of some significant undertaking, like a building project or a peace accord. **Commence** is interchangeable with **begin**, except that it is a shade more formal, while **start** implies a certain urgency: *Drivers – start your engines!*

behest *see* **request, behest**

belabour, labour
Occasionally **belaboured** is used as a synonym for **laboured**, which it isn't. **Belabour** can mean 'physically to beat someone or something', or 'to attack verbally': *He belaboured his opponent with his poor political record.*

believe, feel, think
The usage of these words follows this logic: You **believe** with faith, you **feel** with your senses, and you **think** with your mind: *At first I believed he was telling the truth but felt he was hiding something, and now I think he was lying all the time.* Think about **feel** before using it. *I feel I should leave now,* or usages similar to this example are common enough. But . . . **feel**? In most cases the user means **think**, having worked out that a train must be caught or that the party is becoming boring anyway. On the other hand, if the person is at a party and realises that he or she is a bit under the weather, **feel** would no doubt be appropriate. **Feel** is becoming an overused, if harmless, synonym for **think** – which it isn't.

below *see* **beneath, below, under, over**

bellwether, harbinger
Often seen in the financial pages of newspapers, **bellwether** is sometimes used wrongly in place of **harbinger**, which is someone or something that foretells of an approaching event. A **bellwether**, on the other hand, is traditionally a sheep with a bell hanging from its neck, which was used to lead the flock. The modern meaning is therefore something that others follow blindly, like sheep, or a trend-setter: *The share issue proved to be a mesmerising bellwether which predictably resulted in the usual sacrificial slaughter of incautious punters* is correct (and adroit) modern usage.

bemuse *see* **amuse, bemuse**

beneath, below, under, over
Beneath and **below** mean 'lower than' and are the opposite of **above**. **Under** (and **underneath**) are the opposite of **over**, and both suggest a sense of position and proximity: *His exam marks were well below* (not under) *mine; She slid eagerly under* (not below) *the blankets.* As you can see, the differences are extremely subtle.

benefit *see* **advantage, benefit**

bereft, bereaved
Both words have the broad meaning of loss, of being deprived, but while **bereft** is used in a general sense (*She was suddenly and tragically bereft of sustenance, of hope, of all human dignity . . .*), **bereaved** is reserved for a loss brought about by death.

beside, besides
Beside means 'next to', or 'by the side of'. **Besides** means 'in addition to', or 'moreover': *She asked me to sit beside her; besides, there were no other available seats.* *See also* **as well as, besides**.

best, better
Better applies to a choice of two entities (*Of the two entries Mr Peacock's was the better*) and **best** is used when the choice is wider: *Of the fifteen entries, Mr Peacock's was easily the best.*

biannual, biennial, bimonthly, biweekly
The only unambiguous words in this lot are **biennial**, which as gardeners know means 'once every two years', and **biannual**, which means 'twice a year'. Unfortunately, **bimonthly** and **biweekly** can mean twice a month or once every two months, and twice a week or once every two weeks. To make yourself clear, do not use either – spell it out in full.

Bible, bible, biblical
When referring to the Old and New Testaments, use a capital *B*, but use a lower-case *b* in the context of, for example, *His book on stamp collecting is regarded as the bible of philately.* The word **biblical** uses a lower-case *b*.

biennial *see* **biannual, biennial, bimonthly, biweekly**

billiards *see* **snooker, pool, billiards**

billion
Fifty years ago, the British **billion** equalled a 'million million' and the American **billion** was a 'thousand million'. Now the British billion, too, has become a 'thousand million'. A **trillion** is a million million million (1,000,000,000,000,000,000) . . . for now!

bimonthly *see* **biannual, biennial, bimonthly, biweekly**

birthday *see* **anniversary, birthday, jubilee**

biweekly *see* **biannual, biennial, bimonthly, biweekly**

black, negro, coloured, non-white
Tread warily and sensitively through this linguistic minefield. **Black** has emerged as the most acceptable term to define most dark-skinned ethnic groups (although not all Asians); the other terms are usually only acceptable in an historical sense, for example, when writing dialogue set in a time period when such usage was commonplace. Also extend sensitivity to the use of idioms such as *black sheep* and applications like the verb *to black*, meaning to boycott: *Chief police officers decided unanimously yesterday, after studying a paper highlighting the huge number of timewasting callouts, to black people whose alarms kept going off* (*The Times*) is, on a quick reading, potentially provocative.

blame

I blame that stupid chair for this bruise on my leg is incorrect – blame cannot be attributed to inanimate objects for misfortune: they can't accept it was their fault or feel remorse. **Blame** should not be followed by *on*, as it so often is: *They blamed the disaster on me*. A correct version would be *They blamed me for the disaster*.

blanch, blench

Strange word, **blanch**. Although in cookery books it can mean 'to plunge vegetables briefly into boiling water to preserve their colour', it usually means 'to *remove* colour, to lighten and whiten'. Thus, if someone received a shock, they might **blanch** or go pale: *She shuddered and blanched at the thought*. **Blench** is also strange: from an older meaning of 'to deceive' it now means to 'flinch from in fear'. Many dictionaries unhelpfully list both meanings under both words.

blatant *see* **flagrant**

blaze, blazon

Apart from its use to describe fire and light, to **blaze** means to mark or open up a path or territory: *He helped blaze a new trail across the Rockies*. Occasionally we see the word **blazoned** wrongly substituted for **blazed**. To **blazon** means to 'boldly proclaim something to all and sundry' and, in heraldry, 'to draw up heraldic arms'.

blench *see* **blanch, blench**

bloater *see* **kipper, herring, bloater**

bloc, block

Bloc is used rather than **block** to describe a group of individuals, organisations or nations united in a common cause. A good example is the former *communist bloc*.

blond, blonde

If the subject is a male, use **blond**, if female, use **blonde**. Even less known (and observed) is the male version of **brunette** – **brunet**.

boar, boor, bore, Boer

Although a dictionary soon sorts them out, this quartet is commonly confused: a **boar** is a male pig; a **boor** is a rude, insensitive, uncivilised person; a **bore** is a tiresome, garrulous and fiendishly uninteresting person, and the **Boers** were the original white, mostly Dutch, settlers in South Africa.

bogey, bogie, bogy

A **bogey** in golf is a score of one stroke over par for a particular hole on a course. A **bogie** is a set of wheels, usually four or six, on locomotives or railway carriages; a **bogy** (as in bogyman) is an evil spirit, but confusingly, can be spelled bogey/bogeyman. Finally, a **bogy** (one spelling only) can be something unmentionable ejected from the nose.

bona fide, bona fides
Bona fide, which looks like the singular of **bona fides**, actually isn't. It's the adjectival form: *He judged it to be a* bona fide *complaint,* meaning a genuine one. **Bona fides** is the noun and it is singular: *He hoped his* bona fides *was sufficiently convincing to allow him entry.*

boor, bore *see* **boar, boor, bore, Boer**

born, borne, bourne
Born is used exclusively in relation to birth: *She was born on September 3; He was born of an English mother and a Turkish father.* **Borne** can be used similarly (*The mother had borne the baby over the full term*) but has wider applications: *The pain he had borne was beyond belief; These facts should be borne in mind.* **Bourne** is an old English word for stream that survives in countless place-names such as Littlebourne, Bishopsbourne, etc.

both, each, either
Both embraces two things. **Each** refers separately to one of two or more things: *Both buckets had holes in them; Each of the three buckets was riddled with holes.* Be careful not to mix singular and plural: *Each of the volunteers has a job to do* is all singular and correct. *The volunteers each have a job to do* is also correct; in this case a plural verb (*have*) must follow the plural *volunteers.* The fairly common use of **either**, as in *Two large trees stood on either side of the house,* can be confusing. A clearer version might be: *A large tree stood on each side of the house.*

bourne *see* **born, borne, bourne**

bowdlerise
Bowdlerise is sometimes wrongly used to mean to 'cut and mutilate a text' when it really means 'to remove words or passages considered to be offensive or obscene': *Their edition of The Family Shakespeare had been thoroughly bowdlerised.*

Boy Scouts *see* **Scouts**

brand new, bran new
Believe it or not, confusion exists: *A bran-new population, in a bran-new town, in a bran-new quarter of the city* (*The Guardian*, 1991). What is intended, of course, is **brand-new**, meaning absolutely new.

bravery, bravado, bravura, courage, heroism
Bravery is the readiness to face danger or pain; **bravado** is the ostentatious pretence of bravery; **bravura** is a display of daring brilliance, often in an artistic performance. **Courage** is the quality required to meet confrontation or danger with firm resolve – a quality most of us would like to possess at times of stress or challenge. **Heroism** implies an act of selflessness that transcends normal human behaviour.

breach, breech
To **breach** is to break or violate, as in *a breach* (break or gap) *in a wall*; *a breach* (violation) *of the peace*. **Breech** (remember that breeches is the garment that covers the posterior!) refers to the rear of anything, as in *breech birth* (a baby born feet-first), *breech-loading gun* (loaded from behind).

break *see* **fracture, break**

broach, brooch
To **broach** is to open up: *He eventually broached the delicate subject of marriage.* A **brooch** is a piece of jewellery, usually fixed to the clothing with a pin.

brownie points
Go up in your kids' estimation. Earn some brownie points. A gold star even (advertisement for EuroDisney, 1994). The original **brownie points**, named after an unpopular superintendent, were introduced in the early 1900s on the Canadian Pacific Railway as demerits for breaking regulations.

Britain

Britain and **Great Britain** are synonymous; both mean the union of England, Scotland and Wales. The **United Kingdom** (full title: The United Kingdom of Great Britain and Northern Ireland, abbreviated to the UK) comprises England, Scotland, Wales and Northern Ireland plus various islands. The **British Isles** loosely include the UK, the Republic of Ireland, and the dependencies of the Isle of Man and the Channel Islands. UK citizens are known as **British**, **Britons**, **Britishers** or **Brits**.

---

brunet, brunette *see* **blond, blonde**

buccaneer *see* **pirate, buccaneer, corsair, privateer**

buffet
Buffet (pronounced as spelt) means to batter: *The ship was buffeted by gales all across the Bay of Biscay.* A **buffet** (pronounced *boo-fay*) is a counter from which refreshments are served or an informal meal where guests help themselves.

bug *see* **bacteria, virus, bug**

bulimia, anorexia
Both are psychological eating disorders. With **bulimia**, sufferers compulsively overeat to the point of obesity, then force themselves to vomit (*bulimia nervosa*). With **anorexia**, the sufferer looses all appetite for food to the point of serious wasting – and even death.

bulls and bears

These stock market terms can be confusing. The **bulls** buy shares when they think the price will rise to sell them later at a profit. If enough **bulls** buy, the market becomes buoyant and is called a **bull market**. **Bears** sell shares when they expect the market to go down, hoping to buy them back later at a much lower price. Too much selling activity may drive all share prices down and this may cause a **bear market**.

bumf, bumph

The correct spelling is **bumf**, an abbreviation of 'bum-fodder' (i.e. toilet paper), and refers to useless, time-wasting documents and paperwork.

burgeon, burgeoning

The words are frequently used to indicate rapid and luxuriant growth or increase, but the primary meaning is to bud or sprout, to *begin* growing.

burglar, burgle, burglarise; burglary, robbery, stealing, theft

Stealing is taking or appropriating something belonging to someone else without his or her permission. **Burglary** is entering premises with intent to steal or commit a felony. A **burglar** does the breaking-in to **burgle**. **Burglarise** is not a real word. **Robbery** is stealing that involves violence or the threat of it. **Theft** is synonymous with stealing.

burned, burnt

The two are virtually interchangeable except: *The bushfires burned for several days* rather than *The bushfires burnt for several days*. A rough rule is **burned** when the burning is continuing; **burnt** when everything is ashes.

burro *see* **donkey, ass, burro, mule**

bursar *see* **registrar, bursar, bursary**

bust, burst

Do you **bust** a balloon, or **burst** it? Careful users will **burst** a balloon and use **bust** only in informal contexts: *Joe's firm went bust; That nightclub is busted at least twice a year; It was quite a bust-up.*

cabalistic, cabbalistic

Cabalistic is the adjectival form of **cabal**, a group of plotters or intriguers, or the plot itself, and consequently meaning 'someone by nature a secretive conspirator'. **Cabbalistic** derives from **cabbala**, an ancient Jewish mystical tradition based on an interpretation of the New Testament – so the adjective means 'mystically secretive'.

cache, cachet

A **cache** is a hidden store of treasure, food, documents, etc. A **cachet** is a stamp or seal of approval. The pronunciations are respectively *kash* and *kah-SHAY*.

caddie, caddy
A **caddie** is someone who carries the bag of golf clubs for a player, now often replaced by a **caddie-cart** or **caddie-car**. A **caddy** is a small container for storing tea.

café, cafe, caff
General usage in British now drops the accent and pronounces it *KAF-ay* – despite some inroads by the Cockney affectation *kaff*. American English retains the French pronunciation: *kaf-AY*.

calendar, calender
A **calendar** is a table showing the succession of years, months and days and any phenomena connected with it (phases of the moon, holidays, schedules, etc). A **calender** is a pair or series of rollers through which cloth or paper is pressed.

callous, callus
Callous denotes insensitivity in people: *He had a callous attitude towards his animals*. A **callus** is a hard patch of skin.

candelabra, chandelier
These two are sometimes confused. **Candelabra** (singular = *candelabrum*) are branched candle holders; a **chandelier** is an ornamental hanging light.

cant, hypocrisy
Often used wrongly as synonyms. **Cant** describes a wide span of verbiage from pious platitudes through repetitious, meaningless stock phrases to jargon. **Hypocrisy** is the act of a person purporting to hold beliefs or standards not manifested in that person's actual behaviour.

canvas, canvass
Canvas is a heavy cloth; to canvass is to solicit – votes, opinions or sales orders for double-glazing. But note: *His collection included several canvases (plural) by Hockney; He regularly canvasses the downtown areas*.

capital, capitol
The **capitol** is the legislative building, while the **capital** is the city in which the legislature is situated. The Capitol in Washington DC always has a capital *C*.

cardigan *see* **sweater, jersey, jumper, pullover, etc**

cardinal *see* **crucial, cardinal**

carat, caret, karat
A **carat** (spelt **karat** in the USA and Canada) is the unit of weight for diamonds and precious stones, and also indicates the amount of gold in an alloy. A **caret** is the small inverted-V editorial mark used to show that inserted material is required.

Carousal, carousel

carousal, carousel
A **carousal** is a boisterous, well-lubricated drinking party; a **carousel** is a rotating fairground ride, and also that revolving conveyor at airports on which you vainly search for your luggage. Pronounced *kuh-ROW-suhl* and *kar-ruh-SEL*.

cash *see* **money, monies, funds, cash**

caster, castor
Caster is very fine, ground white sugar, a sweetener; **castor oil** is a purgative. The swivelling little wheels on the legs of furniture can be spelt as either **casters** or **castors**.

casual, causal
A confusing pair of near-opposites. **Casual** denotes something unplanned, happening by chance, relaxed, unconcerned: *Theirs was merely a brief, casual affair.* **Causal** is the relationship between an affect and its cause: *The causal agent for the environmental damage was undoubtedly the build-up of nitrates.*

catholic, Catholic
With a small *c*, **catholic** means 'wide-ranging, comprehensive, near-universal': *She had catholic tastes in music.* With a capital *C*, it is the shortened form for the Roman Catholic religion, and a member of it.

causal *see* **casual, causal**

cause, responsible
Thick fog is not **responsible** for motorway pile-ups; a violent storm cannot be **responsible** for death and damage. Things can **cause** pile-ups, death and damage, but only people can bear responsibility for their actions. *See also* **source, cause**.

cavalry, Calvary
Cavalry are mounted soldiers, on horses, camels or wheels; **Calvary** is the mount near Jerusalem where Jesus Christ was crucified.

ceiling, maximum
Ceiling is a figurative term used to express a limit or maximum, but is often used incorrectly, as in: *The committee agreed that under the circumstances the ceiling would be appropriately increased.* A **ceiling** can be raised or lowered but not increased.

Celsius *see* **centigrade, Celsius**

celibate, chaste
To be **chaste** is to be pure, modest and sexually faithful. To be **celibate** is to abstain from marriage (and sexual intercourse) altogether, as do members of many religious orders.

cement, concrete
Cement is a bonding agent that comes in many forms and can be used to join a variety of materials. **Concrete** is the product of a bond between cement (the powdered grey variety of calcined limestone) and aggregates such as sand and gravel.

censer, censor, censure
A **censer** is the container in which incense is burned during religious ceremonies. A **censor** is a person who, usually by authority, suppresses matter – written, drawn or otherwise expressed – on moral or political grounds. To **censure** is to reprimand severely.

centering, centring
Centring means 'placing in the centre'; **centering** is a temporary structure used to support an archway during construction. Confusion can arise because of the American-English spelling of centring = centering.

centigrade, Celsius
The **centigrade** temperature scale (0 degrees = freezing point of water; 100 degrees = boiling point of water) was invented by the Swede Anders **Celsius** in 1742; the scale is now commonly called Celsius but both mean the same. In the *Fahrenheit* scale, water freezes at 32 degrees and boils at 212 degrees.

centre, middle
Geometrically, the **centre** of something is a focal point, precise and measurable; the **middle** of something is a more general, approximate term.

certainty, certitude
Certainty means 'being certain, without doubt': *The coach relaxed in the certainty of victory.* **Certitude** is a synonym but suggests additionally the feeling of satisfaction in being so certain: *The bishop was now thoroughly convinced and almost rejoiced in his certitude.*

chafe, chaff
To **chafe** is to irritate or make sore by rubbing; to **chaff** is to tease light-heartedly.

chairman, chairwoman, chairperson, chair
Depending upon your committment to political correctness, you can safely use **chairman**, **chairwoman** or **chairperson** as appropriate. **Madam Chairman** is not uncommon in Britain but there remain many who resist calling a person a **chair**: *Will those with questions please now address them to the chair.*

chance *see* opportunity, chance, possibility

chandelier *see* candelabra, chandelier

chaotic, inchoate
These two are wonderful confusables. **Chaotic** needs little explanation: totally disordered, confused and seemingly out of control. Perhaps because in appearance it sits between incoherent and chaotic, **inchoate** appears to be related to these words but isn't. It means 'just beginning, undeveloped, incomplete': *The inchoate nature of the plans made it difficult for the committee to visualise the sculptor's ambitious project.*

character *see* trait, character

charted, chartered
If an area of land or sea is **charted**, it has been explored, surveyed and mapped. It might have been done by a **chartered** surveyor, that is, a surveyor who has passed the examinations of the Institute of Chartered Surveyors – which in turn has been granted a charter to confer such privileges. The same applies to chartered accountants and numerous other professions. In quite another sense, a **chartered** bus, train, aircraft, etc, is one that has been hired for an occasion.

chary *see* wary, chary

chaste *see* celibate, chaste

chemist, druggist, pharmacist
If you want medicine, you go to a **chemist** in the UK and a **druggist** in the USA. In both, you should meet the **pharmacist**, who is qualified to prepare and dispense drugs and medicines. But there are also many varieties of professional chemist: analytical, agricultural, organic, molecular, to name a few.

chequered, checkered
The former is the UK spelling; the latter is standard in American English.

childish, childlike
Childish is usually used in a disparaging way to describe someone who is acting 'like a child': *Every now and then Mrs Hounslow would throw a childish tantrum.*

Childlike is a much kinder term, expressing some aspect of the charm of childhood: *Even as an adult, Emma still retained a childlike trust in others.*

choose, pick
These are synonymous, **pick** being the more idiomatic, as in *take your pick*. *Make a choice* means the same thing but would be considered more elegant.

chords, cords
A **chord** is a group of musical notes played simultaneously. **Cords** are various kinds of string. Vocal **cords** are the vibrating folds at the back of the larynx. *They feared that Miss Caparello's vocal chords might have been damaged by the accident* is incorrect.

Christian name, first name, given name, forename
Strictly speaking, only Christians can have **Christian names**. The other terms – **forenames / given names / first names** – distinguish them from someone's surname.

chronic, acute
Acute means 'sharp and quick', whereas **chronic** means almost the opposite, 'long-lasting and recurring': *The acute pains he suffered were symptoms of a chronic illness.*

chutney *see* **ketchup, catsup, sauce, chutney, pickle**

circumspect *see* **discreet, circumspect, prudent**

cite *see* **quote, cite**

city, town, village, hamlet
It is no longer easy to define these terms precisely. The largest of these communities is a **city**, which, in the UK, was once defined as a town that included a cathedral within its boundaries – not necessarily so any more. A **town** is smaller than a city but larger than a village. A **village** in the UK might consist of a dozen to several hundred homes; a **hamlet**, smallest of all, might include as few as two or three dwellings, probably without a church.

claim, allege, assert, maintain
Just four of a group of words that are often used synonymously and wrongly. To **claim** is to demand or assert a right: *He came to England to claim the crown.* It is, however, frequently used wrongly as a synonym for *declare, assert, protest* and *allege*: *It was claimed in the High Court yesterday*. To **allege** is to assert without proof, and as it nowadays implies guilt (as in the satirical news quiz, *Have I Got News For You*), it should be used with caution: *the alleged bribe; the alleged crime.* **Assert** has a stronger emphasis than *said* and means to declare positively. The primary meanings of **maintain** are to 'hold, preserve and sustain', so it is a supportive word: *In the face of the allegations, she steadfastly maintained her innocence.*

classic, Classics, classical
Classic has by modern usage almost been stripped of any meaning. From TV comedy programmes, horse races, old cars to soft drinks, anything can be a '**classic**'. **Classics** in the plural and upper-case is the study of ancient Greek and Latin: *She read Classics at Oxford.* **Classical** describes the highest attainments of an era (e.g. Greek and Roman) or of literature and art. **Classical music** is usually chamber or orchestral in nature and is distinct from jazz, folk music or rock.

clean, cleanse
As verbs, **clean** and **cleanse** both mean 'to clean', but the latter additionally implies to 'clean thoroughly and to purify': *His mother used to insist that merely cleaning the face did not cleanse the soul.*

clear *see* apparent, evident

climatic, climactic, climacteric
Climatic relates to weather conditions: *The climatic conditions were extremely trying and sometimes unbearable* disposes of that one. **Climactic** relates to a climax, a high point (*After the thunderous applause it was agreed that it was the climactic speech of his career*), while a **climacteric** is a critical period of change (usually physical) in human life, for example, puberty or the menopause.

climb down, climb-down
Inch by heart-stopping inch he climbed down the treacherous ravine. Isn't there a contradiction here? Those who respect the meaning of climb as 'to ascend' may prefer *he descended into the treacherous ravine*. But although **climb down** is now an ingrained phrasal verb (as is **climb up**, where the *up* is redundant), it has acquired a second meaning which is 'a retreat from a position': *By withdrawing her libel action the Duchess suffered a humiliating climb-down.*

coat, jacket
Today's usage accepts that an **overcoat** is a **coat** and the upper half of a suit a **jacket**.

coliseum, Coliseum *see* Colosseum, coliseum, Coliseum

collaborate, cooperate
To **collaborate** is to work jointly with someone, usually on some specific project. To **cooperate** is to work with someone or be willing to help or contribute. Curiously, if you *cooperate* with the enemy, you are a *collaborator*.

collision, collusion
A **collision** is the impact of two moving objects or forces; **collusion** is a conspiracy to deceive: *They were forever colluding against the rightful owners of the land.*

colony, protectorate, dependency
A **colony** is a territory annexed by another power; once numbering more than a

hundred, only a few of these now survive. These include former British Crown Colonies, now termed **dependencies**, which have their own legislatures – Cayman Islands, the Falklands and Ascension are examples. A **protectorate** is a territory administered and defended by a stronger state but whose inhabitants are not granted citizenship of that state.

Colosseum, coliseum, Coliseum
The **Colosseum** is the original (now ruined) amphitheatre in Rome, built in AD 75–80. A **coliseum** now describes any major amphitheatre or stadium, while the **Coliseum** is the landmark theatre of that name in London.

coloured *see* black, negro, coloured, non-white

come, cum
Occasionally, we see a combination such as an *office-come-den*, or *she was a secretary-come-childminder*. These are incorrect as the connecting preposition is **cum** (Latin = with) which is used to connect two nouns: *He showed us into an office-cum-den; She complained she'd become a secretary-cum-childminder.*

comet, meteor
A **comet** is a celestial body of vaporised debris that orbits the sun and from which streams a luminous tail; Halley's comet, for example, completes an orbit every 75 years. A **meteor** is a meteorite that enters the earth's atmosphere with a one-off display of luminosity.

comic, comical
Comic is something that is intended to be funny; a **comical** situation may be hilarious but unintentional; however, the difference between the two words today is almost erased. Where tragedy, real or theatrical, is shared with the humour, the terms are *tragicomic* and *tragicomical.*

commence *see* begin, commence, inaugurate, initiate, start

commensurate, consummate
Commensurate means 'corresponding or roughly proportionate in size, amount or degree': *The guidelines he laid down were commensurate with the laws of the previous administration.* **Consummate** has two meanings: 'highly skilled and accomplished' (*kon-sum-ATE*) and 'to complete' (*KON-sum-ate*): *With consummate ease and considerable enthusiasm, the couple consummated their marriage on the Orient Express between Innsbruck and Venice.*

common *see* mutual, common

commonly, customarily, frequently, generally, habitually, ordinarily, usually
Commonly, **generally**, **ordinarily** and **usually** are virtually synonymous, meaning 'normally as expected'. **Customarily** differs by only a fine degree, meaning 'according to established practice'. **Frequently** means 'often', while **habitually** implies frequency as the result of habit.

Common Market *see* **European Union, European Community**

compare to, compare with
The convention has been to use **compared to** to express dissimilarities to make a point (*She often compared her boyfriend's intelligence to two thick planks*; or, more poetically, *Shall I compare thee to a summer's day?*) and **compared with** to note the differences between two similar things or classes: *You can't really compare Caruso's voice with Pavarotti's; Compared with Australia's, New Zealand's Sauvignons are much more refined.*

compatriot *see* **expatriate, compatriot**

compel, impel
If you are **compelled** to do something, it is because of some outside force or pressure that you can't resist and over which you have little or no control. But if you are **impelled** to do something, the decision is yours, despite the pressure, the urging and all the reasons.

complacent, complaisant
Spelt differently, but pronounced similarly, a **complacent** person is self-satisfied and smug; a **complaisant** person is always rather eager to please others and will do anything to oblige.

complement, compliment, supplement
A **complement** is that which makes something complete: *The hospital finally achieved its full complement of nursing staff; She complemented the dish with a swirl of cream.* A **compliment** is an expression of praise or approval, and a **supplement** is an addition to something already complete: *He complimented her on the meal; The doctor supplemented her diet with a course of vitamins and minerals.*

completion *see* **fruition, completion**

complicated, complex
As adjectives, these are for all practical purposes synonyms, although **complex** tends to be used in more scientific contexts and **complicated** to express something difficult to understand: *The substance turned out to be a complex mixture of rare herbs and spices; Mary felt the affair was becoming absurdly complicated and washed her hands of the matter.* As a noun, **complex** came into fashion to describe a group of units: *The team went to inspect the new sports complex.*

compliment *see* **complement, compliment, supplement**

comply, conform
These are synonyms, but **comply** is followed by **with** (*He always complied with the regulations*) and **conform** by **to**: *The quality of the cloth conformed to the standards laid down by the EU.*

compose, comprise, constitute, include
Comprise means 'consists of' and describes all the parts that make up the whole: *The house comprised five bedrooms, four reception rooms and the usual offices.* The meanings of **compose** and **constitute** are the same but don't necessary imply completeness: *The pudding is composed of some unusual ingredients; She hardly dared list the ingredients that constituted the pudding.* Use **include** when only part or parts of the whole are indicated: *The ingredients included Chinese walnuts and cherry brandy.*

comprehend *see* **understand, appreciate, comprehend**

comprise *see* **compose, comprise, constitute, include**

compulsive, compulsory
Compulsive means 'being subject to some degree of inner compulsion, either psychological, moral or physical': *Ray was a compulsive gambler; The new TV crime series makes for compulsive viewing.* **Compulsory** means 'obligatory by law, regulation or some other force': *Car registration is compulsory.* In both cases, there is an implied inability to resist.

concave, convex
Concave means 'curving inwards' (think of a cave); **convex** means curving outwards (think how vexed you are when you develop a bulge!)

concede, accede
Accede indicates willing agreement; **concede** implies grudging agreement, or 'giving way': *After an hour he conceded the argument to his opponent; The chess team acceded enthusiastically to the idea of a return match.* See also **accede, agree**.

concrete *see* **cement, concrete**

condominium *see* **flat, condominium, apartment, cooperative**

Condone, Approve, Allow

In her bestselling book on sex, *The Hite Report*, the American author Shere Hite fell for a common misconception: *Heterosexual intercourse . . . is the only form of sexual pleasure condoned in our society.* It is doubtful if Ms Hite meant that heterosexual intercourse was overlooked or forgiven or excused, for that is what **condone** means – it is not a substitute for *allowed* or *approved*. Nor is it a synonym for *disapprove: My position is that I neither condone nor condemn fox hunting.*

---

confident *see* **optimistic, confident**

confident, confidant
To be **confident** is to be assured, certain of yourself, without doubts. A **confidant** (pronounced *kon-fih-DANT*) is a trusted friend to whom you confide your closest secrets. If the friend is female, use the feminine **confidante**.

conform *see* **comply, conform**

congenial *see* **genial, congenial, congenital**

conjugal, connubial
These are virtual synonyms. Because its most frequent usage is in the phrase *conjugal rights* – which, legally, denotes the rights to sexual relations with a spouse – **conjugal** tends to relate more to the responsibilities of marriage, while **connubial** ('connubial bliss') rather hints at the joys of the union.

connote *see* **denote, connote**

connubial *see* **conjugal, connubial**

conscience, conscious, conscientious
A **conscience** is a person's sense of what is right and wrong. **Conscious** implies self-awareness, being aware of one's mental and physical state. To be **conscientious** is to act according to one's conscience or to a code of principles.

consecutive, successive
Consecutive means 'following without an interval or break', while **successive** means 'following in order but without emphasis on the intervals': *After winning three consecutive Derbys, he went on to claim six successive Derby wins over 12 years.*

consensus, consensus of opinion
A **consensus** (not *concensus*) is widespread agreement or general opinion. **Consensus of opinion** is a very common waste of words.

consequent, consequential
Consequent means 'following as an effect or direct result'. **Consequential** in this context also means 'following as a result' but usually indirectly: *It was obvious that thirty years down the mines had something to do with his lung problems and consequent death; His behaviour had been scandalous so his consequential abandonment by the party came as no surprise.* In quite another sense, **consequential** can mean 'significant, important' and 'self-important'.

consequently, subsequently
Often confused. **Consequently** (see above) means 'following as a direct result'; **subsequently** simply means 'occurring after'.

conservative, Conservative
With a small *c*, **conservative** means 'opposed to change', 'moderate, cautious

and conventional'; with a capital *C*, it denotes a member or supporter of the **Conservative** political party.

consists of, consists in
These are used differently. **Consists of** means 'comprises, formed of, made up of': *He knew the committee consisted of some pretty unusual characters.* **Consists in** means 'to have its existence in': *Her entire life seemed to consist in those three daily visits to her church.*

constitute *see* compose, comprise, constitute, include

constraint, restraint
Both are forms of restriction but one is often self-imposed and the other arises through outside forces. A **constraint** is something that prevents one from pursuing some action: *Her knowledge of Sir Percy's crime acted as a constraint to her speaking freely on the matter.* **Restraint** is self-control, the ability to check or moderate one's actions, passions or impulses.

consulate, embassy, legation
A nation establishes only one **embassy** in another country to represent its diplomatic and economic interests, usually in the capital or key city, whereas **consulates** can be found in centres where there is a need for them. A **legation** is a diplomatic mission typically headed by a government minister. The key figure in an embassy is the *ambassador* (although in the British Commonwealth it is usually a *High Commissioner*) and in a consulate, the *consul*. A *chargé d'affaires* is, in the absence of an ambassador or minister, the temporary head of a diplomatic mission.

consultant, specialist
In medical language, patients are referred to a **specialist**; a **consultant** is a specialist consulted by doctors on behalf of their patients. However, the term consultant is now freely applied to almost every avenue and level of medical specialisation.

consummate *see* commensurate, consummate

contagious *see* infectious, contagious

contemporary
Contemporary means 'living at the same time, belonging to the same period, existing in the present time'. Modern usage also extends its meaning to 'up-to-date, modern'.

contemptuous, contemptible
To be **contemptuous** means 'to be scornful, arrogant, sneering and insulting': *She was always contemptuous of my plans to make money.* The object of her scorn could very well be **contemptible** and deserving of contempt: *His ridiculous efforts to make a fortune were contemptible.*

contiguous *see* **adjacent, adjoining, contiguous**

continuing *see* **ongoing, continuing**

continual, continuous
Continual means 'repeated at short intervals'; **continuous** means 'uninterrupted': *I've just suffered continual interruptions; I can't possibly work with that continuous racket blaring from next door!*

contrary
Two meanings and two pronunciations. **Contrary** (pronounced *KON-truh-ree*) means to be opposed, opposite: *He invariably held views contrary to everyone else's.* **Contrary** (pronounced *kon-TRAIR-ee*) means obstinate, perverse: *If you remember, Janet was always a contrary child.*

contrast to, contrast with, in contrast with
Usage has rendered these interchangeable. **In contrast** was usually followed by **with**, but even that convention has been dropped and **in contrast to** makes no difference to the meaning: *The progress made in Manchester is in stark contrast to the situation in Liverpool.*

converse, inverse, obverse, reverse
This quartet all mean 'opposite' in some sense. **Inverse** is used in mathematics and **obverse** when refering to the faces of a coin or medal. **Converse** (pronounced *KON-vers*) and **conversely** (which is used loosely as 'on the other hand') denote a reversal of meaning: *Every journalist knows that dog bites man, and its converse, man bites dog; Every journalist knows that dog bites man, and, conversely, that man bites dog.* Note also that to **converse** (pronounced *kon-VERS*) means to have a conversation. **Reverse** is rarely misunderstood: *He maintains that a high-fibre diet makes you fat; the reverse is true.*

convex *see* **concave, convex**

convict, impeach
To **impeach** is to bring a charge or accusation against someone and is often a first step in trying to remove an official from office. To **convict** (pronounced *kon-VICT*) is (for a court) to find a person guilty of an offence against the law. A **convict** (pronounced *KON-vict*) is one who has been found guilty of a crime or someone who has been jailed.

convince, persuade, induce
Convince implies proving something to somebody by argument, by an exposition of the facts: *After hearing John's version he was convinced that Emily was in the wrong.* **Persuade** is a stronger word, meaning 'to urge, encourage, influence and convince a person to the stage where he or she is won over to a point of view or course of action': *After a series of tense discussions they finally persuaded her to stay the night.* **Induce** is a near synonym except that it implies that in return for being

persuaded there may be some reward or penalty: *The promise of peace of mind was the factor that really induced William to agree.*

cooperate *see* **collaborate, cooperate**

cooperative *see* **flat, condominium, apartment, cooperative**

copse *see* **corps, corpse, copse**

copy *see* **replica, copy, facsimile**

coral, corral
Coral consists of the skeletons of marine creatures which form reefs; a **corral** is an enclosure for horses and cattle.

cords *see* **chords, cords**

core
Very much a vogue word that modern usage has rendered into a vague word: *core values, core executives, core missions, soft-core, hard-core* . . . use it carefully if you must use it at all.

co-respondent *see* **correspondent, co-respondent**

corporal, corporeal
In the army, a **corporal** is a *non-commissioned officer*, senior to a private and junior to a sergeant; in the navy, a petty officer under a master-at-arms. **Corporal** also means 'relating to the body', as in *corporal punishment*, that is, punishment of the body, such as flogging. Similarly, **corporeal** refers to the material or physical side of nature as opposed to the spiritual.

corps, corpse, copse
A seemingly simple trio but often confused. A **corps** (pronounced *kor*) consists of two or more army divisions; a **corpse** is, of course, a dead body; a **copse** is a thicket of trees or bushes.

corral *see* **coral, corral**

correspond to, correspond with
If you **correspond with** someone, you exchange letters with him or her. **Correspond to** means 'to be in harmony with', or 'to tally with': *Your version of the affair corresponds to that of Matilda's.*

correspondent, co-respondent
Don't be confused between **correspondent** (one who writes or exchanges letters with another) and **co-respondent** (someone cited as 'the other party' in divorce proceedings).

corsair *see* **pirate, buccaneer, corsair, privateer**

cosmetic *see* **superficial, cosmetic**

council, counsel, councillor, counselor
A **council** is a body of people, usually elected, for the purpose of advising, guiding or administrating; a **councillor** is a member of a council. A **counsel** is an individual qualified in some way to give advice or guidance, especially in law: *The barrister eventually agreed to act as counsel for the defence.* A **counsellor** (**counselor** in American English) is the same as a **counsel**, but the term, with **counselling**, is now fairly widely applied to anyone advising on some aspect of social services or personal problems.

counterfeit *see* **authentic, genuine**

couple, pair
A **couple** is two things that are united or joined together, as in *a couple of drinks,* or *a married couple.* A **pair** is two things of a kind that are mutually dependent, as in *a pair of scissors* (joined) and *a pair of gloves* (not joined). Both words are singular – *a pair of gloves was found* – except when the parts are treated individually: *The couple decided to go their separate ways; The pair were considered to be very odd characters indeed.*

courage *see* **bravery, bravado, bravura, courage, heroism**

covert, overt
Covert means 'concealed, secret, disguised'; **overt** is the opposite: 'open to view, public and free for all to see'.

crape *see* **crepe, crape**

crapulous
In a review of a biography of the poet Dylan Thomas and his wife, Caitlin, the reviewer regarded the tone of much of the account as 'crapulous'. This was not intended as an insult to the biographer. Those familiar with the fact that the couple were ferocious drinkers for most of their lives would have had a clue: **crapulous** means given to extreme intemperance and has nothing to do with bodily functions.

crass, silly, stupid, gross
Of these terms of abuse, **silly** is the mildest, with **stupid** close behind; in fact both are often applied to oneself – *Oh, silly me; How stupid of me!* – whereas one would hardly label oneself as *crass* or *gross.* To be **crass** is to be ignorant and insensitive and, idiomatically, extremely thick. **Gross** is all of these with an overlay of repulsiveness, coarseness and vulgarity. Save it for someone special.

credible, creditable, credulous
Credible means 'believable'; **creditable** means 'deserving credit or praise'; **credulous** is having the naive willingness to believe in something.

crepe, crape
Crepe, the thin crinkly fabric or paper, is the traditional spelling. Also the spelling for the orange-flavoured pancake flambéed in brandy. Note the first *e* has a circumflex: *crêpe suzette*. **Crape** is generally understood to be a heavier fabric than crepe and is used extensively for mourning clothes.

crescendo
Towards the end of the piece the orchestra rose to a crescendo is a commonly heard expression, but it is wrong. **Crescendo** means 'getting louder'. An orchestra can play a *crescendo passage* but can't rise to one.

criterion, criteria
Although **criteria** is today generally used in both singular and plural senses, it is worth keeping them separated, if only to display your superior knowledge: *The committee had always insisted that the criterion for efficient book-keeping was scrupulous honesty; Harvey had never quite understood the criteria used to value Peruvian Railway stocks.*

crotch, crutch, crux
One of the more hilarious Malapropisms on record is *I'm not going to rest until I get to the crutch of the matter*! The word intended, of course, was **crux**, meaning 'the essential or fundamental point (of a problem)'. The **crotch** is the genital area of the human body and also, in tailoring, the inner join of the legs of a pair of trousers. **Crutch** is also sometimes used in this sense but more correctly defines a support, or an aid to standing or walking, its original meaning.

crucial, cardinal
If something is **crucial** it is decisive: *There is no doubt that O'Brien's brilliant tackling will be crucial to our winning the match.* If something is **cardinal**, it is fundamental: *The coach claimed that O'Brien's inclusion in the team was of cardinal importance if it was to win.* And remember the **cardinal virtues**: justice, prudence, temperence and fortitude, to which are sometimes added faith, hope and charity to make up the Seven Virtues.

crutch, crux *see* crotch, crutch, crux

cry *see* weep, cry

cultured, cultivated
In the sense of 'refined, educated, exhibiting good taste', these are now accepted as synonyms.

cum *see* come, cum

curb, kerb
Curb means 'to check or restrain'. In the UK, a **kerb** is the edge of a pavement; in the US, a **curb**.

currant, current
A **currant** is a small, dark dried grape. **Current** has two meanings: 'a flow (of electricity, water, air, etc)'; and 'existing in the present time': *It is difficult to keep up with current events.*

customarily *see* **commonly, customarily, frequently, generally, habitually, ordinarily, usually**

cyclone, hurricane, tornado, typhoon, waterspout
Hurricanes are violent gales with winds of above around 745 miles an hour and are found in the Atlantic and eastern Pacific oceans; a **cyclone** is a hurricane, the winds of which blow spirally towards a centre region of low barometric pressure, found in the Indian Oceans. **Typhoons** are hurricanes found in the western Pacific and Southeast Asia. **Tornados** (and, lately, twisters) are hurricane-speed winds that rotate, creating funnel or cylindrical shapes over land. A **waterspout** is a tornado occurring over water.

cynical, sceptical
A **cynical** person or **cynic** is someone who believes there is little good in anyone or anything; a **sceptic** (**skeptic** in American English) is a doubter who has a problem believing anything without ample proof.

Cyprus, cypress
Cyprus is the former British island colony, now split into Greek and Turkish territories, situated in the Mediterranean; a **cypress** is a coniferous tree.

dais, lectern, podium, rostrum
A **rostrum** is a raised platform, and a **dais** (pronounced *day-iss*) is a rostrum upon which several people can sit or stand. A **podium** is a platform for a single speaker. A **lectern** is the stand on which the speaker's notes are placed.

darkly, darkling
Both mean the same when referring to darkness, but **darkling** has the additional meaning of 'obscure'.

data, datum
Data Affirm Higher Cancer Risk For Female Spouse of a Smoker (headline, *New York Times*) is correct: **data** is the plural form of **datum**. But the tendency to use **data** as a singular word, particularly in the computer industry, is now so widespread as to render the practice acceptable.

debar, disbar
Debar means 'to exclude or shut out'; **disbar** means 'to expel', usually a barrister from a law court.

debate
Dole will debate Clinton on Tuesday is incorrect usage. You may **have a debate, be**

engaged in a debate or **debate a subject**: *Senator Dole will debate the issues with President Clinton on Tuesday.*

deceitful, deceptive
To be **deceitful** is deliberately to mislead or cheat. **Deceptive** describes the effect of a misleading circumstance: *The bright sunshine proved to be deceptive, for it was really quite cold.*

decent, descent, dissent
Decent means 'good, respectable, morally upright'; **descent** is a movement downwards; **dissent** is disagreement. Note also the spelling of the opposites, *descent/ascent* and *assent/dissent*.

deceptive *see* **deceitful, deceptive**

decimate
Decimate, strictly, means to 'kill or destroy one in ten'. Usage, however, has extended its meaning to indicate great destruction and even total annihilation: *He said the blast had cost the firm £150,000 in damage and loss of trade. 'Basically this has decimated us,' he added.*

decry, descry
To **decry** is to disparage or condemn; to **descry** something is to detect or discover it by careful looking: *He decried the use of force in getting the prisoners to cooperate; Then, suddenly, out of the darkness, the lookout descried the vague shape of a conning tower.* Descry is a word hardly ever used today.

deduce, deduct, adduce
The confusion between the first two probably arises because their nouns are spelt the same: *deduction*. But **deduce** means 'to arrive at a conclusion through reasoning', while **deduct** means ' to subtract or take away'. To **adduce** is to present something as an example of evidence or proof: *The hypnotist adduced a series of demonstrations, to the amusement of the audience.*

defective, deficient, defected
Defective means that something is faulty; **deficient** means that something is missing. A notice seen recently on London's Underground advised passengers that *Due to a defected train at Charing Cross there are delays on the Bakerloo Line.* The word the notice was looking for is **defective**. Someone who has **defected** has deserted his or her country or allegiance to join an opposing interest.

defer, delay
There is a subtle difference here: **defer** implies a decision to postpone, while **delay** carries overtones of slowing up a process, of hindering, procrastination: *The final decision was deferred until January; The difficulties with the new computer design will delay completion of the production line.*

deficient *see* **defective, deficient, defected**

definite, definitive
These are not synonymous. **Definite** means 'explicit, exact, clearly defined': *About her views on examination standards she was most definite*. However the word is also widely used to mean 'unquestionably': *Looking at the advance results, I'd say the Berkeley team will definitely win*. **Definitive** means not only 'precise and explicit' but also 'conclusive, absolutely final, the last word': *It took him many years but Professor Abrams produced the definitive essay on the phi-phenomenon*.

defuse, diffuse
Defuse means 'to remove a device or some circumstance likely to cause an explosion or an explosive situation'. **Diffuse** means 'to spread': *Unrest was diffusing among the crowd, and he knew he had to defuse what was becoming an ugly situation*.

deleterious, harmful
These are synonymous, but the trend is to use the simpler and better understood **harmful**.

delusion *see* **illusion, allusion, delusion**

denigration, denegation
Denigration is the disparaging or belittling of someone; **denegation** is the denial or refusal of a request.

denote, connote
Denote means 'to indicate' or 'to designate': *The arrival of that whisper of a breeze around four o'clock always denoted a cool evening*. **Connote** means 'to suggest or imply an association or an idea': *In Joe's mind a Turkish bath invariably connotes something sinful in all that steam*.

deny *see* **rebut, refute, repudiate, deny**

dependant, dependent
The difference here is that **dependant** is a noun and **dependent** an adjective; a **dependant** is someone who is **dependent** upon someone or some form of physical, moral or financial support: *It was well-known that the captain had half a dozen dependants in various ports; The young man was unfortunately dependent on drugs*.

dependency *see* **colony, protectorate, dependency**

deplete *see* **exhaust, deplete, reduce**

depository, repository
A **depository** is more correctly a warehouse used for storage, while a **repository** is generally some place of indeterminate size used for storing or displaying things. *He used the old chest as a repository for his medal collection; Leonardo's notebook*

was the repository of many of the world's most brilliant ideas; The British Museum is one of the greatest repositories of Egyptian artefacts in the world.

deprecate, depreciate
Often confused but easily separated. To **deprecate** is to disapprove or belittle: *She never missed an opportunity to deprecate his efforts.* **Depreciate** means 'to reduce or lessen': *The pound depreciated alarmingly during the 1970s.* Confusion may arise when **depreciate** is used to devalue something by criticism: *His harsh comments were cleverly calculated to depreciate all their hard work on the project.*

derby, Derby
A **derby** is a bowler hat; **Derby** is the county town ('capital') of Derbyshire in England and, more famously, the classic horse race, named after the Earl of Derby, the race held annually at Epsom Downs in Surrey, and also a kind of porcelain made at Derby.

derision, derisive, derisory, desultory
Derision is the act of mocking or derision; **derisive** means 'mocking and scornful': *Henry's knockout in the first round was met with derisive laughter.* To be **derisory** is to be the object of derision and ridicule: *The men regarded the management's latest offer as utterly derisory.* The look-alike word **desultory** is sometimes seen in a context that seems to indicate that it was meant to mean *derisory* – but not so! *Such a massive sum is not only an insult to those victims of crime awarded desultory amounts, it also fails to acknowledge that the woman takes some responsibility for such brainless abuse.* (Lesley White in *The Sunday Times*, 17.5.98). Here the writer uses *desultory* to mean *irresponsibly haphazard.*

descent *see* decent, descent, dissent

descry *see* decry, descry

deserts, desserts
Often confused. Note the correct spelling of the word in the well-known phrase *He got his just deserts,* meaning 'he got what he deserved'. A **desert** is an arid, usually sandy region; **dessert** is the sweet or pudding course of a meal.

derby, Derby

desire, want, need
Of this trio, **need** expresses the strongest requirement and urgency. **Want** implies a less urgent craving, while **desire** involves a degree of wishful thinking: *He desired an easier life, wanted a house to live in, but meanwhile needed the price of a square meal.*

despatch *see* **dispatch, despatch**

desserts *see* **deserts, desserts**

desultory *see* **derision, derisive, derisory, desultory**

detract, distract
To **detract** is to 'take away from,' or diminish: *Her rudeness detracted from the otherwise good impression we'd made of her.* To **distract** is to divert someone's attention away from what they're doing: *It is unlawful to distract the driver while the vehicle is in motion.*

developing *see* **ongoing, continuing**

device, devise
Device is a noun, and is something designed and made for a specific purpose: *The electric potato peeler was one of the most intriguing devices she'd ever seen.* **Devise** is a verb that means 'to plan, work out or create something': *The inventor had spent three years devising the electric potato peeler.*

devil's advocate
A **devil's advocate** is not so much a person who defends an unpopular cause or point of view but rather someone who deliberately and constructively sets out to uncover faults and flaws in an argument: *It became obvious that because of his engineering knowledge Benny was acting as devil's advocate in the heated discussion.*

devise *see* **device, devise**

diagnosis, prognosis
A **diagnosis** is an identification of or an opinion about a problem or disease, while a **prognosis** is a prediction about the outcome: *When the initial diagnosis was confirmed Dr Metcalfe remained very cagey about the prognosis.*

dialect *see* **accent, dialect**

diametric, opposite, opposed
Many of us use the terms **diametrically opposed** and **diametrically opposite** without knowing quite what they mean. **Diametrically** means 'completely, directly and irreconcilably opposite', so the terms are redundancies. The simpler **opposite** and **opposed** should serve for most purposes (or even *violently opposed*).

dice, die

Although **die** is the correct singular for the plural **dice** (*the die is cast*), nobody in his or her right mind today would say to a fellow Ludo player, *'Hey, Bill, hurry up and throw that die!'*

differ from, differ with

To **differ from** suggests a contrast: *Male views usually differ from those of females.* To **differ with** someone is to disagree: *I differed with Frank on just about every point he put forward.*

different *see* disparate, different

different from, different to, different than

Different to has been consistently frowned upon and **different from** is recommended instead. **Different than** is more widely used in American-English, which avoids the clash.

differentiate *see* distinguish, differentiate

dike *see* dyke, dike

dilate, dilatory

To **dilate** something is to expand it; to be **dilatory** is to waste time.

dilemma

A **dilemma** does not mean 'a problem', 'a puzzle' or 'a difficult situation' but a choice between two equal (and often undesirable) circumstances.

dinghy, dingy

A **dinghy** is a small boat; **dingy** means 'grimy, soiled, shabby and gloomy'.

Who's Coming to Dinner, Supper, Lunch or Tea?

Depending upon your background, your work and where you live in Britain, these terms can be very confusing. An invitation to **dinner** from strangers can be social dynamite! Many people eat **lunch** (or, formally, **luncheon**) at about 1 pm and their main meal, **dinner** (sometimes called **supper**), at 7–8 pm. Others have **dinner** as a main meal between noon and 1 pm and a lighter meal, called **tea**, between 5 and 6 pm, with perhaps a light **supper** before bedtime. Yet other families will have a light snack before noon, dinner around 1 pm, tea at about 4 pm and a substantial supper during early evening. **High tea** is a meal replete with meat or fish served late in the afternoon, while **afternoon tea** is a mid-afternoon snack of sandwiches or cake washed down with tea or coffee. And this by no means covers all the confusing gastronomic bizarreries of Britain.

directly

The traditional meaning of **directly** is 'immediately, at once': *She went to him directly she entered the room,* but a confusing secondary meaning is entering the usage scene, meaning 'soon, in a short while, when I'm ready': *Arthur shouted that he'd be down directly, and went on with his work.* Avoid confusion by sticking with the original usage. Also see **soon, presently**.

disabuse *see* **abuse, misuse, disabuse**

disassemble *see* **dissemble, disassemble**

disassociate *see* **dissociate, disassociate**

disbar *see* **debar, disbar**

disc, disk

The two spellings have been slugging it out for a couple of centuries. Although today usage is still far from consistent, we tend to use **disc** to describe flat circular surfaces – *disc brakes, compact disc* – and **disk** in connection with computers, as with *floppy disk* and *disk drive.* But usage is still far from consistent.

discomfit, discomfiture, discomfort, discomfiture

Discomfort means, as the word suggests, 'lack of comfort', pain or distress: *The operation was a success but left her vaguely discomforted.* To **discomfit** someone is to disconcert, frustrate or embarrass them; **discomfiture** is the noun: *There was national sympathy for the miners, who were obviously enjoying the discomfiture of the owners.*

discover, invent

To **discover** something is to find it for the first time – even though that something is already existent: *Benjamin Franklin discovered the electrical properties of lightning; Jane was happy to discover her mother was sympathetic to her case.* To **invent** is to create something that never previously existed: *We will probably never know who invented the wheel; He invents absurd excuses to avoid attending Jane's parties.*

discreet, discrete

Discreet means 'tactful, careful to avoid embarrassment'. **Discrete** means 'separate, unattached, distinct': *The lecturer emphasised that the two subjects were discrete; Her discreet behaviour ensured the two relationships remained discrete.*

discreet, circumspect, prudent

Most people use all three interchangeably, but there are shades of difference. To be **discreet** is to be tactful and sensitive, especially in order to avoid some potential embarrassment. To be **circumspect** or to act **circumspectly** is to combine discretion with caution, whatever the circumstance. **Prudent** has traditionally meant 'to be careful about one's affairs' and also 'to provide against the future', but with recent usage it has also come to mean 'wise': *When he saw the size of the man who'd just knocked the drink out of his hand, he felt it prudent not to make a fuss.*

discriminating, discriminatory
Although they derive from *discriminate*, they have two quite distinct meanings. To be **discriminating** is to have the ability to discern fine distinctions, especially in matters of taste. To be **discriminatory** is to be biased and prejudiced: *Eric held what many regarded as discriminatory views on the subject of women's rights.*

disingenuous *see* ingenious, ingenuous, disingenuous

disinterested, uninterested
These are not synonyms. To be **disinterested** is to be impartial and free from bias; to be **uninterested** is to lack interest altogether, to be bored: *Although he was asked to contribute to the discussion as a disinterested party, he found himself completely uninterested in the proceedings.* Surprisingly, many grammarians and some dictionaries suggest that the difference in meaning between these two words is not worth maintaining in the face of usage, but this is yet another case of yielding to ambiguity and should be resisted.

disk *see* disc, disk

disoriented, disorientated
Both words mean the same – 'to be confused', or 'to lose your bearings' – so opt for the shorter word.

disparate, different
Different means 'not the same' or 'partly or completely unlike something else'. **Disparate** means 'utterly different', with nothing whatsoever in common.

disparity, discrepancy
Both words indicate a 'difference'. **Disparity** highlights a dramatic inequality: *The disparity between the wages of men and women in the plant was hard to defend.* A **discrepancy** is a difference that shouldn't exist at all: *The investigators soon uncovered some glaring discrepancies in the company's recent annual reports.*

dispatch, despatch
Dispatch, meaning to 'send or to do something promptly', is the more common spelling, meaning to send or to do something promptly: *The postmistress promised to dispatch the parcel immediately; He accomplished the tasks with admirable dispatch.*

dissatisfied, unsatisfied
To be **dissatisfied** is to be discontented, displeased, unhappy, disappointed. To be **unsatisfied** is to feel the lack or want of something: *Apart from his dissatisfaction with the menu, the miniscule portions ensured that he left the table quite unsatisfied.*

dissemble, disassemble
Confusingly, the opposite of assemble is not dissemble but **disassemble**, meaning to take apart: *The entire machine could be assembled and disassembled in less than a day*. **Dissemble** means 'to conceal by pretence': *His evil intentions were dissembled by a pious demeanour*.

dissent *see* decent, descent, dissent

dissociate, disassociate
Not only is **dissociate** the opposite of associate – meaning 'to break up an association between two parties' – but so is **disassociate**. The shorter word is preferred.

distinct, distinctive
Distinct means 'readily distinguished from', clear, precise, definite: *That dish had the distinct flavour of fermented cabbage*. **Distinctive** means 'possessing some obvious characteristic or distinguishing feature': *The badger is always easily identified by the distinctive stripes on its back*.

distinguish, differentiate
In the sense of detecting the difference between things, the two are synonymous, but **differentiate** has an additional shade of meaning, which is 'to discriminate': *The assistant then proceeded to differentiate between the genetic clusters using a code of coloured dyes*.

distract *see* detract, distract

distrust, mistrust
Usage maintains a distinction between the two rather than a difference. To **distrust** someone is to suspect strongly that he or she is dishonest or untrustworthy. To **mistrust** is to have doubts, to be wary or sceptical. You can **mistrust** (but not **distrust**) your own feelings and judgement at times.

divers, diverse
Divers, meaning 'several, various and sundry' is an old-fashioned word that is little used now. **Diverse** means 'varied, assorted, of many and different kinds': *We will never cease to be astounded by the diverse creatures of the sea*. Or to use the noun form: *We will never cease to be astounded by the diversity of the creatures of the sea*.

Domesday, doomsday
Though similar in pronunciation, the **Domesday Book** is the survey of England made in 1086; **doomsday** is the biblical day of judgement.

dominate, domineer
To **dominate** is to control or rule over; to **domineer** is to tyrannise.

donate, give
In his *The Complete Plain Words*, Sir Ernest Gowers advises succinctly: 'Use give.'
However, in the context of giving money or time to charity, or organs to medical
science, **donate** is well understood.

donkey, ass, burro, mule
A **donkey** is a hardy, long-eared small horse that originated in Africa. An **ass** is
the same animal although some strains may have originated in Asia, as is the
burro, which is the Spanish/Mexican version. The odd one out here is the **mule**,
which is the sterile progeny of a male donkey and a female horse.

doomsday *see* **Domesday, doomsday**

doubtful, dubious
Doubtful is preferred, unless you wish to suggest something underhand:
*She was very doubtful about the arrangement, especially with so many dubious
characters involved.*

doubtless, undoubtedly
By comparison with the more forceful and unequivocal **undoubtedly**, **doubtless**
is rather passive, but both have their uses for discriminating writers.

douse, dowse
There seems no good reason why these should be interchangable as they are in
some dictionaries. To **douse** is to saturate with fluid or water, as with **dousing** a
fire, or **dousing** (plunging) something into water or some other liquid. **Dowsing**
is what a diviner does with a forked twig or divining rod – locate underground
water.

Draught, Draughts, Draughtsman, Draftsman

The spelling of **draught** is an English survivor – in the USA the spelling
draft is used and even the game of **draughts** is called *checkers*. and
otherwise. In British English the following differences continue to be
preserved:

   draught – a current of air; a quantity of liquid; a dose of medicine;
beer on draught; the depth of a loaded boat or ship; a draught-horse;
draughting a plan or map.

   draft: to compose a preliminary outline of an article, book or speech;
to draw up a parliamentary bill; a banker's order for payment; to
separate, usually sheep or cattle.

   A person who draws maps or plans is a **draughtsman** or **draughts-
woman**; the official who draws up parliamentary bills is the **government
draftsman**.

drawing room *see* **living room, sitting room, lounge, drawing room**

draws, drawers
Draws are small lotteries; **drawers** slide out from cabinets and tables. **Drawers** is also used as a comic alternative to underpants and knickers. All take plural verbs.

dress circle *see* **balcony, circle, dress circle, gallery, stalls**

drier, drily *see* **dryer, drier, drily, dryly**

drowned
Check the difference between these two statements: *The unfortunate young man drowned in the weir; The unfortunate young man was drowned in the weir. The Times* insists that **drowned** means being suffocated, usually accidentally, in water or other liquid; but **was drowned** indicates that another person caused the victim's death by holding the unfortunate's head under water. Few, if any, dictionaries discriminate.

druggist *see* **chemist, druggist, pharmacist**

dryer, drier, drily, dryly
By using **dryer** for drying machines (*spin dryer, hair dryer*), the way is left clear to use **drier** as the comparative adjective to mean 'more dry, lacking moisture'. **Drily** not **dryly** is the correct spelling of the adverb. But note: *dryish, dryness*.

dual, duel
Dual means 'consisting of two' or 'double': a **dual carriageway**, **dual brakes**. A **duel** is a contest or combat between two adversaries.

dubious *see* **doubtful, dubious**

due to *see* **because, since, on account of, owing to, due to**

dwarf, midget, pygmy
A **dwarf** is a human, animal or plant of stunted growth; in a human dwarf, the head may be large and extremities disproportionately short. A **midget** is an extremely small person, normally proportioned, while a **pygmy** (not pigmy) is generally one of several tribes (including the Pygmy tribe), the members of which are undersized by average human standards.

dyke, dike
In the context of female homosexuality, **dyke** (or **dike**), formerly an insulting term for a lesbian, is now being reclaimed – although halfway respectable, use with caution.

dysfunction, malfunction

In the meaning of 'failure to operate properly' because of some disturbance or deterioration of a part or organ, both mean roughly the same. **Dysfunction** tends to be used more to express some organic abnormality, while **malfunction** seems more clearly associated with mechanical failure.

each *see* both, each, either

each other, one another

Many people try to preserve a difference between these, using **each other** for two things and **one another** for more than two. Their usage has, however, become so intertwined that few of us now would appreciate the difference.

eager *see* anxious, eager

earn, paid

Many people strongly object to such statements as *The administrative head of the department earns £105,000 a year*. Perhaps not unreasonably they ask, 'does he really honestly earn that money?' and insist that such statements should read *The administrative head of the department is paid £105,000 a year*. A strong case exists for preserving the difference between something deserved or merited (**earned**) and an amount given in return for imprecise, perhaps even undeserved, services (**paid**).

earthly, earthy

The use of **earthly** can mean 'real, of the world, material' as opposed to 'heavenly', such as *an earthly paradise is virtually confined*, or can be used in a negative context such as: *no earthly chance*. **Earthy** means 'characteristic of the earth' or 'course, crude': *This has an earthy taste; Bill's language can be pretty earthy at times*.

eatable, edible

Both are synonymous, perhaps with the distinction that **eatable** implies something more tasty than merely **edible**: *The mushroom, once thought to be poisonous, is edible although bitter; She was relieved when she found the dish to be quite eatable*.

eclectic *see* esoteric, eclectic, exotic

ecology, environment

Ecology is the study of the relationship between the environment and its inhabitants, human or otherwise. The **environment** defines the external habitat and all the conditions surrounding an individual or group, human or otherwise: *Having studied the ecology of the lichen family for many years Peter concluded that the tiny plant recently found in the Andes lived in the harshest environment imaginable*.

economic, economical, encomium

Economic relates to economics, the principles governing the production and consumption of goods and services and commercial activity: *The government's latest economic policy is founded on optimistic expectations.* To be **economical** is to be thrifty and not wasteful. An **encomium** is a formal eulogy.

edible *see* eatable, edible

educationalist, educationist, educator

There is still debate about these. **Educationalist**, the traditional form, is giving way to the simpler **educationist**, but surely **educator** is the simplest and least pompous of all.

effect *see* affect, effect

effective, effectual, efficacious, efficient

This quartet causes plenty of confusion. **Effective** means 'an action that produces the intended effect': *He found that the threat of detention was effective in keeping control.* **Effectual** (subtle, this one) means 'capable of producing the desired effect': *Detention and demerits were quite effectual in keeping the boys under control.* **Efficacious** means 'having the power to produce the intended effect' or 'the ability to apply a remedy': *He claimed the medicine was the most efficacious cure for sore throats; The efficacy of his so-called sore-throat medicine was in some doubt.* **Efficient** means 'competent': *He was an efficient judge, effective on the bench, with a style that was effectual in clearing up the backlog of cases; and above all, he believed in handing out the sort of sentences that were efficacious.* Watch out for an emerging new meaning for **efficient** in 'management-speak'; in company terms, being more efficient means getting fewer people to do more work. This technique is called 'efficiency savings'.

effectively, in effect

Effectively is sometimes wrongly used to mean 'almost, all but': *The management's tactics effectively routed the demonstrators and only the hard core remained.* **In effect** might be the more precise term here, meaning 'for all practical purposes': *In effect the demonstrators were routed and only the hard core remained.* **Virtually** is a useful synonym.

effete, effeminate

Although **effete** can be used unisexually, it is usually applied to weak, ineffectual, morally and intellectually decadent men. It can sometimes be used otherwise – in biology, for example, where it can refer to animals no longer capable of reproducing. To be **effeminate** is for a man to display unmanly or feminine characteristics.

efficacious, efficient *see* effective, effectual, efficacious, efficient

effrontery *see* affront, effrontery

egoist, egotism
Egoism is a person's undue preoccupation with his or her self, a display of obsessive self-interest. An **egotistical** person is also obsessively self-interested but reveals it to all with excessive boasting and a predominance of 'I' in conversations.

egregious *see* **gregarious, egregious**

Eire *see* **Ireland, Eire, Ulster, Irish Republic**

either, any
Either means 'one or other of two': *Either take it or leave it; There were two movies showing and I didn't like either of them*. **Any** refers to more than two: *There were four movies showing and I didn't care for any of them*. Both **either** and **neither** are singular: *Either you or I am lying*. Although gramatically correct this looks and sounds awkward, so reconstruct: *Either you are lying or I am*. Also remember the *either/or* and *neither/nor* rule. *See also* **both, each, either**.

elapse *see* **lapse, elapse**

elder, older, eldest, oldest
The use of these words is still governed by tradition. **Elder** and **eldest** are used primarily for human family relationships; you would not say: *Toby is the eldest horse in the stables*, but you might say *Mr French is the firm's elder partner*. **Older** is the comparative of **old**: *Esther is the older of the two sisters; I thought that Emily was the oldest member of the family but it turns out that Rebecca is the eldest* (or *elder*).

election *see* **plebiscite, referendum, poll, ballot, election**

elemental, elementary, alimentary
Elemental relates to the primal forces of nature, things basic and fundamental: *She found herself transfixed by the elemental surges of the tide*. **Elementary** means 'basic and simple', and 'returning to first principles': *'As for the reason for Cargill's panic,' Holmes replied, 'it's elementary, my dear Watson.'* **Alimentary** refers to food and eating; hence one's *alimentary canal*.

elide *see* **allude, elude, elide**

elucidate, explain
Elucidate is merely a fancy word for **explain**.

elude *see* **allude, elude, elide** and **evade, elude, avoid**

emaciate, emancipate
A guinea pig was found in an emancipated condition – Matlock Mercury, Derbyshire. The word required is **emaciated**, meaning 'abnormally thin'. To **emancipate** is to free from restriction, usually in a social context: *In most respects she regarded herself as a truly emancipated woman, free to do do as she wanted.*

embassy *see* **consulate, embassy, legation**

emend *see* **amend, emend**

emigrant, immigrant
If John Smith leaves Britain to live in Australia, he's **emigrating** from Britain and **immigrating** to Australia, where he becomes an **immigrant** or, as some Australians have it, a **migrant**.

eminent, imminent, immanent
An **eminent** person is somebody of note, 'distinguished': *He was the most eminent neurosurgeon of his time*. **Imminent** means 'impending, threatening, about to happen': *Everyone felt that war was imminent*. There is also a rarely used word, **immanent**, which means 'inherent'.

emotional, emotive
To be **emotional** is to be affected, sometimes excessively, by emotion: *On the subject of her former partner, David, she invariably became emotional; The boy suffered from a variety of emotional problems*. **Emotive** means 'to arouse emotion': *Discussing missing husbands with their abandoned wives is understandably an emotive issue*.

empathy, sympathy
Sympathy means 'a sharing of emotions and feelings of compassion and pity with another, especially at a time of difficulty'. **Empathy** is a feeling of intimately understanding a person, 'the close identification with the thoughts and feelings of another': *In his latest portrait the artist revealed an unusual empathy with the sitter*.

empirical, imperial
Confusion between these two may arise from the similarity of *emperor* and *empire* to *empirical*, but there is no connection. **Empirical** means 'knowing by observation, facts and experience rather than from theory'. The word that relates to empire is **imperial**.

encomium *see* **economic, economical, encomium**

endemic, epidemic, pandemic
Cholera has been endemic in parts of the Indian subcontinent for the past 200 years; it causes numerous epidemics and from time to time pandemics, when it spreads across the world – The Times 1994. **Endemic** means 'frequently found in a particular area'; **epidemic** means 'affecting many people at the same time'; while **pandemic** means 'affecting many people over a wide geographical area'.

endogenous *see* **indigenous, endogenous**

enervate, energise
Enervate is often used wrongly; it means 'to drain and weaken': *The succession of hot, humid days left them irritable and enervated*. **Energise** means the opposite: *After three large glasses of chilled orange juice, Barry felt bouncy and energised*.

enjoin, join

To **join**, meaning 'to 'bring together', offers few problems. To **enjoin** is 'to 'order, urge or require': *The speaker enjoined the angry gathering to proceed quietly to their homes.*

ensue, ensure

Occasionally confused. **Ensue** means 'to follow subsequently, often as a consequence': *When the prizewinners were announced the usual babble and shouting ensued.* **Ensure** means 'to make certain': *Her powerful serve ensured her place on the tennis team.*

ensure *see* **assure, ensure, insure, promise**

enthralled *see* **thrilled, enthralled**

envelop, envelope

Don't confuse these. To **envelop** (pronounced *en-VEL-up*) something is to wrap it or cover it: *She screamed when she was suddenly enveloped by the poisonous green gas.* An **envelope** (pronounced *EN-vel-lope*) is of course a flat wrapper or other container, usually of paper.

envious, enviable, envy, jealousy

Although one of the seven deadly sins, **envy** can range from being merely a casual longing for something to deep hatred and malice towards someone possessing something that one wants. **Enviable** means 'arousing envy, or to be worthy of envy': *George has got himself an enviable position in the firm.* To be **envious** is to feel or show envy; a near synonym is to *covet*, which is to lust after the possession of something or someone. **Jealousy** is the expression of personal unease or resentment about a situation, often involving rivalry, the transfer of affection or love from one to another, or a suspected infidelity, and can surface as irrational behaviour and vindictiveness.

environment *see* **ecology, environment**

envisage, envision

These are near synonyms, but **envision** tends to imply future possibility rather than an image: *The minister envisioned a day when everyone, regardless of circumstance, would be adequately housed.* To **envisage** is to form a mental image of something in the future: *She envisaged her ideal home – a modernised thatched cottage with an old-fashioned garden and orchard.* Loose usage has tended to extend the meaning of *envisage* (and *envision*) to 'expect, feel, think': *The farmers envisaged/envisioned that next year's crop would be the biggest ever.* Not to be encouraged.

envy *see* **envious, enviable, envy, jealousy**

epicure *see* **gourmand, gourmet, epicure, glutton**

epidemic *see* **endemic, epidemic, pandemic**

epigram, epigraph, epitaph
The playwright Dennis Potter's *The trouble with words is that you never know whose mouths they've been in* is an **epigram**: a pithy, witty slice of wisdom. An **epitaph** is an inscription on a gravestone, as in this example commemorating the 17th-century architect Sir John Vanbrugh: Under this stone, reader, survey / Dear Sir John Vanbrugh's house of clay. / Lie heavy on him, earth! for he / Laid many heavy loads on thee. An **epigraph** is usually a thematic quotation appearing at the beginning of a book, but it can also be an inscription on a statue or building.

epithet
Careful users will observe this word's original meaning: an adjective or phrase expressing some attribute or quality characteristic of a person or thing. Richard the Lionheart, Chubby Checker, Gorgeous Gussy Moran, Babe Ruth are all epithets, none of them necessarily disparaging. Today many, if not most, people regard an **epithet** as abusive: *'Stupid bitch' and other epithets were shouted at her by passing lorry drivers.*

equable, equitable
Equable means 'unvarying and free from extremes' or, as applied to people, 'placid, even-tempered': *As the executive who fields all the complaints, Margaret has the ideal equable temperament.* **Equitable** means 'fair, impartial and just': *The insurance company arrived at an equitable settlement.*

equal to, equal with
These are used for quite different purposes. *He was glad to hear that they felt his skills were equal to the immense task ahead.* Here **equal to** is used to convey 'adequate, equivalent to'. **Equal with** means 'being identical, evenly balanced': *She felt that after her pay rise she was now about equal with the men in the firm.*

equitable *see* **equable, equitable**

erotic *see* **obscene, pornographic, erotic**

erupt, irrupt
To **erupt** is to burst out violently; to **irrupt** is to enter forcibly and violently. The same meanings apply to the nouns, **eruption** and **irruption**.

Eskimo *see* **Inuit, Aleut, Eskimo**

esoteric, eclectic, exotic
Many writers find these hard to separate. Something **esoteric** is confined or restricted to a minority who understand it, such as obscure religious ritual, the peculiar attractions of trainspotting or, these days, Latin. Something **exotic** is strange, unusual and foreign, but it can also mean 'outrageous' and 'thrilling'. An **eclectic** person has the talent and taste to select the best of everything.

especially, specially
Especially means 'really exceptionally'; **specially** means 'out of the ordinary, individual, particular': *The dog was specially chosen for his alertness, but he is especially attentive at mealtimes.*

essentials *see* **necessities, necessaries, essentials**

European Union, European Community, Common Market
Use the first and the abbreviation **EU** rather than **Common Market**, **EEC** or **EC**.

evacuate, vacate
Evacuate means 'to make empty' (e.g. the bowels) or 'to remove from': *The evacuation offrom the threatened town went smoothly.* **Vacate** means 'to give up occupancy': *The squatters vacated the premises with surprisingly little fuss.*

evade, elude, avoid
Avoid means 'to shun, to keep away from'. **Evade** and **elude** are similar and mean 'to avoid by cleverness or deception'. Knowing the difference between **avoidance** and **evasion** could keep you out of jail when paying your tax; **tax avoidance** (by good advice) is legal, while **tax evasion** (by dishonest means) is clearly illegal.

evaluate *see* **appraise, apprise, assess, evaluate**

every day, everyday
As an adjective, **everyday** means ordinary, usual: *Sighting deer during their walks along the cliffs was now an everyday occurrence.* **Every day** means each day: *We saw deer wandering through the garden nearly every day.*

everyone, every one, everybody
There were ten apples and every one was rotten; There were ten people in the pub and everyone was drunk. Here **every one** is used to emphasise individual apples, and **everyone** the whole, as a group, but note that everyone and every one are both singular. Sir Roy Strong's book *The Story of Britain* is described on the cover as: *One man's quest to give to everyone the history of their country.* The publishers should have known better, although the practice of using the plural pronoun instead of, for example, *his/her* is now widespread. **Everybody** and **everyone** are interchangeable.

evidence, proof, testimony
Testimony is the statement of a witness; **evidence** is information presented to support an argument; **proof** is evidence that removes any doubt.

evident *see* **apparent, evident**

evince, evoke
Both are used in relation to abstractions, such as emotions, images and visions.

To **evince** is to 'to show, to make evident': *She evinced little surprise when confronted by her former enemy*. **Evoke** is a near synonym but perhaps a little more active in that it implies 'to summon up, to make clear': *In his speech he evoked the dream of freedom, independence and nationhood*. *See also* **invoke, evoke**.

exacerbate, exasperate, aggravate

All three mean 'to make worse' but are used in different ways. **Exacerbate** is customarily applied to things and conditions: *The almost forgotten feud between the brothers was suddenly exacerbated by family interference*. **Exasperate** is used to express a worsening situation between individuals: *She finally exasperated me to the point of screaming!* **Aggravate,** which many people mistakenly believe to mean 'annoy', is a synonym for **exacerbate** but may sometimes involve a degree of intent and persistence: *Elizabeth's constant sniping at Jack was cunningly calculated to aggravate the already tense situation*. *See also* **aggravate, exasperate**.

exact, extract

In the sense of 'demand, force or compel', these are synonymous: *After winning the lottery, Barney knew it would be only a matter of time before the family would be around to exact their share*. Perhaps **extract** implies a greater degree of removal by extortion than **exact**, but it is a matter of choice.

exasperate *see* **aggravate, exasperate and exacerbate, exasperate and aggravate**

except, unless

Use **except** to express an omission and **unless** to make a condition: *I will work every day except Saturday unless you disagree*. The use of **except** as a synonym for **unless** is an archaism except perhaps in Northern Ireland: *Except [unless] you right now give me a categorical assurance that you believe my word on the constitutional position of Northern Ireland, I will not hold any conversation with you* – Ian Paisley MP, 1994.

except *see* **accept, except**

exceptional, exceptionable

Exceptional means 'out of the ordinary, most unusual', but to be **exceptionable** is to be objectionable: *On the court, he was an exceptional tennis player, but in the clubhouse most found his behaviour quite exceptionable*.

excoriate, execrate

One old meaning of **excoriate** was to 'flay, or to strip the skin' from someone. Today's usage is less physical but no less severe: to denounce or scathingly condemn. To **execrate** is to loathe and detest: *In no uncertain words the President excoriated his former ally as a barbarian traitor; She positively execrated the memory of her late stepmother*.

excuse *see* **alibi, excuse**

exercise *see* **exorcise, exercise**

exhaust, deplete, reduce
Exhaust means 'to drain, empty, remove and to deplete totally'. **Reduce**, in a similar context, means 'to make smaller in size, number or extent'. The odd man out is **deplete**, which, rather unhelpfully, can mean 'to use up or empty partially or completely'. If you intend to write *The local reservoirs were depleted well before the end of summer*, you are inviting confusion. Better to be specific and use *reduced* (partial depletion) or *exhausted* (total depletion).

exigency, exiguous
Two classic confusables, which is perhaps why we don't see them (or even need to use them) very often. An **exigency** is a state of great urgency that requires immediate attention. **Exiguous** means 'meagre, small': *The problem with the Somalis, apart from having to cope with natural and manmade exigencies, was simply their traditionally exiguous incomes*.

exorcise, exercise
Although there cannot be many writers unfamiliar with **exercise**, these two are sometimes muddled. A New South Wales government leaflet advises car buyers to demand the car's history from the vendor, *Otherwise, a finance company could exorcise its rights*. To **exorcise** is to attempt to dispel evil spirits from a person or place (or even a car!).

exotic *see* **esoteric, eclectic, exotic**

expatiate, expiate
To **expatiate** is to elaborate or enlarge upon a topic in speaking or writing: *The doctor expatiated on the dangers of bad dietary habits*. To **expiate** is to make amends or atone for some wrong: *In his desperate efforts to expiate his cruel treatment of his sisters, Joel moaned and tore his hair and banged his head upon the floor*.

expatriate, compatriot
An **expatriate** (often abbreviated to **expat**) is a resident of a foreign country: *All the American expatriates would gather every Friday in their club on the Nanking Road*. To **expatriate** is to expel a person from a country. A **compatriot** is a fellow countryman: *He found several compatriots among the British expatriates in Barcelona*.

expect *see* **anticipate, expect, hope**

expeditious, expedient
Expeditious means 'speedy and efficient', while **expedient** expresses an action that is convenient for the purpose: *It was considered expedient to wind up the firm as expeditiously as possible*.

expertise, skill
Expertise is usually substituted as a posh word for **skill**, although you can differentiate between them if you wish. **Skill** suggests practical ability, as in a

surgeon's skill, while **expertise** conveys (or should convey) the acquisition of specialised knowledge and experience to an exceptional degree.

expiate *see* **expatiate, expiate**

explain *see* **elucidate, explain**

explicit, implicit
To be **explicit** is to be absolutely clear and specific; something **implicit** is not directly expressed but implied or hinted at. Nevertheless, whatever is implied is usually or instinctively understood or taken for granted: *The volunteers were only too keenly aware of the implicit dangers of the task ahead.*

extant *see* **extinct, extant**

extempore *see* **impromptu, extempore**

extinct, extant
Similar looking, but opposites. Something **extinct** no longer exists; something **extant** is still, or thought to be, in existence or surviving: *Everyone knows that the trilobite is extinct, but its distant cousin the woodlouse is still extant throughout the world.*

extract *see* **exact, extract**

Extract, the Extract and Other Lookalikes

A family of words exists that frequently causes people to pause: words that are spelt the same but are pronounced or accented differently where there is one pronunciation for the noun and another for the verb. An example is **extract**. The **extract** of cod-liver oil you may have known in your childhood is pronounced *EX-trakt*, while the process of extracting it from the poor cod is pronounced *ex-TRAKT*.

Here are some other fairly common words where the nouns and verbs look alike but are pronounced differently (noun first, then the verb): **abstract** (*AB-strakt, ab-STRAKT*); **accent** (*AK-sent, ak-SENT*); **attribute** (*AT-trib-yoot, at-TRIB-yoot*); **combat** (*KOM-bat, kom-BAT*); **compound** (*KOM-pound, kom-POUND*); **compress** (*KOM-press, kom-PRESS*); **conduct** (*KON-duct, kon-DUCT*); **consort** (*KON-sort, kon-SORT*); **contest** (*KON-test, kon-TEST*); **contract** (*KON-trakt, kon-TRAKT*); **convert** (*KON-vert, kon-VERT*); **convict** (*KON-vikt, kon-VIKT*); **defect** (*DE-fekt, de-FEKT*); **digest** (*DY-jest, dih-JEST*); **discharge** (*DIS-charj, dis-CHARJ*); **escort** (*ES-kort, es-KORT*); **ferment** (*FER-ment, fer-MENT*); **object** (*OB-jekt, ob-JEKT*); **pervert** (*PER-vert, per-VERT*); **present** (*PRES-ent, preh-SENT*); **project** (*PRO-jekt, pro-JEKT*); **rebel** (*REH-bel, reh-BEL*); **refuse** (*REH-fyoos, reh-FYOOS*); **suspect** (*SUS-pekt, sus-PEKT*).

extraneous, extrinsic, intrinsic

Extraneous means 'external, coming from without' or, in another sense, 'irrelevant, unrelated or not essential': *At the enquiry the business about the missing personal effects was considered to be an extraneous issue.* **Extrinsic** has a subtly similar meaning but is applied in the sense of not being an inherent or essential part of something: *The auctioneer played up the extrinsic contribution of the necklace's previous alleged royal owners to its fame and value.* Its opposite, **intrinsic**, meaning 'an essential part of something', is more common.

fable *see* allegory, fable, myth, parable, legend

facility, faculty

Of the various meanings the one that causes most confusion concerns ability. By **facility** we usually mean 'having the ability to do something with apparent ease': *She had the charming facility to make people relax.* By **faculty** or **faculties** we mean 'natural or inherent powers' (that is, sight, hearing, taste, intuition, intelligence, etc): *The task they set him was going to challenge all his faculties to the hilt.*

facsimile *see* replica, copy, facsimile

facts, true facts, factitious

Facts are verified or observable truths, events that have actually happened or things that have existed or are real. The phrase **true facts** is tautological. Something **factitious**, on the other hand, is false or artificial: *She claimed that most of Deborah's teachers had been seduced by her academic achievements, which turned out to be factitious.*

Fahrenheit *see* centigrade, Celsius

faint, feint

Faint means 'weak, feeble, indistinct' as an adjective, and also 'to lose consciousness' as a verb. A **feint** is a feigned or pretended attack intended to mislead: *The Missouri Kid feinted with his left and then belted Navarro on the chin with a terrific right.*

fair, fayre

Does the current ubiquity of **fayre**, to denote a country or charity fair or fête, indicate a desire to return the word to its Old Saxon root – *fagr* or *fagar*? This doesn't wash because the etymology of **fair**, the holiday or entertainment, derives from the Old French *feire*, or festival. More likely **fayre** is a symptom of 'Ye Olde Syndrome', or the quest for the quaint. Be sensible and use **fair**.

fallacy, misconception

A **fallacy** is not an 'erroneous belief' but a faulty opinion or argument based on inaccurate facts or false reasoning. An erroneous belief is a **misconception**.

familiar with, familiar to

Familiar with indicates 'having a good knowledge of': *James was familiar with the type of engine and had it going in no time*. **Familiar to** implies a lesser degree of familiarity: *As she entered the church Ethel realised that many of the faces in the congregation were familiar to her*.

famously

As in *Canute was the king who famously commanded the tide to turn*, **famously** is an overrated and overused adverb. Use with caution, if at all.

farther, further

Farther is used exclusively to express distance, either literally (*He guessed that Bristol was farther from London than Bath*) or figuratively (*Fred's claims could not be farther from the truth*). **Further** means 'in addition': *She was seriously thinking about further education*.

fatal, fated, fateful

The primary meaning of **fatal** is 'causing or resulting in death'; **fated** means 'doomed'. **Fateful** is the most loaded of this group, suggesting all kinds of ominous portents beyond anyone's control, including death, disaster and ruin: *From that fateful encounter sprang a legacy of hate that engulfed the two neighbouring states*.

fatuity *see* **futility, fatuity, futurity**

fauna *see* **flora and fauna**

fayre *see* **fair, fayre**

faze *see* **phase, faze**

feasible *see* **possible, plausible, feasible**

feel *see* **believe, feel, think**

feint *see* **faint, feint**

ferment, foment

He [Englishman Hugh Ryman] fomented his ultra-ripe grapes in oak barrels . . . (Oz Clarke in *The Daily Telegraph*, 3.5.97). Strange way to make wine! **Fermenting** rather than **fomenting** might be a better way to brew a better vintage. In the sense of 'causing or stirring up trouble' these are synonyms. Otherwise, to **ferment** is the chemical process of fermentation, of converting, for example, grapes into wine, while to **foment** is to apply moist heat to the body to reduce pain.

fervent, fervid, fervour

Fervour is an intense feeling, a passion, from which springs **fervent**, meaning 'to be keenly enthusiastic, ardent and passionate'. **Fervid** is synonymous but tends to be used to suggest a heightened, more passionate, even incandescent fervour for which the little-used **perfervid** is really the correct word.

feud *see* vendetta, feud

few, little, less, fewer

It is not unusual to see on the label of a dietary product an assertion that it is **less** fattening, **less** expensive and has **less** calories. Two correct out of three; what is meant is **fewer** calories. The rule is simple: use **few** and **fewer** with numbers and when what is being described can be counted, and **less** when describing something abstract or uncountable: *In my last driving test I made fewer mistakes than ever before; Although I made fewer mistakes my instructor seemed less pleased with my performance.* Use **little** to indicate 'not much': *Although I have little spare time, I do have a few minutes to spare now.*

fiancé, fiancée

The first is masculine, the second, with the double *ee*, is feminine. Conscientious writers will retain the accent.

fictional, fictitious

Something **fictional** relates to a fiction, a work of the imagination – a novel, play or movie: *He referred to the fictional account of his grandfather's life in 'The Moon and Sixpence'.* Something **fictitious** is untrue or not genuine: *I'm tired of hearing her obviously fictitious excuses for being late each morning.*

filet, fillet

In British English, the noun **fillet** (pronounced *FILL-it*) means a strip of boneless meat or fish, while the verb to **fillet** means to 'remove the bone from meat or fish'. In American- English, the word is **filet** (pronounced *fil-LAY*). The well-known dish *filet mignon* is pronounced *fih-LAY MEEN-yohn* wherever you are.

filial *see* finial, filial

fill in, fill out

There's logic here. When you **fill in** something, you insert: *I filled in the gaps; I filled in the application form.* When you **fill out** something, you add or complete: *He filled out John's speech with some spicy anecdotes.* In American English, **fill out** is used universally.

finalise *see* finish, finalise

find out *see* ascertain, find out

finial, filial
A **finial** is an ornament on top of a spire, gable or piece of furniture. **Filial** relates to sons and daughters: *He expected, and received, daily displays of filial devotion.*

finish, finalise
These are not synonyms. **Finish** means to complete; to **finalise** (or finalize) is to 'settle something, to reach agreement' or 'to put something into a final form': *She finalised the amendments, but the agreement was far from finished.*

first, firstly
It's hardly worth getting into a stew over **firstly**, as many grammarians do in objecting to **firstly**, **secondly**, **thirdly**, etc. Use this pattern if you wish, or even **firstly**, **second**, **third**, and so on. But shorter and neater (and avoiding ninety-ninthly) is the formula: **first**, **second**, **third** . . .

first name *see* **Christian name, first name, given name, forename**

fish, fishes
Both are used as the plural form of **fish**, though **fishes** nowadays appears infrequently.

flagrant, blatant
Flagrant means 'shocking and outrageous'; **blatant** means 'glaringly obvious': *Mavis's flagrant disregard of her mother-in-law upset the whole party; Barrie's accusation was recognised by everyone as a blatant lie.*

flammable *see* **inflammable, flammable**

flare, flair
These are sometimes confused. **Flare** expresses 'bursting with activity' – usually to do with fire and flame: *The sudden gust caused the fire to flare alarmingly; As they explored deeper into the cave they had to light flares; As the temperature rose, tempers flared among the miners.* **Flair** refers to a person's natural ability, talent, elegance and style: *Barbara always dressed with flair.*

flat, condominium, apartment, cooperative
While transatlantic usage is variable, a **flat** in the UK, and in other places like Australia, is an **apartment** in the USA. A **condominium**, a more common description in the USA than elsewhere, is a block of flats whose owners share costs and responsibilities for the upkeep of the building and its facilities. In the USA a **cooperative** is a block of apartments owned by a corporation in which the owners hold shares equivalent to the value of their individual apartments.

flaunt *see* **flout, flaunt**

flautist, flutist
In Britain, a flute player is a **flautist**; **flutist** is the American English term.

flora and fauna

Unlike similar Latin nouns, these aren't plural but collective nouns. The plural forms, rarely used, are *floras* and *faunas*, even more rarely *florae* and *faunae*.

flotsam, jetsam, ligan

These all originate from ships and are items that either float off (**flotsam**), are jettisoned or thrown off (**jetsam**), or sink to the bottom of the sea (**ligan** or **lagan**). The question is, how can you tell which is which when you find them?

flounder *see* **founder, flounder**

flout, flaunt

Flout means to 'disregard, show contempt or to deliberately defy'; **flaunt** means 'to show off boastfully, to display ostentatiously': *In playing the overture the violinist flouted just about every one of the composer's directions; The dancer shamefully flaunted her smouldering sexuality.*

flu, flue

Flu or **'flu** is short for *influenza*; a **flue** is a chimney or pipe to carry off smoke or gas.

fob, foist

Usage seems to favour **foist** as meaning 'to pass off something fake or inferior as genuine and valuable', or 'to impose an unwanted item or task onto someone': *That supervisor deliberately foisted this lousy job on me.* **Fob** means to 'put off by evasion' and is usually followed by **off**: *She won't fob me off with that weak excuse again.*

follow *see* **succeed, follow**

foment *see* **ferment, foment**

forbear, forebear

As nouns, both mean the same: 'an ancestor'. **Forbear** (without the first *e*) is also a verb meaning 'to refrain from': *She could hardly forbear crying out aloud when she heard Frank's voice.*

forceful, forcible, forced

Forcible and **forced** are near adjectival synonyms, the latter more common, to express the use of force: *The evidence indicated a forced entry.* **Forceful** means 'powerful and persuasive': *His advocacy during the trial was both thoughtful and forceful.*

forebear *see* **forbear, forebear**

forego, forgo

Forego means 'to precede, to go before'; **forgo** means 'to do without, or to give up something': *Betsy thought twice about forgoing her morning coffee.*

forename *see* **Christian name, first name, given name forename**

forensic
Many think that **forensic** is a medical term; in fact as an adjective forensic means 'legal'. **Forensic medicine** is medical science applied to the purposes of law.

forever, for ever
These are worth separating, with **forever** meaning 'continuously, at all times' (*The two old dears were forever gossiping*), and **for ever** meaning 'eternally, always' (though in American English, it often appears as one word): *He swore he'd love me for ever (or for ever and ever!).*

foreword, forward
Forward conveys 'moving ahead, towards the front': *Every time he had the chance he moved a little bit forward*. A **foreword** is a preface or introduction to a book: *Max was paid £150 to write a new foreword to the book.*

forgo *see* **forego, forgo**

formally, formerly
Pronounced the same, spelt differently and often confused. **Formally** means 'in a formal, conventional or established manner': *For the wedding they all had to dress formally*. **Formerly** means 'in past or earlier times': *Formerly it was accepted that you'd dress for dinner.*

former, latter
The convention, still healthily maintained, is to use these only when referring to two people or things: *The doctor recommended brandy and lemon for his cold – with plenty of the former; There wasn't much between Harris's and Smith's quotes but Jill felt inclined to choose the latter.*

fortuitous, fortunate
Something that happens by chance or accident is **fortuitous**; if the result is a happy one it is also **fortunate**: *Our meeting at the supermarket was fortuitous but, fortunately, she remembered the money she owed me.*

forward and backward, backwards and forwards
As adjectives, **forward** and **backward** are not spelled with *s*: *She had a very forward attitude*. Otherwise, with or without the *s*, both are acceptable except in some selective usages. You would not say, for example, *Look forwards to a cosy evening by the fireside*. In most cases, your ear should tell you which sounds right.

founder, flounder
Flounder means 'to struggle helplessly': *After a series of interruptions, the speaker floundered for several minutes*. If you **founder**, however, you're in serious trouble; it means 'to sink': *The ill-fated ship foundered in only ten feet of water.*

Founding Fathers, Pilgrim Fathers
The **Founding Fathers** were members of the 1787 US Constitutional Convention. The **Pilgrim Fathers** were the Puritans who sailed on the *Mayflower* to New England in 1620.

fracture, break
There is no difference between a **broken** bone and a **fractured** bone. Medically, the preferred term is **fracture**.

fragile, frail
Although their meanings overlap, careful writers will use these differently. Both mean 'delicate and easily broken', but **fragile** is more aptly applied to things (*a fragile vase, fragile health*), while **frail**, implying physical weakness, feebleness and incapability, is best reserved for people: *Even in her frail state, she always managed the evening trip to the corner pub.*

Frankenstein's monster
Many people think that **Frankenstein** is the monster. Not so. In Mary Shelley's 1818 novel, Baron Frankenstein *created* the monster that destroyed him. If you allude to something that destroys its creator, you can call it Frankenstein's monster.

frantic, frenetic
Someone **frantic** is to some degree, over-excited, hysterical and agitated. **Frenetic** is a close synonym but its roots from both Greek and Latin link it more to the mind and insanity; perhaps best reserved for conveying a wild, deranged frenzy or delirium.

frequently *see* **commonly, customarily, frequently, generally, habitually, ordinarily, usually**

freshman *see* **sophomore, freshman**

frightened, scared, alarmed, afraid
Afraid has a certain permanence about it: *He was afraid of crossing roads.* To be **frightened** or **scared** is a more immediate or passing experience: *The children were frightened/scared by the loud bang.* **Alarm** is a fear or anxiety that can build : *Finding nobody, she began to be alarmed by the eerie silence.*

front *see* **back, behind, backward, backwards**

fruition, completion
Fruition conveys the enjoyment of fulfilment and success. **Completion** is the state of being finished, complete: *The completion of the project signalled the fruition of his life's work.*

funds *see* **money, monies, funds, cash**

furnish, furbish
Furnish means to 'provide, equip, supply, fit out': *By agreement the room was furnished with only top-quality cupboards and appliances*. To **furbish** is to 'polish or restore to brightness'.

further *see* **farther, further**

fustian, fusty
Fustian is used mostly in the literary sense of being pretentious, pompous and bombastic. **Fusty** means 'smelling damp and mouldy' and, thus figuratively, being stale and old-fashioned.

futility, fatuity, futurity
Futility means 'total lack of purpose, point and success'. **Fatuity** is 'complacency, inanity, smug stupidity'. **Futurity** is the odd one out and is a fancy word for 'the future'.

Gaelic *see* **Gallic, Gaelic**

gaff, gaffe
A **gaff** is a fishing pole with a hook on it; a **gaffe** is a social blunder or an indiscreet remark: *Bernard turned a bright red when he realised he'd made a gaffe*.

gale *see* **cyclone, hurricane, tornado, typhoon, waterspout**

Gallic, Gaelic
Gallic (from Gaul, the earlier name of France) relates to France and its people. **Gaelic** refers to Celtic descendants (Scots, Irish, Isle of Man) and their languages.

gallery *see* **balcony, circle, dress circle, gallery, stalls**

Gambia, The Gambia
The latter is the correct name for this tiny country on the West African coast.

gamble, gambol
Occasionally confused but their meanings are miles apart. To **gamble** is to play a game of chance for money; to **gambol** is to frolic about playfully: *He quickly gambled his fortune away; The lambs gambolled happily in the early spring sunshine*.

gaol, jail
Both are correct but the former is alive and well only in Britain.

geezer *see* **geyser, geezer**

gelatin, gelatine
Generally the British prefer **gelatin**, and the Americans **gelatine**.

gender *see* **sex and gender**

generally *see* **commonly, customarily, frequently, generally, habitually, ordinarily, usually**

generous *see* **prodigal, generous**

genial, congenial, congenital
To be **genial** is to be friendly, pleasant and good-tempered; to be **congenial** is to relate to and to share your friendliness with others of similar disposition: *The atmosphere during the whole trip was wonderfully congenial.* **Congenital** relates to any non-inherited abnormality acquired before or during birth.

gentleman, man
Usage of **gentleman** is mostly a social nicety. It can be used in a complimentary way: *That kind gentleman gave me his seat.* Or sarcastically: *That gentleman over there just rudely brushed past me.* The phrase *he's no gentleman* indicates clearly that the man has bad manners and probably a long list of other sins. Its most common usage is in the form of an address to a gathering: *Gentlemen, will you please take your seats?*

genuine *see* **authentic, genuine**

genteel, gentle, Gentile
Two of these are generally well understood: **gentle** means 'tender and kindly', the opposite to 'rough, coarse and violent'; and a **Gentile** is a non-Jewish person. **Genteel** is trickier; it originally meant 'well-bred, respectable and refined' but is now often used in a mildly sarcastic way to send up ordinary people who affect or aspire to middle- or upper-class lifestyles.

geriatric, elderly
Geriatric is not a synonym for elderly. **Geriatric medicine** or **geriatrics** is the branch of medicine that studies and treats elderly people and their diseases.

German shepherd *see* **Alsatian**

get, acquire, obtain, secure
Get is such a powerful, versatile but simple word that we often fall over ourselves trying to find a smarter substitute. Usually there isn't one. Sir Ernest Gower hated **acquire** but you can use it in a sort of shifty sense: *He acquired it from the back of a lorry.* There's not much call for **obtain**. **Secure** is like **get** plus a favour: *I've secured you two tickets for the big match tomorrow.* Many people object to the brutal **have got** as in: *I have got two tickets for the match tomorrow,* preferring the shorter, more mellifluous **have** by itself: *I have two tickets for the match tomorrow.*

geyser, geezer
A **geyser** is an active hot spring and used to be (in the UK) a domestic gas bathroom water-heater. A **geezer** is a slang term for a man, usually any older man, but the **geezer** is 'the boss'.

gibe *see* **jibe, gibe, gybe**

gilt, guilt
Gilt is the result of gilding, that is: covering with gold or a preparation that imitates it. **Guilt** is the product of moral or criminal wrongdoing. In most people, guilt can give rise to feelings of responsibility and remorse.

gipsy *see* **gypsy, gipsy, Romany, traveller**

gist, grist
The **gist** (pronounced *jist*) is the point or substance of an argument: *The gist was, as Mr Peters explained, that there would be no pay rises until after September.* **Grist** is grain intended for grinding. The phrase *it's grist to the mill* means it is something that can be turned to a profit: *To Fred, any old scrap metal, batteries, tyres and so on was all grist to the mill.*

give *see* **donate, give**

given name *see* **Christian name, first name, given name, forename**

glance *see* **scan, glance, scrutinize**

glutton *see* **gourmand, gourmet, epicure, glutton**

god, God
The Greeks had **gods**; Christians have **God**, the supreme being, always with a capital *G*. Similarly, pronouns referring to *God* (*Him, He, Her, Thee, Thou*, etc) should be capitalised. Sometimes a choice is difficult: *If you believe Goldsmith, the shares are a bargain. If you believe the market, disaster lies ahead. Personally, I believe Goldsmith. But god help him if he is wrong.* (*The Sunday Times*, 1993).

good, well
Using **good** as an adverb (*Elizabeth can cook quite good*) is incorrect; use **well**. On the other hand, Elizabeth's cooking can taste *good*. And you can **feel good** and also **feel well** – two different states. Tread carefully to retain clarity.

got, gotten, has got
Gotten travelled with the settlers from Britain to America where it is now standard usage, but the word never returned to its native shores. Here, although we retain *forget/forgotten* and the biblical *beget/begotten*, the use of **gotten** produces furrowed brows and dismissal as American slang: *Fred's gotten to be a smartass these days.* In Britain, **got** is the past participle of to **get** as well as being the form used for the past tense: *She's got a great voice; They've got a nerve!* Used informally in speech there's little to complain about, but when written many people find 'has got' grating: She has got a great voice; They have got a nerve. With **has got** and **have got** the objection disappears when you drop **got**: *She has a great voice*; and *I have to go* instead of *I have got to go*. There are no firm rules for **got**, but sentences often seem more elegant without it.

Gothic, Gothick

Gothic describes the Western European architectural style during the 12th–16th centuries, and the painting and sculpture associated with it. **Gothick** specifically denotes the 18th-century neo-medieval revival in architecture, art and literature.

gourmand, gourmet, epicure, glutton

Deepest in this trough is the **glutton**, who will eat anything and any amount of it. Then comes the **gourmand** who, while appreciating food, just loves to eat. Finally, the **gourmet** and the **epicure**, both of whom appreciate the finer points of eating and drinking except that, to the **epicure**, the joy of food is almost a religion.

gradation, graduation

A **gradation** is a gradual progression of stages, in size, tone, sound or degree, often imperceptible: *The sky was a striking gradation of purples and reds.* In this context, a graduation is a progression of measuring marks or calibrations.

graduate, undergraduate, postgraduate

An **undergraduate** is a student studying for a first degree who becomes a **graduate** when the degree is awarded. A **postgraduate** is, as a wag suggested, a dead graduate. The correct term is **postgraduate student**, who is studying for more advanced qualifications

grammar, syntax

Grammar is the system that binds all the elements that make up a language; **syntax** is the system (within grammar) that controls the order and relationships between words in constructions such as sentences.

gratuitous, gratuity

Sometimes confused with *gratitude*, **gratuitous** means 'something given free and unrequested'. Its use today is increasingly to define something that's unnecessary and uncalled-for: *The two men traded gratuitous insults for half an hour.* A **gratuity** is a gift, usually money, for services rendered.

Great Britain *see* Britain

green paper *see* white paper, green paper

gregarious, egregious

These were once opposites: **gregarious** meaning 'enjoying the company of others and tending to flock together' and **egregious** (pronounced *eh-GREE-jus*) meaning 'separate from the flock, or outstanding'. But while **gregarious** has retained its original meaning, **egregious** is now used almost exclusively to mean 'blatantly, deliberately bad, bald-faced': *I've never met such an egregious liar in all my life.*

grisly, grizzly
Grisly means 'gruesome'; **grizzly**, applied to hair and bears, means 'grey or streaked with grey'.

grist *see* **gist, grist**

gross *see* **crass, silly, stupid, gross**

grow, growing
There is a trend, imported from North America, to a new use of **grow** and **growing** as a substitute for *increase*: *By encouraging communication we will grow the telecommunications market* (*The Times*, Business Section, 30.12.96). It is well-worn nowadays, but nevertheless it's worth pointing out that on all counts it's a cliché and incorrect. If you care about accuracy, remember that we *grow* sweet peas but *increase* markets.

guarantee, warranty
Although somewhat interchangeable, a **guarantee** is an assurance that a product or service will meet agreed standards or specifications; or an agreement to repair or replace. A **warranty** is usually more specifically a promise that what is being sold is the vendor's (for example a car), and is suitable and fit for the use claimed.

guess, suppose, think
To **guess** is to put forward an opinion or estimate based on little or no information. To **suppose** is to assume that something is true, again based on hazy information. To **think** is to arrive at a decision or point of view after conscious thought: *I guess stew will be on the menu again tonight; After his big sale last week, I suppose Jim will be first in line for promotion; We're all very tired so I think we should return home.*

Guides, Girl Guides
The former **Girl Guides** organisation in Britain is now known as the **Guides**. In the USA, their equivalent is the *Girl Scouts*.

guilt *see* **gilt, guilt**

gybe *see* **jibe, gibe, gybe**

gynaecologist, obstetrician
A **gynaecologist** specialises in diseases of the urinary and genital organs of women; an **obstetrician** deals with all aspects of childbirth.

gypsy, gipsy, Romany, traveller
Gypsy (plural *gypsies*) is preferred to **gipsy** but **Romany** is the technically correct term for the true ethnic gypsy, that is, a member of a race of wanderers, originating in India, who came to Britain in the early 16th century. The term **traveller** appears with increasing frequency, but is ambiguous as it not only refers to Romany travellers, but also to more recently formed groups of itinerants.

habit, habitual

A **habit** is an established or usual custom, so the term 'usual habit' is a redundancy – as is 'customary habit'. **Habitual** is the adjective, meaning 'by habit': *Unfortunately, for his job prospects, Tony was an habitual drinker.*

habitually *see* **commonly, customarily, frequently, generally, habitually, ordinarily, usually**

had had

There are times when we all get caught in a construction with the dual **had**: *If I had had the time I would have stayed to watch.* Although grammatical, it's not a pretty sight and best avoided by rewriting: *I would have stayed to watch but didn't have the time.*

hale, hail

These two soundalikes confuse because between them they have four common meanings: **hale** the adjective meaning 'robust and healthy'; **hale** the verb meaning to 'haul or drag'; **hail** the noun meaning 'frozen raindrops or similar particles driven with great force'; and **hail** the verb meaning 'to attract attention' or 'to greet enthusiastically'. Recognise these meanings and you'll know how to use them in such expressions as: *Even at eighty-six Ethel was still hale and hearty*; *Last week Gerry was haled before a judge*; *Under a hail of gunfire they raced for the nearest cover*; *Outside the theatre, they hailed a taxi.*

hallo *see* **hullo, hallo, hello**

hamlet *see* **city, town, village, hamlet**

hanged, hung

A recently published book entitled *How To Get Hung* alarmed some people who thought it might be a do-it-yourself suicide manual; in fact it was by an art gallery owner advising artists how to get their work exhibited. To remove such ambiguity, a person is **hanged** (by the neck until dead); a picture (or your suit) is **hung**.

hanger, hangar

A **hanger** is a wire contraption on which you hang clothes; a **hangar** houses aircraft.

happen *see* **transpire, happen, occur**

harangue, tirade

A **harangue** is a forceful, loud, long and eventually tedious speech: *Mr Oliver harangued the crowd for two interminable hours.* A **tirade** is much the same but angrier.

harbinger *see* **bellwether, harbinger**

Harebrained, hairbrained

harebrained, hairbrained
The first is correct, although the second is also now used, to describe something hastily and very badly thought out: *The proposal to give away free tickets was just another of Mildred's harebrained schemes.*

healthy, healthful
Healthy means 'having good health'; **healthful**, not much used now, means 'giving good health': *Barbara was always careful to eat healthful foods.*

hello *see* **hullo, hello, hallo**

harmful *see* **deleterious, harmful**

Hebrew *see* **Jewish, Jew, Hebrew, Yiddish**

helpmate, helpmeet
Both mean the same: 'a helpful and dependable friend, companion, husband or wife'. The less used **helpmeet** derives from the archaic meaning of *meet*: 'proper, correct and fitting', that is, 'a suitable helper'.

hence, thence, whence
Think of *here*, *there* and *where*: they went **hence** (from here); they advanced **thence** (from there, or that place); **whence** (from where?) came the new arrivals? All are archaisms except hence, when meaning 'therefore, or for this reason': *The Smiths won £2,000 on the lottery, hence the new TV set.*

hereditary, heredity
Hereditary means 'transmitting or passing genetically or by inheritance'; **heredity** is the ability of living things to transmit genetic factors from one generation to another to determine individual characteristics. *Sir Gerald's hereditary title was bestowed upon him at the age of three; Whether his intellectual fastidiousness is a product of heredity or academic environment is anybody's guess.*

heroism *see* **bravery, bravado, bravura, courage, heroism**

herring *see* **kipper, herring, bloater**

hiccup, hiccough
The simpler (and easier spelt) **hiccup** is now generally preferred.

high tea *see* **dinner, supper, lunch, tea**

Hindi, Hindu
A **Hindu** is a person who follows the Indian religion of Hinduism; **Hindi** is the language.

hire, rent, lease, let
Modern marketing has introduced a large degree of interchangeability here: you can now **hire**, **rent** or **lease** cars, vans, rave venues, vacuum cleaners, cement mixers, storage space, even people (*party clowns for hire*; *rent-a-crowd*). Strictly speaking, **rent** is the money you pay. To **let** an apartment or flat means that temporary possession of the property is granted on payment of an agreed **rent** or **rental**. The person who lets is the **lessor**; the person who pays the rent is the **lessee**.

histology, history
History we all know; **histology** is the study of plant and animal tissues.

historic, historical
Something significant that has a place in history is **historic**: *The long-delayed meeting will be one of the great historic events of our time.* **Historical** relates to events of the past: *Emma's novel about Nelson is based on historical evidence.*

hitherto, previously
Hitherto means 'up to this time, until now'; **previously** means 'until then, prior to': *Hitherto the company had succeeded in ignoring all their claims; Previously, the company rule had been simply to ignore their claims.*

HIV *see* **Aids, HIV**

hoard, horde
The magazine *Cumbria Life* is discredited with confusing these: *Wordsworth in particular has brought hoards of visitors invading the very privacy so revered by the poets.* A **hoard** is a store or accumulation; a **horde** is an unruly and often unpredictable crowd of people. Obviously *Cumbria Life* meant hordes.

holiday *see* **vacation, holiday**

holistic, holism, holy
Holistic has nothing to do with God or any sacred deity and thus has no connection with **holy**. **Holism** and **holistic** refer to the doctrine that the whole of a system is greater than the sum of its parts. In treating human disorders, **holistic medicine** considers the whole person and not just individual organs.

Holland *see* **the Netherlands, Holland**

holocaust, Holocaust
A **holocaust** is an act of truly terrible destruction; with its capital letter, it has come to mean and symbolise the Nazi genocide of the Jews during the Second World War. Use with caution.

home, house
Although increasingly regarded as synonyms, a **house**, as the saying goes, is not a **home**. To most people it seems reasonable that you can build, buy or sell a **house**, flat or apartment and live in a comfortable **home**. A **home** implies much more than a house: life, a family, roots, comforts; when we say that a home is 'wrecked', we mean something quite different from demolishing a house.

homicide, manslaughter, murder
Homicide is the killing of one person by another; the killer is also known as a **homicide**. **Murder** is the unlawful premeditated killing of another. **Manslaughter** is the unlawful killing of another but without 'malice aforethought' or premeditation, often under provocation, in the heat of passion, or through negligence.

honorary, honourable
An **honorary** position or title is one that is awarded as a recognition or honour (*an honorary degree*) or one that is unpaid (*honorary club treasurer*). To be **honourable** is to possess high principles or intentions: *Although many regarded him as being rather dim, Arthur was thought by all to be an honourable man.*

hoodoo *see* **voodoo, hoodoo**

hope *see* **anticipate, expect, hope**

hotel: a hotel, an hotel
*She once lived in Paris in **a hotel** on the Boulevarde St Germain: an ideal life, on a scholarship, writing a book. She still goes to Paris, alone, stays in **an hotel**, goes to bookshops and sits in cafés.* While *The Times* in this example has it both ways, the preference leans to the soft *h* sound of *hotel*: **an hotel**.

houmous, hoummos *see* **humus, hummus, houmous, hoummos**

house *see* **home, house**

hullo, hello, hallo
Originally the greeting was **hallo** or **halloo**; modern usage favours **hello** and **hullo** – take your choice.

human, humanity, humane, inhuman, inhumane
Human and **humanity** refer to the human race or humankind, and the words are usually used with favourable intent. To be **humane** is to have one of the

civilising qualities of humankind and means to be considerate, kind and merciful. Conversely, an **inhuman** person lacks the qualities of humankind; to be **inhumane** is to be unfeeling, cruel and brutal.

humanist, humanitarian
A **humanist** believes in the superiority of human concepts and ideals – culture, philosophy, literature, history – over religious beliefs. **Humanitarians** are kind, philanthropic people with the interests of their fellow humans at heart: *The doctor denied he was an atheist but admitted to staunch humanist beliefs; The ship left on its humanitarian mission to Ethiopia.*

humus, hummus, houmous, hoummos
Humus is decayed organic matter in soil; **hummus** (or **houmous** or **hoummos**) is a chick-pea puree that originated in the Middle East.

hung *see* hanged, hung

hurricane *see* cyclone, hurricane, tornado, typhoon, waterspout

hypocrisy *see* cant, hypocrisy

hypocritical, hypercritical
To be **hypocritical** is to pretend to be what you are not or to affect beliefs or views that are contrary to your actions. To be **hypercritical** is to be excessively critical and carping.

idea, opinion
An **idea** is a thought, a mental concept, a creation, an intention or a plan. An **opinion** is a view, judgment, assumption or estimation.

identical to, identical with
Identical with is the originally correct usage, although today little fuss is made about **identical to**.

if, whether
Mostly interchangeable, although **whether** seems to be preferred where alternatives are indicated: *Did you notice whether David returned that book today?* Quite commonly you will hear *I don't know whether or not David returned the book;* here the 'or not' is regarded as redundant, but on the other hand it removes all ambiguity.

ignorant *see* illiterate, ignorant

ilk, of that ilk
The traditional Scottish meaning of **of that ilk** is 'of the same place or name'. **Ilk** refers to a type or class of person: *I really don't like people of that ilk using the clubhouse.*

ill *see* **sick, sickly, ill**

illegal *see* **illicit, illegal**

illegible, unreadable
Illegible is usually taken to mean writing or printing that cannot be deciphered because of some fault, such as fading or other damage. **Unreadable** means that the writing is impossible or very difficult to read because it is badly presented or simply very bad and boring: *They tried to read the markings on the gravestone but time had rendered them illegible; Bruce's essay was so full of errors the teacher pronounced it unreadable. See also* **legible, readable**.

illicit, illegal
Although for most purposes these terms are synonyms, **illicit** is more often used to denote something that is not allowed or approved of by custom or community standards, while **illegal** means unlawful, or forbidden by law: *They admitted they had conducted their illicit love affair over the past four years; Nobody realised that Maria was an illegal immigrant.*

illiterate, ignorant
An **illiterate** person is not necessarily **ignorant** but does not know how to read or write. Many **illiterates** are in fact very knowledgeable and surprisingly clever in surmounting their problem.

illegitimate, natural
An **illegitimate** child or person is born out of wedlock, that is, of parents who were not married at the time of birth. Social service workers now tend to favour **natural**, despite the danger of ambiguity: *The rumour was that he was the natural son of Sir William; He never realised that Martha and Carl were his natural parents.*

illusion, allusion, delusion
An **illusion** is a deception of the mind or eye; a **delusion** is a mistaken idea or false belief; an **allusion** is a passing reference to something: *The magician performed one brilliant illusion after the other; Margaret's dream of an easy life turned out to be a delusion; The speaker's allusion to Bill's enthusiastic attachment to the bottle was regarded as being in bad taste.*

imaginative, imaginary
Imaginary means 'existing in the imagination, unreal'; to be **imaginative** is to possess a heightened or creative imagination: *She loved drawing imaginary animals; Lucinda had always been an imaginative child.*

imbue *see* **inculcate, imbue**

immanent *see* **eminent, imminent**

immigrant *see* **emigrant, immigrant**

impassable, impassible, impasse

imminent *see* **eminent, imminent**

immoral *see* **amoral, immoral**

immunity, impunity
Immunity means 'the ability to resist something, usually harmful', or 'being free from some liability or obligation': *The injections gave him immunity from a range of tropical diseases; The diplomatic plates on the illegally parked car gave it immunity from the usual £50 fine.* **Impunity** means 'exemption from some unpleasant consequence' such as recrimination or punishment: *Carlo's political connections enabled him to rob and extort the native population with arrogant impunity.*

impassable, impassible, impasse
Something **impassable** means something that cannot be passed or travelled over: *During winter the old mountain track is quite impassable.* **Impassible**, an adjective deriving from *impassive*, is not a variant spelling but a different word meaning 'insensibility to injury and pain'. An **impasse** (pronounced *am-pass*) describes an extremely difficult situation in which any progress is blocked: *After three weeks of fruitless negotiation, both sides realised the talks had reached an impasse.*

impeach *see* **convict, impeach**

impel *see* **compel, impel**

imperial *see* **empirical, imperial**

impersonate *see* **personify, impersonate**

implicit *see* **explicit, implicit**

imply, infer
To **imply** means 'to express indirectly, to hint or suggest'; to **infer** is to deduce or suppose by reasoning: *I inferred that they had a bad attitude to working and strongly implied that I wasn't prepared to put up with their behaviour.*

impracticable, impractical *see* **practical, practicable**

impromptu, extempore
Both mean 'spontaneous and unpremeditated', but **extempore** is customarily reserved to describe an off-the-cuff speech: *The children gave a wonderful impromptu performance on the makeshift stage; Lance was noted for the wittiness of his extempore speeches.*

improve, ameliorate
Ameliorate is frequently wrongly used to mean 'alleviate, mitigate, lessen, nullify or neutralise' when it really means 'to improve or to make better': *The new treatment ameliorated his condition immediately.* You can avoid ambiguity by using *improve*.

in, in to, into
In denotes a place and is static: *Elizabeth is in the bathroom.* **Into** expresses motion and direction: *Elizabeth went into the bathroom.* **In to** implies a sense of purpose or 'in order to': *Elizabeth wandered towards the bathroom and then slipped in to powder her nose. See also* **on, on to, onto**.

inapt, inept
In the sense of 'inappropriate and ill-conceived', these are synonymous. But **inept** also means 'clumsy and incompetent': *The inclusion of the jingoistic song in the programme was considered to be decidedly inapt; It had to be admitted that Errol's carpentry skills were embarrassingly inept.*

inaugurate *see* **begin, commence, initiate, start**

incapable, unable
There is a difference between these two for those who wish to preserve it. **Incapable** means 'lacking the ability, capacity or power to accomplish something'; *incompetent* would be a near synonym: *Fred was utterly incapable of singing in tune.* But with a statement like *Fred was unable to climb the stairs* we are left in some doubt as to the reason; Fred might have a physical disability or he might be able to climb them when he sobers up. **Unable** implies an inability to do something at a particular time or because of some special circumstance.

inchoate *see* **chaotic, inchoate**

include *see* **compose, comprise, constitute, include**

incredible, incredulous
Incredible means unbelievable or beyond belief, although it is now widely and wrongly used to mean 'wonderful, astonishing, remarkable, etc'. **Incredulous** describes the inability to believe: *When John had told them the incredible full story they all remained incredulous.*

incubus, succubus

Gendered devilry here: an **incubus** is the demon who in the night lies upon sleeping women to have intercourse with them, whereas a **succubus**, a sister spirit if you like, descends in the night to lie upon sleeping men for the same purpose.

inculcate, imbue

His father had inculcated him in most of the rules of hunting; She was thoroughly inculcated with Theodora's legendary wisdom. Both these usages are common but incorrect. You cannot **inculcate** people, only ideas: *Mr Simmonds inculcated a new sense of purpose in the entire staff.* But you may **imbue** or inspire a person with ideas: *His father had imbued him with a sense of family pride; She was thoroughly imbued with Theodora's legendary wisdom.*

independence *see* interdependence, independence

index, indexes, indices

Both **indexes** and **indices** can be used as the plural of **index**. Interestingly, *The Times* goes along with this but prefers **indexes** in the context of books.

indigenous, endogenous

Indigenous means originating in a given location, or 'native to': *The species of moss is indigenous to the Lakeland region.* **Endogenous**, formerly a rare word indeed, recently emerged as a term in economics, as in *Shadow Chancellor Gordon Brown seemed to be endorsing the post neo-classical endogenous growth theory.* The word means 'developing or originating from within an organism'.

indoor, indoors, outdoor, outdoors

Indoor and **outdoor**, the adjectives, describe physical situations: *The players still preferred the indoor courts to the recently built outdoor complex.* **Indoors** and **outdoors**, the adverbs, are used differently: *During the winter the players naturally preferred to play indoors rather than outdoors.*

induce *see* convince, persuade, induce

inept *see* inapt, inept

inequity, iniquity, inequality

Inequity is injustice; an **inequitable** situation is unjust and unfair. An **iniquity** is also an injustice but one that is grievous and wicked: *James was appalled by the inequity of the judge's remarks; The new demands were little short of iniquitous.* **Inequality** is the state of being unequal, out of balance, irregular: *The difference between the government's treatment of the two families was one of gross inequality.*

inestimable *see* invaluable, inestimable

infect, infest
To **infect** is to cause an infection or to contaminate; to **infest** is to overrun in dangerous numbers: *The infestation of lice was undoubtedly the cause of the infection.*

infer *see* **imply, infer**

infectious, contagious
Contagious diseases are transmitted by physical contact; **infectious** diseases are spread by micro-organisms in the air or in fluids, often disseminated by coughing and sneezing.

infinite, infinitesimal
Two easily confused opposites. Something **infinite** is so great that it has no limit; **infinitesimal** is so small as to be negligible: *It is a mystery why the scientists took such infinite pains to measure such an infinitesimal difference.*

inflammable, flammable
Inflammable means intensely **flammable**, but the ever-present danger is that, thinking the *in* prefix means 'not' in this case, some people might assume that **inflammable** means 'not flammable' or non-combustible. That's why we're seeing more and more **flammable** and **highly flammable** labels on products that are a fire risk.

informant, informer
An **informant** supplies information; an **informer** provides information with the intention of incriminating someone.

infringe, infringe on, infringe upon
The man infringed the law and paid the price is correct usage; **infringe** means 'to break or violate' and thus **infringe on** and **infringe upon** are redundancies. But many of us feel the need for the prepositions when **infringe** is used to mean 'to tresspass or encroach upon': *The farmer's animals constantly infringed upon the municipal park.* Keep your nerve and leave them out.

in heat, on heat, in season
All are acceptable terms (especially to the animals concerned).

ingenious, ingenuous, disingenuous
An **ingenious** person is clever, inventive and resourceful; an **ingenuous** person is someone who is naive and artless and thus more likely to be open, frank and candid. A **disingenuous** person is insincere and not as ingenuous as he or she might appear.

inhuman, inhumane *see* **human, humanity, humane, inhuman, inhumane**

iniquity *see* **inequity, iniquity, inequality**

initiate *see* **begin, commence, initiate, start**

in lieu of, instead of
In lieu means 'instead of, or in place of'. But if you accept the principle of using foreign words and expressions only in the absence of suitable English equivalents, use **instead of**.

inning, innings
In cricket it's an **innings**; in baseball an **inning**.

inoculate, vaccinate
Meaning 'to cause immunity from a disease by the use of a vaccine', these are now synonymous.

insofar as, in so far as
In so far as the inflation rate is concerned, prices will inevitably respond is still general English usage, although the joined-up version is gaining in popularity. It joins similar combinations: *whomsoever, inasmuch, hereinafter, nonetheless* and *nevertheless*.

insolvency, bankruptcy
Insolvency happens when a person can't pay his or her debts when they are due. If sufficient assets can't be realised, the person may be declared **bankrupt**, the official, public state of insolvency, when assets are distributed to creditors. When a company goes bust, it goes into **liquidation**, either compulsorily or voluntarily.

instantly, instantaneous
Both mean the same: 'immediately, at once, without delay'.

instead of *see* **in lieu of, instead of**

instinct, intuition
Instinct is a natural impulse triggered by some stimulus; **intuition** is an unconscious, non-reasoning mental awareness: *Sensing a movement he instinctively stepped back; She intuitively realised she would never really feel comfortable with David.*

institute, institution
In most cases, these are synonymous. The exceptions are when organisations choose either to call themselves **institutions** (*Royal Institution*) or **institutes** (*Massachusetts Institute of Technology*) and in the context of something well known and well established: *The artist was regarded as something of an institution in Dorset.*

insurance *see* **assurance, insurance**

insure *see* **assure, ensure, insure, promise**

intense, intensive
The two are different. **Intense** should be used to describe an extreme degree: *intense heat, intense power, intense aroma*. **Intensive** is about concentration: concentrated medical effort (*intensive care*); a thorough murder investigation (*intensive enquiries*).

interdependence, independence+
These lookalikes are actually opposites. **Independence** is to be free from control, not dependent or reliant upon anything else; **interdependence** means to depend upon each other: *The couple had lived together so long that their interdependence was virtually total.*

interment *see* **internment, interment**

internecine
From its original meaning of 'bloody carnage and slaughter' **internecine** is primarily used now to describe a conflict that is mutually destructive. Beware of a growing usage that implies that internecine merely means 'conflict within a group': *The struggling organisation was a viper's nest of internecine rivalries.*

internment, interment
Internment is detaining and confining someone, usually for security reasons during a conflict or war. An **interment** is a burial.

intrigue, intriguing
Although there still remains some resistance to the wider use of **intrigue**, meaning 'to arouse curiosity and interest', this has now substantially overtaken the original meaning of 'to plot secretly'. The same applies to **intriguing**.

intrinsic *see* **extraneous, extrinsic, intrinsic**

intuition *see* **instinct, intuition**

Inuit, Aleut, Eskimo
The use of **Eskimo** to describe the north Canadian or Greenland peoples has now been generally replaced by the specific tribal names, **Inuit** (sometimes *Innuit*, plural *Innu*) and **Aleut**.

invaluable, inestimable
Invaluable means 'priceless' – something so valuable that its worth is difficult or impossible to estimate. **Inestimable**, meaning 'beyond estimation', is a synonym but tends to be used to describe abstract rather than material qualities: *The chairman praised Jane for her inestimable contribution to the project.* See also **valuable, invaluable, valued**.

invariably, always
Invariably means 'fixed, unchanged, never varying'; **always** means 'uninterruptedly, at all times', but for all practical purposes they are

synonymous. However, many people tend to misuse **invariably** to mean 'almost always': *Although he's missed the train on occasions, John is invariably on the platform five minutes early.*

inveigh, inveigle
To **inveigh** is to denounce or to speak bitterly about something: *The Opposition leader inveighed against the injustice of the Poll Tax.* Note that **inveigh** is followed by **against.** To **inveigle** is to convince or persuade by trickery.

invent *see* **discover, invent**

inverse *see* **converse, inverse, obverse, reverse**

in vivo, in vitro
These terms, now common in the context of artificial insemination, define the two methods. **In vivo** fertilisation is when it occurs or is carried out in the living organism, while **in vitro** fertilisation is a laboratory process (*vitro* = glass) in which the fertilised ovum is reinserted into the womb. Hence the idiomatic 'test-tube baby'.

invoke, evoke
Two well-worn confusables! To **invoke** is to appeal to or to call upon someone – often God or a god – for help or inspiration: *The camel driver fell to his knees and invoked the wrath of Allah upon his enemies.* To **evoke** is to summon or recall some feeling or memory: *The plaintive dirge evoked in her a rush of memories of her Highland childhood. See also* **evince, evoke**.

ion, iron, steel
The confusion probably arises in the UK because **ion** and **iron** are pronounced similarly in the UK (in the USA they stress the *r* in iron). An **ion** is an electrically charged atom or group of atoms; **iron** is, of course, the metal. Much of what we commonly call *iron* is actually **steel**, a much stronger iron-carbon alloy.

Ireland, Eire, Ulster, Irish Republic
Eire is the Irish word for Ireland, or, more correctly, the **Irish Republic** with its government in Dublin. **Ulster**, or Northern Ireland, consists of the six counties outside the Republic.

irony, sarcasm, satire
You are waiting for a bus, the rain is belting down and you are splashed by passing cars. The next person in the queue says, *Lovely day, isn't it?* That's **irony**: saying something the opposite of what you mean with the intention of mocking. **Sarcasm** is a bitter, derisory form of irony: *Well, thanks for telling everyone about our secret!* **Satire** is the witty demolition of stupidity, wickedness and folly, sometimes called **lampoon** or **spoof**.

irregardless *see* **regardless, irregardless**

irreparable, unrepairable
Irreparable means 'beyond remedy or repair': *His mother's criticism over many years had caused irreparable damage to his already fragile self-esteem*. **Unrepairable** is customarily used to describe objects rather than concepts: *The TV engineer said that the set was unrepairable*.

irrupt *see* **erupt, irrupt**

Islam, Islamic *see* **Muslim, Moslem, Islam, Islamic**

It, Its, It's

You can't go through a day without using **it** a few thousand times. Nor, it seems, can you go through a day without seeing **its** and **it's** used wrongly. The only time **its** has an apostophe is when it is used as a contraction for **it is**: *It's raining; If it's not raining it's pouring!* The possessive form of **it** is **its** (no apostrophe): *The parrot fell off its perch*. If in doubt, read the sentence literally and aloud: *The parrot fell off it's perch* would sound like *The parrot fell off it is perch*. It's very simple.

---

iterate *see* **reiterate, repeat, iterate**

it looks like, it looks as though
One of the longest-running sores in the whole of English grammar is – what's correct – *it looks like (it might) . . . it looks as though (it might, . . . it looks as if (it might) . . . it looks possible that (it might) . . .* etc. Editor, columnist and satirist Ian Hislop found himself in such a pile of poo (as he blithely put it) recently, and admitted quite candidly that he found it difficult, if not impossible, to extricate himself from the ordure. It's all a matter of taste, actually.

its, it's *see* **it**

jacket *see* **coat, jacket**

jail *see* **gaol, jail**

jealousy *see* **envious, enviable, envy, jealousy**

jejune
Latin scholars in particular insist that **jejune** should not be used to mean 'naive, simple and unsophisticated' but its original meaning of 'insipid, dull, barren or insubstantial' – the word derives from the Latin for hungry and empty. **Jejune** does not mean 'juvenile': use 'childish', 'puerile', 'infantile' instead.

jetsam *see* **flotsam, jetsam, ligan**

jersey *see* **sweater, jersey, jumper, pullover, etc.**

jewellery, jewelry
Jewellery is the usual British English spelling; **jewelry** is standard in American English.

Jewish, Jew, Hebrew, Yiddish
While there remains a sensitivity about **Jew** being a pejorative term it is preferable to euphemisms such as 'a Jewish person' and is generally preferred by the Jewish community anyway: *My fellow Jews approve it*, wrote one reader of the first edition of *Word Check*. **Jewess** is discouraged, however; **Jewish woman** is preferred. **Hebrew** and **Yiddish** are languages spoken by Jews; **Hebrew** is the official language of Israel, while **Yiddish** is a Hebrew-influenced vernacular version of German. Many Yiddish words have entered the English language via America: *bagel* and *lox, chutzpah, schmooze*.

jibe, gibe, gybe
To **gibe** means 'to taunt or jeer' and that is the favoured spelling in the UK. **Jibe** is an acceptable alternative and general in the USA. **Gybe** (**jibe** in the USA) is a nautical term.

join *see* **enjoin, join**

jubilee *see* **anniversary, birthday, jubilee**

judicial, judicious
Judicial refers exclusively to justice and the law courts; **judicious** means showing good judgement: *Dividing the property between the two brothers proved to be a judicious solution*.

jujitsu, judo, karate, kung fu
Jujitsu is the traditional Japanese samurai form of unarmed martial combat, from which **judo**, a more sports-oriented form, was developed. **Karate** is a similar art which uses sharper blows and chops to the body with hands and feet. **Kung fu** is the Chinese version, in which weapons are sometimes used. Exponents in these arts graduate from a 'white belt' through green, blue and brown to a final 'black belt'.

jumper *see* **sweater, jersey, jumper, pullover, etc.**

junction, juncture
A **junction** is a location where several things meet: roads, railway tracks, electrical cables, etc. A **juncture** is a moment in time, such as a pause, a crisis or a turning point: *At this juncture it is essential that we review the situation*. The frequently used phrase *At this juncture in time* is redundant.

jury, juror, jurist
A **jury** is composed of members of the jury, or **jurors**. A **jurist** is a general term used to describe anyone well versed in law, including legal graduates, scholars and writers.

just, about, just about
It's just about time to go and meet the train is a statement to which few would take exception. However it contains a very common contradiction: **just about**. The word **just** indicates accuracy and precision; **about** means 'near, or close to'. So what do we mean when we combine the two as in *just about*? Little or nothing, because one cancels out the other; either one or the other is redundant. Use **just** if you mean to be exact, **about** if you mean approximate: *There's just time for another drink; It's about time we left.*

just as *see* **like, as, as if, such as, just as**

karat *see* **carat, caret, karat**

karate *see* **jujitsu, judo, karate, kung fu**

kerosine *see* **paraffin, kerosene, kerosine**

kerb *see* **curb, kerb**

ketchup, catsup, sauce, chutney, pickle
Ketchup is a vinegar-based condiment, usually tomato-flavoured, and often distributed directly on to food from a bottle; **catsup** is an alternative spelling usually found in American English. With our modern preoccupation with cooking and restaurant eating, a **sauce** (formerly **gravy**) is increasingly a piquant liquid accompaniment to a cooked dish. **Chutney** consists of coarsely cut fruit and vegetables preserved by cooking with vinegar, salt, sugar and spices. **Pickle** consists of vegetables – onions, cauliflower, etc. – preserved in vinegar or brine.

kiloton *see* **megaton, kiloton**

kind, kind of, sort of, type of
It helps to know that **kind** is a singular noun and to be able to recognise when you need the plural form: *This kind of novel gives publishing a bad name; Many kinds of fruit are in the shops at this time of year.* The same applies to **sort of** and **type of**. Expressions such as *He sort of has a funny effect on me* and *I felt kind of relieved it was all over* are cheerfully informal, as is *I kinda like this town*, but not good written English.

kinky, quirky
Within a couple of decades, **kinky**, originally meaning eccentric or bizarre, has come to mean unusual or abnormal sexual behaviour. **Quirky** is safer if you wish to describe someone or something as peculiar, unconventional or unpredictable.

kipper, herring, bloater
Each of these starts life as a **herring**, the North Sea fish. When split, salted and smoked, it is called a **kipper**; a **bloater** is a herring cured whole without being split.

knave, nave
An area in St Mary's Church in Beverly in North Yorkshire has been known for some time as 'The North Isle Knave'. Nobody is inclined to change it even though most parishioners are aware that it is really 'the north aisle nave.'

knell, knoll
A **knell** is the tolling of a bell to announce a death or a funeral; a **knoll** is a small, usually rounded, hill.

Knell, knoll

kung fu *see* **jujitsu, judo, karate, kung fu**

labour *see* **belabour, labour**

lady, woman
The use of **lady** can convey courtesy and respect or can evoke a sense of sophistication and elegance: *She's a real lady; It's usual to serve the ladies before the men; Mrs Griffiths is a wonderful old lady.* (See **gentleman, man**.) However, **lady** can also carry implications of condescension and should be used carefully: *Nancy Astor was the first lady parliamentarian* has less impact than *Nancy Astor was the first woman to be elected to parliament.*

lagan *see* **flotsam, jetsam, ligan**

lagged, lagged behind
The English purists will say, *For years the Oxford Street store has lagged its rivals,* but the overwhelming majority will say '**lagged behind**', meaning to hang (back) or fall (behind). **Lag** or **lagged** 'behind' is far more knowing and elegant.

laid, lain, lay, lie

The veteran novelist Barbara Cartland described her authorial technique: *My writing day starts at 1.30 when I lay on the sofa and dictate 6,500 words* (interview in *The Times*). One hopes that Ms Cartland was **lying**, not **laying**, on the sofa. Remember the difference between **lay** and **lie** by reciting: *Lay down the law and lie on the floor*. In other words, to **lay** is to put or set down something, while to **lie** is to recline. The same goes for **laid** and **lain**: *After she'd laid the table for dinner she went to lie down; The corpse was lying on the floor; It had lain there for days*. Watch for **lay** when used as **lie** in the past tense: *She simply lay there and cried her eyes out*.

lama, llama

A **lama** is a Tibetan or Mongolian monk; a **llama** is the South American ruminant.

lampoon *see* irony, sarcasm, satire

landslide, landslip

These are synonymous when referring to a mass of earth or rock giving way, but only **landslide** is used to dramatise an overwhelming election victory.

lapse, elapse

Lapse can mean 'a slight slip or failure' (*We all suffer from the occasional lapse of memory*), 'a gradual falling or decline' (*They watched as Sue lapsed into unconsciousness*), or 'to become ineffective or to expire' (*Unfortunately the family's insurance policy had lapsed*). **Lapse** can also indicate the passing of time, which is where it can overlap with the usage of **elapse**: *Time lapses slowly on that particular train journey; Elapsed time at the halfway mark of the race was three hours thirteen minutes and four seconds*.

last, latest

Have you read Salman Rushdie's last book? Sounds a bit ominous. What the speaker meant was, *Have you read Salman Rushdie's latest book?* Use **last** only when you mean to convey finality: *My grandfather travelled on the last horse-drawn tram in London*.

latitude, longitude

The imaginary navigational lines around the earth that meet at the Poles are called meridians of **longitude**; the similar horizontal lines that run around the earth parallel to the Equator are called parallels of **latitude**.

laudable, laudatory

Laudable means 'deserving praise'; **laudatory** means 'expressing praise'. But **laudable** is often used to express worthiness rather than unqualified approval: *The committee's efforts, though laudable, ultimately proved to be a waste of time*.

lavatory, toilet, loo, bathroom

Modern usage now frowns upon the traditional, basic **lavatory** as an upper-class affectation; **toilet** is now more or less standard in the UK, along with the more informal **loo**. In the UK, the **bathroom** is the functional room containing bath, basin and toilet; in the USA, however, it is more often a euphemism for the toilet: *Look, Fido is whining – he wants to go to the bathroom.* Other euphemisms abound: *powder room, rest room, His'n'Hers, bucks & does,* etc.

laver bread
The menu of a prominent Cardiff hotel, before it was hastily corrected, offered diners *'breakfast complete with larva bread'*. This sounded suspiciously like fried bread and weevils. Not to be outdone, the London store Selfridge's tried to sell customers the same delicacy packaged as *'lava bread'* – presumably very crunchy. The real Welsh breakfast dish is **laver bread**, made with a special seaweed.

Law and Lawyers

A **lawyer** is a member of the legal profession and is usually a barrister or a solicitor. A **barrister** pleads on behalf of **defendants** (criminal defence) or **plaintiffs** (civil defence) in the courts; a **solicitor** is a legal adviser to his or her clients, and to barristers. An **attorney** is a practitioner in common law, while a **notary public** verifies contracts and deeds and administers oaths. A **silk** is a barrister who dons a silk gown on becoming a Queen's counsel.

---

lawful, legal, legitimate
Lawful means 'permitted by law'; **legal** means 'related to law'. **Legitimate** has a wider range of meanings – proper, natural, conforming to custom – but commonly refers to children born in wedlock.

lay *see* **laid, lain, lay, lie**

lead *see* **led, lead**

leading question
A **leading question** is phrased in a way that tends to steer or lead the person being asked to give the desired answer. *And what did you see him do next?* is a fair question. *And then did he go to the drawer and bring out the carving knife?* is a leading question. Such questions are regarded as unfair in a law court and usually disallowed.

leak, leakage
A **leak** is the accidental escape of something, often fluid or air but also information, secrets, etc. **Leakage** is the 'instance of leaking' but usually means 'the rate of loss caused by a leak': *Even though they thought they'd fixed the fault, the leakage continued.*

learn, learn of, learn about, understand
Consider this comment from *The Times*: *The sooner some union leaders learn his absolute determination to take Labour into government* . . . There's something wrong about this – perhaps because you can't **learn** 'his absolute determination' because this is a personal quality of Mr Blair's. **Learn** is a transitive verb that has these clear meanings: 1. to gain specific knowledge. 2. to acquire specific skills. 3. to gain by a specific experience. 4. to commit something specific to memory. In the context of the statement above it needs 'learn' in an intransitive mode: *The sooner some union leaders (**learn about**) his absolute determination* . . . or, *The sooner some union leaders (learn of) his absolute determination* . . . Or it could be attacked in another way altogether: *union leaders understand* . . . or *union leaders realise* . . .

learned, learnt
Although **learned** expresses the past tense of **learn**, usage favours **learnt**, leaving the way clear for the adjective **learned** (pronounced *LER-ned*), meaning 'having great knowledge': *Halliday was easily the most learned of all the professors.*

lease *see* **hire, rent, lease, let**

leave alone, let alone
Usage tends to separate the senses that these phrases are meant to convey. *Leave me alone* is a demand to the intruder to depart, to go. *Let me alone*, admittedly a similar command, is nevertheless intended to mean 'stop annoying me!' **Let alone** can also mean 'not to mention': *She could not read or write well, let alone spell.*

lectern *see* **dais, lectern, podium, rostrum**

led, lead
The confusion arises no doubt from their similar pronunciation. **Lead**, the verb, meaning 'to guide, show the way or to take charge', is pronounced *leed*: *The committee asked Joan to lead the special enquiry.* But **lead**, the metal, is pronounced *led*, as is **led**, the past tense of **lead**: *The man promptly led the detectives to the body.*

legal *see* **lawful, legal, legitimate**

legation *see* **consulate, embassy, legation**

legend *see* **allegory, fable, myth, parable, legend**

legible, readable
Legible means 'writing or print that can be read or deciphered'. **Readable** is synonymous in this sense but has another common meaning: *I've always found Chandler's novels most readable*, meaning 'enjoyable'. *See also* **illegible, unreadable**.

legal *see* **lawful, legal, legitimate**

Lend and Loan

A reader's letter to *The Times* complains: *In my post today I received a letter from a local headteacher, offering the use of his school's facilities. Apart from various grammatical and spelling errors, his letter invited my firm to 'loan' his school's video. I do not know whether the concept of borrowing and lending is included in the national curriculum, but if headteachers are unable to master this simple idea, what hope is there for their pupils?* What the headteacher should have known is that the verb **loan** is strictly a financial transaction; you **loan** money but **lend** a video. Perhaps he confused **loan** (the verb) with **loan** (the noun), which is used to describe any sort of lending, financial or otherwise: *Bert thanked him for the loan of the car.* What the headteacher presumably intended was to invite the reader's firm to borrow his school's video: *The headteacher kindly offered to lend his school's video to the local firm* or *The headteacher kindly offered the loan of his school's video to the local firm.* Be warned, however; sloppy usage has effectively smudged the difference between these two words.

less *see* **few, little, less, fewer**

lessee, lessor
A **lessee** leases property from the owner, known as the **lessor**.

let *see* **hire, rent, lease, let**

liable *see* **likely, liable, apt, prone**

libel, slander
A **libel** is something written, published or broadcast that damages a person's character and reputation. **Slander** is a spoken defamatory statement.

liberal, Liberal, libertarian, libertine
If you are **liberal** you're generous, tolerant, progressive, open and receptive to ideas, and a champion of individual freedom. If you are a **Liberal**, you are or were a supporter (in Britain) of the former Liberal Party. A **libertarian** believes in freedom of thought and speech while – careful here – a **libertine** is a thoroughly immoral and dissolute philanderer.

licence, license
The confusion here lies in your ability or otherwise to remember that **licence** is a noun (*your driving licence, TV viewing licence*), and that **license** is a verb (*James Bond was licensed to kill; The vendor claimed he was licensed to sell hotdogs by the Council*). In other words, a **licence** is the piece of paper or evidence of permission granted; **license** or **licensing** is the act of authorising. In American English, the one word **license** is used both as the noun and verb.

licentious, licentiate
Licentious means 'sexually unrestrained'. A **licentiate** is someone who holds a licence or certificate of competence to practise a trade or profession.

lie *see* **laid, lain, lay, lie**

ligan *see* **flotsam, jetsam, ligan**

lightening, lightning
Lightening means 'to become lighter or paler'; **lightning** is the dramatic flash seen in the sky during thunderstorms: *As the sky was lightening at dawn, distant flashes of lightning illuminated the horizon.*

like, as, as if, such as, just as
The so-called misuse of **like** is widespread and the word has the strange capacity to make even alert writers nervous. The problem is that **like** is so easy to use as an all-purpose conjunction: *My mother can't get through a busy day like* (as) *she used to*; *It sounded like* (as if, as though) *she was about to scream the house down*; *I prefer the early German composers, like* (such as) *Bach*; *Like* (just as) *in Pam's case, Liz received no compensation.* When using **like** in a sentence, read it over carefully; in many cases your 'ear' will warn you of possible misuse.

likely, liable, apt, prone
Likely is a useful word to express degrees of probability: *It is likely to be a fine day today.* **Liable** indicates a strong probability but, curiously, is almost always used in a negative sense (*It's liable to rain again today*), derived no doubt from **liability**, the primary meaning of which is 'being exposed to an (unpleasant) obligation'. **Apt** implies suitability, appropriateness or having a tendency to something: *At her age she's apt to tire easily.* **Prone** is a synonym for *apt*, but again is usually used negatively: *After a few drinks Betty was prone to talking rather too frankly about her friends*; *She said that all her children were prone to any germ that came along.*

limbo
Limbo is occasionally misused to indicate a gap or void: *He wondered what to do to fill the limbo between assignments.* A **limbo** is in fact an imaginary place for lost or forgotten things or persons: *The aftermath of the illness had left her in a sort of limbo, disoriented, floating and remote from the real world.*

line *see* **queue, line**

liquidate, liquidise
In the financial sense to **liquidate** means to use assets 'to settle liabilities' or 'to pay off debts'. Most of us are also aware that it means 'to terminate, to kill'. To **liquidise** means 'to pulp food into a liquid': *It took the machine only seconds to liquidise the vegetables into a creamy soup.*

lira, lire

The Italian currency unit **lira** is singular; **lire** is the plural.

litany, liturgy

A **litany** in the Christian religion is a repetitious prayer to which there is a fixed response by the congregation. The **Litany** (upper-case *L*) is the prayer contained in the Book of Common Prayer. If you use **litany** in a non-religious sense to mean 'a long, repetitious and tedious list or speech', use a lower-case *l*. A **liturgy** is the prescribed ritual of public church worship.

literal, literary, literate, literally, littoral

If someone says, *He literally hammered the guy into the ground*, you should expect to see the flattened remains of the victim merging with the earth. But that is rarely what such speakers intend by using **literal**, which really means 'actual or actually'. Unfortunately, many of us use it in the opposite sense; what we really mean is 'figuratively'. But how often would you expect to hear someone say, *He figuratively hammered the guy into the ground*! **Literate** means 'having the ability to read and write', and **literary** means 'pertaining to literature and books'. **Littoral** is the odd one out here: it is a shoreline.

little *see* few, little, less, fewer

liturgy *see* litany, liturgy.

livid, lurid

His angry, livid face blazed with the intensity of a furnace. The imagery is certainly dramatic but **livid**, used here to indicate redness, is the wrong word. **Livid** means 'discoloured', as with a bruise, and if it indicates colour at all it is bluish-grey. **Lurid** is also sometimes misused to describe something red, glowing or fiery; in fact in colour terms it means 'yellowish, pale and wan', quite the opposite. **Lurid** is best used for its primary meaning, which is 'vivid, shocking, sensational': *His lurid accounts of her infidelities alienated her previously adoring public.*

living room, sitting room, lounge, drawing room

Describing a room in a house in which to relax and entertain, the first three are now synonymous and their use is a matter of choice. However, a **drawing room** is understood to be a grander, more formal room for entertaining, of the kind you would expect to find only in a very large house.

llama *see* lama, llama

loan, loaning

*She is director of the Grosvenor House Art and Antiques Fair, to which the Duke of Westminster is **loaning** important items . . .* (*The Times*, 2 June 1998). If this is a word we're still using today then it must be a real antique. If it exists at all today, it is a Scottish or Northern English dialect word meaning a country lane or a cow's milking area. As we have noted earlier under **lend, loan**, 'loan' is the noun (except when used as a verb in the case of financial transactions: *The bank loaned us the money with no objections*) and 'lend' is the verb (though **loan** as a verb is common in American English). Therefore in the quotation above the writer should have reported *the Duke of Westminster is **lending** important items*.

loath, loth, loathe

Commonly confused. **Loath** is an adjective and means 'reluctant and unwilling': *Although he needed the money Robert was loath to accept anything for helping to fix Brian's car*. **Loth** is an alternative spelling but rarely used. **Loathe** is a verb and means 'to detest, to feel hatred and disgust': *She loathed the very idea of going into hospital*.

locale, location, locality

A **locale** is a place that has a relationship with some event, a venue: *After some argument they allowed him to inspect the locale of the gunfight*. A **location** is a place where something is sited: *This is to be the location of the new factory*. A **locality** is a neighbourhood area or district.

loggia, logia

A **loggia** is a gallery or porch supported by columns; **logia** (plural of *logion*) are the collected sayings of Christ.

longitude *see* **latitude, longitude**

look up, look up to

The idiomatic **look up** can mean 'refer to', 'to improve', 'to have respect for' and 'to make contact': *We'll promise to look up the Jones's when we're in Newcastle; Things began to look up for the boy*. Use judiciously to avoid misunderstandings; a sign in the window of a Sydney bookstore urged potential customers of Scottish descent to '*Look up your clan's tartan*'. To **look up to** means 'to have respect for': *John looks up to his intelligent cousin*.

loo *see* **lavatory, toilet, loo, bathroom**

loose, lose

Use **loose** to describe anything free, unrestrained, unfastened: *She hated to wear anything but loose clothing; The vampire was on the loose again*. **Lose** describes loss: *Give him money and he's sure to lose it*.

lounge *see* **living room, sitting room, lounge, drawing room**

low, lowly

Low has a great number of meanings: 'not high; a small supply; coarse and vulgar; quiet and soft; a sound made by cattle'. However, **lowly** has but a single meaning which is 'humble, meek and low in rank': *Despite his wealth Frank always boasted about his lowly origins*.

lubricious, lugubrious
Lubricious means 'lewd and lecherous'; **lugubrious** means 'dismal and mournful'.

lumbago *see* **arthritis, rheumatism, lumbago, sciatica**

lumbar, lumber
The **lumbar** region is at the lower end of the spine; **lumber** is sawn timber – or discarded household items sometimes stored in a *lumber room*. Less well known, a **lumber** can be a prison or a pawnshop, and a **lumberer** a pawnbroker.

lunch *see* **dinner, supper, lunch, tea**

lurid *see* **livid, lurid**

luxuriant, luxurious, luxuriate
Luxuriant means 'prolific, lush, rich and abundant': *Lisa had the most luxuriant hair*. Something **luxurious** is sumptuous and usually costly: *At the hotel they marvelled at the luxurious surroundings*. To **luxuriate** is to revel in pleasure: *She spent most of the evening luxuriating in the Jacuzzi*.

macrocosm, microcosm *see* **microcosm, macrocosm**

madam, madame
Use **madame** when in France; otherwise **madam**. In France, **madame** is the equivalent of the English Mrs; in Britain it is used only formally: *Dear Madam* (in a letter); *If I were you, Madam, I'd complain to the management*.

mad, angry
Mad meaning **angry**: defenders of this usage quote the Bible and Shakespeare to support their cause but the original meaning is worth preserving: 'insane, senseless, foolish'.

mafia, Mafia
The **Mafia** (upper-case *M*) is the infamous international secret organisation founded in Sicily. The word is now used generally to denote a powerful clique or group: *Despite the mergers, the firm is still run by the Glasgow mafia*.

Magdalen, Magdalene
It's **Magdalen College**, Oxford, and **Magdalene College**, Cambridge (both pronounced *maudlin*).

maintain *see* **claim, allege, assert, maintain**

majority, more, most
Maxwell pensioners are to be offered an outline settlement next Wednesday to fill the majority of the £440m hole left by Robert Maxwell's pension fund plundering. (*Daily Telegraph*). Some usages of **majority** can leave you scratching your head; here it

is misused because **majority**, although it means 'most of', is used only of things that can be *counted*. As no part of a hole can be counted, '*majority*' in that sentence should be replaced by '*major part*'. **More** means greater: in quantity, number, extent or importance; so does **most**, except that it implies a greater proportion: *Although more people are now coming to church, most of the villagers still stay at home.*

mannish *see* **masculine, mannish**

malevolent, malicious, malignant
Of this trio, **malevolent** means 'of evil intent'; **malicious** implies a desire to hurt and injure or to create mischief; **malignant**, in this context, means 'capable of causing serious harm to another person'.

malfunction *see* **dysfunction, malfunction**

mall
Three centuries or more ago a **mall** was a long tree-lined alley designed for playing the game of *paille maille* – a combination of croquet, basketball and aerial golf in which a ball was hit into a suspended iron ring. When the game palled, the malls (pronounced *mal*) survived (London's The Mall and Pall Mall are two) along with the name. But today, mall (pronounced *mawl*) describes a creation quite architecturally different: an out-of-town complex all under cover with shops, supermarkets, cinemas, restaurants and vast parking lot.

man *see* **gentleman, man**

manège *see* **ménage, manège**

mannequin, mannikin
A **mannequin** displaying clothes can be ravishingly alive at a fashion show or an inanimate dummy in a shop window. A **mannikin** (or **manakin**, or **manikin**) is a dwarf or very small man, and also a moveable model of the human figure used by artists and sculptors, reduced in scale and usually carved from wood.

mannish *see* **masculine, mannish**

***manqué*, marque**
Manqué means 'unfulfilled, failed, would-be': *As with many members of the Groucho Club Tony was just another writer* manqué. The word, being French, is italicised. A **marque**, also from the French, is a brand or make, usually of a car, and not italicised: *The Stutz marque was noted for its looks, speed and insolence.*

manslaughter *see* **homicide, manslaughter, murder**

mantel, mantle
Mantel is the shortened form of **mantelpiece**, which is the shelf over a fireplace. A **mantle** is a cloak or covering: *The pirates moved towards the ship under a mantle of utter darkness.*

marginal, minimal, slight
Something **marginal** is close to some lower or outer limit: *The farmers complained about the marginal profit yielded by the new season's potato crop.* Although many dictionaries now allow secondary meanings of 'small, insignificant, minimal, slight', the original meaning is worth keeping in mind.

marjoram, oregano
Although there's a lot of cross-fertilisation, *Origanum majorana* is **sweet marjoram**; the wild *Origanum vulgare* is **oregano**. Good cooks are rarely confused.

marriage with, marriage to
The invitation from Buckingham Palace read: *Wedding Breakfast following the Marriage of The Prince of Wales with Lady Diana Spencer.* A marriage is after all a union, which suggests **with** rather than **to** although many prefer the democratic **between**.

marten, martin
The **marten** is a furry, flesh-eating weasel-like animal; the **martin** is a bird of the swallow family.

masochism *see* **sadism, masochism**

masculine, mannish
Masculine refers to typical male characteristics; **feminine** is the opposite. **Mannish** is sometimes used to describe women with masculine looks, habits and qualities, often in a derogatory way: *They're strange, that pair; Judy is so feminine while Lucy is decidedly mannish.*

masterful, masterly
Masterful means 'imperious, domineering, self-willed'. **Masterly** describes someone endowed with extraordinary skill: *With a flurry of masterly strokes Anton finished the charcoal portrait.*

mawkish, maudlin
Mawkish means 'sickeningly sentimental, insipid' . . . yuk! **Maudlin** describes a state of tearful, sentimentality: *Jerome's biography of the bishop was damned by one critic as confused, tedious and mawkish; Harry lapsed into an inarticulate, maudlin account of his early life.*

maxim, axiom
A **maxim** is a concise saying expressing a recognised truth (*pride goeth before a fall; live by the quick and not the dead*); an **axiom** is a generally accepted principle used as a basis for reasoning and argument: *The debating society decided to test the axiom that 'every law has a loophole'.* See also **axiom, axiomatic**.

maximum *see* **ceiling, maximum**

may be, maybe

May be as two words indicates possibility and is used differently from **maybe**, which means 'neither yes nor no, perhaps': *The conclusions may be correct after all; I may be at home tomorrow; Maybe the conclusions are correct after all; Maybe I'll stay at home tomorrow.* You will note that **maybe** expresses slightly more uncertainty and hesitation than **may be** in these examples.

mayday, May Day

Mayday, the international distress signal, is from the French *m'aidez*, meaning 'help me!' **May Day** is the holiday Monday closest to 1 May each year.

mean, mien

Mean has many meanings but **mien** has only one: **mien** is a person's bearing, appearance or expression.

meantime, meanwhile

Meantime is primarily a noun (*In the meantime we'll simply wait*); **meanwhile** is primarily an adverb (*Meanwhile we'll wait as patiently as we can*); but both are fairly interchangeable as nouns and adverbs.

mecca, Mecca

Mecca, birthplace of Mohammed, is the holiest city of Islam; **mecca** (lower-case) is used to describe a centre of aspiration or activity: *St Andrews is the mecca for all true golfing addicts.*

media, medium

The **media** are the agglomeration of newspapers, magazines, television and radio stations, cable and telephone networks whose business is communications. **Media** is the plural of **medium**: *The Times* is a print medium; the BBC is a broadcast medium. However, **media** is increasingly used as a singular noun and attracting less and less criticism: *The mass media has a lot to answer for.*

meddlesome, mettlesome

Two different words although often thought to be merely different spellings of one. **Meddlesome** means 'interfering and intrusive'; **mettlesome** means 'spirited and adventurous': *The landlady was a meddlesome old woman; With a couple of my more mettlesome friends we explored the Turkish baths of the old city.*

mediate *see* **arbitrate, mediate**

megaton, kiloton

A nuclear weapon of one **megaton** would be equal in destructive power to a million tons of TNT; a **kiloton** is equivalent to 1,000 tons of TNT.

melted, molten

The adjective **molten** means 'made liquid by extreme heating' (*Molten lava coursed over the volcano's rim*); a solid that turns liquid through heat **melts**, is **melting**, has **melted**.

ménage, manège
A **ménage** consists of the members of a household; **manège** is horsemanship: the art of training horses and riders. **Manège** is sometimes used as a fancy term for riding school.

meretricious, meritorious
The first means 'superficial and flashy but empty and valueless'; the second means 'excellent and praiseworthy': *The prospective MP made a typically meretricious appeal to the party members; Although Jenny came only third in the race, her effort was considered to be the most meritorious.*

metal, mettle
Surprisingly, these are often confused. **Metal** is the mineral product (gold, copper, iron, etc); **mettle** means 'spirit or courage': *They all realised that the challenge would test his mettle.*

metaphor *see* **simile, metaphor**

meteor *see* **comet, meteor**

meter, metre
In British English, a **meter** is a measuring gauge (*gas meter, speedometer*); a **metre** is the metric unit of length (1.094 yards) and also the **metre** of rhythm in music and poetry. American English uses the single spelling **meter** to cover all meanings.

mettle *see* **metal, mettle**

mettlesome *see* **meddlesome, mettlesome**

microcosm, macrocosm
A **macrocosm** is a whole, an entire unified structure, such as the universe. A **microcosm** is a system on a small scale, a structure in miniature: *In Gilbert White's mind, his village of Selborne was a microcosm of the world as it then existed.*

middle *see* **centre, middle**

midget *see* **dwarf, midget, pygmy**

mien *see* **mean, mien**

militate, mitigate
Near opposites, yet often confused. To **militate** means 'to influence an action or event': *Surprisingly, most of the members were for militating against industrial action.* Note that **militate** is usually followed by **for** or **against**. To **mitigate** means 'to moderate, to soften, to make less severe': *Amy's failure to win the championship trophy was mitigated by her being awarded Best of Breed for poodles.*

millennium, millennia
The third **millennium** is now here, so watch the spelling – note two l's, two n's. It defines a period of 1,000 years. **Millennia** is the plural.

minimum, minimal, minimise, minuscule
Minimum and **minimal** are used to mean 'the smallest, the least possible': *The minimum amount served from this pump is two litres; What problems we faced during the journey were minimal.* To **minimise** is to reduce to the smallest possible amount, degree, extent or size. **Minuscule** describes anything extremely small.

minister *see* **administer, minister**

minority *see* **majority, minority**

misconception *see* **fallacy, misconception**

mistrust *see* **distrust, mistrust**

misuse *see* **abuse, misuse, disabuse**

mitigate *see* **militate, mitigate**

moat, mote
A **moat** is a ditch filled with water to protect a fortification such as a castle; a **mote** is a tiny speck: *The sun made bright yellow shafts through the dust motes.*

mold *see* **mould, mold**

mollify *see* **nullify, mollify**

molten *see* **melted, molten**

momentary, momentarily, momentous
Momentary is the adjective and means 'lasting only a moment'; **momentarily** is the adverb meaning 'just for a moment, for an instant': *She was prone to suffer from momentary lapses of memory; As I went to meet him I was momentarily confused.* **Momentous** means 'of great significance or consequence': *The President's inauguration was a momentous occasion.*

money, monies, funds, cash
Money is a singular noun and it remains singular regardless of how much money is involved: a million pounds or dollars is still just **money**. The plural, **monies**, although archaic, is still in use: *Nearly half the monies set aside for the projects have been spent.* **Cash** is 'ready money'; **funds** are available financial resources including, of course, **money**.

moot, moot point

Although **moot** is usually encountered in the phrase **moot point**, meaning 'a point worth arguing about', **moot** is perfectly capable of acting for itself: *The students agreed unanimously that the issue of alleged immorality at the University was moot.* In other words, the issue was arguable and ripe for debate.

moral, morale

Moral concerns right and wrong in human character and conduct; **morale** is a mental state of confidence and optimism: *The hypocritical moral standards of the officers had a bad effect on the morale of the troops.*

more than *see* over, more than

mortgagee, mortgagor

The **mortgagee** provides the loan on a security, such as a house; the **mortgagor** borrows the money.

most, almost

Because the idiomatic use of **most** to mean **almost** is almost standard in American English (*Most everyone enjoys a good holiday*) it is now thought acceptable for British English to follow suit. It isn't.

motivate *see* activate, motivate

motive, motif

A **motive** is the reason behind a course of action: *It was fairly obvious that Brenda's motive for the attack was pure jealousy.* A **motif** (pronounced *mo-TEEF*) is a theme or idea typically repeated and expressed in graphic, musical or literary form: *The same motif of St Francis and a dove was repeated in all the stained-glass windows.*

mould, mold

For all its meanings ('a shape used to make castings'; 'to shape or form'; 'to influence', 'a fungus' or 'mildew', etc) the spelling is **mould** in British English and **mold** in American English.

mule *see* donkey, ass, burro, mule

murder *see* homicide, manslaughter, murder

Muslim, Moslem, Islam, Islamic

Muslim is preferred to **Moslem**. **Muslims** are followers of **Islam**, the religion. **Islamic** is the appropriate adjective when referring to such things as Islamic writing, Islamic art, etc.

must

The overuse of the word **must**, as in *A visit to the British Museum is an absolute must*, can be discouraged by remembering that, in Anglo-Indian, a **must** is the frenzied state of elephants in heat.

mutual, common
Charles Dickens is held responsible, in *Our Mutual Friend*, for the original misuse of **mutual** to mean **common**. **Common** means 'something belonging equally to two or more or all': *Although they came from widely different backgrounds all the boys had a common interest: football; In the end the lawyers managed to find some common ground*. **Mutual** means 'something reciprocated, something shared, experienced or felt between two or more individuals or groups': *For many years the two partners had enjoyed a mutual trust and respect*. Well-worn terms such as *mutual agreement* (how can you have an agreement without it being mutual?) are considered acceptable through established usage.

myth *see* **allegory, fable, myth, parable, legend**

nadir, zenith
The **nadir** is the lowest point of anything; the **zenith** is the highest point.

natural *see* **illegitimate, natural**

naturalist, naturist
A **naturalist** studies natural history; a **naturist** or **nudist** enjoys natural surroundings too, but without the hindrance of clothing.

naught *see* **nought, naught**

nauseated, nauseous
A *Times* story described how initial irregularities in the motion of *Le Shuttle* trains rendered their drivers **nauseous** – a common error. What *The Times* meant was **nauseated**, the uncomfortable sensation of nausea or feeling sick. Someone or something **nauseous** is obnoxious and repulsive and capable of causing others to feel disgust and revulsion – or **nauseated**. It's worth mentioning here that the Latin term *ad nauseam* is more often than not misspelt *ad nauseum*.

naval, navel
Often confused. **Naval** refers to a navy, a country's seaborne armed force of warships and sailors. Your **navel** is the small depression left by the umblical cord in the skin of your stomach. *See also* **nautical, naval**.

nave *see* **knave, nave**

nautical, naval
Nautical refers to anything concerning ships, shipping, seamen and navigation; **naval** relates only to a country's navy, its ships, personnel and activities.

near by, nearby
Near by is used as an adverb only: *Margaret's mother lives near by*. **Nearby** can also be used adverbially as above, or as an adjective: *Margaret's mother lives in the nearby flats*.

Naval, navel

necessities, necessaries, essentials
Few people preserve the differences here because they are extremely subtle. They have all come to mean the same, which is why we feel the need to add qualifiers to create *bare* **necessities**, *absolute* **essentials**, *the* **necessaries** *of life*, etc.

need *see* **desire, want, need**

negligent, negligible
To be **negligent** is to be careless and indifferent, to neglect something or someone, perhaps to a dangerous degree: *The court found the ship's engineer to have been grossly negligent in policing safety regulations.* **Negligible** means 'unimportant, trivial, insignificant': *Fortunately the effects of the tainted food on the men were negligible.*

negro *see* **black, negro, coloured, non-white**

neither nor, either or
Neither means 'not either of two', and thus, like **either**, is singular: *Neither of his two novels is read much nowadays.* And while **either** is followed by **or**, **neither** is followed by **nor**: *Neither Jane nor Thomas is to go to the cinema today.* However, there can be plural constructions: *Neither Marcia's parents nor Harvey's friends **are** welcome here any more* (where both subjects are plural) and: *Either Marcia's parents or Harvey **have** to decide who is to go to the airport* (one subject plural, one singular).

nemesis
Frequently misused to mean fate or destiny or even some adversary or rival, **nemesis**, derived from Nemesis, the Greek goddess of vengeance, means the prospect of a punishment: *At last the cruel leader became the people's prisoner, awaiting his nemesis alone in his cell.*

net, nett
The first is correct; **nett** is a pointless variant.

the Netherlands, Holland
Use **the Netherlands** in official and political contexts; otherwise **Holland**.

nevertheless, none the less
Nevertheless means 'however, in spite of, yet, notwithstanding': *I was quite ill; nevertheless I felt I should attend the meeting.* **None the less** (written as one word in American English) is a synonym but also covers the meaning 'not any the less': *Although I was none the less eager to attend the meeting, my illness prevented me.*

nicety, niceness
A **nicety** is a subtle point of detail, a delicacy of refinement: *Thomas was a master of the niceties of sarcasm.* **Niceness** is a safe and fresh way of conveying the combination of charm, sympathy, kindliness and modesty: *You couldn't help admiring Emily's niceness.*

Nissan, Nissen, Nisan
Nissan is the Japanese car manufacturer; a **Nissen hut** (called a **Quonset hut** in North America) is the semicircular shelter structure, usually of corrugated steel. **Nisan** is the first month in the Jewish calendar.

noisome, noisy
Noisy needs no explanation, but **noisome** has nothing to do with noise or loudness; it means objectionable and offensive: *The visitors wrinkled their noses as they passed the noisome slurry tanks.*

nominal *see* **token, nominal, notional**

none the less *see* **nevertheless, none the less**

non-white *see* **black, negro, coloured, non-white**

normally, normalcy, normality
Normal once meant 'according to the rule or standard' but for a long while now we have been using **normal** and **normally** to mean 'usual, common, typical': *Today it's quite normal for a woman to sit unaccompanied in a bar.* Although **normalcy** is standard (or normal) in American English; **normality** is preferred in the UK: *At last the situation returned to some semblance of normality.*

notable, noted, noticeable, notorious
If you are **notable**, you are someone distinguished by some aspect of worthiness or character: *Both men came from notable military families.* If you are **noted**, it is usually because of some outstanding skill or achievement: *Henshaw was, among other things, a noted bassoon player.* If you are **notorious**, you are a celebrity for all the wrong reasons: *Dolores was notorious for running away with other women's husbands.* **Noticeable** means 'detectable, easily seen': *The effects of the accident on the patient were noticeable.*

notional *see* **token, nominal, notional**

notwithstanding *see* **pace, according to, notwithstanding**

nought, naught
Nought is the correct British English spelling for zero (the numeral 0); **naught**, meaning 'nothing', is occasionally found in such statements as: *All their efforts came to naught*. In the USA, **naught** is used in both senses and **noughts-and-crosses** is better known as **tic-tac-toe**.

novice *see* **amateur, novice, tyro**

noxious, obnoxious *see* **obnoxious, noxious**

nubile
It would take a brave or foolish writer to use **nubile** in its original meaning to describe a woman: 'suitable or ready for marriage'. Its now well-established meaning is 'female, young and physically and sexually attractive' and is replete with suggestive overtones.

nugatory, nuggety
Something **nugatory** is worthless and trivial; someone **nuggety** is stocky and rugged.

nullify, mollify
To **nullify** means 'to make useless, to cancel out or to render null and void'. To **mollify** means 'to appease and soothe'.

number *see* **quantity, number**

nutritious, nutritional
Certain foods may be **nutritious**, meaning 'nourishing'. **Nutritional** refers to the process of nourishing the body: *The nutritional needs of the patients require at least two nutritious meals a day*.

O, Oh, Ooh!
The single, capitalised **O** is now used only in religious, historic or poetic contexts: *O Thou, that in the heavens dost dwell; O my luve's like a red, red rose*. **Oh** is the usual expression for mild surprise or pause: *Oh, that was close! Oh, I see.* **Ooh!** is reserved for bigger shocks.

OAP *see* **old age pensioner, OAP**

objective, subjective
To be **objective** means 'to be uninfluenced by any prior beliefs, personal feelings or prejudices'. To be **subjective** is to be the opposite: to be over-influenced by personal considerations or relationships.

obligate, oblige
Of the two, **obligate** implies a moral or legal duty, whereas **oblige** means 'to render a favour or to accommodate': *The man had obliged him on several occasions, and now Peter felt obligated to repay his kindness.*

obliterate *see* obviate, obliterate

oblivious to, oblivious of
Although **oblivious to** is commonly seen and also mistakenly used to mean 'ignorant or uncomprehending' (*Bob was completely oblivious to the importance of being polite*), **oblivious of**, meaning 'unaware or forgetful', is correct: *Bob was completely oblivious of the racket going on around him.*

obnoxious, noxious
Obnoxious means 'very unpleasant' and is often applied to aggressive behaviour: *Even though it was his fault, the other driver couldn't have been more obnoxious.* Something **noxious** is potentially injurious.

obscene, pornographic, erotic
Something **obscene** is 'disgusting and offensive to accepted standards of decency' – *Mrs Harris branded the exploitation of children to sell toys on television as obscene* – but more often 'sexually indecent, lewd and lascivious': *They were appalled by the obscene graffiti that adorned all the walls.* **Pornographic** means 'designed deliberately to arouse sexual excitement': *The centre spread of the magazine was dominated by a picture of Miss Behaving in a pornographic pose.* In the context of exciting sexual desire, **erotic** is a near synonym except that **erotica** is claimed to have the redeeming quality of being 'art'.

observance, observation
An **observance** is a ceremony or custom and also the act of complying with a law or custom: *Almost the entire village supported the eleven o'clock observance; Observance of the new dog fouling laws was almost total.* **Observation** is the act of watching, or noting information: *He was awarded the science medal for his observations on the mating of the rare white seal.*

obverse *see* converse, inverse, obverse, reverse

obvious *see* palpable, obvious

obsolete, obsolescent
If something is **obsolete**, it is out of use or out of date; if it is **obsolescent**, it is in the process of becoming obsolete: *It was fairly clear that the trusty old engine was facing obsolescence.*

obstetrician *see* gynaecologist, obstetrician

obtain *see* get, acquire, obtain, secure

obtuse *see* **abstruse, obtuse**

obviate, obliterate
Obviate means 'to prevent in advance, or forestall': *The new car park should obviate the need for people to park in the street*. **Obliterate** means 'to remove or efface by destruction': *The remains of the old town were obliterated in a matter of days*.

occupied, preoccupied
In the sense of using one's time, being **occupied** means being busy; being **preoccupied** means being absorbed, engrossed and oblivious of all around you.

odd, queer
Most people today hesitate to use **queer** in its original meaning of 'strange and unusual' for fear of being misunderstood. Even an innocent remark such as *I'm feeling a bit queer* will provoke sniggers and guffaws. Now that the word's accepted meaning is 'homosexual', it's safer to use alternatives: *peculiar, curious, unreal, suspicious, dotty*, etc. Beware also of **odd** (*He estimated there were 30-odd people in the bus at the time*) in the sense of an unspecified number; in the above example, the hyphenated '*30-odd*' is necessary to remove ambiguity.

odious, odorous
Odious means 'unpleasant and detestable'; **odorous** applies only to smells, not necessarily unpleasant. To describe a bad smell, use **malodorous**.

offence
You can **give offence** (*He [Evelyn Waugh] crafted some exquisite novels, caused much merriment, and gave offence to nearly everyone he met*), **take offence** (*She took offence at the slightest criticism*) and **cause offence**: *Something in the man's psychological makeup prompted him to cause offence at every opportunity*. In American English, the spelling is **offense**.

offer *see* **proffer, offer**

official, officious
Official implies possessing a position of authority: *a government official, an official document*. **Officious** means 'self-important and unnecessarily intrusive, especially where advice is concerned': *The official in charge was officious in the extreme*.

Oh *see* **O, Oh, Ooh!**

okay, OK
As an adjective, **okay** and **OK** are acceptable. As a verb, as in *The boss has just okayed William's idea*, the full spelling is preferred to '*OK'd*'.

old age pensioner, OAP
OAP, **old age pensioner** and just plain **pensioner** are used in British English,

with **pensioner** the preferred usage. **Senior citizen** is usually found in American English.

older, oldest *see* **elder, older, eldest, oldest**

on *see* **upon, on**

one *see* **you (*the reader*) and one**

one another *see* **each other, one another**

ongoing, continuing
Ongoing is an 'in' word (*ongoing dialogue, ongoing situation, ongoing programme*), but there are better choices such as: *continuing, developing*.

onward, onwards
Onward is the adjective: *Despite the hail of gunfire the car maintained its onward course*. But **onwards** and also **onward** are adverbs, with the former more in general use in the UK: *The car kept coming, despite the fierce gunfire, onwards to the escapee's hideout*.

opinion *see* **idea, opinion**

opponent *see* **adversary, opponent**

opportunity, chance, possibility
Chance, as any gambler knows, is a force by which things happen without cause; **opportunity** is a favourable combination of circumstances; **possibility** is the chance for something to happen or exist.

opposed, opposite *see* **diametric, opposite, opposed**

optimal *see* **optimum, optimal**

optimistic, confident
To be **optimistic** is to look on the bright side of things, to expect the best in everyone, to believe that good will triumph over evil, to be always cheerily hopeful. **Optimistic** generates a wide range of meanings, so if you wish to convey feelings of (for example) hope, confidence, expectation, light-heartedness, cheerfulness, idealism and so on, use specific adjectives.

optimum, optimal
Optimum is frequently mistakenly used to indicate 'the most, the greatest, the biggest or best'. In fact **optimum** (and its fancy synonym **optimal**) means 'the best result produced by a combination of factors'. The optimum selling price for a product isn't necessarily the highest or the lowest, but that which will do best for the vendor.

oral, aural, verbal

Oral refers to the mouth, thus spoken; **aural** refers to the ear, thus heard. **Verbal** refers to words but its use is invariably ambiguous because such terms as *verbal abuse* and *verbal agreement* are usually accepted as being of the **oral** kind, i.e. spoken. When you wish to convey that something is written, do not use **verbal**; instead, use *written agreement, in writing*, etc.

orchestrate, organise

In its non-musical sense, **orchestrate** does not mean to **organise** but to arrange something for a special or maximum effect: *Fresh from organising the Budapest Festival, Paul orchestrated a surprisingly well-received event by our rather motley collection of speakers.*

ordinance, ordnance

An **ordinance** is a regulation or decree; **ordnance** means 'military armament, munitions and supplies'.

ordinarily *see* commonly, customarily, frequently, generally, habitually, ordinarily, usually

ordinary *see* average, ordinary

oregano *see* marjoram, oregano

organise *see* orchestrate, organise

oriel, oriole

An **oriel** is a projecting window, usually from an upper storey; the **oriole** is a brightly plumaged songbird.

orient, orientate

Meaning 'to find your bearings', both are, as with their opposites, **disorient** and **disorientate**, synonymous.

oriole *see* oriel, oriole

or, nor *see* neither nor, either or

orotund, rotund

An **orotund** voice is rich and resonant; an **orotund** speech is loud and pompous. **Rotund** can also be applied to speech – meaning sonorous and grandiloquent – but is mostly used to describe the human figure: plump and round.

orthopaedic, paediatric

An **orthopaedist** was once the medical specialist who treated deformities in children, and this is why there remains some confusion with **paediatrician**. Nowadays an **orthopaedist** treats the bone, joint and muscle problems of children and adults; a **paediatrician** treats children only – and for any diseases. In American English the diphthongs are dropped: **orthopedic, pediatric**.

outdoor, outdoors
Outdoor is the adjective: *Jane loved all outdoor activities.* **Outdoors** is the adverb: *Rupert loved to paint outdoors.* **Outdoors** is also a noun: *the great outdoors.* See **indoor and indoors**.

outward, outwards
Outward is the adjective: *Despite all the problems on the cruise ship, they enjoyed the outward journey.* **Outwards** (and also **outward**) is the adverb: *They couldn't help noticing that his rather large feet turned outwards.*

over, more than
Over is a very useful catch-all word, and there's the catch: over-use. Many object to its use in place of **more than**: *He weighed in at over fifteen stone; She collected over six hundred Barbie dolls.* The use of **over** in other contexts is also regarded as sloppy: *The complaint was over lack of redundancy payments* ('caused by'); *The strike was over increased employment guarantees* ('for' or 'about'): *She expressed her worries over the missing child* ('about'). It's worth taking a little care over **over**. *See also* **beneath, below, under, over**.

overcoat *see* coat,jacket

overly
The use of this word is common enough and standard in American English (*Vera was not overly fond of cabbage*) but continues to be frowned upon. Use instead: *Vera was not over-enthusiastic about cabbage.*

overt *see* covert, overt

owing to *see* because, since, on account of, owing to, due to

p *see* penny, pee, pence, p

pace, according to, notwithstanding
Fowler's says forthrightly that the Latinism *pace* 'is one we could well do without in English' because it is so widely misunderstood. Faced with a sentence containing ***pace***: *But in the House of Lords there is no hilarity – pace Lord Salisbury's speech last night* . . . many people are prone to think that ***pace*** means **notwithstanding**. Another guess is that it means 'according to'. In fact, ***pace*** (pronounced *pay-say* or *pah-chay*) is a nicety expressing polite disagreement but with due deference to, and is thus used to acknowledge the author of a quote: *The inscription in E. M. Forster's* A Passage to India, *'God si love' is not,* pace *Andrew Motion, a typographical mistake that was never corrected, but an observation noted at Moghul Sarai railway station and recorded in Forster's diary for January 1913.*

pacific, Pacific

A **pacific** person is against the use of force and thus war. **Pacific** with a capital *P* refers to the Pacific Ocean, its islands and adjoining land masses (for example the Pacific Rim).

paediatric *see* **orthopaedic, paediatric**

paid *see* **earn, paid**

pair *see* **couple, pair**

palate, palette, pallet

The **palate** is the roof of the mouth; a **palette** is an artist's board on which colours are mixed; a **pallet** is many things but most visibly the robust timber tray on which are stacked heavy, bulky goods for easy lifting and transportation, or a small or makeshift bed: *Take up your pallet and walk.*

palpable, obvious

The word **palpable** is frequently misused for 'obvious': *The female buttocks in many of Man Ray's early photographs are so palpable nobody could miss them.* **Palpable** doesn't mean simply 'obvious': it means 'real, capable of being felt' and 'perceived by the sense of the mind or the sense of touch'. As an observer has noted, 'Buttocks in photographs may be breathtaking, obscene, delightful or even obvious, but they are not palpable.'

palpate, palpitate

When a doctor **palpates**, he or she examines by the sense of touch and pressure. **Palpitate** means 'to tremble' but is used most frequently to describe an abnormally fast and uneven heartbeat.

panacea

The team found that common aspirin and several days' rest was the panacea for the latest flu epidemic. Not untypically, **panacea** is used incorrectly here; a **panacea** is a universal remedy for all ills.

pandemic *see* **endemic, epidemic, pandemic**

parable *see* **allegory, fable, myth, parable, legend**

paraffin, kerosene, kerosine

In many countries – the USA, Canada, Australia, etc – what is called **paraffin** in the UK is called **kerosene** or **kerosine**.

parameter, perimeter

A **perimeter** is a boundary or limit: *The prisoners managed to get as far as the perimeter fence.* A **parameter**, a very much misused jargon word, is a mathematical term for a constant, with variable values, used to determine a problem – nothing to do with boundaries at all. Outside higher mathematics you should have no occasion whatsoever to use **parameter**. Instead you may need such words as *limit, confines, frame, boundary, border*: *The new accountant was requested to work within the confines of the previous year's budget.*

paramount, tantamount

Surprisingly, these have been muddled. **Paramount** means 'of the greatest significance and importance': *Of all his ambitions, that of getting into university was paramount*. **Tantamount** means 'as good as, the same as, amounting to': *Wendy's jibe was tantamount to branding Barbara a liar.*

parlay, parley

In betting jargon, **parlay** means 'to stake all the winnings from one bet to the next'; to **parley** is to discuss informally with an opponent terms for ceasing hostilities.

parochial *see* provincial, parochial

parody *see* pastiche, parody

parsimony, penury

Parsimony means 'frugality and stinginess'; **penury** means 'extreme poverty': *The old man was parsimonious, which was why he was never penurious.*

part from, part with

To **part from** someone is to leave; to **part with** something is to give it away or give it up: *He parted from Beryl on the best of terms; The little girl absolutely refused to part with her favourite teddy bear.*

partial, partially, partly

Partial and **partly** both mean 'in part', with **partial** having the additional meaning of either 'prejudiced' or 'incomplete', so use it only when the meaning is clear: a *partial account* of some event could mean either that it is an 'incomplete account' or a 'one-sided account'. **Partly** is more likely to be used to open an explanatory phrase: *Partly because she was ill, Mary cancelled her own birthday party.*

passed, past

Passed is the past tense of to **pass**: *We told the police that the car passed us at great speed*. **Past** can confuse writers because it can be a noun (*All that bitterness is now in the past*); an adverb (*They watched as the car accelerated past*), and a preposition: *They drove past us at great speed*. *See also* **ago, before, back, past**.

pastiche, parody

Pastiche is sometimes used instead of **parody**, but there is a difference. A **pastiche** is a play, painting or some other creation that imitates and borrows styles from other artists and periods. A **parody** is a humorous – intentional or unintentional – or satirical imitation of another individual's work.

pastille, pastil, pastel
After the loss of that tidy sum he [Hattersley] may care to reflect on why he has been discarded like a green fruit pastel. (*Daily Telegraph,* 10 August 1997). **Pastel** is a pigmented stick or crayon specifically manufactured for drawing or colouring. You are not encouraged to suck pastels, although **pastilles** (sometimes misguidedly called **pastils**), or flavoured lozenges, can be chewed or sucked.

pathos, pathetic *see* **bathos, pathos, bathetic, pathetic**

peaceful, peaceable
Peaceful means 'tranquil, calm, undisturbed'; someone **peaceable** is attracted to peace and calm, and abhors aggression: *Jules was above all a peaceable man.*

peal, peel
A letter in *The Times* encouraging campanologists to travel: *Visiting other churches broadens the experience of ringers, as does the occasional peel.* A series of changes rung on bells is of course a **peal**; to **peel** is to remove or strip from a surface – peel from an orange, clothing from a body, etc.

pebble *see* **rock, stone, pebble**

pedlar, peddler, pedaller
Someone who peddles or hawks goods from house to house or person to person is a **pedlar** in the UK and a **peddler** or **pedler** in the USA. A **pedaller** is usually found riding a bicycle.

pee *see* **penny, pee, pence, p**

peel *see* **peal, peel**

peeping, peeking
To **peep** or **peek** is to take a quick or furtive glance – while both are synonyms, **peep** is preferred in the UK, **peek** in the USA. **Peep** is also a more suggestive word in that it can imply 'looking secretly from a hidden place'; hence *peephole* and *Peeping Tom.*

pence *see* **penny, pee, pence, p**

penetrate *see* **permeate, pervade, penetrate**

peninsula, peninsular
A **peninsula** is a piece of land almost surrounded by water, while **peninsular** is the adjective, as in *Peninsular War* and the full name of P&O: The Peninsular & Oriental Company.

pensioner *see* **old age pensioner, OAP**

penny, pee, pence, p
What a quandary! When the British currency was decimalised in 1972, the 240 pennies that made up the old pound became 100 pence to the new (decimalised)

pound. To differentiate between the two values, the new penny coins were called **new pence**, which was quickly abbreviated to '**np**' and, subsequently, to '**p**'. While this looked fine when written (85p) it was a less than mellifluous sound when pronounced – *pee* – with its long usage to mean 'passing urine'. The French don't say *twenty-four eff* for 24 francs, nor are Americans bound to say *ten see* for 10 cents, but the British now fluctuate between **pee** and **pence**.

penury *see* parsimony, penury

people, persons
Where the sense of a group needs to be conveyed or there is an uncountable or indeterminate number of individuals, use **people**: *Hundreds of people hurled themselves at the turnstiles.* Where a sense of individuality needs to be preserved, or the number of individuals is small or countable, **persons** is appropriate: *The number of persons injured in the blast is likely to reach double figures.* However, **persons**, which has had more usage in the USA, is gradually giving way to **people**, as **persons** retreats to semi-legal language: *In person or persons unknown.*

per, a
We worked ten hours per day is considered inferior to the plainer *We worked ten hours a day.* Restrict the use of **per** to commercial or legal contexts (*per annum, per diem*).

per cent, percent, percentage, proportion, part
Percentage and **proportion** are habitually used when neither a percentage nor a proportion is remotely involved in the statement: *A large percentage of the shareholders voted for the changes* (probably meaning 'many'); *The biggest proportion of the profits will be ploughed back into research* (probably meaning 'most'). When a percentage figure or a known proportion is involved, fair enough; otherwise use *part, most, many, few, little,* etc. **Per cent**, as two words, is still maintained in Britain while **percent** is more or less standard in the USA.

perceptible, perceptive, percipient
Perceptible means 'observable or able to be recognised or measured': *The lights on the far shore were barely perceptible.* **Perceptive** and **percipient** mean 'quick to see and understand': *The captain proved to be quite perceptive when he chose Gary for the chess team.*

peremptory, perfunctory
Peremptory means 'final, decisive, allowing no questions and objections'. **Perfunctory** means 'careless, half-hearted, without enthusiasm': *After drilling in such a perfunctory manner, the squad was peremptorily ordered to the cookhouse.*

perimeter *see* parameter, perimeter

permanent, perennial
Perennial does not, as many people believe, mean 'year after year'; its correct meaning is 'permanent, unfailing, unceasing, long-lived'.

permeate, pervade, penetrate

These, together with **saturate** and **impregnate**, are near synonyms, but there are subtle differences. **Permeate** is the action of passing through by diffusion: a gas or smell can *permeate* a room. **Pervade** means to 'spread through, gradually and subtly': a sense of fear can *pervade* a roomful of people. **Penetrate** implies physical or psychological breakthrough: an explorer can *penetrate* a jungle; a counter-espionage agent can *penetrate* a spy ring, etc.

perpetrate, perpetuate

Perpetrate means 'to cause, commit or carry out some act that (usually) is underhand, deceptive or even criminal'; **perpetuate** means 'to continue indefinitely, to preserve by making eternal': *Guy Fawkes perpetrated an assassination plot, the meaning of which is perpetuated by the annual Bonfire Night festivities.*

perquisite, prerequisite

These are easily and often confused. A **perquisite** ('perk') is a benefit or privilege, often regarded as a right: *The company pointed out that high on the list of perquisites were a luxury car, an executive dining room and membership of the Key Club.* A **prerequisite** is a precondition: *One of the prerequisites of membership of the society was total abstinence.*

persecute, prosecute

To **persecute** is to ill-treat, harass or oppress someone; to **prosecute** is to bring a criminal action against a person. **Prosecute** is also sometimes used to mean 'carrying out a task or undertaking': *The parking inspector prosecuted his duties with the utmost vigour.*

personal, personnel

Personal is an adjective relating to a person's private life (*personal hygiene, personal expenses, a personal question*), while **personnel** is a noun describing the staff of a company or organisation: *Jack was the senior personnel officer of quite a large company in the Midlands.*

personify, impersonate

To **personify** is to attribute human characteristics to an object or abstraction: *Old Mr Wilkins was greed personified.* To **impersonate** is to pretend to be another person, usually by copying that person's appearance and mannerisms.

persons *see* people, persons

perspicacity, perspicuity

Perspicacity is the ability to clearly understand; **perspicuity** is the ability to express lucidly, to state clearly. As Eric Partridge put it, *'Perspicacity is needed to grasp the distinction, and perspicuity to explain it'.*

persuade *see* convince, persuade, induce

pertinent, pertinacious
Pertinent means 'relevant'; to be **pertinacious** is to be resolute in purpose, stubborn and unyielding: *The lawyer insisted that the witness's past was entirely pertinent to the case; The case would have been lost but for the pertinacious attitude of the defence team.*

peruse, read
Peruse is often mistakenly believed to mean 'to read casually, at a glance'. In fact it means the opposite, which is to read and examine carefully and critically: *He seemed to take forever as he perused the document.*

pervade *see* **permeate, pervade, penetrate**

perverse, perverted
To be **perverse** is wilfully to deviate from normal expectations, to be persistently obstinate: *You could always count on Agnes to cause trouble but tonight, perversely enough, she was all sweetness and light.* To be **perverted** is to deviate from the norm to abnormal, immoral or corrupt behaviour and standards: *The police charged him with perverting the course of justice when he was discovered to have lied about being at the scene of the crime.*

petition, partition
A **petition** is a request or plea to some authority, usually in the form of a written document signed by a very large number of people supporting the demand: *They all signed the petition to urge the government to abandon daylight saving.* **Partition** means division or something that divides: *The rooms were separated by a very thin partition.*

pharmacist *see* **chemist, druggist, pharmacist**

phase, faze
A **phase** is a state or period in a sequence of events: *Both her children went through the dreaded 'terrible two's' phase.* Surprisingly it is sometimes muddled with **faze**, meaning 'to disconcert, confuse or worry': *The fact that his trousers had split didn't seem to faze him one bit!*

Petrol and Other Hydrocarbons

Petroleum is what comes out of the oil well, and **petrol** (**gasoline** or **gas** in the USA) is refined from it. **Paraffin** (called **kerosine** or **kerosene** in North America, Australia and other countries) is also distilled from petroleum. What comes out of the pumps marked **DERV** (abbreviation for Diesel Engined Road Vehicle) is **diesel** oil, one of the heavier fractions broken down from the crude petroleum.

phlegm, phlegmatic

Apart from being infernally difficult to spell and pronounce (*flem, fleg-MAT-ik*) these two are also hard to relate to each other, but there is a relationship. Rarely, you may come across a remark that a person has **phlegm**. In this case, it is not respiratory mucus of the throat-clearing kind (also called **phlegm**) but meaning that the person is 'self-possessed, imperturbable, cool'. Hence **phlegmatic**: unemotional, indifferent, stolid, not easily excited.

pick *see* choose, pick

picturesque, picaresque

Picturesque means 'visually pleasing and charming'; **picaresque** describes an episodic form of fiction featuring the adventures of a rogue hero.

pidgin, pigeon

Because these are pronounced alike they are occasionally confused. **Pidgin** is a bastardised language, made up of elements of one or more languages, which is understood by people whose own languages render communication with each other difficult or impossible. In Papua New Guinea, **pidgin** linguistically helps to unite over six hundred different tribes and groups, each with its own language.

piebald, skewbald

A **piebald** horse has black and white markings; a **skewbald** horse is brown or fawn and white.

Pilgrim Fathers *see* Founding Fathers, Pilgrim Fathers

pirate, buccaneer, corsair, privateer

Although more reminiscent of the 17th century, these terms are occasionally used in modern contexts. A **pirate** was someone who had committed a robbery, hijacking or other felony not only on the high seas but in any place, port or river under the jurisdiction of the British Lord High Admiral. **Buccaneers** were Caribbean pirates of the 17th century; **corsairs** were pirates or privateers operating in the Mediterranean; **privateers** were captains or ship-owners licensed by the British Admiralty to commit piracy, a proportion of their loot being delivered to the Crown.

pitiful, piteous, pitiable

Pitiful means 'arousing pity' but can also be used to mean 'deserving contempt': *The amount they finally raised for the family was truly pitiful.* **Piteous** and **pitiable** are synonyms, though less used: *They found the old man in a piteous/pitiable state.*

plaid *see* tartan, plaid

plaintiff, plaintive

A **plaintiff** is someone who brings a civil action in a court of law: *Through her barrister, the plaintiff listed a dozen grievances against her neighbours.* **Plaintive** means 'mournful and melancholy': *At night the aid team couldn't escape the plaintive cries of the grieving mothers.*

plane *see* **aeroplane, airplane, aircraft**

platonic, Platonic, plutonic
Platonic (capital *P*) relates to the philosophical teachings of the Greek philosopher Plato; **platonic** (small *p*) is almost always associated with the term **platonic love**, meaning a love or affection that is free from sexual desire: *Despite everyone's suspicions, David and Ruth insisted that their friendship was purely platonic.* **Plutonic** is a geological term pertaining to rocks that have originated from the earth's molten mass.

plausible *see* **possible, plausible, feasible**

plebiscite, referendum, poll, ballot, election
A **plebiscite** is a direct vote by citizens on an issue of supreme national importance such as a change of sovereignty or frontier. A **referendum** is usually accepted to mean a direct vote by citizens to confirm a proposed change in the law or constitution or to vote on an issue of great public importance. A **poll** is the casting and recording of votes in an election, a democratic process in which candidates are approved by the electorate for government or local government office. A **ballot** is the practice of electing candidates or deciding a course of action by marking the choice on a paper that is deposited in a sealed ballot box and afterwards counted.

podium *see* **dais, lectern, podium, rostrum**

poetess *see* **actor, actress, authoress, poetess, sculptress, etc**

point of view *see* **standpoint, point of view, viewpoint**

politic, politics, political
Politic (pronounced *POL-ih-tik*) means 'prudent, sensible, shrewd': *The management decided it was politic to refrain from commenting on the issue.* **Politics,** the noun, describes the practice of government; **political** is the adjective. **Politics** can be singular or plural: *Politics is not a science, but an art* (Bismarck); *The Prime Minister is one reason why politics are so deeply unfashionable these days.*

poll *see* **plebiscite, referendum, poll, ballot, election**

populist, popularist, populariser, spin doctor
Populist derives from the 19th-century US People's Party and is still sometimes used to describe a politician on the side of the 'little man'. A **populariser** is someone who makes causes attractive and acceptable to the public. A **spin doctor** is someone (usually in politics) paid to put a favourable 'spin' on potentially damaging news or policy. **Popularist** is occasionally incorrectly used for populariser but as a word it was pensioned off a century ago.

pool *see* **snooker, pool, billiards**

portable *see* **potable, portable**

Potable, portable

poring, pouring
'*Here is John Major pouring over his newspaper*' reports columnist Richard Ingrams (*The Observer*, 17 July 1998). This particular gaffe often occurs, even in *The Times*: '*There was the lone figure of Sir Charles . . . pouring over plans . . .*' What is obviously intended is **poring**, meaning 'to make a close study or examination'.

pornographic *see* **obscene, pornographic, erotic**

portentous *see* **pretentious, portentous**

position *see* **situation, position**

positive, positively
Some authorities object to using the adjective **positive** to replace the adverb **positively**, as in *think positive* instead of the grammatically correct *think positively*.

possible, plausible, feasible
Possible means that something could exist, happen or be done; **feasible** means that something really can be done. If an argument or statement appears to be true or reasonable, it is **plausible**: *The plan was plausible, for although the river was subject to flooding, it was still feasible to construct the bridge.*

possibility *see* **opportunity, chance, possibility**

postgraduate *see* **graduate, undergraduate, postgraduate**

potable, portable
Potable means 'drinkable'; **portable** describes anything that can be carried easily.

pouring *see* **poring, pouring**

practical, practicable
Practical has a wide range of meanings, including 'useful, usable, sensible, realistic, efficient': *Although it was practicable to scale the wall with a rope, they agreed that a more practical plan would be to find a ladder.* **Practicable** means 'feasible, capable of being done and put into practice'. Both words have opposites: **impractical**, meaning 'although possible, ineffective, inconvenient or useless', and **impracticable**, meaning 'impossible, unfeasible, unattainable': *The idea of combining the two wedding receptions was finally written off as impractical; Everything that science had taught him screamed that a perpetual motion machine was impracticable.* See also **pragmatic, practical**.

practically, virtually
The difference in meaning between these two words is now **practically/ virtually** non-existent. **Practically** used to define 'in practical terms, for practical purposes, in practice', whereas now it is used as a synonym for 'almost, very nearly, as good as, to all intents and purposes'. **Virtually** today means 'nearly, practically, having the same effect' – so that modern meanings of both words have collided as in this example, where either word can be switched: *Living on anything they could find, the people were practically starving, and clean water was virtually non-existent.*

practice, practise
The doctor had practised medicine for over forty years, thirty of them from his practice in Harley Street. **Practice** is the noun: *piano practice, It is not the usual practice to tip, Let's put theory into practice*; while **practise** is the verb: *The tribe practises ritual murder; He's a non-practising Anglican.* In American English, **practice** serves as both noun and verb.

pragmatic, practical
A **pragmatic** individual approaches a problem with **practical** considerations and results in mind rather than with theories. Even so, the **pragmatic** approach is not necessarily practical. A **practical** person is also not too impressed by theories but knows how to do things and actually gets them done. *See also* **practical, practicable**.

prawn *see* **scampi, shrimp, prawn, langoustine**

precede, proceed, supersede
To **precede** is to go before or come before; to **proceed** is to continue or to go forward: *The Archbishop preceded the Queen as they proceeded up the aisle to the altar.* **Supersede** means to displace or replace someone or something: *Many people regretted that the Authorised Version had been superseded by the Revised English Bible.*

precipitate, precipitant, precipitous
All three derive from the Latin *praecipitare* (to throw down headlong), and the first two are concerned with unexpected and hasty action. *She precipitated her dismissal by swearing at the supervisor; You could say that Dawn's swearing at the supervisor was a rather precipitant action.* Here **precipitated** is used to mean 'caused to happen sooner than expected' and **precipitant** to mean 'impulsive and hasty'. The primary meaning of **precipitous** is 'extremely steep'; *She lost her nerve on the mountain's precipitous ascent.*

précis, résumé
A *precis* (in English, appears in italics and the accent is optional) is a brief written summary of the essential points of a text or speech. A **résumé** (retain the accents) is a descriptive summary, usually of some event. In American English, **resume** (no accents) is also a curriculum vitae or CV.

prediction, predilection
Predilection has nothing to do with predicting. To have a **predilection** means 'to have a preference or predisposition for something': *Kathleen confessed to a predilection for old-fashioned sticky puddings.*

pre-empt, prevent
To **pre-empt** is to do something or obtain something beforehand, or to appropriate something in advance of other claims: *John's generous offer pre-empted any further bickering among the family.* To **prevent** is to hinder or stop an action.

premier, premiere
Premier means 'first or foremost' and is often used as a title for a country's leading statesman. **Premiere** is used exclusively to describe the first performances of plays and films, and can be a noun or a verb: *Shortly after its premiere in London next week the musical will premiere on Broadway.*

premise, premises
Premises describes land and buildings: *The firm has just moved to new premises in the High Street.* **Premises** is always plural, whereas **premise** is singular, meaning an 'assumption, theory or hypothesis': *The general's strategy was, in the opinion of many of his officers, rather too heavily based on the premise that the enemy was too weak to attack.*

preoccupied *see* **occupied, preoccupied**

prerequisite *see* **perquisite, prerequisite**

prescribe, proscribe, ascribe
The first two are almost opposites. **Prescribe** means 'to recommend a course of action or to lay down rules'; **proscribe** means 'to banish or forbid': *Bill's doctor had prescribed a course of antibiotics and three days in bed; Smoking is proscribed on the Underground.* **Ascribe** means 'to attribute, to credit with': *The scientists ascribed the unsettled weather to volcanic activity in the Pacific region.*

presently *see* **soon, presently**

pressured, pressurised
The witness told the court that he had been constantly pressurised not to give evidence.
This is an example of very loose usage of a scientific term concerned with the
compression of gas or liquid. **Pressured** is to be preferred.

presume *see* **assume, presume**

presumptuous, presumptive
These are often confused. **Presumptuous** behaviour is arrogant, insolent,
impertinent and unwarranted: *It was presumptuous of the chairman to start the
meeting with only half the members present.* Something **presumptive** is based on a
presumption – the belief that something is or will be true: *The case was
considerably weakened by the presumptive evidence that a body existed even though it
had not been found.*

pretence, pretense, pretext
Pretence (**pretense** in American English) is the act of pretending; its near
synonym, a **pretext**, is a fictitious reason or false excuse: *He abandoned the pretence
of having MI5 connections; He lured her into confessing, on the pretext that he was her
friend.*

pretentious, portentous
A **pretentious** person is showy, self-important and pompous and inclined to
make exaggerated claims. Although one meaning of **portentous** is also 'self-
important and pompous', its primary meaning is 'ominously foreshadowing
some momentous or awe-inspiring event': *James was convinced that his dream was
a portentous warning of what marriage to Annabel would be like.*

pretext *see* **pretence, pretense, pretext**

prevaricate, procrastinate
These are commonly confused. To **prevaricate** is to act falsely or evasively with
the intention of deceiving; to 'be economical with the truth' by deliberately being
misleading: *When asked if the problem would be dealt with immediately the Minister
prevaricated with a barrage of waffle and dubious statistics.* To **procrastinate** is to
waste time – 'never to do something today that you can do tomorrow'; *It was
clear that the Minister was indulging in the gentle art of procrastination on the question
of getting the beef ban lifted.*

prevent *see* **pre-empt, prevent**

preventative, preventive
Both mean 'to prevent something from happening or recurring'. In the medical
sense, **preventative** is increasingly being used as a noun: *The view of the preventive
medicine lobby is that, against the common cold, vitamin C is an effective preventative.*

previously *see* **hitherto, previously**

prima facie see **a priori, prima facie**

principal, principle
A pair of classic confusables! In a recent article in *The Guardian*, the writer managed a confusable 'hat-trick': *There isn't even a principal at stake here . . . Sir Bryan said he still accepted the compensation principal but, as far as BT is concerned, accepting the principal is unlikely ever to translate into actual contributions.* In all three cases the correct word is **principle**. The meanings of **principle** are fairly straightforward: it can be a fundamental truth, a belief or doctrine, an agreed rule of action or conduct. **Principal** can be an adjective (meaning 'of primary importance') or a noun (meaning 'a person who is the leader, the head, first in importance'): *The school principal said that his principal aim was to insist on students observing a code of strict moral principles.* In the financial sense, **principal** is money, capital or property on which interest accrues: *His father had taught him to spend the interest if you must, but never touch the principal.*

prise, pry, prize
To **prise** is to force something open, usually by levering: *After considerable effort she managed to prise the lid from the jar; They finally prised the information from the prisoner.* Although an alternative spelling is **prize**, its use only causes confusion with the long-established meaning of **prize**: the reward or honour given for success or for winning something. The use of **pry open** for **prise** in American English is creeping into the UK and, again, is being confused with the traditional meaning of **pry**, which is to snoop and meddle or poke your nose into someone else's affairs.

pristine
Often misused to mean 'spotlessly clean', **pristine** in fact means 'pure and uncorrupted, original and unspoiled': *The experts hoped to restore the ancient lamp to its pristine state.*

privateer *see* **pirate, buccaneer, corsair, privateer**

prize *see* **prise, pry, prize**

probity, property
The royal family nowadays is a model of property compared with those days (Letter to *The Sunday Times*, 1995). What the writer meant was **probity**, a quality combining honesty, integrity, fairness and open-mindedness.

proceed *see* **precede, proceed, supersede**

proclivity *see* **propensity, proclivity**

procrastinate *see* **prevaricate, procrastinate**

proctor, proctologist *see* **prostates and proctors**

prodigal, generous
To be **prodigal** is to be recklessly wasteful and extravagant, to be **generous** is to be unselfish and ready to give freely.

proffer, offer
What little distinction there was or is between the two is exceedingly fine, but **proffer** is more formal and implies offering or tendering in expectation of acceptance: *The amount proffered by the management was calculated to make the men think twice about calling another strike.*

prognosis *see* **diagnosis, prognosis**

program, programme
Programme is the traditional British spelling; **program** in the USA. However **program** has enjoyed wide use in Britain (mainly because of the computer industry) to the extent that two spellings and two meanings are emerging: **programme** for TV, radio, theatre performances, etc (*Where are tonight's television programmes?*), and **program** for schedule, project, plan, proposition, etc: *The owners finally released details of their building program.*

promise *see* **assure, ensure, insure, promise**

prone *see* **likely, liable, apt, prone**

prone, prostrate, recumbent, supine
All four refer to the action of lying down – but all have different meanings. To lie **prone** is to lie face downwards; **prostrate** assumes the same position but suggests exhaustion and helplessness. **Recumbent** is lying in any comfortable position, while **supine** is lying listlessly (spinelessly?) on the back, looking upwards.

proof *see* **evidence, proof, testimony**

propensity, proclivity
Both mean 'having a natural tendency or inclination' although **proclivity** is sometimes given a twist to imply 'naughty or unnatural', as in: *We all knew about Heather's sexual proclivities.*

prophecy, prophesy
Prophecy is the noun; **prophesy** is the verb: *The old farmer prophesied a hard winter, but his last prophecy about the weather had been totally wrong.*

propitious, auspicious
These synonyms mean 'favourably inclined' although a few writers like to preserve a fine difference of meaning: **auspicious**, meaning 'the circumstances are a good omen pointing to success', and **propitious**, meaning 'the conditions are directly conducive to success': *Everyone felt that the inauguration was an*

auspicious occasion; The chairman judged by the happy tone of the meeting that it would be a propitious time to introduce the subject of increased membership fees.

proportion *see* **per cent, percent, percentage, proportion, part**

proposal, proposition
While both mean 'something suggested', **proposal** is more of an offer, as in *a proposal of marriage*; a **proposition** is a stronger suggestion, even an assertion, that might invite discussion before agreement: *The team looked carefully at the detailed proposition that had been put to them.* That said, they are both fairly interchangeable.

proscribe *see* **prescribe, proscribe, ascribe**

prosecute *see* **persecute, prosecute**

Prostates and Proctors

A not uncommon malapropism is: *He's seeing the doctor because of his prostrate trouble.* **Prostrate** means to lie face down, while the **prostate** is the male reproductive gland that tends to peter out with increasing age. And a **proctor**, perhaps because it rhymes with doctor, is sometimes thought to specialise in diseases of the anus. In fact, a **proctologist** does that; a **proctor** is a university official, one of two elected annually.

---

protagonist, antagonist
Mr Castle-Reeves is fortunate to have two stalwart protagonists to help him in the forthcoming by-election. The use of **protagonist** to mean 'ally or supporter' is a common error; a **protagonist** is the leading character or key player in an event, and thus there can never be more than one: *He was grateful to have the millionaire shipowner as his protagonist for the difficult election ahead.* An **antagonist** is an adversary or opponent.

protectorate *see* **colony, protectorate, dependency**

protest, protest against
Many grammarians object to the use of **protest at**, **protest against** and **protest about**: *The angry students protested against the closing of the cafeteria.* It is customary to use **protest alone** as a verb, as in *She protested her innocence,* but in parallel examples such as *The nurses protested the government's rejection of their pay claim,* it cries out, as Fowler puts it, for the insertion of **against**.

provided that, providing that
Provided and **providing** are conjunctions that traditionally are followed by that: *Provided/providing that Jill and Sue arrive on time we'll just make it to the train.*

However usage is beginning to favour the abandonment of that and little harm seems to have been done: *Provided the company instals the smoke-removing equipment, they should get the licence.*

provincial, parochial
In the UK, **provincial** tends to be applied to anything and anywhere outside London, but strictly speaking it means 'relating to the provinces'. The term is often used (by city dwellers) in a derogatory way: *Her taste in theatre, my dear, is rather provincial.* The compass of **parochial** shrinks to parish boundaries; it also implies a viewpoint that is narrow and limited in outlook and interest.

prudent *see* discreet, circumspect, prudent

prudery, prurience
These are opposites. **Prudery** is the affectation of excessive modesty and primness, especially with regard to sex. **Prurience** is having an excessively morbid interest in sex and eroticism.

pry *see* prise, prize, pry

pullover *see* sweater, jersey, jumper, pullover, etc

pupil, student
Although somewhat interchangeable, a **pupil** is a child at school who is taught in disciplined classes, while a **student** studies at a centre of higher education and is expected to be self-disciplined. However, secondary-school pupils are often referred to as students.

purport, purported
Purport means 'supposed to be, or claims to be': *With its official stamps and seals, the document purports to be genuine.* **Purported** is now often used to mean 'rumoured': *They were intrigued by the purported £15m government subsidy.*

purposely, purposefully
Purposely means 'intentionally, on purpose': *That man tripped me and did it purposely!* **Purposefully** means 'determined and resolute': *Miriam took a deep breath and purposefully rose to address the meeting.*

pursuant to, pursuivant
Pursuant to means 'in accordance with, in agreement with': *Pursuant to regulations, passengers must now disembark from the port exits.* The word is nowadays regarded as legalistic and a bit old-fashioned. **Pursuivant** is a term used in heraldry.

pygmy *see* dwarf, midget, pygmy

quantitative, qualitative
Quantitative refers to measurable quantities and proportions; **qualitative** refers to quality, of characteristics, properties, attributes and singularities: *The agency agreed to commission a qualitative study of the effects of a price rise, while the client would look after the quantitative issues.*

quantity, number
Use **number** only when the items are countable: *To make the juice, you need a large number of oranges and a generous quantity of water.*

queer *see* **odd, queer**

queue, line
A **queue** in British English is a **line** in American English. The use of the latter term in the UK usually attracts objections, as in this letter to *The Times*: *I am disappointed to see that even* The Times's *leader columns are succumbing to the relentless invasion of American English. In your leader on the National Lottery you state that 'stores which sell tickets have lottery-only lines on a Saturday'. Don't you mean 'Shops. . . have lottery-only queues'?*

quietness, quietude, quiescent
Quietness and **quietude** are synonyms describing a state of little or no sound or movement. **Quietude**, however, is commonly used to describe a state of peace and tranquillity: *During her convalescence, Sarah enjoyed the quietude of their Cornwall retreat.* **Quiescent**, the adjective, can also mean quiet, but its primary use is to indicate a state of inactivity or dormancy: *The villagers were relieved to find that the volcano was quiescent.*

quirky *see* **kinky, quirky**

quite, rather
Quite is commonly used in two different ways, and this inevitably leads to ambiguity. First, **quite** can mean 'completely, totally, entirely, absolutely': *The runner flung himself to the ground, quite exhausted.* Then, **quite** can mean 'somewhat, sort of, rather': *The horse was going quite well until the fifth hurdle.* The latter usage is not nearly so common in American English as it is in Britain. If you were to say to an American, *I think the movie is quite good,* he or she would take it that you meant it was really very good, whereas in fact what you meant was that the movie was 'okay, so-so, acceptable'. In most cases any ambiguity can be removed by substituting *rather.*

quorum, quota
A **quorum** is an agreed number of people required to be present before a meeting can be held; a **quota** is 'a proportion, a limit, an agreed number or amount'.

quote, cite
Both overlap in their meaning of 'referring to or repeating something said or written': *To support his argument the MP quoted / cited several authoritative opinions*

on the subject. **Cite** also means 'to summon', especially to be summoned to appear in court: *The new neighbour was cited in Mary and Ralph's divorce case*; and 'to mention or commend', usually for bravery: *During the Vietnam War he was cited on three occasions.*

racism, racialism

The two have in the past been allotted separate meanings by some dictionaries (the *Routledge Dictionary of Race and Ethnic Relations* has **racism** = discriminatory attitudes and beliefs; **racialism** = abuse directed at another race); nowadays, both are viewed as synonyms, with the shorter **racism** being preferred.

rack *see* wrack, rack

racket, racquet

The Times sensibly prescribes **racket** for tennis, for noise and commotion, and for fraudulent enterprise. **Racquet** remains an acceptable alternative spelling for the tennis racket.

rain, reign, rein

Rain we all know about; to **reign** is to rule or exercise supreme authority, and a **reign** (the noun) is a period during which a particular monarch rules: *The reign of George III was a turbulent one.* To **rein in** is to check or control, and a **rein** (the noun) is the strap that controls and guides a horse or other animal. **Rein** is also used in two opposite senses: *to keep a tight rein* (restrain) and *to give free rein* (allow freedom): *The constant rain of criticism did nothing to stop Henry VIII giving full rein to his appetites throughout his entire reign.*

Rain, reign, rein

raise, raze, rise

To **raise** is to elevate; to **raze** is the reverse: 'to destroy completely, to level with the earth', so the well-known phrase *The house was razed to the ground* is tautological. **Raise** is also creeping in to mean 'rear children', but most British parents still seem to prefer to raise sheep and bring up a family. You also **raise** your head but **rise** in the morning and **rise** from your bed. In British English, a **pay rise** is the equivalent of the American **raise**.

rang, rung
The team rung the bells for half an hour is incorrect: *the team rang the bells.* **Rung** is the past participle of the verb *to ring*, so it would be correct to say *The team had rung the bells for half an hour.*

range *see* **spectrum, range**

rapt, wrapped, rapped
Rapt means 'engrossed and absorbed' (*The children listened with rapt attention to the storyteller*); **wrapped** means 'enveloped, enfolded, blanketed': *The trappers were well wrapped against the bitter cold.* **Rapped** describes the act of striking something sharply (*The caller rapped several times on the door*) and also the fast, rhythmic monologue delivered over a music track: *Public Enemy rapped non-stop until well after midnight.*

rather *see* **quite**

ravaged, ravenous, ravished, ravishing
Ravaged means 'extensively damaged, ruined or destroyed', although the word is sometimes used in a romantic sense: *Sheila was swept away by his sunburned, ravaged face.* To be **ravenous** is to be famished, starving. **Ravish** requires some care in usage; its primary meaning is 'to enrapture, to be carried away with great delight', but it is also associated with violence and rape and therefore the possibility of ambiguity is likely. **Ravishing** is safe: it means 'enchanting, delightful, lovely'.

raze *see* **raise, raze, rise**

react, respond
A **reaction** is a spontaneous and immediate **response** to some stimulus, so **react** should not be used as a substitute for feeling, answer, reply, opinion or response – all of which require considered thought. *The mayor's reaction to the crisis was to sleep on it* is the sort of usage that has become acceptable today, but careful writers would use **response**.

readable *see* **legible, readable**

real, really
There should be no problem with the adjective **real**; it means 'existing in the physical world; true, actual, genuine'. But the adverb **really**, which we use constantly, can cause headaches. *The Daily Mirror Style Book* describes **really** as '0.1 per cent colouring matter' but acknowledges its usefulness in providing an artificial boost to otherwise dull statements: *The career of hairdresser Karen, 20, from Middlesex, is really taking off . . .* If you drop the **really**, the announcement does go rather flat. *See also* **actually, virtually, really**.

rebut, refute, repudiate, deny

There are several shades of meaning among this lot. To **rebut** is to contradict by argument with the support of evidence; to **deny** is to merely insist that an allegation or statement is false; to **repudiate** is to disown, reject or refuse to admit a charge or claim; to **refute** – the strongest and most convincing denial of all – is to prove that an accusation is false. Neither **rebut** nor **refute** is a synonym for **deny** or **dispute**.

receipt, recipe

A **receipt** (pronounced *rih-SEET*) is a written acknowledgement that something (money, goods, a letter or document) has been received, although it also has an obsolete meanin as a **recipe** (pronounced *RES-ih-pee*), which is a formula of ingredients and instructions to make something, usually in cookery.

recollect *see* remember, recollect

recount, re-count

To **recount** is to relate or recite the details of a story or event: *Jim recounted his amazing adventures to a fascinated audience.* To **re-count** is to count again: *Because the ballot result was so close, a re-count was demanded.*

recoup, recover

Recoup means to 'regain or replace a loss', usually financial: *The company managed to recoup the previous year's losses with a series of shrewd investments.* **Recover** is synonymous but is used in a broader way: *When she recovered from the fainting spell she also recovered her composure.*

recover, re-cover

To **recover** is to regain or retrieve something after losing it; to **re-cover** something is to cover again: *They decided to have the old suite re-covered in dark red velvet.*

recrudesence *see* resurgence, recrudesence

recumbent *see* prone, prostrate, recumbent, supine

reduce *see* exhaust, deplete, reduce

reduce, lessen

These are mostly interchangeable, except that **lessen** tends to be used where numbers are involved in the quantity: *By reducing his petrol consumption, he lessened the number of weekly trips to the garage.*

redundancy *see* tautology

referee *see* umpire, referee

referendum *see* plebiscite, referendum, poll, ballot, election

refute *see* rebut, refute, repudiate, deny

regardless, irregardless

Although it is occasionally heard (and sometimes written) **irregardless** is not a word. **Regardless** is used in two senses: as an adjective to mean 'unthinking and reckless' (*The two men fought on the balcony, regardless of the danger of the six-storey drop*) and as an adverb meaning 'in spite of everything': *Its rudder damaged, spinnaker gone and sails in shreds, the yacht sailed on regardless.*

register, registry

A **register** can be a record of names, transactions, events, correspondence, data, etc; a **registry** is a place where registers are kept: But watch out: a Register's Office (not Registry) is where births, deaths and marriages are recorded, and civil marriages celebrated.

registrar, bursar, bursary

A **registrar** keeps registers and official records; a **bursar** manages the financial affairs of a school, college or university. A **bursary** is a scholarship awarded by a school or college.

regret, remorse

To **regret** (verb) or to express **regret** (noun) is to feel sorry, sympathetic, upset or repentant about something unfortunate that has occurred. **Remorse** is synonymous except that it implies that the person feeling remorse is the one guiltily responsible.

regretful, regretfully, regrettable, regrettably

The first two mean 'to feel sorry or to express regret', while the second pair is used when sorrow or regret is *caused*: *Regretfully, I am forced to cancel our plans for the visit; The problems caused by the cancellation are regrettable, but I had no other choice.*

regulate, relegate

To **regulate** means 'to adjust, control or restrict'; to **relegate**, as most football fans know, means 'to consign to an inferior position'.

reign *see* rain, reign, rein

reiterate, repeat, iterate

To **repeat** means 'to do, make or say something again'. **Reiterate** is a near synonym but tends to be used to express the repetition of a word, statement, account or request: *He carefully reiterated the terms of the agreement to make sure they were fully understood.* **Iterate** is a little-known and even lesser used synonym for **reiterate**.

relapse, remission

A **relapse** is a return to a previous condition or former state; a **remission** is a respite from or abatement of a detrimental condition or the symptoms of a disease: *About 15 per cent of multiple sclerosis patients have a fairly benign form of the disease, but 80 per cent have remissions alternating with relapses that become successively worse.*

relation, relative
In the context of kinship, the two nouns are synonyms.

relatively, comparatively
Use only when there is something to be relative to, or something to compare with: *Although it appeared to be a most ambitious project, he said it would occupy relatively/comparatively little of his time.*

relegate *see* **regulate, relegate**

remember, recollect
To **remember** means 'to become consciously aware of something forgotten' or 'to retain something in the conscious mind'. To **recollect** is not instantaneous but requires some, often considerable, conscious mental effort: *Little by little she recollected the terrors she'd experienced on the journey.*

reminiscence, reminiscent
Some writers have difficulty using these. A **reminiscence** (noun) is a memory of some event or past experience: *The old sea captain was full of fascinating reminiscences.* **Reminiscent** (adjective) means 'stimulating memories' or 'stimulating comparisons with someone or something': *The paintings were reminiscent of the murals she'd seen in Venice many years before.*

remission *see* **relapse, remission**

remorse *see* **regret, remorse**

remuneration *see* **salary, wages, remuneration**

renascence, renascent, renaissance, Renaissance
Renascence is an alternative spelling of **renaissance**, meaning 'revival' or 'rebirth', usually in the context of culture or learning: *The professor claimed that the world was witnessing the renaissance of the art of hieroglyphic communication.* **Renascent** is more often seen than **renascence** and means 'growing and becoming active again'. The **Renaissance** (capital *R*) is the period, from the 14th to the 16th century, marking the European revival of art and classical scholarship, the end of the Middle Ages, and the rise of the modern world.

rent *see* **hire, rent, lease, let**

reparation *see* **retribution, restitution, reparation**

repeat *see* **reiterate, repeat, iterate** and **replicate, repeat**

repel, repulse, repellent, repellant
Although both **repel** and **repulse** mean 'to force or drive back', they have other meanings, the usage of which can cause confusion. The related word **repulsive**,

for example, means 'causing distaste or disgust', but we do not say *His filthy, drunken state repulsed the other passengers* – instead we use **repelled**. Nor is **repel** appropriate when the meaning is 'to drive away or reject'; here usage demands **repulse**: *She repulsed his proposal by flinging the flowers to the floor*. **Repellent** can appear as a noun or adjective: *She found his behaviour repellent; The insect repellent seemed to be effective*. **Repellant** is also used for the noun.

replace *see* substitute, replace

replica, copy, facsimile
It is generally accepted that a **replica** is a duplicate made by the original artist or maker, or made under his or her supervision. A **facsimile** is a copy of something, exact in every respect and detail. A **copy** is the most general term and can be a mechanically produced duplicate (a photocopy, for example, or a printed reproduction), a written word-for-word transcription or a hand-made imitation.

replicate, repeat
Although increasingly used as a synonym for **repeat**, **replicate** means rather more than that. Technically, a **replication** is a repetition of a study or of research, using the same data and methods, to confirm whether the results will be the same.

repository *see* depository, repository

repudiate *see* rebut, refute, repudiate, deny

repulse *see* repel, repulse, repellent, repellant

request, behest
A **request** is a demand or expression of desire: *The hostess had requested that all the men wear black tie*. **Behest** is a near synonym meaning 'authoritative request' and is used mostly in a formal context: *The children had attended the service at their late father's behest*.

requisite, requirement
These are near synonyms, broadly meaning 'something required'. But **requirement**, a noun, suggests an obligation or something demanded: *One of the requirements for the job was absolute punctuality*, while **requisite**, an adjective, implies 'something essential or indispensable': *Emily knew she had the requisite qualifications for the job*.

resin, rosin
These should not be regarded as alternative spellings or synonyms. **Resin** is a gummy exudation from certain trees and plants (for example, amber, copal), but the word is now also applied to a wide range of synthetic plastics. **Rosin** is the residue from the distillation of turpentine used in varnishes, paints and for treating the bows of stringed instruments.

resister, resistor
A **resister** is a person who resists, or who fights against something; a **resistor** is a component that introduces resistance into an electrical circuit.

resolve, solve
Resolve is often mistakenly used to mean **solve**. Sherlock Holmes did not resolve the case of the 'Crooked Man', he solved it. You **solve** a problem or mystery when you find an explanation for it: *Jim took less than two hours to solve the Rubik cube puzzle*. To **resolve** means 'to firmly decide something, or to determine a course of action': *The meeting resolved to petition the Home Secretary*.

respectably, respectfully, respectively
Respectably means 'in a way that is honest, decent and deserving respect': *Although desperately poor the family was always dressed respectably*. **Respectfully** means 'with respect': *The men doffed their hats respectfully as the cortege went past*. **Respectively** means 'in the order given': *John, Amy and Sarah are aged twelve, nine and five respectively*.

respect of, in respect to, with respect to
In respect of and **with respect to** are pseudo-formal phrases commonly used to mean 'with reference or relation to'. **In respect to** is sometimes seen but is meaningless and should not be used.

respond *see* **react, respond**

responsible *see* **accountable, responsible** and **cause, responsible**

restful, restive, restless
Restive and **restless** are the opposite of **restful**, which means 'peaceful, calm, inviting rest': *Aunt Elizabeth looked forward to the restful atmosphere of the lakeside hotel*. A **restless** person is one who cannot be still and quiet, while someone **restive** frets under restraint. The latter is mostly applied to animals: *The horses grew restive as the storm drew closer*.

restaurant, restaurateur
The latter owns or manages the former; note the spelling.

restitution *see* **retribution, restitution, reparation**

restraint *see* **constraint, restraint**

result *see* **upshot, result**

résumé *see* ***précis*, résumé**

resurgence, recrudesence
Resurgence means 'revival, reinvigoration, new life': *The huge numbers at the rally were a strong indication of the resurgence of nationalist feeling*. **Recrudescence** is

sometimes wrongly used as a synonym that it most emphatically isn't; although it means 'to reappear or break out', it means this only in the sense of worsening: *The doctor was dismayed by the recrudescence of the wound, which they thought had healed weeks ago.*

retort *see* **riposte, retort**

retribution, restitution, reparation
Reparation is the act of making amends, or redressing a wrong, or repairing or restoring some damage or injury. **Restitution** can have an identical meaning but it also has recognition in law as the act of compensating for loss or injury, especially by returning something to its original state, for example, the removal of graffiti by the perpetrator. The meaning of **retribution** (from the Latin *retribuere,* which means 'to repay') carries with it overtones of punishment and revenge, as well as a Divine judgement and should be used only to mean the act of punishing or taking revenge for some sin or injury.

revenge, avenge, vengeance
Revenge is personal retaliation: *I eventually got my revenge by having him arrested for harassment.* To **avenge** a wrong, the punishment is meted out by a third party as a form of rough justice: *They avenged my father's murder.* **Vengeance** is interchangeable with **revenge**.

reverse *see* **converse, inverse, obverse, reverse**

review, revue
In a theatrical context, a **revue** is a performance of sketches, comedy routines, songs and dancing; a **review** is a critical assessment of any public performance: *Although the revue was enthusiastically received by the audience, the cast was shattered by the theatre critic's savage review.*

rheumatism *see* **arthritis, rheumatism, lumbago, sciatica**

rigour, rigorous, rigor
Rigour is a state of strictness, inflexibility, severity and hardship; **rigorous** is the adjective: *The monks were subjected to three years of rigorous discipline.* **Rigor** is the medical term for a violent attack of shivering, and also for the stiffness and rigidity of body tissues, as in *rigor mortis*. Both are spelt **rigor** in American English.

rime, rhyme
Rime is a rather archaic word for frost, used almost exclusively in a poetic context perhaps because it **rhymes** with *clime, climb, lime, mime, time,* etc.

riposte, retort
A **riposte** is a quick, sharp, sometimes witty reply. A **retort** is much the same, but is usually reserved to indicate a degree of anger and sarcasm.

rise *see* **raise, raze, rise**

roast *see* **roost, roast**

robbery *see* **burglar, burgle, burglarise; burglary, robbery, stealing, theft**

rock, stone, pebble
Boys throw **stones** in Britain; in the USA they throw **rocks**. The separate words and their meanings (a **stone** is a small lump of **rock**; a **pebble** is even smaller, and rounder) are worth preserving.

Roman Catholic *see* **catholic, Catholic**

roost, roast
The battle between **rule the roost** and **rule the roast** is a long and noble one, dating from 13th-century France. In the 1920s Fowler's *Modern English Usage* and *Chambers Dictionary*, two of a number of authorities, still opted for **roast**, although, by the 1950s, Fowler for one had switched allegiance to **roost**. Today, **roost** is the most accepted.

Romany *see* **gypsy, gipsy, Romany, traveller**

rosin *see* **resin, rosin**

rostrum *see* **dais, lectern, podium, rostrum**

rotund *see* **orotund, rotund**

round robin
Many believe this term means a document that's distributed to or signed by a number of people who are agreed about a certain cause. Specifically, however, a **round robin** is a document signed in such a way (with the signatures arrayed in a circle, for example) to disguise the order in which they signed. In sporting terminology, a **round robin** is a tournament in which each player plays against every other player.

rouse, arouse
Both mean 'to awaken, to stir out of inactivity', but **rouse** tends to imply a physical response (*The sergeant roused the men from their bunks*) while **arouse** suggests a more emotional reaction: *Sally's frequent disappearances began to arouse his suspicions*.

rout, route
A **rout** (pronounced *rowt*) is a disorderly retreat; an overwhelming defeat; to **rout** (verb) is to cause a defeat or retreat: *The rabble was promptly routed by the well-trained guards*. **Rout** also has the less used meaning of 'to dig, to turn over'; today's usage prefers **root**: **The pigs rooted among the leaves for acorns**. A **route** (pronounced *root*; *rowt* in the USA) is the course planned or taken from

one place to another during a journey. And watch the spelling of **routeing**: *Fred was in charge of routeing the buses.*

rule the roost *see* **roost, roast**

run, runs, manages, operates, directs
Grace runs a women's fashion shop in the High Street. The use of **run** and **runs** in this sort of context is sloppy, especially when there is no shortage of more specific substitutes such as *manages, operates, directs, conducts,* etc.

rung *see* **rang, rung**

rustic, rusticate
Something **rustic** is associated with the country or rural life, supposedly simple, peaceful and unsophisticated. To **rusticate** can mean 'to banish to the country', but its common meaning is to be sent down from a university as a punishment. In the architectural sense, to **rusticate** means 'to carve or cast deeply textured designs in masonry'.

saccharin, saccharine
Saccharin is the sugar substitute; **saccharine** means excessively sweet: *After a while the singer's saccharine voice began to get on my nerves.*

sacred, sacrosanct
Sacred means 'dedicated to religious use: holy, and not to be profaned'. **Sacrosanct** is more intensive, meaning 'pure and incorruptible, incapable of being violated'.

sadism, masochism
Sadism is the abnormal desire to inflict physical pain on others for (usually) sexual pleasure; **masochism** is the abnormal desire to be physically abused or humilated by another, again usually for sexual gratification.

salary, wages, remuneration
A **salary** is usually fixed as an annual rate and paid by the month or week; **wages** are rates usually paid by the hour, day or week. **Remuneration** is payment for work or for services provided, not necessarily on a regular basis.

salon, saloon
Salon survives almost exclusively as a *hairdressing salon* or a *beauty salon*. A **saloon** in Britain is one of two or three drinking bars in a pub; in North America it is commonly a sleazy establishment serving alcohol. In the context of automobiles, a **saloon** in Britain is a **sedan** in the USA.

same, similar
Harry sold six cars last week, and a similar number this week. What is meant here is *the **same** number this week;* **similar** means 'resembling something or someone'.

Salon, saloon

sanatorium, sanitarium, sanatarium

A **sanatorium** is a hospital or establishment for the treatment of invalids and convalescents; **sanitarium** is the American English spelling. **Sanatarium** is incorrect.

sanguine, sanguinary

Writers find this pair confusing to use. **Sanguinary** has one bloody meaning: 'attended with much bloodshed, bloodthirsty, flowing or stained with blood'. **Sanguine** also has its bloody aspect; it means 'blood-red and ruddy'. But it is also frequently used to mean 'optimistic, cheerful and confident': *Charles was quite sanguine about the team's prospects*. Use both with care.

sank, sunk, sunken

Sank is the past tense of **sink**, as is **sunk**: *With great relish Wilbur sank/sunk his teeth into the hamburger.* **Sank** is correct as an active verb: *She sank with all hands.* **Sunk** is correct as a passive verb: *The ship had been sunk by a torpedo.* **Sunken** is mostly encountered as an adjective: *sunken spirits, sunken cheeks, sunken treasure.*

sarcasm, satire *see* irony, sarcasm, satire

sauce *see* ketchup, catsup, sauce, chutney, pickle

scampi, shrimp, prawn, langoustine

Scampi are prawns fried in breadcrumbs or batter. **Prawns** are the crustaceans that grace prawn cocktails and range from the 1–4-inch Atlantic deepwater or Greenland prawns to the giant (up to 12-inch) Tiger prawns from Southeast Asia. **Shrimp** are a large family of marine decapods fished around Britain, of which the *Crangon vulgaris* is the main edible member. **Langoustine** to the French are **Dublin Bay prawns** to the British and look like miniature lobsters.

scan, glance, scrutinize

Scan can have opposite meanings. It can mean 'to look over in a casual manner': *Mr Hewitt picked up the newspaper and scanned the headlines*. However, **scan** can also mean 'to examine closely and thoroughly' and electronic scanners have been designed to minutely and systematically **scrutinize** objects. Make sure that your usage of **scan** is unambiguous. In this context, a **glance** is a quick look: *She had only time to glance at the table before the train left the station.*

scare, scarify
To **scare** is to frighten; to **scarify** is to scratch, abrade, break up or wound: *The general launched into a scarifying denouncement of the behaviour of his troops.*

scared *see* frightened, scared, alarmed, afraid

sceptic, septic
A **sceptic** (in American English, **skeptic**) is a doubter who is unwilling to believe anything without superabundant proof. Something **septic** causes infection and putrefaction; in a **septic tank**, sewage is broken down by bacteria.

sceptical *see* cynical, sceptical

sciatica *see* arthritis, rheumatism, lumbago, sciatica

Scotland, Scotsman, Scot, Scotch, Scottish
Natives and institutions of Scotland are **Scottish** or **Scots**: *Scotsman, Scotswoman, Scottish smoked trout, Scots language, Scottish writers,* etc. The use of **Scotch** is mostly confined to *Scotch broth, Scotch mist* and, of course, *Scotch whisky*.

scotch
To **scotch** a rumour is to suppress it. Plans can be **scotched**, too, when the word means 'to put an end to, to prevent, to block': *The overnight rain scotched plans to resume play this morning.* **Scotch** in these contexts is not a slang expression but a word deriving from the Old French *escocher*, 'to cut'.

Scouts, Boy Scouts
The former Boy Scouts are now known in Britain simply as **Scouts**; Wolf Cubs are just **Cubs**; Girl Guides are **Guides**.

scrimp, skimp, skimpy
Both **scrimp** and **skimp** mean 'to be sparing, frugal, stingy': *Their mother scrimps / skimps on food for the family but smokes like a chimney.* **Skimp** has a second meaning, which is 'to do something carelessly, hastily and in a slapdash manner': *The builder skimped on the job so we're suing him.* **Skimpy** means 'brief and scanty' and is usually applied to clothing: *Wearing only a skimpy dress, she nearly froze while waiting for the bus.*

Scripture, scriptural
When used as a shortened form of Holy Scripture, **Scripture** and the **Scriptures** are capitalised. The adjective **scriptural** is lower-case.

scrutinize *see* **scan, glance, scrutinize**

scull, skull
Scull can be a single oar, a long, narrow racing boat, or the action of pulling on one or a pair of oars: *To the cheers of the crowd, Watson sculled his way to victory.* The **skull** is the bony skeleton of the head.

Scull, skull

sculptress *see* **actor, actress, authoress, poetess, sculpress, etc**

scuttle, scupper
These are not interchangeable. A **scupper** is an opening on the deck or side of a ship for draining off water. A **scuttle** is also an opening, but it is a covered hatchway for access. If such openings are made below the waterline, the ship can be scuttled, or sunk. Away from seafaring, **scuttle**, but more usually **scupper**, are both used to mean 'to wreck or ruin': *The arrival of half a dozen other ice-cream vans scuppered Bert's plans to make a killing.*

seasonal, seasonable
Seasonal means 'occurring at a certain season' as in *seasonal storms* and *seasonal labour*. **Seasonable** means 'suitable to' or 'in keeping with the season': *The weather was seasonable for April.*

secure *see* **get, acquire, obtain, secure**

sensitive, sensual, sensuous
Sensitive means 'acutely susceptible to influences, highly responsive to stimuli, or easily offended'. Except that it shares the meaning of 'the ability to perceive and feel', **sensibility** is not a synonym but means 'having the capacity to respond to emotion, moral feelings and intellectual and aesthetic stimuli'. **Sensual** pleasure derives from physical indulgences such as eating, drinking and sex. Something or someone **sensuous** is capable of arousing or pleasing the senses: *She closed her eyes as she listened to the sensuous progression of Ravel's 'Bolero'.*

Sex and Gender

It is first of all essential to grasp the fact that there are only two sexes (male and female) and three genders, which apply to words (masculine, feminine and neuter). Despite this, **sex**, once exclusively used to denote the difference between male and female, has now through usage gained new meanings. This one – *The couple claimed they had sex five times a day* – to mean 'sexual intercourse' – has virtually levered the word away from its primary meaning. Because of the biological connotations of **sex** (the word), many writers and feminists in particular have nominated **gender** as its substitute to mean the difference between being male and masculine, and female and feminine. **Gender** now covers the social functions, status and expectations of males and females: **gender roles** instead of **sex roles** and **gender gap** instead of **sex gap** are now standard terms. There exists also a quest for **gender-free language** (lawyer, dentist, doctor, student are okay; chambermaid, barmaid, businessman, chairman and clergyman aren't).

septic *see* **sceptic, septic**

sew *see* **sow, sew**

sewage, sewerage
Sewerage is the sewer system, and **sewage** is what passes through it.

shear, sheer
Shear means 'to cut off' (hair), 'break off' (metal, etc), or 'strip off' (privileges, powers, authority). **Sheer** can mean 'fine and transparent' (silk, stockings, underwear), 'steep' (road, cliff) or 'absolute' (*The woman laughed for sheer joy*). **Sheer** also means 'to deviate or swerve', but in this sense **veer** is a less ambiguous choice.

shewn *see* **shown, shewn**

shop, store
A **shop** in Britain is a **store** in the USA. In the UK, however, **department store** describes a large shop with many departments.

shortage, shortfall
A **shortage** is an insufficient amount or a deficiency; a **shortfall** is the failure to meet some requirement or target, and the extent of it: *The fundraising goal suffered a shortfall of some £15,000.*

shown, shewn
Shewn is an archaic spelling of **shown**, but some people still persist in using it.

shrimp *see* **scampi, shrimp, prawn, langoustine**

sick, sickly, ill
To be **sick** is a euphemism for to **vomit**, so **ill** is usually substituted for **sick** to mean a state of sickness or being unwell. The usage is about evenly divided because we still say *sick pay, sick leave, sickness benefit, sick child,* etc. A **sick/ill** Australian resolves the dilemma by saying *I'm crook*. A **sickly** person is unhealthy, weak and disposed to frequent ailments.

silicon, silicone
Silicon is the chemical element that, as silicon oxide, is all about us in the form of quartz and sand; **silicone** is a synthetic silicon compound that is used to make lubricants, water repellants and a range of other products.

silly *see* **crass, silly, stupid, gross**

similar *see* **same, similar**

simile, metaphor
Both are figures of speech. A **simile** makes a comparison or indicates a similarity, usually preceded by *as, as if,* or *like*: *He is as thick as two short planks; The party went like a house on fire*. A **metaphor** makes a more direct analogy: *You're a doll; She's a pain in the neck*. A **mixed metaphor** combines two incompatible comparisons: *We've got a real headache on our hands; This decision is a very hard blow to swallow*.

simple, simplistic
The two are not synonyms. **Simplistic** means 'excessively simplified to the point of naivety'. The difference is made clear here: *Dalton's deductions were brilliantly simple, but the solution put forward by Keene was just too simplistic*.

since *see* **ago, before, back, past** and **because, since on account of, owing to, due to**

sitting room *see* **living room, sitting room, lounge, drawing room**

Situation, Position – It's a Problem Situation

A **situation** is, simply, a position, a location, or a state of affairs. But more often than not **situation** is used to inflate the importance of a statement: *It was a typical confrontational situation* for *It was a typical confrontation is a fair example*. A *crisis situation* is simply a crisis; an *emergency situation* is just an emergency. But with overuse threatening to topple **situation** from fashion, its cousin **position** seems to be taking over: *The position in regard to the need to increase railway fares is that it is being kept under review*. This again is gobbledegook, which, when translated, could mean: *The possibility of increasing railway fares is being considered*. Use **situation** and **position** with care and discrimination.

size, sized

A **large-size** pumpkin or a **large-sized** pumpkin? Both usages are acceptable although the adjective **sized** is usually preferred.

skewbald *see* **piebald, skewbald**

skill *see* **expertise, skill**

skimp, skimpy *see* **scrimp, skimp, skimpy**

skull *see* **scull, skull**

slander *see* **libel, slander**

sleight, slight

Sleight means dexterity, as in the *sleight of hand* displayed by a magician, but as a word it is rarely used by itself. **Slight** means 'small, slim, insignificant' and also a 'snub or insult'. *See also* **marginal, minimal, slight**.

slow, slowly

Remorseless usage has converted the adjective **slow** into a substitute for the adverb **slowly**: *Drive slow past the school; Doesn't Thomas walk slow?; Is the train running slow again?* The adverbial use of **slow** is now widespread, but you will be recognised as a writer of discernment if you use **slowly** where it should be used: *Drive slowly past the school.*

smelled, smelt

Smelled, not **smelt**, is preferred as the past tense and past participle of **smell**.

snook, snoot

Because **snoot** is slang for the nose, the rude gesture made by placing a thumb on the nose with the fingers outstretched is not uncommonly called **cocking a snoot**. It seems a shame therefore to point out that this is completely wrong. The name for this particular gesture is in fact a **snook**, and the correct phrase is **cocking a snook**.

snooker, pool, billiards

Snooker is played on a billiard table with a white cue ball, fifteen red balls and six other coloured balls, which are all potted in a certain order. **Pool** is essentially an American game and is played with coloured and numbered balls plus a cue ball. In **eight-ball pool** players must sink their own balls before those of an opponent, plus the black eight-ball, to win the game. **Billiards** is played with two white balls and a red ball with players scoring by potting the red ball, the opponent's ball, or another ball off either of these two.

so-called

This is regarded as a put-down or sneer term, such as **self-styled** or **soi-disant**,

would-be and **self-proclaimed**. It indicates that what follows is to be held up to doubt, question or ridicule: *The so-called animal lovers claimed they had collected a petition of ten thousand names.*

solecism, solipsism, sophism, sophistry

In linguistic terms, a **solecism** is a violation of conventional usage, such as breaking a grammatical rule, misusing a word, mixing metaphors or mispronouncing a word. **Solipsism** is the belief that only the self is real and knowable, and the denial of the existence of any knowledge beyond one's own existence. **Sophism** is clever and persuasive but nevertheless specious argument. **Sophistry** is an example of this type of argument, or the art of specious reasoning.

solve *see* resolve, solve

somebody, someone *see* anybody, anyone, any one

sometime, some time, sometimes

Some time and to a lesser extent **sometime** are used to indicate 'at some unspecified time or another': *The Smith family moved away some time ago; We promised we would meet sometime.* Fowler makes a point that **sometime** should be reserved for its adjectival sense, meaning 'former': *The sometime president of the Board of Trade was at the meeting* – but usage will undoubtedly ignore this advice. **Sometimes** means 'occasionally, now and then'.

somewhere, someplace

The traditional and perfectly adequate **somewhere** appears to be standing up rather well to the American English import **someplace**.

soon, presently

Although the original meaning of **presently** (immediately) was supposed to have been obsolete for couple of centuries, it is still in evidence, which causes confusion with its contemporary meaning of 'soon, in a while'. Curiously, the old meaning never died out in Scotland, so the Scots should win some points for consistency. In American English, too, **presently** is accepted as meaning 'now, at the moment': *James Mahoney is presently one of the key advisers to the President.* If you wish to avoid ambiguity, use **soon**, **now**, **currently**, **shortly**, etc. *See also* **directly**.

sophism, sophistry *see* solecism, solipsism, sophism, sophistry

sophomore, freshman

In the USA, a **freshman** is a student of either sex in the first year of secondary school or is a first-year undergraduate at a university. A **sophomore** is the second-year equivalent.

sort of *see* kind, kind of, sort of, type of

sorted out, sorted

It's time to get that personal pension sorted! exhorted a recent financial services advertisement (*Daily Telegraph*, 1996). Only a year or two before the headline would have exclaimed, more traditionally, *It's time to get that personal pension sorted out!* Dropping the **out** (the blame is placed on East End London speech: *Okay, let's ge' i' saw-hid*) is a recent fashion but the abbreviated phrase is sticking like glue to current usage. You have been warned.

soul, sole

Kielder Ferries is a profitable family-run cruise business that enjoys the soul ferrying rights on Kielder Water, now one of Northumberland's largest tourist attractions (advertisement in *The Newcastle Journal*, 1994). Not only a profitable business but a classical one, ferrying souls across the water! What the ad intended to say was '**sole** ferrying rights' – meaning exclusive or unshared.

sow, sew

You **sew** with a needle and thread (**sewed**, **sewn**) and **sow** seeds (**sowed**, **sown**). A **sow** (pronounced to rhyme with *how*) is a female pig.

spasmodic, sporadic

Spasmodic means 'happening in short, irregular and unexpected bursts or spasms' (*His displays of academic excellence tended to occur spasmodically*), while something **sporadic** occurs intermittently, at scattered intervals: *The thunder continued sporadically throughout the afternoon.*

specialist *see* consultant, specialist

specially *see* especially, specially

specialty, speciality

These are interchangeable, although **specialty** is standard in American English and **speciality** is preferred in the UK.

specie, species

Specie defines coins and coinage, as distinct from paper money. A **species** is 'a kind, or variety' or, most commonly in biology, 'a group within a genus which can interbreed and which may contain subspecies and varieties'.

specious, spurious

Both words share the basic meaning of 'being false and not genuine', but they are not synonymous. Something **specious** may appear to be superficially genuine, true or correct but in fact turns out to be false, untrue or wrong: *It took them a while to see through Brett's specious claims about his medical qualifications.* Something **spurious** makes little effort to mask its falseness.

spectrum, range

Spectrum is often used as a synonym for **range**: *He enthused over the spectrum of possibilities.* Use **range** in such contexts; it's plainer and clearer.

spelt, spelled
Spelt is generally found in British English, and **spelled** in American English: *The judge spelt out the alternative to prison.*

spilt, spilled
Spilt is generally found in British English, and **spilled** in American English: *The overturned tanker spilt an estimated three thousand litres of milk over the road.*

spin doctor *see* **populist, popularist, populariser, spin doctor**

spoilt, spoiled
Spoilt is generally found in British English, and **spoiled** in American English, but remember that there is no such word as *despoilt* – it's **despoiled**.

spoof *see* **irony, sarcasm, satire**

sporadic *see* **spasmodic, sporadic**

spurious *see* **specious, spurious**

stalactite, stalagmite
A **stalactite** (*c* for ceiling) hangs down; a **stalagmite** (*g* for ground) projects up from the ground. Remember that 'tites' come down.

stalls *see* **balcony, circle, dress circle, gallery, stalls**

stammer, stutter
Although through usage and abusage, these are now regarded as synonyms, the technical difference is still worth preserving. A **stammer** is a speech disorder characterised by involuntary repetitions, hesitation and silences as the speaker attempts to utter the next word. A **stutter** is a similar disorder in which the speaker repeats the beginnings of words, particularly consonants, before being able to complete them.

stanch, staunch
Both are correct, but as a verb meaning 'to stem the flow of blood', **stanch** is more widely used, leaving **staunch** as an adjective meaning 'firmly loyal and steadfast'.

standpoint, point of view, viewpoint
Some object to **standpoint** but it is a respectable word deriving from the German *Standpunkt*, meaning 'a position from which something is viewed', either in a physical or abstract sense: *From the client's standpoint the construction so far was a mess.* **Point of view** and **viewpoint** have the same meaning.

start *see* **begin, commence, inaugurate, initiate, start**

stationary, stationery
Stationary means 'fixed, not moving, standing still'; **stationers** sell writing material, which is called **stationery**. A useful mnemonic is 'stationary = stand; stationery = letter'.

statistic, statistics
Statistics can be singular or plural, depending on the sense: *Statistics is an inexact science; The statistics are indicating a Conservative victory.* But **statistic** is always singular: *The one statistic that impressed the voters was the low inflation index.*

stealing *see* **burglar, burgle, burglarise; burglary, robbery, stealing, theft**

steel *see* **ion, iron, steel**

stimulant, stimulus, stimuli
Both nouns mean 'something that produces an arousal or increase in activity' and are near synonyms. However, a **stimulant** is almost always used in a physiological context (*Jane could never get going in the morning without strong coffee or some other stimulant*) while **stimulus** is used to indicate something that arouses action or acts as an incentive: *There was little doubt that the overtime payment served as an effective stimulus to increasing production.* **Stimuli** is the plural of stimulus.

stile *see* **style, stile**

stolid, solid
Stolid means 'impassive, dull, showing little feeling or perception'. **Solid**, used in a similar context, means dependable: *When it comes to supporting the school, John's as solid as a rock.*

stone *see* **rock, stone, pebble**

store *see* **shop, store**

storey, story, storeys, stories
A **storey** (**story** in American English) is a floor or level in a building: *Jim lost his wallet in the multi-storey car park.* The plural is **storeys**. A **story** (plural **stories**) is a tale, a narrative.

straight, strait, straightened, straitened
Phrases and combinations that include these words require care: *straight and narrow* (although it's *strait and narrow* in the Bible!), *straight-edge, straight-faced, straightforward, straight bat; dire straits, strait-laced, straitjacket, straitened circumstances.* You **straighten** something by making or bending it **straight**; **straitened** means 'restricted'. A useful mnemonic is *The Hunchback of Notre Dame didn't live in straightened circumstances.*

strategy, stratagem, tactics
Strategy is the planning of an operation; **tactics** involve putting the strategy into effect. A **stratagem** is a scheme designed to deceive.

stricken *see* **struck, stricken**

struck, stricken
Stricken is sometimes mistakenly used as the past tense and past participle of **strike**: *Adverse comments on behaviour should be stricken from the records of a dyslexic student*. The intended word is **struck**. **Stricken** means to be 'affected or laid low by an illness'.

student *see* **pupil, student**

stupid *see* **crass, silly, stupid, gross**

stutter *see* **stammer, stutter**

style, stile
A **stile** is the arrangement of wooden steps to help you climb over a fence; **style** embraces a wide range of meanings: 'the manner in which something is done; a form of appearance or design; a refinement of dress and manners', etc.

subconscious, unconscious
Subconscious has two meanings: that of being only partly aware, and, more commonly, the thoughts that occupy the hidden level of the mind and influence our actions: *The analyst concluded that subconsciously Helen had a deep hatred for her sister*. To be **unconscious** is to be unaware: *She was unconscious of the danger she was in*. It can also mean total loss of consciousness: *After the accident the young man was unconscious for three days*.

subjective *see* **objective, subjective**

subnormal *see* **abnormal, subnormal**

subsequently *see* **consequently, subsequently**

substitute, replace
These are subtly different. **Substitute** means 'to put in the place of', while **replace** means 'to put back again in place': *He carefully replaced the candlesticks but substituted a cheap imitation for the priceless bowl*.

succeed, follow
These are often regarded as synonyms but they are not. To **follow** means 'to go or come after and in the same direction': *Almost every child in the neighborhood followed the marching band*. To **succeed**, in this context, means 'to come next in order or sequence': *It was expected that Charles would succeed his father as senior partner in the business*.

successive *see* **consecutive, successive**

succubus *see* **incubus, succubus**

such as *see* **like, as, as if, such as, just as**

suit, suite
Although pronounced differently (*sut, sweet*), confusion between the two is not unknown: a **suit** of clothes but a **suite** of furniture; strong **suit**, follow **suit**; a **suit** of cards; a **lawsuit**; but a presidential **suite** (of rooms in a hotel), a musical **suite**, a **suite** of attendants.

summoned, summonsed
You can be **summoned** to appear at a public enquiry, or to a court hearing. If, however, you are presented with a **summons**, you are therefore **summonsed**.

sunk *see* **sank, sunk, sunken**

superficial, cosmetic
We've made a few changes but they're only cosmetic is a usage now very much in vogue. **Superficial** is more to the point and preferred.

supersede, surpass
Supersede means 'to supplant or replace with something or someone superior to the original'. Note: **supersede** is often misspelled *supercede*. To **surpass** is to be better or greater than or superior in excellence or achievement: *Her results at the last Olympics surpassed even her own previous records. See also* **precede, proceed, supersede**.

supine *see* **prone, prostrate, recumbent, supine**

supper *see* **dinner, supper, lunch, tea**

supplement *see* **compliment, complement, supplement**

suppose *see* **guess, suppose, think**; also **assume, presume**

surge *see* **upsurge, surge**

surpass *see* **supersede, surpass**

surplice, surplus
A newspaper in southwest England recently reported that *students at Salisbury Cathedral School who, after becoming full choristers, were presented with* **surpluses** *to wear over their cassocks*. These, presumably, were not surplus stock, but the real thing – **surplices**.

swam, swum
Harry and Peter swum out to the buoy is wrong. The past tense of **swim** is **swam**: *Harry and Peter swam out to the buoy.* **Swum** is the past participle of **swim**: *The water was so warm and inviting they could have swum all day.*

swap *see* **swop, swap**

swingeing, swinging
Swingeing (pronounced *swin-jing*) means 'severe in degree': *People tend to forget that the so-called Swinging Sixties also saw swingeing tax increases.*

swop, swap
Meaning 'to exchange', **swap** is universal and preferred; **swop** is a purely British variant.

swot, swat
These are two different words. To **swot** is to study or cram for an examination; to **swat** is to smack or hit sharply: *We did little all day but swat flies and mosquitoes.*

swum *see* **swam, swum**

sympathy *see* **empathy, sympathy**

Sweater, Jersey, Jumper, Pullover, etc

In matters of clothing, usage departs from often vague or out-dated dictionary definitions, so it's difficult to describe precisely what a jumper is, or a sweater, or any similar upper garment. Here's a cross-section of opinion: A **sweater** is knitted, neither tight nor loose, either with or without sleeves, and is a synonym for **jumper**, the latter term being used more to describe a child's garment. A **jersey** or **guernsey** was originally a heavy woollen sweater made for warmth; the same garment, in lighter material, is now fashionably called a *maillot*. A **pullover** can be with or without sleeves and is loose enough to slip easily over the head; it tends to be a male garment. The **cardigan** is distinguished by having buttons up the front and is long-sleeved; in a **twinset** it is worn over a matching short-sleeved sweater. A **T-shirt** (or **tee-shirt**) is usually short-sleeved, usually made of cotton, and with no collar or buttons. A **tank-top**, extremely fashionable in the 1970s, is a lightweight vest-like garment with wide shoulder straps. The trade or generic term for all of the above is simply **tops**.

---

syndrome, synergy, symbiosis
Each of these is about relationships. A **syndrome** is a combination of symptoms or signs that suggests some disease, disorder or problem. **Synergy** is now popularly used to mean 'productive relationship' or 'mutually beneficial relationship', but what it really means is the action of two groups or entities that when combined produce an effect of which each is incapable alone. **Symbiosis** is a biological term defining the interdependency of two animal or plant species.

syntax *see* **grammar, syntax**

synthesis *see* **analysis, synthesis**

tactics *see* **strategy, stratagem, tactics**

tantamount *see* **paramount, tantamount**

tantalise, tease
To **tease** means 'to light-heartedly annoy someone', or 'to arouse desire with no intention of satisfying it' or 'to offer something with no intention of supplying it'. To torment or irritate means substantially the same, so how different is **tantalise**? There is a subtle difference, and it derives from the frustrating experience of the ancient Greek king Tantalus. He was condemned to stand in a pool of water which receded every time he stooped to drink, and under trees which drew back every time he reached to pick the delicious fruit that hung from them. To be tantalised is to be tormented and frustrated by the sight of something dearly desired but inaccessible.

tartan, plaid
Tartan is the distinctive patterned cloth used for certain Scottish garments, including the kilt and the plaid – the length of cloth worn over the shoulder.

tasteful, tasty
Tasteful is something that embodies or employs aesthetic discrimination and good taste: *The reception rooms were tastefully furnished.* **Tasty** means 'flavourful to the palate', although colloquially it has also come to mean 'sexually attractive'.

tea *see* **dinner, supper, lunch, tea**

tease *see* **tantalise, tease**

temerity *see* **timidity, temerity**

temporal, temporary
Temporal relates to real life, to the secular as opposed to the spiritual, to earthly time rather than to eternity. **Temporary** means 'impermanent, lasting for a limited time only'.

tendency, trend
A **tendency** is an inclination, a leaning, a disposition towards something: *When he'd had a few too many, George had a tendency to fall asleep.* A **trend** is a general movement: *The current trend is for people to book their holidays early.*

tenterhooks
There are no such things as 'tender hooks' or 'tenderhooks', yet these mysterious objects keep surfacing in ill-informed sentences. The word is **tenterhooks**, traditionally the nails or hooks on a frame for stretching canvas or cloth: *She's on tenterhooks waiting for her exam results* means she's in an agony of suspense waiting for the outcome.

testament, testimony, testimonial
A **testament** is a will, the document by which a person disposes of his or her estate after death, as in *last will and testament*. **Testimony** is evidence, proof or confirmation, sometimes given under oath: *Fred's rapid climb up the company hierarchy was testimony to his 24-hour-a-day charm offensive*. A **testimonial** is a personal endorsement of a person's character, ability and experience: *Sam said he'd be delighted to provide a testimonial for David's youngest son*. *See also* **evidence, proof, testimony**.

theft *see* **burglar, burgle, burglarise; burglary, robbery, stealing, theft**

their, there, they're
A confusing trio – they look different but sound the same. **Their** is a possessive pronoun, the possessive of **they**: *This is their car*. **There** means 'in or at that place': *She left the car there but now it's gone*. **They're** is a contraction of 'they are': *They're trying to break into our car*.

thence *see* **hence, thence, whence**

think *see* **guess, suppose, think**; *also* **believe, feel, think**

though *see* **although, though**

thrilled, enthralled
To be **thrilled** is to experience tingling excitement, an intense wave of emotion. To be **enthralled** (held in thrall) is to be captivated, spellbound, in a state of fascinated attention: *Julie almost stopped breathing, enthralled by the sheer poetry of the ballet*.

tight, tightly
The adjective (**tight**) and adverb (**tightly**) are regarded as often interchangeable: *He held her tight/tightly*. But whereas **tight** suggests a condition (*The cork was jammed tight*), **tightly** implies action: *James held him tightly around the neck*.

till, until
Till is the informal and short form of **until**, meaning 'up to the time when': *I'll love you till the end of time*. Both are interchangeable but **until** is preferred, especially at the beginning of a sentence: *Until Jim arrives we'll just have to twiddle our thumbs*.

timidity, temerity
Timidity is the tendency to be easily frightened, shy and fearful – or **timorous**. **Temerity** means almost the opposite: 'foolish, reckless boldness': *Only Felicity would have had the temerity to question the consultant's judgement*.

tirade *see* **harangue, tirade**

titillate, titivate
Titillate means 'to tickle or excite'; **titivate** means 'to smarten up'.

TNT, dynamite, gelignite
Dynamite, a compound of liquid nitroglycerin and absorbent material, was the invention of Alfred Nobel in 1866; he followed this with blasting gelatin, or **gelignite**, in 1875. **TNT**, or tri-nitro-toluene, is the most recently developed of the trio and safest from friction and shock.

toilet *see* lavatory, toilet, loo, bathroom

token, nominal, notional
All three are frequently misused to mean 'minimal'. In the sense of 'symbolic gesture', **token** and **nominal** are closely related: a nominal payment and a token payment, meaning 'partial payment', are the same thing. **Token** also means 'slight, or of no real account': *The Party regarded his contribution of £20 as merely token support.* **Nominal** means 'not in fact, in name only'; a nominal charge is one removed from reality in that it is small compared to its real value: *Brian was allowed to buy his company car for the nominal payment of £100.* Something **notional** relates to concepts and hypotheses rather than to reality: *The engineers' notional cost for a single unit was thought to be in the region of £150.*

ton, tonne
A British **ton** is 2,240 lbs; a short or American **ton** is 2,000 lbs; a metric **tonne** is 1,000 kilograms or about 2,200 lbs.

tornado *see* cyclone, hurricane, tornado, typhoon, waterspout

tortuous, torturous
Tortuous means 'twisting, winding, devious'; **torturous** means 'inflicting torture and pain': *Following the dark tortuous underground passages became a torturous nightmare.*

toward, towards
Both, meaning 'in the direction of' or 'in respect of', are interchangeable. Use according to taste, sound and appearance: *He steered the yacht toward/towards the harbour; The storm broke towards dawn.*

town *see* city, town, village, hamlet

toxin, tocsin
Toxin is poison caused by bacteria; a **tocsin** is a bell rung to raise an alarm.

trait, character
Character – of a person, object or group – is the combination of qualities that distinguishes them: *Fred was rather a weak character; It was not in Trudy's character to be aggressive.* A **trait** is some aspect or feature of a person or that person's behaviour: *One of Auntie's most endearing traits was her boundless optimism.*

transpire, happen, occur
Transpire does not mean happen or occur but to 'become known gradually, or come to light': *It transpired that, because she had accidentally overheard some gossip, Jean at last grasped the probability that John and Julie were having an affair.*

trauma
This word has become debilitated by misuse and overuse. Originally restricted to mean 'extreme pathological or psychological shock severe enough to have long-lasting effects', **trauma** has for some time been trivialised: *I simply couldn't stand the trauma of going for another job interview.* Return **trauma** and **traumatise** to the medical cabinet.

traveller *see* **gypsy, gipsy, Romany, traveller**

trend *see* **tendency, trend**

triple, treble
Meaning threefold, both are interchangeable except in the terms **treble clef** (in music) and **treble chance** (football pools); and **triple jump** (the hop, step and jump event in athletics).

triumphal, triumphant
Triumphal means 'celebrating a triumph or victory'; **triumphant** means 'victorious or successful, and rejoicing in the glory': *The team returned home, tired, drunk and triumphant.*

troop, troupe
Riverdance – the dance troop that took the Eurovision Song Contest by storm – is now beset with ego clashes and petty squabbles (*The Sunday Times*). A **troop** is a large assembly or a flock but more usually a military formation, hence **troops**. What the writer intended was **troupe**: a group or company of performers.

true facts *see* **facts, true facts, factitious**

truism, truth
A **truism** is not something that is merely true but a glaring self-evident truth, often expressed as a platitude: *Every man was once a boy*. See also **veracity, truth**.

T-shirt *see* **sweater, jersey, jumper, pullover, etc.**

turbid, turgid
Turbid means 'clouded, muddy, opaque', turgid means 'swollen, bloated, inflated'. A river in flood can be both turbid and turgid.

type *see* **kind, kind of, sort of, type of**

typhoon *see* **cyclone, hurricane, tornado, typhoon, waterspout**

tyro *see* **amateur, novice, tyro**

U and non-U

In Britain, **U** means 'upper class' or associated with it, while **non-U** means not upper-class. The terms are not creations of Nancy Mitford as is popularly supposed, but of the linguist Professor Alan Rose who first used them in *Neuphilologische Mitteilungen*, a Finnish-language journal.

Ulster *see* Ireland, Eire, Ulster, Irish Republic

umpire, referee

Both undertake the same duties (conducting a game according to the rules) but attend different games: **umpire** for tennis, hockey, cricket and baseball; **referee** for football, ice hockey, rugby and boxing.

unable *see* incapable, unable

unaware, unawares

Lookalikes but actually two different words and meanings. If you are **unaware** (adjective), you are not aware or you are ignorant of something (*Betty was unaware of the danger*); if you are caught **unawares** (adverb), something has happened without warning and you are surprised: *Betty was caught unawares in her nightgown*.

unclear *see* apparent, evident

unconscious *see* subconscious, unconscious

under *see* beneath, below, under, over

undergraduate *see* graduate, undergraduate, postgraduate

underlay, underlie

To **underlay** is to place something beneath or to support something from beneath – think of carpet underlay. To **underlie** means 'to lie under something or to act as a foundation': *Deep and complex analysis underlies the champion's every move*.

understand, appreciate, comprehend

I appreciate the reasons for your refusal demonstrates the questionable use of **appreciate** as a substitute for **understand**; **appreciate** really means 'to feel grateful or thankful'. **Comprehend** is a synonym for **understand** but with the inference of 'complete understanding': *Joe eventually comprehended my warning*.

undoubtedly *see* doubtless, undoubtedly

unexceptional, unexceptionable

Something **unexceptional** is normal, ordinary or commonplace; something **unexceptionable** is beyond criticism or objection: *He remarked that the jury's verdict might seem severe in some respects but was generally unexceptionable*.

uninterested *see* **disinterested, uninterested**

United Kingdom *see* **Britain**

universal
An obituary in the *Arundel and Brighton News* began: 'Father Gerry', *as he was universally known in the Reigate and Red Hill area* . . . Unfortunately, Father Gerry's fame was rather more suburban than universal, the meaning of **universal** being 'typical of the whole of humankind . . . existing or prevailing everywhere' or 'unlimited'. Better choices for the obituarist would have been *always, generally, invariably*, etc.

unless *see* **except, unless**

unreadable *see* **illegible, unreadable**

unrepairable *see* **irreparable, unrepairable**

unsatisfied *see* **dissatisfied, unsatisfied**

until *see* **till, until**

unwanted, unwonted
Unwanted means 'not wanted': *The last thing she intended was to make the child feel unwanted*. **Unwonted** means 'unusual, out of the ordinary': *She was fascinated by him and followed his every move with unwonted curiosity*.

upon, on
With a couple of exceptions, **upon** and **on** are interchangeable: *She sat on/upon the chair*. However you would hardly begin a fairy story by intoning, *Once on [upon] a time*; nor does the ear respond favourably to *The suburbs stretched for mile on [upon] mile* . . .

upper circle *see* **balcony, circle, dress circle, gallery, stalls**

upshot, result
The two are synonymous except that **upshot** can suggest a 'surprise, final result': *After all the arguments and appeals the upshot was that they awarded Abbot the gold medal*.

upsurge, surge
To **surge** is to swell, bulge, well up, gush, rush, heave or flow (or in any combination of these): *The increasingly uncontrollable crowd surged towards the exits*. **Upsurge** suggests a rising or increasing surge: *The police attributed the upsurge of violence to the growing presence of drug dealers on the estate*.

upward, upwards
Upward is an adjective (*upward mobility, an upward slope*), and while it is also an adverb the alternative, **upwards**, is preferred in this role: *They climbed upwards for what seemed like an eternity*.

urban, urbane

Urban refers to the city, as in *urban living, urban architecture*; **urbane** means 'poised and sophisticated: *Ten years of urban life had transformed the country boy into a witty, urbane gentleman.*

use, utilise, usage

Use is synonymous with the other two words in most cases and should be preferred. **Utilise** (or **utilize**) also has the narrower meaning of 'making useful or turning to profitable account': *The company utilised the old factory to manufacture office furniture.* **Usage** – especially in the context of the English language – is the recognised practice of something: *The Professor was an expert in English usage; Such old usages are now forgotten.* It is also applied where quantities are involved: *Domestic water usage in Kent rose 30 per cent last month.*

usually *see* commonly, customarily, frequently, generally, habitually, ordinarily, usually

vacant, vacuous

Vacant means 'empty or unoccupied'; **vacuous** means not only 'empty' but 'blank, bereft and mindless': *The stranger unsettled everyone with his vacuous stare.*

vacate *see* evacuate, vacate

vacation, holiday

In British English a **vacation** is a **holiday**; in American English a long holiday break is known as a **vacation** and one-day breaks (Thanksgiving, Labor Day, etc) are called **holidays**.

vaccinate *see* inoculate, vaccinate

valuable, invaluable, valued

Valuable means 'having great value, or being worth a lot of money'. **Invaluable** means 'priceless, precious beyond valuation': *Her friendship at this difficult time was invaluable to him.* Apart from its use in contexts such as *I'm going to have my watch valued*, **valued** means 'esteemed and highly regarded': *Of all the things David valued, her friendship was paramount. See also* **invaluable, inestimable**.

venal, venial

To be **venal** is to act dishonestly and to be readily and easily corrupted and bribed. **Venial** also comes from the Latin and means 'pardonable' – as of a wrongdoing that is of a minor nature and is of little or no consequence.

vendetta, feud

A **feud** is a dispute or quarrel between two people, families or groups. It can be bitter and prolonged and even involve killing, when it is called a **blood feud**. Or it can merely amount to competitive rivalry: *The two newspapers were always feuding over their distribution areas.* A **vendetta** (from the Italian, meaning 'to avenge') is a rather more serious conflict, usually involving one family (typically Sicilian or Corsican) against another, and revenge killings.

vengeance *see* **revenge, avenge, vengeance**

veracious, voracious
Veracious means 'habitually truthful and careful with facts'; **voracious** means 'greedy, rapacious, insatiable'.

veracity, truth
Truth is something that is true, that is fact. **Veracity** is the capacity for being truthful, accurate and honest: *We can depend upon his admirable veracity for the truth to come out.*

verbal *see* **oral, aural, verbal**

via
It is fairly common to see **via** used like this: *They travelled from Victoria to Tower Hill via the Underground.* Purists prefer to see the use of **via** restricted to mean 'by way of' and not 'by means of': *They travelled on the Underground to Tower Hill from Victoria via the Embankment.*

viable, workable
The true meaning of **viable** (from the Latin *vita* = 'life') is 'the capability to maintain independent existence in life'. The word has, however, become an overworked and inaccurately used buzzword, to the extent that a doctor once claimed, *'Suicide is a viable alternative to painful terminal illness'.* Try to limit its use to mean 'capable of surviving and thriving independently': *The Channel Tunnel is expected to be operationally viable by the year 2010.* **Workable** means 'something or some plan that is practicable and can be made to work'. See **practical, practicable**; also **possible, plausible, feasible**.

vicious, viscous
Vicious implies a propensity for vice, hatred, spite and violence; **viscous** means 'thick and sticky', and is usually used to describe liquids.

viewpoint *see* **standpoint, point of view, viewpoint**

village *see* **city, town, village, hamlet**

virtually *see* **actually, virtually, really**; also **effectively, in effect**; also **practically, virtually**

virus *see* **bacteria, virus, bug**

visible, visual
Visible means 'capable of being seen'; **visual** relates to anything involving the sense of sight: *visual arts, visual aids, visually handicapped, VDU (visual display unit),* etc.

vocal cords

They are not chords, the musical notes, but vocal *cords* – the vibrating folds at the back of the larynx.

vocation, avocation

Although these are increasingly regarded as synonyms, they are not, and it is worthwhile preserving their separate meanings. A **vocation** is a person's regular occupation, profession or trade; an **avocation** is a diversion from a person's regular employment – a hobby or part-time job.

vomit *see* sick, sickly, ill

voodoo, hoodoo

Voodoo is a Caribbean variety of witchcraft; a **hoodoo** is something or someone that brings bad luck: *After crashing his car, breaking an ankle and losing his girlfriend, all in one week, Peter was convinced he was the victim of a hoodoo.*

voracious *see* veracious, voracious

wages *see* salary, wages, renumeration

wait *see* await, wait

waive, wave

These two are often confused. Waive means 'to relinquish, not to insist upon something': The accused man waived his legal right to speak.

want *see* desire, want, need

warranty *see* guarantee, warranty

wary, chary

There's not much between these although some writers discern a shade of difference: **wary** = 'watchful and wily'; **chary** = 'careful and choosy': *In her old age Ethel had become very chary of her friends.*

was *see* were, was

waste, wastage

Waste is the wanton, careless or useless squandering of resources, money or time. **Wastage** is accidental or unavoidable loss through evaporation, leakage, wear or decay. The term **natural wastage** is sometimes euphemistically applied when a workforce is reduced in size by voluntary resignation, retirement, etc.

waterspout *see* cyclone, hurricane, tornado, typhoon, waterspout

wave *see* waive, wave

way, weigh
When a ship **weighs** anchor, it then gets under **way**.

weep, cry
It used to be maintained that children cried and adults wept, but this hardly applies today as the two are almost synonymous. **Weeping**, however, suggests a deeper grief and sometimes bitterness. Mourners, for example, weep rather than cry, while a child who scratches a knee will cry – often loudly and tearfully.

well *see* **good, well**

were, was
The use of **were** / **was** in sentences describing a hypothetical situation often causes hesitation: *He acted as though he were one of Bill's friends* is grammatically and stylistically correct; the informal alternative, *He acted as though he was one of Bill's friends* sounds decidedly dodgy, but many people would still use **was** rather than **were** in such instances. Remove the hypothetical situation and **was** is correct: *The man told us he was one of Bill's friends.*

wet, whet
Wet means 'moistened, covered or saturated with water or a liquid'; **whet** means 'to sharpen': *He whetted the knifeblade on the grindstone; The smell of cooking whetted their appetites.*

whatever, what ever, whatsoever
What ever is that funny thing over there? and *Whatever you do, don't miss the movie on Channel Five tonight* are two examples of legitimate usage of **what ever** and **whatever**. **Whatever** means 'no matter what' (*Whatever the problems, I promise to finish the job*). **What ever** is used as an interrogative: *What ever is the matter with you?* **Whatsoever** is vaguely synonymous in the context of 'at all': *Have you no manners whatsoever?* But the usage that has grown into a monster has resulted from the hijacking of **whatever** to mean 'and so on and so forth and who cares anyway?': *On Sundays I usually do some shopping, wash my hair, empty the cat litter, generally slob around and, you know, whatever. . .*

whence *see* **hence, thence, whence**

whet *see* **wet, whet**

whether *see* **if, whether**

while, a while, awhile, whilst
While is a notoriously ambiguous word. In its sense of 'at the same time', there is little confusion (*You can talk to me while I iron these shirts*) but watch out for ambiguity when the meaning is 'whereas, although or but': *My wife likes a good laugh, while I watch the news; While he sleeps like a log, I like to party all night; James spent his childhood in Devon, while his parents grew up in Scotland.* **A while** is the

noun and this can be tricky, too. Make sure you indicate whether it is a **long while** or a **short while**. *We only waited for a while* implies a short time and *We waited for quite a while* indicates a longer time, but both are imprecise. **Awhile** is the adverb, which means 'a short while': *We waited awhile*. **Whilst** is an old-fashioned form of *while* and ought to be avoided.

whisky, whiskey
Traditionally, **whisky** is produced in Scotland (*Scotch whisky*), whereas **whiskey** is the equivalent Irish, American and Canadian liquor.

white paper, green paper
A **white paper** is a published report that states the [British] Government's policy on legislation that will come before Parliament. A **green paper** sets out proposals for legislation for discussion and comment by interested parties.

whoever, who ever
Whoever you are, you are not welcome uses **whoever** in its correct sense of 'no matter who you are'. The two-word version is used when **ever** is used for emphasis and usually in the interrogative: *Who ever could have done this?*

whose, who's
Whose always relates to possession; it can ask, for example, *Whose book is this?* or it can act as a relative pronoun: *That's the man whose car was stolen*. **Who's** is an abbreviation of **who is** or **who has**: *Who's [who is] knocking at the door?*; *Who's [who has] been using my paint brushes?*

woman *see* lady, woman

wont, won't
Won't is a contraction of 'will not': *Young Tom simply won't do as he's told*. If you omit the apostrophe you have **wont**, either as an adjective meaning 'accustomed' (*He was wont to break into song after his fourth pint*) or as a noun meaning 'habit': *After lunch she read, pottered in the garden or dozed as was her wont*.

workable *see* viable, workable

worthwhile, worth while
Worth while is almost always a redundancy: *Marcus said that the concert was worth while going to*. If you drop the 'while' there is no loss of meaning, so drop it: *Marcus said that the concert was worth going to*. **Worthwhile** is an adjective meaning 'sufficiently rewarding or important': *They all agreed it was a worthwhile concert*.

wrack, rack
'*Wracked on the wheel of growth*' is a classic (and common) mistake. **Wrack** has the following meanings: 1. seaweed or other floating vegetation 2. wreck or piece of wreckage. **Rack**, on the other hand, has a plethora of meanings, not one of them

having anything to do with seaweed or wreckage: a frame or framework for storing objects; an instrument of torture; mental or bodily stress; a snooker triangle for holding the balls; to rack a bottle of wine; to rack one's brain, and a dozen or so more.

wrapped *see* rapt, wrapped, rapped

wreath, wraith
A **wreath** is a circular band of flowers offered as a memorial at funerals; a **wraith** is a ghost or apparition.

Yiddish *see* Jewish, Jew, Hebrew, Yiddish

yoke, yolk
Both are pronounced the same and there is occasional confusion. The **yolk** is the yellow part of an egg; a **yoke** is traditionally the collar and bar worn by oxen but is now mostly used figuratively: *The peasants had suffered under the yoke for too long and were ready to revolt.*

you (*the reader*) and one
The use of the pronoun **one** to represent an indefinite person (*One doesn't do that kind of thing*) is stylish and elegant but can be regarded as affected. **You** is the democratic substitute and has the additional advantage of informally but directly addressing the reader: *You simply don't do that kind of thing.* Choose one or the other but don't mix them in mid-sentence as in this example: *Soon one phones one's publisher to see if one's year of birth can be removed from the [dust] jacket. Presumably, as one gets older, one gets asked instead whether the reason no one will touch you with a bargepole is because you keep writing books detailing the foul personal habits of your former boyfriends* (novelist Rachel Cusk in *The Times*).

your, yours, you're
Your means 'belonging to you or belonging to an unspecified person': *I love your house. Is this your own house? Is that your opinion?* **Yours** identifies a particular entity belonging to you: *Is this jacket yours? That son of yours is a real tearaway.* It is never spelt with an apostrophe. **You're** is frequently confused with **your**, but it is a contraction of **you are**: *You're [you are] all quite mad!*

Yours faithfully, Yours sincerely, Yours truly
Yours does not have an apostrophe. **Yours faithfully** is the traditional formal closing at the end of, say, business communications or letters to strangers, while **Yours sincerely** has been preferred when the writer is addressing a named or known person. Now the difference is smudged. If you want to indicate a degree of friendliness or closeness, use *sincerely* or *truly* or some other variation. **Yours aye** is a charming Scottish sign-off.

5

EXPANDING YOUR VOCABULARY

A-Z Series of Tests

To widen your word use, plus clues to meaning, recognising word elements

A

Choose the Correct Meaning

Which one of the three alternatives, **a**, **b** or **c**, most accurately fits the meaning of the word? Circle your choices (while trying not to make wild guesses!) and then check the answers on page 436.

aberration	**a.** excessive sneezing; **b.** a departure from the normal; **c.** airline navigators' allowance for polar magnetism.
abeyance	**a.** a state of being suspended; **b.** the Muslim law of parental respect; **c.** humiliation.
abnegation	**a.** to be resigned to one's fate; **b.** to renounce upon oath; **c.** renouncing or denying oneself a privilege.
abrogate	**a.** to coarsely insult someone; **b.** to formally revoke or abolish; **c.** to condense or abridge a text.
abstruse	**a.** to be argumentative; **b.** hard to understand; **c.** hopeless.
accede	**a.** to agree; **b.** to abandon; **c.** the steepest part of a slope.
accolade	**a.** a meritorious award; **b.** the plumage on a governor's ceremonial headgear; **c.** a fizzy yoghurt-style drink.
accrue	**a.** to turn sour; **b.** to attack bitterly; **c.** to increase by addition or growth.
accretion	**a.** to increase by external growth; **b.** the components of concrete; **c.** residue left by high tides.
Achilles heel	**a.** an athlete's complaint; **b.** fashionable shoes by a Greek designer; **c.** a vulnerable spot.
acolyte	**a.** a devoted attendant; **b.** an ancient Egyptian hand-held oil lamp; **c.** a pinkish gemstone.
acquiesce	**a.** a wine-making process reducing sweetness; **b.** to agree without protest; **c.** to motivate unconsciously.
acrid	**a.** a bluish hair colouring; **b.** excessively solemn; **c.** unpleasant pungent smell.

acrimonious   **a.** caustic or bitter in manner; **b.** inclined to drunkenness; **c.** following bad advice.

actuary   **a.** a hospital volunteer helper; **b.** part of a library where religious books are kept; **c.** an insurance statistician.

acuity   **a.** keenness or sharpness in thinking; **b.** brilliance with maths and numbers; **c.** the pain experienced by gout sufferers.

acumen   **a.** a pepper-like substance from South America; **b.** penetrating insight; **c.** the ability to tolerate giddy heights.

adamant   **a.** easily adaptable; **b.** hard and inflexible; **c.** ant-like.

ad hoc   **a.** for a particular purpose; **b.** very occasionally; **c.** a last-minute invitation.

adjunct   **a.** a fracture of the wrist; **b.** something incidental or not essential added to something else; **c.** a cancelled advertisement.

adroit   **a.** left-handed; **b.** very skilful; **c.** easily manipulated.

adventitious   **a.** appearing accidentally or unexpectedly; **b.** prone to take extreme risks; **c.** reluctance to take risks.

aegis   **a.** the provision of protection or sponsorship; **b.** the overuse of commas and other punctuation marks; **c.** racial harmony.

affidavit   **a.** a solicitor's instruction; **b.** a written statement made on oath; **c.** a judge's direction to the jury.

aficionado   **a.** the sword thrust that kills in a bullfight; **b.** a large wine barrel for aging sherry; **c.** a keen devotee or follower.

aggrandise   **a.** to withhold information from an official enquiry; **b.** to increase one's wealth or power; **c.** to marry late in life.

agnostic   **a.** a religious hermit; **b.** a severe sinus irritation; **c.** someone who holds that knowledge of the existence of God is impossible.

agronomy   **a.** the study of grasses; **b.** the study of river pollution; **c.** the study of soil and cultivation.

akimbo   **a.** sitting with legs crossed; **b.** standing with hands on hips, elbows pointing away; **c.** standing with legs wide apart.

alacrity   **a.** liveliness and cheerful briskness; **b.** withdrawn and uncommunicative; **c.** argumentative.

alfresco   **a.** famous New York salad containing walnuts; **b.** a refreshing wine-based drink; **c.** in the open air.

allude   **a.** a composition for the harp; **b.** to refer to something indirectly; **c.** the first stage of drug rehabilitation.

alter ego   **a.** a mind-bending drug; **b.** one's other or second self; **c.** an overwhelming desire to be someone else.

altruism   **a.** unselfish concern for and generosity towards others; **b.** in horses a tendency to lameness; **c.** an inability to form conclusions from overwhelming evidence.

amalgam   **a.** a compound of different metals; **b.** ash left from burnt ivory; **c.** fool's gold.

amanuensis   **a.** a nurse specialising in tubercular care; **b.** a secretary; **c.** a sewing machine attachment that makes buttonholes.

Altruism (c)

ambidextrous   a. the ability to juggle with hands and feet; b. the ability to jump long distances; c. the ability to use both hands with equal facility.

ambience   a. the glow from a fire; b. the natural warmth of a human body; c. the feeling or atmosphere of a place.

ambivalent   a. not complete; b. exhibiting conflicting or contradictory attitudes; c. inability to walk although physically capable.

ameliorate   a. to blend oil and water; b. to improve or make better; c. to initiate a person into a religious order.

amenable   a. open to suggestion; b. easily succumbing to temptation; c. keen to apologise, even when unnecessary.

amoral   a. overly prone to sexual excitation; b. lacking normal moral standards; c. sleeping with two partners simultaneously.

amortise   a. to reduce or pay off a debt; b. to fix two pieces of wood together without nails or screws; c. to die leaving two or more wills.

anachronism   a. type of lobster; b. passion for collecting old clocks; c. a person or event misplaced in time.

analgesic   a. a non-mercuric dental filling; b. a substance that reduces pain; c. a family of drugs that reduces inflammation.

analogous   a. capable of being analysed; b. similar in some respect; c. a process for waterproofing leather.

anathema   a. something detested; b. a love-hate relationship; c. a diagnostic technique for lung diseases.

ancillary   a. doubtful in meaning; b. shapeless; c. subsidiary.

angst   a. fleeting mental instability; b. an unfounded sense of anxiety or remorse; c. obsessional need to seek revenge.

annuity   a. the period between Christmas and New Year; b. a stipend paid each year to Church of England vicars; c. a fixed sum paid annually.

If, after checking the answers, you find that you failed to identify the correct meanings of all these 50 words beginning with A, you'll find it worthwhile revisiting those that caused you to stumble and to commit them to memory. If you scored 40 correct you did well – and in the process you will add a further 10 words to your growing vocabulary. Now for another 50 A words . . .

Identify the Word

From the meanings given, fill in the gaps and identify the words:

1. To abolish, or cancel the validity of something   *a _ _ u l*
2. Deviating from the norm or usual   *ano _al _us*
3. Obsessional fear of becoming fat by refusing food   *a _ _ r _ xia*
4. A collection of literary works, excerpts or passages   *anth _ _ _ gy*
5. A course of hors d'oeuvres in an Italian meal   *an _ ip _ sto*
6. A feeling of intense dislike or hatred   *ant _ pa _ _ y*
7. Something that's the exact opposite   *ant _ th_ s _ s*
8. A word that means the opposite of another word   *an _ o _ ym*
9. A laxative   *aper _ _ nt*
10. A short pithy saying expressing a general truth   *aph _ r _ sm*
11. Someone who keeps bees   *api _ _ ian*
12. Extreme self-confidence or self-possession   *ap _ _ mb*
13. A prophetic revelation or disclosure   *apo _ _ lyp _ e*
14. Of questionable authenticity   *apo _ _ _ phal*
15. The highest point   *ap _ _ ee*
16. Abandonment of one's faith or religion   *ap _ sta _ y*
17. A short cryptic remark containing an accepted truth   *apo _ _ egm*
18. The elevation of a person to the status of a god   *ap _ theo _ _ s*
19. Ideally suited for the purpose   *app _ _ ite*
20. Praise and commendation   *app _ _ bation*
21. A less significant part or thing   *app _ _ ten _ nce*
22. Appropriate or pertinent   *apr _ _ os*
23. The domed or vaulted recess at one end of a church   *a _ se*
24. Having the curved shape of an eagle's beak   *aq _ _ line*
25. Describing land capable of being cultivated for crops   *ar _ _ le*
26. The scientific group name for spiders   *ar _ ch _ id*
27. Subject to personal whims and prejudices   *arb _ _ r _ ry*
28. Requiring secret knowledge to be understood   *a _ cane*
29. The jargon peculiar to a group, often thieves   *a _ _ ot*
30. A catastrophic conflict; a war to end all wars   *Arma _ _ ddon*
31. A large French-style chest or cabinet   *ar _ _ ire*
32. To bring a prisoner before a court to answer an indictment   *ar _ a _ gn*
33. Someone unscrupulously ambitious   *arr _ vi _ te*
34. Someone who abstains from worldly pleasures   *as _ _ tic*

35. Acting obstinately or stupidly	*as _ _ine*
36. A malicious or disparaging remark	*as _ _ r _ ion*
37. A sharp temper	*asp _ r _ ty*
38. Persevering and hard-working	*ass _ _ uous*
39. To soothe and relieve pain or grief	*ass _ _ ge*
40. The wasting away of part of the body	*atro _ h _*
41. To extend and make thin, or to weaken	*att _ _ u _ te*
42. Wearing away to weaken or destroy	*att _ i _ ion*
43. Not conforming to type; not typical	*at _ _ i _ al*
44. In touch and fully informed	*au f _ _ t*
45. Describing a situation that's favourable	*aus _ _ c _ ous*
46. Independent of others	*auton _ _ ous*
47. A person's job or career	*a _ oc _ tion*
48. Resembling or concerning a helpful uncle	*av _ _ cular*
49. Askew or twisted	*aw _ y*
50. Self-evident; aphoristic	*ax _ _ m _ tic*

A few spaces unfilled? With the aid of the answers on pages 436, fill in the gaps and your knowledge at the same time. If you scored 35 or more, well done.

Clues to Meaning: Recognising Word Elements

A vast number of English words have been built from Greek and Latin roots and other elements: prefixes, suffixes and combining forms. Recognising these can provide instant clues to the meanings of thousands of otherwise unfamiliar words. Here is a selection of A words.

Word, Element	Origin	Meaning	English words
amor, am, amat	Latin	love	*amour, amorous, enamoured, amicable*
annus, annu, enni	Latin	year	*annual, annuity, annals, perennial*
audire, audi, audit	Latin	to hear	*audio, audible, audience, audition, audit, auditor, auditorium, auditory*
arkhaio, archae	Greek	beginning	*archaeology, archaic, archaism, Archaeozoic*
autos, aut, auto	Greek	self	*autobiography, autograph, autocrat, autocracy, autologous*
ante-	Latin	before	*antecedent, antechamber, antedate, antebellum, antenatal, antediluvian, anterior, ante (stake)*
-able, -ible	Latin	capable of suitable for	*watchable, eatable forcible, edible, payable*

A Little Light Revision

No doubt by now you've had your fill of A words. But before we leave them, how sure are you that your vocabulary's digestive system is in good working order? Hand on heart, do you remember the meanings of these words?

acolyte, ad hoc, adventitious, angst, approbation, avuncular, asinine, adamant, agnostic, anathema.

B

Right or Wrong?

Knowing the meanings of a lot of words can be very useful. But knowing how to use words in their proper context, expressively and precisely, can be even more rewarding and profitable. Here's an exercise to test your knowledge of certain words.

Are they being used correctly? Answer right/wrong and then check the answers on page 436.

		Right	**Wrong**
1.	The rave ended on a distinct *bacchanalian* note, for those who could remember the next morning.	___	___
2.	Senior surgical nurses had to undergo a stiff examination in *badinage* before graduating.	___	___
3.	For Rockefeller, the $16 million donation was a mere *bagatelle*.	___	___
4.	The giant fixed a *baleful* eye on the two children.	___	___
5.	They leaned on the *balustrade*, watching the crowd beneath.	___	___
6.	In his finest ceremonial robes the chief led the solemn *banal* to the sacrificial temple.	___	___
7.	The *barmitzvah* holiday is the one enjoyed most by Jews.	___	___
8.	Kitty's designs exhibited all the extravagance of the *baroque*.	___	___
9.	The director's interpretation of *Uncle Tom's Cabin* was spoiled by the *bathos* of the final scene.	___	___
10.	The rustlers rode cautiously through the parched *bayou*.	___	___

		Right	**Wrong**
11.	Edith returned from her visit to the cathedral in a state of *beatitude*.	——	——
12.	The *behemoth* spread her pretty wings and flew from his hand.	——	——
13.	They listened in silence as the church team rang the *bel canto*.	——	——
14.	The document *belied* the sister's claim to the estate.	——	——
15.	The red-faced driver assumed a *bellicose* manner and refused to allow them on the bus.	——	——
16.	They decided to sail, as the *bellwether* indicated good conditions.	——	——
17.	The comedian from Manchester left them *bemused* and rolling in the aisles.	——	——
18.	Mr and Mrs Drayton were the most gentle and *benign* couple you could ever hope to meet.	——	——
19.	Left mostly to themselves in the decrepit orphanage, the children were *bereft* of all hope.	——	——
20.	The factory was immensely profitable, turning out millions of *bespoke* garments every month.	——	——

You've made 20 choices, but are you absolutely sure about all of them? You'll find the correct meanings of those words used incorrectly in this exercise on page 436. If you are in doubt about any of the others, be smart and look them up in your dictionary.

Choose the Correct Meaning

Which of the alternatives, **a** or **b**, most accurately defines the meaning of the word? Circle your choices (wild guesses should count as a blank!) and then check your answers on page 437.

bête noire	**a.** a liquorice-based sweetmeat from southern France; **b.** someone or something regarded with fear and loathing.
bibelot	**a.** a trinket; **b.** a French sailor.
biennial	**a.** twice a year; **b.** every two years.
bifurcate	**a.** to fork or divide into two parts or branches; **b.** to make an iron bar with two flat, parallel surfaces.
bijou	**a.** an object that is small and elegant; **b.** a style of two-piece swimsuit fashionable in the 1960s.
bilateral	**a.** an underground stream that surfaces as a spring; **b.** involving two sides or parties.
billabong	**a.** An Australian bushman's cooking gear; **b.** a branch of a river that forms a separate lagoon or pool.
billet-doux	**a.** a love letter; **b.** a small Parisian apartment for two.

binary **a.** a mathematical system based on two numbers; **b.** a machine that renders corn into flakes.

biodegradable **a.** describing the breakdown of biological mechanisms in the human body; **b.** capable of being decomposed by bacteria.

biopsy **a.** a state of giddiness and nausea caused by sudden change of temperature; **b.** removal of tissue from a body for examination.

bisque **a.** a French game played on a court with rope rings; **b.** a soup made from crustaceans and shellfish.

Black Maria **a.** a police van for transporting prisoners; **b.** a type of highly destructive typhoon generated in the Caribbean.

blag **a.** to wheedle or con a favour or advantage from someone; **b.** to boast, especially about one's sexual prowess.

blandishments **a.** violent threats; **b.** flattery intended to acquire something.

blasé **a.** the glaze on fine porcelain; **b.** indifferent and bored.

blench **a.** to flinch or shrink back; **b.** to feel suddenly ill.

blithe **a.** outwardly friendly, but with the purpose of cheating; **b.** casual, happy and cheerful.

bombastic **a.** using pompous, boastful language; **b.** using sarcastic, hurtful language.

Bombay duck **a.** Indian duck dish reputed to generate enormous amounts of wind; **b.** Indian fish curry dish.

bona fide **a.** real or genuine; **b.** the law governing sworn oaths in court.

bonhomie **a.** contents of Christmas crackers; **b.** exuberant friendliness.

bon vivant **a.** have a pleasant voyage; **b.** one who loves food and drink.

boondocks **a.** remote rural areas; **b.** deserted, former wharves.

boreal **a.** an evening sky flushed with red; **b.** relating to the north.

bourgeois **a.** middle-class; **b.** radical working class.

bowdlerise **a.** to cut words and passages from a book on prudish grounds; **b.** to force women to cover their legs and ankles.

boycott **a.** a handkerchief with knotted corners used as a makeshift head covering for sun protection; **b.** to protest by refusing to deal with or buy from a person or organisation.

braggadocio **a.** bragging and boasting; **b.** an Italian veal and onion dish.

braise **a.** to cook lightly in a closed pan; **b.** a bruise caused by subcutaneous inflammation.

brasserie **a.** a bar serving drinks and cheap food; **b.** a foundry specialising in making pewter and brassware.

bravura **a.** the automatic cry from a Spanish crowd after the killing of a bull in the ring; **b.** a display of artistic boldness and brilliance.

breccia **a.** a style of mosaic with blue shades predominating; **b.** a rock with angular fragments embedded in it.

breviary **a.** the closed-off part of some churches devoted to reverence for royalty; **b.** a book of psalms, hymns and prayers.

bric-a-brac	**a.** small collectable objects and curios; **b.** discarded half-bricks.
brioche	**a.** a woman's hairstyle with a bun; **b.** a light yeasty roll or loaf.
Brobdingnagian	**a.** huge; **b.** tiny.
brouhaha	**a.** a commotion or uproar; **b.** the fancy decoration on a gable.
brusque	**a.** blunt or abrupt in manner or speech; **b.** a ballet movement in which the male dancer spins his female partner.
bucolic	**a.** a viral disease in cattle; **b.** relating to the countryside.
bulimia	**a.** chronic boils on the neck; **b.** compulsive over-eating followed by self-induced vomiting.
bumptious	**a.** extremely clumsy; **b.** unpleasantly self-assertive.
bum steer	**a.** misleading information; **b.** a deformed male calf.
burgeoning	**a.** vigorously sprouting and growing; **b.** overflowing.
burgher	**a.** an upright, respectable citizen; **b.** a disgraced parson.
burlap	**a.** a prickly bush, originally from South Africa; **b.** a coarse canvas or sacking.
burnish	**a.** to polish and make smooth and shiny; **b.** a deep gold colour that displays iridescence in certain light.
buttress	**a.** a wooden press that squeezes whey from curds in butter-making; **b.** a construction that supports a masonry wall.
Byronic	**a.** romantically melancholic; **b.** the birth defect of a shrunken foot, after Lord Byron's disability.
Byzantine	**a.** inflexible, complex and baffling; **b.** uniquely bizarre.

If, after checking the answers on page 437 you find you've scored 40 correct, then you've done well. Those you missed out on are worth checking, too, in your dictionary, and committing to memory.

A Spot of Revision

Revision is a chore, but it's really worthwhile checking to see if you've absorbed and can remember the majority of the B words you've learned. Can you correctly define the following:

baroque, bemused, biopsy, bulimia, burgeoning, bucolic, behemoth, biennial, bonhomie, brouhaha.

C

What's the Appropriate Word?

From the description given in brackets, substitute the appropriate word in each sentence. For example, in the sentence *The intention of the [group of plotters] was to bring down the government*, the word that fits the description closest is *cabal*. Although some might claim that *gang* is just as good a fit, the smarter among you will realise that *gang* doesn't begin with *c* and therefore won't score. Answers on page 437.

1. They both admired the 18th-century chair with the [*gracefully curved and tapering*] legs.
2. Mark was delighted when he came across the [*hidden store*] of ancient coins.
3. She did everything to [*wheedle or persuade by flattery*] him into buying her the oriental carpet she coveted.
4. Apart from the strict diet, he also embarked on a course of [*light exercises designed to promote fitness, strength and beauty*].
5. The poor professor was a victim of [*malicious and defamatory utterance of false statements*] put about by his departmental enemies.
6. It was delightful to observe the [*spirit of familiarity and loyalty between friends*] among the new officers.
7. In Venice they managed to climb the 275 steps to the top of the [*bell tower*].
8. The village church was noted for its excellent training in [*the art of bell ringing*].
9. Dr Phillips energetically refuted the [*rumour or false report*] that he had faked his medical credentials.
10. Although the board was deeply disappointed by his financial report, they all thanked him for his [*honesty, openness and frankness*].
11. Now in his late 70s, Mr Needham was a kindly, incredibly knowledgeable but [*irascible, disagreeable and crotchety*] old man.
12. Priscilla hated walking in the city on the grounds that the traffic fumes were [*liable to produce cancer*].
13. The selectors believed that the inclusion of a spin bowler in the team was of [*fundamental, principal, prime*] importance.
14. The company decided to give their chief executive [*complete discretion and authority*] in the forthcoming merger negotiations.
15. The Consumer Council accused the oil companies of operating a [*collusive association intended to monopolise distribution and pricing*].
16. The house was rather pretentious, with a [*having battlements, like a castle*] facade and a fake turret.
17. Jeremy felt outraged at being [*severely rebuked and criticised*] by Mr Peters in front of all the staff.
18. Annabel's presence no doubt acted as a [*a substance, object or person that causes change*] in the love affair between Joe and Margaret.
19. The young man's confessions obviously acted as a much needed [*the bringing of repressed and buried experiences into consciousness*].
20. The injured driver was tethered to his bed by a mass of drip tubes and a [*tube inserted into the bladder for draining fluid*].

There are no apologies for the aforegoing 20 vocabulary posers. They are designed to make you think a little harder about words and their meanings, and to enhance their memorability. A score of 10 or more is passable; 15 or more correct is excellent. But the point of the exercise is to cement 20 useful words into your vocabulary.

Complete the Word

From the meanings given, fill in the missing letters to complete the words.

1. Universal, liberal, all-inclusive — *cath _ _ ic*
2. A closed meeting or committee of members of a political party — *c _ _ cus*
3. To carp and quibble and raise petty objections — *ca _ il*
4. Involving intelligence rather than emotions or instinct. — *cereb _ _ l*
5. Ceasing or stopping — *ce _ _ ation*
6. The area around the altar of a church reserved for theclergy — *chan _ _ l*
7. Having exceptional personal qualities and power to influence and inspire many others — *char _ _ matic*
8. A person falsely claiming to have knowledge and expertise — *charl _ tan*
9. Smug, aggressive belief in the superiority of one's country, sex, race or cause — *ch _ _ vinism*
10. Dishonest or sharp practice — *chican _ _ y*
11. A sideboard, often with shelves and mirror above — *chi _ _ onier*
12. An imagined monster or horror — *c _ imera*
13. Bad-tempered, irascible, touchy — *ch _ leric*
14. Audacity and impudence (from the Yiddish) — *chut _ pah*
15. A serious movie enthusiast — *cin _ aste*
16. Prudent, cautious, discreet — *c _ _ cumspect*
17. To outwit, evade or bypass — *circum _ _ nt*
18. Furtive, secretive, concealed — *clandest _ _ e*
19. A team of people hired to applaud a performance — *cla _ ue*
20. Weather that's mild and gentle — *clem _ _ t*
21. Causing or involving a climax — *clim _ _ tic*
22. To merge, blend, come together in one body or mass — *c _ _ lesce*
23. An addition revoking or modifying a will — *c _ dicil*
24. To compel or restrain, disregarding individual wishes or rights — *co _ rce*
25. Forcefully convincing, authoritative, to the point. — *cog _ _ t*
26. Connoisseurs with informed appreciation of the fine arts — *c _ _ noscenti*
27. Security pledged for the repayment of a loan — *coll _ _ eral*

28.	Describing informal speech or vocabulary	*collo _ _ ial*
29.	Stupefied, sluggish, lethargic	*com _ tose*
30.	Proportionate, or corresponding in amount, degree or size	*commen _ _rate*
31.	Able to exist harmoniously together	*c _ _ patible*
32.	Easy-going, careless, self-satisfied	*c _ _ placent*
33.	Eager to comply, oblige and be polite	*compl _ _ sant*
34.	Being an accomplice in an intrigue or criminal act	*complic _ _ y*
35.	Occurring or existing together	*conc _ _ itant*
36.	The quality of being brief and concise	*conc _ sion*
37.	Extremely lustful erotic desire	*concupi _ cence*
38.	Parallel or taking place at the same time and location	*concu _ _ ent*
39.	Fitting and well-deserved (e.g. punishment)	*condi _ n*
40.	Combining or blending two things to form a whole	*con _ lation*

Check the answers on pages 437. A score of 30 for this round would indicate that you already possess a serviceable vocabulary. Still, the exercise will help you enlarge it by a further ten new words. Now for a final assault on C words:

Choose the Correct Meaning

Which, of the two definitions given for each word, **a** or **b**, is correct? Circle your choices (and once again, try not to make wild stabs) and then check the answers on page 437.

congenital   **a.** describing an abnormal condition existing at birth; **b.** a hereditary disease or disability.

congeries   **a.** an accumulation or collection; **b.** the area of a town or city once reserved for a fish market.

congruence   **a.** the state of marital disharmony; **b.** the state of agreeing or corresponding.

connotation   **a.** an idea or association suggested by a word or phrase; **b.** the ability of human and animal tissue to heal naturally.

consanguinity   **a.** unlawful acts between humans and animals; **b.** being related by birth or blood.

construe   **a.** to draw out or lengthen; **b.** to interpret or deduce the meaning of something.

consummate   **a.** to bring to completion or perfection; **b.** to achieve an orgasm.

contiguous   **a.** joining or adjacent; **b.** every alternate page of a book.

contrapuntal   **a.** contradicting expectations; **b.** describing music that combines two or more melodic lines.

contretemps   **a.** an embarrassing mistake or situation; **b.** a situation in which two sides at first disagree, then find agreement.

contrite   **a.** unlawful severing of a contract; **b.** full of remorse.

contumacious   **a.** readily submitting to flattery; **b.** stubborn and obstinate and resistant to authority.

contusion   **a.** a bruise or injury where the skin is unbroken; **b.** a wound in which bone or bone fragments break through the skin.

convoluted   **a.** spiral-shaped; **b.** twisted, involved, hard to comprehend.

corollary   **a.** a deduction or result; **b.** the angle formed by the meeting of two converging lines or surfaces.

corroborate   **a.** to be eaten away; **b.** to confirm or prove correct.

corrugated   **a.** describing material formed into alternate curved furrows and ridges; **b.** cardboard made from recycled pulp.

coruscate   **a.** to fiercely admonish; **b.** to sparkle and flash.

costive   **a.** cheating by altering prices; **b.** sluggish and constipated.

coterie   **a.** an exclusive group of people sharing common interests; **b.** a Caribbean dance performed by four people.

crapulous   **a.** grossly and repulsively untidy; **b.** given to overindulgence in eating and drinking.

credo   **a.** a formal statement of beliefs; **b.** the decorative strip on a wall parallel to floor and ceiling.

credulity   **a.** readiness to believe anything; **b.** lack of financial creditworthiness.

crepuscular   **a.** relating to dimness and twilight; **b.** knobbly and lumpy.

criterion   **a.** an army flag-bearer; **b.** a standard by which something can be judged or decided.

cruciform   **a.** a deep clay pot for smelting metal alloys; **b.** shaped like a cross.

culpable   **a.** blameworthy, deserving censure; **b.** left-handed.

cupidity   **a.** eagerness to please; **b.** greed for money and possessions.

curmudgeon   **a.** a surly, crabby, miserable person; **b.** a person who avoids any form of work and leaves chores to others.

cursory   **a.** hasty and superficial; **b.** bad-tempered.

cynosure   **a.** a distrust of people and ideas; **b.** someone or something that attracts unusual interest and attention.

It's worth pointing out that all the C words in these vocabulary-building exercises, far from being esoteric examples, were chosen from two national British newspapers, where they appeared over a two-month period. How did you fare? A score of 25 or more would be a result to be proud of. But if yours fell below that you have all the more reason to increase and sharpen your vocabulary.

Clues to Meaning: Recognising Word Elements

We've already noted that an awareness of Greek and Latin roots and elements such as prefixes and suffixes can often help identify the meanings of words that are unfamiliar to you. Here is a selection of Cs.

Word, Element	Origin	Meaning	English words
caro, carn	Latin	flesh	*carnal, carnivorous, carnivore, carnage, carnival*
cognitio, cogn	Latin	to know	*cognisant, cognisance, cognitive, recognise, incognito*
corpus, corp	Latin	body	*corpse, corporation, corporate, corps, corporal, corpulent, corporeal, corpuscle, corpus*
creditum, cred,	Latin	to trust	*credible, credibility, credit,*
credo	Latin	believe	*credentials, incredulous, creed, discredit, credulous*
circum-	Latin	around, on all sides, surrounding	*circumnavigate, circumference, circumlocution, circumvent, circumcise, circumstance*
contra-	Latin	opposite	*contradict, contravene, contraband, contraception*
counter-	Latin	against	*counteract, counterattack, counterfeit, countermand*
centum, cent-	Latin	hundred	*century, centenary, centimetre, centipede, centigrade*
chroma, chrom-	Greek	colour	*chromatic, chrome, chromosome*
chronos, chron-	Greek	time	*chronology, chronicity, chronic, chronometer, synchronise*
cosmos, cosmo-	Greek	universal	*cosmic, cosmopolitan, cosmology*
-krates, -crat,-cracy	Greek	ruler	*democrat, autocrat, bureaucracy*

Revision Time

A sure test of your understanding of a word's meaning is: can you use the word in the context of a sentence? For example, one of our C words was *chutzpah*. If you knew, or learned, the meaning of this word (and of all the others), don't just file it away in your memory – make an attempt to use it:

Emily had the necessary chutzpah to talk the radio station into giving her a job as a programme director.

Now try your hand at putting the following words into sentences. If you're in any doubt about the appropriateness or accuracy of your usage, check your dictionary.

cerebral, charismatic, clandestine, compatible, complaisant, connotation, contiguous, contretemps, coterie, cynosure.

D

Choose the Correct Meaning

Which one of the three choices, **a**, **b** or **c**, most accurately fits the meaning of the word? Circle your choices and then check the answers on page 437.

dado	**a.** early 20th-century surrealist movement; **b.** the decorated or panelled lower part of the walls of a room; **c.** a drink made from almonds.
dalliance	**a.** flirting; **b.** sparkling; **c.** long-winded oratory.
dearth	**a.** a plague; **b.** scarcity; **c.** frightening appearance.
debacle	**a.** an ornamental silver buckle; **b.** a large garden party; **c.** a complete rout and collapse.
debilitate	**a.** to nourish; **b.** to wound; **c.** to weaken.
decant	**a.** to pour from one receptacle to another; **b.** to confess one's sins; **c.** to sing in a monotone voice.
déclassé	**a.** having lost social status; **b.** to act superior to one's status; **c.** to offer wine in the wrong glass.
declivity	**a.** an abrupt drop; **b.** a gradual slope downwards; **c.** a sudden drop in barometric pressure.
décolletage	**a.** a decorative fringe on curtains; **b.** sediment sometimes found in red wine; **c.** a woman's revealing neckline.
decrepitude	**a.** persistent drunkenness; **b.** the state of being enfeebled and worn out; **c.** old age.
de facto	**a.** existing, though perhaps not legally; **b.** in defiance of the law; **c.** with the permission of the court.
deferential	**a.** showing respect; **b.** sullen; **c.** habitually careless.
déjà vu	**a.** old-fashioned; **b.** a person acquainted with witchcraft; **c.** the illusion of having previously experienced a present event.
deleterious	**a.** noxious; **b.** extremely sweet; **c.** wholesome.
deliquescent	**a.** a substance that dissolves in moisture absorbed from the air; **b.** a substance capable of burning the skin; **c.** a substance that can explode on contact.
Delphic	**a.** of dark appearance; **b.** always smiling; **c.** ambiguous
demagogue	**a.** a person who hates religion; **b.** a person with an urge to degrade others; **c.** an agitator who plays on the passions and prejudices of the mob.
demeanour	**a.** manner of behaviour and appearance; **b.** the art of arguing a cause; **c.** prone to easy seduction.
demimonde	**a.** objects and clothing made in the 1920s; **b.** women of dubious character; **c.** a jewelled cloche hat.
demotic	**a.** relating to the common people; **b.** staring wildly; **c.** a student of the black arts.
demurrer	**a.** an objection; **b.** a writ; **c.** a demand for payment.

denigrate   a. to use cosmetics excessively; b. to belittle or defame; c. to remove teeth unnecessarily.

denouement   a. a foiled elopement; b. a military surrender; c. the unravelling and solution of a mystery.

depilatory   a. for preventing bleeding; b. for removing hair; c. for controlling perspiration.

deprecate   a. to attack someone in a cowardly way; b. to express disapproval of someone or something; c. to harass.

depreciate   a. to reduce the value of someone or something; b. to cause a false alarm; c. to lose one's social position.

derogatory   a. the part of a church tower that contains the bells; b. a church service for the sick; c. offensively disparaging.

deshabille   a. only partly dressed; b. wanton; c. in mourning.

desiccated   a. chopped finely; b. dried or dehydrated; c. bleached.

desuetude   a. the condition of being unused or abandoned; b. relaxation; c. tiredness.

desultory   a. fish able to live in fresh and sea water; b. casual and unmethodical; c. to feel inferior.

determinism   a. belief that determination will solve all problems; b. belief that the father more than the mother determines a child's features; c. belief that all events and human actions are predetermined.

devolution   a. the transfer of powers from central to regional authority; b. the process of one state being absorbed by another; c. the political aftermath of a revolution.

dextral   a. left-handed; b. right-handed; c. colour-blind.

dharma   a. Indian cooking based on lamb and hot spices; b. Hindu religious and moral duty; c. silk sash worn with a sari.

dialectic   a. a debate intended to resolve differences; b. a religious belief based on self-analysis; c. relief through electrolysis.

Diaspora   a. the circlet of rubies in the British royal crown; b. the dispersal of the Jews; c. the Russian Orthodox hierarchy.

diatribe   a. cross-breeding between communities; b. a bitter verbal denunciation; c. folk medicine.

dichotomy   a. the second hymn in a church service; b. an operation on the joints of the foot; c. division into two parts.

didactic   a. inclined to teach; b. inclined to avoid problems; c. inclined to depend on others.

Check your choices against the answers on page 437. There are some toughies in this round so don't be too disappointed if your score is around or below 30. The really important point in vocabulary building is follow-up – double-check your wrong choices in a dictionary and commit the words and their meanings to memory.

Now for a second round . . .

What's the Word?

From the definitions given, fill in the missing letters to identify the words:

1. Shy, timid, and lacking in self-confidence. *diff _ dent*
2. Wasting time and putting off tasks until later *dil _ tory*
3. An art-loving person whose interests are rather superficial *dile _ _ ante*
4. Describing the philosophy of spontaneity and irrationality *Dion _ sian*
5. A person with an uncontrollable desire for alcohol *_ _ _ somaniac*
6. To rid someone of a misguided idea *dis _ buse*
7. To cause inconvenience to someone *disco _ _ ode*
8. To disturb the composure of someone *disconc _ _ t*
9. Disappointed, dejected, sad beyond comforting *discons _ _ ate*
10. An inconsistency between facts or figures *discr _ _ ancy*
11. Consisting of quite distinct or separate parts *discr _ te*
12. Describing speech or writing that jumps from one subject to another *discur _ ive*
13. Insincere and lacking in frankness *dis _ ngenuous*
14. Objective and impartial *disinter _ _ ted*
15. Utterly different and distinct *dis _ ara _ e*
16. To conceal by pretence, to hide one's intentions *di _ semble*
17. Discordant combination of sounds *dissona _ ce*
18. Happening daily or during the day *d _ urnal*
19. A prima donna; a world-class female singer *d _ v _*
20. A brief entertainment, usually between acts of a play *div _ _ tissement*
21. Stubbornly theoretical, with no regard for practicality *doctrin _ _ re*
22. Humorous verse *do _ _ erel*
23. Causing or involving pain or sorrow *dolor _ us*
24. One's dwelling place or legal residence *d _ _ icile*
25. A word or phrase that can be interpreted in twoways *dou _ le entend _ e*
26. Tough and resolute *doug _ _ y*
27. The senior member of a group, profession or society *do _ en*
28. Extremely harsh *Drac _ nian*
29. A coarsely woven mat *drug _ et*
30. Doubtful and uncertain *dubi _ _ s*
31. Describing a metal that can be beaten or stretched thinly *du _ tile*
32. Sullen anger and resentment, often 'high' *dud _ eon*
33. Describing pleasant and soothing music or sounds *d _ lcet*
34. The first section of the small intestine *duod _ num*
35. A market shared by only two producers or suppliers *du _ poly*
36. Deceptive double-dealing *duplici _ _*
37. Compulsion by the use of force or threats *d _ _ ess*
38. A sequence of hereditary leaders, rulers or heads of a family *dy _ asty*

39. The impaired ability to read   *d _ slexia*
40. Suffering from indigestion or upset stomach   *dyspe _ tic*

The completed words in this final set of words beginning with D are on page 438. A score of 30 or more correct would confirm that you have an above-average vocabulary and one well worth improving. Use your dictionary to check the meanings of those words that stumped you.

Have you Understood? Time for Revision

Before we depart from D territory it would be wise to test your understanding of some of the more unfamiliar words, but words you may nevertheless find useful in your everyday conversation and reading. In your mind, try using each of the following words, appropriately and accurately, in a sentence:

disinterested, debilitate, déjà vu, denouement, desultory, disabuse, disingenuous, Draconian, desiccated, décolletage.

E

Right or Wrong?

When you're truly familiar with a word you can use it confidently in its correct context in a sentence. Are you that familiar with the following 20 words? Are they being used correctly? Answer right/wrong and then check the answers on page 438.

	Right	Wrong
1. At John's stag party, Edmund was even more *ebullient* than he usually was.	____	____
2. Lorna's *eclectic* and notorious shyness made it impossible for her to enjoy social occasions.	____	____
3. The bishop was regarded as the most liberal and *ecumenical* of all his church colleagues.	____	____
4. They peered in vain at the old gravestone but all the markings had been *effaced* long ago through time and weather.	____	____
5. Shirley had always been a bright and *effervescent* girl.	____	____
6. The sky, *effete* with crisp, billowing clouds, promised a fine day	____	____

	Right	Wrong

7. The prescribed medicine unfortunately proved to be
    efficacious and Mr Gower expired that night.   ____   ____

8. The neighbours even had the *effrontery* to leave their
    car parked right across our driveway.   ____   ____

9. After the meal Bernie felt distinctly bloated and
    effulgent.   ____   ____

10. Despite his aristocratic background and undoubted
    wealth, Lord Mayberry was *egalitarian* at heart.   ____   ____

11. The discus soared overhead in a perfect *egocentric*
    arc.   ____   ____

12. It was well known that Mark was an *egregious*
    liar and thief.   ____   ____

13. The young boy performed the piece with tremendous
    élan.   ____   ____

14. The *elegiac* strains of evensong drifted across the
    fields.   ____   ____

15. Because the material of the carving looked
    elephantine the expert pronounced it to be
    genuine ivory.   ____   ____

16. The investigator did his best to *elicit* the truth
    from the woman.   ____   ____

17. Harold had formerly belonged to the *élite* Horse
    Guards.   ____   ____

18. John had inherited the family's tendency to
    elliptical fits   ____   ____

19. Abigail's psychological state caused her to *elucidate*
    and to recall the most remarkable dreams.   ____   ____

20. He fondly recalled the *Elysian* days of their
    Greek holiday.   ____   ____

Having only a hazy idea of a word's meaning can lead you into error if you use it in your speech or writing. The result can be an embarrassing malapropism. So check your 20 responses against the answers on page 438 and double-check your dictionary to nail those words whose meanings you didn't know or misunderstood.

Top and Tail the Words

The following round lists words with their first and last letters missing – which you are asked to replace. As the meanings of the words are supplied you shouldn't have too much trouble.

1. To issue or flow from   _ *manat* _
2. To free from restraint, to liberate   _ *mancipat* _

3.	To weaken, to deprive of masculine properties	_ masculat _
4.	To prohibit or restrict	_ mbarg _
5.	The blocking of an artery or vein by a blood clot	_ mbolis _
6.	In an early stage; undeveloped	_mbryoni _
7.	To correct by removing errors or faults	_ mendat _
8.	Retired from full-time work (usually academic or professional) but retaining one's title on an honorary basis	_ meritu _
9.	A substance that causes vomiting	_ meti _
10.	A preparation that sooths and softens the skin	_ mollien _
11.	The quality of understanding and sympathising and sharing another person's feelings	_ mpath _
12.	Describing conclusions based on experiment, experience or observation	_ mpirica _
13.	Heavenly and sublime; relating to the heavens or sky	_ mpyrea _
14.	To equal or surpass by imitation	_ mulat _
15.	A citation of very high praise	_ ncomiu _
16.	Found in or exclusive to a localised area	_ ndemi _
17.	To invigorate	_ nergis _
18.	To weaken or debilitate	_ nervat _
19.	An embarrassing child or discomfortingly indiscreet person	_ fant terribl _
20.	To cause or bring about something	_ gende _
21.	Something unexplainable	_ nigm _
22.	To order or instruct someone to do something	_ njoi _
23.	A feeling of hostility or ill will	_ nmit _
24.	A feeling of listlessness and boredom	_ nnu _
25.	Something outrageous, of extreme wickedness	_ normit _
26.	To implore, beg or plead	_ ntrea _
27.	To articulate clearly	_ nunciat _
28.	Transient or short-lived	_ phemera _
29.	A person devoted to sensual pleasures, especially eating and drinking	_ picur _
30.	A witty or paradoxical saying or short verse	_ pigra _

The answers are on page 438. You should have had very little trouble replacing the first letter of each word! So for this round a score of 25 or more would be appropriate for someone making good progress with his or her vocabulary building.

Choose the Correct Meaning

Which of the two choices, **a** or **b**, most accurately fits the meaning of each word? Circle your choices – the result of knowledge, not guessing! – and then check the answers on page 438.

epitome   **a.** a typical or ideal example of something; **b.** the first volume of a three-volume set of books.

eponymous   **a.** describing a word or name derived from the real name of a person or place; **b.** someone who attempts to remain anonymous but fails.

equable   **a.** capable of being balanced by an equal mass or amount; **b.** placid and even-tempered.

equanimity   **a.** closeness; **b.** calmness of mind or temper.

equinox   **a.** When the orbit of the moon is farthest from the earth; **b.** The two annual occasions when day and night are of equal length.

equitable   **a.** fair and just; **b.** a desire for revenge.

equivocal   **a.** ambiguous and uncertain; **b.** loud-mouthed and rude.

ergonomics   **a.** the study of the efficiency of human muscles; **b.** the study of the relationship between workers and their environment.

erogenous   **a.** sensitive to sexual stimulation; **b.** fatty tissue.

ersatz   **a.** a rare variety of mink fur; **b.** an artificial or inferior substitute.

eructation   **a.** a painful erection of the penis; **b.** belching.

erudite   **a.** well-read and well-informed; **b.** blackened.

eschatology   **a.** taboo expressions in the Bible; **b.** the branch of theology concerned with the end of the world.

eschew   **a.** processing nuts into a cream; **b.** to avoid or abstain from.

esoteric   **a.** obscure and restricted to an initiated minority; **b.** a style of art that blends erotic and religious subjects.

esprit de corps **a.** sense of comradeship and shared purpose; **b.** the principle of 'fighting to the death'.

ethos   **a.** the distinctive character or spirit of a culture or era; **b.** the difference between races of humans.

etymology   **a.** the origin and history of food; **b.** the origin and history of words.

eugenics   **a.** the study of selective breeding in humans; **b.** a form of dancing for fitness introduced in the 1920s.

eulogise   **a.** to weep over the dead; **b.** to praise highly.

euphemism   **a.** a stifled sneeze or cough; **b.** an inoffensive word or phrase substituted for one considered to be hurtful or obscene.

euphonious   **a.** pleasing to the ear; **b.** feeling great joy.

euphoria   **a.** a feeling of extreme elation; **b.** goods sold in bargain stores.

Eurasian   **a.** relating to the kingdom of Eurasia; **b.** of mixed European and Asian blood.

euthanasia   **a.** partial anaesthesia; **b.** killing someone painlessly to relieve suffering.

evanescent   **a.** fading away; **b.** saturated with the perfume of flowers.

eviscerate   **a.** to disembowel; **b.** to produce excessive saliva.

exacerbate   **a.** to abrade or roughen; **b.** to aggravate or make worse.

excoriate   **a.** to remove the core or middle of something; **b.** to severely censure or denounce.

exculpate   **a.** to free from blame or guilt; **b.** in surgery, to remove the top of the skull.

execrable   **a.** of very poor quality; **b.** of doubtful parentage.

exegesis   **a.** the last three books of the Old Testament; **b.** explanation or interpretation of a text, particularly of the Bible.

exemplary   **a.** fit to serve as an example to be imitated or as a warning; **b.** severely restrictive.

Extempore (a)

exigency   **a.** an urgent or pressing demand or requirement; **b.** a state of self-inflicted poverty.

exonerate   **a.** to incriminate an innocent party; **b.** to clear or absolve from blame or criminal charges.

exorcise   **a.** to remove subcutaneous tissue; **b.** to drive out evil spirits.

expatiate   **a.** to elaborate on a subject at great length; **b.** a person living temporarily in a foreign country.

expiate   **a.** to atone for or make amends; **b.** to return stolen money.

exponentially   **a.** with great and ever-increasing rapidity; **b.** the discovery of hidden possibilities.

expropriate   **a.** to illegally transfer public property to private ownership; **b.** to seize possession of private property for public use.

expunge   **a.** to delete or obliterate; **b.** to moisten lightly.

expurgate   **a.** to threaten a defendant in court with a custodial sentence; **b.** to remove supposedly offensive passages from a book.

extempore   **a.** outdoor classical ballet; **b.** impromptu or unprepared.

extenuating   **a.** qualifying or justifying **b.** broadening or fattening.

extraneous   **a.** non-essential or irrelevant; **b.** relating to the outdoors.

exuberant   **a.** rotund; **b.** abounding in vigour and high spirits.

This round contained some interesting and useful E words and perhaps a few that prompted some head-scratching. Check the answers on page 438 and if you scored 35 or more correct you did very well.

Element of Words Give Clues to Meanings

Let's tune in again to our serialisation about the roles played by prefixes and suffixes in word formation. You doubtless already know that when you see a word ending in *ess* it's likely to describe the female or feminine of something or someone: an *actress* is an actor, but a female one. Likewise you probably instinctively know that a word ending in *et*, *ette* or *let* is most likely a smaller version of someone or something: a *booklet*, for example, is a small book. But what about *trumpet*, you teasingly ask. The same principle applies, albeit disguised. The English word *trumpet* is derived from the Old French *trompette*, or 'little trompe', a diminutive version of a larger instrument. But *strumpet* – a 'little strump'? We'll never know. Although the word has been around for half a millennium its origin is unknown.

Word, Element	Origin	Meaning	English words
epi-	Greek	upon, on, over, above	*epicentre, epidermis, epitaph, epidemic, epidural*
ex-	Latin	out of, from	*exit, exclude, exhume, excuse, exhale, extort*
extra-	Latin	beyond, outside	*extraordinary, extramarital, extraterrestrial*
-ee	Latin	involved	*addressee, employee, escapee, licensee*
-ess	Greek	female	*hostess, lioness, baroness, laundress, princess*
-et, -ette, -let	Old French	lesser, small, minor	*cigarette, islet, maisonette, flatlet, midget, droplet*

It's Revision Time Again!

Spend a few minutes brushing up on the E words you've learned. Here are a dozen words which, although you may not use them or come across them every day, are in fairly common use. Hand on heart – can you instantly and accurately define them?

eclectic, egalitarian, empirical, enormity, epitome, equivocal, ersatz, exacerbate, extempore, extraneous, effete, empathy.

F

Increase your Word Power!

Circle or tick the word or phrase you believe is nearest in meaning to the key word. The answers are on page 438.

facetious   **a.** long-winded; **b.** inclined to be secretive; **c.** making jokes at inappropriate times; **d.** self-pitying.

facile   **a.** superficial; **b.** rapid; **c.** sporting; **d.** left-handed.

facilitate   **a.** to hesitate; **b.** to interfere; **c.** to be sympathetic to another's troubles; **d.** to make things easier.

factotum   **a.** a bookmaker's clerk; **b.** a 'jack of all trades' servant; **c.** an undertaker's assistant; **d.** a weather summary.

fait accompli   **a.** a clueless crime; **b.** a willing accomplice to a crime; **c.** something already accomplished and beyond alteration; **d.** having faith only in practical matters.

fallacy   **a.** a false belief or argument; **b.** a papal law; **c.** a deliberate lie; **d.** a hidden truth.

Falstaffian   **a.** argumentative; **b.** belligerent, looking for a fight; **c.** thin as a pikestaff; **d.** plump, jovial and dissolute.

farcical   **a.** painfully unfunny; **b.** funny, but hurtful to others; **c.** a 17th-century comic play; **d.** ludicrous and absurd.

farinaceous   **a.** food containing starch; **b.** inclined to be sticky; **c.** any grain that's imported; **d.** having the appearance of corn.

farrago   **a.** invective; **b.** an overlong speech; **c.** a hotchpotch or jumble; **d.** a West African sailing vessel.

fascism   **a.** an art movement; **b.** an authoritarian and undemocratic ideology or government; **c.** a left-wing movement that preceded communism; **d.** a branch of the Italian mafia.

fastidious   **a.** smartly dressed; **b.** over-critical and hard to please; **c.** excessively tidy; **d.** punctual.

fatuous   **a.** complacently foolish; **b.** complacently overweight; **c.** complacently smug; **d.** complacently idle.

fatwa   **a.** Muslim teacher; **b.** the shawl headdress of certain Muslim priests; **c.** one of the key Muslim holy books; **d.** a decree issued by a Muslim leader.

faux pas   **a.** cunning like a fox; **b.** a social indiscretion; **c.** a false ballet step; **d.** a doomed failure.

fealty   **a.** bravery; **b.** foolhardiness; **c.** cowardice; **d.** loyalty.

febrile   **a.** lukewarm; **b.** itching; **c.** feverish; **d.** decaying.

feckless   **a.** a person without purpose, plan or principles; **b.** a horse impossible to train; **c.** a clear skin; **d.** a young criminal.

fecund   **a.** one millionth of a minute; **b.** muddy; **c.** fertile; **d.** a natural ability for playing sport.

feign   **a.** a pretender to a royal crown; **b.** to pretend; **c.** a boxer's move to avoid a punch; **d.** to remove impurities from gold.

A score of 15 or more would be above average. But don't be discouraged if you scored less – just keep working at it and revise, revise, revise!

Fill in the Missing Letters

Each of the words in this set has a letter missing. From the meanings given, can you replace the letters to form the complete and correct words? The answers are on pages 438-9.

1.	Lively and quick-tempered	*fe _ sty*
2.	Happy and agreeable	*felici _ ous*
3.	Involving a criminal act	*f _ lonious*
4.	Describing an animal or plant that reverts to its wild state	*fer _ l*
5.	A subversive infiltrator	*fifth col _ mnist*
6.	Pertaining to sons and daughters	*f _ lial*
7.	To obstruct legislation by making long speeches and other delaying tactics.	*fili _ uster*
8.	The ornament on top of a spire or gable	*fin _ al*
9.	Flabby, soft and limp	*flac _ id*
10.	Blatant and outrageous	*fla _ rant*
11.	Showy and extravagant	*flambo _ ant*
12.	Inappropriately frivolous	*flip _ ant*
13.	Having a red or flushed complexion	*flo _ id*
14.	To treat with contempt	*fl _ ut*
15.	Smelling of nauseating decay	*foet _ d*
16.	A peculiarity or idiosyncrasy	*fo _ ble*
17.	To instigate or stir up trouble	*f _ ment*
18.	Trivial and silly	*fo _ tling*
19.	A raid, an incursion or a first attempt	*fo _ ay*
20.	Self-control and patience	*forbear _ nce*
21.	Relating to or connected with a court of law	*fore _ sic*
22.	To anticipate or to take action to delay or stop an event	*fo _ estall*
23.	Something at which a person excels	*f _ rte*
24.	Accidental or unplanned	*fort _ itous*
25.	A rowdy quarrel or brawl	*frac _ s*
26.	Restless and irritable	*fra _ tious*
27.	Someone who admires France and things French	*Franco _ hile*
28.	The act of killing one's brother	*fratr _ cide*
29.	Distracted and frantic	*fre _ etic*

30.	Easily broken up and crumbled	*fr _ able*
31.	The realisation or fulfilment of something worked for	*fr _ ition*
32.	To denounce noisily and explosively	*fu _ minate*
33.	Obviously and embarrassingly sincere	*ful _ ome*
34.	Belief in the literal truth of sacred texts and in their strict observance	*funda _ entalism*
35.	Gloomy, mournful and suggestive of a funeral	*fune _ eal*
36.	Showy ornamental trimming on women's clothing	*furbe _ ow*
37.	A public protest or outburst of rage	*furor _*
38.	Pompous or bombastic speech or writing	*fus _ ian*

The idea behind these 'missing letters' rounds is not so much to allow you to gleefully reinstate the missing letters (relatively easy) but to pause sufficiently long enough to allow the accompanying meanings to attach themselves to your memory. So how successful were you? Check the answers on pages 438-9 and, as always, look in your dictionary for the full meanings of those words that tripped you up.

Developing a really good vocabulary depends very much on the two *i's* – *inquisitiveness* and *initiative*. Always be inquisitive about the words you read and hear, especially those you don't quite understand; and have the initiative to find out what they really mean.

Word Elements: Clues to Meaning

Here are some more word elements, suffixes and prefixes, derived mostly from Latin and Greek, that can often help you recognise the meanings of words. From the Latin word *ferrum*, for example, meaning iron, we get the combining form *ferro*. Once we know this, we can safely assume that any word beginning with *ferro* (*ferrocyanide, ferromagnetism, ferruginous, ferrule, ferrous,* etc) has something to do with iron.

Word, Element	Origin	Meaning	English words
for-	Old English	rejection, prohibition	*forbid, forswear, forlorn, forfend*
fore-	Old English	before; in front	*foresight, forefather, foreman, forecast, forestall*
-fy, -ify	Latin	making, becoming	*pacify, gratify, falsify, nullify, testify, notify*
-fer, -ferre	Latin	to bring	*offer, proffer, prefer, confer, refer, transfer, suffer*

Revision, Revision, Revision!

Know your F words? Here's a baker's dozen* worth revisiting. Do you know their meanings precisely?

facile, fastidious, faux pas, flaccid, flout, forensic, forte, fortuitous, fracas, fulsome, furore, facetious, farrago.

* An interesting old term, meaning 13, and deriving from a baker's anxiety not to be accused of giving light weight; if someone ordered a dozen rolls he would pop in one extra.

G

Replace the Missing Words

Below are ten words and ten sentences. A word is missing from each of the sentences. Can you place the appropriate words in all ten sentences?

gaffe	galaxy	galleria	Gallic	galvanised
gambit	gamine	gamut	gangrene	garrulous

1. Audrey Hepburn always played the role of _____ to perfection.
2. The horrific news _____ the team into action.
3. Malcolm apologised for his unfortunate _____ at the party.
4. The husband could hardly get a word in edgeways; his wife was easily the most _____ woman they'd ever met.
5. The Milky Way, consisting of millions of stars, forms part of our _____.
6. Dorothy Parker wrote that the actress's _____ of emotions ran all the way from A to B.
7. Both Arctic explorers suffered badly from _____ caused by frostbite.
8. He used the old joke about Churchill as a _____ to soften the audience.
9. Edouard was decidedly _____ when it came to charming women.
10. The new shopping mall featured a spectacular _____ of four storeys.

Understanding words and their meanings enables you to use them appropriately and expressively. The more extensive your vocabulary, the more choice you have when looking for 'just that right word'. Or, put another way, the greater the choice, the clearer your voice. So if, in this exercise, you placed all the words in their correct contexts, you're well on the way to an eloquent vocabulary. Just the same, check the answers and the meanings of the words on page 439 to make sure you're 100 per cent correct.

What's the Correct Usage?

On the same theme, here are some more useful G words. In each case one is used correctly and one is not. Can you identify the sentences, **a** or **b**, that are correct in sense and meaning?

gauche **a.** The artist presented her with a framed gauche. **b.** The young girl was beautiful but gauche.

gazebo **a.** They loved sitting in the gazebo for hours and hours. **b.** The orchestra played a tuneful gazebo in Margaret's honour.

gazumped **a.** The house hunters complained to the agent that this was the second time they'd been gazumped. **b.** The fullback was carried from the rugby field after he'd been gazumped.

generic **a.** The vicar said that the couple's idea of a wedding was too generic for his church. **b.** He explained that aspirin was a generic drug and could be marketed by any firm.

genre **a.** Jacob's family had a genre stretching back to the 16th century. **b.** He preferred the realistic fiction of Dickens and works of that genre.

genuflect **a.** As she entered she genuflected briefly towards the altar. **b.** The three-year sentence gave him ample time to genuflect upon his crime.

geriatric **a.** Poor old grandad was confined to the geriatric section of the hospital. **b.** The newly developed antiseptic had a beneficial geriatric effect on most patients.

germane **a.** The ochre shade was attractive, but in the end she preferred the germane. **b.** Mark insisted that consideration of salaries was germane to the factory's inefficiency problem.

gerrymander **a.** The sitting candidate realised too late that the gerrymander could cost him the election. **b.** The gang boss threatened to gerrymander the FBI by fleeing to a neighbouring state.

gestation **a.** The average gestation time for a heavy meal is five hours. **b.** It was obvious the mare's gestation was in its final weeks.

gesundheit **a.** 'Gesundheit!' he said to his friend, after a whole-hearted sneeze. **b.** Angrily, he sat down. 'Gesundheit!' he swore under his breath.

gibe **a.** Fred had long learned to suffer the gibes from his mates. **b.** One day, thought Wendy, he's going to gibe me in the ribs once too often.

gigolo **a.** You could tell by his effeminate manner that he was a gigolo. **b.** The widow had plenty of money and a string of eager gigolos.

gilt-edged **a.** He was one of the partners who'd invented the gilt-edged safety razor. **b.** He regarded the house purchase as a gilt-edged investment.

gimcrack   **a.** The antique armchair lost its value because it was riddled with gimcracks. **b.** Beryl had no taste at all, addicted as she was to gimcrack jewellery.

glasnost   **a.** The new chairman felt that the normally secretive company would benefit from a dose of glasnost. **b.** After the heavy snowfall the windows were glazed with a veil of glasnost.

glitterati   **a.** The famous actress never really cared about being part of the London glitterati. **b.** When in Venice they bought a superb carnival mask, ornamented with glitterati.

gloaming   **a.** As dusk approached, Sir Bernard suggested they follow the old song and do some 'roaming in the gloaming'. **b.** In Scotland the gloaming is a favourite haunt of lovers.

glutinous   **a.** The plant trapped insects in its glutinous nectary. **b.** He came up and spoke to my aunt in his usual glutinous manner.

gobbet   **a.** His body hung for days beneath the evil, creaking gobbet. **b.** The starving prisoners clamoured for the gobbets of rancid flesh.

gobbledegook   **a.** Among Lewis Carroll's creations were the Cheshire Cat, the snark, the boojum and the gobbledegook. **b.** The management's baffling memo was utter gobbledegook.

gossamer   **a.** The dress's fabric was as fine as gossamer. **b.** The leaves of the tree turned as purple as gossamer.

gourmandise   **a.** The factory was built to gourmandise milk into cheese. **b.** Her dream was to gourmandise on fancy Swiss chocolates.

Grand Guignol   **a.** With constant violent arguing, living in the Taylor household must have been pure Grand Guignol. **b.** Having won the lottery, our neighbours thought they were Grand Guignol.

grandiose   **a.** The garden party was a grandiose affair. **b.** Lord Wainscott was always grandiose with his money.

gratuitous   **a.** Not all the diners were gratuitous to the waiters. **b.** The movie was marred by the scenes of gratuitous violence.

gravamen   **a.** The gravamen of the case was the premeditated nature of the attack. **b.** The vicar finally delivered his gravamen to the happy couple.

gregarious   **a.** Jem was a gregarious person and invariably became restive when alone. **b.** When the gregarious mood hit him he would lie in wait for some casual prey.

gremlin   **a.** They hated the painted gremlins in their neighbour's garden. **b.** When the mower kept stalling he blamed the gremlins in the carburettor.

grenadine   **a.** The ex-guardsman had a grenadine manner about him. **b.** The cocktail called for a generous splash of grenadine.

gullible   **a.** Seagulls are so expertly gullible they can swallow a kilo of fish in less than a minute. **b.** Brian was so gullible he was a favourite target of the street traders.

gumption   **a.** The brick pillars were topped with weathered stone gumptions. **b.** The teacher told them that with a bit of gumption they could achieve anything.

gunge   **a.** When all the gunge was finally removed the brasswork looked like new. **b.** The designer favoured the new gunge fashion style so admired by students and ravers.

Slogging through that set might have seemed like a lot of hard work, but if after checking the answers on page 439 you marked 25 or more correct, then surely it was worth it. Reflect a little on the words you missed and explore their full meanings in your dictionary. When you're satisfied that you fully comprehend their meanings, add them to your growing vocabulary.

Word Roots: Guides to Meaning

As with prefixes, suffixes and combining forms (linguistic elements that help form compound words: e.g. *dia* + the combining form *gram* = *diagram*), the ancient roots of many of our words often hint at their meanings. Here are some 'G' examples:

Word, Element	Origin	Meaning	English words
gamos	Greek	marriage	*monogamous, bigamy, gamete, polygamous, monogyny*
generare	Latin	to beget	*gender, generate, gene*
genus	Latin	kind, type	*genre, genealogy, gentry*
gradus	Latin	a step	*gradual, gradation, graduate*
gravis	Latin	heavy	*gravitas, gravity, grave*
grex, gregis	Latin	flock	*gregarious, congregate*
gune	Greek	woman	*gynaecology, misogynist*

Review, Reappraisal, Reassessment = Revision

Revision by any other name is still revision, but don't dismiss its importance in helping you to enrich your vocabulary. Do you fully understand the meanings of the following words? Can you use them meaningfully in mental sentences?

gauche, gibe, grandiose, gratuitous, gregarious, gullible, garrulous.

H

Choose the Correct Meaning

Which one of the three alternatives, **a**, **b** or **c**, most accurately fits the meaning of the word? Circle or mark your choices (trying not to be tempted into making wild guesses!) and then check the answers on page 439.

habeas corpus **a.** murder case lacking a body; **b.** demand for a prisoner to appear before a court; **c.** appeal to dismiss a case through lack of evidence.

habitué **a.** a regular visitor to a place; **b.** a drug addict; **c.** a very stylishly dressed person.

hackneyed **a.** to be transported by a horse-drawn carriage; **b.** stale and trite; **c.** tired and listless.

hagiography **a.** a stream of invective; **b.** a catalogue of complaints; **c.** a biography that idolises its subject.

ha-ha **a.** a sunken fence; **b.** a fountain; **c.** a summer house.

haiku **a.** a Japanese ceremonial sword; **b.** a 17-syllable Japanese verse form; **c.** the wide sash worn over a kimono.

halation **a.** the coating of dried salt left by sea-spray; **b.** a greenish deposit on neglected teeth; **c.** a halo effect seen in some photographs caused by pointing the camera at a light.

halcyon **a.** peaceful and pleasant; **b.** a thick crayon used for stage makeup; **c.** the fringe on an oriental carpet.

halitosis **a.** body odour; **b.** smelly feet; **c.** bad breath.

hapless **a.** clumsy; **b.** angry and irritable; **c.** unfortunate and unlucky.

harangue **a.** the muscle at the back of the tongue; **b.** ornamental brassware on a horse's harness; **c.** to address someone in a loud, abrasive and persuasive way.

harbinger **a.** someone or something that foretells an event; **b.** a rowboat used for hunting whales; **c.** a species of honey-eating bird.

hauteur **a.** high fashion; **b.** pride; **c.** causing or deserving hate.

hearsay **a.** gossip and rumour; **b.** a broken promise; **c.** a method for teaching young children to read and write.

hector **a.** to tease and bully; **b.** to act strangely in public; **c.** a stage direction in which the actors directly address the audience.

hedonism **a.** the denial of bodily pleasures; **b.** the pursuit of pleasure as a principle; **c.** the belief that everyone goes to Heaven.

hegemony **a.** property passing from a mother to her children; **b.** the dominance of one country or power over others; **c.** the state's inherent right to tax its citizens.

heinous **a.** horse-loving; **b.** evil and atrocious; **c.** rural interests.

helix   **a.** a spiral shape or form; **b.** a four-pronged spear or weapon; **c.** the gold headband of a royal crown.

hellebore   **a.** a rude and tiresome person; **b.** a group of plants; **c.** a type of ship's figurehead.

herbivorous   **a.** plants that are fleshy rather than woody; **b.** plants with medicinal uses; **c.** grass- or plant-eating animals.

heresy   **a.** an unorthodox belief; **b.** a wicked lie; **c.** a traitorous act.

hermetic   **a.** self-love; **b.** an aversion for other people; **c.** sealed so as to be airtight.

heterogeneous **a.** a group made up equally of males and females; **b.** not of the same kind or type; **c.** a preference for the opposite sex.

heuristic   **a.** learning by inquiry and investigation; **b.** an obsession with time; **c.** an admirer of holy artifacts.

hiatus   **a.** a break or gap; **b.** a summer holiday; **c.** acute hiccups.

Hibernian   **a.** pertaining to Scotland; **b.** pertaining to Ireland; **c.** pertaining to the Isle of Man.

hierarchy   **a.** the ruling group of a religion; **b.** persons or things arranged in a graded order; **c.** the chiefs of Scottish clans.

hindsight   **a.** all-round vision; **b.** the part of a gunsight nearest the eye; **c.** the ability to be wise after an event.

histology   **a.** the study of organic tissue; **b.** the study of ancient burial sites; **c.** the study of hay fever.

histrionic   **a.** excessively melodramatic; **b.** referring to the early Victorian period; **c.** the inability to pronounce sibilant letters.

hoary   **a.** covered with cobwebs; **b.** red-faced as a result of Christmas revelry; **c.** white or whitish-grey in colour.

Hobson's choice **a.** the best out of three; **b.** a selection so rich that often the worst choice is made; **c.** no choice at all.

hoi polloi   **a.** the toffs and aristocrats; **b.** arrogant public officials; **c.** the common people.

hologram   **a.** a message from the Vatican; **b.** printing by means of gelatin; **c.** a three-dimensional photographic image.

homily   **a.** a religious painting intended for the home; **b.** a moral lesson; **c.** a coarse flour made from barley.

homogeneous   **a.** all of the same kind; **b.** all different; **c.** mixed.

honorarium   **a.** a minor award made to civil servants; **b.** a collection of military medals; **c.** a fee paid for a nominally free service.

hortatory   **a.** pertaining to clocks and time-keeping; **b.** a sleep-walking condition; **c.** giving encouragement.

To score in this round of interesting and useful words, check your choices against the answers on page 439. A score of 35 or more correct would be excellent, but don't feel too put out if yours was around the 30 mark. Just keep revising, that's all.

Supply the Missing Words

Below are ten words and ten sentences. A word is missing from each of the sentences. Can you place the appropriate words in all ten sentences? Each word can be used only once.

hubris	humane	humdrum	husbandry	hybrid
hydrofoil	hyperactivity	hypochondriac	hyperbole	hypothetical

1. The _____ took only half an hour to travel from Dover to Calais.
2. Many philologists regard English as a _____ language.
3. David's brilliant career was predictably destroyed by his own _____.
4. Despite having a famous father and a socialite mother, Wayne himself led a _____ existence.
5. Since her stroke, grandmother has developed into a veritable _____.
6. Although he had a poor view of humans, the farmer had a _____ side when it came to his animals.
7. Louis was always good fun, even though his claims as a womaniser were generously laced with _____.
8. Although the Ryans were a large low-income family they lived very well, no doubt largely due to Edith's expert_____.
9. Although entirely _____, Sopwith's contention that the firm was cheating them was probably true.
10. Young Robert fell off the wall and broke a tooth, the victim, unfortunately, of uncontainable _____.

It's worth spending a little thought over exercises like this one because if you replace the words correctly the resulting sentences demonstrate their actual usage. And if you get the odd one wrong, then you're forced (if you're serious about building your vocabulary) to check the meaning of the word and to try again. (Answers page 439.)

More Word Elements: Combining Forms

Combining forms, as we discussed earlier, are elements that can be married to other word roots to form new words: *hydro* + *electric* = *hydroelectric*. Or take another example, *dehydrate*, which is made up of a prefix, a combining form, and a suffix:

Prefix	*Combining form*	*Suffix*
de-	**hydro, hydra**	**-ate**
meaning to remove	meaning water	meaning possessing

If you translate this, the verb *dehydrate* can be understood to mean 'the removal of water possessed by the substance'. This once again underlines the usefulness of a knowledge of word roots in helping you to figure out the meanings of many words.

Here are some combining forms beginning with H:

Word, Element	Origin	Meaning	English words
haemo-, haema-	Greek	blood	*haemoglobin, haemophilia, haemorrhoids, haemostasis, haemorrhage*
helio-	Greek	sun	*heliograph, heliosphere, heliotrope, heliocentric, helium*
hetero-	Greek	other	*heterodoxy, heterogeneous, heterosexual, heteronym*
homo-, homeo	Latin	the same	*homogeneous, homosexual, homeoeroticism, homogenise*
hydro-	Greek	water	*hydrolysis, hydroelectric, hydrofoil, hydraulic, hydrogen, hydrocephalus, dehydrate*
hypno	Greek	sleep	*hypnotise, hypnosis, hypnogenesis*

Time for Revising

A few minutes revising your 'H' words will be time well spent. Do you, right off the cuff, know the meanings of the following?

habitué	**halcyon**	**harbinger**	**hearsay**	**hegemony**
heresy	**hiatus**	**histrionic**	**hoi polloi**	**hubris**

I

Choose the Correct Meaning

Which of the alternative meanings most accurately fits the word? Mark or circle your choice, **a** or **b**, and then check the answers on page 439.

iconoclast   **a.** one who attacks established beliefs; **b.** one who believes only in material things.

idiomatic   **a.** describing expressions common to a particular group or in a particular region; **b.** writing that consists predominantly of slang.

idiosyncrasy **a.** a slip of the tongue; **b.** a personal mannerism or habit.

idolatry **a.** worship of idols and images; **b.** desecration of churches.

ignominious **a.** extreme shyness; **b.** disgraceful and dishonourable.

imbroglio **a.** a love affair between a husband and sister-in-law; **b.** a complex and confused state of affairs.

imbue **a.** to instil or inspire with ideas or principles; **b.** to subtly introduce an opposing point of view into an argument.

immolate **a.** to kill by sacrifice; **b.** to make a generous gesture by giving away all one's material possessions.

immured **a.** to be declared an outcast; **b.** to be imprisoned.

immutable **a.** unchanging and unalterable; **b.** a metal able to combine with other metals to form an alloy.

impartial **a.** fair and not prejudiced; **b.** relaxed and uncaring.

impasse **a.** a narrow opening or ledge; **b.** an insurmountable object or situation.

impeach **a.** to accuse a US president of immoral, although not criminal, conduct; **b.** to accuse a person of a crime, especially treason.

impeccable **a.** faultless and flawless; **b.** dressed in the latest style.

impenitent **a.** close to bankruptcy; **b.** unrepentant and not sorry .

imperturbable **a.** dour and small-minded; **b.** calm and unruffled.

impervious **a.** unable to be penetrated; **b.** partly water-resistant.

implacable **a.** unrelenting and not to be appeased; **b.** someone consumed by deep jealousy.

implausible **a.** most unlikely, prompting disbelief; **b.** a stage variety act that begins well but ends in disaster.

importune **a.** unfortunate timing; **b.** to demand urgently and persistently.

imprimatur **a.** sign of good breeding; **b.** a mark of approval.

impromptu **a.** offhand, without preparation; **b.** amateurish.

impugn **a.** to challenge the word of someone; **b.** to incite a crowd.

inane **a.** lazy and slovenly; **b.** senseless and stupid.

incandescent **a.** glowing white-hot; **b.** to lose one's temper.

incapacitate **a.** to decrease by a small amount; **b.** to disable or deprive of power or physical capacity.

incipient **a.** just beginning to happen; **b.** an inherited problem.

inconsequential **a.** placed in correct numerical order; **b.** insignificant or trivial, not worth worrying about.

incontrovertible **a.** incapable of being contradicted; **b.** an event that is predicted to end in disaster.

inculcate **a.** to impress on the mind by repetition and force; **b.** to raise classroom success levels by lowering academic standards.

incumbent **a.** heavy and bulky; **b.** someone who is currently holding an office or position.

incursion **a.** a surgical incision involving skin only; **b.** a sudden attack.

indefatigable **a.** tireless and unflagging; **b.** impossible to defeat.

indigent **a.** destitute; **b.** the child of an inter-tribal marriage.

ineffable	**a.** too overwhelming to be expressed in words; **b.** incapable of being flustered and upset.
ineluctable	**a.** unworthy to be elected; **b.** unable to be avoided.
inertia	**a.** a disinclination to move or act; **b.** reverse gravity.
inexorable	**a.** unbending and unmoved; **b.** a prediction that turns out to be true.
ingenuous	**a.** inclined to be mean; **b.** open, candid and frank.
ingratiate	**a.** to position oneself so as to invite favours; **b.** to wriggle out of a difficult situation by lying and subterfuge.
inherent	**a.** an inseparable part; **b.** the eldest son in a family.
inimitable	**a.** extremely funny; **b.** unique.
iniquitous	**a.** someone who refuses to take part in a legal inquiry; **b.** an unjust and wicked act.
innate	**a.** an inborn quality; **b.** leaf-shaped.
innocuous	**a.** natural resistance to disease; **b.** harmless.
insalubrious	**a.** unhealthy; **b.** passion for keeping clean.
insular	**a.** imperious; **b.** isolated, narrow-minded, looking inwards.

If you're not too exhausted after that round, check your choices with the answers on page 439 and tot up your score. If you achieved 40 or more correct (with not too many wild guesses) your vocabulary is well above average.

More Merry Pop-Ins

Fifteen words, fifteen sentences with holes in them. Simply pop each of the words in the appropriate hole so that all the sentences make perfect sense. The words are used once only. The answers are on page 439.

inter alia	interdict	intransigent
intrinsic	inviolable	inured
inveighed	inveterate	invidious
iota	irascible	iridescence
irreparably	irrevocable	itinerant

1. The store told us that the CD player was _____ damaged.
2. Mr Jacob is one of the most mulish and _____ clients I've ever had to deal with.
3. Muriel's decision, she apparently told her boyfriend, was _____.
4. We get our knives sharpened by the _____ handyman who calls here every couple of months or so.
5. By the government's _____ of 1985, fireworks cannot be sold to anyone under the age of 15.
6. Grandfather's will went on to say that, _____ , his personal possessions were to be divided between us.
7. As for studying and revision, young John couldn't care one _____.
8. He found himself in the _____ position of trying to placate the family.

9. Difficulty in starting the engine was an _____ part of the charm of the classic sports car, Malcolm insisted.
10. For nearly an hour the MP _____ against the government for its lack of policy on banning fox hunting.
11. Our neighbour, Mr Twine, was an _____ old man and it didn't pay to upset him.
12. They admired the spectacular display of _____ thrown off the male peacock's feathers.
13. Having spent a good part of his life begging and sleeping rough, the man was _____ to hardship.
14. The young couple idealistically regarded their union as _____.
15. Despite all the medical evidence, Beryl was an _____ smoker and would never easily give it up.

There may be instances here where you've popped a word in its right place without precisely knowing its meaning. But only you will know that, and only you will know that, if your working vocabulary is to benefit, you have to check its meaning in your dictionary. Is your dictionary showing any signs of wear yet?

Word Roots: Inter- and -Itis

You cannot avoid these two common word roots: the prefix *inter-* and the suffix -*itis*. Let's spend a few moments studying their roles in the formation of our words.

Word, Element	Origin	Meaning	English words
inter-	Latin	between, among, together	*interact, interbreed, interactive, interchange, international, intercontinental, intercept, interference.*
-itis	Greek	inflammation	*tonsillitis, appendicitis, meningitis, Mondayitis.*

Five-Minute Revision

You've just learned or reacquainted yourself with 100 or so I words – all of them eminently employable in an active working vocabulary. But just to satisfy yourself that you have their meanings nailed down, why not run through the lot again, pausing to check those pernickety words that continue to confuse you. And, at the very least, try putting the following words into mental sentences of your own:

ineluctable	indigent	interdict	iconoclast	importune
incipient	irrevocable	ingenuous	insular	irascible

J

Choose the Correct Meaning

Which of the three choices, **a**, **b** or **c**, most accurately fits the meaning of the word? Tick or circle your choices (if you have to make a guess it's best to be honest and pass) and then check the answers on page 440.

jalousie   **a.** a small commuter bus; **b.** a summer house in the mountains; **c.** a window shutter made from angled slats.

jaundiced   **a.** having a distorted, pessimistic point of view; **b.** an optimistic outlook; **c.** a process for making jam from stone fruits.

jejune   **a.** bright and sparkling; **b.** immature, uninteresting and insipid; **c.** young and sexually innocent.

jeopardy   **a.** danger and uncertainty; **b.** the legal status between bail and remand; **c.** the hours between midnight and 6 am.

jeremiad   **a.** an extremely unlucky person; **b.** a lament; **c.** a traitor.

jerry-built   **a.** foreign-made; **b.** a manufacture of German origin; **c.** sloppily built using cheap materials.

jettison   **a.** to throw things overboard; **b.** to crash a boat into a dock; **c.** to recover items lost at sea.

Jezebel   **a.** a young girl who loves to dance; **b.** a shameless and wanton woman; **c.** an excessively made-up and ornamented woman.

jihad   **a.** the ruling council of a Muslim state; **b.** a Muslim holy war against infidels; **c.** the confederation of Muslim states.

jingoism   **a.** a compulsion to tell jokes; **b.** chauvinistic, aggressive patriotism; **c.** belief in witch doctor healing.

Job's comforter **a.** a woollen cardigan of many colours; **b.** the bell or whistle indicating the end of the day's work; **c.** someone who, while claiming to sympathise, only adds to the distress.

jobsworth   **a.** a minor official who sticks to the letter of the law regardless of circumstances; **b.** a particularly ambitious employee; **c.** a job that turns out to be onerous and low-paid.

jocose   **a.** red-faced; **b.** humorous and facetious; **c.** loose-limbed.

joie de vivre   **a.** delight in being aggressive; **b.** addicted to wearing perfume; **c.** joy at being alive.

jubilee   **a.** a 100th anniversary; **b.** a royal anniversary occasion; **c.** any special anniversary occasion.

A short round for which a score of 12 or more correct would be reasonable. Now for the rest of the J words that should form part of your vocabulary.

Words in Use – Right or Wrong?

If you're truly familiar with the following words you'll have no trouble deciding which of them are being used correctly and which are not. Answers on page 440.

		Right	Wrong
1.	They felt they had been disgracefully deceived and vowed that they would never forgive Tom's *judicial* behaviour.	____	____
2.	Mr Hare decided it might be *judicious* to avoid controversy and to delay the visit for another week.	____	____
3.	At this *juncture* the meeting broke up in wild disorder	____	____
4.	Mrs Siddons, admirably *Junoesque*, swept into the theatre in a swish of skirts and perfume.	____	____
5.	The senior tribal members entered the temple to worship the sacred *junta*.	____	____
6.	Their eldest daughter had decided to study *jurisprudence*.	____	____
7.	The prisoner complained to his lawyers that because the trial was *jury-rigged* he was certain to be convicted.	____	____
8.	Old Mrs Thomson was becoming increasingly *juvenescent*, frail and forgetful.	____	____
9.	Even though the drawings were obviously *juvenilia* they nevertheless fetched high prices at the studio sale.	____	____
10.	In flower arranging, the art is skillfully to *juxtapose* contrasting colours, shapes and textures.	____	____

In that set, four words were incorrectly used – did you spot them? It's a good idea when you are reading and come across a word unfamiliar to you, to look up its meaning – and also note *how* it was used.

Revision: A to J

At this point in your vocabulary-enlarging programme it would be an excellent idea to look back over your newly acquired word stock. Of the thousand or so words you've perused so far, perhaps a hundred may have been new to you. You may also have been hazy about the precise meanings of another hundred. And you may have had a little difficulty using as many again in their appropriate context.

That's the real test of a working vocabulary – whether it consists of words you understand fully and can use with ease and familiarity. So how about putting your new words to work? Flip back over the previous sections, A-J, and select a dozen or two words that were new to you but which you think will be useful in your speech and writing. In turn, write them into actual sentences. Let's say the word you select is *abstruse*. It's a word that you could have used a number of times if you had known it existed and what it meant. So have a go now:

*I found some of the words in this book **abstruse** and hard to understand.*

How's that? Well, we're not quite there; the sentence is tautological. What? Yes, the sentence uses the word *abstruse* correctly, but then it pointlessly repeats the meaning – because *abstruse* itself means 'not easy to understand'. So let's rewrite it:

*I found some of the words in this book **abstruse**.*

Now try working words into your own sentences. If you're in doubt about how a word should be used, check its meaning or meanings again in the dictionary, which should also provide some grammatical guidance: whether a word is a noun, verb, adjective or some other designation. Take that word *tautological*. Your dictionary will show it as a noun (*tautology*), a verb (*tautologise*), an adjective (*tautologous, tautological*) and as an adverb (*tautologically, tautologously*). All that will help you not only to use the word appropriately in the context of meaning but grammatically correctly as well.

K

Choose the Correct Meaning

Words beginning with K are somewhat scarce in the dictionary but there are some that you should know. Which of the three choices, **a**, **b** or **c**, most accurately fits the meaning of the word? Mark or circle your choices and then check the answers on page 440.

Kafkaesque	**a.** a story with a twist at the end; **b.** middle-European in outlook; **c.** dehumanising and nightmarish.
kaftan	**a.** a hammock made of woven cane; **b.** a long, loose dress; **c.** the ceremonial headwear of an Indonesian chief.
kamikaze	**a.** an action that is suicidally foolhardy; **b.** a long and persistent artillery blitz; **c.** the cloud that hangs above Fujiyama in Japan.
karaoke	**a.** popular Japanese raw fish and rice dish; **b.** publicly singing songs over a prerecorded backing tape; **c.** fortitude.

kaput	**a.** lost; **b.** irreplaceable; **c.** broken or not functioning.
karma	**a.** the sum of a person's actions that are transferred from one life to the next; **b.** spiritual well-being; **c.** spiritual guidance that cannot be ignored.
kedgeree	**a.** wind-dried whale flesh; **b.** a dish of cooked fish, rice and eggs; **c.** a seabird common in Norway.
Keynesian	**a.** describing a doctrine that recommends government spending to counter economic failure and unemployment; **b.** describing a doctrine that favours a free market and with no government intervention; **c.** describing a doctrine that favours a return to the gold standard.
keystone	**a.** the large carved stone that dedicates a building; **b.** the wedge-shaped stone at the top of an arch; **c.** a large masonry block that acts as the base for a pillar.
kibbutz	**a.** Israel's democratic party; **b.** a desert war of attrition, used by Israel to occupy the Left Bank; **c.** an Israeli communal collective settlement.

We're shifting gear here into examples of usage. So keep going! Just select the usage, **a** or **b**, that you think is appropriate and correct. The answers are on page 440.

kinetic	**a.** Brendan thought that kinetic energy was mainly concerned with heat. **b.** Jerry thought that kinetic energy was mainly concerned with motion.
kismet	**a.** The young woman accepted widowhood as her kismet. **b.** To secure her love he promised her his eternal kismet.
kitsch	**a.** It was well known that he published nothing but kitsch. **b.** As a family friend he undertook to act as the children's kitsch.
kleptomaniac	**a.** After a dozen convictions for theft she was finally diagnosed as a kleptomaniac. **b.** His chronic sleepwalking confirmed him as a kleptomaniac.
knell	**a.** The lifeboatmen were pleased to see the knell at last. **b.** The family filed out of the church to the mournful knell of the church bells.
Knesset	**a.** It was a genuine Knesset rug, so obviously very expensive. **b.** The Knesset sat all night to resolve the border problem.
knock-for-knock	**a.** The argument developed into a nasty knock-for-knock confrontation. **b.** Both owners had knock-for-knock insurance agreements so the accident claims were settled quite promptly.
kosher	**a.** The new woollen kosher fitted Elaine perfectly. **b.** Three passengers on the flight had ordered kosher meals.
kowtow	**a.** Lucy had never seen a Chinese with the traditional kow-tow. **b.** Bert hated to kow-tow to his landlord in the big house.
kudos	**a.** Trevor's sales figures brought him plenty of kudos. **b.** They would spend countless hours playing kudos.

If you find that you tripped up on one or two of these examples of usage, make sure you look up the meanings of the words. Then you can add them to your growing vocabulary.

L

Replace the Missing Words

Below are ten words and ten sentences. A word is missing from each of the sentences. Can you place the appropriate words in all ten sentences? Each word is used only once. Answers on page 440.

| labyrinthine | lachrymose | lackadaisical | lacklustre | laconic |
| lacuna | laissez faire | laity | lambent | lamentable |

1. The coach was unamused by the team's _____ performance, its worst in ten years, losing by four goals to an inferior side.
2. Many economists blamed the market's free-fall on the Government's uncaring, _____ attitude to imports.
3. With his expert knowledge of public life, Sir Gregory was the ideal man to penetrate the _____ workings of the Foreign Office.
4. Although George was an avid churchman he'd always been perfectly satisfied to remain among the _____.
5. Although she didn't lack intelligence, Deborah's _____ efforts when it came to exams almost spelt disaster.
6. The couple chatted for hours in the _____ light of the candles.
7. She loved the strong, silent type of actor, which is probably why Robert Mitchum's _____ style appealed to her.
8. When they read Aunt Hilda's confessional letter it wasn't the contents that intrigued them but the puzzling _____ towards the end.
9. As though she had all the time in the world, Jenny sauntered down the lane in her typically _____ manner.
10. Two days after the funeral Jim had had enough of the _____ household, and headed for the pub.

If you fitted all the pieces of that verbal jigsaw together then you did very well, as several of the words would hardly qualify as common. But all ten would be useful in any person's vocabulary so make sure you're familiar with their meanings and usage.

Chose the Correct Meaning

From the alternatives, **a** or **b**, mark or circle which one you think represents most accurately the meaning of each word. The answers are on page 440.

lampoon   **a.** a sailing ship's lantern; **b.** a satirical attack in prose or verse.

landau   **a.** A French provincial cottage; **b.** a horse-drawn carriage

langoustine   **a.** a small spiny lobster; **b.** a soup made from pork offal.

languorous   **a.** sleekly beautiful; **b.** feeling sluggish and drowsy.

lapidary   **a.** a doctor specialising in surgery of the abdominal wall; **b.** a worker or dealer in gemstones.

largesse   **a.** a generous gift, usually money; **b.** water that gathers in the hull of a ship.

lascivious   **a.** lustful and lecherous; **b.** given to excessive laughter.

lassitude   **a.** physical and mental weariness; **b.** the relief of escaping from a hurtful emotional situation.

latent   **a.** a temperature just prior to boiling point; **b.** existing but not noticeable or explicit.

lateral   **a.** relating to the top or bottom of something; **b.** relating to the side or sides.

laudable   **a.** praiseworthy; **b.** drugged with opium.

lectern   **a.** a junior university lecturer or assistant; **b.** a raised reading desk or support.

leger-de-main   **a.** chain-mail jacket worn by medieval knights; **b.** deception or sleight of hand.

leitmotif   **a.** a recurring theme in music, art or literature; **b.** the Berlin subway system.

lese-majesty   **a.** high treason, or an offence committed against the Crown; **b.** the act of bending the knee in the presence of a monarch.

lessee   **a.** a tenant to whom a lease is granted; **b.** an owner who grants a lease of property.

lethargic   **a.** suffering from lead poisoning; **b.** drowsy and apathetic.

leviathan   **a.** monstrously huge and powerful; **b.** small, weak and puny.

lexicography   **a.** the study of mathematical puzzles; **b.** the profession of compiling dictionaries.

liaison   **a.** a disastrous relationship; **b.** communication or contact between groups or individuals.

libertarian   **a.** a believer in free thought and expression; **b.** an advocate of 'free love' and polygamous relationships.

libidinous   **a.** having excessive sexual desire; **b.** being a consummate liar.

libretto   **a.** the soprano section of a choir; **b.** the text of an opera or vocal work.

licentious   **a.** involved in piracy; **b.** sexually unrestrained.

lickspittle   **a.** a person who insists on being uncomfortably close when speaking to others; **b.** a fawning, servile person.

Lilliputian   **a.** very tiny or trivial; **b.** outrageously imaginative.

limbo   **a.** a vague place or condition of uncertainty; **b.** an area used by athletes to warm up before performing.

limpid   **a.** soft and malleable; **b.** clear and transparent.

linchpin   **a.** a person or thing regarded as absolutely essential for a successful outcome; **b.** the lever that operates the trapdoor of a gallows.

lingua franca   **a.** a syrupy cure for hangovers; **b.** a common language used for communication by people with many different mother tongues.

lionise   **a.** to treat someone as a celebrity; **b.** to monopolise a conversation.

lissom   **a.** golden-haired; **b.** lithe and supple.

litany   **a.** the curtains that screen off a crematorium furnace; **b.** a long and tedious recital or speech.

livid   **a.** in red blotches; **b.** greyish discoloration as from a bruise.

lobbyist   **a.** a person who attempts to influence legislators on behalf of a particular interest; **b.** a newspaper reporter specialising in political stories.

locum tenens   **a.** a professional stand-in, usually for a doctor or chemist; **b.** the technique used to locate fractured bones.

logistics   **a.** the management of the supply and flow of materials within an organisation; **b.** forestry science and management.

logorrhoea   **a.** bad breath; **b.** excessive talkativeness.

longevity   **a.** ancestor worship; **b.** long life.

longueur   **a.** the train of a wedding dress; **b.** a period of utter boredom.

loquacious   **a.** excessively talkative; **b.** having red-rimmed eyes.

Lothario   **a.** a seducer of women; **b.** swarthy and crude-mannered.

louche   **a.** calm and laid-back; **b.** shifty and devious.

loupe   **a.** the magnifying eyepiece used by jewellers; **b.** an intrauterine contraceptive device.

lubricious   **a.** obviously effeminate; **b.** lewd and lecherous.

lucid   **a.** brittle and easily breakable; **b.** clear and easily understood.

lugubrious   **a.** excessively mournful; **b.** fulsome and persuasive.

lumpen   **a.** people who are grossly overweight; **b.** deprived and stupid.

luxuriant   **a.** lush, rich and abundant; **b.** devoted to luxury.

That was quite a round, so take a breath and check your choices with the answers on page 440. A score of more than 40 correct would be an excellent achievement, and one of 35 or more very respectable. But shame on you if you missed lexicography!

Revision: All the Way from K to L

Just when you thought it was safe to assume that revision had been forgotten or abandoned, here we are with a reminder that some K words might require revisiting, along with the L words you've just learned. So spare a few minutes to assure yourself that you've really assimilated those vital new words into your vocabulary. How about these, for example:

Keynesian	**kudos**	**kleptomaniac**	**kitsch**	**Kafkaesque**
lachrymose	**laconic**	**lascivious**	**leitmotif**	**louche**

M

Words in Use: Right or Wrong?

There are two good tests to see if a word is well embedded in your vocabulary. One is, 'If I hear a word or come across it in my reading, do I know immediately what it means?' And the other is, 'Can I use it spontaneously to express my thoughts?' That's what a working vocabulary is all about: instant recognition; easy erudition.

Try the tests on the following words. If you're comfortable with their meaning and usage you'll have no trouble deciding which of them are being used correctly and which are not. Answers on page 440.

		Right	Wrong
1.	He placed the thin tissue of *macrocosm* under the microscope.	___	___
2.	With some trepidation they walked into the council chamber and a *maelstrom* of bitter and violent argument.	___	___
3.	She found herself subjected to the *magisterial* gaze of the widely admired but much feared choirmaster.	___	___
4.	True to his *magnanimous* reputation, Sir Richard made sure all the silver was counted before the guests departed.	___	___
5.	After the concert they all agreed that the concerto was undoubtedly his *magnum opus*.	___	___
6.	Although the professor was brilliant with his students he was distinctly *maladroit* when it came to the simplest household tasks.	___	___

	Right	Wrong

7. Bernard could not shake off the *malaise* that had affected him since his return from Nigeria.   ___   ___

8. Mrs Hilton committed the gross *mulapropism* of laying out the dinner cutlery in quite the wrong order.   ___   ___

9. Of the two seafood dishes, Claude preferred the *mal de mer*.   ___   ___

Mal de mer

10. After hearing the evidence it was clear who the *malefactor* was.   ___   ___

11. It was unfair of Charles to *malign* Mrs Hardcastle, especially as she had been so kind to him.   ___   ___

12. Robert held the *Malthusian* viewpoint that the Far East would ultimately drain the world's resources to the point of disaster.   ___   ___

When you check the answers on page 440 you'll find that four words were used wrongly. Did you spot them? Did you approve the eight correct examples of usage?

Choose the Correct Meaning

Which of the two alternatives, **a** or **b**, most accurately fits the meaning of the word? Mark or circle your choices (you know now that wild guesses don't count) and then check the answers on page 441.

mandatory	**a.** obligatory or compulsory; **b.** officially sanctioned.
manifest	**a.** promising; **b.** obvious, easily noticed.
manifold	**a.** to accumulate; **b.** multiple or many different kinds.
manna	**a.** the remains of a meal; **b.** an unexpected windfall or gift.
manqué	**a.** unfulfilled, would-be; **b.** the dust and detritus in an abandoned habitation.

mantra	**a.** the sacred cape worn by a Buddhist priest; **b.** a sacred word repeated endlessly as an aid to prayer.
maquette	**a.** highly glazed and ornamented ceramic tile; **b.** sculptor's small preliminary model for a larger piece.
marmoreal	**a.** resembling marble; **b.** relating to small monkeys.
materfamilias	**a.** family consisting of all daughters; **b.** female head of family.
maudlin	**a.** tearfully sentimental; **b.** easily convinced.
maunder	**a.** to receive alms on Maundy Thursday; **b.** to talk or act incoherently.
maverick	**a.** an independent, unorthodox person; **b.** an injured cow or bull that becomes dangerous.
mawkish	**a.** falsely sentimental; **b.** excessively nosey.
maxim	**a.** a general truth or rule, briefly expressed; **b.** a rule prescribing a limitation.
mea culpa	**a.** the drink is poisoned; **b.** it is my fault.
mealy-mouthed	**a.** crudely outspoken; **b.** hesitant, afraid to speak plainly.
median	**a.** a hidden mountain plateau; **b.** a middle point or value.
mediate	**a.** to intervene in order to bring about agreement in a dispute; **b.** to separate disagreeing parties in the belief that time will heal their differences.
megalomania	**a.** fear of spots; **b.** delusions of grandeur or power.
megrim	**a.** a migraine headache; **b.** a horrific, realistic dream.
melange	**a.** a confused mixture; **b.** a milk jelly dessert.
melee	**a.** a lady's long silk dressing gown; **b.** a noisy fight or brawl.
mellifluous	**a.** smooth and honeyed; **b.** soft and billowing.
memorabilia	**a.** manuscripts produced prior to the 15th century; **b.** objects connected to famous people or events.
ménage	**a.** a stable of horses; **b.** members of a household.
mendacious	**a.** prone to lying and deception; **b.** miserly and grasping.
mendicant	**a.** a holistic doctor; **b.** someone dependent on begging.
mephitic	**a.** foul-smelling and poisonous; **b.** a substance that makes the eyes water.
mercenary	**a.** practical: 'act first, think later'; **b.** motivated primarily by greed or gain.
meretricious	**a.** annoyingly repetitive; **b.** vulgarly or superficially attractive.
mesmerise	**a.** to hypnotise; **b.** to cure by immersion in water.
messianic	**a.** having or imitating the appearance of Christ; **b.** describing an orator who promises salvation or an ideal life of peace and prosperity.
metabolism	**a.** the bodily process that converts food to energy; **b.** the theory that base metals like lead can be converted into gold.
metaphorical	**a.** symbolic, illustrative; **b.** relating to philosophical theory.
métier	**a.** one's natural vocation; **b.** a group of art students.
metronymic	**a.** music with a steady beat; **b.** a name or qualities derived from the mother or other female ancestor.

mettle	**a.** decency and honesty; **b.** courage and spirit.
mezzanine	**a.** a basement bar; **b.** an intermediate storey between ground and first floor.
miasma	**a.** a noxious, foreboding atmosphere; **b.** a mass flight of bees, wasps or other insects.
microcosm	**a.** a miniature version of something that is regarded as representing the qualities of the larger original; **b.** extremely thin slices of material prepared for microscopic viewing.
micturate	**a.** preserving crystals in oil; **b.** to urinate.

From that round of 40 a score of 35+ or would be excellent, while one of 30 or more would be above average.

Fill in the Gaps: Identify the Word

From the meanings given, fill the gaps with the missing letters and identify the words. Then check the answers on page 441.

1. One's normal surroundings or setting   *mili* _ _
2. To influence some decision or event   *milita* _ _
3. The act or art of mimicking or copying   *mimic* _ _
4. Threatening or menacing   *minato* _ _
5. A servile, fawning employee or dependant   *mini* _ _
6. Describing something, often writing or printing, that is very small   *minuscu* _ _
7. Small, inconsequential, trifling details   *minuti* _ _
8. Someone who dislikes and distrusts everyone   *misanthro* _ _
9. The interbreeding of different races   *miscegenati* _ _
10. To interpret incorrectly, to arrive at a wrong conclusion *misconstr* _ _
11. An incorrect or unsuitable name   *misnom* _ _
12. Hatred of women   *misogy* _ _
13. To moderate, or make a condition less severe   *mitiga* _ _
14. An aid to the memory   *mnemon* _ _
15. An attribute that denotes mode, mood or manner   *modali* _ _
16. A small amount or portion   *modic* _ _
17. One of two parts or shares of something   *moie* _ _
18. To soothe and pacify   *molli* _ _
19. Reclusive, like a monk or nun   *monast* _ _
20. The theory that inflation is caused by an excess supply of money in the economy   *monetari* _ _
21. A book, treatise or study concerned with a single subject *monogra* _ _
22. Mounds and hills of rock debris deposited by former glaciers   *morai* _ _
23. An agreed suspension of an obligation or activity   *moratori* _ _
24. The fundamental values and customs of a society   *mor* _ _

25. Describing a marriage between a man and woman of
    vastly dissimilar position in which the offspring of the
    lower-ranked partner have no rights to titles and
    property of the higher-ranked partner   *morganat* _ _
26. Without force or vitality; stagnant   *moribu* _ _
27. Ill-tempered and peevish   *moro* _ _
28. The perfect, most appropriate word or expression   *mot jus* _ _
29. Civilian attire, worn instead of a military uniform   *muf* _ _
30. Having many parts of great variety   *multifario* _ _
31. Ordinary, everyday, unexciting and banal   *munda* _ _
32. Extremely generous and liberal   *munifice* _ _
33. Having the ability to change; adaptable   *mutab* _ _
34. Common to or shared by two or more people or groups   *mutu* _ _
35. Shortsighted or unable to see distant objects clearly   *myop* _ _

An easier round, wouldn't you agree? If, after checking the answers on page 441
you find you have completed 30 or more words correctly, congratulate yourself.
A lesser score is no disaster, but it tends to indicate that you need to work with
determination and enthusiasm to achieve that A1 vocabulary!

Word Roots and Building Blocks

Here are some more word roots which, between them, have provided vital
building blocks for dozens, if not hundreds, of our words. Learning their basic
meanings will often help you identify the meanings of many words unfamiliar
to you.

Word, Element	Origin	Meaning	English words
macro-	Greek	large, long	*macrobiotics, macrocosm, macro lens, macroscopic.*
malus, mal-	Latin	bad	*malevolent, malignant, malady, maladroit, malign.*
manus, man-	Latin	hand	*manual, manicure, manuscript.*
mater, matri-	Latin	mother	*maternal, matron, matrix, matrimony, matrimonial.*
mega-	Greek	great	*megabyte, megalith, megalopolis, megastar.*
meta-	Greek	change	*metabolism, metamorphosis*
-meter	Greek	measuring	*metre, barometer, metrication, gasometer.*
micro-	Greek	very small	*microcosm, microscope, microfilm, micrometer.*

Word, Element	Origin	Meaning	English words
milli-	Latin	thousand	*milligram, millimetre, millibar, millennium.*
mis-	Old English	bad, wrong	*misunderstand, misfortune, mistake, misspell, mislead.*
monis, mono-	Greek	one, single	*monocle, monody, monograph, monochrome.*
-morph	Greek	shape, form	*amorphous, morpheme, morphology.*
-most	Old English	superlative	*uppermost, utmost, hindmost, foremost.*
multi-	Latin	much, many	*multistorey, multimillion, multiple, multifarious.*

A Reminder to Revise

Revision should be instinctive by now. With an urge to move forward, it's understandable that lingering on M words could be irksome when new N words beckon from the next page. But before you wrap up this section, double-check your comprehension of the following selection:

macrocosm	*magnanimous*	*mantra*	*mea culpa*	*ménage*
meretricious	*misogyny*	*mollify*	*moratorium*	*mores*

Satisfied? If you are, then by all means move on. But if not . . . you know what you have to do . . .

N

Are They being used Correctly?

You've probably encountered the following ten words in your reading at some time or other. You may know all their meanings – but are you conversant with their usage? Here are the words integrated into sentences, several of which are completely meaningless. Can you separate the good from the garbage? Simply answer **right** or **wrong**. Answers on page 441.

Answers on page 441.

	Right	**Wrong**
1. She could hardly express the exhilaration and joy she felt at reaching the *nadir* of her ambition.	___	___

2. The interminable silence extended for several
    nanoseconds.   ___   ___

3. Camilla was very fond of June except for her
    narcissistic streak.   ___   ___

4. A **nascent** spark of anger ignited in Jack's righteous
    breast.   ___   ___

5. Dennis hated the dense, **nebulous** atmosphere of
    the tropics.   ___   ___

6. After his release from gaol, Victor returned to his
    nefarious ways.   ___   ___

7. The two old men liked nothing more than to yarn
    by the fire, long into the night, fuelled by their
    mugs of **negus**.   ___   ___

8. After hours and hours of disastrous betting, Sir
    Randolph prayed that his **Nemesis** would arrive
    soon in the shape of a huge win.   ___   ___

9. The trendy lecturer confused a good many of his
    audience by his relentless use of **neologisms**.   ___   ___

10. Hilary admitted that she was a **neophyte** in the
    auction business.   ___   ___

Your score should read Right = 6; Wrong = 4. If it doesn't, spend a minute or two
more on this exercise before consulting the answers on page 441.

Choose the Correct Meaning

Which one of the three choices, **a**, **b** or **c**, most accurately fits the meaning of the
word? Mark or circle your choices and then check the answers on page 441.

ne plus ultra   a. that extra effort; **b.** perfection; the highest point attainable;
                  c. a place of peace and privacy.

nepotism   a. pertaining to the kidneys; **b.** the Muslim principle that the
                  grandmother becomes head of a family; **c.** favouritism shown
                  to relatives and friends by those in positions of power.

nexus   a. a link or bond between a group or series; **b.** the central point
                  of a spiral; **c.** a partial vacuum.

nicety   a. ridiculous social mannerism; **b.** well-ordered and organised;
                  c. a subtle point or distinction.

nihilism   a. the rejection of all established authority and institutions;
                  b. the doctrine that man is imprisoned by his environment;
                  c. the belief that despite superficial circumstances, all men are
                  really equal.

noblesse oblige   **a.** the obligation of the ruled to their rulers; **b.** the supposed obligation of the nobility to be fair and generous; **c.** the obligation of an aristocrat to share his title with his wife.

noisome   **a.** offensive behaviour; **b.** smelly and disgusting; **c.** very loud.

nominal   **a.** theoretical, or token; **b.** a pre-appointment to an office or an official position; **c.** one-tenth of any amount.

nonage   **a.** people enjoying life after 90 years of age; **b.** a woman of 'a certain age'; **c.** the legal state of being a minor.

nonce word   **a.** any term describing homosexuality; **b.** a word coined for a single occasion; **c.** a word invented by Lewis Carroll.

nonchalant   **a.** indifferent, calm and cool; **b.** with a chip on the shoulder; **c.** habitually lazy.

nonentity   **a.** an insignificant person or thing; **b.** a pseudonym; **c.** a stateless person; someone with no known nationality.

nonpareil   **a.** something unmatched or unsurpassed; **b.** something that is out of line with everything else; **c.** any gemstone weighing more than 20 carats.

nonplussed   **a.** to have one's trousers taken away; **b.** to be utterly perplexed; **c.** a person who continually 'misses out'.

non sequitur   **a.** an illogical conclusion; **b.** an unfortunate misunderstanding; **c.** a misunderstanding because of bad timing.

nostrum   **a.** the beginnings of a moustache; **b.** a violent headache or migraine; **c.** a dubious cure-all.

nouveau riche   **a.** a gaudy style of architecture; **b.** a person vulgarly displaying newly acquired wealth; **c.** a ceremonial procession of lawyers.

nuance   **a.** a subtle difference; **b.** a barely discernible breath or breeze; **c.** a lullaby sung to a baby.

nubile   **a.** a startlingly statuesque woman; **b.** with a shiny, dark skin; **c.** describing a young woman of marriageable age.

nugatory   **a.** of little or no value; **b.** hard-headed and hard-hearted; **c.** a gold alloy containing very little precious metal.

numinous   **a.** crackling with light; **b.** arousing spiritual or religious emotions; **c.** dismissive, arrogant.

nymphet   **a.** a freshwater mermaid; **b.** a young, sexually precocious girl; **c.** a winged cherub, symbolic of water.

For this quick round, with few challenges, a score of less than 12 would be rather disappointing – but, please, not discouraging! Check your dictionary to make sure you have all the meanings mastered and then add them to the growing number of N words in your vocabulary.

Neologisms, or New Words

Throughout a millennium or more the English language has borrowed, purloined, adapted and remodelled words from just about every language that ever existed around the globe. It has also invented quite a few: often, seemingly, instantly and out of thin air. It's a continuing, seamless process. The day you read this an estimated 20 to 40 new words will be coined to help us describe or explain or express something that never existed before, or to describe, explain or express something familiar in quite a different way. These new words are called *neologisms* and their importance is such that publishers are engaged in a Forth Bridge-painting operation to include them in their dictionaries, the irony being that by the time they are listed they are out of date (or worse, out of use) – as is the following selection coined in the 1990s. Are these in your dictionary?

acquaintance rape	rape by a person well-known to the victim.
all gone pear-shaped	something that has gone wrong.
andropause	male menopause.
bad hair day	a day when everything goes wrong.
big girl's blouse	a weak, ineffectual or pathetic person.
blag	to dupe or 'con' an advantage from someone.
Blairism	the policies and style of government associated with British Prime Minister Tony Blair.
bobbitt	to sever a man's (usually a husband's) penis.
brollability	the probability of rain.
cereologist	someone investigating the phenomena of crop circles.
cybersex	sexual activity or information available through computer networks.
designer stubble	facial hair on men midway between clean-shaven and bearded.
dumbing down	the policy of excessively appealing to popular taste.
dweeb	a person who is boringly conventional, dull and studious.
firkinised	off-the-shelf designer pubs, with names such as Flock & Firkin; Falstaff & Firkin, etc.
gonzo	a crazy, unorthodox person.
jones	Black personification of the male member; penis.
pink pound	homosexual spending power.

rollover	an unclaimed lottery jackpot that is added to the prize money for the following lottery draw.
saddo	a dull, unsociable person.
scuzz	an unpleasant person.
siblicide	the killing of a young bird by a fellow nestling.
to give it some welly	extra effort or enthusiasm applied to a task.
wally	an ineffectual, stupid, despised person.
white-knuckle	describing an amusement-park ride experience that absolutely terrifies.
wysiwyg	a term indicating that what you see on a computer screen is what you get in a printout: *what you see is what you get.*

Numbers, Sizes and Amounts from Word Roots

Although our names for numbers, sizes and quantities are derived from Greek and Latin roots, we chose Arabic numerals rather than Roman. But even though our numerals are Arabic (5, 6, 7) the way in which we express their applications is a glorious mixture of Greek and Latin. For example:

7 = hepta (Greek) and **septem** (Latin). From the former we get *heptagon, heptameter* and *Heptateuch*, while from the latter comes *septuagenerian, septet* and *September* (it was the seventh month of the year in ancient Rome).

6 = hex (Greek) and **sex** (Latin). From the former comes *hexagonal* and *hexagram*, while from the latter derive *sextuple, sextet, sextant* and *sextuplets*.

And so on. This helps to explain why words describing applications of the same numeral often share two different prefixes. The number four has the Greek root **tetra-** (*tetrahedron, tetradactyl, tetralogy, tetragram*) and also the Latin **quad-** (*quadrant, quadrangle, quadrilateral, quadrille, quadroon, quadruped, quadruplet, quadruple*), all expressing some form of the number four. This is a classic case of the English language being unable to make up its mind!

Here's a quick guide to numerical prefixes:

Number	Greek root	Latin root
1	oine	unus
2	duo	duo
3	treis, tri	tres
4	tetra	quad
5	pente	quinque
6	hex	ex
7	hepta	septem
8	okto	octo
9	ennea	novem, non
10	deca	decem
100	hecto	centum
1000	kilo	milli

Five Minute Revision

Spend a worthwhile five minutes looking back over your N words. Are you satisfied, for example, that you are fully conversant with the meanings of *nebulous* and *Nemesis, neophyte* and *nepotism*? Can you use *nominal, non sequitur* and *nugatory* appropriately in sentences? If you're satisfied you can, then let's move on.

O

Complete the Sentence

Below are 12 words and 12 sentences. A word is missing from each of the sentences. Can you place the appropriate words in all 12 sentences? Each word is used only once. Answers on page 441.

obdurate	obeisance	obfuscate	oblique	obloquy	obsequious
obsolescent	obstreperous	obtuse	obviate	occidental	occlude

1. To the Chinese, confronted by the first Western adventurers, _____ clothing and habits must have seemed totally alien.
2. The professor complained that all his students were equally barbarian, ignorant and _____.
3. They were all of the view that Miss Bertram had gained her various promotions through her grovelling and _____ manner.

4. Despite Emma's pleading, her father remained _____ .
5. The dirt road ran off the highway at an _____ angle.
6. The effect of the nest was to _____ the passage of the smoke up the chimney.
7. Even though he'd served his sentence, Mark found the _____ of his crime too much to bear and withdrew from all public life.
8. As she entered the room Rebecca bowed hesitantly in _____ to the chief on his makeshift throne.
9. The most unruly and _____ boys in the class were moved to the front row of desks.
10. The farmer agreed with the agent that the tractor was _____ and would soon need to be replaced.
11. They felt that installing the new computers would _____ the need for the extra staff the office manager had been requesting.
12. The new handbook only served to _____ the already bewildering maze of unintelligible instructions.

Check the answers on page 441 and feel pleased with yourself if you scored eight or more correct. Now for some more useful O words.

Choose the Correct Meaning

Which of the three choices, **a**, **b** or **c**, most appropriately fits the meaning of the word? Mark or circle your choices (remember, blind stabs with a pin shouldn't count!) and then check your answers on page 441.

odium   **a.** bad breath; **b.** intense hatred; **c.** gold amalgam dental filling.

odontologist   **a.** cares for the feet; **b.** cares for the nose; **c.** cares for the teeth.

odyssey   **a.** any long poem; **b.** a long eventful journey; **c.** a search for the ideal woman.

oeuvre   **a.** a dish of quail's eggs; **b.** a list of soldiers killed in battle; **c.** the whole work of a writer or artist.

officious   **a.** over-ready to offer advice or services; **b.** helpful and obliging; **c.** unable to work with others.

olfactory   **a.** a branch of industrial archaeology; **b.** abuse of unionism; **c.** relating to the sense of smell.

oligarchy   **a.** an unbroken line of female descendants; **b.** a government controlled by a privileged few; **c.** a communal olive grove in Mediterranean countries.

omnipotent   **a.** having great or unlimited power; **b.** one whose statements are always true; **c.** one who foresees the future.

omniscient   **a.** knowing everything; **b.** being ruled or overawed by astrology; **c.** fear of the dark.

omnivorous   **a.** eating only herbaceous matter; **b.** eating only animals; **c.** eating anything.

onerous   **a.** arduous and oppressive; **b.** selfish; **c.** given to making sarcastic remarks.

opprobrium   **a.** disgrace; **b.** a dark place; **c.** an eye disease.

optimal   **a.** well-balanced eyesight; **b.** having the most favourable or advantageous situation; **c.** the unachievable.

opulent   **a.** stout and podgy; **b.** abundant, wealthy; **c.** showing off.

oracular   **a.** roughly elliptical; **b.** prophetic; **c.** squinting.

Orcadian   **a.** the ideal; **b.** sea-loving; **c.** a native of the Orkney islands.

ordure   **a.** excrement; **b.** money distributed to peasants by aristocrats; **c.** the human remains in unmarked graves.

ormolu   **a.** an exquisite black gemstone; **b.** fancy scrollwork in wood; **c.** a gold-coloured alloy used in furniture decoration.

oscillate   **a.** to move up and down; **b.** to swing regularly from side to side; **c.** to vibrate at intervals.

osmosis   **a.** evaporation by use of artificial heating; **b.** diffusion through a porous barrier; **c.** the process of a body turning to dust.

ossified   **a.** transformed into a paste; **b.** turned into rubber; **c.** turned into bone.

ostensibly   **a.** seemingly; **b.** obviously; **c.** incautiously.

ostentatious   **a.** silent and secretive; **b.** pretentious and showy; **c.** using bright, dazzling colours.

osteopathy   **a.** treatment using water and sea products; **b.** using nerve stimulation; **c.** using massage and bone manipulation.

ostracise   **a.** to make a quadruped walk on two legs; **b.** to exclude or banish someone; **c.** to blend various ingredients.

otiose   **a.** useless and futile; **b.** fat and lazy; **c.** slow and lumbering.

ottoman   **a.** a small oriental carpet; **b.** a low padded seat; **c.** a tall brass long-spouted teapot.

overly   **a.** randomly; **b.** excessively; **c.** lately.

overt   **a.** hidden and secret; **b.** open and public; **c.** shy and retiring.

overtone   **a.** an additional meaning or nuance; **b.** the sound from a wrongly tuned stringed instrument; **c.** mild sunburn.

oxymoron   **a.** someone consistently using meaningless expressions; **b.** a calf born on Christmas Day; **c.** an expression that combines contradictory terms.

An interesting round and one that should add some fresh words to your vocabulary. A score of around 20 would be average, but if you managed to select 25 or more as correct, allow yourself an indulgent smile.

The 'Ology Department

There must be by now, since the combining forms *-logy* and *-ology* were introduced in the early 19th century, some thousands of *'ologies*. Many of them you certainly know, but there may be some that remain unfamiliar to you. Here's a selection:

anthropology	the study of man, his origins and physical characteristics.
cardiology	the study of the heart.
cetology	the study of whales.
chronology	the determination of proper sequences of time, dates and past events.
conchology	the study of shells.
cosmology	the study of the origin and nature of the universe.
cytology	the study of plant and animal cells.
dermatology	the study of skin and its diseases.
ecology	the study of the relationships between living creatures and their environment.
gastroenterology	the study of diseases of the stomach and intestines.
haematology	the study of diseases of the blood and blood-forming tissue.
histology	the study of animal and plant tissues.
horology	the art of making clocks and measuring time.
ichthyology	the study of fish.
immunology	the study of biological immunity.
mycology	the study of fungi.
odontology	the study of diseases of the teeth, gums and jaw.
oenology	the study and art of making wine.
oncology	the study and treatment of tumours, especially cancers.
ontology	the theory of the nature of being.
ophthalmology	the study of the eye and its diseases.
ornithology	the study of birds.
palaeontology	the study of fossils and the structure and evolution of extinct animals and plants.
parapsychology	the study of telepathy and mental phenomena.
pathology	the study of the cause, origin and nature of disease.
petrology	the study of the origin and formation of rocks.
pharmacology	the study of drugs, their actions and uses.

philology	the study of the evolution of language.
phrenology	the study of human brain function according to its parts.
pomology	the study of fruit and its cultivation.
primatology	the study of the ape and monkey tribes.
proctology	the study of the anus and rectum.
radiology	the use of radioactivity in diagnosis and treatment of diseases.
seismology	the study of earthquakes.
sociology	the study of the development, functioning and classification of human societies.
speleology	the study of caves.
toxicology	the study of poisons and their antidotes.
volcanology	the study of volcanoes.

O, Revision! Revision!

Do you think you know your O words sufficiently to safely stow them in your vocabulary? Just try these again by fitting them into mental sentences:

obsequious obsolescent oeuvre orotund optimal overt

Make sure you fully understand *obsolescent*: it doesn't mean 'defunct' – that is *obsolete* – but 'in the process of becoming obsolete, defunct or dead'. And *orotund*? Oops! Sorry about that. When applied to the voice, it means 'booming and resonant'; with writing, it means 'pompous and bombastic'.

P

Choose the Correct Meanings

Which one of the pair of alternatives, **a** or **b**, most accurately fits the meaning of the word? Mark or circle your choices and then check the answers on page 442.

pacifist **a.** supporter of inter-Pacific Islands economic union; **b.** a person who refuses to undertake military service.

paediatrician **a.** a specialist in bone diseases; **b.** a specialist in children's diseases.

palaver **a.** a drawn-out discussion; **b.** a Mexican Indian woven cape.

palimpsest **a.** a text that has been erased and written over; **b.** a word game in which the player tries to make as many different words as possible from the original.

palliative **a.** an effective drug but one that has severe side-effects; **b.** a treatment that relieves but without curing.

palpable **a.** evident and obvious; **b.** barely eatable.

palpitate **a.** to massage violently; **b.** to flutter or tremble.

panacea **a.** wishful thinking; **b.** a universal remedy.

panache **a.** dash and verve; **b.** a vague, irritating ache.

panegyric **a.** any bitter medicine; **b.** an elaborate, very flattering expression of praise.

panjandrum **a.** a Punjabi feast; **b.** a self-important official.

pantheism **a.** the doctrine that the universe is a manifestation of God; **b.** the theory that all souls exist until eternity.

paparazzi **a.** a long row of marble columns; **b.** tenacious freelance photographers of celebrities.

paradigm **a.** a model example; **b.** a tongue-twisting phrase.

paragon **a.** a person held up to ridicule; **b.** a model of excellence.

paramour **a.** an occasional lover; **b.** the lover of a married man or woman.

paranoia **a.** fear of criticism or attack; **b.** delusions of persecution.

paraphrase **a.** a restatement in different words intended to clarify; **b.** a passage rewritten to disguise its real meaning.

pariah **a.** a West African tribal chief; **b.** a social outcast.

pari mutuel **a.** a banking system that guarantees depositors a fixed interest rate; **b.** a betting system that divides the total stakes among the winners, less a percentage.

parity **a.** equality of rank and pay; **b.** an agreed currency exchange rate between two countries.

parlance **a.** a marble facade of a building; **b.** a particular or idiomatic manner of speaking.

parlous **a.** poor and embittered; **b.** difficult and perilous.

parodic **a.** amusingly mimicking the style of another's work; **b.** arriving at an unexpected time or in an unusual way.

paroxysm **a.** a fatal disease caught from parrots; **b.** a convulsive fit or outburst.

parsimonious **a.** being frugal; **b.** being unfriendly.

partiality **a.** prejudice or bias; **b.** sly greediness.

partisan **a.** any division into two parts; **b.** a person devoted to one party or cause.

parvenu **a.** a newly rich social upstart; **b.** a leading patron of the arts.

passé **a.** up-to-the-minute; **b.** behind the times.

pastiche **a.** a work that imitates the style of another; **b.** a slow movement for orchestral strings.

paterfamilias **a.** male head of a household; **b.** the collective uncles of a family.

pathogenic **a.** pertaining to autopsies; **b.** capable of causing disease.

patina **a.** circumference of the retina of the eye; **b.** an oxidised layer or the sheen of wear on a surface.

patisserie **a.** a shop selling pastries; **b.** a shop selling preserved meats.

patois **a.** a stepped patio; **b.** a regional dialect of a language.

patrial **a.** pertaining to a person's country of birth; **b.** a person with an unknown father.

patrician **a.** a fluent speaker of French, Italian or Spanish; **b.** an aristocrat or person of refined tastes.

Pauline **a.** relating to Pope Paul and his papal bulls; **b.** relating to St Paul or his doctrines.

Pecksniffian **a.** an admirer of the works of Charles Dickens; **b.** a hypocrite who advocates moral behaviour but behaves otherwise.

That's the first round of five – P is an extremely productive generator of words – and a lot of interesting and essential ones, too. For this first set of 40 words a score of around 25 would be satisfactory, 30 very good, and one of 35+ excellent.

Words in Use: Right or Wrong?

In some of the following sentences the P word is used correctly; in others incorrectly, resulting in nonsense. Which usages are right and which are wrong? Mark your decisions and then check the answers on page 442.

		Right	**Wrong**
1.	He puffed out his chest and the audience admired his *pectorals*.	——	——
2.	The old trader was always on the lookout for a *pecuniary* advantage	——	——
3.	He was a fanatical *pedagogue*, always travelling, never arriving.	——	——
4.	Joanne was always breathlessly **pedantic** and in a hurry.	——	——

		Right	**Wrong**
5.	Her hair was invariably tied in a crowning *peignoir*.	___	___
6.	The man was thoroughly unpleasant and could never refer to anyone other than in a sneering, *pejorative* manner.	___	___
7.	In the *pellucid* water the divers could see for 50 metres.	___	___
8.	They were all envious of the beautiful *penchant* she wore that night.	___	___
9.	Harry jumped all the hurdles but tripped on the *penumbra*.	___	___
10.	Old Lady Markham was surprisingly alert and *percipient*.	___	___

Five are right and five are wrong – did you sort them all out correctly? Two or three misses would be no great disaster.

Choose the Correct Meanings

Another substantial round in which you are asked again to choose which of the alternative definitions, **a** or **b**, most accurately fits the word. Mark or circle your choices and then check the answers on page 442.

peregrination   **a.** an extensive voyage; **b.** travelling pointlessly in circles.

peremptory   **a.** cautious and hesitant; **b.** decisive and final.

perennial   **a.** annual; **b.** everlasting.

perfunctory   **a.** careless and half-hearted; **b.** vigorous and positive.

peripatetic   **a.** prone to indigestion; **b.** always travelling.

periphrasis   **a.** a roundabout way of speaking or writing; **b.** an obsession with words.

permeate   **a.** to penetrate or pass through a substance; **b.** to beat two substances together to form a blend.

pernicious   **a.** irritating; **b.** harmful.

peroration   **a.** a memorial address; **b.** the summing up at the end of a speech.

perquisite   **a.** unearned money, favour or benefit; **b.** a service that is required before a payment is made.

persiflage   **a.** frivolous, teasing banter; **b.** embarrassing flattery.

perspicacious   **a.** unduly suspicious; **b.** having the ability to understand things clearly.

pertinacious   **a.** indolent and cheeky; **b.** stubbornly persistent.

pervasive   **a.** persuasively persisting; **b.** spreading subtly and gradually.

philanderer   **a.** a womaniser; **b.** a travelling salesman.

philippic   **a.** a letter expressing deep regret; **b.** a bitter speech of denunciation.

philanthropist   **a.** a charitable and benevolent person; **b.** a postage stamp collector.

Philistine   **a.** a person indifferent to learning and the arts; **b.** someone who attacks established values.

phlegmatic   **a.** excessively pessimistic; **b.** unemotional and unexcitable.

physiognomy   **a.** the study of cranial bumps and depressions; **b.** a person's facial features.

picaresque   **a.** relating to fictional episodic adventures; **b.** cute and appealing.

picayune   **a.** petty and niggling; **b.** bright and sparkling.

pied-à-terre   **a.** an apartment for secondary or occasional use; **b.** a dish featuring stewed snails.

pinchbeck   **a.** a frugal person; **b.** a cheap alloy imitating gold.

pinnate   **a.** a flagless flagpole; **b.** having the shape or arrangement of a feather.

piquant   **a.** having a stimulating tart taste; **b.** sly joking.

pique   **a.** resentment because of wounded pride; **b.** extreme envy.

pixilated   **a.** slightly dotty; **b.** obsessed with garden gnomes.

placate   **a.** to firmly put someone in their place; **b.** to appease.

placebo   **a.** a neutral substance given in place of an effective medicine; **b.** a glass-walled garden summer house.

plagiarism   **a.** falsely attributing genuine documents to fake paintings, manuscripts or antiques; **b.** stealing and using another's work or ideas and passing them off as one's own work.

plangent   **a.** a deep and resonant sound; **b.** a small, square pill.

Platonic   **a.** a blood-bond between two men; **b.** a friendship that's non-sensual and free from physical desire.

plebeian   **a.** a layman who pleads before a court; **b.** common and vulgar.

plenary   **a.** complete and absolute; **b.** intermediate and ongoing.

plethora   **a.** superabundance; **b.** an operation for gallstones.

podiatry   **a.** the art of speechmaking; **b.** the treatment of the feet and its disorders.

poetaster   **a.** a degraded person; **b.** a writer of bad verse.

pogrom   **a.** persecution or extermination of an ethnic group; **b.** a coup that leaves a family ruling a government.

poignant   **a.** sad-looking; **b.** distressing and painful to the feelings.

Having consulted the answers on page 442, did you fare any better in this round? It has to be said, however, that there is a fair sprinkling of 'difficult' words in this set, so you should be pleased with any score of 25 or more.

Complete the Sentence

Here are ten words and ten sentences. A word is missing from each of the sentences. Can you place the appropriate words in all 12 sentences? Each word is used only once. Answers on page 442.

| *polemic* | *polyglot* | *polymath* | *poltergeist* | *portentous* |
| *potable* | *pragmatic* | *precocious* | *preclude* | *predatory* |

1. The campers spent a whole day searching for clean, _____ water.
2. The distant _____ rumbling threatened even further earthquakes.
3. Convinced they'd heard a _____, Margaret and Aunt Edith refused to stay in the old house a moment longer.
4. With an expert knowledge of botany, history, chess and astronomy, and with an amazing talent for writing and painting, William was a true _____.
5. Naturally argumentative, Mark loved to engage in long _____ discussions.
6. Because of the varied ethnic mix, _____ signs were everywhere.
7. Perhaps because most of his family had been convicted for theft at some time or another, the lad could never shake off his _____ instincts.
8. The onset of the rainy season would _____ any further exploration.
9. With make-up, short skirts and high heels, the child looked dangerously _____.
10. The partners feared bankruptcy, but Mr Peters took the _____ view that a rescue package could be arranged without difficulty.

With a little thought, a score of seven or eight should be possible even though you may not have been familiar with half the words. But check them all so that you'll instantly know their meanings in the future. Now for the fifth and final P round!

Choose the Correct Meanings

Once again, which one of each pair of alternatives, **a** or **b**, most accurately fits the meaning of the word? Mark or circle your choices and then check the answers on page 442.

predicate	**a.** to assert or imply; to proclaim; **b.** to predict firmly, based on fact.
predilection	**a.** a vague dislike for something; **b.** a special liking for something.
prehensile	**a.** in a primitive state; **b.** capable of grasping.
preponderance	**a.** a great amount or number; **b.** a greater amount or number.
prerogative	**a.** a privilege or right; **b.** a person's first public speech.
prescient	**a.** possessing foresight; **b.** easily irritated.
pretentious	**a.** loud and bombastic; **b.** claiming undeserved importance.
prevaricate	**a.** to evade and mislead; **b.** to argue fiercely.
prima facie	**a.** unfounded allegations; **b.** apparently self-evident.
primordial	**a.** pertaining to swamps; **b.** existing from the beginning.
probity	**a.** serious and analytical; **b.** proven integrity.

proclivity	**a.** a tendency or inclination; **b.** a feature of rising ground in a landscape.
procrastinate	**a.** to think things over very carefully; **b.** to defer or postpone until later.
profligate	**a.** wildly wasteful and debauched; **b.** a financier who takes a profit before everything is accounted for.
prognosis	**a.** the determination of a disease and its treatment; **b.** a prediction of the outcome of a disorder or disease and the chances of recovery.
prolapse	**a.** a recurrence of a disorder; **b.** the downward displacement of an internal organ.
prolix	**a.** tediously long-winded; **b.** the centre of an ellipse.
propensity	**a.** strong and robust; **b.** a natural tendency or disposition.
prophylactic	**a.** germ-free milk; **b.** anything that protects from or prevents disease.
propinquity	**a.** subtle warning signals; **b.** nearness in place or time.
propitious	**a.** prone to lose one's balance; **b.** favourable.
prosaic	**a.** flat and lacking in imagination; **b.** one given to making faintly ridiculous flowery statements.
proscribe	**a.** to condemn or forbid; **b.** to agree under duress.
proselytise	**a.** to translate thoughts into words; **b.** to convert someone from one religious belief to another.
prosthesis	**a.** replacement of a body part with an artificial substitute; **b.** an unwelcome medical opinion.
protean	**a.** versatile and changeable; **b.** of vast size and girth.
protégé	**a.** a legally appointed guardian; **b.** someone who is helped and protected by another.
provenance	**a.** proof of authenticity; **b.** place of origin.
proviso	**a.** legal advice attached to a document; **b.** a condition or stipulation.
prurient	**a.** highly moral in thought and deed; **b.** inquisitive about the smutty and obscene.
psychosomatic	**a.** describing a physical disorder caused by or influenced by the emotions; **b.** a terminal illness.
puerile	**a.** silly and childish; **b.** offensively smelly.
puissant	**a.** self-mocking; **b.** powerful.
pulchritude	**a.** innocence and reverence; **b.** physical beauty.
pullulate	**a.** to vibrate and sway; **b.** to breed abundantly.
punctilious	**a.** paying strict attention to details of conduct; **b.** having an obsession with time and time-wasting.
purlieu	**a.** the fashionable clothes of high society; **b.** a neighbourhood or its boundaries.
pusillanimous	**a.** tending to favour members of one's family; **b.** timid and lacking in courage.
putative	**a.** supposed or reputed to exist; **b.** emerging and growing.

Pyrrhic victory a. a victory in which the victor's losses are as great as those of the defeated; **b.** a victory that has emerged from the ashes of defeat.

If you've stayed the P course for all five rounds you'll have mulled over the meanings of no fewer than 120 words – a lexicographical marathon! – and, surely, in the process, added considerably to your vocabulary. As with similar rounds, a score for this one of 25 or more would be commendable. If it's any consolation, the low-quota Q section is next.

Words from Ancient Beginnings

If you look at the pair of words *suspend* and *pendulum* for a few moments, you'll see that they are connected by a common syllable, **pend** – as a suffix in *suspend* and as a prefix in *pendulum*. The source for **pend** is the Latin *pendere*, meaning 'to hang', and if you think for a minute you'll probably come up with some more words containing the same element, such as *pendant, pendulous* and *pending*. You might also wonder about *depend* – and, yes, that too derives from the old Latin word. If you were, for example, to ask a favour of a friend, he might reply, 'Well . . . that **depends** . . . ' In other words, he's letting your request hang for a while before making up his mind or inventing some conditions. You can thus see that even a flimsy knowledge of word elements can often help you suss out the approximate meaning of words not in your vocabulary. Here are a few more worth thinking about.

Word, Element	Origin	Meaning	English words
pan-	Greek	all, everything	*panacea, pan-American, pantheism, panchromatic*
para-	Latin	protection	*paramedic, parachute*
ped-	Latin	foot	*pedestrian, pedal, pedestal, quadruped, centipede*
per-	Latin	through	*pervade, percolate, persist*
phon-	Greek	voice, sound	*phonetics, phonograph, telephone*
poly-	Greek	many, much	*polygon, polygamy, polyglot*
port-	Latin	to carry	*portable, porter, support*
post-	Latin	after, behind	*postpone, posterior, postwar, pm (post meridian)*
pre-	Latin	before	*preface, predate, preschool, premedication, pre-eminent*
pro-	Latin	forward in place of in favour of	*proceed, progress, prologue, pronoun, proactive, project, pro-European*

Revision Suggestion

For a change, try DIY revision – browse through the P section and spend a minute or two with any words whose meanings don't instantly spin out of your memory.

Q

Select the Correct Usage

For each word there are two examples of usage: one in which the word is used in its correct sense, and one in which it is not. Obviously, the example of incorrect usage will make no sense at all. Try to select, in each case, the example of correct usage. Circle or mark your choice, **a** or **b**, and then check the answers on page 442.

qualm   **a.** Miranda sailed in and, without a *qualm*, commanded the dogs to be quiet. **b.** John grew more restless as evening approached, and the eerie *qualm*, which usually presaged a violent storm, was almost palpable.

quandary   **a.** With the majority unexpectedly voting against him, Councillor Evans found himself in a *quandary*. **b.** Guy was always confused between the one-humped *quandary* and the two-humped Bactrian camel.

quango   **a.** Sir Edward seemed always to be running from one *quango* meeting to another. **b.** Although it has to air-freighted from the Pacific, the *quango* has become a popular delicacy in Britain.

quantum   **a.** She decided that perhaps half a *quantum* would be better than none. **b.** There wasn't a *quantum* of evidence to support the case against him.

quasar   **a.** It wasn't until 1963 that the rare *quasar* jelly was extracted from the queen bee's honey. **b.** One *quasar* has been detected up to 10 billion light years away from earth.

querulous   **a.** The matron was fed up with her patient's *querulous* attitude. **b.** The teacher was delighted with Anne's *querulous* approach to difficult problems.

quiddity   **a.** They were both amused and appalled by the poor man's *quiddity*. **b.** The *quiddity* of a pun is its wit.

quidnunc   **a.** His snobbishness, vanity and *quidnunc* passion for uniforms was well known. **b.** Being a hairdresser and thus the confidante of several dozen women, Mrs Mount was in the ideal situation to hone her talents as the village *quidnunc*.

quiescent	**a.** The volcano last erupted in 1878 and was now *quiescent*. **b.** The doctor said that Bill would recover; his heartbeat was now steady and *quiescent*.
quietus	**a.** The bell tolled its long and lonely *quietus*. **b.** The coup d'état celebrations were short-lived, silenced by the inevitable, even bloodier, *quietus*.
quintessence	**a.** Jason thought himself to be the *quintessence* of the modern male. **b.** Lingering in the air was that faint *quintessence* typical of early apple blossom.
quisling	**a.** The man was completely unaware that his grovelling, *quisling* manner made him an object of derision. **b.** The suspicion never died that Mr Bender was some sort of *quisling* during the war.
quixotic	**a.** Albert's face reddened with *quixotic* anger. **b.** He lived rough in the country most of the time, trying to stop bypasses and motorway extensions in his usual *quixotic* style.
quoin	**a.** He pointed to the huge *quoin* and claimed to have laid it when he was working on the building fifty years ago. **b.** The machine counted the sheets and stacked them in *quoins* of twenty-five.
quondam	**a.** In exchange for the pawned rings he received a *quondam* note as a receipt. **b.** The horse cantered up to us and nuzzled its *quondam* owner.
quorum	**a.** The conductor surveyed the orchestra and the enormous *quorum* of singers. **b.** Satisfied that a *quorum* was present, the chairman announced the start of the meeting.
quotidian	**a.** The neighbours were maddened by the *quotidian* uproar from the boarding house. **b.** Jules was a polished *quotidian* from Milton to Wordsworth.

Of the 17 Q words offered here, how many were strange to you? Or, more to the point, how many – from your knowledge and experience – were you able to immediately confirm were being used correctly? Check the answers on page 442 and also your dictionary to make sure you have this tiny Q section well buttoned-up in your vocabulary.

Qantas, Qintar and Other U-less Q-words

Lurking outside the selection of words listed under Q in most dictionaries is an exclusive and exotic tribe of words beginning with Q – but without the customary following '*u*'. **Qantas** (it's not so much a word as an acronym formed from the original company – Queensland And Northern Territory Air Services), **qintar** (Albanian currency unit,

100 to a lek) and *qwerty* (the standard typewriter keyboard layout) aside, it's debatable whether these are acceptable as English words or simply just foreign words. Addicts of the game *Scrabble* welcome them; dictionary-makers generally refuse admission. Here are a few for the record:

qabbala	secret and mystical versions of the scriptures.
qawwali	an Islamic religious song.
qadi	a Muslim judge of religious law.
qaf	a letter in the Arabic alphabet.
qaid	a Muslim official.
qantar	a unit of weight.
qat	a narcotic Arabian shrub.
qazaq	a brightly coloured Caucasian woollen rug.
qiblah	the direction Muslims turn to during ritual prayer.
qinah	a traditional Hebrew elegy.
qiviut	wool from the undercoat of the Arctic musk ox.
qobar	a dry fog affecting the Upper Nile.
qoph	the 19th letter of the Hebrew alphabet.
qvint	a Danish measurement of weight.

R

Pop the Word in Place

Below are ten words and ten sentences with holes in them. Simply pop each of the words in the appropriate hole so that all the sentences make sense. Each word is used once only. The answers are on page 443.

Rabelaisian	*raconteur*	*raffish*	*raillery*	*raison d'être*
rapprochement	*rancour*	*rapport*	*rara avis*	*ratiocination*

1. Never able to forgive, the resentful old colonel was still full of _____ towards his former superiors.
2. Lucas was that _____, a farmer who genuinely loved all animals, both his own and all the wild creatures too.
3. Their boisterous and ribald sessions at the pub took on an even more _____ flavour as closing time approached.
4. After a decade of hostility, Britain and Iran were keen to seek a _____ .

5. Most of his listeners would agree that 40 years of mixing with the rich and famous had a lot to do with Philip's urbane skills as a _____ .

6. The _____ for the impromptu party was Fiona's engagement.

7. Although Mr Bennett took his time, his partners appreciated that his unflappable _____ invariably resulted in the right solution.

8. Along with his knowledge of antiques, Basil had the kind of _____ manner and appearance that seems to make a successful dealer.

9. Dressed in that outrageously sexy gear it was little wonder that June attracted a good deal of _____ from the backstage staff.

10. A lot of their success as a comedy act was due to the long-established _____ between the two men.

Despite a couple of head-scratchers in that batch, a little thought should have resulted in a score of at least seven correct. Eight would be good and the perfect score of ten, of course, excellent!

Complete the Words

From the meanings given, supply the missing letters to complete the words. The answers are on page 443.

1. It sounded harsh and hoarse and loud   *r _ _ cous*

2. He was hostile to change and progress   *react _ _ nary*

3. The whole atmosphere of the place was repellent
    and forbidding   *re _ arbative*

4. The old horse proved to be stubborn and uncontrollable   *recalci _ rant*

5. She decided to publicly retract her former opinions   *rec _ _ t*

6. To make sure they all understood, he decided to restate
    the main points of his argument   *re _ _ _ itulate*

7. She was always searching for the rare, strange and
    exquisite   *re _ herché*

8. His habitual relapse into criminal behaviour was not
    unexpected   *recidiv _ sm*

9. Having won, she was the delighted owner of a new
    fridge   *re _ ipient*

10. In return for their help they decided to give their
    neighbours a party   *recip _ _ cate*

11. The two families were always at war, with a constant
    barrage of charge and counter-charge and mutual
    accusations   *recrim _ _ ation*

12. Professor Home's speciality was obscure and
    profound philosophies   *rec _ _ dite*

13. After nearly a year the dreadful disease broke out afresh   *recru _ escent*

14. Mr and Mrs Jones were models of moral integrity   *rectit _ _ e*

15. The vandalism occurred repeatedly, on an almost regular basis — *recu _ _ ent*
16. The house smelled of something that stirred her memory — *red _ lent*
17. He was still a formidable figure, commanding respect — *redou _ table*
18. They decided to invite the electorate to vote on the issue — *ref _ _ endum*
19. As a child he was always obstinate and unmanageable — *refra _ tory*
20. In the clear sky the stars were radiant and shining brightly — *reful _ ent*
21. With the fresh evidence he was able to prove that all the charges against him were false — *ref _ _ e*
22. The doctor decided to put him on a new course of treatment — *reg _ men*
23. The man was repeating it over and over again — *re _ _ erate*
24. It was obvious he was negligent and lacked attention to duty — *remi _ s*
25. She went outside to object strongly about their noisy behaviour — *remon _ trate*
26. Although he liked the job, the pay was poor — *remun _ _ ation*
27. The lovers agreed to meet at a certain place — *rende _ vous*
28. Should he go back on his promise? — *ren _ ge*
29. After the bombing he sought compensation for the damage — *re _ _ ration*
30. After a few drinks he was a master of the sharp and witty response — *repart _ _*

After a few drinks . . .

There was surely nothing too *recondite* or *recherché* in that round, so a score of 25 correct would be a reasonable effort. But in any case consult your dictionary for the meanings of any of the words that tripped you up.

Choose the Correct Usage

Which one of the alternatives, **a** or **b**, most accurately expresses the usage of the word? Circle or mark your choices (a reminder: don't count 'correct' wild guesses!) and then check the answers on page 443.

repertoire   **a.** Bill's *repertoire* of jokes was getting a bit thin. **b.** Lucy enjoyed an enviable *repertoire* with her two sisters.

replicate   **a.** The judge decided to *replicate* the publican and withdraw his licence. **b.** The professor decided to *replicate* the experiment to make sure the initial findings were correct.

reprehensible   **a.** Mandy found it difficult to overcome her *reprehensible* feelings towards George. **b.** Larry's awful behaviour towards his parents was utterly *reprehensible*.

reprobate   **a.** Uncle's will was the subject of a *reprobate* for the third time. **b.** Archie was a confirmed *reprobate* for whom there was little sympathy among his few exasperated friends.

repudiate   **a.** The breakaway group threatened to *repudiate* the latest agreement with the council. **b.** The court agreed to *repudiate* the prisoner on compassionate grounds.

repugnant   **a.** The patient's breathing was becoming *repugnant* to a dangerous degree. **b.** Although driven by her Christian principles, Marcia found her work at the old men's home undeniably *repugnant*.

rescind   **a.** The board agreed to *rescind* the total ban on smoking. **b.** After the fire they sifted through the *rescind* for anything of value.

resonant   **a.** When he tapped the gourd the *resonant* sound indicated it was empty. **b.** The hive was *resonant* with honey, and in minutes he was up to his elbows in it.

respite   **a.** The old lady was full of bitter *respite* and accusations. **b.** They fully deserved the unexpected but welcome *respite* from the searing heat.

resplendent   **a.** The governor at last appeared, *resplendent* in his white uniform and plumed helmet. **b.** Harold was fearful that he would be cited as a *resplendent* in Lady Hatfield's divorce case.

resurgent   **a.** Her father had signed up as a *resurgent* in the Spanish Civil War. **b.** After the war everyone looked forward to a *resurgent* nation with a fair deal and prosperity for all.

reticent **a.** Harvey was always *reticent*, so on the few occasions he did speak, everyone listened in surprise. **b.** Josephine was not *reticent* when it came to knowing the sleazy bars in the city.

retrench **a.** With an empty order book and a poor economic outlook ahead, the firm decided to *retrench*. **b.** The man was asked to *retrench* his allegations or face legal action.

retrograde **a.** We sped through the chicane and then down the steep *retrograde*, with the other car in pursuit. **b.** Motorists agreed that changing to the one-way system was a *retrograde* step.

retroussé **a.** His smart suits and immaculate grooming were marks of his *retroussé* charm. **b.** With her wide blue eyes and pert, *retroussé* nose, Dawn had all the attributes of a natural model.

reverberate **a.** The sound of the explosion continued to *reverberate* through the town. **b.** Although the attack was moderating, the man's limbs continued to *reverberate*.

reverie **a.** Martha was accustomed to falling on her knees and reciting her *reverie* twelve times every day. **b.** Leonard was a dreamer and we would often find him lost in a *reverie*.

rhetorical **a.** Trevor was fascinated by the *rhetorical* past and loved poking around in ruins. **b.** As a speechmaker, he was rather too *rhetorical*, and facts were few and far between.

rictus **a.** The *rictus* that affected his legs was painful to see. **b.** After the shocking apparition he glanced around and saw the *rictus* on Ellen's horror-stricken face.

riparian **a.** The country house came with nearly a mile of *riparian* rights and privileges. **b.** Joyce hated *riparian* creatures such as snakes and lizards.

riposte **a.** The jockey sensed that he was in a *riposte* position and certain to win. **b.** The stand-up comedian responded to the jeering with a withering *riposte* that silenced the audience.

risible **a.** His dramatic performances on stage were unintentionally *risible*, often causing an undercurrent of giggling. **b.** The skin of the porpoise has a smooth, slithery *risible* quality.

rococo **a.** The disease that hit *rococo* plantations in the 1960s threatened chocolate production for nearly a decade. **b.** The interior was decorated in the elegant *rococo* style.

roué **a.** For the sauce the chef first prepared a *roué* to which he added the stock and herbs. **b.** Although handsome in his youth Brendan today was a decrepit old *roué*.

rubicund **a.** The gardener's *rubicund* face creased with amusement. **b.** Hilda's thoughts turned to *rubicund* musings, of former lovers and love's regrets.

rumbustious **a.** The rugby team were undoubtedly a *rumbustious* lot. **b.** Larry closely searched the old musician's *rumbustious* features for some sign of appreciation.

ruminate   **a.** Jack went away to *ruminate* upon his defeat. **b.** The recipe called for the beef to *ruminate* in the wine sauce for several hours.

rusticate   **a.** The surface of the desk was subtly *rusticated*, a sure sign of many years of use. **b.** His parents decided to *rusticate* and began looking for a suitable property in Hampshire.

The point about usage exercises such as the above is that they make you think about the word, its meaning, and its application in the context of the sentence. But there is a problem with words whose meanings you simply don't know. In such cases, consult the answers on page 443 or, better still, look up the more complete meaning (or meanings) in your dictionary, then refer back to the example of usage to see how the word is actually employed.

Three Word Elements: Re, Retro and Rupt

Word, Element	Origin	Meaning	English words
re-	Latin	back, again	*return, renew, recall, re-do, reuse, refresh, remarry*
retro-	Latin	backwards	*retroactive, retrograde, retrospective, retrorocket*
rupt	Latin	break	*disrupt, interrupt, rupture, eruption, corrupt*

Revision: Q to R

Take a breather and spend a few minutes reviewing any of the Q and R words that were unfamiliar to you – and also words the meanings of which you were a little hazy about. For example, can you, without too much hesitation, mentally place the following words appropriately in sentences?

querulous   *quiescent*   *rapprochement*   *rebarbative*   *redolent*
refute   *repudiate*   *retroussé*   *rhetorical*   *riposte*

The five minutes required to tuck these ten words securely away in your expanding vocabulary is surely worth it.

S

What's the Correct Meaning?

Which of the two choices, **a** or **b**, most accurately fits the definition of the word? Mark or circle your choices before checking the answers on page 443.

sacrilegious	**a.** taking something regarded as sacred for secular or inappropriate use. **b.** excessive deference to the church hierarchy.
sacrosanct	**a.** shaped like the head of an arrow. **b.** sacred and inviolable.
sagacious	**a.** circumspect and proper. **b.** wise and perceptive.
salacious	**a.** obscene and bawdy. **b.** obsessively jealous.
salient	**a.** highly conspicuous. **b.** favoured with a following wind.
salubrious	**a.** prone to catch infections easily. **b.** wholesome and favourable.
salutary	**a.** intending to have a beneficial effect. **b.** a well-earned rest.
sanctimonious	**a.** pretending to be generous but in actuality very mean. **b.** making a display of piety and purity.
sang-froid	**a.** composed and self-possessed. **b.** a haughty manner.
sanguine	**a.** gloomy and despondent. **b.** cheerful and optimistic.
sardonic	**a.** sneering and scornful. **b.** shy and retiring.
sartorial	**a.** relating to shooting stars and comets. **b.** relating to tailoring.
Sassenach	**a.** a primitive Scotsman, from an English point of view. **b.** an Englishman, from a Scots point of view.
saturnine	**a.** having a mane of black hair. **b.** having a gloomy temperament.
savoir-faire	**a.** extremely witty. **b.** a fine sense of what's right and wrong socially.
scatology	**a.** having a great knowledge of trivia. **b.** an unhealthy interest in excrement.
sceptic	**a.** a cut or bruise that becomes infected. **b.** a person who habitually questions accepted beliefs.
schadenfreude	**a.** delight in another's misfortune. **b.** to remain calm in a heated argument.
schism	**a.** the division of a group into opposing factions. **b.** a fissure that threatens to deepen and become wider.
scintilla	**a.** a group of bright stars. **b.** a tiny, minute amount.
scion	**a.** a descendent, heir or young member of a family. **b.** a small, shallow-gabled porch.
scrupulous	**a.** obsessively clean. **b.** careful and precise.
scurrilous	**a.** obscenely abusive and defamatory. **b.** in a hurried manner.
sebaceous	**a.** prone to skin complaints. **b.** fatty and greasy.
secular	**a.** pertaining to sacred things. **b.** pertaining to worldly things.

sedentary	**a.** involving little or no exercise, such as sitting about.
	b. involving work that requires extreme concentration.
sedulous	**a.** assiduous and diligent. **b.** casual and uncaring.
semantics	**a.** concerned with the sounds of words. **b.** concerned with the meanings of words.
semiotics	**a.** the study of signs and symbols in communications; **b.** the study of American Indian languages.
senescent	**a.** becoming young again. **b.** growing old.

If after checking the answers on page 443 you find that you failed to identify the correct meanings of some of the words, you'll find it worthwhile to revisit those that caused you to stumble and to commit their meanings to memory. If you scored 25 or more correct you did very well.

Words into Spaces

Below, 12 words and 12 incomplete sentences. Each of the sentences has a space for a missing word. Which word goes into which space? Take your time and with a little thought a perfect score should be possible. Each word is used only once. The answers are on page 443.

sententious	*sequestered*	*serendipitous*	*serpentine*
serrated	*servile*	*shibboleths*	*sibilant*
sidereal	*simian*	*similitude*	*simulacrum*

1. With his long arms and grossly hairy chest the man looked positively _____.

2. Archie looked the man over and decided there was a certain _____ that reminded him of an old school friend – and who turned out to be his twin.

3. Judith had always been fascinated by astrology and the stars and her _____ interests eventually led to a lucrative newspaper column.

4. He thought the philosopher's lectures, loaded with aphorisms, sound bites and moralising, were just a lot of _____ nonsense.

5. The road wound its _____ way around the sides of the canyon.

6. Colin declined to join the society, saying that the members could keep its ridiculous and secret _____ to themselves.

7. The old couple were quite content with their quiet and _____ life.

8. After nearly half a century as a butler to the household it was understandable that Mr Nobbs' demeanour was _____ and unassertive.

9. The _____ edge of the knife cut deeply into the assailant's bare arm.

10. Linda's _____ discovery of the kind and helpful Bailey family undoubtedly changed her life.

11. The ghostly image that began to emerge from the gloom was a _____ of his grandmother.

12. The gap between Bernard's two front teeth gave his speech a pronounced
_____ sound that put paid to his disc jockey ambitions.

Some tough ones in that lot, admittedly, so a score of nine or more correct would
be quite an achievement. Words beginning with S are prolific in the English
language, so prepare yourself for another extended round of Choose the Correct
Meaning.

Choose the Correct Meaning

As before, choose one of the alternatives, **a** or **b**, that most accurately fits the
meaning of the word. Wild stabs that turn out to be correct shouldn't score, so try
not to guess. Mark or circle your choices before checking the answers on page 443.

sinecure	**a.** a cushy, well-paid and secure job. **b.** the inability to bend an arm at the elbow.
sinistral	**a.** a hot wind that blows off the Mediterranean. **b.** left-handed.
Sisyphean	**a.** someone who will attempt anything regardless of the consequences. **b.** describing an activity or task that is endless and futile.
skulk	**a.** to lurk unseen with wrongdoing in mind. **b.** to run away from trouble.
slander	**a.** false or defamatory words spoken about somebody. **b.** false or defamatory words written about somebody.
sobriety	**a.** the state of drunkenness. **b.** the state of being sober.
sobriquet	**a.** flowers presented to a singer after a performance. **b.** a humorous epithet or nickname.
sodality	**a.** malicious scheming. **b.** fellowship and fraternity.
soi-disant	**a.** a devil-may-care attitude. **b.** so-called or self-styled.
soignée	**a.** an elegantly groomed woman. **b.** a jewelled clasp for the hair.
soiree	**a.** an evening of conversation and music. **b.** a gathering of female friends.
solecism	**a.** a recorded sun-spot. **b.** a grammatical or social mistake.
solicitous	**a.** excessive use of legal means to achieve one's ends. **b.** showing concern and consideration.
soliloquy	**a.** a speech made to oneself. **b.** a poem full of musings.
solipsism	**a.** the denial of the possibility of all knowledge except that of one's own existence. **b.** an unforgivable social gaffe.
sommelier	**a.** a brandy warehouse. **b.** a wine waiter.
somnambulism	**a.** communicating with the spirit world. **b.** sleep-walking.
somnolent	**a.** in a depressive mood. **b.** feeling drowsy and sleepy.
sonorous	**a.** giving out a full, rich sound. **b.** a person with a knowledge of the Spanish and Portuguese languages.
sophistry	**a.** the use of fallacious and deceptive argument to win a point. **b.** having a preference for one's own sex.

soporific	**a.** unpleasantly oily. **b.** sleep-inducing.
sotto voce	**a.** slightly inebriated. **b.** in an undertone.
soupçon	**a.** the lowliest, poorest-paid employee in a restaurant kitchen. **b.** a tiny amount.
spasmodic	**a.** happening at sudden and brief intervals. **b.** any drug or preparation that induces vomiting.
spatial	**a.** existing or happening in space. **b.** exhausted.
spavined	**a.** worn out and broken down. **b.** split in two.
specious	**a.** undersized. **b.** seemingly true and correct but actually false and wrong.
splenetic	**a.** a tendency to be constantly ill. **b.** spiteful and bad-tempered.
spoonerism	**a.** the wrong placement of cutlery on a formal dining table. **b.** the inadvertent transposition of consonants or words often resulting in confusion and ambiguity, sometimes with comical results.
sporadic	**a.** at regular intervals. **b.** occurring intermittently or irregularly.
spurious	**a.** not genuine or real. **b.** a freshly broken or trained horse.
staccato	**a.** abrupt and clipped. **b.** a long kettle-drum roll or solo.
stasis	**a.** a static or stagnant state. **b.** an irregular heartbeat.
statutory	**a.** held down by force. **b.** authorised by legislation.
stentorian	**a.** an excessively strict teacher. **b.** uncommonly loud.
stigmatise	**a.** to identify as bad or to be avoided. **b.** to cross-fertilise plants.
stoical	**a.** resigned to bearing problems and pain. **b.** rejecting pleasures of the flesh.
stolid	**a.** massively built. **b.** showing little emotion or interest.
stringent	**a.** highly aromatic and stinging. **b.** requiring strict attention to rules and detail.
stultify	**a.** to make useless or ineffectual. **b.** to check growth.
Stygian	**a.** bottomless depths. **b.** dark and gloomy.
subjugate	**a.** to make subservient or submissive. **b.** to divide equally.
sublimate	**a.** to drift into very deep sleep. **b.** to refine and make pure.
subliminal	**a.** describing a brief or subtle stimulus of which the individual is unaware. **b.** so deeply buried in the unconscious as to be irretrievable.
subservient	**a.** deferential and submissive. **b.** in any series, the second number, place or position.
substantiate	**a.** to be bold. **b.** to establish as valid or genuine.
subsume	**a.** to incorporate or absorb into. **b.** to reduce or diminish.
subterfuge	**a.** a major underground tunnel for conveying water supplies. **b.** a stratagem designed to conceal or evade.
succinct	**a.** easily dissolved. **b.** sharp and concise.
supercilious	**a.** extremely superficial. **b.** arrogant and indifferent.
superfluity	**a.** an oversupply or excess of what is needed. **b.** an officious and superior manner.
supernumerary	**a.** any number greater than a billion. **b.** a person or something that exceeds normal requirements.

supplant   **a.** to take the place of. **b.** an alternative or emergency supply.
suppurate   **a.** to vibrate. **b.** to fester.
surrogate   **a.** a person appointed as a substitute for another person.
                  b. a person wholly dependent upon charity or public funds.

Sisyphean? *Spoonerism*? *Stygian*? Surely these shouldn't be expected to be in an average vocabulary? But the record shows that these unlikely words occur in print with surprising regularity, no doubt intriguing or irritating a few million 'average' readers. So perhaps, after all, there's a good case for knowing what they mean.

Sisyphean is an old word now in vogue: an example from *The Times*: 'The painters who undertook the Sisyphean work on the mile-long Forth Rail bridge will down brushes for a year because of spending cuts by ScotRail.' It derives from Greek mythology and the story of King Sisyphus who was punished in Hades by having to roll an enormous boulder eternally up a hill. As it neared the top the boulder was always fated to roll down again. Is there another word in the language that combines the definitions of an endless task and utter futility? Search and ye may find. Or not.

Spoonerism derives from a real person, the Rev William Archibald Spooner, one-time warden of New College, Oxford. Dr Spooner suffered from the rare condition of *metathesis*, or the inadvertent transposition of sounds. Thus, intending to say 'Is the Dean busy?' he would say, 'Is the bean dizzy?' or 'Three cheers for the queer old Dean' instead of the intended 'Three cheers for the dear old Queen'. Anyone can utter these mirthful slips of the tongue, or *spoonerisms*, and there doesn't seem to be another word that so engagingly describes them.

Stygian, like *Sisyphean*, also derives from Greek mythology – in this case the infamous Underworld River Styx whose water killed everybody who drank it and corroded any vessel that tried to contain it. *Stygian*, therefore, means dark and hateful and hellish – and words don't come with meanings much more frightening than that!

But notwithstanding this curious trio, a score of 30 correct would be commendable.

Words in Use: Right or Wrong?

Here are ten sentences, each containing a highlighted word. In some sentences the words are used correctly and appropriately, but in others they are not and the resulting sentences make no sense at all. Can you identify correct and incorrect usage? In each case make your choice by marking Right or Wrong. The answers are on page 443.

		Right	**Wrong**
1.	By *surreptitious* means the landlord had managed to prove that the family had broken their lease agreement.	___	___

		Right	Wrong
2.	Ravishingly *svelte*, Priscilla showed off the designer ball gown to perfection.	____	____
3.	Mr Marlar was a reputed worshipper of Satan and other dark *sybaritic* cults.	____	____
4.	The lawyer was so *sycophantic*, constantly niggling over relatively unimportant details.	____	____
5.	From the argument that mice are just small rats, and that all rats are pests, David produced the *syllogism* that all mice are pests.	____	____
6.	They concluded that the small bird, by cleansing the rhino of ticks and other insects, had a *symbiotic* relationship with its host.	____	____
7.	The *synchronous* material allowed the fluid to permeate through it and to be completely absorbed.	____	____
8.	The directors felt that the merger would result in productive *synergies* and enhanced profitability.	____	____
9.	Hugh might have been a competent writer had he had a better understanding of *syntax* and the importance of correct spelling.	____	____
10.	Thinking it might be poisonous the doctor decided to ask the laboratory to *synthesise* the substance in the bottle.	____	____

A rather tricky lot, so if after checking the answers on page 443 you managed a score of seven or more correct choices, you can feel reasonably pleased with your effort.

Word Elements: Script to Syn

Once again, a glance at some ancient word elements that can often help to identify the meanings of words.

Word, Element	Origin	Meaning	English words
script, scrib	Latin	to write	*inscription, scripture, postscript, description*
se-, separare	Latin	apart	*separate, segregate, secede, select*
sect	Latin	cut	*intersect, section, sector, sectile, vasectomy*
sed	Latin	seat, situated	*sediment, sedate, resident, sedentary, sedan chair*
sequ, secut	Latin	to follow	*sequence, consecutive, sequel, consequence*

Word, Element	Origin	Meaning	English words
soph	Greek	wise	*sophistry, sophisticated, sophomore, philosophy*
spec	Latin	look	*spectacle, spectrum, spectre, spectator, conspicuous*
-some	Old English	tendency	*awesome, wholesome*
sub-	Latin	under, beneath	*subterranean, subordinate, submarine, sub-editor*
super-	Latin	above, over	*supervisor, superior, superman, supermarket*
syn-	Greek	with, together	*synchronise, synagogue, syndicate, synchromesh*

A Little Light Revision

Yes, it may be tiresome, but periodical revision does help you to remember. What's the point of filing useful and interesting words in your vocabulary if you can't, or only vaguely, remember the meanings? So cast your eyes – and memory – over this selection of S words.

sanctimonious	*sanguine*	*savoir-faire*	*sequestered*
sinecure	*soi-disant*	*solecism*	*stoical*
stultify	*subsume*	*surrogate*	*sacrosanct*

T

Complete the Word

Here's a round of 30 words. Each word is incomplete, with one or more letters missing. Your task is to fill in the missing letters to complete the words. To help you, the meaning of each word is given. Answers on page 444.

1. An instrument, often seen in cars, that measures speed of rotation — *ta _ _ ometer*
2. Indirectly expressed: implied or inferred — *tac _ t*
3. Habitually silent and uncommunicative — *tacitu _ n*
4. Relating to the sense of touch — *t _ ctile*
5. A small object believed to protect the wearer from evil — *ta _ isman*
6. Real, capable of being seen and touched — *tan _ ibl _*
7. As good as, or equivalent in effect — *tantam _ _ nt*

8.	A brownish-grey colour	ta _ pe
9.	Using words that unnecessarily repeat a meaning already conveyed	tautolog _ _ al
10.	Moving things without touching them, as though through willpower	te _ ekinesis
11.	Rashness or boldness	temer _ ty
12.	Relating to earthly rather than spiritual or religious affairs	tempora _
13.	To delay in order to gain time or arrive at a compromise	temp _ rise
14.	Showing an intentional bias	tendent _ ous
15.	A belief, dogma or opinion	te _ et
16.	Insignificant, flimsy or delicate	ten _ ous
17.	A 300th anniversary	te _ centenary
18.	Relating to the earth, as opposed to the sea and air	te _ _ estrial
19.	There's primary, then secondary, and then . . .	tert _ ary
20.	Paved or inlaid with a mosaic of small tiles	te _ sellated
21.	Any person who makes a will	testa _ or
22.	A steroid hormone secreted in the male	testost _ _one
23.	A private conversation between two people	tête-à-t_ _ e
24.	The belief in one God as creator of the universe	the _ sm
25.	Relating to maintaining health and the treatment of disease	the _ apeutic
26.	Relating to drama, the theatre, and to actors	thesp _ _ n
27.	Being subjected to the power and control of another person	thra _ l
28.	Fearful and timid	timor _ _ s
29.	A ringing, hissing or booming sensation in the ears	ti _ _ itus
30.	An alarm or warning signal, especially the ringing of a bell	to _ sin

Not too difficult, was it? Therefore a score of 25 or more correct should be expected. Make sure you double-check the meanings of the words that tripped you.

What's the Correct Meaning?

Another round of T words. This time each word has three definitions, only one of which is correct. Choose the one option from **a**, **b** or **c**, that you think is the correct meaning.

torpid	**a.** apathetic and sluggish. **b.** uncomfortably warm. **c.** slithery.
tort	**a.** a junior judge. **b.** a civil wrong or injury, liable for a claim for damages. **c.** the laws regarding criminal offences.
tortuous	**a.** causing physical and mental agony. **b.** twisted and winding. **c.** writhing and wriggling.

touché **a.** the acknowledgement of a witty response. **b.** a challenge. **c.** a gentle warning of a problem ahead.

tractable **a.** something easily traced. **b.** something easily swallowed. **c.** docile and easily controlled.

traduce **a.** to defame someone. **b.** to pursue the favours of an older woman. **c.** to subtly persuade.

tranche **a.** a French government bond. **b.** a portion or instalment of something, usually money. **c.** divided into three parts.

transcend **a.** to gradually disappear. **b.** to rise above or go beyond a limit. **c.** to travel across difficult territory.

transient **a.** speedy. **b.** fleeting or temporary. **c.** a lover of travelling.

translucent **a.** semi-transparent. **b.** having the appearance of opal. **c.** dull.

traumatic **a.** the effects of a shock or injury. **b.** lapsing into unconsciousness. **c.** loss of memory or absentmindedness.

travail **a.** uncomfortable travelling. **b.** painful toil or exertion. **c.** the sound of wailing at a funeral.

travesty **a.** a ceiling-to-floor wall hanging. **b.** a farcical imitation or parody. **c.** a deep disappointment.

tremulous **a.** lisping. **b.** singing in a low register. **c.** trembling, wavering.

trenchant **a.** forceful and incisive. **b.** eating with greedy gusto. **c.** living underground.

trepidation **a.** the magical art of suspending a person without support. **b.** rapidly vibrating. **c.** a state of fear or anxiety.

trichology **a.** the study of shells. **b.** the study of combustible matter. **c.** the study of hair.

tridactyl **a.** having a long tail. **b.** having three fingers or toes. **c.** having armoured scales.

triptych **a.** a painting on three panels. **b.** a religious sculpture, especially of the Madonna. **c.** a three-handled vase or urn.

triumvirate **a.** a gathering of cardinals. **b.** joint rule or the sharing of power by three individuals. **c.** an 18th-century three-cornered hat.

troglodyte **a.** a dwarfish gargoyle. **b.** a large toad. **c.** a cave dweller.

trompe l'oeil **a.** lavender bath oil. **b.** a painting that portrays a convincing illusion of reality. **c.** a resounding victory.

trope **a.** a figure of speech that uses words in a figurative way. **b.** a malarial infection. **c.** a pith helmet worn in Africa.

truculent **a.** someone who prefers to be last rather than first. **b.** defiantly sullen and aggressive. **c.** rowdy and attention-seeking.

truism **a.** a falsehood masquerading as truth. **b.** an obvious truth. **c.** a proverb the truth of which is in doubt.

truncate **a.** to cut off or shorten. **b.** to divide into many parts. **c.** to reduce by more than half.

tsunami **a.** an assortment of Japanese raw fish delicacies. **b.** the sash worn by geishas in Japan. **c.** a huge, destructive sea wave produced by earthquakes or volcanic eruptions.

tumescent   **a.** decaying. **b.** gently dozing. **c.** becoming swollen.

turbid   **a.** muddy or clouded. **b.** distended. **c.** sexually aroused.

turgid   **a.** red-faced. **b.** swollen and congested. **c.** over-active.

turpitude   **a.** inherent depravity. **b.** moral uprightness. **c.** admirable strength of character.

tyrannise   **a.** a process to protect timber from rotting. **b.** to rule in a cruel or oppressive way. **c.** to habitually steal.

tyro   **a.** a notorious seducer. **b.** a lazy good-for-nothing. **c.** a novice or beginner.

A score of 25 or less for this round (answers on page 444) would indicate the need for some serious revision. If you scored 30 or more you can relax a little – but don't relapse into complacency!

Word Elements: Tact to Tude

Some of these word elements – *trans* meaning 'across' for example, giving us words such as *trans-Siberian* and *transcend* – may seem too familiar to bother about, but they are worth parking away in your memory as useful pointers to the meaning of words that are not so familiar. Here are some word elements beginning with T.

Word, Element	Origin	Meaning	English words
tactus, tact	Latin	touching	*tact, tactile, contact, tangible*
tele-	Greek	far, distance	*telepathy, telephone, telegram, telescope, telecommunication*
temp, tempore	Latin	time	*temporary, contemporary, temporise, extempore*
terr, terra	Latin	land	*terra firma, territory, terrestrial*
theo	Greek	god	*theology, theocracy, theomancy, apotheosis, pantheon*
topo, topos	Greek	place	*topography, toponym, topology*
tract, tractus	Latin	to drag, pull	*attract, traction, tractor, protract, distract, extract*
trans-	Latin	across, beyond	*transgress, transact, transcribe, transform, translate*
-tude	Latin	state	*solitude, magnitude, plenitude, exactitude*

Time to Revise

Yes, revision time again. Just to make sure your vocabulary has assimilated its full intake of T words, take a little time to refresh your memory with this sampling. In each case, preferably without hesitation, try to frame the word in a sentence.

tacit	*tendentious*	*traduce*	*truism*	*turpitude*
turbid	*trenchant*	*transient*	*temporise*	*tantamount*

U

Select the Correct Usage

Opposite each of the following words are two sentences. In one sentence the word is used correctly and appropriately; in the other it is used wrongly, with the result that the statement makes no sense at all. Your task is to select the sentence, **a** or **b**, in which the usage is correct. The answers are on page 444.

ubiquitous	**a.** In summer the *ubiquitous* dandelions and daisies dazzle the eye. **b.** The *ubiquitous* landlord extracted ferocious rents from his tenants.
ullage	**a.** The shipowner was fined for discharging *ullage* in the docks. **b.** The wine merchant complained about the excessive *ullage* in the barrels.
ululation	**a.** The crowd gasped at the dancer's incredible *ululations*. **b.** The *ululation* of the mourners was almost too much to bear.
umbrage	**a.** Lucy took *umbrage* at the slightest criticism. **b.** The cellar was dark and damp and reeked with *umbrage*.
unanimity	**a.** The choir sang with a *unanimity* that was sometimes even off key. **b.** There was, for once, *unanimity* among all members.
unconscionable	**a.** John took an *unconscionable* time to walk to the rostrum. **b.** On occasions Roberta would lapse into *unconscionable* dreams.
unctuous	**a.** After the sermon a good many felt decidedly *unctuous*. **b.** He addressed them in his usual *unctuous* tone.
unequivocal	**a.** The bank's message was *unequivocal*: pay up or face legal action. **b.** Unable to get his views across, the man felt he was the victim of an *unequivocal* action.
unguent	**a.** The victim's room was in a terrible state, filthy and *unguent*. **b.** The herbalist prepared an *unguent* incorporating comfrey and camomile.

unilateral   **a.** The convoy steered on a *unilateral* course. **b.** the governor made a *unilateral* decision to suspend the constitution.

uninhibited   **a.** Always *uninhibited,* Sabrina was, predictably, the life of the party. **b.** In his *uninhibited* way, Silas made sure all his valuables were securely hidden away.

unison   **a.** The chairman felt that at last there was *unison* between all the parties. **b.** The family was affected by the hereditary *unison* of only ever having male children.

unmitigated   **a.** After the storm and flooding, the landslip was an *unmitigated* disaster for the village. **b.** The agreement was *unmitigated* at the lawyer's request.

unprecedented **a.** The document was *unprecedented* and had no legal standing. **b.** The celebrations were *unprecedented* in the history of the city.

unreconstructed **a.** The minister felt that the hill farmers were an *unreconstructed* lot and would never accept the EU ruling. **b.** Most critics felt that the book was a collection of *unreconstructed* nonsense.

unseemly   **a.** The committee concluded that the machinery was *unseemly* and should be replaced. **b.** Gordon was suspended because of his *unseemly* behaviour at the Christmas party.

untenable   **a.** The consensus was that the professor's theory was *untenable*. **b.** The patient's condition was *untenable* and probably terminal.

untoward   **a.** Harry was fundamentally *untoward*, with no sense of direction. **b.** The boy had been missing for nearly two days and everyone hoped that nothing *unto*ward had happened to him.

unwonted   **a.** The Queen's visit to the village was a most *unwonted* event. **b.** As a child he spent many *unwonted* hours in sad isolation.

urbane   **a.** Georgina arrived with her new, rich, *urbane* escort. **b.** The man looked utterly *urbane* in his string vest and seedy jacket.

usurious   **a.** The upheaval left them all anxious and *usurious*. **b.** He had no alternative but to borrow the money at *usurious* rates.

usurp   **a.** The old tyrant was afraid to leave the country as he knew his son would *usurp* the presidency. **b.** Lord Southwell knew that by leaving the property to Robert it would *usurp* his wife and other children.

utilitarian   **a.** The chairs were plain and strictly *utilitarian*. **b.** The former colonel still retained his *utilitarian* views on discipline.

Utopian   **a.** Jacob lived in fear of having to return to his old *Utopian* existence of begging and homelessness. **b.** As they left for the island the family wondered if life on Desmonia would be the *Utopian* paradise everyone said it would be.

Revision: In a Word

A quick revision exercise. From the single-word meanings, can you recognise the words listed in the U section?

1. wailing	2. ointment	3. unusual	4. insupportable
5. offence	6. unconstrained	7. oily	8. everywhere

V

Choose the Correct Meaning

Which of the alternatives, **a** or **b**, most accurately fits the meaning of the word? Mark or circle your choices and then check the answers on page 444.

vacillate   **a.** to be indecisive and inclined to waver. **b.** to become increasingly angry.

vacuous   **a.** talking interminably. **b.** empty and mindless.

vagary   **a.** an inveterate wanderer. **b.** a whim, an erratic idea or notion.

vainglorious   **a.** vain and boastful. **b.** excessively patriotic.

valedictory   **a.** a collection of biographies of only dead people. **b.** a farewell occasion or speech.

valetudinarian   **a.** a chronically sick invalid. **b.** a person aged between 90 and 100.

vanguard   **a.** the leading position. **b.** a position at the back or rear.

vapid   **a.** insipid, dull and lifeless. **b.** a faint musky smell.

variegated   **a.** too many to count. **b.** displaying a variety of colours.

vegetate   **a.** to believe in the healing power of vegetables and fruit. **b.** to lead a life of mental inactivity.

vehement   **a.** vigorously emphatic. **b.** narrowness of viewpoint.

venal   **a.** easily bribed and corrupted. **b.** slyly envious.

vendetta   **a.** a small boat, used on the Italian lakes. **b.** a prolonged personal feud or quarrel.

veracity   **a.** habitual lying. **b.** consistent honesty and truthfulness.

verbatim   **a.** using exactly the same words. **b.** an exact translation from one language to another.

verbose   **a.** speaking nasally, sneering. **b.** describing a boring and long-winded speech.

verisimilitude   **a.** the appearance or quality of seeming to be true. **b.** a ghostly apparition that resembles a recognisable person.

vernacular	**a.** a long flight of steps. **b.** the common language or dialect of a particular people or place.
vernal	**a.** pertaining to or occurring in spring. **b.** a temperate climate.
vertiginous	**a.** extremely steep. **b.** producing the sensation of imbalance and dizziness.

Nothing too demanding in that lot, so a score of 15 or more would be respectable and one of 18+ exceptional. But watch out for *venal* (listed above) and its rather rarely seen lookalike *venial*, which means 'easily excused or forgiven': *In the vicar's view it was merely a venial error.*

Complete the Sentence

Here are ten words and ten sentences. A word is missing from each of the sentences. Can you place the appropriate words in all ten sentences? Each word is used only once. Answers on page 444.

viable	*vicarious*	*vicissitudes*	*vilify*	*vindicate*
vindictive	*virago*	*virulent*	*virtu*	*vis-à-vis*

1. Mr Hornby said that, _____ the matter discussed yesterday, it would be dealt with as soon as possible.
2. When he married Edna, Bill never had a clue she'd turn out to be an embarrassing and embittered _____.
3. Over the years the couple had accumulated a fine display of objects of _____ .
4. The farmer wondered if raising turkeys would be a _____ business.
5. Looking at the old fisherman's craggy face I could see he'd had his share of life's _____ .
6. Marcia disliked her sister's resentful and _____ nature.
7. Why do you ridicule and _____ your boss just because you didn't get your expected promotion?
8. The infection was so _____ that it laid him low for three weeks.
9. We suspected that Brian's colourful accounts of his Sahara adventures were mostly _____ experiences culled from library books.
10. The barrister produced a file of documents that would _____ his client's claim to the property.

If after checking the answers on page 444 you find you scored eight or more correct, well done.

Identify the Word

From the meanings given, fill in the gaps to identify the words. Answers on page 444.

1. Intuitive or instinctive, rather than intellectual   *visce _ al*
2. Thick and sticky   *vis _ ous*
3. To debase, spoil or make faulty   *v _ tiate*
4. Relating to or made of glass   *vitre _ _ s*
5. Caustic and acrimonious   *vitr _ olic*
6. Abusive and defamatory language   *vit _ peration*
7. Lively and full of high spirits   *vi _ acious*
8. Performing experiments on animals involving surgery   *vivi _ ection*
9. Clamorous, loud and noisy   *vocif _ _ ous*
10. The faculty of exercising one's own choice or decision   *vo _ ition*
11. A reversal of attitude or opinion   *volte-fa _ e*
12. A person addicted to luxury and sensual pleasures   *volu _ tuary*
13. A whirling, spiralling mass or motion   *vor _ ex*
14. A person who dedicates himself or herself to religion   *vota _ y*
15. To agree or condescend to give or grant something   *vouch _ afe*
16. The voice of the people   *vox po _ uli*
17. A Peeping Tom   *vo _ eur*
18. Crafty and clever: relating to or resembling a fox   *vulp _ ne*
19. Predatory and rapacious: relating to or resembling a vulture *vult _ rine*

For that round a score of 15 or more would be a reasonable attainment. But don't
be despondent if your score was lower: after all, you don't come across words
such as *vit _ peration*, *vouch _ afe* and *visce _ al* every day.

The Penultimate Revision

Yes, the end is near! But all the more reason to make sure your V words
are neatly and securely stored away in your vocabulary. Very quickly,
right or wrong?

	Right	**Wrong**
To *vacillate* is to become increasingly angry	____	____
A *vainglorious* person is excessively chauvinistic or patriotic.	____	____
A *vernal* climate is a pleasant, temperate climate.	____	____
Have you ever climbed up a *vertiginous* mountain slope?	____	____
The *vortex* is the highest point of any structure.	____	____
A *votary* is the church helper who lights the candles.	____	____
To *vitiate* something or someone, you bring it to life.	____	____
To be *virulent* is to act foolishly and irresponsibly.	____	____

If you marked any of those definitions or usages as being right, then you
need even further revision. Every one is, in fact, wrong.

WXYZ

Choose the Correct Meaning

Yes, the final round at last! Which of the three choices, **a**, **b** or **c**, most accurately matches the true definition of the word? Mark or circle your answers (last warning: blind guesses shouldn't count!) and then check them on page 444.

wagon-lit　　**a.** a coach lamp. **b.** a sleeping car on a continental train. **c.** the driver's seat at the front of a coach.

waive　　**a.** to set aside or relinquish a privilege. **b.** a circumambulatory walk in the country. **c.** a choice between two similar options.

wanton　　**a.** a Chinese dumpling served with soup. **b.** an orphan. **c.** dissolute, capricious, unnecessarily destructive.

whet　　**a.** a short canal barge. **b.** to sharpen or stimulate. **c.** a cause of worry or anxiety.

winsome　　**a.** sweet singing voice. **b.** charming and engaging. **c.** attractively chubby.

wizened　　**a.** enlightened after years of experience. **b.** shrivelled and wrinkled. **b.** relating to wizards and wizardry.

wraith　　**a.** a thin, swirling mist. **b.** a long, thin silken women's scarf. **c.** a deathly apparition of someone still living.

wunderkind　　**a.** a child prodigy. **b.** the doctrines of the Lutheran church. **c.** a former pupil of Winchester College.

xanthic　　**a.** yellowish in colour. **b.** ability to thrive with little water or moisture. **c.** easily bleached by sunlight.

Xanthippe　　**a.** an army general of commanding stature. **b.** a nagging, peevish, irritable woman. **c.** a person who can speak in a language with which they are totally unfamiliar.

xenophobic　　**a.** hating or fearing foreigners. **b.** hating or fearing aliens and UFOs. **c.** hating and fearing bodily tissues, even one's own.

yahoo　　**a.** a brutish, half-human creature. **b.** a type of lemur found in Madagascar. **c.** a tin whistle with a vibrating reed.

yashmak　　**a.** cheese made from yak's milk. **b.** the veil worn by Muslim women in public. **c.** a colourful blanket woven from yak's wool.

yclept　　**a.** called, or having the name of. **b.** stone stairs leading down to a crypt. **c.** any yew tree over 500 years old.

zealot　　**a.** a fanatic. **b.** an ornamental brass tray. **c.** an Arab horseman.

zeitgeist　　**a.** the spirit of an age or period. **b.** the collective spirits of the dead. **c.** a spirit that keeps returning to haunt.

zenith　　**a.** the farthest point. **b.** the lowest point. **c.** the highest point.

zwieback　　**a.** a wild boar. **b.** a type of twice-baked bread. **c.** a spinal defect in cattle.

zygote　　**a.** the cell resulting from the union of an ovum and sperm. **b.** an instrument used for measuring the intensity of mirrors. **c.** the small skullcap worn by dignitaries of the Catholic church.

zymotic   **a.** frozen with fear. **b.** relating to or causing fermentation. **c.** fervent, fanatical religious zeal.

A tough final round. But *yclept*! What sort of a word is that, many of you may complain. But as with *xanthic*, *Xanthippe* and *zymotic*, such words did turn up on several occasions in the national press in a 12-month period, so who's to say they're not coming back into vogue? As this last test was undeniably tough, why don't we settle on a score of 12 correct out of 20 as a better than passable attempt, and any score greater than that, a real lexicographical achievement.

Word Roots: Final Dig

Here's a final selection of word elements that, as has been noted many times, can help in identifying the meanings of words that are unfamiliar to you.

Word, Element	Origin	Meaning	English words
un-	Old English	not, contrary to	*unable, unaware, unbend, unclean, undated, unbuilt*
ver, verax	Latin	truth	*veracity, veracious, verify, verily, veritable, verity*
vert, versum	Latin	change, turn	*reverse, invert, convert, versus, version, diversion*
vict, vinc	Latin	win, defeat	*victory, victim, convict, convince*
vid, visus	Latin	to see	*vision, visage, visit, vista, evident, video, television*
viv, vit	Latin	live, life	*vital, vivacious, vitamin, vivid, vivify, vivacity*
voc, vocare	Latin	call, voice	*vocal, vocalist, vociferous, evoke, provoke, vocation*
volvare, volt	Latin	to turn	*revolve, evolve, volte-face, revolt, convolvulus*
-wise	Old English	way, manner	*businesswise, clockwise, otherwise, likewise*
-y, -ey, -ie	Old English	smallness	*daddy, granny, bunny, mummy, doggie*
zoo	Greek	animal	*zoology, zoological*

A Final Revision

The mere 20 words in the WXYZ section hardly need revision: they should still be iceberg-fresh in your memory. Just the same, are you sure about the precise meanings of *zeitgeist*, *xenophobic* and *Xanthippe*? If not, your dictionary beckons.

How to Buy a Dictionary

Ask Yourself These Questions before Buying a Dictionary

1. **Is it up to date?** Check the reverse of the title page to see when it was first published and whether it has been revised since.

2. **Does it list the words I want to look up?** It's a good idea to collect some words that you've had to look up recently. Nothing can be more irritating than owning a dictionary that lets you down – a scaled down 'bargain' dictionary that predictably lists all the words you know but in which those you don't know are frustratingly absent.

3. **Does it contain encyclopedic references?** If you want biographical, geographical, cultural and scientific facts, check it for such information: e.g. *Harrier* (British vertical takeoff jet aircraft); *Koran* (sacred book of Islam); *Lapsang Souchong* (variety of China tea); *Lusatian* (relating to Lusatia, a region of Central Europe); *Planck's constant* (a fundamental constant equal to the energy of any quantum of radiation divided by its frequency).

4. **How comprehensively does it explain words with many meanings?** Remember that some words have a hundred or more shades of meaning and usages.

5. **Does it cover American and Commonwealth English?** Ideally, international variations of English words should be included.

6. **Does it give examples of usage?** These can be very useful, especially with abstract and difficult concepts. Are the examples real (i.e. from existing published works) or invented? The former are preferable.

7. **Does it provide information about variations?** The average user wants information and guidance on spelling variations, plural forms, capitalisation, hyphenation, etc.

8. **Can you follow the guide to pronunciation?** Most dictionaries use the International Phonetic Alphabet (IPA) to illustrate the pronunciation of words. This alphabet, with its baffling symbols, is pretty much the standard these days, so you don't have much choice. Does the dictionary provide pronunciation variants?

9. **Does it include slang, idioms and phrases?** These are part of our everyday language and should be comprehensively listed.

10. **Has it a system of cross-referencing?** Does it provide cross-references to words with related or relevant meanings?

11. **Does it give etymological information?** It is interesting and sometimes useful to know the story or origin of the words you are looking up.

12. **Is it a well-made, practical book?** Whether hardback or softback, your dictionary should be built to withstand daily use and abuse. Will it open flat, and stay open (an important consideration)? Is the type legible? Are the entries well laid out and appealing to the eye? Does the look and feel please you? Is it value for money?

More than ten out of twelve? ***Then buy it!***

How to Use a Dictionary

Your first thought about the word *hard* would probably be: 'It's one of the earliest words I ever learned! Why should I want to look it up in a dictionary?'

But look again. Like many seemingly simple words *hard* has many meanings, shades of meanings and usages – in fact, over 40. Its entry also provides a good example of the lexicographical bounty a dictionary has to offer. Our example, on page 434, is from a previous edition of the *Collins English Dictionary*.

Let's analyse the entry:

1. **Headword or main entry.** This is typically flagged in a bold or different typeface to catch your eye.

2. **Pronunciation.** This is illustrated with the symbols of the International Phonetic Alphabet and won't mean much to you until you consult the key, usually found at the front of the dictionary and sometimes at the foot of each page.

3. **Grammatical designation or part of speech.** The main part of the entry treats *hard* as an adjective (its main use) but if you look further down the entry you will see that the word is also used as an adverb and as a noun.

4. **The first of 25 definitions.** These are usually listed in order of usage. The first definition, *'firm or rigid'*, is the most common; its use to describe a type of nuclear missile defence (definition **23b**) is technical and fairly rare.

5. **The first of four related phrases and idioms.** An up-to-date dictionary will include these.

6. **The first of several definitions with *hard* as an adverb.** These are illustrated with examples of usage, e.g. *hard up for suggestions; hard on his heels; prejudice dies hard.* This facility is invaluable to understanding.

7. **A definition with *hard* as a noun.**

8. **Slang form.** Up-to-date dictionaries include slang as it is irretrievably part of our everyday language.

9. **Taboo form.** Again, it is a mark of modernity to include so-called taboo applications of the headword.

10. **Etymology.** This explains the origin of the word – in the case of *hard* we are told that it derives from the Old English *heard*. More expensive dictionaries give more comprehensive details about a word's history.

11. **Cross-reference to related words and meanings.** Here we are directed, if we wish, to look up the separate entry for the noun *hardness*.

That entry isn't the last we see of *hard*, however. Following entries will typically include **hardback, hard-bitten, hardboard, hard-boiled, hardcore, hard-edge, harden** (the verb form), **hardened** (another adjectival form), **hardener** (noun), **hard hat, hard-headed, hard-hitting, hardly** (adverb), **hardness** (noun), **hard-nosed, hard rock, hard sell, hard shoulder, hardware**, and many more.

While all dictionaries provide explanatory meanings to words, some include synonyms, which is useful if you have a poor memory and are forever searching for precisely the word you want yet have no wish to invest in a thesaurus or a dictionary of synonyms.

How Does Your Dictionary Do?

Having reached this far, and been diligent in your pursuit of a wider and more rounded vocabulary, you will have needed to consult a dictionary on many dozens of occasions. Now is the time to ask yourself: *Has my dictionary provided the answers to all my queries about words and meanings, spelling and pronunciation? Instantly and unambiguously? Has it relieved my doubts and hesitations about using certain words? Is it a pleasure to use?*

1.   *2.*   *3.*   *4.*

hard (hɑːd) *adj.* **1.** firm or rigid. **2.** toughened; not soft or smooth: *hard skin.* **3.** difficult to do or accomplish: *a hard task.* **4.** difficult to understand: *a hard question.* **5.** showing or requiring considerable effort or application: *hard work.* **6.** demanding: *a hard master.* **7.** harsh; cruel: *a hard fate.* **8.** inflicting pain, sorrow, or hardship: *hard times.* **9.** tough or violent: *a hard man.* **10.** forceful: *a hard knock.* **11.** cool or uncompromising: *we took a long hard look at our profit factor.* **12.** indisputable; real: *hard facts.* **13.** *Chem.* (of water) impairing the formation of a lather by soap. **14.** practical, shrewd, or calculating: *he is a hard man in business.* **15.** harsh: *hard light.* **16. a.** (of currency) in strong demand, esp. as a result of a good balance of payments situation. **b.** (of credit) difficult to obtain; tight. **17.** (of alcoholic drink) being a spirit rather than a wine, beer, etc. **18.** (of a drug) highly addictive. **19.** *Physics.* (of radiation) having high energy and the ability to penetrate solids. **20.** *Chiefly U.S.* (of goods) durable. **21.** short for **hard-core. 22.** *Phonetics.* (not in technical usage) denoting the consonants *c* and *g* when they are pronounced as in *cat* and *got.* **23. a.** heavily fortified. **b.** (of nuclear missiles) located underground. **24.** politically extreme: *the hard left.* **25.** *Brit. & N.Z. inf.* incorrigible or disreputable (esp. in **a hard case**). **26. a hard nut to crack. a.** a person not easily won over. **b.** a thing not easily done or understood. **27. hard by.** close by. **28. hard of hearing.** slightly deaf. **29. hard up.** *Inf.* **a.** in need of money. **b.** (foll. by *for*) in great need (of): *hard up for suggestions.* ~*adv.* **30.** with great energy, force, or vigour: *the team always played hard.* **31.** as far as possible: *hard left.* **32.** earnestly or intently: *she thought hard about the formula.* **33.** with great intensity: *his son's death hit him hard.* **34.** (foll. by *on, upon, by,* or *after*) close; near: *hard on his heels.* **35.** (foll. by *at*) assiduously; devotedly. **36. a.** with effort or difficulty: *their victory was hard won.* **b.** (*in combination*): *hard-earned.* **37.** slowly: *prejudice dies hard.* **38. go hard with.** to cause pain or difficulty to (someone). **39. hard put (to it).** scarcely having the capacity (to do something). ~*n.* **40.** *Brit.* a roadway across a foreshore. **41.** *Sl.* hard labour. **42.** *Taboo sl.* an erection of the penis (esp. in **get** or **have a hard on**). [OE *heard*] —'**hardness** *n.*

5.   *6.*   *7.*

11.   *8.*   *9.*   *10.*

Or has it given you a hard time? Made you want to fling it out of the window when you can't find a word or its meaning eludes you? Or given you the queasy feeling that you're not getting the full monty? (does it, in fact, explain the meaning of *the full monty*?).

Before you proceed any further with your vocabulary building, now's the time to decide whether to keep your dictionary or to replace it. Acquiring a new, up-to-date comprehensive dictionary could be one of the best investments you'll ever make.

Searching for Synonyms: The Thesaurus

Back in 1852 an Anglo-Swiss doctor in Edinburgh, taking pity on 'those who are painfully groping their way and struggling with the difficulties of composition', published his now world-famous *Roget's Thesaurus of English Words and Phrases*. Since then, despite many influential detractors, it has sold some 35 million copies worldwide.

The contents of a thesaurus are arranged, not in alphabetical order, but according to the ideas they express. In Roget's book, words were divided into six classes: **abstract**, **space**, **matter**, **intellect**, **volition** and **affections**. These were further subdivided; **affections** was split up into **general**, **personal**, **sympathetic**, **moral** and **religious**. These headings were then reduced to a third division; for example under **moral** were listed **obligations**, **sentiments**, **conditions**, **practice** and **institutions**; and, finally, to a fourth layer.

Writers patient enough to familiarise themselves with *Roget* and similar thesauruses swear by this system of finding synonyms, but there are plenty of critics who regard this type of reference book (or CD) as nothing more than a bluffer's guide.

Because other more modern thesauruses have appeared, *Roget* attempts to update itself every ten years or so. The result is a curious mix of archaic and often ephemeral contemporary slang words, giving rise to its reputation as a browsing book rather than a serious work of reference.

If you are not familiar with a thesaurus then by all means inspect one at a library or bookstore to see if you think one might be useful to you. But a quicker and more straightforward way into alternative words is a plain synonym dictionary. To use one of these effectively, you must either know the word you wish to find a substitute for or a word approximating to its meaning. The words following the main entries of most synomym dictionaries overlap in shades of meaning, so with a little work you can usually find the word you want.

If the elusive word is missing from such an entry, the reader can select the one nearest to the meaning required and look that up; this cross-referencing process means the desired word can usually be found.

Most writers are inclined to defy the purists and have a good synonym dictionary on their desk. But use it with care and discretion and guard against that most despised of literary vices, **elegant variation**!

By constantly using dictionaries, you're bound to increase your vocabulary or word power, and the more words you know, and the better you know how and where to use them, the more effectively you'll be able to communicate.

Answers, Definitions and Meanings

Keep in mind that many, if not most, words have more than a single definition, and that they can also convey various subtleties of meaning according to the context of their use.

In this book only one definition is given for each word, but this will reflect the usual, most commonly accepted meaning.

So it is important that if you are in doubt about what a word means, check its precise meaning or meanings and, if possible, its usage, in your dictionary.

A

CHOOSE THE CORRECT MEANING aberration **b**; abeyance **a**; abnegation **c**; abrogate **b**; abstruse **b**; accede **a**; accolade **a**; accrue **c**; accretion **a**; Achilles heel **c**; acolyte **a**; acquiesce **b**; acrid **c**; acrimonious **a**; actuary **c**; acuity **a**; acumen **b**; adamant **b**; ad hoc **a**; adjunct **b**; adroit **b**; adventitious **a**; aegis **a**; affidavit **b**; aficionado **c**; aggrandise **b**; agnostic **c**; agronomy **c**; akimbo **b**; alacrity **a**; alfresco **c**; allude **b**; alter ego **b**; altruism **a**; amalgam **a**; amanuensis **b**; ambidextrous **c**; ambience **c**; ambivalent **b**; ameliorate **b**; amenable **a**; amoral **b**; amortise **a**; anachronism **c**; analgesic **b**; analogous **b**; anathema **a**; ancillary **c**; angst **b**; annuity **c**.

IDENTIFY THE WORD 1. annul; 2. anomalous; 3. anorexia; 4. anthology; 5. antipasto; 6. antipathy; 7. antithesis; 8. antonym; 9. aperient; 10. aphorism; 11. apiarian; 12. aplomb; 13. apocalypse; 14 apocryphal; 15. apogee; 16. apostasy; 17. apothegm (sometimes apophthegm); 18. apotheosis; 19. apposite; 20. approbation; 21. appurtenance; 22. apropos; 23. apse; 24. aquiline; 25. arable; 26. arachnid; 27. arbitrary; 28. arcane; 29. argot; 30. Armageddon; 31. armoire; 32. arraign; 33. arriviste; 34. ascetic; 35. asinine; 36. aspersion; 37. asperity; 38. assiduous; 39. assuage; 40. atrophy; 41. attenuate; 42. attrition; 43. atypical; 44. au fait; 45. auspicious; 46. autonymous; 47. avocation; 48. avuncular; 49. awry; 50. axiomatic.

B

RIGHT OR WRONG? 1. right; 2. wrong – *badinage* is teasing banter or repartee; 3. right; 4. right; 5. right; 6. wrong – *banal* means trite or commonplace; 7. wrong – a *barmitzvah* (or *Bar Mitzvah*) is the celebration when a Jewish boy assumes his religious obligations; 8. right; 9. right; 10. wrong – a *bayou* is a marsh and certainly not parched; 11. right; 12. wrong – a *behemoth* is a gigantic beast, something huge; 13. wrong – *bel canto* is a style of singing; 14. right; 15. right; 16. wrong – a *bellwether* is a leader (usually a sheep) others follow blindly; 17. wrong – *bemused* means bewildered and confused; 18. right; 19. right; 20. wrong – something *bespoke* is individually made, so cannot be mass-produced.

CHOOSE THE CORRECT MEANING bête noire **b**; bibelot **a**; biennial **b**; bifurcate **a**; bijou **a**; bilateral **b**; billabong **b**; billet-doux **a**; binary **a**; biodegradable **b**; biopsy **b**; bisque **b**; Black Maria **a**; blag **a**; blandishments **b**; blasé **b**; blench **a**; blithe **b**; bombastic **a**; Bombay duck **b**; bona fide **a**; bonhomie **b**; bon vivant **b**; boondocks **a**; boreal **b**; bourgeois **a**; bowdlerise **a**; boycott **b**; braggadocio **a**; braise **a**; brasserie **a**; bravura **b**; breccia **b**; breviary **b**; bric-a-brac **a**; brioche **b**; Brobdingnagian **a**; brouhaha **a**; brusque **a**; bucolic **b**; bulimia **b**; bumptious **b**; bum steer **a**; burgeoning **a**; burgher **a**; burlap **b**; burnish **a**; buttress **b**; Byronic **a**; Byzantine **b**.

C

WHAT'S THE APPROPRIATE WORD? 1. cabriole; 2. cache; 3. cajole; 4. calisthenics; 5. calumny; 6. camaraderie; 7. campanile; 8. campanology; 9. canard; 10. candour; 11. cantankerous; 12. carcinogenic; 13. cardinal; 14. carte blanche; 15. cartel; 16. castellated; 17. castigated; 18. catalyst; 19. catharsis; 20. catheter.

COMPLETE THE WORD 1. catholic; 2. caucus; 3. cavil; 4. cerebral; 5. cessation; 6. chancel; 7. charismatic; 8. charlatan; 9. chauvinism; 10. chicanery; 11. chiffonier; 12. chimera; 13. choleric; 14. chutzpah; 15. cineaste; 16. circumspect; 17. circumvent; 18. clandestine; 19. claque; 20. clement; 21. climactic; 22. coalesce; 23. codicil; 24. coerce; 25. cogent; 26. cognoscenti; 27. collateral; 28. colloquial; 29. comatose; 30. commensurate; 31. compatible; 32. complacent; 33. complaisant; 34. complicity; 35. concomitant; 36. concision; 37. concupiscence; 38. concurrent; 39. condign; 40. conflation.

CHOOSE THE CORRECT MEANING congenital **a**; congeries **a**; congruence **b**; connotation **a**; consanguinity **b**; construe **b**; consummate **a**; contiguous **a**; contrapuntal **b**; contretemps **a**; contrite **b**; contumacious **b**; contusion **a**; convoluted **b**; corollary **a**; corroborate **b**; corrugated **a**; coruscate **b**; costive **b**; coterie **a**; crapulous **b**; credo **a**; credulity **a**; crepuscular **a**; criterion **b**; cruciform **b**; culpable **a**; cupidity **b**; curmudgeon **a**; cursory **a**; cynosure **b**.

D

CHOOSE THE CORRECT MEANING dado **b**; dalliance **a**; dearth **b**; debacle **c**; debilitate **c**; decant **a**; déclassé **a**; declivity **b**; décolletage **c**; decrepitude **b**; de facto **a**; deferential **a**; déjà vu **c**; deleterious **a**; deliquescent **a**; Delphic **c**; demagogue **c**; demeanour **a**; demimonde **b**; demotic **a**; demurrer **a**; denigrate **b**; denouement **c**; depilatory **b**; deprecate **b**; depreciate **a**; derogatory **c**; deshabille **a**; desiccated **b**; desuetude **a**; desultory **b**; determinism **c**; devolution **a**; dextral **b**; dharma **b**; dialectic **a**; Diaspora **b**; diatribe **b**; dichotomy **c**; didactic **a**.

WHAT'S THE WORD? 1. diffident; 2. dilatory; 3. dilettante; 4. Dionysian; 5. dipsomaniac; 6. disabuse; 7. discommode; 8. disconcert; 9. disconsolate; 10. discrepancy; 11. discrete; 12. discursive; 13. disingenuous; 14. disinterested; 15. disparate; 16. dissemble; 17. dissonance; 18. diurnal; 19. diva; 20. divertissement; 21. doctrinaire; 22. doggerel; 23. dolorous; 24. domicile; 25. double entendre; 26. doughty; 27. doyen; 28. Draconian; 29. drugget; 30. dubious; 31. ductile; 32. dudgeon; 33. dulcet; 34. duodenum; 35. duopoly; 36. duplicity; 37. duress; 38. dynasty; 39. dyslexia; 40. dyspeptic.

E

RIGHT OR WRONG? 1. right; 2. wrong – *eclectic* means broad-based and comprehensive; 3. right; 4. right; 5. right; 6. wrong – *effete* means weak and enfeebled; 7. wrong – *efficacious* means effective; 8. right; 9. wrong – *effulgent* means radiant and shining; 10. right; 11. wrong – to be *egocentric* is to be selfish and self-centred; 12. right; 13. right; 14. right; 15. wrong – *elephantine* means huge; 16. right; 17. right; 18. wrong – *elliptical* is having the curved shape of an ellipse; 19. wrong – to *elucidate* is to make clear and intelligible; 20. right.

TOP AND TAIL THE WORDS 1. emanate; 2. emancipate; 3. emasculate; 4. embargo; 5. embolism; 6. embryonic; 7. emendate; 8. emeritus; 9. emetic; 10. emollient; 11. empathy; 12. empirical; 13. empyrean; 14. emulate; 15. encomium; 16. endemic; 17. energise; 18. enervate; 19. enfant terrible; 20. engender; 21. enigma; 22. enjoin; 23. enmity; 24. ennui; 25. enormity; 26. entreat; 27. enunciate; 28. ephemera; 29. epicure; 30. epigram.

WHICH IS THE CORRECT MEANING? epitome a; eponymous a; equable b; equanimity b; equinox b; equitable a; equivocal a; ergonomics b; erogenous a; ersatz b; eructation b; erudite a; eschatology b; eschew b; esoteric a; esprit de corps a; ethos a; etymology b; eugenics a; eulogise b; euphemism b; euphonious a; euphoria a; Eurasian b; euthanasia b; evanescent a; eviscerate a; exacerbate b; excoriate b; exculpate a; execrable a; exegesis b; exemplary a; exigency a; exonerate b; exorcise b; expatiate a; expiate a; exponentially a; expropriate b; expunge a; expurgate b; extempore b; extenuating a; extraneous a; exuberant b.

F

INCREASE YOUR WORD POWER! facetious c; facile a; facilitate d; factotum b; fait accompli c; fallacy a; Falstaffian d; farcical d; farinaceous a; farrago c; fascism b; fastidious b; fatuous a; fatwa d; faux pas b; fealty d; febrile c; feckless a; fecund; c; feign b.

FILL IN THE MISSING LETTERS 1. feisty; 2. felicitous; 3. felonious; 4. feral; 5. fifth columnist; 6. filial; 7. filibuster; 8. finial; 9. flaccid; 10. flagrant; 11. flamboyant; 12. flippant; 13. florid; 14. flout; 15. foetid; 16. foible; 17. foment; 18. footling; 19. foray; 20. forbearance; 21. forensic; 22. forestall; 23. forte;

24. fortuitous; 25. fracas; 26. fractious; 27. Francophile; 28. fratricide; 29. frenetic; 30. friable; 31. fruition; 32. fulminate; 33. fulsome; 34. fundamentalism; 35. funereal; 36. furbelow; 37. furore; 38. fustian.

G

REPLACE THE MISSING WORDS 1. gamine; 2. galvanised; 3. gaffe; 4. garrulous; 5. galaxy; 6. gamut; 7. gangrene; 8. gambit; 9. Gallic; 10. galleria.

WHAT'S THE CORRECT USAGE? gauche **b**; gazebo **a**; gazumped **a**; generic **b**; genre **b**; genuflect **a**; geriatric **a**; germane **b**; gerrymander **a**; gestation **b**; gesundheit **a**; gibe **a**; gigolo **b**; gilt-edged **b**; gimcrack **b**; glasnost **a**; glitterati **a**; gloaming **a**; glutinous **a**; gobbet **b**; gobbledegook **b**; gossamer **a**; gourmandise **b**; Grand Guignol **a**; grandiose **a**; gratuitous **b**; gravamen **a**; gregarious **a**; gremlin **b**; grenadine **b**; gullible **b**; gumption **b**; gunge **a**.

H

CHOOSE THE RIGHT MEANING habeas corpus **b**; habitué **a**; hackneyed **b**; hagiography **c**; ha-ha **a**; haiku **b**; halation **c**; halcyon **a**; halitosis **c**; hapless **c**; harangue **c**; harbinger **a**; hauteur **b**; hearsay **a**; hector **a**; hedonism **b**; hegemony **b**; heinous **b**; helix **b**; hellebore **b**; herbivorous **c**; heresy **a**; hermetic **c**; heterogeneous **b**; heuristic **a**; hiatus **a**; Hibernian **b**; hierarchy **b**; hindsight **c**; histology **a**; histrionic **a**; hoary **c**; Hobson's choice **c**; hoi polloi **c**; hologram **c**; homily **b**; homogeneous **a**; honorarium **c**; hortatory **c**.

SUPPLY THE MISSING WORDS 1. hydrofoil; 2. hybrid; 3. hubris; 4. humdrum; 5. hypochondriac; 6. humane; 7. hyperbole; 8. husbandry; 9. hypothetical; 10. hyperactivity.

I

CHOOSE THE RIGHT MEANING iconoclast **a**; idiomatic **a**; idiosyncrasy **b**; idolatry **a**; ignominious **b**; imbroglio **b**; imbue **a**; immolate **a**; immured **b**; immutable **a**; impartial **a**; impasse **b**; impeach **b**; impeccable **a**; impenitent **b**; imperturbable **b**; impervious **a**; implacable **a**; implausible **a**; importune **b**; imprimatur **b**; impromptu **a**; impugn **a**; inane **b**; incandescent **a**; incapacitate **b**; incipient **a**; inconsequential **b**; incontrovertible **a**; inculcate **a**; incumbent **b**; incursion **b**; indefatigable **a**; indigent **a**; ineffable **a**; ineluctable **b**; inertia **a**; inexorable **a**; ingenuous **b**; ingratiate **a**; inherent **a**; inimitable **b**; iniquitous **b**; innate **a**; innocuous **b**; insalubrious **a**; insular **b**.

MORE MERRY POP-INS 1. irreparably; 2. intransigent; 3. irrevocable; 4. itinerant; 5. interdict; 6. inter alia; 7. iota; 8. invidious; 9. intrinsic; 10. inveighed; 11. irascible; 12. iridescence; 13. inured; 14. inviolable; 15. inveterate.

J

CHOOSE THE CORRECT MEANING jalousie **c**; jaundiced **a**; jejune **b**; jeopardy **a**; jeremiad **b**; jerry-built **c**; jettison **a**; Jezebel **b**; jihad **b**; jingoism **b**; Job's comforter **c**; jobsworth **a**; jocose **b**; joie de vivre **c**; jubilee **c**.

WORDS IN USE – RIGHT OR WRONG? 1. wrong – *judicial* relates to the law courts and justice; 2. right; 3. right; 4. right; 5. wrong – a *junta* is a ruling group of military officers; 6. right; 7. wrong – nautically, a *juryrig* is a makeshift mast or sail; 8. wrong – *juvenescent* means regaining youth and vitality; 9. right; 10. right.

K

CHOOSE THE CORRECT MEANING Kafkaesque **c**; kaftan **b**; kamikaze **a**; karaoke **b**; kaput **c**; karma **a**; kedgeree **b**; Keynesian **a**; keystone **b**; kibbutz **c**; kinetic **b**; kismet **a**; kitsch **a**; kleptomaniac **a**; knell **b**; Knesset **b**; knock-for-knock **b**; kosher **b**; kowtow **b**; kudos **a**.

L

REPLACE THE MISSING WORDS 1. lamentable; 2. laissez faire; 3. labyrinthine; 4. laity; 5. lacklustre; 6. lambent; 7. laconic; 8. lacuna; 9. lackadaisical; 10. lachrymose.

CHOOSE THE CORRECT MEANING lampoon **b**; landau **b**; langoustine **a**; languorous **b**; lapidary **b**; largesse **a**; lascivious **a**; lassitude **a**; latent **b**; lateral **b**; laudable **a**; lectern **b**; leger-de-main **b**; leitmotif **a**; lese-majesty **a**; lessee **a**; lethargic **b**; leviathan **a**; lexicography **b**; liaison **b**; libertarian **a**; libidinous **a**; libretto **b**; licentious **b**; lickspittle **b**; Lilliputian **a**; limbo **a**; limpid **b**; linchpin **a**; lingua franca **b**; lionise **a**; lissom **b**; litany **b**; livid **b**; lobbyist **a**; locum tenens **a**; logistics **a**; logorrhoea **b**; longevity **b**; longueur **b**; loquacious **a**; Lothario **a**; louche **b**; loupe **a**; lubricious **b**; lucid **b**; lugubrious **a**; lumpen **b**; luxuriant **a**.

M

WORDS IN USE: RIGHT OR WRONG? 1. wrong – a *macrocosm* is a large and complex structure, such as the universe, or human society, as opposed to a *microcosm*; 2. right; 3. right; 4. wrong – a *magnanimous* or *generous* person wouldn't bother to count the silver; 5. right, although more usually applied to literary works; 6. right; 7. right; 8. wrong – a *malapropism* is a verbal gaffe, such as 'He's at his wick's end' or 'You could have knocked me down with a fender'; 9. wrong – *mal de mer* is French for seasickness; 10. right; 11. right; 12. right, if Robert's view was that the increasing population in the Far East would eventually exceed its means of subsistence.

CHOOSE THE CORRECT MEANING mandatory **a**; manifest **b**; manifold **b**; manna **b**; manqué **a**; mantra **b**; maquette **b**; marmoreal **a**; materfamilias **b**; maudlin **a**; maunder **b**; maverick **a**; mawkish **a**; maxim **a**; mea culpa **b**; mealy-mouthed **b**; median **b**; mediate **a**; megalomania **b**; megrim **a**; melange **a**; melee **b**; mellifluous **a**; memorabilia **b**; ménage **b**; mendacious **a**; mendicant **b**; mephitic **a**; mercenary **b**; meretricious **b**; mesmerise **a**; messianic **b**; metabolism **a**; metaphorical **a**; métier **a**; metronymic **b**; mettle **b**; mezzanine **b**; miasma **a**; microcosm **a**; micturate **b**.

FILL IN THE GAPS: IDENTIFY THE WORD 1. milieu; 2. militate; 3. mimicry; 4. minatory; 5. minion; 6. minuscule; 7. minutiae; 8. misanthrope; 9. miscegenation; 10. misconstrue; 11. misnomer; 12. misogyny; 13. mitigate; 14. mnemonic; 15. modality; 16. modicum; 17. moiety; 18. mollify; 19. monastic; 20. monetarism; 21. monograph; 22. moraine; 23. moratorium; 24. mores; 25. morganatic; 26. moribund; 27. morose; 28. mot juste; 29. mufti; 30. multifarious; 31. mundane; 32. munificent; 33. mutable; 34. mutual; 35. myopic.

N

ARE THEY BEING USED CORRECTLY? 1. wrong – the *nadir* is the deepest or lowest point; 2. wrong – it must have been an extremely short silence; a *nanosecond* is one thousand-millionth of a second; 3. right; 4. right; 5. wrong – *nebulous* means lacking in form, shape and content; 6. right; 7. right; 8. wrong – *Nemesis* is an agent not of good fortune but of vengeance and retribution; 9. right; 10. right.

CHOOSE THE CORRECT MEANING ne plus ultra **b**; nepotism **c**; nexus **a**; nicety **c**; nihilism **a**; noblesse oblige **b**; noisome **b**; nominal **a**; nonage **c**; nonce word **b**; nonchalant **a**; nonentity **a**; nonpareil **a**; nonplussed **b**; non sequitur **a**; nostrum **c**; nouveau riche **b**; nuance **a**; nubile **c**; nugatory **a**; numinous **b**; nymphet **b**.

O

COMPLETE THE SENTENCE 1. occidental; 2. obtuse; 3. obsequious; 4. obdurate; 5. oblique; 6. occlude; 7. obloquy; 8. obeisance; 9. obstreperous; 10. obsolescent; 11. obviate; 12. obfuscate.

CHOOSE THE CORRECT MEANING odium **b**; odontologist **c**; odyssey **b**; oeuvre **c**; officious **a**; olfactory **c**; oligarchy **b**; omnipotent **a**; omniscient **a**; omnivorous **c**; onerous **a**; opprobrium **a**; optimal **b**; opulent **b**; oracular **b**; Orcadian **c**; ordure **a**; ormolu **c**; oscillate **b**; osmosis **b**; ossified **c**; ostensibly **a**; ostentatious **c**; osteopathy **c**; ostracize **b**; otiose **a**; ottoman **b**; overly **b**; overt **b**; overtone **a**; oxymoron **c**.

P

CHOOSE THE CORRECT MEANINGS pacifist **b**; paediatrician **b**; palaver **a**; palimpsest **a**; palliative **b**; palpable **a**; palpitate **b**; panacea **b**; panache **a**; panegyric **b**; panjandrum **b**; pantheism **a**; paparazzi **b**; paradigm **a**; paragon **b**; paramour **b**; paranoia **b**; paraphrase **a**; pariah **b**; pari mutuel **b**; parity **a**; parlance **b**; parlous **b**; parodic **a**; paroxysm **b**; parsimonious **a**; partiality **a**; partisan **b**; parvenu **a**; passé **b**; pastiche **a**; paterfamilias **a**; pathogenic **b**; patina **b**; patisserie **a**; patois **b**; patrial **a**; patrician **b**; Pauline **b**; Pecksniffian **b**.

WORDS IN USE: RIGHT OR WRONG? 1. right; 2. right; 3. wrong – a *pedagogue* is not an enthusiastic traveller but a teacher or educator – see *peripatetic*; 4. wrong – *pedantic* means to be excessively concerned with details; 5. wrong – a woman's *peignoir* is her dressing gown; 6. right; 7. right; 8. wrong – to have a *penchant* is to have a taste or liking for something; 9. wrong – the *penumbra* is the vague area of shadow between light and dark; 10. right.

CHOOSE THE CORRECT MEANINGS peregrination **a**; peremptory **b**; perennial **b**; perfunctory **a**; peripatetic **b**; periphrasis **a**; permeate **a**; pernicious **b**; peroration **b**; perquisite **a**; persiflage **a**; perspicacious **b**; pertinacious **b**; pervasive **b**; philanderer **a**; philippic **b**; philanthropist **a**; Philistine **a**; phlegmatic **b**; physiognomy **b**; picaresque **a**; picayune **a**; pied-à-terre **a**; pinchbeck **b**; pinnate **b**; piquant **a**; pique **a**; pixilated **a**; placate **b**; placebo **a**; plagiarism **b**; plangent **a**; Platonic **b**; plebeian **b**; plenary **a**; plethora **a**; podiatry **b**; poetaster **b**; pogrom **a**; poignant **b**.

COMPLETE THE SENTENCE 1. potable; 2. portentous; 3. poltergeist; 4. polymath; 5. polemic; 6. polyglot; 7. predatory; 8. preclude; 9. precocious; 10. pragmatic.

CHOOSE THE CORRECT MEANINGS predicate **a**; predilection **b**; prehensile **b**; preponderance **b**; prerogative **a**; prescient **a**; pretentious **b**; prevaricate **a**; prima facie **b**; primordial **b**; probity **b**; proclivity **a**; procrastinate **b**; profligate **a**; prognosis **b**; prolapse **b**; prolix **a**; propensity **b**; prophylactic **b**; propinquity **b**; propitious **b**; prosaic **a**; proscribe **a**; proselytise **b**; prosthesis **a**; protean **a**; protégé **b**; provenance **b**; proviso **b**; prurient **b**; psychosomatic **a**; puerile **a**; puissant **b**; pulchritude **b**; pullulate **b**; punctilious **a**; purlieu **b**; pusillanimous **b**; putative **a**; Pyrrhic victory **a**.

Q

SELECT THE CORRECT USAGE qualm **a**; quandary **a**; quango **a**; quantum **b**; quasar **b**; querulous **a**; quiddity **b**; quidnunc **b**; quiescent **a**; quietus **b**; quintessence **a**; quisling **b**; quixotic **b**; quoin **a**; quondam **b**; quorum **b**; quotidian **a**.

R

POP THE WORD IN PLACE 1. rancour; 2. rara avis; 3. Rabelaisian; 4. rapprochement; 5. raconteur; 6. raison d'étre; 7. ratiocination; 8. raffish; 9. raillery; 10. rapport.

COMPLETE THE WORDS 1. raucous; 2. reactionary; 3. rebarbative; 4. recalcitrant; 5. recant; 6. recapitulate; 7. recherché; 8. recidivism; 9. recipient; 10. reciprocate; 11. recrimination; 12. recondite; 13. recrudescent; 14. rectitude; 15. recurrent; 16. redolent; 17. redoubtable; 18. referendum; 19. refractory; 20. refulgent; 21. refute; 22. regimen; 23. reiterate; 24. remiss; 25. remonstrate; 26. remuneration; 27. rendezvous; 28. renege; 29. reparation; 30. repartee.

CHOOSE THE CORRECT USAGE repertoire a; replicate b; reprehensible b; reprobate b; repudiate a; repugnant b; rescind a; resonant a; respite b; resplendent a; resurgent b; reticent a; retrench a; retrograde b; retroussé b; reverberate a; reverie b; rhetorical b; rictus b; riparian a; riposte b; risible a; rococo b; roué b; rubicund a; rumbustious a; ruminate a; rusticate b.

S

WHAT'S THE CORRECT MEANING? sacrilegious a; sacrosanct b; sagacious b; salacious a; salient a; salubrious b; salutary a; sanctimonious b; sang-froid a; sanguine b; sardonic a; sartorial b; Sassenach b; saturnine b; savoir-faire b; scatology b; sceptic b; schadenfreude a; schism a; scintilla b; scion a; scrupulous b; scurrilous a; sebaceous b; secular b; sedentary a; sedulous a; semantics b; semiotics a; senescent b.

WORDS INTO SPACES 1. simian; 2. similitude; 3. sidereal; 4. sententious; 5. serpentine; 6. shibboleths; 7. sequestered; 8. servile; 9. serrated; 10. serendipitous; 11. simulacrum; 12. sibilant.

CHOOSE THE CORRECT MEANING sinecure a; sinistral b; Sisyphean b; skulk a; slander a; sobriety b; sobriquet b; sodality b; soi-disant b; soignée a; soiree a; solecism b; solicitous b; soliloquy a; solipsism a; sommelier b; somnambulism b; somnolent b; sonorous a; sophistry a; soporific b; sotto voce b; soupçon b; spasmodic a; spatial a; spavined a; specious b; splenetic b; spoonerism b; sporadic b; spurious a; staccato a; stasis a; statutory b; stentorian b; stigmatise a; stoical a; stolid b; stringent b; stultify a; Stygian b; subjugate a; sublimate b; subliminal a; subservient a; substantiate b; subsume a; subterfuge b; succinct b; supercilious b; superfluity a; supernumerary b; supplant a; suppurate b; surrogate a.

WORDS IN USE: RIGHT OR WRONG? 1. right; 2. right; 3. right; 4. wrong – a *sycophantic* lawyer would use fawning and flattery to win his case; 5. right; 6. right; 7. wrong – *synchronous* means 'occurring at the same time'; 8. right; 9. right; 10. wrong – the laboratory would have been asked to *analyse* the substance – that is to break it down into components to find out what it is; to *synthesise* is to combine substances to form something more complex.

T

COMPLETE THE WORD 1. tachometer; 2. tacit; 3. taciturn; 4. tactile; 5. talisman; 6. tangible; 7. tantamount; 8. taupe; 9. tautological; 10. telekinesis; 11. temerity; 12. temporal; 13. temporise; 14. tendentious; 15. tenet; 16. tenuous; 17. tercentenary; 18. terrestrial; 19. tertiary; 20. tessellated; 21. testator; 22. testosterone; 23. tête-à-tête; 24. theism; 25. therapeutic; 26. thespian; 27. thrall; 28. timorous; 29. tinnitus; 30. tocsin.

WHAT'S THE CORRECT MEANING? torpid **a**; tort **b**; tortuous **b**; touché **a**; tractable **c**; traduce **a**; tranche **b**; transcend **b**; transient **b**; translucent **a**; traumatic **a**; travail **b**; travesty **b**; tremulous **c**; trenchant **a**; trepidation **c**; trichology **c**; tridactyl **b**; triptych **a**; triumvirate **b**; troglodyte **c**; trompe l'oeil **b**; trope **a**; truculent **b**; truism **b**; truncate **a**; tsunami **c**; tumescent **c**; turbid **a**; turgid **b**; turpitude **a**; tyrannise **b**; tyro **c**.

U

SELECT THE CORRECT USAGE ubiquitous **a**; ullage **b**; ululation **b**; umbrage **a**; unanimity **b**; unconscionable **a**; unctuous **b**; unequivocal **a**; unguent **b**; unilateral **b**; uninhibited **a**; unison **a**; unmitigated **a**; unprecedented **b**; unreconstructed **a**; unseemly **b**; untenable **a**; untoward **b**; unwonted **a**; urbane **a**; usurious **b**; usurp **a**; utilitarian **a**; Utopian **b**.

V

CHOOSE THE CORRECT MEANING vacillate **a**; vacuous **b**; vagary **b**; vainglorious **a**; valedictory **b**; valetudinarian **a**; vanguard **a**; vapid **a**; variegated **b**; vegetate **b**; vehement **a**; venal **a**; vendetta **b**; veracity **b**; verbatim **a**; verbose **b**; verisimilitude **a**; vernacular **b**; vernal **a**; vertiginous **b**.

COMPLETE THE SENTENCE 1. vis-à-vis; 2. virago; 3. virtu; 4. viable; 5. vicissitudes; 6. vindictive; 7. vilify; 8. virulent; 9. vicarious; 10. vindicate.

IDENTIFY THE WORD 1. visceral; 2. viscous; 3. vitiate; 4. vitreous; 5. vitriolic; 6. vituperation; 7. vivacious; 8. vivisection; 9. vociferous; 10. volition; 11. volte-face; 12. voluptuary; 13. vortex; 14. votary;15. vouchsafe; 16. vox populi; 17. voyeur; 18. vulpine; 19. vulturine.

THE PENULTIMATE REVISION As noted at the end of the exercise, all eight usages are wrong. Check the definitions of those that tripped you up!

WXYZ

CHOOSE THE CORRECT MEANING wagon-lit **b**; waive **a**; wanton **c**; whet **b**; winsome **b**; wizened **b**; wraith **c**; wunderkind **a**; xanthic **a**; Xanthippe **b**; xenophobic **a**; yahoo **a**; yashmak **b**; yclept **a**; zealot **a**; zeitgeist **a**; zenith **c**; zwieback **b**; zygote **a**; zymotic **b**.

6

How to Improve Your Writing

From Here to Obscurity

If language can be like a jungle sometimes, officialese is the minefield laid among the thorny thickets and clinging creepers. And despite the successes of the Plain English teams, officials in government, local councils and other bureaucratic organisations still too often try to lure us into their baffling word mazes.

The language of officialdom can obliterate all meaning. Feel the undergrowth closing in as you try to fight your way out of this trap dug by the former Department of Health and Social Services . . .

The Case of the Crippled Sentence

A person shall be treated as suffering from physical disablement such that he is either unable to walk or virtually unable to do so if he is not unable or virtually unable to walk with a prosthesis or an artificial aid which he habitually wears or uses or if he would not be unable or virtually unable to walk if he habitually wore or used a prosthesis or an artificial aid which is suitable in his case.

This would-be 'sentence' first of all reflects the legalistic terror of official punctuation: the full stop or comma which, if misplaced, might lead the Department all the way to a House of Lords appeal. And, second, it ignores or offends half the population – women – by exclusively using the masculine pronouns *he* and *his*.

So let us take our machete to the undergrowth, bring in the mine detectors and wire-cutters, and try to discover what, if anything, this passage struggles to convey. A step at a time, too, for fear of booby traps.

A person shall be treated as suffering from physical disablement . . . treated?

This is not intended as medical advice, but since the context is medical the reader may, however briefly, be confused. Lift out *treated* and replace with *considered*. Throw *treated* into the shrubbery.

Suffering from physical disablement. Why not simply *physically disabled*? And while we are at it, we don't need *as* after *considered*. Toss that into the shrubbery too.

So far, in our cleaned-up version, we have 'A person shall be considered physically disabled' – and we don't seem to have lost any of the intended meaning.

Such that he is either unable to walk or virtually unable to do so. Wrench away the clumsy *such that he is* and replace it with *which makes him* (we'll come to the offending pronouns later). Next, we cut out *either*, because we don't need it.

We now have *which makes him unable to walk, or virtually unable to do so.* This can be more tightly expressed as *which makes him, unable, or virtually unable, to walk.*

Peering into the darkening thicket we next tackle *if he is not unable or virtually unable to walk with a prosthesis or an artificial aid which he habitually wears or uses . . . Stop!* The rest is just the gibbering of jungle monkeys. This seems to mean that the person can get around, but only with the help of a prosthesis or other artificial aid. The word *even*, before *if he is not*, would have helped. But we really do not need this tangled heap of words at all.

The entire 'sentence', if it means anything, must surely mean this:

> *A person is regarded as physically disabled if he or she always needs an artificial aid to walk.*

We can of course replace the masculine and feminine pronouns with *that person*:

> *A person is regarded as physically disabled if that person always needs an artificial aid to walk.*

As you can see, the meaning remains clear. But what about the prosthesis, you may ask. Well, there are thousands of people with prostheses in the form of replacement hips and knees and other artificial body parts who are bounding about without the least need of any artificial aids – wheelchairs, zimmers and walking sticks – so the amended versions are perfectly valid.

The Case of the Crippled Sentence is a prime example of the need to think 'What do I want to say?' And then to say it, the simple way.

A Serious Case of Effluxion

Here's a verbal smokescreen from a London borough council:

> *And take further notice that under the provisions of Section 47(2) of the said Housing Act 1974 in relation to any land consisting of or including Housing Accommodation in a Housing Action Area a landlord must not less than four weeks before the expiry by effluxion of time of any tenancy which expires without the service of any Notice to Quit, notify the council in writing that the tenancy is about to expire in accordance with the said Schedule 4 . . .*

This is a model of mixed officialese and legalese: you can almost see the glint of watch-and-chain on the Town Clerk's egg-stained black waistcoat. How do we turn it into something like English, without losing any legal force the passage might be required to have?

For a start, there appears to be no need for *And take further notice*. If the reader is not going to take notice, there seems little point in the writer's finishing this masterwork. Next: *under the provisions of Section 47(2) of the said Housing Act 1974* – the words *the provisions of* are redundant. Let's lose them. The same goes for *said*.

And next: *in relation to any land consisting of or including*. The lawyers can keep their *consisting of or including*, just in case they are struggling to cover, say, a backyard or front garden where someone lives in a caravan. But *in relation to* can be shortened to *concerning*. We have now brought *concerning* clumsily close to *consisting*, so let us replace *consisting of* with *that consists of*. The word *Accommodation* after *Housing* is not needed. And once *Housing* is left standing by itself, the capital *H* becomes even more obviously unnecessary.

Plodding on: *a landlord must not less than four weeks before the expiry by effluxion of time* . . . Quickly to the dictionary – to seek out the meaning of this excitingly unfamiliar word, *effluxion*. We find:

> **Efflux, n.** Flowing out (of liquid, air, gas; also fig.) That which flows out. Hence *effluxion*, **n.** See *effluence*, **n.**

From its meaning the word certainly suits the prose style, if nothing else. But we can do without *effluxion*. And we can also do without *expiry*.

Now, what is the rest of the message? It seems that in a Housing Action Area, if a landlord knows that a tenancy is running out and no notice to quit is needed, he must warn the council, in writing, at least four weeks before that tenancy is due to end. So let's tack that information on to our earlier repair:

> *Under Section 47(2) of the Housing Act 1974, concerning any land that consists of or includes housing in a Housing Action Area, if a landlord knows that a tenancy is due to end without need of a notice to quit, he or she must tell the council, in writing, at least four weeks before the tenancy runs out.*

The passage is no nail-biter and is still scarcely slick or smooth. But it *is* quite readable and clear and certainly less forbidding than the original mess.

How Axiomatic is Your Bus Shelter?

Here's a letter from the West Yorkshire Passenger Transport Executive:

> *I refer to your recent letter in which you submit a request for the provision of a bus passenger shelter in Ligett Lane at the inward stopping place for Service 31 adjacent to Gledhow Primary School. The stated requirement for a shelter at this location has been noted, but as you may be aware shelter erection at all locations within West Yorkshire has been constrained in recent times as a result of instructions issued by the West Yorkshire Metropolitan County Council in the light of the Government's cuts in public expenditure and, although it seems likely*

that the Capital Budget for shelter provision will be enhanced in the forthcoming Financial Year, it is axiomatic that residual requests in respect of prospective shelter sites identified as having priority, notably those named in earlier programmes of shelter erection will take precedence in any future shelter programme.

Let us briefly mop our brows and try to fathom what the poor, befuddled author intended to say, before we set about helping him say it in plain English.

At a guess, the passage could be summed up like this:

I refer to your request for a bus shelter in Ligett Lane . . . Unfortunately, because of Government spending cuts, West Yorkshire Metropolitan County Council has in turn ordered a curb on bus-shelter building. Although there may be more money for such work in our next financial year, shelters already on the waiting list will obviously be built first.

This seems simple enough, so where did the author go wrong? Let us lay his Frankenstein's monster on the dissecting slab:

I refer to your recent letter in which you submit a request for the provision of a bus passenger shelter in Ligett Lane . . . If the writer identifies the subject clearly enough, there is no need to remind his correspondent of all the details. The correspondent wants a straightforward Yes, No, or even Maybe – with an explanation, if the answer is No or Maybe.

The stated requirement for a shelter at this location has been noted . . . Of course it has. Otherwise the official would not be writing at all.

but as you may be aware . . . This is word-wasting. It doesn't matter if the correspondent is aware or not. The official's job is to make sure the correspondent knows the facts now.

shelter erection at all locations within West Yorkshire has been constrained in recent times . . . No purpose is served by *at all locations*. There is no reason to use *within* rather than *in*, no matter how widely this particular verbal fungus has spread.

constrained should be replaced by the easier to understand *restricted*; and *in recent times* is a redundancy. So is *as a result of instructions issued by*.

West Yorkshire Metropolitan County Council is rendered with a rare and forceful clarity, with not a syllable wasted. But then we slide back . . . *in the light of the Government's cuts in public expenditure . . .* The only meaning of *in the light of*, here, is *because of*. Your reader, rightly or not, will still blame the government for the lack of a bus shelter, whether you use the clear or the foggy expression. So why head into the fog?

and, although it seems likely that the Capital Budget for shelter provision will be enhanced in the forthcoming Financial Year . . . The reader is less interested in what the bus shelter fund is called than what it will do for him, and when. So ditch *the Capital Budget*. And since a shelter is a shelter, *provision* is yet another unneeded word.

enhanced, in this context, means *increased*; there seems to be no reason to evade the more commonly used word.

it is axiomatic that . . . Your dictionary will tell you that an *axiom* is a self-evident statement, a universally accepted principle established by experience; *axiomatic* here is presumably meant to convey *self-evidently true*. If something is that obvious, the official is wasting paper and his correspondent's time in saying it.

residual requests in respect of prospective shelter sites identified as having priority, notably those named in earlier programmes of shelter erection . . . Thrusting the dissecting knife into the middle of this lot, we are left with *shelter requests not met by earlier building programmes* to which we add *will take precedence in any future shelter programme*. There's not a lot to argue about here, for once – apart, perhaps, from the repetition of *shelter programme*.

The deskbound, wordbound Frankenstein who created our monster may be saddened, even angry, at the way we have slimmed down his offspring. But at least he – and more importantly, his correspondent – can now discover what he really meant to say.

Missives such as our bus shelter letter don't have to be long to lose their way. Here's a paragraph from an insurance policy, hunted down by the Plain English Campaign:

> *The due observance and fulfillment of the terms so far as they relate to anything to be done or complied with by the Insured and the truth of the statements and answers in the Proposal shall be conditions precedent to any liability of the Company to make any payment under this Policy.*

Follow? Perhaps after five minutes' concentration you might feel that you have fully understood it. The Campaign's recommended version would no doubt leave the insurance company gasping for words:

We will only make a payment under this policy if:

- *you have kept to the terms of the policy; and*

- *the statements and answers in your Proposal are true.*

Almost all officialese can be analysed, dissected and rendered into clear and readily understood English but some is so dense as to resist the sharpest and most probing of scalpel blades. Here's an example, quoted by the *Daily Telegraph*, that consigns itself forever in the limbo of lost understanding:

> *ANY lump sum paid in accordance with Provision 7 of the Second Schedule shall be an amount equal to the Basic Nominal Fund that would be applied to calculate the Alternative Annuity under Provision 5 or Provision 12 of the Second Schedule on the assumption that the Annuitant had elected under Provision 4 of the Second Schedule that the date of his death was the Alternative Vesting Date or if greater an amount equal to the premiums received by the Society.*

This is the sort of verbal hurdle that is still likely to confront average citizens at any time. Are we really expected to understand this guff? Or are we expected to hire a specialist or consultant to help us? Yet none of the sorry examples quoted here need have happened, if only the writers had held this conversation with themselves:

Q and A can Save the Day

Q What's it all about?

A It's about when somebody is classed as disabled/the special duty of a landlord in a Housing Action Area/someone wanting a bus shelter built.

Q What do we want to say?

A We want to say that someone who can't walk unaided is officially disabled; that a Housing Action Area landlord has to warn the council when there's about to be a tenancy available; that we can't afford the requested bus shelter just now.

Q Very well. So why don't we just SAY it!

There is no excuse for obscurity. The English language, with its lexicon of nearly half a million words, is there to help any writer express any thought that comes into his or her head – even the virtually inexpressible. If we can't manage this, we should give up and leave it to others. Or admit our faults and learn how to do better.

THE NO-GOOD, THE BAD AND THE UGLY:

Obstacles to Clear Communication

The Long, Long Trail A-winding: Circumlocution

Bournemouth was on Monday night thrown into a state of most unusual gloom and sorrow by the sad news that the Rev A M Bennett – who for the last 34 years has had charge of St Peter's Church and parish, and who has exercised so wonderful an influence in the district – had breathed his last, and that the voice which only about a week previously had been listened to by a huge congregation at St Peter's was now hushed in the stillness of death . . .

Lymington Chronicle, 22 January 1880

When a writer or speaker fills you with the urge to shout 'Get on with it!', he or she is probably committing the sin of **circumlocution** – roundabout speech or writing, or using a lot of words when a few will do. In most of today's newspapers the prose above would be a collector's item.

Politicians, of course, are notable circumlocutionists; perhaps it's an instinct to confuse, to prevent them from being pinned down. A few years ago a British political leader went on television to explain his attitude to the introduction of a single currency for all countries in the European Community.

Before you continue reading, you should probably find a comfortable seat . . .

> *No, I would not be signing up: I would have been making, and would be making now, a very strong case for real economic convergence, not the very limited version which the Conservatives are offering, so we understand, of convergence mainly of inflation rates, important though that is, but of convergence across a range of indicators – base rates, deficits and, of course, unemployemt – together with a number of indexes of what the real performance of economics are . . .*

(Perhaps a brief tea-break would be in order here.)

> *. . . the reason I do that and the reason why that is an argument that must be won before there is any significant achievement of union is not only a British reason, although it is very important to us, it is a European Community reason: if we were to move towards an accomplished form of union over a very rapid timetable without this convergence taking place it would result in a two-speed Europe, even to a greater extent than now – fast and slow, rich and poor – and the fragmentation of the Community, which is the very opposite of what those people who most articulate the view in favour of integration and union really want; when I put that argument to my colleagues in, for instance, the Federation of Socialist Parties, many of whom form the governments in the EC, there is a real understanding and agreement with that point of view . . .*

So what, precisely, might the gentleman have been hoping to convey? Probably this:

> *I do not want a single European currency until various other factors affecting the question have been dealt with. The factors are these . . .*

A former US President, George Bush Snr, was famous for his bemusing circumlocution, as in this speech defending his accomplishments:

> *I see no media mention of it, but we entered in – you asked what time it is and I'm telling you how to build a watch here – but we had Boris Yeltsin in here the other day, and I think of my times campaigning in Iowa, years ago, and how there was a – I single out Iowa, it's kind of an international state in a sense and has a great interest in all these things – and we had Yeltsin standing here in the Rose Garden, and we entered into a deal to eliminate the biggest and most threatening ballistic missiles . . . and it was almost, 'Ho-hum, what have you done for me recently?'*

Circumlocution (also called **periphrasis**) typically employs long words, often incorrectly or inappropriately, and probably derives from a need to sound learned (a policeman referring to a bomb as *an explosive device*) or a desire not to offend (asking, for example, 'I wonder if you would mind awfully moving to one side' instead of the more direct 'Get out of my way!'. Some forms of circumlocution may be excusable, but most are the result of unthinking use of jargon and clichés in place of more precise (and usually briefer) expressions. Typical is the use of *with the exception of* for *except*; *with reference to/regard to/respect to* for *about*; *for the very good reason that* for *because*, and so on.

To avoid being accused of circumlocution, **stick to the point**! If you intend to drive from London to Manchester in the most direct way possible you'd hardly wander off every motoway exit and then dither about along country lanes. The same principle applies to effective communication.

It also pays to be aware of persistent offenders – circumlocutory phrases many of us are inclined to utter when the exact, simple word we want fails to turn up. Here's a short list.

The Circumlocutionist's Lexicon

apart from the fact that – *but, except*
as a consequence of – *because of*
as yet – *yet*
at the time of writing – *now/at present*
at this moment/point in time – *now/at present*
avail ourselves of the privilege – *accept*

be of the opinion that – *think, believe*
because of the fact that – *because*
beg to differ – *disagree*
by means of – *by*
by virtue of the fact that – *because*

consequent upon – *because of*
consonant with – *agreeing/matching*
could hardly be less propitious – *is bad/unfortunate/unpromising*

due to the fact that – *because*
during such time as – *while*
during the course of – *during*

except for the fact that – *except/but*

few in number – *few*
for the reason that/for the very good reason that – *because*

give up on (it) – *give up*
go in to bat for – *defend / help / represent*

in accordance with – *under*
in addition to which – *besides*
in a majority of cases – *usually*
in all probability – *probably*
in anticipation of – *expecting*
inasmuch as – *since*
in association with – *with*
in close proximity to – *near*
in connection with – *about*
in consequence of – *because of*
in contradistinction to – *compared to / compared with*
in excess of – *over / more than*
in isolation – *alone*
in less than no time – *soon / quickly*
in many cases / instances – *often*
in more than one instance – *more than once*
in order to – *to*
in respect of – *about / concerning*
in spite of the fact that – *although / even though*
in the absence of – *without*
in the amount of – *for*
in the event that – *if*
in the light of the fact that – *because*
in the near future – *soon*
in the neighbourhood of / in the vicinity of – *near / about*
in the recent past – *recently*
in view of / in view of the fact that – *because*
irrespective of the fact that – *although*

large in size / stature – *large / big*

make a recommendation that – *recommend that*

nothing if not – *very*
notwithstanding the fact that – *even if*

of a delicate nature / character – *delicate*
of a high order – *high / great / considerable*
of the opinion that – *think / believe*
on account of the fact that – *because*
on a temporary basis – *temporary / temporarily*
on the grounds that – *because*
on the part of – *by*
owing to the fact that – *because*

pink / purple / puce, etc, in colour – *pink / purple / puce, etc*
prior to – *before*
provide a contribution to – *contribute to / help*

regardless of the fact that – *although*

subsequent to – *after*

there can be little doubt that – *no doubt / clearly*
there is a possibility that – *possibly / perhaps*
to the best of my knowledge and belief – *as far as I know / I believe*

until such time as – *until*

with a view to – *to*
with reference to – *about*
with regard to – *about*
with respect to – *about / concerning*
with the exception of – *except*

People prone to pompous long-windedness can be gently reminded of their sins by quoting to them a well-known nursery rhyme rewritten in circumlocutory style:

> *Observe repeatedly the precipitate progress of a trio of sightless rodents: together they coursed apace on the heels of the agriculturalist's consort, who summarily disjoined their caudal appendages with a cutler's handiwork. One had never witnessed such mirth in one's existence as the incident involving those hemeralopic and nyctalopic mammals.*

The rhyme is, of course, *Three Blind Mice*.

An Utterly Unique Added Extra: Tautology

Mr and Mrs David Smith are proud to announce the birth of a baby girl, Sarah Anne.

Now, like 'Dog Bites Man', this isn't really news. But what if Mrs Smith had given birth to an *adult* girl? That would be news! Obviously Mrs Smith had given birth to a baby; it happens all the time. The newsy bit is that it was a girl.

The use of the word *baby* here is what is known as **pleonasm**, the use of redundant words. The same would apply if Mrs Smith invited the neighbours in to see her 'new baby'. Are there any *old* babies? Of course all babies are new!

When a word repeats the meaning of another word in the same phrase it is called **tautology** and, usually, all verbal superfluities are known by this term.

Free gift! Added extra! Added bonus! These are exciting claims. And also wasted words: classic examples of tautology, the use of more than one word to convey the same thought.

A gift, if not free, is not a gift – except perhaps in the slang usage, 'That car was an absolute gift at £6,000'.

Something *extra* is clearly something *added*. And a *bonus* is normally an *addition*. Even if the word is used to describe something apart from money, an *added bonus* is an *added addition*. Nonsense, obviously. Yet we hear and read phrases such as *added bonus* every day, from people who have not thought what they are saying or writing, or do not care.

So accustomed are we to tautology in everyday speech and reading that this form of language misuse can pass unnoticed:

Will David's income be sufficient enough for you both?

How many of us would normally detect that *enough* is a wasted word?

Avoiding redundant words and expressions is a sign of a caring writer and here, to help you, is an A to Z of some of the more common superfluities.

An A to Z of Tautology

absolute certainty
actual facts (and its cousin, *true facts*)
added bonus / extra
adequate / sufficient enough
a downward plunge
advance warning
appear on the scene
arid desert
attach together
audible click

burn down, burnt up (*burn* and *burnt* by themselves are usually better)

circle round, around
collaborate together
connect together
consensus of opinion (it's simply *consensus*)
couple together
crisis situation

divide it up, divide off

each and every one
early beginnings
eat up
enclosed herewith, enclosed herein
end result

file away
final completion
final upshot
follow after
forward planning
free gift
funeral obsequies
future prospects

gather together
gale force winds
general consensus
grateful thanks

have got (a common one, this. Simply *have* is fine)
the hoi polloi (as *hoi* means 'the', *the* is obviously redundant)
hoist up
hurry up

important essentials
in between
inside of
indirect allusion
I saw it with my own eyes (who else's?)

join together
joint cooperation
just recently

lend out
link together
lonely isolation

meet together
merge together
mix together, mix things together
more preferable
mutual cooperation

necessary requisite
new beginner, new beginning
new creation
new innovation, new invention

original source
other alternative
outside of
over with (for *ended, finished*)

pair of twins
past history
penetrate into
personal friend
polish up
proceed onward

raze to the ground (*raze* by itself means exactly that)
really excellent
recall back
reduce down
refer back
relic of the past
renew again
repeat again
revert back
rise up

safe haven
seldom ever
set a new world record
settle up
sink down
still continue
sufficient enough
swallow down

this day and age
totally complete
totally finished
tiny little child

unique means the only one of its kind. You can't get much more unique than that.
Not even *quite unique, absolutely unique* and *utterly unique*
unexpected surprise
unite together
unjustly persecuted
usual habit

very pregnant
viable alternative

warm 75 degrees (of course 75 degrees is *warm*!)
whether or not
widow woman

There are other forms of repetition, some intentional and some not. Writers have often used it for effect, for example in Samuel Taylor Coleridge's *The Rime of the Ancient Mariner*:

> *Alone, alone, all, all alone,*
> *Alone on a wide wide sea!*

Or in this equally famous passage from a speech of Winston Churchill's:

> *We shall go on to the end, we shall fight in France, we shall fight on the seas and oceans, we shall fight with growing confidence and growing strength in the air, we shall defend our island, whatever the cost may be, we shall fight on the beaches, we shall fight on the landing grounds, we shall fight in the fields and in the streets, we shall fight in the hills; we shall never surrender.*

Then there are those instances when, in writing, we manage to box ourselves into a corner with such irritating repetitions as, 'Her opinion *is, is* that it will never work'; 'The dealer admitted he *had had* the sideboard in his shop for two months'; 'Not *that that* would bother her in the least' and so on.

Finally, take care with **double negatives**, distant cousins of pleonasm. Although they can be useful they are also often confusing. *The bomb attack* was not unexpected. If you lived in a terrorist-ridden area, where to be bombed sooner or later would be no great surprise, the double negative *not unexpected* is better for conveying a suspended kind of expectation than *was expected* or *was no surprise*.

The puzzle for many writers is, why is *I* **don't** *know* **nothing** *about it* considered to be unacceptable, while *the Prime Minister is* **not unmindful** *of the damage already suffered* . . . is grammatically respectable? The answer lies in the modifying power of the combination; *not uncommon*, for example, does not mean exactly the same as *common* but something between *common* and *uncommon* – 'a little more common than you might think'. The trouble is that often double negatives can leave the readers trying to work out what is meant, so they are probably best avoided.

Witter + Waffle = Gobbledegook

> *They never shorten anything – that would make it less important –*
> *they inflate the language in a way they certainly oughtn't*
> *to, indeed everything goes into officialese, a kind of gobbledygook*
> *invented by the sort of people who never open a (hardcover) book.*

That comment by poet Gavin Ewart refers to the propensity of ignorant people to witter and waffle and to inflate plain language into a meaningless, pretentious form of expression we recognise as **gobbledegook** (or **gobbledygook**).

all things being equal by and large having said that I am of the opinion in the final analysis last but not least the fact of the matter is more than enough with all due respect

'Witter words' are a key ingredient of gobbledook. Our language is liberally sprinkled with them – expressions that clog a sentence and add neither information nor meaning.

In this, wittering and witter words differ from circumlocution, which adds information, but in the wrong order – usually delaying the main point.

In our death notice for the Rev A M Bennett (see page 450) the reader has to plod through 53 words before arriving at 'breathed his last'. But those 53 words did at least tell us the place and time of death, how long he had been a vicar, the name of the church, the extent of his influence and the reaction in his parish to the news.

Witter words, on the other hand, tell us nothing. Some are more often heard in speech (especially speeches by pundits and politicians) but many appear in writing.

For a classic example of wittering, loaded with witter words, we could hardly do better than this passage from a speech by former Australian Prime Minister Bob Hawke. Mr Hawke had so perfected his ability to say almost nothing in the maximum number of words that the style became known as 'Hawkespeak':

> *And that tends to mean at times if you want to put it, there is no point in running away from it, it tends to mean at times that there's a lack of specificity, or if you want to put it another way, there's a range of options which are put which are there to accommodate that indisputable fact about the social democratic parties such as ours.*

National Times, 22 November 1985

The second ingredient of gobbledegook is **waffle**; vague and wordy utterances that wander aimlessly along a path of meaning but effectively obscure it. In its extreme form it's called **verbal diarrhoea** or, more correctly, **logorrhoea**. When you combine this affliction with a good helping of witter words and a tendency to tangle your syntax, the result is total obfuscation, or gobbledegook.

The former US President George Bush Snr was an acknowledged master of gobbledegook – of using language (perhaps not intentionally, given his difficulties with English), not to reveal, but to obscure. Here he is, chatting with one of the astronauts on the space shuttle Atlantis: 'How was the actual deployment thing?' he asks. And again, this time in full flow when asked if he would look for ideas on improving education during a forthcoming trip abroad:

Well, I'm going to kick that one right into the end zone of the Secretary of Education. But, yes, we have all – he travels a good deal, goes abroad. We have a lot of people in the department that does that. We're having an international – this is not as much education as dealing with the environment – a big international conference coming up. And we get it all the time, exchanges of ideas. But I think we've got – we set out there – and I want to give credit to your Governor McWherter and to your former governor, Lamar Alexander – we've gotten great ideas for a national goals programme from – in this country – from the governors who were responding to, maybe, the principal of your high school, for heaven's sake.

In 1944, a Texas congressman named Maury Maverick became so angry about the bloated bureaucratic language in memos he received that he described it as 'gobbledegook'. Explaining the name he said it reminded him 'of an old turkey gobbler back in Texas that was always gobbledy-gobbling and strutting around with ludicrous pomposity. And at the end of of this gobble-gobble-gobble was a sort of a gook'. Maverick was also the head of a federal agency, and promptly issued an order to all his subordinates: 'Be short and say what you are talking about. Let's stop *pointing up* programs, *finalizing* contracts that *stem from* district, regional or Washington levels. No more *patterns, effectuating, dynamics*. Anyone using the words *activation* or *implementation* will be shot'.

Half a century later it seems that the Maverick Edict has had little effect. The art world certainly never heard of it:

The spontaneous improvisation of trivial and fictional roles means a frame for social and communicative creativity which, by going beyond mere art production, understands itself as an emancipated contribution towards the development of newer and more time-appropriate behavior forms and a growth of consciousness . . .

Studio International, 1976

In a fit of liberalism you may excuse such babblings because writing about art is often incomprehensible anyway. But it is harder to excuse organisations supposedly dedicated to the art of human *communication*. Here is an extract from the Stanford University Press catalogue (1994) touting a forthcoming title called

Materialities of Communication, edited by Hans Ulrich Gumbrecht and K. Ludwig Pfeiffer:

> *Converging with a leitmotiv in early deconstruction, with Foucauldian discourse analysis, and with certain tendencies in cultural studies, such investigations on the constitution of meaning include – under the concept 'materialities of communication' – any phenomena that contribute to the emergence of meaning without themselves belonging to this sphere: the human body and various media technologies, but also other situations and patterns of thinking that resist or obstruct meaning-constitution.*

Of course, to the normal person the first few words of a passage like this flash warning signs of impenetrability; to proceed would be to enter a mental maze from which there is no escape. But not all gobbledegook is that obliging. Much of it can entice you all the way through a wide and welcoming thoroughfare until, at the very end, you realise you are in a blind alley.

All the examples quoted in this section are real although it may seem at times that some genius made them up. Let them be a warning! Next time you are tempted to lapse into what reads or sounds like gobbledegook, remember that Texas turkey.

Smart Talk, but Tiresome: Jargon

> *The increase in £M3 was approximately equal to bank lending plus the PSBR minus net sales of gilt-edged securities other than sales to the banks themselves.*

> Nigel Lawson, *The View from No.11*, 1992

> *. . . the cognitive-affective state characterised by intrusive and obsessive fantasising concerning reciprocity of amorant feelings by the object of the amorance.*

> US sociologist's definition of love, 1977

Most people recognise jargon when they see it: words and phrases that may have begun life within a particular circle of people, trade or profession, but which spread among others who merely wish to appear smart or up-to-date.

The *Collins English Dictionary* defines jargon as 'language characterised by pretentious synatax, vocabulary or meaning; gibberish'.

But not all jargon is pretentious or gibberish. It includes the shop talk of technical terms, understood by those who need to know and who have no need to explain it to outsiders. It is for millions of people a form of time-saving professional shorthand. It is a specialist's language designed for accurate and efficient communication between members of a particular group.

Fair enough, but too often jargon and arcane verbiage are used by people to trick others into believing they know more than they actually do; or exploited as a security blanket to give them the feeling of belonging to an elite. This use – or misuse – can only interfere with meaning and understanding.

Hundreds of former valid scientific, technical. legal and technical terms have become more widely used as vogue or buzz words, and many of them are not properly understood. How many of us can hold hand to heart and say that we know precisely what these vogue words mean: *parameter, symbiosis, quantum leap, synergy, dichotomy, post-modern*? Yet despite our doubts we're still tempted to use them.

In spite of the efforts of the Plain English Campaign, jargon is still very much alive and kicking when we read of:

a visitor uplift facility	=	a tourist mountain train
ambient non-combatant personnel	=	war refugees
enthusiasm guidance motivators	=	cheer leaders
an unpremised business person	=	a street trader
festive embellishments (illuminary)	=	Christmas lights *
an ambient replenishment assistant	=	supermarket shelf stacker
wilderness recreation	=	camping and hiking
frame-supported tension structures	=	tents
unselected rollback to idle	=	aircraft engine failure in mid-flight

* True. This is how the politically correct Northampton Council described them.

The Job Ads Jargon Jungle

It is something of a paradox that where plain language is needed most, jargon is often used instead. This is perhaps best illustrated in job recruitment, where companies offering jobs have created their own hideous non-language:

> *Moving from hierarchical structures to a process-based architecture, our success has been based on consistent, integrated teamwork and quality enhancement through people. By ensuring consistency in the development and integration of process plans, you will facilitate the management processes to develop implementation plans for the processes they manage. You will also be involved in business plan modelling, rolling plan methodologies and the measurement of process effectiveness. As Integration Planner, your position will be at the interface of the personal, planning, implementation and measurement matrix.*

This example, quoted by the Plain English Campaign, prompts one to ask: 'Did anyone get the job, and if so, what are they doing?'

Here are some more cautionary examples of jargon from the same swampy jungle:

cultivational – fortunately a rare sighting, in an English National Opera advertisement for a 'Development Officer – Events', to be responsible for *co-ordinating and administering cultivational and fundraising events*. It is just possible that *cultivational* really means something. Our guess is that it is something to do with sucking up to people to get them to put money into a project. Your guess will be just as good.

driven – as in *quality-driven service organisation*. As with *orientated* (see under separate entry), this is merely meant to indicate the firm's sense of priority – in this case to offer high-quality services.

environment – meaning, usually, the place where the worker will do the job. The firm that boasted of a *quality-driven* organisation also promised . . . *a demanding and results orientated environment*. Another company required the applicant to have a background of *progressive sales or marketing environment*. In this case *environment* presumably meant *experience* or *business* – in which case *sales* or *marketing* would have sufficed. *Progressive* can only mean 'forward-looking' – and few firms would be looking for backward-looking candidates! Yet another employer advertised for a worker who *should have experience in a fast-moving, multi-assembly environment*.

Assuming that *multi-assembly* has its own meaning in the business concerned, why not simply require *experience in fast multi-assembly*?

human resources – This term has now supplanted *personnel*, which in turn replaced *employees* or *workers*. *Personnel*, though also bureauspeak, at least does not have the ghastly pretentiousness and pseudo-caringness of *human resources*.

motivated – one of the most hard-worked jargon words in job advertisements . . . *the ability to motivate, lead and be an effective team player; management and motivation of the sales force; should be self-motivated*. In the first two examples, we can substitute *inspire* and *inspiration*. In the third, it is harder to guess what the applicant will be required to prove. *Enterprising*, perhaps, or *to show initiative*. Or, if these sound too revolutionary for the company's taste, *able to work unsupervised*.

orientated – as in *results-orientated environment* or *profits-orientated system*, is a high-profile jargon word (as is *high-profile*). The word is presumably meant to convey what a firm considers to be important. In these examples its use is *nonsense-orientated*. A company that is not keen on getting results or profits will not be placing job advertisements for much longer, so the phrase is redundant. Another jargon version is *success-orientated* for the far simpler *ambitious*. And in any case *orientated* is wrongly used for the shorter, original *oriented*.

pivotal role – Fancier version of *key role*. Neither helps much to explain a job. If the importance of the position needs to be stressed, what's wrong with *important*?

positive discrimination – in politically correct speak this means providing special opportunities in training and employment for disadvantaged groups and ethnic minorities. However the term is still widely misunderstood and perhaps best avoided. *Favoured* or *give preference to* might be better.

proactive – mostly found in social services advertisements describing the approach to a particular job. It means initiating change where and when needed as opposed to merely responding to events: *reactive*. Although a jargon word, it is difficult to resist as there is no crisp single-word equivalent.

remit – meaning responsibility: *an experience-based understanding of multi-level personnel relationships will be within your remit*. Although *remit* may be shorter it is not otherwise commonly used and is pompous.

remuneration package – simply means *salary and other benefits*.

skills – at first sight this is a reasonable word to expect in job advertisements, but there are some abuses, as in *interpersonal skills*, which presumably means *good at dealing with people*.

specific – as in *the key duties of the post will include developing country-specific and/or product-specific marketing activity plans*. Amazingly, that passage is from an advertisement placed by the personnel department of the University of Cambridge Local Examinations Syndicate. They could have said: . . . *developing plans for selling our products to particular countries*. But perhaps that sounded too boring.

structured – as in *it is likely that you will have worked successfully in a sizeable, structured organisation*. You would hardly go seeking recruits in an *un*-structured organisation, would you?

Not so long ago, schools had teachers, councils had social workers and everyone seemed to understand what they did. Now it is not so simple, and advertisements for jobs in education and social welfare contain more verbocrap than in any other field of human endeavour. Here's some impenetrable prose about a home for teenagers:

> *The aim of the home is to enable older young people who still have substantial emotional and personal deficits to make planned progress towards personal autonomy.*

Even among social workers this is garbled nonsense. Surely no professional catastrophe will happen if we simply say: *to enable teenagers with troubled personalities to learn to cope for themselves* . . . However, lacking in fashionable jargon, the rewrite would probably result in the original writer having a *job security deficit*.

The following example, from a publication of the former Inner London Education Authority, characterises the worst kind of jargon abuse:

Due to increased verbalisation the educationist desires earnestly to see school populations achieve cognitive clarity, auracy, literacy and numeracy both within and without the learning situation. However the classroom situation (and the locus of evaluation is the classroom) is fraught with so many innovative concepts (e.g. the problem of locked confrontation between pupil and teacher) that the teaching situation is, in the main, inhibitive to any meaningful articulacy. It must now be fully realised that the secondary educational scene has embraced the concept that literacy has to be imparted and acquired via humanoid-to-humanoid dialogue. This is a break-through. [and a load of jargon!]

Multicultural Muddle

. . . experience of managing a multicultural urban environment and the ability to integrate equalities considerations into areas of work activity.

This passage, from an advertisement for a Deputy Director of Social Services, is a real polysyllabic mess. *Multicultural urban environment*, despite modern delicacies, simply means *racially mixed part of town. Integrate* here may mean *build in*, or it may have been misused to mean *include.*

Every trade and profession is entitled to its own jargon – up to a point. So let us allow that *equalities* is readily understood among social services people as meaning equal treatment regardless of race, sex and, probably, physical handicaps – although the singular *equality* serves the purpose as well, or better.

That passage, converted into plain English, could read:

. . . experience of dealing with a racially mixed town area and ability to ensure that equality is part of departmental life.

The same advertisement also required *ability to organise intervention in the community to establish the needs of potential service users.* Meaning, presumably, *ability to go out to discover what people need us to do.*

Social workers do not have the field to themselves when it comes to jargon. An advertisement for a health worker in Brazil announced:

You will assist the team in formulating and implementing a health policy, evaluating and developing appropriate responses to specific health problems in indigenous areas . . .

Meaning? Let's try to translate: *You will help to plan and carry out a policy to deal with health problems among local people.* Such a simplification may create a problem, however; to jargon-hardened health workers the revised job description sounds as though it's less important and so worth only half the salary of the inflated version.

Computerspeak and Psychobabble

As computing has evolved from cult to mass culture we can no longer ignore the jargon that computers have generated. Even quite young children are now familiar with dozens of terms: *floppy, prompt, menu, boot, megahertz, toolbar, drag* and *drop* hold no terrors for them. However, some of the worst offences against the English language pour in an unending stream from the computer world:

> *Driven and focused by seeing the world from the customer's perspective, we continue to build an organisation where quality is embedded in every aspect of endeavour . . . our continued growth in the network computing industry mandates that we now identify and attract the most talented and creative sales and marketing professionals . . .*

Mandates? This announcement sounds as if it were written by someone whose dictionary had a bad coffee stain on the relevant entry.

Is writing jargon and management-speak more difficult than writing plain English? Many examples suggest that it is, yet its devotees persist in working harder than they need to. Whoever wrote this job description in an advertisement for a BBC position deserved his Golden Bull award: *The BBC seeks a Human Resources Assessment Technologist, Corporate Management Development.* But jargonising also offers a lazy way out. Here's a press release about a forthcoming conference, put out by the Association for Humanistic Psychology in Britain, which deserves full marks for sloth:

> *Conjoint Family Therapy, demonstration/participation workshop. This is a demonstration/participation workshop illustrating 20 to 30 'ways of being' as therapist (i.e. 'self as instrument'/strategies/techniques) presented from an experiential-Gestalt/communications skills/learning theory/whatever else philosophical viewpoint. Emphasis is on experiencing. . . family/therapist/ participant/self, the several modalities, strategies, values, processes, procedures, goals, dangers, fears, avoidance, growth and excitement of conjoint interaction.*

The author of that psychobabble should be made to stand in a corner and study an advertisement written in 100 per cent plain English:

> *KITCHEN DESIGNER (Trainee considered) for thriving Chelsea studio. Drawing experience essential. Salary negotiable dependent on experience. If you are aged 20-30, educated to at least A-level standard, have a bright personality, thrive on hard work and are happy to work Saturdays, tell me about yourself by leaving a message on my Ansaphone, not forgetting to leave your name and phone no, or write a brief CV to . . . .*

Bright. Unpompous. Direct. And, above all, *clear*!

The Jargonaut's Lexicon

Here's a list of jargon words and phrases that comply with the former US president Harry S Truman's decree: 'If you can't convince 'em, confuse 'em'. The entries are graded with [J] symbols; the more elusive and impenetrable the jargon, the more [JJJs] it earns. Learn to recognise jargon, and avoid it if you can.

accentuate [j] stress

accessible [j] as in *We intend making Shakespeare accessible to the millions.* Use *understandable, attractive*

accommodation [j] use *home, where you live*

accomplish [j] as in *accomplish the task.* Use *complete, finish, do*

accordingly [j] use *so*

accountability [j] use *responsibility*

acquiesce [j] use *agree*

acquire [j] use *get, buy, win*

activist [j] as in *Liberal Party activist.* Use *worker, campaigner*

address [j] as in *we must address the problem.* Use *face, tackle, deal with*

adequate [j] use *enough*

axiomatic [j] use *obvious*

belated [j] use *late*

blueprint [jj] as in *the proposal is a blueprint for disaster.* Use *this will end in, means / could mean disaster*

chair / chairperson [jj] use *chairman, chairwoman*

challenged [jjj] as in *physically challenged.* One of a growing range of euphemisms for personal problems and disabilities. Even in these politically correct times it is more acceptable to be frank but sensitive. Also avoid *differently abled.*

come on stream [jj] as in *the new model will come on stream in April.* Oil producer's jargon usually misapplied. Use *begin production, start working, get under way*

come to terms with [j] use *accept, understand*

concept [j] use *idea, plan, proposal, notion*

core [jjj] as in *core curriculum, core concepts.* Use *basic*

creative accounting [jj] not necessarily illegal but a vague and troubling term best avoided or left to the financial professionals.

cutback [j] a needless expansion of *cut*

de-manning [jjj] use *cutting jobs*

de-stocking [jj] use *running down stocks, shrinking*

downsizing [jjj] usually meant to mean cutting jobs, or reacting to a bad financial year by cutting back production or services

downplay [jj] as in *he tried to downplay the gravity of the case.* Use *play down, minimise*

end of the day [j] as in *at the end of the day, what have we got?* Use *in the end*

final analysis [j] as in *in the final analysis it makes little difference.* Use *in the end*

front-runner [j] use *leading contender, leading* or *favoured candidate*

funded [j] use *paid for*

geared [jj] as in *the service was geared to the stockbroker belt*. Use *aimed at, intended for, connected to, suited to*

generate [j] use *make, produce*

hands-on [jj] as in *he adopted a hands-on policy with the staff*. It makes you wonder what he was paid to do – massage them? Has been replaced by another jargon word, anyway – *proactive*

heading up [jj] as in *Smith will be heading up the takeover team*. Use *heading* or *leading*

hidden agenda [jjj] top-rank jargon. Use *hidden / disguised purpose*

identify with [jj] as in *he was identified with the activists*. Use *associated with, linked with*

implement [jj] use *carry out, fulfil*

inaugurate [jj] as in *she will inaugurate the new policy*. Use *introduce, start*

in-flight / in-house [j] part of the language now but still jargon. When carried further, as in *in-car entertainment*, it can sound faintly ridiculous

input [jjjj] as in 'A core post is available for a Senior Research Associate to take a leading role in the programme. The first projects involve relating nursing *inputs* to patient outcomes in acute hospitals' (University of Newcastle upon Tyne ad). A verbal germ picked up from the computer world where it is used as a verb meaning *enter* or *insert*, as in *he inputted the entire file*. Outside computing the word can mean *contribute* or, as a noun, *contribution*, or . . . nothing at all. Avoid

interface [jjjj] another refugee from computing. As a noun, it means *contact*. As a hideous verb, *interface with* can mean *work with, negotiate with, cooperate with* or simply *meet*. Any of these is preferable

jury is still out [jj] as in *whether the move has saved the pound, the jury is still out*. Use *is not yet known / decided / certain / clear*

meet with, meet up with [jj] use *meet*

methodology [j] often used in error for *method*. It really means *a system of methods and principles*

name of the game [jj] as in *the name of the game is to make money*. Use *object*

new high, new low [j] use *new / record high level; new / record low level*

non-stopping [jjj] as in *the eastbound service will be non-stopping at the following stations* . . . Use *will not stop*

operational [j] as in *the service is now operational*. Use *now running / now working*

outgoing [j] use *friendly*

overview [j] use *broad view*

on the back of [jj] as in *the shares rose sharply on the back of the board's profit forecast*. Use *after / because of / as the result of*

ongoing [jjj] as in *we have an ongoing supply problem*. Use *continuing / continual / persistent / constant*

precondition [jjj] a condition is something that has to happen before something else will happen. A *precondition* is therefore nonsense unless you wish to impose a condition on a condition! *There must be no preconditions for the peace talks* is questionable usage. Best to avoid and use *condition*

put on the back burner [jj] colourful, but jargon nevertheless. Use the more precise *postponed / delayed / deferred / suspended*, etc

scenario [jj] as in *worst case scenario*. Originally meaning an outline of a play or film, its usage has been extended to mean *outcome* or *prediction*. Use the more specific words, or *result / plan / outline*, depending on context.

spend [jj] as in *their total advertising spend will exceed £7m.* A sloppy shortening of *expenditure* or *spending*

state of the art [jj] use *latest / newest*

take on board [jj] use *understand / comprehend / accept*

terminal [j] use *fatal / mortal*

track record [j] except for an athlete, perhaps, *track record* means nothing more than *record*. The next time you are tempted to use *proven track record*, be a brave pioneer and write *experience*

user-friendly [jj] use *easy to use*

venue [j] use *place / setting*

viable alternative [jj] use *alternative / choice / option*

whitewash [j] as in *they'll certainly want to whitewash the incident.* Use *hide, gloss over, cover up, suppress, conceal*

Saying it Nicely: Euphemism

My father did not like the word fart. The first time I heard the word was when I was about three. I was watching a cowman milking and the cow farted. I said 'What was that?' and he said 'That was a fart'. It was just a word; as if I'd said 'what's that on the tree?' and he'd said 'bark'. I had a dog called Tuppy, because I bought him for tuppence. One day as I walked by him, I heard this same noise and I said 'Tuppy farted'. My father said, 'Where did you hear that?' and I said 'It came from his bottom'. However my father had a way of getting around the word. He would say, 'Who whispered?' and we totally accepted this euphemism until one day my granny says, 'Come, David, and whisper in granny's ear'.

Dave Allen, 1990 interview.

That's the trouble with euphemisms – they tend to be self-defeating because they paint a thick veneer over clarity and understanding.

Euphemisms – words and phrases people use to avoid making a statement that is direct, clear and honest – are often used out of kindness when the direct expression might give needless offence. For example a deaf person is often described as *hard of hearing* and a part-blind person as *partially sighted*. Unfortunately, in recent times these traditional and harmless euphemisms have been extended and replaced with such terms as *aurally* or *visually challenged*.

Have you ever admitted that you might have been, well, to put it bluntly – drunk? How often have you heard someone honestly admit they were drunk? No, they might admit to having been *one over the eight, high-spirited, squiffy, happy, a bit merry, worse for wear, tired and emotional* or any one of several hundred other euphemisms for drunkenness, but *drunk* – never!

Any user of the English language has to become something of an expert in understanding the true meaning of euphemisms, so much are they a part of our everyday lives. We need these seemingly innocent terms as replacements for those that are embarrassing, unpleasant, crude or offensive. We begin in the nursery with coy substitutions for organs and functions (*willy, winkle, thingy, botty, potty, tinkle, whoopsie, poo-poo, wee-wee, pee-pee*) and, from there, naturally graduate to adult equivalents: *John Thomas, old feller, down below, the loo* (or worse, *the bathroom*), *naughty bits, sleep with someone, nookie, jollies, hanky-panky, rumpy-pumpy*, and so on.

Our euphemistic skills are honed by the media which, though much franker nowadays, still maintain some taboo areas: *intimacy occurred* (had sex); *she was strangled and mutilated but had not been interfered with* (killed but not raped); *abused* (today's vague catch-all euphemism for any form of questionable physical, psychological or sexual activity). It is, as you can see, a very short journey from *sex-change operation* to *gender reassignment*.

The language of prudery also surprisingly invades that sanctum of directness, the doctor's surgery. Physician-speak is a growth area. *How're the waterworks? The ticker/tummy? Your stool? The back passage? The little lump?* All this prepares the way for *negative patient care outcome* to describe someone who dies in hospital.

The poor, in our euphemistic world, are *in a lower income bracket, under-privileged* or *fiscal under-achievers*. Slum homes are *inner-city housing*. When a city decides to clear away the slums the process is called *urban renewal* rather than slum clearance. And of course the same city calls its rat catchers *rodent operatives*.

Death has no dearth of euphemisms. Shakespeare might well ask today, 'Death, where is thy sting?' *Senior Citizens* and *Golden Agers* no longer simply die, they *pass on, pass away, depart, sleep with the angels, go to their just reward, go to a better place, take a last bow, answer the final call, pop off, go on a final journey, fade away* or, more jocularly, *kick the bucket*.

Euphemism is particularly effective for disguising crime – especially the crimes we might commit ourselves. *Tax fiddling, meter feeding, fare dodging, joy-riding* and *being economical with the truth* all sound like commendable streetwise skills, whereas in fact they all amount to cheating and criminal activity.

Euphemism is also useful to help to make tedious-sounding jobs seem grand. Those people we used to know as insurance salesmen are now variously *financial advisers, investment consultants, fiscal analysts, savings strategists, liquidity planners, pensions counsellors* and *endowments executives*.

Again, the euphemistic traps are laid early in the career paths of young people. Consider these job descriptions and what, in real working life, they probably mean:

Pleasant working manner essential	Must be subservient
All the advantages of a large company	Nobody knows anyone else's name
Perfect opportunity for school leavers	Pathetically low pay
Salary negotiable	But only downwards
Earn money at home	Be exploited under your own roof
Earn £££££s!	But only through commission
Must have a sense of humour	Must not be a complainer

Euphemism and Political Correctness

The fertile breeding ground for euphemism today undoubtedly lies in the quest for what is popularly known as political correctness, or PC. The self-appointed guardians of political correctness quite commendably seek to banish stigmatising and dehumanising terminology from our speech and writing. They have been successful in removing from our everyday language such thoughtless and hurtful terms as *nigger, coon, cripple* and *OAP*; and no thinking person would now use the term *mongoloid* to describe a child suffering from Down's Syndrome. And they have been especially successful righting the centuries-old imbalance between the sexes in the popular perception: the use of *man* as a suffix or prefix (*manhandle, mankind, man-made, manpower, man in the street; foreman, chairman, one-man show, alderman, salesman,* etc), sexist generalisations (*doctors* are usually thought of as being 'he', *nurses* as 'she'; *home helps* are always female, etc) and making writers, editors and broadcasters aware of the problem connected with the dominant male pronoun.

While much of this is desirable rethinking, and even necessary, the PC police have unfortunately taken a few steps too far and are consequently ridiculed by many reasonable people. The campaign to expunge the *E* from *V-E Day* (Victory in Europe Day), in order not to offend our near neighbours during the 50th anniversary of the end of World War II celebrations, succeeded only in offending millions of British families who had lost loved ones in the conflict.

The international campaign for so-called non-sexist language has led to what many people regard as euphemistic excess. Consider these recommendations from a recently published manual from The Women's Press:

a grandfather clock	*should be called*	*a longcase clock*
a granny knot	"	*an unstable reef knot*
an old master painting	"	*a classic painting*
the Old Lady of Threadneedle Street	"	*the Bank of England*
a Johnny come lately	"	*an upstart*
Tom, Dick and Harry	"	*any ordinary person*

Recommendations to end the masculine tyranny of chess are even more controversial – or preposterous. Knights are to be renamed *defenders* or *horseriders*; kings become *sovereigns* and queens are *deputy sovereigns*.

Such bizarre examples should be ample warning to every aspiring writer. Be sensible and sensitive towards people and institutions, whether minorities or majorities, but say what you mean!

A Word to the Wise about Clichés

All Things Considered, Avoid Clichés like the Plague

We have all met people who have the extraordinary ability to talk in clichés:

> *Y'know, not to beat around the bush or hedge your bet, this section is a must-read because it calls a spade a spade and in a nutshell leaves no stone unturned to pull the rug from under those off-the-cuff, old-hat bête noires called clichés.*

These are the people who've given the **cliché** its bad name. We all tend to use them, of course. Sometimes that familiar phrase is the neatest way of expressing yourself and most of us can, *in a flash* (cliché), unconsciously call up a few hundred of them to help us out in writing and conversation. But how aware are we of the irritation (or worse, sniggering) that the overuse of clichés can cause?

Most clichés begin life as someone's incredibly neat, timely or witty way of expressing or emphasising a thought. Because it is clever, a lot of people steal the phrase as their own. Multiply that by a few million and you have the desperately tired and overused husk of somebody's originality.

Many clichés are centuries old. If we say of a jilted bride-to-be that she *was left in the lurch* we are echoing a comment made by the English poet Gabriel Harvey in 1576. Thirty years earlier saw another writer, John Heywood, recognise that he knew *what side his bread's buttered on* (1546). Clichés date from the Bible and more are minted, *waiting in the wings* (cliché) for clichédom, every day. These days a cliché can be born, adopted and be worn out in a matter of mere months.

The grammarian Eric Partridge identified four kinds of cliché. There is the idiom that becomes so indiscriminately used that its original meaning becomes lost (*to the manner born* has become *to the manor born* because of the widespread belief that it means born to wealth and luxury, whereas it originally meant 'following an established custom, or accustomed to a situation' as in Shakespeare's *Hamlet* 4:14). His second type includes phrases that have become so hackneyed that only the laziest writers and speakers ever use them (*to nip in the bud*; *beyond the pale*; *down to the last detail*).

Partridge's third group consists of foreign phrases (*terra firma*; *in flagrante delicto*; *plus ça change*) while his fourth comprises snippets and quotations from literature (*a little knowledge is a dangerous thing* from Pope, and Shakespeare's *a thing of beauty is a joy for ever*).

However we haven't yet rounded up *all the usual suspects* (cliché). One *serial offender* (very modern cliché) is the 'stock modifier' – a *Darby and Joan* (cliché) combination of words that, often for no reason, are always seen together. A person isn't moved; he or she is *visibly moved*; a person isn't merely courteous, he or she is *unfailingly courteous*. These parasitic partners are really sly clichés and you should watch for them. To help you know these partners better, try matching these:

1	*over-riding*	A	*consequences*
2	*woefully*	B	*apparent*
3	*far-reaching*	C	*inadequate*
4	*no-holds-barred*	D	*importance*
5	*increasingly*	E	*interview*

Answers: 1D; 2C; 3A; 4E; 5B

If you make up your mind to watch out for clichés creeping into your speech and writing and to try to avoid them you'll be surprised how easy it becomes to do without them – and how much fresher your writing becomes as a result.

Here are a few you might remove from your vocabulary:

An A to Z of Clichés to Avoid like the Plague

*a*ccidentally on purpose
accident waiting to happen
actions speak louder than words
act of contrition
acid test
add insult to injury
after due consideration
all intents and purposes
all in the same boat
all over bar the shouting
all things considered
almost too good to be true
angel of mercy
angry silence (classic *Darby & Joan*)
as a matter of fact
as luck would have it
as sure as eggs is/are eggs
at the end of the day
at this moment/point in time
auspicious occasion
avid reader

baby with the bathwater, don't throw out the
backseat driver
back to basics/to the drawing board
bag and baggage
bag of tricks
ballpark figure
ball's in your court, the
bang your head against a brick wall
barking up the wrong tree
bat an eyelid (try wink and surprise everyone)
batten down the hatches
beavering away
beer and skittles, it's not all
before you can say Jack Robinson
beggars can't be choosers
be good (and if you can't be good, be careful!)
be that as it may
between a rock and a hard place
bite the bullet
blessing in disguise
blind leading the blind
blissful ignorance
blood out of a stone, it's like trying to get
bloody but unbowed
blow hot and cold
blot on the landscape
blow the whistle
blue rinse brigade
blushing bride
bone of contention
borrowed time
bottom line
breath of fresh air
bright eyed and bushy tailed
brought to book
brownie points
bruising battle/encounter
bumper to bumper traffic jam
by the same token

call it a day
callow youth
calm before the storm
camp as a row of tents
can of worms

captive audience
card up his sleeve
cards stacked against us
cardinal sin
carte blanche
cast of thousands
Catch 22 situation
catalogue of errors/misery/disaster/misfortune
cat among the pigeons, put the
catholic tastes
caustic comment
cautious optimism
centre of the universe
chalk and cheese, as different as
champing at the bit
chapter and verse
chapter of accidents
cheek by jowl
cheque's in the post, the
cheap and cheerful
cherished belief
chew the cud/fat
chop and change
chorus of approval/dispproval
chosen few
circumstances beyond our control
cold light of day, in the
cold water on, pour
come home to roost
comes to the crunch, when it
common or garden
compulsive viewing/reading
conspicious by his/her absence
cool as a cucumber
cool, calm and collected
copious notes (and, if made by a reporter, usually scribbled notes)
crack of dawn
crazy like a fox
crème de la crème
crisis of confidence
cross that bridge when we come to it, we'll
cry over spilt milk
current climate, in the
cut a long story short, to
cut and dried

cut any ice, it doesn't/won't
cutting edge

damn with faint praise
Darby and Joan
darkest hour is just before dawn
dark secret
day in, day out
dead as a dodo
dead in the water
deadly accurate
dead of night, in the
dead to the world
deafening silence
deaf to entreaties
death's door, at
death warmed up, like
depths of depravity
desert a sinking ship
despite misgivings
devour every word (and then there are none left to hang on to)
dicing with death
dim and distant past, in the
dog eat dog
donkey's years ago, it was
don't call us, we'll call you
don't count your chickens before they're hatched
doom and gloom merchants
dot the i's and cross the t's
drop of a hat, at the
dry as a bone
dyed in the wool

each and everyone
eager beaver
eagerly devour
ear to the ground
easier said than done
eat humble pie
eat your heart out
economical with the truth
empty nest, empty nesters, empty nest syndrome
enfant terrible
eternal regret/ eternal shame, to my
every dog has his day

every man jack of them
everything but the kitchen sink
every little helps
every stage of the game, at
explore every avenue

face the facts/music
fact of the matter, the
fair and square
fair sex, the
fall between two stools/by the wayside
fall on deaf ears
far and wide
far be it from me
fast and furious
fast lane, in the
fate worse than death
feel-good factor, the
few and far between
field day, having a
fighting fit
final insult
fine-tooth comb, go/went through it with a
finger in every pie
finger of suspicion
firing on all cylinders
first and foremost
first things first
fish out of water
fit as a fiddle
fits and starts, in/by
flash in the pan
flat as a pancake
flat denial
flavour of the month
flog a dead horse
fly in the ointment
fond belief
food for thought
footloose and fancy free
forlorn hope
fraught with danger/peril
free, gratis and for nothing
frenzy of activity
from the sublime to the ridiculous

from the word go
fudge the issue
fullness of time, in the
funny ha-ha or funny peculiar?
F-word

gainful employment
gameplan
generous to a fault
gentle giant
gentleman's agreement
gentler sex, the
girl Friday
give a dog a bad name
give him an inch and he'll take a yard
give up the ghost
glowing tribute
glutton for punishment
goes without saying, it
goes from strength to strength
golden opportunity
good as gold
go off half-cocked
gory details, the
grasp the nettle
greatest thing since sliced bread
great unwashed, the
green with envy
grim death, like
grin and bear it
grind/ground to a halt
grist to the mill
guardian angel

hale and hearty
hand in glove with
handle with kid gloves
hand over fist
hand to mouth existence
handwriting is on the wall
hanged for a sheep as a lamb, we might as well be
happy accident/event/hunting ground/medium
happily ensconced
hard and fast rule
has what it takes

having said that
have a nice one
have got a lot on my plate, I've
have I got news for you?
head and shoulders above
heaping ridicule
heart and soul
heart's in the right place, his/her
hell or high water
high and dry
hit or miss
hit the nail on the head
hit the panic button
hive of activity
Hobson's choice
hold your horses
hoist with his own petard
honest truth, the
hope against hope
horns of a dilemma, on the
horses for courses
howling gale
how long is a piece of string?
how time flies

if the worst comes to the worst
if you can't beat 'em, join 'em
if you can't stand the heat get out of the kitchen
if you've got it, flaunt it
ignorance is bliss
ill-gotten gains
ill-starred venture
impossible dream, an/the
in all conscience/honesty
in a nutshell
inch-by-inch search
in less than no time
in one ear and out the other
inordinate amount of
in the pipeline
in this day and age
iota, not one
it never rains but it pours
it's a small world
it's not the end of the world

it stands to reason
it will all come out in the wash
it will all end in tears
it will soon blow over
ivory tower

jack of all trades (but master of none)
jaundiced eye
jewel in the crown
Johnny-come-lately
jockey for position
jump on the bandwagon
jump the gun
just deserts
just for the record
just what the doctor ordered

keep a low profile
keep a straight face
keep my/your head above water
keep the wolf from the door
keep your chin up
keep your nose clean
keep your nose to the grindstone
kickstart
kill two birds with one stone
kill with kindness
kiss of death
knee-high to a grasshopper
knocked into a cocked hat
knocked/knocks the spots off
know the ropes
know which side your bread's buttered on
knuckle under

labour of love
lack-lustre performance
lap of luxury
large as life/larger than life
last but not least
last straw, it's the
late in the day
laugh all the way to the bank
laugh up your sleeve
lavish praise/hospitality/ceremony

lay it on with a trowel
leading light
leave/left in the lurch
leave no stone unturned (or as the bird hater said, leave no tern unstoned)
let bygones be bygones
let's get this show on the road
let sleeping dogs lie
let well alone
lick his/their wounds
level playing field
light at the end of the tunnel
like a house on fire
little the wiser
little woman
live and let live
local difficulty, a little
lock, stock and barrel
long arm of the law
long hot summer
long time no see
loose end, at a
lost cause
lost in admiration
lost in contemplation
love you and leave you, I must

made of sterner stuff
made/make a killing
make a mountain out of a molehill
make an offer I can't refuse
make ends meet
make hay while the sun shines
make no bones about it
make my day
make or break
make/making short work of it
make/making the best of a bad job
make/making tracks
man after my own heart, a
make/making waves
manna from heaven
man of straw/man of the world
man to man
many hands make light work
mark my words

matter of life and death
method in his madness
Midas touch, the
millstone around your neck
mind boggles, the
mixed blessing (and a variation, it was not an
    unmixed blessing . . .)

model of its kind/propriety
moment of truth
moot point
more haste, less speed
more in sorrow than in anger
more than meets the eye
more the merrier, the
mortgaged to the hilt
movers and shakers
move the goalposts
much-needed reforms
much of a muchness
muddy the waters
mutton dressed as lamb

nail in his coffin, put/drive a
name of the game, the
nearest and dearest
necessity is the mother of invention
neck and neck
needle in a haystack
needless to say
neither here nor there
new lease of life
nick of time, in the
nine-day/day's wonder
nip it in the bud/nipped in the bud
nitty-gritty
no expense spared
no names, no pack drill
no news is good news
no peace for the wicked
no problem
no skin off my nose
no spring chicken
nothing to write home about
nothing ventured, nothing gained
not just a pretty face

not out of the woods yet
not to be sneezed at
not to put too fine a point on it
now or never

odd man out
odds and ends
off the beaten track
off the cuff
old as the hills
older and wiser
once bitten, twice shy
once in a blue moon
one fell swoop
one in a million
only time will tell
on the ball
on the level
on the spur of the moment
on the tip of my tongue
out of sight, out of mind
out of the blue
out on a limb
over and done with
over my dead body
over the top
own goal, score an
own worst enemy

packed in like sardines
painstaking investigation
pale into insignificance
palpable nonsense
paper over the cracks
par for the course
part and parcel
pass muster
past its/his/her sell-by date
patter of tiny feet
pay through your nose
pecking order
picture of health
piece de resistance
pie in the sky
pinpoint accuracy

plain as a pikestaff
plain as the nose on your face
play your cards right
pleased as Punch
point of no return
poisoned chalice
pound of flesh
powers that be, the
practice makes perfect
press on regardless
pride and joy
pride of place
proof of the pudding
pull out all the stops
pure as the driven snow
put on hold/the back burner
put two and two together
put up or shut up
put your best foot forward
put your foot down
put your money where your mouth is
put your nose out of joint

quality of life
quantum leap
queer the pitch
quick and the dead
quid pro quo
quiet before the storm, the

race against time
rack and ruin, going to
raining cats and dogs (and hailing taxis)
rat race, the
read my lips
red rag to a bull, like a
reinventing the wheel
reliable source (the reporter's friend)
resounding silence
right as rain
rings a bell
rings true
risk life and limb
rock the boat, don't
Rome wasn't built in a day

rose by any other name, a
rotten apple in a barrel, one
rough diamond, a
ruffled feathers
ruled with a rod of iron
run it up the flagpole (and see who salutes)
run of the mill
run to seed

safe and sound
sailing close to the wind
sale of the century
salt of the earth
saved by the bell
search high and low
second to none
seething cauldron
see eye to eye

see how the land lies
see the wood for the trees, can't
sell like hot cakes
serial gossiper/meddler/bullshit artist etc
serious money
set in stone/concrete
shape or form, in any
share and share alike
ships that pass in the night
shoot yourself in the foot/ shot himself in the foot
short and sweet
shot across the bows
sick and tired
sick as a parrot

sight for sore eyes
signed, sealed and delivered
silent majority, the
simmering hatred
sitting duck
sixes and sevens
six of one and half-a-dozen of the other
skating on thin ice
skin of his teeth
slaving over a hot stove all day, I've been
slowly but surely
smell a rat
snatch defeat from the jaws of victory (and, of course, vice versa!)

so far so good
solid as a rock
so near and yet so far
sorely needed
sour grapes
splendid isolation
square peg in a round hole
straight and narrow, stick to the
straight from the shoulder
strange as it may seem/ strange to relate
strike while the iron's hot
suffer fools gladly, he/she doesn't
suffer in silence
survival of the fittest
sugar the pill
sweetness and light, all
swept off his feet
swings and roundabouts

tail between his legs, he went off with his
take it with a grain of salt
take the bull by the horns
take the rough with the smooth
tarred with the same brush
teach your mother/grandmother to suck eggs
technological wizardry
teething troubles
tender loving care (TLC)
tender mercies
terra firma
thankful for small mercies, be
that's life
that's the way the cookie crumbles
there but for the grace of God go I
thereby hangs a tale
there's no such thing as a free lunch
this day and age
throw in the towel
thunderous applause
tighten our/your belts
time flies
time heals everything/ all ills
time waits for no man
tip of the iceberg, the
tired and emotional

tireless campaigner/crusader
tissue of lies
to all intents and purposes
tomorrow is another day
too little, too late
to my dying day
too awful/terrible/horrible to contemplate
too many cooks (spoil the broth)
too numerous to mention
torrential rain
towering inferno
tower of strength
trials and tribulations
turn a deaf ear
turn over a new leaf
twenty-twenty hindsight
twinkling of an eye, in a
twisted him around her little finger
two's company, three's a crowd

u*ltra-sophisticated*
unacceptable face of capitalism (or any other institution you want to knock)
unavoidable delay
unalloyed delight
unconscionable time, taking an/unconscionable liar
under a cloud
under the weather
unequal task
university of life
unkindest cut of all
unsung heroes
untimely end
untold wealth
unvarnished truth
up to scratch/not up to scratch
upper crust

v*anish into thin air*
variety is the spice of life
vested interest
vicious circle
vote with their feet

w*ages of sin (is death)*
waited on hand and foot

walking on air/eggs
walking on broken glass
warts and all
waste not, want not
water under the bridge
wealth of experience/material/knowledge
wedded bliss
weighed in the balance and found wanting
well-earned rest
wheels within wheels
when the cats away the mice will play
when the going gets tough (the tough get going)
whiter than white
winter of discontent
with all due respect
with bated breath
with malice aforethought
without a shadow of a doubt
without fear of contradiction
woman scorned, hell hath no fury like a
wonders will never cease
word to the wise, a
work my fingers to the bone, I
world's your oyster, the
writing's on the wall, the
wrong end of the stick, you've got the

*y*awning gulf
year in, year out
you can bet your bottom dollar/last penny
you can lead a horse to water but you can't make him drink
you can't make a silk purse out of a sow's ear
you can't teach an old dog new tricks
you can't win 'em all
you could have knocked me down with a feather
you get what you pay for
you pays your money and takes your choice
your guess is as good as mine
you're breaking my heart
you're only young once

CLARITY BEGINS AT HOME:

How to Improve Your Powers of Expression

Circumambulate the Non-representational:

Avoid the Abstract

Humans are of the type of matter that constitutes dreams and their relatively brief existences terminate, as well as taking their inception, in a state of unconsciousness.

William Shakespeare, *The Tempest* 4:1

Shakespeare? Never! Well, yes, but not quite. The quote is from Prospero's retort to Ferdinand, the son of the King of Naples, in *The Tempest*:

> *We are such stuff*
> *As dreams are made on, and our little life*
> *Is rounded with a sleep*

. . . except that it was rewritten by Oxford University Professor Richard Gombrich to parody the overblown, tedious writing style of many literary editors and critics.

Sentences consist of many parts of speech (which we'll discuss later) but will almost certainly include one or more nouns. And, again, there are several kinds of nouns, but the two kinds that concern us here are **concrete nouns** and **abstract nouns**.

A concrete noun is something that is perceptible, tangible – something real that you can touch and see and smell: *wood, table, hair, blood*. An abstract noun refers to ideas, concepts, qualities, states of mind: *beauty, fascism, doubt, truth, fear*. Using one without care can knock the stuffing out of what you are trying to express. But there is nothing wrong with the words themselves when used properly.

Aspect, for example, is correctly used to mean the way in which a landscape, a problem or a situation may be viewed: *When looked at from the aspect of Britain's interests the proposal is unsatisfactory*. But when the word is used to mean part or consideration, a sentence can suddenly become soggy: *The government must consider the economic aspect*. Readers' minds always have to work harder when confronted by abstract nouns, adverbial and adjectival phrases.

Look again at our Shakespearean rewrite and note the abstract nouns: *type, matter, existences, inception, unconsciousness*. They outnumber the concrete nouns (*humans, dreams*) by two to one, and as a result you have a sentence that can send the reader's brain into a spin trying to work out the meaning. Shakespeare's original text, even though expressed in antique prose, is much simpler to grasp.

The novelist and playwright Keith Waterhouse found Lincoln's Gettysburg Address to be a model of balance between abstract and concrete nouns. The President's speech is all about abstract, philosophical thoughts which a lot of us would have trouble understanding. But Lincoln solved the problem by anchoring to simple things that most people could readily understand. The passage is well worth studying as an exercise in the intelligent use of abstract and concrete nouns. In the speech the concrete nouns are highlighted in bold type, and the abstract nouns are underlined:

> *Fourscore and seven* _years_ *ago our* **fathers** *brought forth on this* **continent** *a new* **nation** *conceived in* _liberty_ *and dedicated to the* _proposition_ *that all* **men** *are created equal. Now we are engaged in a great civil* _war_ *testing whether that* **nation***, or any* **nation** *so conceived and so dedicated, can long endure. We are met on a great* **battlefield** *of that* _war_*. We have come to dedicate a* _portion_ *of that* **field** *as a final* **resting-place** *for those who here gave their* _lives_ *that that* **nation** *might live. It is altogether fitting and proper that we should do this. But, in a larger* _sense_*, we cannot dedicate, we cannot consecrate, we cannot hallow this* **ground***. The brave* **men***, living and dead, who struggled here have consecrated it far above our poor* _power_ *to add or detract. The* **world** *will little note or long remember what we say here, but it can never forget what they did here. It is for us the* **living** *rather to be dedicated here to the unfinished* _work_ *which they who fought here have thus far so nobly advanced. It is rather for us to be here dedicated to the great* _task_ *remaining before us – that from these honoured* **dead** *we take increased* _devotion_ *to that* _cause_ *for which they gave the last full* **measure** *of* _devotion_ *– that we here highly resolve that these* **dead** *shall not have died in vain, that this* **nation** *under* _God_ *shall have a new birth of* _freedom_*, and that* _government_ *of the* **people***, by the* **people***, for the* **people***, shall not perish from the* **earth***.*

You can easily see how the 18 abstract nouns expressing ideas and concepts (*liberty, power, devotion, God,* etc) are brought down to earth – and understanding – by the 21 concrete nouns (*nation, men, resting-place, the people,* etc).

If, on re-reading something you've written you find it a bit tortuous, a bit difficult to follow, the fault may lie in your over-use of abstract nouns. So look at your piece again, identify the culprits, and try to do without them.

Here is a short list of everyday abstract nouns and adjective/adverb phrases with suggestions on how they might be replaced.

Some Awful Abstracts

(in) abeyance – in *the fitness classes were in* **abeyance**. Try *the fitness classes were suspended/interrupted/discontinued.*

amenity – as in *the school has gymnasium and swimming* **amenities**. Try *the school has a gymnasium and swimming pool.*

aspect – as in *the major* **aspect** *of the campaign*. Try *the important part of the plan.*

attitude – as in *he adopted a menacing* **attitude**. Try *he looked menacing.*

availability – as in *supplies will be subject to limited **availability***. Try *supplies will be limited / scarce*.

basis – as in *she worked on a part-time **basis***. Try *she worked part-time*. This word can sensibly be used when it really means basis: a foundation, a beginning, or main ingredient, as in *the general marshalled his troops on the basis of the spy's information; the basis of their romance was a shared love of music*.

capability, capacity – as in *Iraq has a chemical warfare **capability / capacity***. Try *Iraq has chemical weapons*.

cessation – as in *a **cessation** of hostilities was hoped for*. Try *it was hoped hostilities would end / cease / stop*.

character – as in *the parcel was of a suspect **character***. Try *the parcel was suspect*.

degree – as in *she displayed a high **degree** of restraint*. Try *she showed great restraint*.

description – as in *they had no plans of any **description***. Try *they had no plans*.

desirability – as in *he questioned the **desirability** of the proposals*. Try *he asked whether the proposals were desirable*.

element – as in *there was a rebel **element** in the village*. Try *there were rebels in the village*.

expectation – as in *the government's **expectation** was for an optimistic outcome*. Try *the government expected an optimistic outcome*.

factor – as in *don't forget the unemployment **factor***. Try *don't forget unemployment*.

level – as in *the general **level** of conduct was satisfactory*. Try *generally / in general, conduct was satisfactory*.

manner – as in *he drove in a reckless **manner***. Try *he drove recklessly*.

nature – as in *they made arrangements of a temporary **nature***. Try *they made temporary arrangements*.

operation – as in *the automatic doors were not in operation*. Try *the automatic doors were not working*.

participation – as in *there was enthusiastic **participation** on the part of the members*. Try *the members took part enthusiastically*.

persuasion – as in *Joyce was of the strict Methodist **persuasion***. Try *Joyce was a strict Methodist*.

situation – as in *please let me know about the present state of the **situation***. Try *please let me know how things are / stand*.

Overloading can Sink Your Sentence

We recommend an average sentence length of 15-25 words to make any text easy to read.

Plain English Campaign

By now, if you have been eliminating euphemism, jettisoning jargon, cutting out clichés and showing the gate to gobblegook, your writing should be looking leaner and meaner. But there still remains a curious human impulse to overcome: the tendency to let the moving finger write, and write, and write . . . on and on. In short, to pack as much into a sentence as possible.

Consider this passage from the *Daily Telegraph*:

> *Seven of the 33 buildings in St James's Square, in the heart of one of the most expensive parts of London, display For Sale or To Let signs.*

Nothing wrong there. But then:

> *The sight of some of the capital's most exclusive business addresses languishing empty – when not long ago they were snapped up as corporate headquarters – brings home the impact of the recession as financial controllers cut costs by letting out spare space vacated by staff who have been made redundant or exiled to less costly locations.*

Now, readers of the national 'quality' newspapers may be perfectly able to wind their way through that sentence. But why should they have to?

Let's count the items of information that the author has loaded in:

1. *some of the capital's most exclusive business addresses*
2. *are empty*
3. *when not long ago they were snapped up*
4. *as corporate headquarters*
5. *impact of the recession*
6. *financial controllers cutting costs*
7. *by letting out spare space*
8. *. . . which was left empty when staff either were made redundant*
9. *or moved*
10. *to somewhere cheaper*

Clearly, the structure of this overloaded sentence ought to be dismantled and reassembled in a more manageable form. The major items of information are:

(a) the situation is caused by an economic recession;

(b) the recession meant that offices were emptied because staff were sacked or moved to cheaper accommodation;

(c) companies also saved money by renting out offices they once occupied themselves.

What could the author have done instead? Well, he or she could have written:

> *The sight of some of the capital's most exclusive business addresses languishing empty brings home the impact of the recession. Offices have been left empty as staff were made redundant, or moved to cheaper accommodation. Financial controllers have cut costs by letting out the space their firms no longer need.*

Overloaded sentences do not have to be long. Here's one with an unremarkable 47 words but it is still well above the Plimsoll Line of saturated sentences:

A man living alone was approaching his house when he was attacked by seven armed robbers who forced him at gunpoint to open the front door of his secluded country cottage in Kent before leaving him so badly beaten that he is now afraid to return home.

The main news points in this opening sentence seem to be:

(a) a man was badly beaten by robbers in his secluded cottage in Kent;

(b) he was beaten so badly that he is now afraid to return home – presumably from hospital.

The additional facts – that he was approaching his house when the attack took place, that there were seven robbers, that they were armed, that they forced him at gunpoint to open the front door, can wait a moment. The vital principle in a story like this is to put the main facts first. And if you think there are just too many facts for a single sentence, turn it into two sentences:

A man living alone in a secluded cottage in Kent was beaten so badly by robbers that he is afraid to go home. Seven armed men struck as he approached the house, and forced him at gunpoint to open his front door.

Even though we now have two sentences, we have managed to save five words. But more importantly, the reading task is easier and the meaning is clearer.

Nowhere is overloading more pronounced than in bureaucratic documents – they are so weighed down with circumlocution, jargon and gobbledegook.

Here's a typical passage from a booklet called *Frameworks for the Future*, about the Northern Ireland settlement proposals. It won the 1994 Golden Rhubarb Trophy for the most confusing government document of the year:

Where either government considers that any institution, established as part of the overall accommodation, is not properly functioning within the Agreement or that a breach of the Agreement has otherwise occurred, the Conference shall consider the matter on the basis of a shared commitment to arrive at a common position or, where that is not possible, to agree a procedure to resolve the difference between them.

You should have quickly spotted some Awful Abstract nouns in this 66-word sentence (*breach, matter, basis, commitment, procedure*) and sensed that there are far too many facts and thoughts in it for comfortable digestion.

Let's see if we can render it in plain English in a single sentence:

If either government feels that any institutions established by the Agreement are not working properly, or breaching the Agreement, the Conference will try to find a common position or agree a procedure to resolve any differences.

This version seems to retain the intended meaning of the original and at 36 words is shorter and clearer. But a 36-word sentence is still suspect (remember the Plain English Campaign's recommended 25-25 words). So let us try again, this time with two sentences:

> *The governments may feel that institutions established by the Agreement are either not working properly or breaching the Agreement. In such cases the Conference will try to find either a common position or a procedure that will resolve any differences.*

We've used four more words than the single-sentence rewrite, but the meaning sticks out a mile. If any proof were needed that shorter sentences help understanding, this exercise should have provided it.

The No-no Non Sequitur

A common feature of many overlong, overweight sentences is the presence of non sequiturs. A non sequitur is a statement that has little or no relevance to what preceded it – a sentence that attempts to join the unjoinable:

> *the egg-and-spoon race was won by Julia Jones whose parents taught her to sing and tap dance.*

You might well ask, what does singing and tap dancing have to do with winning an egg-and-spoon race? That is a non sequitur. These are usually caused by a writer's hankering to compress information with a minimum of punctuation, but the inevitable consequence is confusion:

> *Mr Pearson was a star graduate of the University of Birmingham's highly regarded science faculty and he travelled widely throughout Eastern Europe as a part-time tennis instructor.*

Although fairly short this sentence still suffers from overload – in this case two quite different, even opposing, sets of facts:

(a) Mr Pearson was a star science graduate from Birmingham University

(b) He was a part-time tennis instructor in Eastern Europe

If the two sets of facts were relevant to each other, the problem wouldn't exist:

> *Mr Pearson was a star graduate of the University of Birmingham's highly regarded science faculty, and he quickly found a high-paying position with ICI.*

In other words, he quickly found a job because he was a star graduate. Or the second set of facts might be related to the first because they were surprising:

Mr Pearson was a star graduate of the University of Birmingham's highly regarded science faculty despite his having no previous grounding in any science subjects.

Here we have no trouble with the two sets of facts because they are joined (despite) by a common interest.

But returning to our original example, if the two sets of facts about Mr Pearson are all we have, we could remove the and separating faculty and he to form two sentences. But they would be irritatingly short – and still confusingly irrelevant to each other. If you are faced with a situation like this your options are so limited that a rewrite is probably the best way out. For example:

After leaving the University of Birmingham's highly regarded science faculty as a star graduate, Mr Pearson decided to to travel throughout Eastern Europe as a tennis instructor.

To avoid overload, re-read and rewrite. Or as someone once said – but not about over-long sentences – divide and conquer.

Avoiding the Minefield of Muddle

Any person not placing dog litter in this receptacle will be liable to a fine of £100.

Sign in Kensington Gardens

If, walking in the park without a dog and lacking any dog litter (or for that matter, dogshit), would we be required to search for some to deposit in the bin to avoid the £100 fine?

That ambiguous sentence is the victim of muddled thinking and, consequently, muddled writing. There's a lot of it about. Perhaps it's because we're trained in logical leapfrog by a diet of newspaper headlines:

Police Discover Crack in Devon
MARS BARS PROTEST
Milk Drinkers Are Turning To Powder
VIRGIN TAKES RECORD BOOKINGS
General Flies Back To Front
POLICE FIND CONSTABLE DRAWING IN ATTIC

Most people can translate muddled mind-benders like those without even thinking. Longer passages, however, can cause momentary confusion:

The witness told the commissioners that she had seen sexual intercourse taking place between two parked cars in front of her house.

US newspaper report

You can't imagine how out of things I feel, never to be able to discuss how my husband hasn't touched me in months, the way all my girlfriends do.

Letter to a women's magazine agony column

Not all such muddled writing is funny; most of it is simply confusing, irritating and, in some cases, potentially harmful. But it all has a common origin: muddled writing occurs when the author is not really thinking about what he or she is putting on paper.

Disaster at Lunchtime

The lunch hour is not what it appears to be for the majority of workers.

An hour is more likely to be fewer than 30 minutes for two in every five workers, while a mere 5 per cent take a more leisurely attitude and admit to exceeding the traditional time limit.

The Independent

The apparent attempt at being jokey turns the first part of paragraph two into a muddle of statistics likely to dissuade most readers from finishing the sentence.

Mixing ordinary numbers with percentages is another annoyance; the reader has to stop and try to work out how the two sets of statistics (two in every five; 5 per cent) compare. But perhaps the passage can be rescued:

For 40 in every 100 workers, that 'hour' is likely to be under 30 minutes. Only five in 100 take a more leisurely attitude and admit to exceeding the traditional time limit.

An Ugly Mess in the Vestibule

The high for the day was achieved for a marble Georgian chimney-piece circa 1770 with superbly carved tablets of Diana and her hounds. It went on estimate for £23,650 to Bartlett, the Bermondsey dealer in architectural fittings who paid £330 for three piles of marble at Castle Howard last year which he has since sold to America for about £150,000, reconstructed as a 15ft vestibule by Sir John Vanbrugh.

Eaton Hall Estate auction report in the *Daily Telegraph*

This is a thorough mess, breathtakingly muddled. Ignoring the jargonaut's *high* in the first sentence, we are violently wrenched from the latest doings of Bermondsey Bartlett to an entirely different event, year and place.

What exactly was it that Bartlett from Bermondsey 'sold to America'? The marble? Castle Howard? Last year itself? Did he sell it to the American

Government? And what exactly was reconstructed as a 15ft vestibule by Sir John Vanbrugh? Marble? Castle Howard?

And wasn't Sir John Vanbrugh, by then, rather old to be reconstructing anything, having died in 1726?

With a minimum of research we find that Sir John was an architect besides being a playwright. Castle Howard, in Yorkshire, was the first building he designed. So could it be that the three piles of marble had originally been a 15ft vestibule which he'd designed? If we assume it is, it now becomes possible, with heavy lifting-gear and wearing our hard hats, to reconstruct this pile of literary rubble – not, perhaps, as a grand 15ft vestibule but at least as a piece of clear English:

> . . . It went at the estimated price, £23,650, to Bartlett, the Bermondsey dealer in architectural fittings. Last year, at Castle Howard, the same dealer paid £330 for three piles of marble, originally a 15ft vestibule by the castle's architect, Sir John Vanbrugh. Bartlett has since sold the marble in America for around £150,000, where it has been used to reconstruct the vestibule.

And not a scrap of Vanbrugh's valuable verbal marble vandalised!

Doorstep Body Horror

This absurdity, taken from an American newspaper, is a masterpiece of muddle:

> A Texan undertaker left the body of a man on the doorstep of his son because he could not afford a cremation.

Let's try to decode this one. Whose son owned the doorstep? The dead man's son? The undertaker's son? Who could not afford a cremation? The dead man? His son? The undertaker?

At first sight, this dreadful sentence (in other circumstances it would deserve the adjective *deathless* = immortal) appears easy to rewrite without confusion or any loss of meaning. But try doing it also without repetition, which the writer may have been desperate to avoid:

> A Texan undertaker dumped a dead man on the man's son's doorstep because the son could not afford a cremation.

Although the meaning is now quite clear the sentence is clumsy and repetitive. It's worth another try:

> A dead man was dumped on his son's doorstep by a Texan undertaker because the son could not afford a cremation.

Again, the facts are crystal clear but the sentence is still repetitive. Another try:

A dead man whose son could not afford a cremation was dumped on the son's doorstep by a Texan undertaker.

Many writers would settle for this version but perfectionists would recognise that the order of facts is a bit muddled. And it still repeats son, perhaps unnecessarily. It's worth a final shot, but this time let's take a small liberty by introducing the word *family*, which in this context would be acceptable usage:

A Texan undertaker who found that a dead man's family could not afford a cremation dumped the body on the son's doorstep.

To Visit, or not to Visit?

Trust staff, the report discloses, have been advised that they should only visit the area after midday in the event of an emergency.

What can this snippet mean? It could be saying: *Trust staff have been advised that if there is an emergency, they should not visit the area in the morning.* But it could also be saying: *Trust staff have been advised that the only time to visit the area is after midday – and even then, only if there is an emergency.*

If we look closely at the original sentence we can narrow the search for the source of confusion to the word *only*, or rather its placing. Does the writer mean only visit that area? Or visit that area only after midday? Or visit after midday only if there is an emergency?

There is also another problem that adds to the confusion: the piece of verbiage, *in the event of*, meaning, in clearer English, *if there is* or *unless there is an emergency*.

What the sentence so clumsily failed to convey was this:

Trust staff have been advised not to visit the area after midday, unless there is an emergency.

When you use *only*, make sure that you have it in the right place. *Professor Hawking only published his book after years of deep thought*. Does this mean that all the Professor ever did was to publish this one book? It seems so, but it's not true. What the sentence intended to convey was *Professor Hawking published his book only after years of deep thought*. When using the adverb *only* in circumstances like these, ensure that it is placed next to the word it modifies.

Like as Not

Another source of muddle and obscurity is the word *like*. One of the most common ways in which *like* is misused is to introduce examples:

It included stars like Frank Sinatra, Bob Hope and Michael Jackson.

Who were these lookalikes? Or do we really mean *stars such as*? Fortunately this form of misuse is so common that it rarely causes misunderstanding.

My mother can't get through a busy day like (as) she used to; It sounded like (as if, as though) she was about to scream the house down; Like (Just as) in Pam's case, Liz received no compensation are examples of *like* used as an all-purpose conjunction. When using it read the sentence over carefully; in many cases your 'ear' will warn you of possible misuse.

Might or May

The misuse of *may* instead of *might* is also common and can confuse. *May* is correct when an outcome is still unknown. *Might* is right when an *if* is lurking in the background – when we discuss something that was likely or possible on some past occasion.

RIGHT:	*If it had not been for the paramedics, I **might** have died. (but I didn't)*
WRONG:	*If it had not been for the paramedics, I **may** have died.*
RIGHT:	*I accept that I **may** have been mistaken. (I am still not sure)*
WRONG:	*I accept that I **might** have been mistaken.*
RIGHT:	*It **might** have been a mistake to turn right, so I didn't. (at the time I wasn't sure)*
WRONG:	*It **might** have been a mistake to turn right, because I finished up hitting another car.*
RIGHT:	*It **may** have been a mistake, but I turned right. (I still don't know whether it was a mistake or not)*
WRONG:	*It **may** have been a mistake to turn right, so I didn't.*

Remember to use may in the present and future tense; might in the past. The boss may leave for New York tomorrow; The boss might have left last night.

Danglers and Floaters

These are the somewhat colourful descriptions for what are more boringly known as **unattached** or **hanging participles**. You may not be familiar with the technical term and you may not immediately recognise them, but you have probably experienced the head scratching they cause when you come across them in print:

After the first day, sleeping after a 1,000 ft climb, my underpants were eaten by warrior ants.

In recounting his trip to the Andes, *The Times* columnist Matthew Parris upstages the scenery when he introduces us to his incredible underpants, with their ability to climb mountains and sleep. Millions would have paid good money to see these but unfortunately they succumbed to an attack by warrior ants.

Danglers like that one can often be found somewhere in the middle of a muddled passage, of which this is a typical example:

> *However, the optimistic forecasts by the societies have repeatedly been disappointed over the past few years and they are again having to admit that the market is still on its back.*

Richard Thomson in The Observer

Well, we get the drift, so it's not seriously ambiguous, but why should part of our minds gave to grapple with forecasts that appear to possess the human abilities to be disappointed, and to make admissions?

And how can you suppress the exotic, Dali-esque and distracting mind-picture evoked by the blurb on this book jacket:

> *She lives in London with a large Scotsman, their daughters Georgia and Holly, a nanny and a goldfish, where she now writes full time.*

As with many other traps waiting to trip us up and muddle our prose, danglers and their like can be avoided by the following ways:

• Take some time to think out what you want to say before you begin to write.

• While you are writing, test your prose phrase by phrase, sentence by sentence, to make sure you are expressing exactly what you want to say.

• When you have finished, re-read every sentence carefully and ensure that nothing can be misunderstood.

Writing Elegant, Expressive English:
The Elements of Style

> *The apples on the tree are full of wasps;*
> *Red apples, racing like hearts. The summer pushes*
> *Her tongue into the winter's throat.*

From The Pelt of Wasps by David Constantine

We've been lectured on shoddy workmanship. We've been hammered on grammar and punctuation. We've worked like navvies with the nuts and bolts and girders of the language. We've done the hard labour.

Now the paint job, to cover all the construction. The magic bit, when at last you're allowed to throw the verbs and nouns in the air and juggle the adverbs and adjectives to produce some inspirational prose, and – *Pouf!* Well, perhaps we're not quite there yet.

So far we've concerned ourselves with what is correct and acceptable and advised and what is not. All that information will, in various ways, contribute something towards your writing style. But now we're going to look at style in its broadest sense, examining the elements that help to hide the hard labour. One of the greatest stylists in English, Somerset Maugham, put it this way: 'A good style should show no sign of effort. What is written should seem a happy accident'.

Another eminent stylist, the novelist and playwright Keith Waterhouse, noted that although there have been great blind writers, from Homer to Milton and beyond, there have been no great deaf ones in the sense of 'being unable to hear one's composition in one's head, as Beethoven heard his music'. Waterhouse insisted that while the mind dictates what is to be written, the ear monitors what is going down on paper – or at least it should. Writers with a tin ear are never likely to write with precision, brevity and elegance – or with style.

Just as certain blends of musical notes stir us deeply in some mysterious way, so certain combinations of words possess the strange power to freeze us in our tracks, to inspire us, to echo in our minds for a lifetime. How is it done? Of course, everbody would like to know. But for the present we are earthbound, dependent still on our box of grammatical tricks for the magic. Some writers – perhaps you – will transcend the box of tricks and create real magical prose, but at least the rest of us have the opportunity to learn to write good, crisp, clear English, which is no mean accomplishment.

Style is the way in which writers use the language to express themselves. The three-line excerpt from a poem at the beginning of this section evokes an autumnal mood with a combination of words that is unique to that writer. Unless we allow the most bizarre coincidence, no other writer on earth, no matter how much he or she learns about grammar and style, will at any time now or in the future throw those words together in that particular way.

Meanwhile, though, we should be getting on with the job – polishing, burnishing, simplifying, colouring our writing, developing a critical ear and learning from writers who please and thrill us, practising our box of tricks.

Remember the Basics

Achieving good writing is a learning process. And like all learning, start with the simple. In our case, start with simple, clear prose – no pyrotechnics, no words or expressions you don't quite understand – just tell it like it is. Take Dr Samuel Johnson's advice, quoting what an old college tutor said to a pupil: 'Read over your compositions, and wherever you meet with a passage which you think is particularly fine, strike it out'.

Plain writing need not be dull writing. On the contrary, a good writer always keeps the reader foremost in mind, thinking constantly, 'Will the reader grasp what I'm writing . . . enjoy reading it . . . laugh at this joke . . . learn something? If the warning bell rings a good writer unhesitatingly changes a word, switches a phrase around, rewrites and reviews again . . . and again. Sounds like hard work. But the end product is worth it and can be very satisfying.

Go down to the 'word gym' and practise some exercises. Writing directions will get rid of the flab. Try writing directions for tying a granny knot. Or how to drive a car, or make a cheese omelette. Every good writer needs some humility!

Build on Brevity

The Americans Strunk and White, in their 20 million copy bestseller *The Elements of Style*, distilled an essay on the beauty of brevity into one paragraph:

> *Vigorous writing is concise. A sentence should contain no unnecessary words, a paragraph no unnecessary sentences, for the same reason that a drawing should have no unnecessary lines and a machine no unnecessary parts. This requires not that the writer make all his sentences short, or that he avoid all detail and treat his subjects only in outline, but that every word tell.*

By brevity we do not mean the extreme terseness of telegram-speak. That can rebound, as a showbiz reporter once discovered when he wired the actor Cary Grant, then in his sixties: 'How old Cary Grant?' The actor replied, 'Old Cary Grant fine'.

Few people these days want to write more words than necessary, or to be forced to read two hundred words when the information could have been conveyed in a hundred.

Earlier we saw how, by combining simple sentences into compound sentences, we can economise on words and even enhance clarity; but there is another grammatical convention that allows us to trim away words we don't need, or 'sentence fat'. It's called ellipsis, and it works like this:

WITHOUT ELLIPSIS   *When the children were called to the dinner table they came to the dinner table immediately.*

WITH ELLIPSIS   *When the children were called to the dinner table they came immediately.*

The reason we get away with this trimming is that, if the reader is paying attention (or you, the writer, have won his or her attention!) he or she will automatically supply the missing words from the context of what is written.

Alexander Pope's advice on brevity is as sound today as it was nearly three centuries ago:

> *Words are like leaves; and where they most abound,*
> *Much fruit of sense beneath is very rarely found.*

Or, to further encapsulate the thought: lean is keen.

Change up a Gear: Active and Passive

Would you rather do something, or have something done to you? With the first choice, you are in control; in the second you are the subject of somebody's whim. That's about the difference between what is known grammatically as the **active voice** and the **passive voice**. Being aware of the difference between active and passive expressions will make an enormous impact on your writing. Look at these sentences:

ACTIVE   *The favourite **won** the 3.30 hurdle event.*
                    *Her boyfriend **bought** the ring.*

PASSIVE   *The 3.30 hurdle event **was won** by the favourite.*
                    *The ring **was bought** by her boyfriend.*

It's easy to see why one kind of sentence is called active and the other passive; active sentences are direct and personal and seem more interesting, while passive sentences tend to be detached and impersonal by comparison.

If you are writing a scientific or academic article, then passive would be appropriate; otherwise use the active voice. And when you do, be careful not to slip into the passive mode, which will only result in discord:

My father painted those pictures which were left to me.

That sentence begins with the active voice (*My father painted those pictures*) but then switches to the passive (*which were left to me*). What the sentence should have said is: *My father painted those pictures and left them to me.* Follow the logic: my father did both things – painted the pictures and (presumably) left them to me.

. . . and up a Gear Again

Mixing active and passive expressions isn't the only source of discord in a sentence. Perhaps the most prevalent form of discord is the sentence which fails to recognise that a singular noun takes a singular verb and a plural noun takes a plural verb:

WRONG   *We **was** furious with the umpire's decision.*
                    *The four houses **isn't** for sale.*

CORRECT   *We **were** furious with the umpire's decision.*
                    *The four houses **aren't** for sale.*

These are glaringly apparent examples but less obvious traps lie in wait in longer sentences:

The Harris Committee has just a week (to January 17) to announce their initial findings.

Clearly either *has/its* or *have/their* are required.

Shifting from personal to impersonal pronouns in the same sentence (and vice versa) is another common mistake:

If one is to keep out of trouble, you should mind your own business.

Either stay with *one* or the personal (preferred) *you*.

Accentuating the positive (as they say) will vastly improve your writing style:

That dog is not unlike the one I saw in town yesterday.
That dog is similar to the one I saw in town yesterday.

Using the *not un-* construction is very fashionable today, but if you heed George Orwell's advice (from his *Politics and the English Language* of 1946) you'll desist:

A not unblack dog was chasing a not unsmall rabbit across a not ungreen field.

In fact it pays to have a 'not unuseful warning device' attached to your writing; too much negativism can have a depressing effect on the reader. Sometimes it is more tactful to express a negative thought in a positive way. *She is not beautiful* is negative and also vague: she could be *statuesque* or *handsome*, *obese* or *pimply*.

Add Colour to Your Word Palette

Are you conscious that you may be writing in monochrome? Without the vibrancy, the variety, the sensuality and fun of colour? Then what you need is a paintbox of verbal effects, a word palette of literary devices called figures of speech: **metaphor**, **simile**, **hyperbole**, **alliteration** and **wordplay**.

Metaphor

We're surrounded by everyday **metaphors**: *raining cats and dogs, mouth of the river, stony silence, he sailed into him, over the moon* . . . thousands of them are irrevocably part of the language. The difficulty is in inventing new ones, and writers who can, and can inject them at appropriate places in their texts, are a step ahead of the rest of us.

The beauty of metaphor is that it has the ability to bring a dull expression vividly to life and explain a difficult concept with startling clarity. We still use Dickens's 'The law is an ass' probably because nobody else has come up with a better pithy description for the odd and illogical decisions that can issue from our courts.

As you can see, metaphor is describing something by using an analogy with something quite different. If we hear that a person 'has egg on his face' we are expected to know that he wasn't the victim of a phantom egg-thrower but has been left in a very embarrassing situation. *Egg* and *embarrassment* are connected only by a wild flight of imagination (metaphor and cliché!).

By all means invent new metaphors but try to avoid creaky old ones. And in particular, watch out for mixed metaphors such as *They were treading in uncharted waters* and *I smell a rat but I'll nip him in the bud*.

Simile

A **simile** makes a direct comparison between two dissimilar things: *as fit as a fiddle, as good as gold, as sick as a parrot, he's crazy like a fox, ears like jug handles*. You'll note that invariably similes are introduced by the conjunction *as* or the preposition *like*.

A simile can enliven a piece of writing, but it should preferably be original; as with metaphors, creating apt similes is a special art. If your skill is on a par with that of Robert Burns (*My love is like a red, red rose*), Wordsworth (*I wandered lonely as a cloud*) or Cecil Day Lewis (*a girl who stands like a questioning iris by the waterside*), or an anonymous Aussie (*she was all over me like a rash*) then have fun with similes. But most of us need to employ tired simile-avoidance techniques to prevent our writing being clogged by such hoary chestnuts as *sharp as a razor, dull as ditchwater, pleased as Punch, plain as a pikestaff* and *mad as a March hare*.

Hyperbole

Hyperbole is deliberate overstatement: wild exaggeration used to make an emphatic point. Someone who complains that *I'm dying of hunger* or *I could eat a horse* would probably be perfectly satisfied with a hamburger. A person who offers you *a thousand apologies* would be somewhat taken aback if you insisted on having them.

As with other figures of speech, hyperbole has to be witty or outrageous to succeed. It's a stylistic area that leaves us envious of the writers who first coined such hyperbolic classics as *I got legless last night; couldn't fight his way out of a paper bag; couldn't organise a piss-up in a brewery* and *a diamond that would choke a horse*.

If you think you can beat 'em, then join 'em.

Alliteration and Wordplay

Making mischief with words is a way of having fun with the language, and it's something every writer feels the urge to do at some point. However, intruding drollery into prose can fall *as flat as a pancake* (**simile**, **cliché**) if it isn't up to scratch, and even when it is, it should be used sparingly.

Here are some more pastel shades you can squeeze on to your palette.

- **Alliteration** *Sing a song of sixpence* and *Peter Piper picked a peck of pickled peppers* are examples of alliteration from the nursery – the repetition of stressed sounds in words adjacent or near one another. Here's another example, in verse form, from the Gilbert and Sullivan opera, *The Mikado: To sit in solemn silence in a dull, dark dock / In a pestilential prison, with a life-long lock / Awaiting the sensation of a short, sharp shock / From a cheap and chippy chopper on a big, black block!*

  Alliteration that's been clumsily shoe-horned into your writing will *stick out like a sore thumb* (simile, cliché) so don't strive for alliterative effect. Mellifluous alliteration involving at most two or three words in a sentence will, with the least assistance from you, often occur naturally if your writing is flowing well.

- **Colloquialism and Idiom** Knowing when and where to use colloquial, idiomatic and slang expressions is a matter of style and experience. Their occasional use can certainly take the stuffiness out of some writing. They include such expressions as *get cracking, don't drop your bundle, go for it, give us a break, it'll be all right on the night, d.i.y* (colloquialisms); *part and parcel, keep a straight face, pass the buck, how's tricks?, odds and ends* (idioms); *bimbo, ankle biter, sprog, muttonhead, ballbreaker, jollies, tosser* (slang).

- **Litotes** (pronounced *ly-toe-tees*) Litotes is understatement, the opposite of hyperbole . . . so what's the point? Some examples may help: *this is no easy task, he was not a little upset, not uncommon, not a bad writer.* In other words litotes is a way of asserting a statement by denying its opposite: *not bad* means *good, fine, okay.* Litotes can convey fine shades of meaning, so use this device carefully; it can go off in your hand.

- **Synecdoche** This is a figurative device in which a part is substituted for the whole, or the whole for a part. Follow? Some examples: *We sent twenty head to France today.* (i.e. *We sent twenty cattle.* The expression uses part of the cow to indicate the whole). *England beat Australia by three wickets.* (Here the whole – *England* and *Australia* – is used to indicate a part – the English and Australian cricket teams). The device is useful in achieving brevity and avoiding repetition. One of the most common – and contentious – synecdochic expressions is *man*, which, in the sense of *mankind*, is only part of a whole, *man and woman.*

Don't Come Down with a Crash!

Perhaps learning to write fluently is a bit like learning to fly. Once you experience the heady feeling of being airborne and solo, the sky's the limit. Barrel rolls, loops, dives, Immelmann turns, you can do it all. And maybe you can. But you can also stall, lose direction, run out of gas . . . even the most thoroughly trained flyer can have a *bad air day*. So learn to temper your new-found skills with caution.

Enough has been said about long-windedness, clichés, tautology, gobbledegook, jargon and euphemism for an amber light to flash every time you stray in their direction. But there are still a few more amber, if not red, light districts awaiting the adventurous but unwary writer.

- **Elegant Variation** In a review of a biography of Abraham Lincoln by David Donald, the novelist Martin Amis wrote: 'Although Donald may be as methodical as Lincoln, he is his junior not least in literary talent. The prose is continually defaced by that scurviest of all graces, Elegant Variation. Here is but one example of Donald's futile ingenuity: "If the president seemed to support the Radicals in New York, in Washington he appeared to back the Conservatives."' Although many might think that Amis was being a bit picky, he was surely justified, in defending the principles of style, in criticising the author's obvious recourse to a 'strained synonym'; rather than repeat *seemed to support*, the author substituted *appeared to back*. This practice, abhorred by stylists, was first identified by the grammarian H. W. Fowler, who scornfully called it 'Elegant Variation'.

  Every writer can face the problem of dealing with identical words appearing in the same sentence or an adjoining one. In writing dialogue, for example, the word *said* is likely to be endlessly repeated at the risk of annoying the reader. The quick solution is to substitute near-synonyms: *uttered, replied, responded, answered, retorted, remarked, announced, added,* etc. If such substitutions are used judiciously and with restraint, the reader will probably not realise what is going on; fluency and readability will not be impaired.

  Running to the thesaurus or synonymn dictionary for a replacement word can trap the rookie writer, who will proceed merrily, unaware of the smell left behind to be picked up by the fastidious reader. Rewriting the sentence might be a better solution, or even, if allowing the repeated word if it doesn't jar, leaving it in.

- **Puns and Humour** Attempts at humour can be the downfall of the adventurous but incautious writer. Perhaps that's why there are very few writers able to make their readers laugh. Although newspapers will pay the earth for them, they still remain only a handful internationally. Are you likely to be one of them?

  This is not to say that your writing should be uniformly po-faced. A light touch is appreciated by more readers and it is no bad thing to aim at being amusing from time to time. A well-placed witty turn of phrase, a funny but apt quotation, a waggish allusion or mischievous irony – all these are within reach of writers who may have to be hypercritical of their work.

Except for national tabloid headlines, puns are regarded with deep suspicion by many writers. They can be verbal banana skins. The pun towards the end of the opening paragraph of this section (*a bad air day* for *a bad hair day*, itself a metaphor) is a calculated risk, as all such puns must be.

- **Adjectival economy** In discussing adjectives, we demonstrated how they can be accumulated to form an accurate description of an object, person or idea. One example showed a pile-up of seven consecutive adjectives, which is rather too many.

   Such overloading can cause confusion; by the time the reader has reached the last one the first may have been forgotten.

   But, more importantly, make sure that every adjective you use adds something essential to the description: *Her skis sliced through the powdery white snow on her downward trajectory*. Most of us know that snow is white, and believe it is very difficult to ski uphill, so the adjectives *white* and *downward* could well be returned to the dictionary.

- **Plagiarism** In their pursuit of rapid progress, some ambitious writers are led up the dodgy path of plagiarism – words, ideas, stories or texts copied from the work of other writers. Very few writers have the gall to copy a work in its entirety and claim it as their own, but it has been done. More common is the practice of 'borrowing' someone else's work without indicating this by the use of quotation marks or crediting its source. This can lead to complaint and legal action: every year in Britain there is at least one serious – and sometimes costly – accusation of plagiarism.

   As a cautionary tale, here is the case of two books, one a biography of the Empress Eugenie published in 1964 by Harold Kurtz, and the other about royal brides by the Princess Michael of Kent, published 1986:

The Empress Eugenie	*Crowned in a Far Country*
Harold Kurtz	Princess Michael of Kent
All her life Eugenie placed very little	*All her life Eugenie placed very little*
importance on sex, not as something	*importance on sex; not as something*
wicked, just unimportant and cheap.	*wicked, just unimportant and cheap.*
'You mean,' she would say in tones of	*'You mean,' she would say in disbelief,*
incredulity, 'that men are interested	*'that men are interested in nothing but*
in nothing but that?' when her ladies	*that?' when her ladies were chatting*
were chatting about the infidelities	*about infidelities.*
of men.	

On the face of it, this looks pretty incriminating. But do bear in mind that finding the same thought expressed by a later writer does not *necessarily* mean that the later writer has plagiarised the original. Coincidences do happen; and never forget that lawyers are always vigilant for rash accusations. All one can say is that there comes a point in the course of a book when it becomes obvious to all (even lawyers) that a later writer is simply copying what an earlier writer has written, so be warned about purloining prose! And if you have heard that there is no copyright in literary ideas, concepts, structure and titles, take care also, because if it can be proved that you are 'passing off' another's original work you could find yourself at the wrong end of a lawsuit.

To Sum Up . . .

- Brevity is beautiful. So is simplicity. Short words too. And short sentences.
- Prefer concrete to abstract words
- Prefer the active voice to the passive
- Prefer positive expressions to negative
- Keep sentences harmonious – in voice, tense and number
- Listen to your sentences
- Remember that it is your job to attract and keep the reader's attention
- Think precision
- Think poetry

HOW TO WRITE A BETTER LETTER:

Say What You Mean, Get What You Want

Communicate Better with a Well-Written Letter

In a man's letter his soul lies naked.

Dr Samuel Johnson

The Post Office in Britain handles over two billion items of personal correspondence a year; in the same period *The Times* receives just under an astonishing 100,000 letters from readers.

Telecommunications and electronic transmissions have risen exponentially, of course, but it would be a brave pundit who predicted the demise of letter writing. After all, faxes and e-mails still have to be written.

There may be a sound reason for the letter's lusty survival in the face of progress. A telephone call has the advantage of immediacy, with a minimum of preparation, but that is also its weakness. A letter allows the writer to weigh thoughts, plan strategies of approach and persuasion, withdraw cruel and rash statements, refine and sharpen arguments, and, having done all that, decide after a period of rumination not to send it at all. A well-written letter also allows the shy and retiring writer to stand tall alongside the silver-tongued telephone speaker. And there are other advantages. A letter is tangible; it carries weight, it is a record you can keep and it makes a pleasant change.

But a problem remains: the scourge of postman's block. What does one say? How does one say it? How does one coordinate paper, pen, envelope, stamp and address?

Let's face it: most of us are a bit rusty when it comes to writing letters. Some of us never really learnt. Once, it was normal for children who had received a gift to write a short, neat and closely supervised thank you letter to the benefactor; sadly, this is not so common nowadays. And even though we may rattle off chirpy letters to friends or relatives with ease, how do we suddenly change gear to plead for more time to pay an overdue account, or complain to neighbours about their barking dog, without causing World War Three; or write to an ombudsman seeking redress over bad pension advice?

The essence of an effective letter is its individuality; every letter, in wording and tone, must be unique to the circumstances and its recipient. So it can't be stressed enough that the sample letters that follow are simply guides to how various letter-writing problems might be tackled. Many have been adapted from real letters that achieved results, gleaned from colleagues, correspondents, companies and public institutions, but it would be a mistake to regard them as models to copy.

Preparation and Planning

Always have writing materials around the house; a pack of good-quality A4 lightly lined bond paper if you write by hand, or standard bank, copier or computer paper if you use a word processor or typewriter; a supply of POP (Post Office Preferred) envelopes in a couple of sizes, 1st and 2nd class stamps. You will never carry through your self-improvement letter-writing plan if you have to concern yourself about materials every time.

Next, familiarise yourself with one of the accepted layouts for most letters:

The essentials are (1) your address (2) the date (3) the recipient's name and address.

The following can be dispensed with in personal letters to those you know well: (4) the introduction (5) the contents (6) the sign-off, your signature, and, in non-personal letters, your printed name. Sometimes it's a good idea to include a reference, which may summarise the content: *Repairs to garden tractor*; or identify previous correspondence. Such references are usually underlined and go under the introduction (*Dear Mr Holmes*) and above the first line of the contents.

> The Willows,
> 26 Long Barn Lane,
> Wilmardenden,
> Kent
> CT8 5TW
>
> 1 July 1999
>
> Mr G W Holmes,
> Managing Director,
> Gnome Garden Engineering Ltd,
> Forklift Road,
> Romford, Essex RM7 2DYT
>
> Dear Mr Holmes,
>   Begin your letter here. If you don't know who the managing director is you could hazard a 'Dear Sir or Madam'; or, better still, phone the firm's switchboard and ask for the managing director's name and initials.
>   Indent each subsequent paragraph similar to the first, like this. When you come to the end of your letter, close with either 'Yours sincerely' if you know the recipient, or 'Yours faithfully' if you don't. If you are writing to an official whom you've never met and are not likely to meet, sign off with 'Yours truly'. None of these sign-offs is set in stone, however.
>
> Yours faithfully,
>
> [sign here]
>
> [your name here]

Now, the planning. This is really another term for thought. In fact, three thoughts:

- Think about the **reason** you're writing the letter. If there are several reasons, separate them clearly and logically in your mind. Put them in order of importance.

- Separate **facts** from your **opinions**. State the facts first, then add your opinions or comments if you must.

- Focus sharply again on your reason for writing. What **result** do you want? What do you want the recipient to do? In an extreme case, what will you do if the recipient doesn't do as you wish?

If you write by hand or use a typewriter, then it pays to do a draft which gives you the opportunity to correct and change and polish the text. Does it make the points clearly? Does it flow? Is every word spelt correctly? (Quick! The dictionary!) As with all writing, try to put yourself in the shoes of the intended reader and imagine the reaction. Is it what you intended? Take your time and get it right.

If you use a word processor, you will be familiar with the 'edit as you go' technique which allows you to make corrections and revisions at will. When you are satisfied with what you see on your screen, then print. Check the printout carefully: it's amazing how many errors you pick up when reading the printed word!

Your final version should be free of errors, well laid out and inviting to read. If you write more than one letter a week (that's 50 a year) it would make sense to have a letterhead printed. A neat letterhead undoubtedly adds a touch a gravitas to any correspondence. Most towns have a franchised fast printing and copying centre that will print a couple of hundred letterheads for you at competitive prices. Or a good wordprocessor will let you create your own, very easily. Alternatively you could have a self-inking name and address stamp made for less than £10. These last several years with normal use and have the added advantage of allowing you to letterhead any size paper and have your name and address on the backs of envelopes.

When addressing an envelope be sure it bears all the information necessary for sure and safe delivery, including the vital postcode. If you are unsure of how to address a person, there's a guide to forms of address on page 584.

Finally, in this section on generalised advice:

- When writing business or non-personal letters, be clear and concise.

- In personal correspondence to those you know and love, be yourself (but preferably personable and as informal and honest as you dare!)

Relationships by Post: Strictly Personal

We may be the last generation to write to each other.

Philip Larkin

Personal Letters

Personal correspondence runs parallel to one's life, from birth announcements and thank-you notes for christening gifts through love letters, apologies and get-well cards to letters of condolence. For all of this you need to cultivate a personal voice in your correspondence: light and friendly, sincere and sympathetic, affectionate and loving, according to the occasion and the recipient.

Personal letters will inevitably convey your thoughts and emotions, but you need to measure your emotions with care. There will be moments in your life when you're tempted to open the floodgates of your heart to a correspondent. Just remember that your outpourings will be on permanent record, which is fine if they remain in safe and discreet hands but emotionally scarring if they don't.

Perhaps the most common of personal communications is the thank-you note. As simple a concept as it is, many people, intending to lay on thick slabs of rapturous gratitude, finish up with a terse, flat 'Fred and I wish to thank you for the knitted tea cosy'. Yet gift-givers are almost always so delighted to receive grateful acknowledgements that it's worthwhile honing your thank-you skills, and some pointers are given in this section.

An oft-heard question is: should a personal note be handwritten? The short answer is yes – if your handwritting is neat enough. Handwritten notes are certainly appreciated. But if your handwriting is semi-legible, typescript is perfectly acceptable.

And it is even more acceptable if the introduction – Dear John/Judy/ Mrs Smith – and perhaps the close – Ever yours/With much love, etc – are handwritten. Because thank-you letters are so prized, it's worth remembering that these need not be limited to acknowledging presents and hospitality. If somebody has helped you in some way, and given generously of his or her time or support, a gracious thank-you note is not only likely to be appreciated but also remembered and treasured.

Monday

My dear Anne,

What a wonderful weekend! Can I hope that you enjoyed it as much as I did? For me it will always remain one of the most deliriously exciting occasions of my life.

The real reason for this letter is to say, once again, that I love you. It gives me a thrill just to write that down. Let me throw caution to the winds – do you love me? I can't tell you how happy I'd be to know that you feel the same way about me as I do about you. All I can say is, I've never felt anything like this before in all my life.

I know it's a big step making such a commitment and I will understand your hesitation. But something tells me, excuse the cliché, that we're made for each other. In just under a week we'll be together again and when you look into my eyes (and my heart) you'll know, you'll really know, that I speak the truth. My beautiful Anne, is it our fate to become the two happiest people in all the world?

I think of you constantly. I love you.

Billy

Love Letters

- Handwritten letters are preferred and advised, as is best quality stationery. In your fervid state, don't forget the postage stamp.

- Don't lapse into mushiness. Be gentle, tender and understanding.

- Don't give the impression that you're doing the object of your desire a great favour. A little humility can work wonders.

- Note the simple, sincere-sounding **I love you** at the end.

  Monday

Dear Pansy,
    I got the news this morning and can't wait to congratulate you
and Freddie on your engagement.
    Although we have known each other most of our lives I have only
known Freddie for the six months since he came into your life.
But even in that short time I have come to realise what an ideal
couple you make! You must be over the moon, and your parents
must be delighted.
    Let's meet soon – I want to hear it all. And please give my love
and congratulations to Freddie.

Your devoted friend,

Millie

Congratulations on an Engagement/Marriage

- These are among the most pleasant forms of personal correspondence, so
  don't hold back on your goodwill or enthusiasm.

- A letter like this will help cement your friendship to the couple, who'll value
  and remember your supportive and affectionate response.

- Letters similar in tone can also be sent to the couple's parents, although some
  might regard this as cynical networking.

---

30 June

Dear Pat and Don,

 I can't tell you how thrilled we were when we unwrapped your most generous gift.

 How could you have known that Jamie is a fiend for toast? He almost fainted with joy when he tried out the automatic individual slice pop-up control. And you chose green! How did you know that that will be perfect in our kitchen-to-be?

 It was lovely seeing you both at our wedding, and when we settle down (we're temporarily in Jamie's old flat) I'll let you know. Once again, many thanks.

Love,

Margaret

Thanks for the Present

- Undoubtedly over the top but think of the warm glow you'll give the recipients! Although the use of 'Thanks for the Gift' cards is increasing, a personal, preferably handwritten, note wins hands down for sincerity.

- A personal note can soften the rather calculated way in which such gifts are solicited nowadays (tick off the list of suggestions, phone the store, etc).

- Unsolicited gifts from those who were not invited to the wedding deserve a very special letter of thanks.

- In all such letters be sure to acknowledge what the present actually is.

- If the gift is money, the donors might get enjoyment from knowing how you intend to spend or use it.

Sunday

Dear Mrs Morgan,

It was most thoughtful and kind of you to visit me yesterday.

Thoughtful, because through a mutual friend you found out that I was rather lonely and feeling sorry for myself, and kind because you took a couple of hours from your very busy schedule to come and see me.

Your visit cheered me up immensely, and you'll be pleased to know that I spent most of this morning in the garden because of your encouragement.

You have my heartfelt thanks,

Yours sincerely,

Elizabeth Curzon

Saying Thanks

- Who could fail to be touched and rewarded by the gratitude so sincerely and graciously expressed in a note like this? Handwritten, of course.

- Similar thank you letters (for gifts, visits, hospitality, a timely note of sympathy or support, some special effort) should pay tribute to thoughtfulness, kindness, generosity, forbearance, compassion, solicitude, etc.

- A teacher who'd spent out-of-hours time helping your child, a neighbour who towed your crippled car to a garage, a colleague who took the trouble to check on your family's needs while you were hospitalised – all would be pleased to be thanked but more than pleased to receive a thank-you letter.

2 September

Dear Uncle Ernest,

I remember that when you were down here last Christmas you asked me to keep you posted about my new business. You told me then that you thought the 'Ezy Bulb Planter' I was developing should be a big commercial success.

Unfortunately this has turned out not to be the case. The two firms I hired to manufacture the item struck problems and abandoned the project and although contractually I am in the right they cost me nearly £30,000 with nothing to show for it.

As a result I face losing my business and everything I've sunk into it. Ironically, I've now found a new manufacturer who's solved the problems, but unless I can find £6,000 within two weeks I will face bankruptcy – at 27!

You know I've put everything I have, physically, mentally and financially, into the business. I've worked an average 16 hours a day for two years. I've borrowed to the limit (Mum and Dad have helped, of course). Uncle Ernest, it's not easy making this appeal, and I apologise unreservedly for writing to you, but you are my last resort, my final hope. If you can manage to lend me the £6,000 you will see every penny back.

I will understand totally if you can't see your way to helping me financially. And regardless of what you decide, I would in any case welcome any advice you can give me.

Your affectionate nephew,

Michael

Saying Please

- The outcome of begging letters is notoriously difficult to predict. Instead of producing the desired effect (money) they can result in misunderstanding, hostility, family quarrels and total estrangement. So beware!

- Give a brief background to the crisis but also stress the positive outcome (if there is one) if £x will solve the problem. A would-be benefactor might consider being a rescuer but balk at throwing good money after bad.

- A flattering end-note (asking for advice) might help hit the right button.

Sunday

My dear Toby,

We've just heard from your mother about your graduation, and Aunt Josie and I are just as thrilled as she is.

What a wonderful achievement – and you've worked so hard for it, too. We're particularly pleased that you've proved yet again that there are brains in the family!

Obviously we're keen to know about your plans for the future, so make sure you write, and also visit us soon.

Once again, our wholehearted congratulations.

Love from us both,

Albert

Congratulations

- Being offered congratulations is a life-enhancing experience.

- For many people it doesn't happen too often, so when some achievement (graduating, having a baby, getting a first job or a promotion, learning to fly, passing a driving test) is greeted with written congratulations, it can make someone's day.

- Make it short and sweet, on a card if you like, and preferably handwritten.

Stonefield,
Cherrytree Lane,
Marstone,
Bath
BA2 7CV

Day of Atonement

My dearest Abigail,

How can I apologise for my behaviour at your luncheon party yesterday? Although my recollections are muddled I now realise that I must have upset your guests, embarrassed you and Bill and generally made an obnoxious fool of myself.

It was completely unforgivable, but I hope you will find the generosity to forgive and forget. The thought of losing your friendship over my display of stupidity is more than I can bear. Can I assure you that what happened was untypical and will never, never happen again.

With fond regards to you both,

Ted

Apologies

- A difficult letter to write and demanding a high order of courage, but should you decide to write an apology, don't hold back. To work, it must be an all-out, grovelling, hand-wringing, reproachful confessional.

- Ask for forgiveness and pray that the transgression will be deeply buried and forgotten.

- Write promptly and arrange to see the victims soon to avoid having the incident fester in their minds.

- Don't rely entirely on written words. Accompany them with flowers.

Thursday

Dear Arthur,

Ellen told me that you were spending your holidays this year at St Catherine's, you lucky thing – warm bed, loads of pretty women eager to do anything for you (anything??), just lying about all day doing nothing – where can I buy a ticket?

I'm told also that everything went well and that you're doing fine, so keep up the good work. And don't be too impatient – on the outside it's wet and cold and grey, and last night Jack was caught in a five-mile motorway tailback because of fog. And my car's in the garage; I spun on the ice last week, hit a brick wall and demolished the front end and lights – such fun!

Sam also has car troubles – his was stolen and although it was eventually found it was minus the radio and his favourite leather jacket.

But the good news is that Heather's young man has asked her to marry him (do you remember Trevor? He has an engaging lisp) and I won the bridge prize last week.

Anyway, Arthur, relax and enjoy your holiday and you'll be well and fit in no time. We think of you all the time.

Love from us all at No. 36,

Deborah

Get Well

- When you hear of a friend or colleague in hospital the knee-jerk reaction is to send off one of the thousands of cards published specifically for the occasion. But after a week or two, when the clutter of cards has been cleared from the bedside unit, a letter can be a godsend to a bed-bound patient.

- Avoid dwelling on medical matters, keep it cheerful and pack it with news and gossip that can be recycled during visiting hours.

15 June

My dear Carol,

We are deeply saddened by your mother's death and our sympathies and condolences go out to you and your family.

Although we hadn't seen your mother during the last few years our memories of her will always remain. She was so big-hearted and generous that just thinking of her gives us a warm glow of deep and lasting affection.

We will miss her terribly but the loss to you must be incalculable.

There must be ways in which we can help you at this most painful time. Lauren will call you next week, and I hope to see you very soon.

You are constantly in our thoughts.

In sorrow and sympathy,

Lauren and Roy Green

Condolences (intimate and informal)

- Avoid cards; write a brief, comforting hand-written note as soon as you can after hearing about the death. Offer help as well as sympathy.

- Write from your heart; feelings honestly expressed, however clumsily, will always be appreciated. But contain your emotions or you risk sounding mawkish.

- Offer a recollection of the deceased if you wish: fond memories, a particular occasion, a summary of the person's outstanding qualities.

- Don't dwell on the circumstances surrounding the death; rather try to take the recipient's mind forward – to some future event or meeting.

134 Haywood Drive,
Marling, Nr Picton, Kent
Tel. 01899 221216

12 December

Dear Mrs Long,

   I would like to express my sincere condolences to you over your sad loss of Harry.

   You may have difficulty remembering me but I met you on a couple of occasions at Harry's firm's golf days.

   I would like you to know that Harry will always have an important place in my memory. I owe him an enormous debt of gratitude for his unfailing help in my career. He was both wise and generous, as I'm sure you know. He also guided me through a distressing and emotional period when I lost my little daughter and, a short while later, when my wife left me.

   Losing Harry is a grievous blow to me, so I know his loss must be overwhelming for you.

   Please accept my deep sympathy, and if there is any way in which I can help you, please let me know.

Yours sincerely,

Richard Milton

Condolences (to a non-acquaintance)

- Sending condolences to a relative or close acquaintance can be a matter of duty. Expressing your sympathy to a bereaved person who doesn't or hardly knows you is an act of compelling unselfishness.

- Your duty in such cases is to provide a personal testament to the deceased, simply and sincerely. Coming 'out of the blue', as it were, such letters are invariably valued by the bereaved and may even offer new insights on the life of the loved one.

Jane Bush,
12 Potsdam Road,
Mercator,
Bolton
BL2 9QR
01720 045671
22 June

Dear Mr Parish

Please accept my thanks for your kind letter and your very kind words about Jeremy.

I have been deeply touched by the dozens of letters and cards I've received, and comforted to know how much Jeremy was admired and loved.

Thank you for your thoughts and for you offer to help. It is exceedingly generous of you, and I shall contact you should the need arise.

Yours sincerely

Jane Bush

Responding to Sympathy and Condolences

- Although it is quite common to acknowledge letters of sympathy and condolences with cards, writing a letter, when the emotional landscape has cleared a little, can be cathartic.

- It is an unfortunate fact that after a death many bereaved people find themselves facing an unexpectedly lonely existence. Part of the reason is that friends and acquaintances are sometimes hesitant to make contact, perhaps feeling that they might be intruding on the person's privacy and grief. Writing letters can provide a vital link to continuing relationships.

Sunday

Dear Mick,

I was sorry to hear that you and Margot have decided to separate. I know that you've had your difficulties lately so it wasn't a total surprise; nevertheless I had hoped you would find a way to rediscover your former happiness.

Is there anything I can do to help? As you know, I love and care for you both, so it's a double dilemma for me.

Would it help if I spoke to Margot? At the risk of being thought an interfering so-and-so I will do anything I can to help you two back together again. But if it is not to be, then you know you will always have my love and friendship and that you can pick up the phone any time and call –

Your devoted friend,

Judy

Commiseration

- Certain misfortunes can be soul-destroying: separation and divorce, bankruptcy and redundancy; sudden disablement, a shop-lifting or drunk-driving charge . . . personal catastrophes that can wreck the life of a friend, relative or colleague. Do you comfort, or walk away?

- Writing a letter of comfort to someone caught up in a personal tragedy can be like walking over broken emotional glass and is never without its dangers, but knowing that someone cares can help restore that person's shattered self-confidence and hope for the future.

14 April

Dear Arnold,

I'm sorry to have to write this letter, but I see no other way of appealing to you to pay back the £400 I lent you last December.

As you know, this is not the first time I've asked you for repayment but now I really must have the money as I'm way overdrawn at the bank, all because of that loan. Our agreement, by the way, was that you would repay it all within six weeks. So it's long overdue.

I know you've had problems, and from our long acquaintance I know you to be completely honest and a person of integrity, so I have no doubt you will pay me. And if, for any reason you cannot right now, I'm sure you would tell me so that we could work something out.

Arnold, I desperately need that money, and now. It would be crazy if this matter ended a long and enjoyable friendship, wouldn't it? So please call or write urgently.

George

The Gloved Fist

- When a friend or relative won't pay back a loan and goodwill is running low, you want to send out a lynching party, not a letter. But confrontational anger is a last resort and can result in legal action, shattered relationships – and still no money.

- Letters that express your disappointment and anger can be written without intemperate language and wild threats. Make your points firmly, of course, but allow that the misdemeanour is untypical and forgivable.

- Cool reason and an appeal to the person's sense of fairness is more likely to be productive than hostile fireworks.

Announcements and Invitations

Announcements and invitations hardly aspire to be personal letters, but even these can benefit from a knowledge of the principles of written etiquette. A good many still retain, probably unintentionally, the pomposity of a more formal age, whereas today we generally prefer a more relaxed approach to such correspondence.

There are cards for all occasions, of course, in an almost overwhelming choice.

Beginning at the beginning, with births, the news of the happy arrival is usually spread via a card, the appropriate columns of the local newspaper, or by word of mouth.

There isn't a lot to say about a baby other than that it has arrived and that it is a boy or a girl with such and such a name, so to announce it with a letter seems excessive.

More appropriate to a letter is the baptism:

---

12 Abbot's Parkway,
Arnott's Grove,
Belford,
Notts
NG4 TH8

Dear Margaret and Toby,

Holly Mae will be christened on Sunday 4 June at St Stephen's Church, Centre Street, Tonborough.

The service will begin at 4 pm but before then we are having drinks at home from 2.30 and we would love you to be there.

After the service you are also welcome to return here for further celebrations!

Love,

Joan and Ken

Although many people like copperplate formality for parties and receptions, others prefer a lighter, more informal touch for their invitations. Whatever the tone, though, don't forget the essential information.

Bowing to tradition and convention, wedding announcements invariably take on a formal tone and appearance – almost always in the form of an elegantly printed card. Bucking the custom with something more original and cheerful could mean a lighter, less formal touch. Remember, however, that this is the bride's (or her parents') department. The usual formula is:

> *Lucinda and Geoffrey Barnes*
> *would be delighted if you could join them*
> *to celebrate the engagement of their daughter*
> *Pauline*
> *at a party in the Admiralty Room, Nelson Hotel,*
> *Wharf Crescent, Port Abington,*
> *on Saturday, September 20, at 8.00 pm.*
>
> *RSVP*   *Party frocks*
> *'The Grove', Elm Tree Drive,*   *Lounge suits*
> *Abington (01447) 320 432*

The invitation has a similar style:

> *Mr and Mrs Hugh Blake*
> *request the pleasure of the company of*
>
> _____
>
> *at the marriage of their daughter Susan Emily*
> *to Mr James McNicholl*
> *at St Swithin's Church, Normanville,*
> *on Saturday, May 3, at 3 o'clock*

An RSVP should be appended to the invitation or, more thoughtfully, an addressed reply card could be included for the guest's response.

When replying to invitations, a good rule is to match the style of your reply to that of the invitation. If handwritten, it is a courtesy to reply similarly; on the other hand a formal invitation suggests a formal reply. While that's straightforward enough some people have a problem finding the words to gracefully decline an invitation.

There are two things to remember: be complimentary, disappointed and apolgetic, and explain the reasons for your inability to attend:

6 March

Dear Lynne and Charles,

We're distraught! We were delighted to get your kind invitation until we checked the family diary and were dismayed to find that we have a long-standing engagement to spend the day with June's parents in Norwich that weekend. We only visit them a couple of times a year so we can't let them down. It's a great shame.

So please accept our apologies – and our best wishes for a great party!

Yours in tears,

Jack and Bernice

Of all announcements, a letter advising relatives and friends of a death is the saddest and probably the most difficult to write. Unsurprisingly many bereaved people prefer to send out a simple, formal card, or use the telephone, not least because the days surrounding a death are confused and chaotic. However there may be circumstances that require a personal letter to convey the news with greater sensitivity. This solemn duty may, if you are a close relative or friend of the deceased, fall to you.

10 August

Dear Mr and Mrs Howard,

It is my sad duty to inform you that Mary's mother died yesterday, 9 August.

Her life ended painlessly and peacefully after her long illness.

Mary has asked me to thank you both for your devotion to her mother and for your many visits and gifts, which Ellen always looked forward to with eager delight.

Ellen's funeral will take place at the East Chapel, Fulham Crematorium, at 11 am, Friday 13 August.

Yours sincerely,

Adam Santangelo

Protecting Your Interests:
Complaining with Effect

Caveat emptor – Let the buyer beware.

Even the most careful consumer occasionally gets lumbered with a defective appliance, a bodged plumbing job, a phantom delivery, an inaccurate bank statement.

In the great majority of cases the supplier is only too happy to set things right. But there are always the sloppy, intransigent or plain crooked traders who'll evade their responsibilities, and they can make your life hell.

If you let them.

Knowing how to complain effectively when you're a victimised consumer is one of life's essential arts. Knowing who to complain to is also important.

First in your sights should be the person or firm who actually sold you the faulty goods or services. It is worth remembering that if you have paid with cash or by credit card, your claim is not against the manufacturer, importer or wholesaler, but the retailer or seller. If you used a credit card you are further protected by the Consumer Credit Act, which makes the credit card company responsible.

A further line of defence is the Sale and Supply of Goods Act, which stipulates that goods or services must be 'as described', must be of good quality and work satisfactorily, and must be fit for the purpose for which they are sold. The seller or supplier is legally bound to make sure that all of these apply; if not, you must be compensated.

Other legislation that protects your interests includes the Consumer Protection Act, which prohibits labels or advertisements with misleading prices; the Trade Descriptions Act, which forbids traders to make false claims about the goods or services they sell; the Unfair Contract Terms Act, which protects purchasers' rights from the 'small print' in contracts; and the Food Safety Act, which protects consumers from unsafe or sub-standard foodstuffs.

If you fail to get redress, you can turn to various consumer watchdogs, including municipal advice bureaux, regional Departments of Fair Trading, the Department of Trading Standards, a number of trade regulatory authorities and ombudsmen, the addresses and telephone numbers of which you can get from your nearest Citizens' Advice Bureau. Finally, you can consult your local MP or a solicitor.

But first, the letter. It is absolutely vital to keep and copy all receipts, documents and relevant correspondence. However aggrieved you may feel, don't begin your complaint by antagonising the supplier. State the facts clearly and concisely. Make it clear what it is you want: a replacement, a refund, a repair or compensation. Keep cool and calm, and you'll collect.

You may find that your first letter fails to achieve the desired response. Try again. Perhaps it didn't make your case strongly enough or it was read by the wrong person.

Maybe it found its way on to the 'too hard' pile. More likely, you were being fobbed off: 'Sorry, your complaint should have been made within 30 days . . . it is our policy not to make refunds . . . we do not guarantee that product . . . it's the manufacturer's problem, not ours.' None of these responses is legally valid, so try again. This time, get some advice and quote the relevant Act so that they know they're not dealing with an innocent.

In the following pages, you'll find suggested letter formats designed to deal with some of the more common areas of complaint. It would be rare for two causes of complaint to be exactly the same, so each must be adapted to the circumstances.

But before getting down to details, here are some tips:

- If you've been unable to get anywhere by complaining in person or over the telephone, a letter backed by solid facts is hard to ignore.

- Rather than address your letter to some anonymous executive, call the firm's switchboard and ask for the name of, say, the general manager, sales manager or marketing director. In larger firms, senior management may be surprised to learn that their company is treating its customers unfairly.

- Don't attach original receipts or documents to your letter – always use copies. Originals can sometimes get 'lost'.

- Don't threaten legal action in your initial correspondence; it is always taken with a grain of salt. Save it for a final showdown.

- If you are forced, at last, into taking legal action, either use a solicitor or make sure you know the working of the procedures of Small Claims Courts (for amounts under £5,000 in England and Wales; £750 in Scotland; £1,000 in Northern Ireland). Apply directly to the courts for advice and information.

16 Newark Street
Chelmsford
Essex

Monday, 12 May

Mr H. O'Brien
18 Newark Street
Chelmsford
Essex

Dear Mr O'Brien,

Every day and evening during the past week (4–11 May) we have been disturbed by excessive noise from your garage adjoining this house. The noise is, I understand, due to your automotive engine-tuning business.

On three occasions I have asked you to eliminate or reduce the noise to an acceptable level but it has continued unabated. I have explained to you that the noise is distressing and is affecting our health. Mrs Burns has suffered almost continual headaches during this past week.

I am therefore forced to give you notice that if the nuisance continues beyond today I will instruct my solicitor to initiate legal proceedings against you, including a restraining order and a claim for compensation.

Yours faithfully,

Gordon H. Burns

Fighting Environmental Pollution

- Installing proper sound reduction baffles is going to cost Mr O'Brien a packet, so don't expect him to give in easily. But give in he must, because today noise pollution is widely recognised as one of the main environmental actors that can make people's lives a misery.

- When appeals and warnings have gone unheeded, a no-nonsense letter is called for – one that makes the consequences clear. But you must be prepared to carry out your threat, or any future warnings and letters will ring hollow – the worst noise of all.

32 Assize Court,
Pemberton Road,
Glaston,
Mouton,
Exeter
EX2 4NG

9 December

Planning Officer,
Highways Department,
Exeter City Council,
42 High St,
Exeter
EX1 2CE.

Dear Sir,
    The paving outside the above address and along Pemberton Road is broken and dangerous. I have stumbled on it several times and at least one other resident, an old lady, is afraid to risk walking on the pavement for fear of an accident.
    Will you please have the paving repaired, urgently.

Yours faithfully,

R. J. Thomas

Writing to the Council

- As above, keep it simple, factual and unemotional, no matter how many times you've twisted your ankle. Councils know by now that they are liable for compensation if you have an accident attributable to their lack of maintenance and care, so a letter like this will get action.

- Make a phone call to find out to whom you should be writing and get a name. If you don't, your letter could ricochet around the corridors of local power for months.

Mrs A. W. Wilson,   2 October
Tour Booking Director,
Sunset Holidays,
High Street,
Bath.

Dear Mrs Wilson,

I wish to make a complaint about the holiday I booked at your office on 19 July this year (Ref: MAJ20232677).

Your booking assistant confirmed then that we would have a large, air-conditioned double room with a spacious balcony directly overlooking the beach. The ensuite bathroom was to have both a shower and bath.

We also chose the 'A' class accomodation because it gave us access to the garden pool.

Instead, what we got was a cramped room without air-conditioning. The bathroom had no bath. The balcony overlooked a drab apartment block with washing lines. The beach and sea were not to be seen. The garden pool was empty.

I pointed all this out to your courier, Mr Sanchez, who was sympathetic but could do nothing. Our annual holiday was completely spoiled.

Quite clearly your firm failed to discharge its contractural and legal obligations, and this letter is to inform you that I hold you liable for our failed holiday and that I am seeking compensation. Please let me have your proposals for compensation within seven days.

Yours faithfully,

G. N. Hampton

Holiday Woes

- Complaints about miserable holidays are unfortunately fairly routine, and many operators have a fairly slick routine to deflect or minimise them. So it is important to be specific: set out exactly what you were promised and what was really delivered, but keep in mind that most holiday brochures come laden with hectares of fine print. [*See* following letter]

14 July

Tour Booking Director,
Sunset Holidays Ltd,
High Street, Bath
BA3 4YW

Dear Sir/Madam,

Your Ref: CR2A11568
    This will confirm that I have booked the 10-day Tuscan Holiday
(Ref as above) with you, departing Gatwick 18 August and returning
28 August, for which I have paid £740 for two adults including all
supplements.
    Please note that I have also booked the following special
requirements:

(1) Spacious second-floor room with double bed and ensuite
bathroom and uninterrupted landscape views;

(2) Baby cot suitable for a two-year old child.

    If for any reason you cannot confirm any of the above please
advise me immediately.

Yours faithfully,

(Mrs) Joyce Mitchell

Confirming Holiday Arrangements

- An increasing number of holiday makers are ensuring that any special
  requirements agreed upon when making the booking are confirmed by both
  parties before departure.

- Although this procedure won't guarantee that things won't go wrong, it
  should certainly make everything easier if you have to complain when you
  return.

- If this safeguard fails to protect you and your letters seeking compensation
  are ignored or disputed, you should write to the Association of British Travel
  Agents (ABTA), 55 Newman Street, London W1P 4AH.

10 Arcadia Lane,
Bushampton,
Kilmarnock KA6 4BV

The Manager,
Historic Art & Artifacts Ltd,
Brayville Road,
Edinburgh EH14 8NY

Dear Sir/Madam,

Order No. HAA2356

I wish to complain about the delivery of the pair of Clarice Cliff brooches (Cat. No. 2136, £47.50 plus £2.95 postage) I ordered on 2 December but which did not arrive until Christmas Eve, 24 December.

Your catalogue clearly stated that Christmas orders placed before 5 December would be guaranteed delivery in the UK within 14 days.

Thus my order should have been delivered by 16 December at the latest. The brooches were intended as a Christmas gift for a friend in Germany, but they arrived far too late to be forwarded in time. Instead I had to buy an alternative gift.

I am deeply disappointed. The items are enclosed, and I request a full and prompt refund (£47.50 plus £2.95 postage plus my return postage).

Yours faithfully,

(Miss) Josephine Barber

Late or Non-Delivery

- The Sale of Goods Act requires suppliers to deliver ordered goods 'within a reasonable time'. The period is rather arbitrary but any delivery taking longer than 28 days should be challenged. In the case above the supplier is definitely in breach of the Act.

- It is important that you act promptly and supply all the relevant order and delivery documentation.

- NB: If it is a damaged or faulty mail order item, the carriage for its return should also be paid by the supplier. Quite often they will send you a pre-paid postage label or arrange for a carrier to collect it.

26 Afton Way,
Banferrie,
Belfast

12 September

The Manager,
Mercury Motors Ltd,
Market Estate,
Lisburn
RU7 8HJ

Dear Sir,

On 30 August I purchased an Avant 1.9TDi 210SE red Audi from you. Within three days it developed a serious gear-change problem and severe squealing from the steering mechanism. It is obvious that the car was defective at the time of purchase.

Under the sales agreement you are clearly in breach of contract and bound to make whatever repairs or replacements as are necessary, free of charge. If these take longer than 24 hours I will require a courtesy car during the repair period.

I will call you tomorrow to arrange for the car to be restored to 100 per cent as new roadworthy condition. I reserve my rights under the amended Sale of Goods Act 1979.

Yours faithfully,

Michael Singer

Buying a Lemon

- Buying a lemon when acquiring a car is every driver's nightmare. Heaven forbid if you are caught up in an ill-starred transaction, but if you are, a blunt letter like the above should help put the calamity on a businesslike basis.

- Despite guarantees there is no guarantee that any amount of repair work and replacements will restore the machine to the car it should have been. That's why it's important always to reserve your rights under the amended Sale of Goods Act, which enables you to claim compensation if the repairs prove to be faulty or ineffectual.

56 Zurich Place,
Athelstone Park,
Tonbridge,
Kent TN3 6HY

Service Manager   13 October
Overway Motor Services Ltd
Dale St,
Tonbridge

Dear Sir,

On 5 October you serviced my Mercedes Estate 230SE, Reg. GKT 984. After driving it home I noticed the automatic steering was unusually stiff and the wheels very difficult to turn. When I asked my local garage what they thought was wrong they found that the steering fluid reservoir had been topped up with gear-box oil. This, they said, would severely damage many automatic steering components. It has rendered the car impossible to drive safely.

You have obviously failed to service my car to the standards required by the Supply of Goods and Services Act, under which I am entitled to compensation for breach of contract.

You can either undertake to repair and restore the car to its previous condition, or I will have it done elsewhere and send you the bill.

I await your prompt response.

Yours faithfully,

A. T. Michaels

Faulty Car Repairs and Servicing

- Next to buying a faulty car, faulty auto repairs produce a veritable *hors concours* of classic complaints. But you can seek protection under the Supply of Goods and Services Act 1982, which requires contracted work to be carried out with 'reasonable skill and care'.

- Most problems of this kind are dealt with in person or over the phone. But the writer probably forsees trouble ahead, hence the precautionary letter.

Duntree Cottage,
Fourbush Lane, Allandale
Notts NG7 4PR
19 September

Mr Peter Price-Williams,
Goulez & Spindler,
Financial Consultants,
Headway House,
Nottingham NG1 8BU

Dear Sir,

Biltmore Pension 96/665/GS2001

About three years ago (23/7/96) I asked you to recommend a pension plan suitable for my retirement at 60, on a monthly budget of £120. In the event you recommended that I transfer my current pension plan into a 20-year Biltmore Personal Insurance plan towards which I have been paying £113 per month.

My accountant has just analysed my current outlay with the expected return and finds that if I had stayed with my former plan I would enjoy the same or better pension benefits on retirement yet I would be paying only £72 per month. This means that I am needlessly paying nearly £10,000 more for my pension.
In recommending the above product you have given me bad advice which will leave me severely out of pocket. My accountant estimates my loss to be £9,456.00 over the 20-year period.

As you know, you are bound by the Financial Services Act 1986 to deal promptly with my complaint and offer appropriate compensation.

I expect your reply within 14 days and, if not forthcoming, I will forward my complaint to the relevant authorities.

Yours,

Bill Forbes

Bad Pension and Financial Advice

- Financial advisers aren't infallible, and it is always wise to get a second opinion. If you suspect that the advice you've been given has been over-optimistic or appears to involve you in loss, arrange to meet the adviser and ask for an explanation

- If not satisfied, write a letter demanding restitution, which, if your complaint is justified, should lead to negotiations for compensation. Your adviser is regulated by the Personal Investment Authority to whom you should apply if your complaint remains unresolved.

Jane Saunders,
45 Hay Farm Rd,
Cardling,
Bristol
BS8 2GJ

26 August

The Manager,
Consumer Bank Ltd,
114 Portside Street,
Bristol
BS1 4QP

Dear Sir,

Last month at your suggestion I transferred £600 from my current account into a 'Golden Key' 30-day account as it pays an extra 1 per cent interest.

On my first statement I note that you have charged me £16 for the transfer. No mention was made of this charge at the time, so I would like an explanation.

I also note that your monthly fee for July on my current account was increased from the usual £8 per month to £22, even though the account has always been in credit. Please explain this.

Yours,

Jane Saunders

Querying a Bank Statement

- It may seem laughable but many people go through life believing their bank to be infallible. Not so. Anyone who fails to examine their bank statements closely deserves to lose money from a bank account, not make it.

- In the recent years of intense competition, banks have introduced all kinds of charges, fees and penalties to maximise revenues, so beware.

- That cynical appraisal aside, banks are usually only too ready to put things right if a mistake has been made – but only if you complain.

12 Parkway Close,
Helmsdale,
Worcester
WR5 2KM

30 September

Mr Bert Jordan,
Jordan, Tanner & Co,
Apple Industrial Estate,
Mordern,
Worcs.

Dear Mr Jordan,
    I wish to complain about the extension and other work you carried out at my house at the above address during July.
    I am sorry to say that some of the work is of an unsatisfactory standard, which has led to serious defects in the walls (damp patches), the plumbing (leaking radiator) and floor (bad squeaking). A detailed list of these faults is attached.
    I must request that you rectify these faults as soon as possible as we cannot use the extension in its present condition.

Yours faithfully,

Edward Byrnes

Defective Building Work

- This letter underlines the importance of having a firm, detailed estimate, counter-signed by both parties, before work commences. This will be of enormous value should there be a dispute later.

- Payment arrangements should also be agreed at this time: how much up front, progress payments and, most important of all, the sum to be held over for a period (1–3 months is common) to ensure that the builder will make good any defects.

Apt 14F,
Juillard Mansions,
44 Tanner Rd,
Bexton,
York

12 June

Telford Construction Co,
Railway Yards,
23 Beatty Road,
York

Dear Mr Knight,

Thank you for the work you recently completed in our flat and also for keeping to the fairly demanding timetable. However, I was shocked to note that your final invoice for the work is almost £1,500 more than you quoted. I accept that you found more rot in the floors than you anticipated and had to instal a larger load-bearing beam, but you quoted a fixed price for the work and that constitutes our contract. Your quote made no mention of allowances for any extra work.

I therefore enclose my cheque for the balance of the original quoted amount.

Yours sincerely,

Alan G. Glover

Disputing a Builder's Bill

- A common situation: a builder, having quoted a fixed price without reservations, is involved in extra time or expense during the work. Not surprisingly, he tries to claw it back from the client. But for all the client knows, such contingencies could (and should) have been included in the quote anyway.

- So you are wise to resist such try-ons and unless you agreed during the progress of the work to pay extra amounts, pay only the sum set out in the original contract.

Witherdale,
Church Lane,
Myrecroft,
Peterborough
PE3 5AY

8 March

The Manager
Consumer Service Division,
SouthElec,
12 Oswald Way,
Peterborough.

Dear Sir/Madam,

Ref: A/c No. A8923/0049
    I wish to query my last two accounts for electricity used between 1 October and 28 February.
    The amounts shown on the invoices are higher than usual, despite this house being empty from 15 December to 28 January, when all power was shut off.
    It would seem that the meter is faulty, or there is an electricity leakage of some kind. Would you be good enough to have the meter tested so that the charges can be adjusted?

Thank you,

(Mrs) Tessa Bayliss

Querying Electricity, Gas, Water and Phone Bills

- If you think you are being overcharged or paying for electricity, gas, water or telephone services you haven't used, phone first to find out to whom in the company you should complain, then write.

- If you have a suspected faulty meter, you may be required to pay for a test, usually refunded if the meter is proved to be defective. If it is, you can have your bill reduced or compensation paid. For all the utility services there are scales of compensation payments made for interrupted supply. If the company is tardy in dealing with your complaint, your nearest Citizens' Advice Bureau will point you in the direction of the appropriate watchdog.

42A Roper Road,
Folly Lake Estate,
Newport
NP12 5AR

15 August

Credit Manager,
Newmarket Securities Ltd,
Field House,
Newport

Dear Sir/Madam,

On 2 July last year I purchased an Escoma 75 Multimedia Computer (Invoice DX23-7561; Credit Agreement NS/DX 7561–96934) on a hire-purchase agreement with Newmarket Securities Ltd from Computer Supermarket, Wharf St, Newport.

Since then the computer has developed serious faults which, despite several service calls, have not or cannot be rectified. The machine does not function as it should, and I now wish to return it and have all my instalments refunded in full, a total to date of £456 plus service charges of £72.45. I give notice that no further instalments will be paid.

I understand that my rights in this matter are protected by the 1973 Supply of Goods (Implied Terms) Act, under which I terminate my hire-purchase agreement with you on the grounds stated above.

Yours faithfully,

Harold Shields

Terminating a Hire-Purchase Agreement

- Getting goods replaced or your money back from a finance or hire-purchase company can be a messy business. However you are protected from faulty or misdescribed goods by the Supply of Goods (Implied Terms) Act 1973.

- Remember that when you buy something on a hire-purchase agreement, your contract passes from the seller to the finance or lending company.

---

22 Wakefield Drive,
Hazel Park,
Lawen,
Glasgow
G17 6TN

14 December

The Manager,
Hilltower Building Society,
Suchard St,
Glasgow
G1 3AX

Dear Sir,

Account 0214572

I note from my latest statement (Sheet 223) that the monthly Direct Debit payment to Marlborough Technics has increased from £21.80 to £23.

I authorised no such increase and therefore request that (1) you supply an explanation for the change and (2) reinstate the monthly payment to £21.80.

Yours sincerely,

James Speakman

Direct Debits and Standing Orders

- This letter will get a result but unfortunately not the one the writer might expect. Perhaps the writer thought he'd arranged to pay the monthly amount by standing order, an arrangement by which the account holder instructs the bank to pay a certain amount at specific intervals. Only the account holder can alter this arrangement.

- With a direct debit, however, the account holder makes an agreement with the payee and authorises the bank to pay those amounts requested by the payee. As you can see, the payee may vary these amounts without seeking permission from the account holder.

- If the DD agreement is abused, however, the account holder can claim reimbursement from the bank.

12 Abbott Lane,
Purcell Park,
Perth
PH2 6TG

18 March

Sales Manager,
Trent Glazing Services,
146 Main Terrace,
Perth PH1 7CM

Dear Sir/Madam,

Two days ago, on 16 March, I signed a contract for your firm to double-glaze four windows of my house for a sum of £1,230. Since then I have decided that I do not want the work done and wish to cancel the contract.

I was originally called by your firm and told that my house qualified as a 'show home' in this district and that half the work would be done free. When I agreed to discuss this, I did not realise a salesman would call. As a result I found myself signing a contract for work costing the same as it would have with any other firm. This was not what was originally discussed.

This letter is a formal notice to cancel the contract I signed within the 7-day cooling-off period provided by the Consumer Protection (Cancellation of Contracts Concluded away from Business Premises) Regulations 1987. Accordingly, I request the prompt return of the £230 deposit I paid.

Yours faithfully,

(Mrs) Mona Anderson

Cancelling a 'Signed-at-Home' Contract

- The provisions of the 1987 Consumer Protection Regulations has saved tens of thousands of householders kissing goodbye to money committed by contract in a moment of weakness or under pressure from salesmen.

- To qualify for this protection, however, you must not have invited the salesman to your home. In the case above the householder did not realise that she had agreed to have a salesman call and should therefore benefit from the 7-day cooling-off period.

- Be sure to send the letter by Recorded Mail with Proof of Delivery.

76 Egerton Street,
Tranmore,
Telford
TF5 8RR

23 August

Hilton Credit & Investment Ltd,
Harboard House,
Brass Street,
Birmingham,
B16 3ER

Dear Sirs,

Account HCI/247/E880B

On 16 March 1998 I signed the above hire purchase agreement to help me purchase a camper van. Since then I have met the monthly payments of £196.50 on time and expected to do so for the remainder of the three-year agreement.

Unfortunately, owing to an unforseen financial problem and my wife being declared redundant last week, I will be unable to meet the repayments in full, at least for the time being. I must stress that I have no intention of defaulting on the debt but I must ask you to consider reducing the monthly amounts over a longer repayment period.

I sincerely hope you will consider this request favourably and look forward to discussing revised terms with you.

Yours faithfully,

Andrew Wyatt-Smith

Please Sirs, I Can't Pay . . .

- Although credit companies prefer clients to pay their hire-purchase commitments in full and on time, they also welcome honesty from debtors who find that they can't keep up payments. If you're caught in a payment trap, be cooperative and make whatever offer you can reasonably afford.

79 Ivorsen Crescent,
Renfree Park,
Blackpool
FY5 8BK

4 January

Claims Division,
Century Insurance Co,
Chronicle Buildings,
Gate St,
Manchester
M2 4BW

Dear Sirs,

Policy No. CI/10041/C887C

I refer you to our previous correspondence regarding my claim on the above policy. In your latest letter you advise that your offer of £3,400 will not be increased, despite my submitting to you an independent loss assessor's estimate of £4,850 for the damage.

Unless I receive a more realistic offer from you within 14 days I regret to advise that our correspondence will be forwarded to the Insurance Ombudsman Bureau, of which you are a signatory, for arbitration.

Yours faithfully,

Guy Robertson, MD

Disputed Insurance Claim: the Last Resort

- There are occasions when an insurance company and a policy holder fail to see eye to eye. If you feel the company's offer (or perhaps non-offer if it argues that damage or loss is not covered by a policy) isn't fair you can pay for an independent assessment, which may help your case.

- If not, you can, as a last resort, appeal to the Insurance Ombudsman Bureau in London. This won't help you, though, if your insurer isn't a signatory to the scheme, so it pays to check on this before you sign any insurance policy.

24 Virginia Street,
Motherwell
ML15 4DV

19 December

Mr Derek N Baines,
42 Chalker Avenue,
Motherwell
ML8 5GB

Dear Mr Baines,

Re: Accident on North Parade

On November 12 an accident on North Parade involving your Ford van G25 RSB resulted in considerable damage to my Volvo Estate P24 GBM.

I have claimed for the damage covered by my comprehensive insurance policy but this still leaves me liable for £640 not covered by the policy, namely for the insurance excess amount, loss of no-claim bonus, a day off work and transport incurred while the car was being repaired.

You have admitted that the accident was caused solely by your negligence and so far I have heard nothing from you or your insurers.

As you are legally responsible for the £640 I look forward to receiving this amount. If I do not receive it within 14 days a county court summons will be issued against you.

Yours faithfully,

Arthur Ableman

Claiming Uninsured Expenses from a Negligent Driver

- Claiming on car insurance policies is a complex business, mostly achieved by a plethora of form-filling. But there often remains the even more complex business of claiming compensation for uninsured expenses from a negligent driver or the driver's insurance company (if he or she is comprehensively covered).

- This can require considerable patience and persuasion, and you may well be driven to recover your loss through a small claims court.

14 October

Mr Bertram Clifford,
Wrangle, Tryon & Clifford,
Solicitors,
22 Beecham Chambers,
Old Road,
Belfast
BT6 5JK

Dear Mr Clifford,

Your Ref: 98/Best vs Gruner/078002

While I appreciate your firm's work on my behalf in the above action I feel bound to question your charges as shown on your invoice of 7/10/98.

While I fully understand that estimates for legal work can never be precise, your final account is almost double the £ 2,020 estimate you gave me on 16/6/98.

Would you please supply me with a detailed itemisation of the charges?

Yours sincerely,

Anthony G Best

Querying a Solicitor's Bill

- This firm of solicitors is bound by the Solicitors Act 1974 (Section 64) to supply the information requested.

- Complaints about alleged overcharging by legal firms is common enough although in many cases unjustified. Nevertheless it pays to query charges for legal work and also for what you feel is incompetent work and undue delay. If you fail to get satisfaction you have recourse to a battery of complaint and reassessment bodies, beginning with the Law Society.

Avery Crombie & Partners, Architects,
Broadman Place,
Carlisle CA2 3TU

18 February

Mr Gene McIvor,
Ackerman Publishing Ltd,
27 Parkway,
Dundee DD5 4NN

Dear Mr McIvor,

It has come to our notice that in the December issue of your newsletter *Fabrication & Construction Calendar*, in an article entitled 'Architects on the Take', you referred to this firm as 'one of the most rapacious in the northern architectural community' and that 'Avery Crombie & Partners benefited from a non-returnable fee arrangement to the tune of over £150,000'.

Both statements are untrue and completely without foundation, libellous and seriously damaging to the reputation of this firm, to its profitability and to the livelihoods of its employees.

We therefore request that you immediately send to our solicitors, Lawnside & Partners, a letter of retraction to be approved by them and to be published in the five leading fabrication and construction trade journals at your expense and to be published prominently in the next issue of your Newsletter.

The alternative is swift and unconditional legal action to retrieve our good reputation and to seek substantial damages.

Yours faithfully,

David P. Crombie
Managing Director

Threatening Legal Action

- Letters containing the threat of legal action for non-compliance must be just that: threatening, unequivocal, and with clear demands. The reader must be left in no doubt that you mean business and mentioning the name of your lawyers will help give sharp legal teeth to your threat. Remember: this is a once-only or final shot that might save you from entering the potentially expensive portals of the law courts.

27 Sandy Lane,
Towbridge,
Kent TN1 2CD

22 July

Mr Paul Madeson,
Green Landscapes
Robinia Lane, Letram,
Kent
TN10 4RF

Dear Sir,

I have received your letter of 15 July threatening me with legal action for non-payment of your invoice for £142.50.

As I have already stated (my letter of June 30), I deducted that amount from your original invoice for landscaping because (a) untreated timber in the pergola had to be replaced and (b) I had to pay an extra £50 in labour costs for the reconstruction. The amount deducted was entirely due to your negligence.

There is no question of my paying the £142.50. However, to bring this matter to a close and without prejudice, I will offer you a final payment of £50. If this is not acceptable to you, please address all future correspondence to my solicitor, Miss J Barnes, 78 Horsefield Rd, Tonbridge TN2 8BC.

Yours faithfully,

John P. Rutger

Avoiding Legal Action

- Whatever the merits of your case, it is always worthwhile (and usually cheaper in the end) to avoid legal proceedings. Winning in the courts is no guarantee of winning financially as costs can be awarded against both sides.

- If reasoning fails, bury your pride and consider making a compromise offer.

- To protect your right to withdraw or change your offer, insert the words 'without prejudice' which helps to keep your legal options open.

- Directing future correspondence to a solicitor is usually an effective ploy to make your correspondent think twice about taking legal action.

5 March

Mr Harold Woolfson,
MP for Upper Craddock,
House of Commons,
Parliament Square,
London SW1

Dear Mr Woolfson,

As one of your constituents (and supporters) I hope you can help in the following matter.

Last December it was learned that funding for the Special Needs Department of Lambert Comprehensive School was to be frozen at the 1997 level despite a 40 per cent increase in students requiring special educational needs help. Although normally funding is the responsibility of the East Sussex Education Department it seems to have no control over the situation.

As the chairwoman of an ad hoc committee of concerned parents I have been unsuccessful, despite three months of trying, in identifying which government department is responsible for effectively cutting the funding for a vital educational service.

Copies of all correspondence is attached, and I would appreciate it if you could help us understand what is going on and whom to approach to correct this absurd situation.

Yours faithfully,

Emma Clarkson

Writing to a Member of Parliament

- Your Member of Parliament is a kind of court of last resort so it is expected that you will have exhausted every avenue before approaching him or her.

- Keep your submission short and to the point, and attach copies of relevant documents. It saves time if you are sure of your facts. Try to make clear what it is you want your MP to do.

- An MP may not be able, or in the position, to change the course of history but most will do what they can to help; their jobs, after all, depend upon people like you.

Staying Alive: Employer and Employee

Work is accomplished by those employees who have not yet reached their level of incompetence.

The Peter Principle

In the workplace, employer and employee face a two-way trial. When a job advertisement appears these days, the odds are that it will attract dozens, sometimes hundreds, of applications. The employer (or the personnel manager) then faces the task of sifting through the mass of paper trying to pick a winner. The would-be employee, on the other hand, is an entrant in a race that is not necessarily won by the swift but more often by ingenuity and guile.

For the employer, knowing what he or she wants makes the task easier. The wise employer will advertise a precise job description and all applications will be compared to that. People who seem closest to the ideal will be ahead in the race.

If you're an applicant whose qualifications, experience and personal profile fit the job description you're in there with a chance. You might be among the final half-dozen, but there is only one vacancy. So what are the factors – the 'special extras' – that will provide that surge to get you to the finishing line first?

At the interview stage there is a good chance that, of several equally qualified finalists, the applicant with a pleasant appearance, exuding self-confidence and a winning charm is most likely to get the job. But less presentable applicants can do quite a lot about more subtle presentational skills, such as writing enviably clear, persuasive, attention-getting letters. In short, expressing and enhancing their personalities through the written word. Qualities such as enthusiasm, clarity of thought, confidence and know-how can all be conveyed to a reader by a well-written letter.

Enlightened employers know how fewer and fewer recruits can communicate well. Perhaps illiteracy has been largely overcome, but semi-literacy is all around us. So be assured that good speakers and skilled writers will always be in demand.

If you are a jobseeker, this section will try to help you develop some basic writing skills that should help you get a job, and keep it. The section also includes tips on preparing and presenting a CV (or curriculum vitae – your resumé of education, professional or vocational training and work experience).

Getting that Job – Some Preliminaries

Before starting on your written application, find out as much as you can about the firm or organisation, and its business. Ask for any brochures they may have. A knowledgeable applicant will win hands down over one who has no idea what the employer actually does.

Don't waste your time, or the employer's, by responding to an advertisement for a job if it requires qualifications you don't really have.

Send your CV with a covering letter explaining why you think you are suitable for the job and state where you saw the job advertised. It is customary to offer references, although not to enclose them with your initial application.

Ask to be considered for an interview.

Don't make claims that won't stand up. By all means emphasise your strong points, especially those relevant to the job, but don't lie. Don't claim extensive experience if your lack of it will soon become embarrassingly apparent. If you do lack experience, emphasise your enthusiasm, adaptability and willingness to learn.

Before dispatching your application, check it thoroughly – several times – for neatness and correctness. This applies particularly if you are communicating by e-mail, when the speed of the process and the need to go nowhere near a letter box can create the temptation to be over-hasty. Make sure there are no spelling errors, especially in the firm's or organisation's name: these can make many employers grind their teeth and toss your application on the reject pile. Keep copies of your covering letter and CV.

Your application may not be a response to an advertised job but a letter inquiring if there is a vacancy. In this case, make sure your covering letter is addressed to the right person, by name or title or both. If in doubt, call the firm's switchboard. Emphasise your willingness to be interviewed and that you are prepared to wait until an appropriate job does become vacant. Enclose your CV and ask if it can be filed to await a vacancy.

Be specific about your training, qualifications and work experience. A 'course in cookery' could mean anything to a hotel wanting a trainee chef; a 'Master Chef's Federation Catering Certificate' could attract serious attention. Don't claim to have 'worked for several electrical contractors': name them and also say when they employed you.

32 Woodlands Road
Aberdeen AB8 9DT

16 February

Personnel Manager
Bush Paper Products Ltd,
Saxon Industrial Estate,
Aberdeen AB3 7UU

Dear Sir,
I am responding to your advertisement in the 13 February edition of
the 'Sunday Post' for a Technical Support Manager.

The position is just what I have been looking for, and from the job
description I am sure I have the requisite training and experience.
My CV is attached.

Although I am happy and reasonably well paid in my present job,
there are few opportunities for advancement. I have studied at night
for an Grade 2 Supervisor's Diploma and now feel I am ready for a
fresh challenge.

I am aware that your company is highly innovative and growing,
and I am sure I can play a part in its future success.

I live locally, am happily married with two children and
genuinely see my future in the paper products industry.

I look forward to hearing from you and can make myself available
for interview any day except Fridays.

Yours faithfully,

Richard McCormick

Applying for an Advertised Job

- This would be regarded as an intelligent covering letter for a CV. Without
  frills, it projects ambition, enthusiasm, conscientiousness and stability –
  presumably the qualities in a job applicant every employer is looking for.

- If you think it helps, a brief paragraph about your family status (stability) and
  interest in the employer's industry (devotion) can be included, as above.

- Always explain why you wish to leave your present job.

25 Regent Terrace,
Plymouth,
Devon
PL8 4GH

22 July

The Personnel Manager,
Balcombe Industries Ltd,
Maybank Road,
Torquay
TQ2 9JR

Dear Sir,

I am writing to inquire whether there are any openings in your company for a Packaging Materials Technical Officer, either now or in the near future.

At present I am employed as a Technical Trainee at a packaging materials firm but feel that my training and experience now qualify me for advancement opportunities not available from my present employer.

My CV is attached, and you will see that I have spent the past six years on materials courses and training seminars.

I now feel I am ready for a position of greater responsibility with opportunities for growth which I hope might be available at Balcombe Industries.

I look forward to a favourable reply and can make myself available for interview at almost any time.

Yours faithfully,

Simon Masters

Inquiring about Job Opportunities

- The big hurdle facing a letter like this is simply that there may be no immediate job prospects at all. But there may be in the future – and there is always the chance that your letter might be filed and referred to if that happy situation should come about.

- Keep your letter short, snappy and, above all, optimistic. Try to convey an impression of a person who is well qualified, hard-working and eager to face the challenge of a new and more rewarding job.

7 Park Road,
Great Melton,
Norfolk NR 23 7ST
14 January

Mr Brian Haydon,
Managing Director,
Haydon & Bright Opticians,
High St,
Norwich NR1 6TD.

Dear Mr Haydon,

I understand there may be a vacancy in your firm for an experienced optical assistant.

I have spent 12 years working as an optometrist's assistant, both in the front of the shop and in optical labs. I also have extensive experience in dealing with the public and their optical problems and hold an optometrist's testing certificate. The attached CV gives a detailed account of my qualifications and experience.

Although I have not worked full-time for nearly nine years (raising my family of three girls) I have tons of energy and enthusiasm.

I also think I can prove I am conscientious and reliable and I get on famously with people whether they are colleagues or customers.

I look forward to hearing from you soon.

Yours sincerely,

Janet Macpherson

Rejoining the Work Force

- For complex and obscure reasons many employers are biased against people who are over 40, declared redundant or otherwise out of work. Perhaps they're thought to be losers. On the contrary, most are industrious and enterprising, and undeserving of their plight.

- So your letter must defuse this latent hostility by painting a picture of an employee bubbling with the energy and enthusiasm of youth but with the wisdom and experience of maturity.

12 Upper Town Street,
Luton
LU23 7GN

31 August

Mrs Belinda Penney
Personnel Department,
Cross Department Stores Ltd,
Draper Rd,
Luton
LU4 4RD

Dear Mrs Penney,
Thank you for your letter inviting me for an interview for the
position of Systems Analyst at your Luton head office.
    I am pleased to confirm that I am available for the interview at
10 am on Tuesday 8 September.
    I look forward to meeting you then.

Yours sincerely,

Sarah Addison

Confirming an Interview

- If you get as far as being offered an interview, don't assume it's all over. It's not. You may be the only candidate, or you may have a dozen or more rivals. That's why it's worthwhile making a good impression when accepting or confirming your interview.

- Make it crisp and businesslike and perhaps just a touch – but just a touch – grateful.

18 April

Mr George Bashford,
General Manager,
Cranbrook Hilton Hotel

Dear Mr Bashford,

I would like to ask for a review of my salary which, as you know, has remained unchanged during the three years I have worked as Booking Manager of the hotel.

In that time I believe I have worked hard and competently.

My range of duties has also grown: on Mondays and Tuesdays I have the extra responsibilities of the switchboard and opening the cocktail bar in the afternoons and I often fill in for absent staff at weekends. I believe you have never heard a complaint against me and after three years here I am now an experienced and more efficient employee.

However, none of the above has been rewarded even although our room occupancy rate has increased by 18 per cent in that time.

I hope you will recognise my worth to the hotel with an appropriate increase in my salary.

Yours sincerely,

Harry Adams, Front Desk

Asking for a Salary Increase

- It shouldn't happen of course, but it does: many employers don't grant salary increases unless they're really pressed. If you find yourself in the position of a salary supplicant, here are some points that may help your case:

- Stress the length of time your salary has remained static.

- List any extra responsibilities you've taken on in that time.

- Point out that in that time you've gained the experience which has made you more efficient and productive at your job.

- If your employer is doing well in terms of sales or profit, point out that you, as an employee, helped contribute to that and should be rewarded.

30 June

Mr David Black,
Chief Executive,
Forward & Thomas Engineering plc,
Oldham

Dear David,

I regret to tell you that I have decided to resign from my present position of Senior Designer in the Fabrication Unit. I wish to leave at the end of July and therefore give you the four weeks' notice as required by the terms of my contract.

Although I am accepting a position with one of our competitors I have genuinely enjoyed my six years working with you and hope I've given the company as much as it's given me in experience and creative satisfaction. However, the new position gives me a wider range of responsibilities with appropriate financial rewards and I simply could not pass up the opportunity.

Thank you for your past support and a friendship that I hope will endure beyond this parting of the ways.

Yours sincerely,

Simon Felstead

Tendering Your Resignation

- Unless the circumstances leading to your decision to quit are acrimonious, don't burn any bridges. Often a polite and sincerely felt letter of resignation will make management think again, perhaps leading to your reappointment on much more favourable terms.

- If you've enjoyed working for the company, say so. You might also refer to your reasons for leaving. And if your departure leaves the company in the lurch, an offer to train a replacement will go down well.

- Retaining goodwill keeps the door open for the possibility of returning to the firm in the future and also helps when you ask for a reference.

14 Flanagan Drive,
Hopetown Park,
Hull
HU5 2TG

March 20

Rev Walter McDonnell,
The Rectory,
Hopetown Parade,
Hull HU5 9SX

Dear Rev. McDonnell,

I am applying for the position of deputy retail manager at Carson's Electrical Stores in Hull and wonder if you would be kind enough to supply me with a reference.

Although I am not a regular churchgoer, I am one of your parishioners and we have met on several occasions at social events.

I enclose my CV for your reference so you will see that I am a hard-working father and that I have worked on several community projects. The new job means a lot to me, especially the higher pay, as I have been very hard-pressed financially during the past few years.

Yours sincerely,

Trevor Evans

Asking for a Reference

- Employers and recruitment professionals are generally agreed on the importance of references, which can act as a kind of 'proof of existence' for the candidate's virtues. A job application accompanied by several references will usually be taken seriously.

- If asking for a reference, give the referee some guidance on what should be stressed. In the above example the writer has enclosed his CV which gives the referee some meat to work on.

Stein Electronics Pty Ltd,
Border Leas,
Chelmsford,
Essex CM2 7AY

Executive Offices

12 May

TO WHOM IT MAY CONCERN

I have known Miss Joanna Patrick for six years, since she came to work for Stein Electronics, Chelmsford, in April 1992, as personal assistant to the sales director.

During this time she has been an enthusiastic, supportive and hard-working executive – the complete professional. Her personal contribution to this company has been considerable, and she will be missed both as a valued colleague and friend.

Any organisation fortunate enough to recruit Joanna will find her a highly intelligent, fast-thinking, loyal and devoted employee. Joanna is energetic and ambitious and intends to widen her experience in electronics sales, and she leaves with our best wishes.

Sincerely,

Jeremy Woodstock, Executive Chairman

Writing a Reference or Testimonial

- Most references are coded; enthusiasms tend to be muted, flaws are glossed over and weaknesses of character are expressed in the best light. So if you really want to praise someone you have to break the mould to try to ensure that your reference is read as sincere and truthful.

- Rather than write a potentially damaging though truthful reference – which could result in a libel action – make an excuse and leave the testimonial writing to others.

Selling Yourself: Creating a Persuasive CV

Avoid what we call a 'Carmen Miranda' CV – like the words of her famous song it has too much 'I, I, I, I'. . .

Recruitment Consultant

Most people would find it extremely difficult to tell his or her life story to a complete stranger. To tell it on paper could prove to be even more difficult. So it isn't surprising that many jobseekers respond to ads in the recruitment columns of newspapers and to websites on the Internet and turn to professional writing services to create their CVs. Even then, results can be uncertain and sometimes a waste of time and money.

Yet you can write an effective curriculum vitae by following some simple rules.

First, **presentation**. A CV should be well laid out, attractive to the eye; typed or prepared on a word processor using either a 12pt or 14pt typeface; and preferably not more than two pages long. Good quality paper can help to give a good initial impression. You'll probably need a dozen or so clean, clear copies.

Second, **stick to the facts**. Divide the CV into essential sections: **personal details**, **education and training**, **employment and career**, **professional profile**, **useful talents** and **attributes**. The order of these sections is a matter of taste. Some prefer personal details (name, age, address, marital status, etc) at the beginning of a CV; others at the end. However, your employment record – the jobs you've held, right up to your present one – is of most interest to an employer and should command pride of position. Including the names and contact addresses or telephone numbers of referees is optional but you should certainly say that references can be supplied on request if you have them.

Personal Details:
Full name, address, phone number.

Employment and Career:
Lead off with details of your present or most recent job. If you have had several jobs over a period of years, give more details about the most recent, less information about your earlier employment. Supply start and end dates of each of your jobs. Keep the summaries brief: name of employer, location, type of work involved, and possibly the reason you moved on.

Education and Training:
Include brief details of secondary education, names of schools, colleges, dates of attendence, exam passes from GCSE/Standard Grade upwards, any special merits. Add to this details of any university courses or degrees, and any other qualifications – for example, business school courses, technical or vocational training, etc.

Personal and Professional Profile:
While your employment record and educational qualifications provide an objective summary of your current status as a jobseeker, a prospective employer also needs to have an analysis of your personality and skills. If you believe yourself to be pleasant, optimistic, competitive and cooperative with good communication abilities, then say so. Are you recognised as a good team worker? A leader? Are you creative and outgoing, or do you possess a quieter, more analytical nature? If you think certain qualities are relevant to the job you're applying for, stick them in. Then outline the skills you've learned during your work experience – flesh out your job descriptions with instances of specific attainments, workplace innovations, sales records, management commendations and so on.

Other Attributes:
Here you could list such lifestyle bonuses as having a clean driving licence, fluency in a foreign language, computer proficiency, etc.

Other Personal Details:
List your age and birth date, nationality, marital status and number of children, state of health and, if you really must, personal interests, preferably intellectual (chess); cultural (choir singing); sport (rugby referee, golf); relaxation (gardening). Don't say you're a theatregoer even if you are – everybody does.

Try to cover all this in two pages if you can. If you can't, revise; deciding what to leave out can be as important as what you put in. Check and double-check for spelling errors and grammatical gaffes. Don't make moral judgments about yourself; passages such as 'I am kind and considerate with an unblemished record of honesty' are out. Don't lie: you'll eventually be rumbled. Don't belittle previous employers or reveal confidential information such as sales figures and production plans. E-mailing or faxing your job application and CV as well as mailing them can help you get noticed.

Remember that you are marketing *you*. You're both salesperson and product. You have an intimate knowledge of the product and how good it is. Now get out there and sell yourself!

Marianne Jane Craig
42 Nettlehome Drive, Curnow Park,
Bournemough BH8 5TG
01202 566 876

CURRICULUM VITAE

Employment:
- March 1996 to present:
  Sales Director, Floor Coverings Division, Viscose Corporation, London.
  Responsible for national sales team of 16 reps and overseas agents in 22 countries.
- January 1992–March 1996: Sales Manager, Heritage Furnishings, Leeds.
  Responsible for national sales of all company products; led sales team of 7.
- April 1991–January 1992: Senior Sales Representative, Heritage Furnishings.
- May 1990–April 1991: Sales Representative, Heritage Furnishings.
- September 1988–May 1990: Sales Trainee, Optimum Fabrics Ltd, Manchester.

Education:
St Stephen's College, Manchester 1979–86; 8 O-levels; 2 A-levels (History B;
English B)
Manchester Union Art College 1986–88; Design Diploma; Fabric Design Certificate.

Career Profile:
My interest in design and fabrics led me into the furnishings trade where, because
of my technical and art training, I was offered a trainee sales position. From that
point my career has grown to the point where I am now responsible for national
and international sales of a range of innovative floor coverings (sales in 1997
£31.6m); building the brands; marketing strategy and advertising agency liaison
(three accounts billing £2.8m) – all figures on trade record. I now believe my
experience and success have prepared me for a broader-based executive sales
position, preferably with an international home products company.

Personal Profile:
I have always been regarded as a good team worker, which I believe has helped
me to lead and inspire sales teams. I enjoy my work, and it never worries me that I
put in many extra hours a week of my own time. I am computer literate and write
and design most of the company's sales literature. I am quite competitive and have
won several sales awards during my career.

Other:
I have a clean driver's licence. I have no problem relocating either in the UK or
overseas. I am at present halfway through a part-time MBA course with the Open
University.

Personal:
Age 31. Born 16/10/1967
British nationality
Formerly married six years; now divorced; one five-year old child (girl)
Health excellent
Interests: tennis, patio gardening

Documentation:
Full sales history and detailed responsibilities can be supplied on request.
References available on request.

That's a fairly straightforward CV, with lots to shout about and nothing to hide. It portrays a bright and talented young woman who'd be an asset to any sales-oriented company, and she shouldn't have to wait too long before she's snapped up.

But not everyone is so fortunate. Let's take a young man whose CV, if it's to be an honest document, has to reflect some knocks: a period of illness, say, another of unemployment, and an incomplete education. The challenge here is, in the words of the popular song, to 'accentuate the positive' while not completely 'eliminating the negative'. See how it looks.

Charles Timothy Renwick
23A Vaucluse Road,
Portergate, Slough SL5 7JK

CURRICULUM VITAE

October 1995–March 1999. ASSISTANT PRODUCTION MANAGER
Rickard & Packer Industrial Lithographers, Slough. Supervised work-flow through 4 AB Mann 6-colour units, plus folders, binding, finishing, packing, store and despatch. Was due to be made Production Manager (have reference to this effect) but because of lack of orders two units were closed down and I was made redundant.

September 1992–October 1997. DEPUTY PRODUCTION MANAGER
Clayburn & Son, Book Printers, Reading. Responsible for all book throughput and quality control, binding, finishing and dispatch. Volume ranged from 2m to 2.7 million units per month. Was offered temporary Assistant Production Manager position at Rickard & Packer, and promised Production Manager position there at end of 1998.

February 1991–September 1992. DEPUTY MANAGER, BINDERY
Clayburn & Son, Book Printers, Reading. Took over from former Deputy Manager who was promoted. This gave me almost two years valuable experience in case-binding and paperbacking techniques. Responsible for maintenance and staff of 23.

April 1990–February 1991. GENERAL ASSISTANT, BINDERY
Clayburn & Son, Book Printers, Reading. Relocated to Reading. Although could not get a job in line with my printing trade skills I was keen to add bookbinding to my work experience.

December 1989–March 1990. CLEANER
Southern Printers Pty Ltd, Southampton. Best job I could get after my illness but it did keep me in touch with the printing trade.

From March to December 1989 I suffered from a severe back injury sustained during my employment with Industrial Packaging. In this time I was unable to work but managed to complete a home study course on Computer Data Processing.

September 1985 - December 1989. STORE CLERK
Industrial Packaging Printers Ltd, Southampton. Moved to Southampton to improve employment prospects but the store job was the best offering. Printing trade generally very depressed. During July 1984 to September 1985 I was unemployed, apart from some part-time work on local farms. I completed a one-year night course on Computing at Maidstone Technical College.

September 1980–July 1984. LEADING HAND LITHO PRINTER
Otway Greeting Cards Ltd, Maidstone, Kent. Responsible for pre-prep and running of Butler colour web press. Won commendation and bonus for increasing volume 20% two years running. Firm was taken over by Hanways in 1984 and all operations moved to Bristol. Was made redundant.

January 1980–September 1980. LITHO PRESS TRAINEE
Otway Greeting Cards Ltd, Maidstone, Kent.

EDUCATION
Paddock Wood Comprehensive 1972–78, 2 O-levels. 1978–1980 Youth Training Centre, Maidstone, General Printing Course Certificate. Vocational Training, Maidstone Technical College, Lithographic Press Operator Proficiency Diploma.

PERSONAL AND CAREER PROFILE
I am an optimistic person, enjoy working hard, and am motivated to improve myself. I am particularly interested in printing and new printing technology including digital processes. I have moved three times in order to stay in the trade which is where I believe my future lies. I now have the knowledge, experience and maturity to enable me to take on management responsibilities in all phases of print production.

PERSONAL DETAILS
Age: 36. Born January 13, 1962.
Married 1984; four children, aged 13, 11, 8, 5.
Health: Good. Wear supportive brace for back injury.
Nationality: British
Clean driving licence; Commercial Vehicle licence.
Personal Interests: Coach Slough Central High football team; fly fishing.

Mr Renwick's CV plainly states the bald truth that during his working life he's had six months off work through injury and a spell of unemployment lasting over a year. And, having recently been made redundant, he's out of work now.

But despite what might be considered by some employers as drawbacks, the CV manages to depict Mr Renwick as a conscientious worker determined to make good in his chosen field, the printing industry. It demonstrates how he used his time off work usefully by undertaking computer courses and how he overcame employment setbacks by moving to where work for a printer was available. And, if you follow the ups and downs of his career, there is a steady upward line of progress from trainee to middle management. A thoughtful employer, reading the CV carefully, could hardly fail to be impressed by the qualities of this perhaps unspectacular, but industrious artisan.

Could a real-life Charles Renwick write such a document? Why not? If you analyse the CV it is really nothing more than a collection of facts – employers, job descriptions, dates, educational and personal details, arranged in logical order and presented so that it is easy to read and absorb.

Anyone can do it – and, if ever the need presents itself – so can you.

Getting It and Keeping It: Money Matters

That money talks, I'll not deny, I heard it once: it said 'Goodbye'.

Richard Armour

Previous sections have touched on money matters (chasing a loan, page 526; querying a bank statement, page 540; terminating a hire-purchase agreement, page 544; pleading inability to pay, page 547, etc) but here we'll take a closer look at how the stuff that dominates our lives can be made, lost and kept with the help of the written word.

Losing it is distressingly easy. Losing it when it isn't your fault is just plain distressing. Unless you're a hermit it's almost impossible these days to live without a favourable credit rating, and gathering and supplying information about a citizen's creditworthiness is a huge business. Naturally, they can get it wrong, and every day several thousand people suddenly have the feeling that they're walking around with a big sign over their heads saying: 'Won't Pay, Don't Lend', even though they've never reneged on a debt in their lives. The salesperson who's about to wrap up your purchase makes a phone call and shakes her head. The bank manager's frostiness matches the glass panels of his office. The word is out: you're a financial pariah.

If this Kafkaesque situation ever happens to you, start writing. First, to whoever refused your application for credit – whether a store, credit card organisation, bank or hire-purchase company – requesting to be told the specific reason for being turned down.

No organisation offering credit need give any reasons for refusing credit, but you do have some protection under the Consumer Credit Act 1974 (Sections 157–160) if they have based the refusal on information supplied by a credit reference agency, which it commonly is. Your letter might look like this:

27 Mount Street
Leeds
LS10 2AH

14 December

The Manager,
Credit Control Office,
Sanders, Sachs Finance Co Ltd,
London
E1 5BD

Dear Sir/Madam,

Yesterday my application to buy a 28-inch colour TV from Mason's Electronics through a two-year hire-purchase agreement with your firm was refused.

I would like to know the reason for the refusal because I have no unpaid debts and my current bank account is in credit.

If the refusal is related in any way to information supplied by a credit reference agency, you are bound by the Consumer Credit Act 1974 to advise me of the name of that agency in order that the information may be checked.

I would appreciate your prompt cooperation in this and look forward to hearing from you.

Yours faithfully,

Arnold L Travers

Credit Refusal

- A letter like that, providing it is delivered within 28 days of the refusal, is the first step in banishing the bête noire of uncreditworthiness.

- The urgency is quite real, because even the fact that you were refused a hire-purchase loan (perhaps based on misinformation) can finish up as a blot on your credit record.

- The second step is to write to the agency concerned to request a copy of the file they keep of your your credit record:

27 Mount Street
Leeds
LS10 2AH

20 December

The Manager,
Credit Report Services Ltd,
Bishopsgate,
London
E2 4RF

Dear Sir/Madam,

On December 13 I was refused credit through a hire-purchase agreement by Sanders, Sachs Finance Co Ltd. They have informed me, as required by the Consumer Credit Act 1974, that their refusal was based on credit information about me that was supplied by you.

As there is nothing in my financial history that could warrant such a refusal I believe your records are wrong, and under the terms of the above Act I request a copy of my complete credit file, held by you, without delay.

If any charges are involved please let me know.

Yours faithfully,

Arnold L Travers

Requesting Your Credit History

- Under the Consumer Credit Act 1974, credit reference and investigation agencies are required to give you all the information about you that they have on file. If this information is incorrect you can take steps to have it withdrawn or revised. With your credit rating restored there will be thousands of lenders out there only too willing to give you money.

Next to losing your reputation as an A-class credit risk, losing or having your credit cards stolen – along with the probability that someone is having a shopping spree at your expense – can induce justified panic. Depending upon the fine print on your credit card agreement, you are liable for all or most of the pecuniary damage if you don't notify the issuers of its loss. The important point here is, of course, to phone the issuing organisation immediately, but then to follow up with a confirmatory letter with all the details:

The Manager,   15 July
Card Services,
Standard Northern Bank plc,
PO Box 23,
Brighton BN2 6TG

Dear Sir/Madam,

Standard Northern Bank Payment Card 6802 8492 2241 5144
This will confirm my advice by phone this morning that the above card, in my name, is missing.
I last used it for purchasing petrol at the Phoenix Garage, Whitstable, Kent, at about 6.30 pm on 14 July and first noticed it missing at 9.30 am on 15 July.
I would appreciate it if you would arrange to send me a replacement card as soon as possible.

Yours faithfully,

George N Wheedon

So much for trying to keep your money. Spending it is easy. Buying is child's play. But selling . . .

One of the laws of life is that, sooner or later, you have to sell something, to become a salesperson. Perhaps it's flogging your ageing car, or the abandoned greenhouse, in the local freesheet. Or finding customers for a child-minding service . . . tempting people out on a cold winter's night to attend a fund-raising event, or to bring and buy at a church fête . . . finding buyers for your self-published history of the village, or for your dried herbs and flowers . . . whether it's persuading someone to do something or buy something, it all requires salesmanship. Some of us are good at it ('he's a natural salesman . . . could sell refrigerators to Eskimos') but most of us are not. Which prompts the question: can salesmanship be taught?

The existence of thousands of sales training books, programmes, classes, seminars, colleges and even degree courses suggests that it can be. Certainly the principles of successful selling can be learned and put to use, either in direct selling (one-to-one personal contact), 'cold calling' or telesales, or by the written word.

The Sales Letter

Whether you are a one-off, part-time, semi-professional or professional salesperson the aim is the same – to sell. But before we embark on the theory and practice of selling, there are some preliminaries. Are there people out there who might want what you have to sell? And if so, who are they? Where are they?

Unless you get satisfactory answers to these questions, you could be wasting your time, no matter how wonderful your product or service, or how brilliant your prose.

Most businesses try to establish the saleability of a product or service by test-marketing. This especially applies to selling by mail and is usually done by sampling, or sending out mailshots to selected targets – to different residential areas, for example; or to people grouped by occupation; or to commercially available lists of people who have previously purchased a similar product or service. The results of these sample mailshots are monitored; eventually a picture emerges of the kind of person most likely to become a buyer. This testing process helps to define the market for the particular product or service and eliminates the waste of sending expensive mail to households who wouldn't be interested.

With the help of test-marketing you, as the writer, should have a clear idea of whoever you hope to win as a customer. As with any letter, a sales letter – although it might finish up in a million homes – must make the readers feel that it is personally addressed to him or her. To touch a nerve, hit an emotional soft spot, appeal to the senses or the mind, to give your arguments any conviction, you must write as an individual to an individual. And what you write must be relevant to the recipient's interests. If your targets are, say, busy mothers with children, to whom you intend selling a vacuum cleaner, it will be pointless to confuse them with the diameter of the wheels or the horsepower of the motor. You would stress qualities such as efficiency, lightness in weight, clever accessories, attractiveness and lack of maintenance problems.

Whether your sales pitch is in the form of a letter, circular, brochure, poster or advertisement, the structure usually consists of three elements:

THE HEADLINE – to attract attention and interest

THE ARGUMENT – the description, need, usefulness, value

THE ENDING – the personal appeal, the deal, the clincher.

Each of these elements is capable of endless variation. The approach can be gently persuasive or about as subtle as a steamroller; pleading or deliberately off-hand; understated or extravagant. But whatever the approach, the piece should be attractive and inviting to the eye. This helps but is far from fool-proof. Every writer of sales literature has to get used to the brutal fact that 98 per cent of the population abhors unsolicited sales bumpf and bins it without a second glance. The average response (not necessarily sales) to unsolicited mail or leaflets is less than 2 per cent – that is, two people out of every 100 might be sufficiently interested in your proposition to respond at all. So how can you beat the odds?

Your chances of beating those odds are governed by your choice of approach. There are no rules, which is why mail order and leafleting is largely a matter of trial and error; if one approach doesn't succeed, you try another. If it does score some success, you continue to refine your approach, to see if you can improve results even further. It's trial, trial and trial again.

So let's see how all this vague theory can actually be applied to real situations. Let's take three products:

- A home-gym muscle-toning machine costing £249

- A grow-your-own herbs window box costing £19.99

- A local news-oriented radio station, CHAT-FM.

The Opening – and the Selling Concept

With each product we'll try various approaches, first with the opening, or headline:

The Challenge
Home Gym: *How would you like to feel fitter, look better, in just 14 days?*
Herb Box: *Like to grow herbs – without ever getting your hands dirty?*
CHAT-FM: *Become a smarter, more interesting person!*

The Amazing Fact
Home Gym: *You have 436 muscles. Half of them are probably out of shape.*
Herb Box: *Now you can grow the 'Secret of Life' herb.*
CHAT-FM: *CHAT-FM carries more news than 7 national newspapers.*

The Invitation
Home Gym: *Try this Home Gym for two weeks – at our expense.*
Herb Box: *You can own a unique scented garden for just £19.99.*
CHAT-FM: *Talk direct to your MP on CHAT-FM this week.*

The Case History
Home Gym: *Frank: 'I lost 5 pounds in just a week with Home Gym.'*
Herb Box: *'I can open my window on to a perfumed garden.'*
CHAT-FM: *'CHAT-FM is my constant companion.'*

Remember When . . .
Home Gym: *When did you last run up three flights of stairs?*
Herb Box: *Herbs to bring the old-style taste back into your cooking.*
CHAT-FM: *Remember when people actually listened to radio?*

You're Number One
Home Gym: *You know you want to be fitter, leaner, sharper, better.*
Herb Box: *You've always wanted a herb garden. Here it is, £19.99.*
CHAT-FM: *Phone us any time. We want to hear your opinion.*

The Bribe
Home Gym: *Two free home fitness videos with every Home Gym.*
Herb Box: *Free copy of 'Herb Gardening' with every order.*
CHAT-FM: *Listen to CHAT-FM 'News Clues' – win a Summer Holiday.*

Many copywriters begin with a 'concept' approach to their task, jotting down a selection of selling lines each representing a different appeal, a different approach. Which one is likely to fit the product or service best? Which is likely to appeal to the target market? Who, for example, are we likely to be talking to about the Home Gym?

Probably health-conscious, 24–44-year-old people, both male and female, prepared to spend £249 and an hour or two a day toning up their bodies. So forget the nostalgic approach. Would this group respond to a challenge? Possibly. Would they believe a testimonial? Possibly. Or are we looking at people who think about themselves a lot, who are conscious of their wellbeing and appearance? Probably – in which case the 'You're Number One' approach would seem to be a good fit: 'You know you want to be fitter, leaner, sharper, better!'

Who's likely to buy the window-box herb garden? Here we can picture a woman, probably a housewife, who spends a lot of time captive in the kitchen and who might like to nurture a mini-garden of herbs outside her kitchen window. She would also be likely to have £19.99 in disposable income to buy it, too. So why don't we pitch to her? The 'invitation' approach seems appropriate, or we might idealise our prospect in a fictional case history (for they are rarely true!) as a glamorous young woman reaching out to her prolific kitchen window garden and picking a bunch of scented herbs to flavour an exotic meal she's cooking: *Mmm! I just open my kitchen window to a Mediterranean garden.*

A radio station has to sell its service to as many listeners as it can reach. CHAT-FM is a news and talk station, but not over-serious or ponderous. It's looking for listeners who want to be up-to-date with the news and to be informed, but who also enjoy light, chatty content and even involvement in the station's phone-in sessions. How can we best reach these potential listeners and win them over from other radio stations?

If CHAT-FM possesses a USP (unique selling point) then we should use it; in this case it is the claim that the station carries more news in a day 'than seven national daily newspapers'. Sounds good, but will it be enough? Perhaps we should add a bribe to persuade people to switch: CHAT-FM gives you more news than seven national newspapers – plus a summer holiday in Bermuda!

With the selling approach settled, we must now see if it fits the product or service – and the argument or proposition. Don't get the idea that creating winning sales copy is a matter of writing-by-numbers. It isn't. Although you are dealing with lots of separate elements, the finished product must be a seamless, unified creation.

The Steak – and the Sizzle

Now we come to the product or service itself – what it is, what makes it better than similar products, what benefits will be derived from it, why it is good value for money, why buying it represents little or no risk. Here, there is no substitute for a thorough knowledge, understanding and appreciation of the product or service; it's very difficult to write credible, convincing sales copy if you don't know what you're talking about.

After not only studying the Home Gym but also using it, you may note that it has some interesting, if not unique, advantages. Exercising with it is almost a pleasure: it can adapt to over 40 exercises for the body's muscles. It is light to transport but sturdily built and stows away easily. It has a built-in timer and electronic weight scales. It can adjust to people of different heights and weights. Compared to other, similar apparatus, it is excellent value for money. And it can be bought with easy payments over 12 months.

Some of these attributes might be more important to our target market than others, which may affect the way you give prominence to them in your copy, but they are all worth developing. The manufacturer claims that although most features can be found on other home-gym machines, the electronic weighing platform is unique, allowing the user to tell, within a gram, how much weight is lost after each session. It sounds like the kind of extra that could tweak a potential customer's arm enough to want to buy it.

The maker is also willing to allow a free two-week trial; if the buyer isn't satisfied, the machine can be returned for a full refund. That's worth highlighting, too, because it demonstrates the manufacturer's faith in the product. Present it as a copper-bottomed, no-risk guarantee. It all adds up to a valid, serviceable, value-for-money item with plenty of interesting selling points.

The Herb Garden Window Box is a deep, green-painted aluminium tray with 20 small packets of different herb seeds, a bag of special compost and a booklet of growing instructions – not really much to look at. What you are selling here is not the steak, but the sizzle – the dream of a summer windowsill lush with fragrant herbs that can be plucked fresh for the table.

So, develop the benefits: the visual delight of the mini-garden, the different characters and uses of the herbs, the perfume redolent of hot Mediterranean lands, not to mention how the oregano will perk up meat dishes and how a few sprigs of spearmint will add dash to a salad. All this for just £19.99 – plus a free book on herbs and herb gardening if you buy early.

Radio stations try to 'position' themselves to appeal to a particular market – to forge a union of product and image designed to appeal to the kind of listener they wish to attract and retain. CHAT-FM Radio is a new local station, competing against the national BBC stations, Classic-FM and several regionals. It has set out to provide strong local services: hourly news, market, traffic and weather reports, plus national and international news updates. Music is minimal and listeners can phone in to daily discussions. The format is unhurried but ordered and efficient. But is that enough to entice listeners to switch from other stations? Probably not.

Now the writer has to become a detective, to search for that elusive unique selling point. If it can't be found or doesn't exist, it can be created. With CHAT-FM, success may come in the form of a team of bright, young presenters, devoted and enthusiastic. So why don't you sell 'The Chat Team'? Like the Spice Girls or the Teletubbies, each member of the team has a distinct personality that can be developed. Encourage listeners, potential and existing, to get to know the presenters and to love them. Identify and then develop certain aspects of their personalities and lifestyles. Who's the Lothario? The agony aunt? The presenter with the Robin Reliant? The weather girl who hates getting her hair wet? Now you're giving flesh and faces to the radio station. Now you have something concrete to sell.

The Close – and the Clincher

You have their attention, you've whetted their interest, you've described the product or service, you've presented the benefits, you've convinced them of the extraordinary value and alerted them to a unique opportunity. Then you lose them. What's gone wrong?

Preventing that from happening is the job of the finale, the close, the clincher. A hundred thousand people might see an advertisement for a theatrical play. Ten thousand might express interest. A thousand of these might read a favourable review of the play and decide they'd like to see it. Of these, eight hundred, for one reason or another, can't go. Things are pretty desperate! How do you persuade the remaining two hundred?

Advertising copywriters generally agree that it's not difficult to plant an idea in a person's mind. The idea might be, 'Yes, I really like that watch. I'd love to have one. Not all that expensive, either? Mmm . . .' The difficulty is to provoke action.

Try to look into the mind of the health-conscious, 35-year-old shoe-store manager who's read your mailshot on the Home Gym. She's thought about acquiring such a machine for some time. She has the space, and the money to buy it. She likes the look of the Home Gym and appreciates all its features. So why . . . why doesn't she complete the coupon or phone up with her credit card number? If you, the writer, were the salesman, face-to-face with this woman, you'd instinctively know that you were within a hair's breadth of making the sale. What would you do to close the deal? That's how you have to think if you're writing sales copy. So, what would you do?

Well, you could try offering a 10 per cent discount, which would translate in a sales letter as something like: 'If we receive your order within seven days we'll give you 10 per cent discount – you'll save £24.90!' Or you could throw in a gift, or bonus: 'Get a free pair of Easigrip hand weights worth £21!' Marketers and advertisers know that the well-chosen clincher can increase response by 200 per cent and more.

With an item such as the herb-garden window box you are, as we noted, selling a dream rather than a tray of soil and some seeds. So offering a discount isn't what it's really about here – you need to expand and embroider the dream. A small, romantic, illustrated book about the mystery of herbs could work. Or perhaps a free pomander or sachet of pillow herbs to promote sleep. Let's see how this might look: 'For the first 1,000 orders – FREE! – this Victorian pomander of fragrant pillow herbs to transport you to a deep, dreamy slumber.'

A broadcasting service is already free to its listeners, so you can't exploit the freebie option. So what device will be capable of motivating a radio listener to tune to CHAT-FM? A candle-lit dinner with one of the presenters? A £100 shopping spree at a supermarket? Let's take another look at the listeners that CHAT-FM's format is designed to attract. With the accent on news and views you're most likely looking at an older age group, probably 35–65, with local businesses or interests – not an easy group to bribe. But this group is settled and fairly affluent and an important target market for a number of products and services – new vehicles, for example; home improvements – and holidays, especially cruises. You have your bribe: if you're a CHAT-FM listener you're automatically entered in a draw for the Cruise of a Lifetime.

Putting it all Together

It shouldn't take a lot of imagination to apply the critical principles illustrated in those three examples into any kind of sales pitch for almost every kind of product or service. The same principles are employed whether your task is to attract 100 people to a church fête or a thousand fans to a pop concert; or to sell a used mountain bike or your farm's organic produce.

But principles, however correct, are by themselves cold concepts.

Of course it is necessary to get to know what it is you're selling, to define your market, your strategy and approach, your USP and other selling points, and your clincher – the offer they can't refuse. Having done all that you have then to put your writing skills to work, to add heart and conviction and emotion, weaving all the elements into a hypnotically persuasive and irrestible pattern of words.

If you've followed the nuts and bolts of preparing to write the sales copy for the home gym, the herb window box and CHAT-FM, you couldn't do better than to sit down and as a writing exercise put it all together – whether as a sales letter, leaflet or brochure or as an advertisement.

Three young advertising copywriters were each asked to do just this, and here are their quite creditable attempts. Keep in mind that the finished work would almost certainly incorporate typography and illustration, and, where appropriate, a reply coupon.

Deep Down You Want to be Fitter, Leaner, Sharper, Better . . .

What you want is **HOME GYM**.

Want to be fit and healthy and look your best? But don't have the time to drive to a gym? Object to paying the ever-increasing fees? Hate exercising in front of others?

Then think seriously about HOME GYM – a newly developed muscle-toning machine designed so you can exercise in the privacy of your home or flat.

40 DIFFERENT EXERCISE PROGRAMMES

HOME GYM is programmed to give you 40 different exercise regimes. Each exercise can be customised to your height and weight and stamina. A timer lets YOU be the gym instructor! It's the ultimate, scientifically personalised exercise machine for men, women and children – all the family!

UNIQUE ELECTRONIC WEIGHT CONTROL

HOME GYM is so complete it even includes a highly accurate electronic weighing platform that tells you instantly how much weight you've lost – to a gram!

A GYM IN YOUR HOME FOR JUST £249

A family subscription to the average gym is about £250 a quarter. Yet you can own this true 'gym in your home' for just that – £249 – and it's yours for life. But although it's sturdy it's amazingly light, so you can carry and use it anywhere – in your living room, the basement, the attic, the bedroom. And it dismantles quickly and easily for storage. HOME GYM is the modern miracle muscle-toning machine.

TWO FREE FITNESS VIDEOS

Every HOME GYM comes with two one-hour health and fitness videos with special exercise music tracks and full illustrated instructions.

TWO-WEEK FREE HOME TRIAL

We have no hesitation in offering you a two-week trial of HOME GYM. If you're not delighted just return it for a full refund. No risk!

QUALIFY NOW FOR OUR 10 PER CENT DISCOUNT

Apply within 14 days and get 10 per cent discount – it's as simple as that but it can't last. That's almost a £25 saving on your Home Gym! Don't put it off, send for your Home Gym now!

•

MMM . . . I OPEN MY KITCHEN WINDOW – AND THERE'S A SCENTED MEDITERRANEAN GARDEN!

The amazing herb window box that transports the delights of a Mediterranean summer garden to your windowsill.

Although herbs are surrounded by history and mystery, the **Herb Garden Window Box** allows you to grow 20 different herbs easily, quickly and without any fuss.

This exotic, fragrant garden is contained in green rust-resistant trays that come in three sizes to suit any windowsill. The compost is scientifically balanced to feed your garden for a whole season. All you do is water it occasionally.

A Window-box Herb Garden for just £19.99 complete

For just £19.99 and so little effort you can have a herb garden that will waft all the scents of summer into your home. You get:

*Fresh herbs for **salads** – chives, parsley, lovage, tarragon*

*Fresh herbs for **cooking** – thyme, sage, oregano, basil, rosemary*

*Fresh herbs for **drinks** – mint, borage, lemon balm*

*Fresh herbs for **health** – chamomile, evening primrose, feverfew*

*Fresh herbs for **pure pleasure** – verbena, lavender, pennyroyal*

Plus this FREE Edwardian-style pomander filled with traditional pillow herbs to help you sleep . . . and dream. And when your own garden ripens you can refill the pomander with your own dried, fragrant herbs! Just £19.99 buys you a beautiful, practical mini-garden from which you can pluck a variety of herbs fresh for the table. Plus the Edwardian Pomander, worth at least £10.

BUY A GARDEN FOR YOURSELF AND ONE AS A UNIQUE GIFT FOR A FRIEND – and get both herb gardens carriage free!

•

CHAT-FM NOW REACHES ALL YOUR FAVOURITE PLACES – Miami, Bermuda, Bahamas, San Francisco, Hawaii

CHAT-FM is your very own radio service, bringing you local news, weather, traffic and market reports plus hourly national and international news updates on the hour.

BUT NOW CHAT-FM also reaches places you usually only dream about – Miami, Bermuda, the Bahamas . . . San Francisco, Hawaii, Tahiti . . .

BECAUSE over the next 10 weeks you could win the CHAT-FM **CRUISE OF A LIFETIME** to all those fabulous places aboard the luxury cruiseliner *Artemia*. To enter is simple – just call the CHAT-FM Cruise Line (we broadcast the number throughout day and night) and you're automatically entered for the prize draw.

And every week you're in an additional free draw for a trip for two to Paris via Eurostar First Class. Yes, CHAT-FM is giving away **10 free luxury breaks to Paris**.

And while you're waiting for your prize you can be informed, entertained and delighted by CHAT-FM's witty team of presenters who bring you the news and views of your neighbours, besides the rich and famous. So tune in now to **CHAT-FM 106.8**.

CHAT-FM. YOUR LOCAL STATION THAT TAKES YOU ROUND THE WORLD.

Writing in the New Millennium:
Word Processing and E-mail

It came as a boon and a blessing to men,
The peaceful, the pure, the victorious PEN!

J. C. Prince, 1891

If letter-writing was on the wane towards the end of the 20th century (and dozens of pundits insisted that it was) then the word processor has given it new life. For the millions who despaired of their handwriting (or typing, for that matter), their lack of verbal organisation or their spelling, but who never quite lost the urge to correspond, the word processor is a gift.

With editing facility, there need be no more crossing out, no more Tippexing, no more misunderstandings, and the spell-checker can correct your howlers. So the result can look like the work of a craftsman typesetter. A click or two of your mouse, and it's printed. A couple more clicks and it's also filed – on the computer's hard disk, on a Zip disk, a CD or on a small floppy disk that itself can store as much as you could get into a whole old-fashioned filing cabinet. There seems little doubt that the personal computer will encourage the art and craft of writing, not depress it still further.

Another revolution is the arrival of e-mail (electronic mail) and the fax (telephone facsimile transmission). Many messages are sent by fax, to print out at the receiving end. And the use of e-mail, sent over the Internet, grows enormously every day.

You can send a fax – an A4 page should take no more 30 seconds – to most parts of the world for less than the cost of first-class post. Today's e-mail users can send a fax, too, through their Internet service.

The darker side of the electronic revolution is a creeping, atrocious misuse of the English language. Putting material into the computer becomes *inputting*, a connection between two bits of hardware or software becomes an *interface*, the way a system works becomes its *functionality*. Computer professionals are entitled to their particular jargon: anyone hoping to write decent English will have nothing to do with it.

The jargon apart, we can certainly hope for a revival in letter-writing as more and more people realise how well the technology can help to improve your prose. The spell-check can be invaluable, as long as you remember that it will let through a wrong word if that word is in its dictionary – for example: *He through the ball straight at the window*. Your word-processing software may have a grammar check, too, but do not let it cramp your flowing style with some over-academic objection. Consider the suggestion that is offered and then, if you prefer your own version, ignore the checker.

No matter what the computer professional may say, no combination of technological checks and suggestions will ever create a simple sentence, in good, clear English, better than an old-fashioned human being can.

However rapid its spread, access to the Internet and the availability of e-mail are still new methods of communication and a few words of warning are necesssary. First a word on the Internet. Access to it and its plethora of websites poses exactly the same problem as being faced with a library full of books, a bookstall full of magazines and newspapers or an array of TV channels advertising all kinds of programmes – which to trust? There is no requirement for a website to be 'honest, decent and truthful', so, as with all other sources of information, make sure you know something about the website before trusting information that you obtain from it.

Nor has the decline of the apostrophe been arrested by the computer – quite the opposite. Many operating systems (notably Microsoft) do not allow the use of apostrophes in filenames and the same is now true of Internet addresses. The result is that website names that cry out for an apostrophe do not have them, one of these being BBC Radio 4's Woman's Hour website, www.bbc.co.uk/radio4/womanshour.

E-mail

As users of mobile phones have discovered – you are not alone. In an electronic system, you have to be prepared for Big Brother listening in.

Software is now available that permits employers, worried about viruses and pornography on employees' computers, to spy on staff, including reading their e-mails. The Regulation of Investigatory Powers (Rip) Act, which came into force in 2000, was set up to reconcile employers' genuine worries and the rights of employees under the terms of the Data Protection Act of 1984 and the Human Rights Act of 2000. There have been instances of staff in a merchant bank being dismissed when racist e-mails were discovered circulating in its e-mail system during a routine check, and one phone company sacked staff whom it found downloading pornography from the Internet onto their computers. While the employers' motives in these cases may be commendable, civil rights groups and trade unions, among others, fear that the advent of Rip has given employers a licence to spy on employees' electronic communications. Information obtained in this way could then be used to sack staff who may have been critical or who have been deemed to be spending to much time 'surfing the Net' for private purposes. In the words of Will Hutton, Chief Executive of the Industrial Society, quoted in *The Guardian*, 25 November 2000, 'Employers are increasingly aware of "cyberliability" and e-mail abuse and are using more covert and intrusive methods of surveillance. While employers have legitimate interests to protect, over-zealous monitoring can undermine employees' dignity and autonomy within the workplace.'

So, be warned – despite the temptation offered by the sheer speed of e-mailing, keep your head and your views in check. Think of your e-mails as letters in wartime from soldiers at the front – liable to be opened by censors, but in this case it is not information of use to the enemy that will be made indecipherable by the censor's pen but information that can be acted on by political enemies within the system.

Technical limitations in the early days of e-mailing encouraged conciseness in communication, leading to the widespread use of abbreviations and acronyms, such as IYSWIM ('if you see what I mean') and BAK ('back at keyboard'). And punctuation marks were used to devise symbols, called *emotional icons* or *emoticons*, such as the famous :-), created with the colon, dash and right parenthesis; look at it sideways and you'll see why it's called 'smiley'. Technological improvements have obviated the need for these shortcuts but many linger on. Use them with care and only with friends.

The speed with which e-mails can be sent and the degree of anonymity that can be observed bring their own problems, but these can be overcome by observing *netiquette*, which is a set of good behaviour rules intended to make Internet communications (particularly in newsgroups or online chat areas) more friendly and to avoid offending users who seem determined to be offtended. For example, the term *flame bait* is used to describe an insulting message that is intended to provoke a *flame response*, possibly leading to a *flame war*. The three basic rules of netiquette are:

1. Be polite, particularly to new users – everyone has to start somewhere.

2. Be brief and to the point;

3. DON'T SHOUT – that is, don't use capital letters unncessarily. Words can be emphasised by *enclosing them between asterisks*, and the lesser than and greater than symbols can also be used to express emotions or actions, <said he knowingly>.

Forms of Address

Royalty

The Queen
Envelope: The Private Secretary to Her Majesty the Queen
Salutation: Dear Sir (or Madam if the Private Secretary is a woman)

The Duke of Edinburgh
Envelope: The Private Secretary to His Royal Highness, Prince Philip, Duke of Edinburgh
Salutation: Dear Sir (or Madam if the Private Secretary is a woman)

Royal princes and princesses
Envelope: His/Her Royal Highness, The Prince/Princess [first name]
Salutation: Your Royal Highness

Royal dukes and duchesses
Envelope: His/Her Royal Highness, The Duke/Duchess of [place name]
Salutation: Your Royal Highness

Aristocracy

Dukes and Duchesses
Envelope: The Duke/Duchess of [place name]
Salutation: Dear Duke Duchess

Earls and countesses
Envelope: The Earl/Countess of [place name]
Salutation: Dear Lord/Lady [place name]

Barons and their wives
Envelope: The Lord/Lady [place name]
Salutation: Dear Lord/Lady [place name]

Honourables (children of aristocracy)
Envelope: The Honourable (or The Hon) [full name]
Salutation: Dear Mr/Miss [surname]

The married daughter of an aristocrat retains the title Honourable, becoming The Hon. Mrs [husband's name]

Knights and their wives
Envelope: Sir/Lady [full name]
Salutation: Dear Sir [first name]; Dear Lady [surname]

Dames
Envelope: Dame [full name]
Salutation: Dear Dame [full name]

Government Ministers

The Prime Minister
Envelope: The Rt Hon. [full name] MP
Salutation: Dear Prime Minister

The Chancellor of the Exchequer
Envelope: The Rt Hon. [full name] MP
Salutation: Dear Chancellor

Secretaries of State
Envelope: The Rt Hon [full name] PC, MP or by appointment only, e.g. The Foreign Secretary
Salutation: Dear Secretary of State or Dear [appointment]

Ministers
Envelope: [full name], Esq., MP or by appointment
Salutation: Dear Minister

Members of Parliament
Envelope: [full name] Esq., MP
Salutation: Dear Mr [surname]

The Clergy

Church of England

Archbishops
Envelope: The Most Reverend and Rt Hon the Lord Archbishop of [place name]
Salutation: Dear Archbishop

Bishops

Envelope:	The Right Reverend the Lord Bishop of [place name]
Salutation:	Dear Bishop

Deans

Envelope:	The Very Reverend the Dean of [place name]
Salutation:	Dear Dean or Dear Mr Dean

Archdeacons

Envelope:	The Venerable the Archdeacon of [place name]
Salutation:	Dear Archdeacon or Dear Mr Archdeacon

Vicars and rectors

Envelope:	The Reverend [full name]
Salutation:	Dear Mr [surname]; Dear Father [surname]

Roman Catholic Church

The Pope

Envelope:	His Holiness the Pope
Salutation:	Your Holiness or Most Holy Father

Cardinals

Envelope:	His Eminence the Cardinal Archbishop of [place name]; or (if not an archbishop) His Eminence Cardinal [surname]
Salutation:	Dear Cardinal [surname] or Your eminence

Archbishops

Envelope:	His Grace the Archbishop of [place name]
Salutation:	Dear Archbishop [surname] or Your Grace

Bishops

Envelope:	The Right Reverend [full name], Bishop of [place name]
Salutation:	My Lord Bishops or Dear Bishop [surname]

Monsignors

Envelope:	The Reverend Monsignor [full name] or The Reverend Monsignor
Salutation:	Dear Monsignor [surname]

Church of Scotland

Ministers

Envelope:	The Reverend [full name]
Salutation:	Dear Mr/Mrs [surname] or Dear Minister

Jewish

The Chief Rabbi
Envelope: The Chief Rabbi Dr [full name]
Salutation: Dear Chief Rabbi

Rabbis
Envelope: Rabbi [full name]
Salutation: Dear Rabbi [surname] or Dr if applicable

Legal Dignitaries

The Lord Chancellor
Envelope: The Rt Hon [full peerage title], The Lord Chancellor
Salutation: Dear Lord Chancellor or My Lord

The Lord Chief Justice
Envelope: The Rt Hon, The Lord Chief Justice of England, PC
Salutation: Dear Lord Chief Justice or My Lord

Lord Justice-General (of Scotland)
Envelope: The Rt Hon, The Lord Justice-General
Salutation: Dear Justice-General or My Lord

Master of the Rolls
Envelope: The Master of the Rolls
Salutation: Dear Master of the Rolls

High Court Judges
Envelope: The Hon Mr/Mrs Justice [surname]
Salutation: Dear Judge/Madam

Circuit Court Judges
Envelope: His/Her Honour Judge [surname]
Salutation: (Dear) Sir/Madam

Queen's Counsel
Envelope: [full name], Esq., QC/Mrs [surname], QC
Salutation: Dear Mr/Mrs [surname]

Local Government/Civic Officials

Lord or Lady Mayoress
Envelope: The Right Worshipful the Lord Mayor of [place name]/The Lady
Mayoress of [place name]: except for London, York, Belfast and
Cardiff, which is The Rt Hon the Lord Mayor of [place name]

Salutation: Mr Lord Mayor (formal), Dear Lord Mayor (social); My Lady
                   Mayoress (formal), Dear Lady Mayoress (social)

Mayors and Mayoresses
Envelope: The Right Worshipful the Mayor/Mayoress of [place name]
Salutation: Sir/Madam

Councillors
Envelope: Councillor Mr/Mrs/rank [full name]
Salutation: Dear Councillor

Ordinary People

Married Women
Envelope: Mrs [first and surname]
Salutation: Dear Mrs [married surname]

Daughters
Envelope: Miss [first and surname]; the eldest daughter may be just Miss
                   [surname]
Salutation: Dear Miss [surname]

Widows
Envelope: Mrs [husband's first and surname]
Salutation: Dear Mrs [married surname]

Divorcées
Envelope: Mrs [own first name, married surname]
Salutation: Dear Mrs [married surname]

7

FOREIGN WORDS AND PHRASES

A Note on Pronunciation

The English or Continental pronunciation of Roman spelling has been used to convey, as far as possible, the sounds of words belonging to languages with non-Latin alphabets: Russian, Greek, Hebrew, Arabic, Japanese and Chinese (Pinyin).

Words and phrases that are often used orally amidst the English language (*après-ski*, *fruits de mer*, *nisi*, *repêchage*, etc) are accompanied by an indication of their pronunciation. As this guide is intended for English speakers, pronunciation is indicated by simple letter combinations like STY, HAY, GO, BOO and AK:

adieu	*ah-DYUR*
ex gratia	*eks GRAH-shuh*
mêlée	*meh-lay*
sine die	*see-nay dee-ay*

There are some traps. Words ending in '-y' may be pronounced differently:

early	*UR-lee*	*(the 'long e' sound)*
layby	*LAY-bye*	*(the 'long i' sound)*

To make the difference clear, the 'long e' sound is indicated by '*ee*' to rhyme with *glee*, and the 'long i' sound by a '*y*' to rhyme with *eye*.

A stressed syllable is capitalised:

kaffeeklatsch	*KAF-ay-klatsch*

Perhaps the biggest problem facing English speakers is French nasalisation. 'Nasalisation' is required to pronounce correctly words such as vin and blanc de blancs. Most people manage to produce a sound like 'vang' for the former, which isn't too far off the mark, and 'blonk duh blonk' for the latter, which all but pedants find acceptable. But if you wish to do better you could try to nasalise the relevant vowels, and to indicate this we have used the following device:

blanc de blancs	*blah(n) duh blah(n)*
en passant	*ah(n) PAS-sah(n)*
coquilles St Jacques	*koh-kee sah(n) zhahk*

The (n) indicates that the preceding vowel sounds should be followed by an 'ng' sound that somehow gets lost up the nose. If you listen to a fluent French speaker, or to a language tape, you should get the idea fairly quickly.

Guide to Abbreviations

Abor	Australian Aborigine	*Jap*	Japanese
Arab	Arabic	*Lat*	Latin
Ch	Chinese	*Mao*	Maori
Dut	Dutch	*Pers*	Persian
Fr	French	*Port*	Portuguese
Gael	Gaelic	*Rus*	Russian
Ger	German	*Sans*	Sanskrit
Gk	Greek	*Scand*	Scandinavian
Haw	Hawaiian	*Scot*	Scottish
Heb	Hebrew	*Sp*	Spanish
Hind	Hindustani	*Swa*	Swahili
Hun	Hungarian	*Swed*	Swedish
Ir	Irish	*Turk*	Turkish
It	Italian	*Yidd*	Yiddish

A-Z Listing of Common Foreign Terms

A

à bas [*Fr*] down with.

abat-jour [*Fr*] skylight; lampshade; an arrangement for reflecting light into a room.

à bientôt [*Fr*] (*ah byah(n)-toh*) goodbye – see you again soon.

abonnement [*Fr*] a subscription; season ticket.

abseil [*Ger*] (*AB-seyl*) descending a steep or vertical surface using a double rope which is recovered by the last climber down.

absit omen! [*Lat*] touch wood!

a cappella [*It*] unaccompanied choral music, literally chapel style.

Accents Make a Difference

Would you wipe your sweating pâté? Spread your pate on a crusty roll? That demonstrates the seriousness of accents – marks indicating a special pronunciation and usually, therefore, a special meaning. English doesn't possess any so we're not as *au fait* with them as perhaps we should be. Foreign languages, however, make up for that and to make anything of them we should at least know the roles of the most common accents and marks.

There's a view that, when foreign words are 'naturalised' into English their accents are customarily dropped. But when is a word naturalised? The French word *café* is seen more without its accent (which tells us what it is and how it should be pronounced: *kaf-FAY*) than with, but is this sensible? Perhaps it's fashionable for wideboys and Eastenders to pronounce it *kayf*, but it is nevertheless glaringly wrong. The same applies to words such as *cliché*, *façade*, *protégé* and hundreds of others; even in English the accents still provide a valuable guide to their correct pronunciation.

Accents also supply an even more vital steer to clarity and meaning. Peter, for example, is a common English forename offending nobody. But cross the Channel and add an accent – *péter* – and you have the French word meaning farting. There was an actual incident when the royal family forced Princess Margaret to abandon her love affair with the divorced Commander Peter Townsend. This was duly reported in the French newspapers but one mischievous scandal sheet headlined the event: PRINCESS MARGARET RENONCE A PETER – or, PRINCESS MARGARET GIVES UP FARTING.

Foreign languages based on the Latin alphabet often have fewer characters than the English alphabet but more than make up the difference with a multitude of accented vowels, marks and diphthongs. In German, all nouns and words used as nouns are capitalised. French is fly-specked with a range of accents. Spanish has inverted question and exclamation marks. Spanish and Portuguese have the sweet little tilde. To help you understand the roles of pronunciation marks here are those that you will encounter on your voyages through the major foreign languages:

Accents make a difference

Acute accent [´] usually indicates a rise in the voice or some other quality.

Breve [˘] indicates a short vowel

Cedilla [ç] placed under a *c*, before *a*, *o*, or *u*, to indicate it should be pronounced with a soft *c*, not as a hard *k*.

Circumflex [^] usually indicates the vowel should be pronounced with a rising or falling pitch.

Diaeresis [¨] placed over the second of two adjoining vowels (e.g. naïve, Noël) to indicate that they should be pronounced separately.

Grave accent [`] usually indicates a fall in the voice, or to be pronounced with a certain quality.

Hácek [ˇ] Czechoslovakian mark to indicate, for example, Dvorák is pronounced *DVOR-zhak* and not *DVOR-rak*.

Macron [⁻] indicates a long vowel sound.

Stød [ø] in Scandinavian languages indicates an unwritten sound or glottal stop.

Tilde [~] indicates a nasal sound achieved by touching the tongue against the palate, as in the Spanish *señor*.

Umlaut [¨] warning that the marked vowel is affected by the preceding or following syllables.

---

accouchement [*Fr*] (*ah-koosh-mah(n)*) period of confinement for childbirth.

acushla [*Ir*] (*ah-koosh-luh*) darling; term of endearment. The term *macushla* (my pulse, my heartbeat) is an anglicism.

Adeste fideles [*Lat*] (*ad-EST-tay fih-DAY-lees*) first line of the hymn known in English as 'O come all ye faithful'.

à deux [*Fr*] (*ah-DUR*) for two; a meal for two; a meeting for two people.

ad hoc [*Lat*] for a particular purpose only; something hastily arranged.

ad hominem [*Lat*] relating to a certain person; in an argument, appealing to the prejudices or emotions of the listener rather than to reason.

adieu [*Fr*] (*ah-DYUR*) farewell.

ad infinitum [*Lat*] to infinity; without end.

ad interim [*Lat*] for the meantime; meanwhile.

adiós [*Sp*] farewell.

ad libitum, ad lib [*Lat*] at a speaker's discretion; to improvise and speak or perform without preparation.

ad majorem Dei gloriam [*Lat*] for the greater glory of God. Motto of the Jesuits.

ad nauseam [*Lat*] to a sickening degree.

affaire [*Fr*] affair; scandal.

affaire d'amour [*Fr*] love affair.

affaire de coeur [*Fr*] love affair; affair of the heart.

affaire d'honneur [*Fr*] (*uh-FAYR doh-NUR*) a matter of honour.

affiche [*Fr*] a poster; pasted wall notice or advertisement.

aficionado [*Sp*] (*ah-fees-yuh-NAR-doh*) An ardent enthusiast; in Spain, of bullfighting.

à fond [*Fr*] thoroughly; to the end; to the bottom.

a fortiori [*Lat*] all the more; for similar but sounder reasons.

agent provocateur [*Fr*] (*ah-zhah(n) prov-ok-uh-TUR*) someone who provokes another to commit a crime to provide evidence for a conviction.

à gogo [*Fr*] in abundance; galore.

agrégation [*Fr*] (*ag-ray-GAS-yor(n)*) the *concours d'agrégation* is the French competitive examination for teaching posts.

agunot [*Heb*] in Orthodox Jewry, legally divorced women who cannot get a religious divorce and who wish to remain in the faith are called *agunot*, or 'chained women'. If they remarry in a Reform or Liberal synagogue their children are called *mamzerin*, or illegitimates.

à huis clos [*Fr*] in private; in secret.

aide-de-camp [*Fr*] (*ay-duh-kah(n)*) personal assistant to a senior military officer.

aide-mémoire [*Fr*] notes to help the memory.

aîné [*Fr*] (*ay-nay*) elder; always preceded by a name.

aïoli [*Fr*] a widely used garlic and oil sauce.

akvavit [*Scand*] see *aquavit*.

à la [*Fr*] In the manner of.

à la carte [*Fr*] dishes chosen individually from the bill of fare rather than as part of a set menu.

à la mode [*Fr*] fashionable.

à l'anglaise [*Fr*] In the English style.

à la recherche du temps perdu [*Fr*] literally 'in quest of the past', Marcel Proust's seven-part novel, usually known in English as *Remembrance of Things Past*.

al dente [*It*] (al-DEN-tay) cooked to retain firmness (usually pasta); not too soft.

al fresco, alfresco [*It*] in the open air.

allée [*Fr*] an avenue or path; usually through trees or shrubs.

allemansrätten [*Swed*] a Swedish citizen's right to enter private land.

Alles was geschieht, vom Grössten bis zum Kleinsten, geschieht notwendig [*Ger*] everything that happens, from the greatest to the least, happens of necessity – Schopenhauer's philosophy of life.

Alles zu seiner Zeit [*Ger*] everything in its proper time.

allumeuse [*Fr*] a flirt; a woman who wilfully inflames male passions only to deny them satisfaction.

alma mater [*Lat*] 'bounteous mother'; chummy title given to ex-student's former school, college or university.

aloha [*Haw*] Hawaiian for hello and goodbye.

à l'outrance, à outrance [Fr] (*ah-loo-TRAH(N)S*) to the bitter end; to the death.

alte Wunden bluten leicht [Ger] old wounds quickly bleed anew.

alumnus (pl *alumni*) [Lat] former pupil or graduate of a school or university.

amah [Port] (*AH-mah*) strictly speaking, a wet-nurse, but now generally used in the East to mean a maid, servant or children's nurse.

amende honorable [Fr] a public apology for an insult.

amie [Fr] a mistress.

amorino [It] a cupid statue.

amor mío, mis amores [Sp] my love, my darling.

amor patriae [Lat] Patriotism; love of one's country.

amour [Fr] (*ah-MOOR*) A secret love affair.

amour de voyage [Fr] a cruise or shipboard romance.

amourette [Fr] a trivial love affair.

amour propre [Fr] (*ah-MOOR PROP-ruh*) self-respect, self-esteem; inclined to vanity.

amuse-gueule [Fr] an appetiser served before a meal.

ancien régime [Fr] an old regime; specifically, the government of France before the Revolution.

Anglia [Lat] England.

angst [Ger] acute feelings of anxiety, fear and remorse, usually for no accountable reason.

anguis in herba [Lat] a snake in the grass.

angulus terrarum [Lat] a special or favourite corner of the earth.

animateur [Fr] someone able to present complex and abstruse concepts in clear and accessible ways.

an-neel [Arab] the Nile.

Anno Domini [Lat] in the year of our Lord; in the Christian era. The date is usually preceded by the abbreviation AD.

anno regni [Lat] In the year of the reign.

annus horribilis [Lat] awful year; used by Queen Elizabeth II to describe nosediving Royal Family fortunes in 1992.

annus mirabilis [Lat] remarkable, wonderful year.

Anschauung [Ger] a philosophical intuition or insight.

Anschluss [Ger] a political and economic union; specifically the annexation of Austria by Nazi Germany in 1938.

ante bellum, antebellum [Lat] the period before a war; used widely to refer to the period before the American Civil War.

ante meridiem [Lat] before noon. Abbreviated to am.

antipodes [Gk] those parts of the globe opposite our own; a term widely applied to Australasia.

apartheid [Afrikaans] (*a-PART-ayt*) former South African policy of racial segregation.

aperçu [Fr] (*ap-er-soo*) an insight; an intuitive understanding.

apéritif [Fr] alcoholic drink, often fortified wine, taken before a meal.

apocrypha [Lat] writings or documents of doubtful authenticity or authorship.

apologia [*Lat*] a written defence of a person's (usually one's own) opinions.

Apologia pro vita sua [*Lat*] Cardinal Newman's 1864 account of his spiritual journey, now used to describe any significant autobiography.

a posteriori [*Lat*] Logical reasoning from facts and effects to cause; a principle requiring factual evidence to validate it.

apparat [*Rus*] Communist bureaucracy in the former USSR; its members and agents were *apparatchiks*.

appeler un chat un chat [*Fr*] call a cat a cat.

appliqué [*Fr*] (*ap-PLEE-kay*) designs made by stitching one material upon another.

après moi, le déluge [*Fr*] the usual English version, but the correct phrase is *après nous, le déluge*, meaning 'after us, the deluge'; when we're gone let the heavens fall. In other words, nothing now is likely to survive for much longer.

après-ski [*Fr*] (*ap-ray-skee*) socialising after a day's skiing.

a priori [*Lat*] deductive reasoning from cause to effect, which without supporting observation leads to a conclusion. Such reasoning can, of course, lead to wrong conclusions.

apropos [*Lat*] (*ap-pruh-POH*) pertinent; with regard to; appropriate.

aquavit, akvavit [*Scand*] flavoured grain or potato-based spirit.

arabesque [*Fr*] in music and art, a form of complex decoration; a ballet pose.

arak, arrack [*Arab*] a coarse spirit distilled from rice, palm-tree sap and sugar.

arcanum (pl *arcana*) [*Lat*] hidden secrets; deeply mysterious.

à rebours [*Fr*] perversely; against the grain.

arête [*Fr*] sharp mountain ridge formed by erosion.

argot [*Fr*] (*AH-goh*) originally thieves' cant, now generally used to describe the insider jargon of any class or group.

arrivederci [*It*] farewell (until we meet again).

arma virumque cano [*Lat*] of arms and the man I sing (Virgil).

armoire [*Fr*] a tall cupboard or wardrobe.

arrière-pensée [*Fr*] (*ari-ayr-pah(n)-say*) an unrevealed or reserved thought; an ulterior motive.

arriviste [*Fr*] (*ar-rih-VEEST*) someone dedicated to ambition and determined to succeed; self-seeking.

arrondissement [*Fr*] (*ah-roh(n)-DEES-mah(n)*) administrative subdivision of a *département* in France; subdivision of Paris.

arroyo [*Sp*] a steep gully or watercourse.

ars gratia artis [*Lat*] art for art's sake.

ars longa, vita brevis [*Lat*] art is long, life is short.

assiette [*Fr*] a plate or platter of prepared food.

à tâtons [*Fr*] tentative; groping; feeling your way.

atelier [*Fr*] studio; workshop, especially of an artist or craftsman.

à tort et à travers [*Fr*] haphazardly; confused.

à trois [*Fr*] (*ah-TRWAH*) for three; a meal for three; a meeting between three.

attaccabottoni [*It*] a 'buttonholer'; a bore.

attentisme [*Fr*] the philosophy of 'wait and see'.

auberge [*Fr*] A French inn.

auch das Schöne muss sterben [*Ger*] even the beautiful must die (Schiller).

au contraire [*Fr*] (*oh-koh(n)-trare*) on the contrary.

au courant [*Fr*] (*oh-koo-rah(n)*) up-to-date on current affairs.

au fait [*Fr*] (*oh-FAY*) fully informed.

au fond [*Fr*] fundamentally; basically; essentially.

auf Wiedersehen [*Ger*] (*ow-FVEE-duh-zayn*) goodbye; until we meet again.

au grand sérieux [*Fr*] in all seriousness.

au grand galop [*Fr*] at full gallop; at full tilt.

au gratin [*Fr*] (*oh grah-ta(n)*) food covered and baked with breadcrumbs and sometimes grated cheese.

auguste [*Fr*] a circus clown.

auld lang syne [*Scot*] old times; times past.

au mieux [*Fr*] at best.

au naturel [*Fr*] (*oh-natch-yoo-REL*) natural; naked.

au pair [*Fr*] (*oh-PAIR*) commonly used in Britain to describe young people from other countries who help with housework and childcare in exchange for board and pocket money.

au pied de la lettre [*Fr*] literally, to the last detail. Often abbreviated to *au pied*.

au poivre [*Fr*] cooked with pepper.

au revoir [*Fr*] (*oh-ruh-VWAHR*) goodbye; until we meet again.

aurora australis [*Lat*] the southern lights of the Antarctic regions.

aurora borealis [*Lat*] the northern lights of the Arctic regions.

aus den Augen, aus dem Sinn [*Ger*] out of sight, out of mind.

au sérieux [*Fr*] seriously; earnestly.

Auslander [*Ger*] to Germans, an outsider or foreigner.

auteur [*Fr*] a film director who so powerfully influences a film (departing from the original story, script or source) that he is considered its author.

Autobahn [*Ger*] German motorway.

auto-da-fé [*Port*], *auto-de-fé* [*Sp*] a public burning (formerly of people, now books and objects such as flags).

autoestrada [*Port*] Portuguese motorway.

autopista [*Sp*] Spanish motorway.

autoroute [*Fr*] French motorway.

autostrada [*It*] Italian motorway.

autres temps, autres moeurs [*Fr*] (*oh-truh-tah(n), oh-truh-muhrs*) other times, other ways; customs change with the times.

avant-courier [*Fr*] a precursor; a forerunner.

avant-garde [*Fr*] (*av-var(n)-GARD*) pioneering, especially in the arts; innovative; experimental.

avant la lettre [*Fr*] before a word was created to define an event, object, etc.

ave atque vale [*Lat*] hail and farewell!

Ave Maria [*Lat*] Hail Mary! The angelic greeting to the Virgin; the prayer that begins with these words; the bell summoning the faithful to devotion.

avoirdupois [*Fr*] from *aver de peis* (goods of weight), the system of weights (tons, hundredweights, pounds and ounces) still used in some English-speaking countries.

avoir les cuisses légères [*Fr*] literally, 'to possess light thighs'; colloquial expression for a woman of easy virtue.

a vuestra salud [*Sp*] your good health.

ayah [*Port*] a maid, nursemaid or governess, usually to Europeans in Africa and the East.

ayurveda [*Sans*] ancient Indian medical system for healing and prolonging life.

azan [*Arab*] the five-times-daily Muslim call to prayer by a muezzin from a minaret.

azotea [*Sp*] A flat roof used as a terrace for living and entertaining.

B

baas [*Dut*] boss or employer, in some African countries.

babu [*Hind*] literally 'father', now an Indian official or clerk who writes in English.

babushka [*Rus*] a grandmother; also a headscarf worn by peasant women.

baccalauréat [*Fr*] French pre-university school-leaving examination.

bagarre [*Fr*] A scuffle; brawl.

bagno [*It*] originally a prison or slave-house; brothel; bath-house.

baguette [*Fr*] the long French bread stick.

baignoire [*Fr*] a theatre box at stalls level.

bain-marie [*Fr*] large pan of boiling water into which saucepans are placed for simmering food or keeping it hot.

baklava [*Turk*] Mediterranean pastry made with honey and nuts.

baksheesh [*Pers*] a tip or gratuity.

bal costumé [*Fr*] a fancy dress ball.

The Language of Ballet

The language of ballet is French. They got there first even though the style of dance itself derived from the Italian *balletto*, meaning 'a little dance'. Balletomanes are welcome to the terms, but in recent years many of these have overflowed into ordinary writing and conversation. Here are a few you might meet.

adagio slow movements to emphasise grace and line. In the classic *pas de deux* a partner supports the dancer for an even greater display of grace.

allegro fast movement (opposite of *adagio*) with leaps and turns.

arabesque the dancer stands on one leg, the other leg and arms extending in the longest possible lines.

ballet d'action a ballet that tells a story in pantomime.

battement the tapping of one leg with another.

bourrée very fast little steps that give the illusion of the dancer gliding.

cabriole the dancer leaps and taps the lower leg with the upper.

écarté a position in which an arm and a leg on the same side of the body are extended, almost spreadeagled.

entrechat a leap in which the dancer's legs are quickly crossed and uncrossed at the lower calf.

grand jeté a spring from one foot to the other.

jeté a forwards, backwards, or sideways spring.

pirouette a turn on one foot.

sur les pointes on the very tips of the toes.

---

ballon d'essai [*Fr*] a 'trial balloon' to test opinion.

bal masqué [*Fr*] a masked ball.

bal musette [*Fr*] a popular type of dance hall, usually with accordion music.

bambino [*It*] a young child.

banco [*It*] a card gambler's offer to place a stake equal to that of the banker.

bandeau [*Fr*] a ribbon or cloth to bind a woman's hair.

banderilla [*Sp*] the dart with streamer attached that is thrust into the neck of a bull in bullfighting. The *banderillero* is the bullfighter who places it.

banlieue, banlieues [*Fr*] the suburbs.

banquette [*Fr*] cushioned seat with a cushioned back, especially in restaurants.

banshee [*Ir*] a wailing female spirit presaging death.

banzai [*Jap*] originally a greeting to the Japanese emperor; a battle cry.

barcarole [*Fr*] a song of the kind sung by Venetian gondoliers.

bar mitzvah [*Heb*] (*bar-MITS-vuh*) initiation ceremony for Jewish boys. See *bat mitzvah*.

barre [*Fr*] the waist-high rail around the wall of ballet school practice rooms.

barrette [*Fr*] hair slide.

barrio [*Sp*] a ward of a Spanish city or town; Spanish-speaking quarter of a non-Spanish town, especially in the USA.

bas bleu [*Fr*] (*bah-bluhr*) French equivalent of a bluestocking; a seriously academic woman.

basho [*Jap*] a sumo wrestling tournament.

bateau-mouche [*Fr*] passenger boat on the Seine around Paris.

batiste [*Fr*] fine linen or cotton fabric, similar to cambric.

bat mitzvah [*Heb*] Jewish girl's initiation ceremony into her religious majority at the age of twelve.

batterie de cuisine [*Fr*] a complete set of cooking utensils.

Bauhaus [*Ger*] (*BOW-howss*) influential Weimar design school (1919–33) founded by Walter Gropius.

béarnaise [*Fr*] (*bay-uh-NAYS*) widely used sauce made from egg yolks, butter, vinegar and tarragon.

beatae memoriae [*Lat*] of blessed memory.

beau geste [*Fr*] (*boh zhest*) a magnanimous gesture.

beau idéal [*Fr*] an ideal of anything in beauty and excellence.

beau monde [*Fr*] the world of fashion and society.

beauté du diable [*Fr*] superficial beauty.

beaux arts [*Fr*] (*boh-ZAR*) the fine arts.

beerah [*Arab*] beer.

béguin [*Fr*] infatuation; a passing fancy.

bel canto [*It*] singing in the traditional Italian manner with rich tone, perfect phrasing and clear articulation.

bel esprit [*Fr*] (*bel-es-pree*) a brilliantly witty person.

belle époque [*Fr*] the prosperous period from the late 1890s to the outbreak of World War I.

belle laide [*Fr*] see *jolie laide*.

belles-lettres [*Fr*] letters or essays that are serious studies, usually of literature, of a critical or philosophical nature.

Benedictus [*Lat*] God bless you; the part of the Mass that begins (in English) 'Blessed is he that comes in the name of the Lord'.

ben trovato [*It*] a story or account that, invented or untrue, nevertheless is appropriate anyway. *Se non e vero, e molto ben trovato* (if it is not true, it is a happy invention).

berceuse [*Fr*] a cradle song or lullaby.

bergère [*Fr*] (*ber-zhair*) a deep, comfortable armchair.

beschlafen Sie es [*Ger*] sleep on it; look before you leap.

bête noire [*Fr*] someone or something that is especially dreaded and disliked.

bêtise [*Fr*] a tactless act or remark.

bettschwere [*Ger*] without the energy to get out of bed.

bey [*Turk*] Governor of a Turkish town or district.

bhang [*Hind*] Indian hemp.

bibelot [*Fr*] (*beeb-loh*) Small trinket or curio.

bien entendu [*Fr*] (*bih-yahn ah(n)-tah(n)-doo*) naturally; of course; understood.

bien-pensant [*Fr*] (*bih-yahn pah(n)-sahn*) conformist person holding all the accepted opinions and beliefs.

bien sûr [*Fr*] (*bih-yahn soor*) Of course; naturally.

bien trouvé [*Fr*] (*bih-yahn troo-vay*) a happy invention.

bijou [*Fr*] (*bee-zhoo*) Small and beautiful; a trinket.

bijouterie [*Fr*] (*bee-zhoo-teh-ree*) Very delicate jewellery.

Bildungsroman [*Ger*] a novel about someone's formative experiences.

billet doux [*Fr*] (*bih-lay-doo*) a love-letter.

biru [*Jap*] beer.

biretta, berretta [*It*] Roman Catholic clerical square cap worn by priests (black), bishops (purple), cardinals (red) and other orders (white).

bis dat qui cito dat [*Lat*] he gives twice who gives quickly; from the aphorism: 'He who gives alms to a poor man quickly, gives it twice'.

bisque [*Fr*] (*beesk*) Soup made from shellfish, mainly lobster.

bitterje [*Dut*] Dutch jenever (gin) with bitters.

blague [*Fr*] pretentious nonsense; humbug. One who talks such nonsense or boasts is a *blagueur*.

blasé [*Fr*] (*blah-zay*) bored and indifferent because of surfeit.

Blaustrumpf [*Ger*] bluestocking. See *bas bleu*.

blini seekroy [*Rus*] caviar with pancakes.

Blitzkrieg [*Ger*] an intense military attack designed quickly to overwhelm the enemy.

bloembollen [*Dut*] bulbs.

Blut ist dicker als Wasser [*Ger*] blood is thicker than water.

Blut und Eisen [*Ger*] blood and iron: coined by Bismarck.

Boche [*Fr*] derogatory term for Germans.

bodega [*Sp*] (*boh-DEG-uh*) wine shop.

bois [*Fr*] (*bwah*) wood; *boiserie* is woodwork.

boîte, boîte de nuit [*Fr*] (*bwaht de nwee*) a disreputable club, dance hall or dive; a nightclub.

bolas [*Sp*] two or three heavy balls joined by cord, first used by Argentine gauchos to entangle the legs of cattle to single them out from the herd.

bollenveld [*Dut*] a bulb field.

bombe surprise [*Fr*] (*bom soor-preez*) a dessert coated to hide its contents, usually ice cream and meringue.

bonae memoriae [*Lat*] the pleasant memory of someone.

bona fide [*Lat*] (adj) (*BOH-nuh FYdeh*) in good faith; genuine.

bona fides [*Lat*] (noun) good faith; honest intention.

bon appétit [*Fr*] enjoy your meal.

bon goût [*Fr*] (*boh(n) goo*) good taste.

bon marché [*Fr*] (*boh(n) mar-shay*) cheap; also a famous bargain department store in Paris.

bon mot [*Fr*] (*boh(n) moh*) a witty, clever remark.

bonne amie [*Fr*] (*bon ah-mee*) a close woman friend, who may also be more than just a friend.

bonne à tout faire [*Fr*] (*bon ah too fair*) a maid-of-all-work.

bonne bouche [*Fr*] (*bon boosh*) a tasty morsel.

bonne chance [*Fr*] (*bon shah(n)s*) good luck!

bon ton [*Fr*] (*boh(n) toh(n)*) sophisticated.

bon vivant [*Fr*] (*boh(n) vee-vah(n)*) a person who enjoys all the luxuries but especially eating and drinking. The term *bon viveur* means the same but is not used in France.

bon voyage [*Fr*] (*boh(n) vwah-yazh*) have a good journey!

bor [*Hun*] wine.

bordel, bordello [*It*] brothel. In French *un bordel* is slang for a cock-up, a mess.

bordereau [*Fr*] a memorandum. The word is indelibly associated with the fake *bordereau* used to convict Dreyfus of treason.

bore da [Welsh] good morning.

borkostolo [*Hun*] wine cellar.

borné [*Fr*] narrow-minded; short-sighted.

borozo [*Hun*] wine bar.

borsch, borsh, borscht [*Rus*] vegetable and beetroot soup widely consumed in Russia and Poland.

bottega [*It*] a café and wine shop.

bouchée [*Fr*] (*boo-shay*)a small pastry served hot as an hors d'œuvre.

bouclé [*Fr*] (*boo-klay*) a shaggy fabric produced by looped woollen yarn.

bouffant [*Fr*] (*boo-fah(n)*) puffed-out, back-combed hairstyle.

bouillabaisse [*Fr*] (*boo-yuh-bes*) Provençal soup or stew of fish, vegetables and spices.

bouillon [*Fr*] (*boo-yoh(n)*) thin beef or chicken broth.

boules [*Fr*] game played with heavy metal balls tossed at a target ball, usually on a sand court.

boulevardier [*Fr*] (*bool-vah-dee-ay*) a fashionable man who takes care to be seen in all the right places.

bouquet garni [*Fr*] (*boo-kay gar-nih*) Bunch of mixed herbs often in sachet form, used in cooking.

Bourse [*Fr*] (*boorss*) the French stock exchange in Paris.

braccae tuae aperiuntur [*Lat*] your fly is open.

brasserie [*Fr*] an informal restaurant.

brioche [*Fr*] (*bree-osh*) a small, sweet yeast cake.

brique [*Fr*] slang for 10,000 francs.

brise-bise [*Fr*] a net curtain for the lower half of a window.

broderie anglaise [*Fr*] open embroidery on white cotton or fine linen.

brûlé [*Fr*] flavoured with burnt sugar; *brûler* also means to get 'burned' or taken advantage of.

buenas noches [*Sp*] (*bwey-nas noh-ches*) goodnight.

buenos días [*Sp*] (*bwey-nos dee-as*) good morning; good day.

buffo [*It*] (*BOO-foh*) burlesque; comic.

bureau à cylindre [*Fr*] a roll-top desk.

burn [*Scot*] a stream.

bushido [*Jap*] the feudal code of the samurai.

buvette [*Fr*] roadside café.

bwana [*Swa*] Master; form of East African address equivalent to 'Sir'.

C

cabaña [*Sp*] beach hut.

cabotin [*Fr*] a show-off; ham actor.

cabriole [*Fr*] a type of curved furniture leg used from the 18th century.

cachou [*Fr*] (*kash-ooh*) breath-sweetening lozenge.

cacique [*Sp*] originally an American Indian chief in Spanish-speaking regions, now used to mean a local political boss.

cacoethes loquendi [*Lat*] (*kah-koh-EETH-ees loh-KWEN-dee*) an irresistible urge to talk. *Cacoethes scribendi* is a compulsive urge to write.

cadeau [*Fr*] (*kah-doh*) a gift.

cadit quaestio [*Lat*] there is nothing more to discuss.

caeteris paribus [*Lat*] other things being equal.

café [*Fr*] (*kaff-ay*) coffee. *Café au lait* (*kaff-ay oh lay*) coffee with milk; *café crème* white coffee; *café noir* black coffee.

cahier [*Fr*] (*kah-yeh(r)*) originally a notebook; a written or printed report of a meeting or conference.

camino real [*Sp*] the best way to achieve a result.

campo santo [*It*] a burial ground.

canaille [*Fr*] (*kan-eye*) the crowd, the mob, hoi polloi.

ça ne fait rien [*Fr*] it is of no importance.

cantina [*Sp*] bar or wine shop.

capable de tout [*Fr*] unpredictable in behaviour; likely to stop at nothing.

capo d'opera [*It*] a masterpiece.

caporal [*Fr*] a type of light tobacco.

capote anglaise [*Fr*] English hood, a Gallic tilt at the French letter, French slang for condom.

carabiniere [*It*] (*karah-bin-YAIR-ih*) armed Italian policeman.

caramba [*Sp*] a rare exclamation.

carità pelosa [*It*] literally, 'hairy generosity': generosity with some ulterior motive.

carnet [*Fr*] (*kar-nay*) small booklet, usually a document.

carpe diem [*Lat*] (*KAR-pay DEE-em*) make the most of today; eat, drink and be merry for tomorrow we die.

carreras de caballos [*Sp*] horse-racing.

carretera [*Sp*] road; highway.

carte blanche [*Fr*] (*kart blah(n)sh*) complete freedom and authority; full discretionary power.

carte de visite [*Fr*] a small 19th-century visiting card.

carte d'identité [*Fr*] an identity card.

cartonnier [*Fr*] a cabinet with flat drawers for storing prints, drawings and plans.

cartouche [*Fr*] inscription on an ornamental scroll.

casa [*It*] a villa or detached house.

ça saute aux yeux [*Fr*] it's obvious; it cannot be missed.

cassis [*Fr*] (*kah-seess*) syrupy blackcurrant cordial.

cassoulet [*Fr*] a meat and bean dish.

casus belli [*Lat*] an event used to justify a war or quarrel.

catalogue raisonné [*Fr*] (*kat-uh-log ray-zon-ay*) a systematic descriptive listing, usually of a collection or an artist's work.

catholicon [*Gk*] a panacea; universal remedy.

caudillo [*Sp*] (*kow-DEE-yoh*) a military or political leader in a Spanish-speaking country.

cause célèbre [*Fr*] (*kauz se-leb-ruh*) a famous trial, lawsuit or controversy.

causerie [*Fr*] a chatty literary essay or discussion.

ça va? [*Fr*] (*sah-vah*) everything okay?

ça va sans dire [*Fr*] that is obvious; it goes without saying.

cave [*Lat*] (*KA-vih*) slang for 'look out!'; 'beware!'.

caveat [*Lat*] 'let him beware'; a warning or caution.

caveat emptor [*Lat*] 'let the buyer beware'; a warning that it is the buyer, not the seller, who must take the risk.

cavoli riscaldati [*It*] literally, 'reheated cabbage', a lapsed love affair, difficult to revive.

céad míle fáilte [*Ir*] Irish welcome: 'a hundred thousand welcomes!'

ceilidh [*Gael*] (*KAY-lee*) an entertainment in Scotland and Ireland, usually consisting of dancing, folk music, singing – and talking.

cercare il pelo nell'uovo [*It*] to seek the hair in the egg; to pick faults where none exists.

cerveja [*Port*] beer.

cerveza [*Sp*] beer.

c'est la guerre [*Fr*] (*say-lah-gair*) that's war; it happens.

c'est la vie [*Fr*] (*say-la-vee*) that's life.

ceud mile fàilte [*Gael*] (*kood meel-uh FAL-chuh*) Scottish Gaelic welcome: 'a hundred thousand welcomes!'

ch'a [*Ch*] tea. The British slang term is *char*.

chacun à son goût [*Fr*] (*shah-kuh(n)-ah-soh(n)-goo*) everyone to his own taste.

chacun à son métier [*Fr*] (*shah-kuh(n)-ah-soh(n)-may-tyay*) everyone to his own trade.

chacun pour soi [*Fr*] (*shah-kuh(n) poor swahr*) everyone for himself.

chagrin d'amour [*Fr*] misery from an unhappy love affair.

chaise-longue [*Fr*] (*shayz-lor(ng)*) a sofa with a back and one end open.

chambrer [*Fr*] (*shahm-bray*) to bring a wine to room temperature.

chamise [*Jap*] tea-house.

Changcheng [*Ch*] the Great Wall of China.

Changjiang [*Ch*] the Yangtse River.

chapati, chapatti [*Hind*] a flat cake of unleavened bread.

charcuterie [*Fr*] a shop selling cooked meat; cold cuts of pork.

chargé d'affaires [*Fr*] (*shar-zhay da-fair*) a diplomatic representative below the rank of ambassador.

charivari [*Fr*] [*ka-ree-VAR-ee*] a demonstrative racket or celebration.

charpoy [*Urdu*] an Indian bed, usually of woven hemp.

chasse [*Fr*] (*shass*) a liqueur following coffee.

Châteaubriand [*Fr*] (*sha-toh-bree-ah(n)*) thick steak cut from a fillet of beef.

chaud-froid [*Fr*] (*shoh-frwah*) cold meat or chicken covered with a savoury jellied sauce.

chef de mission [*Fr*] organiser or leader of a team.

chef d'équipe [*Fr*] manager of a team.

chef d'oeuvre [*Fr*] (*shay durv-ruh*) a masterpiece.

chemin de fer [*Fr*] a game of cards like baccarat.

cheongsam [*Ch*] a long straight oriental dress with a high collar and a slit on one side of the skirt.

cherchez la femme [Fr] (*shair-shay la fam*) 'look for the woman'; there's always a woman involved.

chère amie [Fr] (*shair ah-mee*) a mistress or sweetheart.

chéri, chérie [Fr] (*sheh-ree*) darling of, *mon chéri, ma chérie*.

che sarà sarà [It] (*kay suh-RAH suh-RAH*) what will be, will be.

chevaux de frise [Fr] iron spikes or some other sharp deterrent on the tops of fences and walls.

chez [Fr] (*shay*) at the house of; e.g.: Chez Humperdinck.

chez moi [Fr] (*shay mwah*) at my house; at home.

chez nous [Fr] (*shay noo*) at our house; at home.

chiasse [Fr] slang term for 'the runs' induced by fear.

chi bestia va a Roma bestia ritorna [It] he who goes to Rome a fool returns a fool.

chignon [Fr] (*shee-nyo(n)*) the roll or coil of hair at the back of a woman's head.

chikatet [Jap] Japanese underground railway systems.

chin-chin, ch'ing ch'ing [Ch] informal greeting, farewell or toast.

chronique scandaleuse [Fr] a scandalous story or gossip.

chuddar [Hind] a garment worn by Muslim women that covers them from head to foot.

chun jie [Ch] Chinese New Year.

ciabatta [It] (*chee-BAT-tah*) slipper; bread made with olive oil.

ciao [It] (*chow*) hello; goodbye.

cicerone [It] a guide, especially at sites of antiquities.

ci-devant [Fr] formerly; that which used to be.

cinéma-vérité [Fr] a style of making films in which the aim is to make the result look as much like real life as possible.

cinquecento [It] (*ching-kweh-CHEN-toh*) the period from 1500 to 1600.

circa [Lat] (*SER-kuh*) approximately; at the approximate time of. Abbreviated to *c.* or *ca* and used before a date: c.1990.

ciré [Fr] (*see-ray*) smooth, usually waxed, fabric

clachan [Gael] a rural village in the Scottish West Highlands.

claque [Fr] (*klak*) originally a group hired to applaud in a theatre, now used in a derogatory way to describe a group of sycophants blindly applauding their leader. Such people are *claqueurs*.

cocotte [Fr] prostitute; also a fireproof cooking dish.

cognoscenti [It] (*kon-yoh-SHEN-tih*) people who are in the know about something; connoisseurs.

coitus interruptus [Lat] contraception method involving withdrawal during sexual intercourse. In Australia it is called 'Getting off at Redfern' (the station just before the terminus, Sydney Central).

colleen [Ir] a girl or young woman.

Comédie Française [Fr] the French national theatre in Paris.

comédie humaine [Fr] (*kom-uh-dee ooh-men*) the comedy of life. *La Comédie Humaine* is the title of Balzac's fictional social history of France.

comédie noire [Fr] (*kom-uh-dee nwahr*) black comedy.

comme ci, comme ça [*Fr*] neither good nor bad; so-so.

commedia dell'urte [*It*] (*kom-AY-dyah del'AH-tay*) the well-known characters of Columbine, Harlequin and Punchinello are from this stylised Italian comedy genre established in the 16th century.

comme il faut [*Fr*] (*kom eel foh*) correct; how things are done; in accordance with acceptable manners.

commère [*Fr*] a female *compère*.

commis [*Fr*] (*kom-mih*) an assistant or apprentice waiter or chef.

commune [*Fr*] the smallest administrative division in France (also in Belgium, Switzerland and Italy), governed by a mayor and council.

compère [*Fr*] the host or commentator of an entertainment, contest or programme. See *commère*.

compos mentis [*Lat*] sane; of sound mind. See *non compos mentis*.

con amore [*It*] (of music) to be performed lovingly.

con brio [*It*] (of music) with energy; to be performed with spirit.

concours d'élégance [*Fr*] (*koh(n)-koor day-lay-gah(n)s*) beauty parade of vintage, veteran or exotic motor cars.

confrère [*Fr*] (*ko(n)-frair*) a professional colleague.

connard [*Fr*] extremely rude expression for a fool, an idiot, someone stupid or dumb.

consommé [*Fr*] (*kohn-soh-may*) clear meat or chicken soup.

contra mundum [*Lat*] against the world; in the face of accepted wisdom.

contrat social [*Fr*] (*ko(n)-trah soh-syal*) the surrender of certain personal liberties to the community in return for an organised society (from title of a book by the philospher Jean-Jacques Rousseau)

contretemps [*Fr*] a small disagreement.

conversazione [*It*] (*kon-ver-sat-sih-OH-nay*) a social gathering at which people discuss the arts or literature.

coq au vin [*Fr*] (*kok oh vah(n)*) chicken cooked in red wine.

coquilles St Jacques [*Fr*] (*koh-kee sah(n) zhahk*) scallops cooked in sauce and served in scallop shells.

coram populo [*Lat*] in full view of the people; in public.

cordon bleu [*Fr*] (*kor-doh(n) blur*) meaning the blue ribbon; a very high distinction; first-rate; food prepared to the highest culinary standards.

cordon sanitaire [*Fr*] a buffer zone or boundary to keep a danger at bay, such as an infectious disease or enemy power.

corniche [*Fr*] (*kor-neesh*) coastal road, typically cut into steep mountains. The road between Nice and Monte Carlo is a famous example.

cornuto [*It*] literally, 'horned'; a male insult to another, implying he has been cuckolded. Even worse, *cornuto e contento* – happy cuckold.

corps d'élite [*Fr*] (*kor day-leet*) people who are the best at something; crack corps.

Corpus Christi [*Lat*] the festival of the Blessed Sacrament or Holy Eucharist.

corpus delicti [*Lat*] the sum of the facts that constitute an offence in law. Often incorrectly used to describe the corpse or body in connection with a crime.

Corrida: the running of the bulls

corrida, corrida de toros [*Sp*] bullfight; the running of bulls.
corroboree [*Abor*] (*koh-ROB-uh-ree*) an Australian Aboriginal dance ceremony.
cortège [*Fr*] (kor-tezh) a procession, especially one following a funeral.
Cosa Nostra [*It*] US branch of the Sicilian Mafia, meaning 'our thing'.
Così fan tutte, ossia la scuola degli amanti [*It*] All women do it; that is the way of all women, or *The School for Lovers*, Mozart's opera.
Côte d'Azur [*Fr*] (*koht dah-zoor*) the French Riviera.
Côte de Beaune [*Fr*] (*koht duh bone*) southern part of the Côte d'Or Burgundy region from Dijon to Nuits-St-Georges.
Côte d'Or [*Fr*] (*koht dor*) the Burgundy region of France, 300 kilometres southeast of Paris.
côtelette [*Fr*] a chop or cutlet.
couilles [*Fr*] testicles; used commonly and vulgarly and with infinite variety. ***Mes couilles!*** – bollocks!
coulant [*Fr*] easy-going; easy to get on with.
couleur de temps [*Fr*] whichever way the wind blows; according to circumstances.

Countries, Cities and Place-names

For a century and a half the British have freely anglicised foreign place-names. If you asked a citizen of Beijing (we've perversely called it Peking for generations) if you were in China you'd be met with an uncomprehending stare; there the country is called **Zhongghuó**. We say Athens and Corfu; the Greeks say – and they should know – **Athena** and **Kerkira**. The country we know as Sweden is really **Sverige**; Brussels is **Bruxelles**; Italy is **Italia**; Hungary is **Magyarország** where, to be fair, they call Great Britain **Nagy-Britannia**.

But, slowly, English speakers are becoming more internationalised, and many of us can now work out that **Firenze** is Florence, **København** is Copenhagen and **München** is Munich.

coup de foudre [*Fr*] (*koo duh food-ruh*) love at first sight; a sudden and surprising event.

coup de grâce [*Fr*] (*koo duh grahs*) a final and decisive stroke; a mortal blow that ends a victim's suffering.

coup de main [*Fr*] (*koo duh ma(n)*) a surprise attack.

coup d'essai [*Fr*] (*koo day-say*) a trial or first attempt.

coup d'état [*Fr*] (*koo day-tah*) a violent seizure of power, usually the illegal overturning of a government.

coup de maître [*Fr*] (*koo duh mehtruh*) a masterstroke; performance worthy of a master.

coup de théâtre [*Fr*] (*koo duh tay-art-ruh*) a sudden and dramatic action; a sensational stage success.

coup d'oeil [*Fr*] (*koo duh-ee*) a quick glance; comprehensive view taken by a quick glance.

coureur (de jupons) [*Fr*] a skirt-chaser; a womaniser.

couscous [*Fr* from *Arab kouskous*] spicy North African dish of steamed semolina served with stew.

coûte que coûte [*Fr*] (*koot kuh koot*) no matter what the cost; at all costs.

couvert [*Fr*] a set place at a meal table; a restaurant 'cover' for which a charge is made.

craquelure [*Fr*] crazing on the surface of old oil paintings and on pottery glazing.

crème de la crème [*Fr*] (*krem duh lah krem*) cream of the cream; the very best.

cri de cœur [*Fr*] (*kree duh kur*) a cry from the heart.

crime passionnel [*Fr*] (*kreem pass-yuh-nel*) a crime motivated by the passions: often murder, usually sexual passion.

crise de conscience [*Fr*] an attack of moral doubt; an awakening of one's scruples.

crise de cœur [*Fr*] an emotional crisis; a catastrophic love affair.

crise de nerfs [*Fr*] (*krees duh nair*) a hysterical attack; a brief nervous breakdown.

Croix de Guerre [*Fr*] (*krwah duh gair*) French military decoration for gallantry first awarded in 1915.

croûte [*Fr*] (*kroot*) crust; fried bread used as a base for savouries.

croûtons [*Fr*] (*kroo-toh(n)*) cubes of toasted or fried bread usually served in soup.

crudités [*Fr*] (*kroo-dee-tay*) appetiser of sliced, raw mixed vegetables served with dips or sauces.

csarda [*Hun*] (*char-duh*) a country inn.

csárdás, czárdás [*Hun*] (*char-duh*) Hungarian national dance.

¡cuéntaselo a tu abuela! [*Sp*] tell that to your grandmother!

cui bono? [*Lat*] (*kwee boh-noh*) for whose benefit? Who will profit by it?

cui malo? [*Lat*] (*kwee mah-loh*) whom will it harm?

cum grano salis [*Lat*] with a grain of salt; not to be taken literally; treat with caution.

cum laude [*Lat*] (*kum LOW-day*) with praise; an above-average examination pass; a pass with distinction. (*See also* **magna cum laude** and **summa cum laude**).

curé [*Fr*] (*kyoor-ray*) French parish priest.

currente calamo [*Lat*] writing that is dashed off without pause.

cwm [*Welsh*] (*koom*) a valley.

Cymraeg [*Welsh*] (*kuhm-RA-eeg*) the Welsh language.

Cymru [*Welsh*] (*KUHM-ree*) Wales.

Cymry [*Welsh*] (*KUHM-ree*) the Welsh people.

D

dacha [*Rus*] (*DAH-tshuh*) Russian country house or villa.

Dáil [*Ir*] (*doyl*) parliament of the Irish Republic in Dublin.

damnosa hereditas [*Lat*] a disastrous inheritance; one that brings problems rather than benefits.

da multos annos [*Lat*] a wish for someone's long life.

danke schön [*Ger*] (*dank-kuh shern*) thank you very much.

danse du ventre [*Fr*] variety of belly dancing.

danse macabre [*Fr*] (*dah(n)s muh-karb-ruh*) the dance of death.

darunter und darüber [*Ger*] topsy-turvy.

Das fragt sich [*Ger*] that remains to be seen.

das kleinste Haar wirft seinen Schatten [*Ger*] the smallest hair casts a shadow. Attributed to Goethe.

de bene esse [*Lat*] subject to certain conditions; without prejudice; provisionally.

déboutonné, déboutonnée [*Fr*] unbuttoned; careless; sloppy.

déclassé [*Fr*] having lost one's social status.

décolletage [*Fr*] (*day-kol-tahzh*) a revealing low-cut neckline on a woman's dress. *Décolleté* describes a garment having such a neckline.

de die in diem [*Lat*] from day to day.

de facto [*Lat*] (*day FAK-toh*) in reality; in fact.

défense d'entrer [*Fr*] (*day-fah(n)s dah(n)-tray*) no entry.

défense de fumer [*Fr*] (*day-fah(n)s duh foo-may*) no smoking.

dégagé [*Fr*] (*day-gah-zhay*) relaxed; unconstrained; detached.

dégueulasse [*Fr*] disgusting. Used vulgarly: *c'est un dégueulasse!* – he's a rotten sod!

de gustibus (non est disputandum) [*Lat*] there's no accounting for tastes.

de haut en bas [*Fr*] (*duh oh ah(n) bah*) consciously superior; in a condescending way.

Dei Gratia [*Lat*] By the grace of God.

déjà vu [*Fr*] the feeling or conviction that an experience is being repeated: a journey, a place revisited, an event, etc.

de jure [*Lat*] (*day YOO-ray*) ln law, by right but not necessarily happening.

delineavit (abbreviation *del*) [*Lat*] (he/she) drew it. Used with the name of the artist: Hogarth *del*.

delirium tremens [*Lat*] in slang, *the DT's*, psychotic condition exhibiting delirium, tremor and hallucinations, induced by excessive intake of alcohol.

démarche [*Fr*] (*day-mahsh*) a new move in political or diplomatic affairs.

demi-mondaine [*Fr*] a woman of the *demi-monde*, of low repute.

demi-pension [*Fr*] half-board, i.e. bed, breakfast and one main meal.

demi-tasse [*Fr*] a small coffee cup; a small cup of coffee.

démodé [*Fr*] outdated, or no longer fashionable.

démon de midi [*Fr*] reawakening of sexual appetite in middle-age.

de mortuis (nil nisi bonum) [*Lat*] say nothing bad about the dead.

de nos jours [*Fr*] (*duh noh zhoor*) of our time, used after a name: 'She was the George Sand *de nos jours*'.

dénouement [*Fr*] (*day-noo-moh(n)*) the unravelling of a mystery and its solution.

de nouveau [*Fr*] (*duh noo-voh*) again; once more.

Deo gratias [*Lat*] thanks to God.

Deo Optimo Maximo [*Fr*] To God the greatest, motto of the Benedictine order; the initials DOM are seen on the labels of Benedictine liqueur.

Deo volente (abbreviation *DV*) [*Lat*] God willing; unless something prevents it.

département [*Fr*] (*day-pahrt-moh(n)*) one of the administrative divisions of France.

dépaysé [*Fr*] (*day-pay-zay*) disoriented; feeling out of place, like a fish out of water.

de profundis [*Lat*] (a cry) from the depths of despair. The first two words of the Latin version of Psalm 130 and the title of Oscar Wilde's apologia published in 1905.

député [*Fr*] (*day-puh-tay*) member of the French lower house of parliament.

dérailler [*Fr*] slang for 'to go off the rails'.

de règle [*Fr*] (*duh rehg-luh*) required by rule or convention.

der ewige Jude [*Ger*] the eternal Jew.

de rigeur [*Fr*] (*duh rih-gur*) required by etiquette.

dernier cri [*Fr*] (*der-nyay kree*) latest fashion; trendy.

dernier ressort [*Fr*] a last resort.

derrière [*Fr*] buttocks; backside.

der Schuster hat die schlechtesten Schuhe [*Ger*] the cobbler's children are always the worst shod.

déshabillé [*Fr*] (*day-za-bee-yay*) in a state of undress; a dressing-gown.

désoeuvré [*Fr*] (*day-zoo-vray*) idle; not doing anything.

détente [*Fr*] (*day-tah(n)t*) relaxation of a state of tension, usually between two countries.

détraqué [*Fr*] unbalanced; insane; out of order.

de trop [*Fr*] (*duh troh*) superfluous or unwanted.

deus ex machina [*Lat*] (*DAY-uhs eks MAK-ee-nuh*) a god or unlikely character who appears, in a play or novel, to solve the mystery or resolve the plot.

Deus vobiscum [*Lat*] God be with you.

Deuxième Bureau [*Fr*] French counterpart of Britain's MI5, the Military Intelligence Department.

dharma [*Hind*] social custom that is religious and moral duty in Hinduism. For Buddhists it is the truth as taught by Buddha.

dharna [*Hind*] the practice of obtaining justice by sitting or fasting on the doorstep of the home of the offender.

dhobi [*Hind*] a washerman or washerwoman in India.

dhoti [*Hind*] male loincloth as worn in India.

dialogue de sourds [*Fr*] discussion in which neither party listens to the other.

Dies Irae [*Lat*] day of wrath. Judgment Day; a hymn describing this.

Dieu et mon droit [*Fr*] (*dyur ay mo(n) drwah*) God and my right. The motto of the Royal Arms of Great Britain.

Directoire [*Fr*] (*dih-rek-twahr*) the fashions of the French Directory period, 1795–99, following classical lines which in turn inspired English Regency fashions.

dirigisme [*Fr*] state control of an economy or society.

dis aliter visum [*Lat*] the gods decided otherwise.

disjecta membra [*Lat*] scattered fragments of a writer's literary work.

distingué [*Fr*] (*dees-tah(n)-gay*) distinguished in manner and appearance.

djellabah See also jellaba [*Arab*] a hooded cloak with wide sleeves worn in North Africa.

djibbah [*Arab*] a long open coat worn by Muslims.

djinn [*Arab*] a spirit in Muslim mythology able to assume human and animal form. Sometimes spelt *jinnee, jinni*.

dolce far niente [*It*] enjoyable idleness.

dolce vita [*It*] (*DOL-chay VEE-tah*) life of luxury and sensuality.

dolmades, dolmathes [*Gk*] traditional Greek dish of vine leaves stuffed with savoury rice.

Dominus illuminatio mea [*Lat*] the Lord is my light, motto of Oxford University.

donné [*Fr*] a basic assumption; accepted fact.

Donner und Blitzen [*Ger*] thunder and lightning. An expression of amazement.

Doppelgänger [*Ger*] an apparition identical to a living person.

douane [*Fr*] (*dwan*) customs office.

douanier [*Fr*] (*DWAN-yay*) customs officer.

double entendre [*Fr*] (*doo-blah o(n)-tah(n)-druh*) a word or phrase having two interpretations, one of them indelicate. The phrase *double entente* is used in France instead.

Drachenfutter (*Ger*) literally, 'dragonfodder', a guilty husband's present to his wife.

droit de cité [*Fr*] freedom of a city, club or organisation.

droit de seigneur [*Fr*] in feudal times, the right of a lord to sleep with his tenant's bride on her wedding night.

duae tabulae rasae in quibus nihil scriptum est [*Lat*] 'two minds without a single thought' – the motto of movie comedians Laurel and Hardy.

d'un certain age [*Fr*] euphemism for 'middle aged'.

dydd da [*Welsh*] good day!

E

eau-de-nil [*Fr*] (*oh-duh-neel*) a tint of pale green.

eau-de-vie [*Fr*] literally, 'water of life'; any strong liqueur or spirit.

ébauche [*Fr*] (*ay-bohsh*) a writer's rough outline for a novel; a quick sketch.

Ecce Homo [*Lat*] (*ek-kee hoh-moh*) 'Behold the Man'; the image of Christ crowned with thorns.

ecce lacunar mirum! [*Lat*] 'now, that's a ceiling!'; to be murmured approvingly in
    the Sistine Chapel.

echt [*Ger*] genuine; pure; unadulterated.

éclaircissement [*Fr*] (*ay-klair-sees-mah(n)*) a revelation; an explanation.

éclat [*Fr*] (*ay-klah*) a great success; a dazzling effect.

école [*Fr*] (*ay-kol*) a school; a group of artistic disciples.

écrase! [*Fr*] shut up!

écritoire [*Fr*] (*ay-krih-twahr*) writing desk.

écrivain maudit [*Fr*] (*ay-krih-va(h)n moh-dee*) accursed, or damned, writer.

écru [*Fr*] (*ay-kroo*) greyish-yellow; the colour of unbleached linen.

écurie [*Fr*] (*ay-kyoo-ree*) a works motor racing team.

Edelweiss [*Ger*] a small white Alpine flowering plant.

editio princeps [*Lat*] the first printed copy of a book.

eekra [*Rus*] caviar.

effendi [*Turk*] an important person; a gentleman.

egeszsegeunkre! [*Hun*] cheers!

Egri Bikaver [*Hun*] Bull's Blood red wine.

eine Schwalbe macht keinen Sommer [*Ger*] one swallow doesn't make a summer.

ein unmütz Leben ist ein früher Tod [*Ger*] a wasted life is premature death (Goethe).

eisteddfod [*Welsh*] (*aye-STETH-vod*) Welsh cultural festival.

élan [*Fr*] (*ay-lah(n)*) vivacity; style and vigour.

Elatha [*Gk*] Greece.

elinikos kafes [*Gk*] Greek coffee.

embarrass de choix [*Fr*] so many options it's difficult to make a choice.

embarrass de richesses [*Fr*] embarrassment of riches; so many options to choose
    from.

embonpoint [*Fr*] (*ah(n)-bo(n)-pwah(n)*) attractive plumpness.

embouchure [*Fr*] (*ah(m)-boo-shoor*) the correct application of the lips and tongue
    when playing a wind instrument.

emeritus [*Lat*] retired, but retaining the title, often on an honorary basis. Usually,
    an emeritus professor.

éminence grise [*Fr*] (*eh-meen-ah(n)s greez*) literally, 'grey eminence'. Someone who
    wields considerable power behind the scenes.

empressement [*Fr*] enthusiastic display of cordiality.

en avant [*Fr*] (*ah(n) ah-vah(n)*) move ahead! forward!

en bloc [*Fr*] (*ah(n)-blok*) in a body; all together.

en brochette [*Fr*] food grilled on a skewer.

en brosse [*Fr*] (*ah(n) bros*) hair cut short and bristly. In Britain, once referred to as
    the 'bog-brush' style.

en cabochon [*Fr*] describes a gem that is rounded and polished but does not have
    facets cut in it.

enceinte [*Fr*] (*ah(n)-sah(n)t*) pregnant.

enchiridion [*Gk*] a handbook; manual, work of reference.

enculé [*Fr*] a very vulgar insult, equivalent to bugger or sod.

endimanché [*Fr*] dressed in Sunday best.

en famille [*Fr*] (*ah(n) fah-mee-uh*) as one of the family; informal.

enfant chérie [*Fr*] a favoured, pampered child.

enfant gâté [*Fr*] a spoiled child; an adult who behaves like a spoiled child.

enfant terrible [*Fr*] (*ah(n)-fah(n) teh-reeb-luh*) someone who embarrasses by being unconventional, indiscreet, opinionated and loud.

en fête [*Fr*] in festive mood.

en garde [*Fr*] on guard; a call to a fencer to adopt a defensive stance; in readiness for attack.

en l'air [*Fr*] up in the air; vague; left for discussion.

en masse [*Fr*] all at once; in a group.

en öl [*Swed*] (*an url*) beer.

en passant [*Fr*] (*ah(n) pas-sah(n)*) in passing; a chess move for capturing a pawn.

en paz descanse [*Sp*] may he rest in peace.

en pension [*Fr*] living in lodgings as a boarder.

en plein air [*Fr*] (ah(n) plen err) in the open air.

en plus [*Fr*] (*ah(n) ploos*) in addition.

en principe [*Fr*] a very common colloquial expression roughly meaning 'in theory' or 'as a rule' but conveying a strong note of scepticism.

en rapport [*Fr*] (*ah(n) rah-por*) in sympathy; in harmony.

en revanche [*Fr*] in return; as an act of retaliation.

entente cordiale [*Fr*] (*ah(n)-tah(n)t kor-dyahl*) a friendly understanding between countries.

en-tout-cas [*Fr*] (*ah(n)-too-kah*) an umbrella-style sunshade.

entr'acte [*Fr*] (*ah(n)-trakt*) interval between theatrical acts.

entrecôte [*Fr*] tenderloin or rib steak.

entre deux guerres [*Fr*] the period between World War I and World War II.

Entre-Deux-Mers [*Fr*] (*ah(n)-truh-dur-mair*) large wine area of the Gironde, between the Dordogne and Garonne rivers.

entre la espada y la pared [*Sp*] literally, 'between the sword and the wall'; means 'between the devil and the deep blue sea'.

entremets [*Fr*] (*ah(n)-truh-may*) side dish served between the main courses of a meal.

entre nous [*Fr*] between ourselves; in strict confidence.

entrepôt [*Fr*] (*ah(n)-truh-po*) a commercial warehouse; a trading centre or port.

en un clin d'oeil [*Fr*] in the twinkling of an eye.

en villégiature [*Fr*] holidaying or staying in the country.

envoi [*Fr*] a postscript; a concluding verse or stanza.

épatant [*Fr*] (*ay-pah-tah(n)*) astounding; mind-boggling.

e pluribus unum [*Lat*] one out of the many, the motto of the USA.

épris [*Fr*] in love; enamoured.

è pur troppo vero [*It*] it is only too true.

eretz ha-kodesh [*Heb*] Holy Land.

eretz Israel [*Heb*] the modern state of Israel.

ergo [*Lat*] therefore; hence.

Er hat Bohnen in den Ohren [*Ger*] he has beans in his ears; none are so deaf as those who will not listen.

Er hat Haare auf den Zähnen [*Ger*] he has hairs on his teeth; he is a sharp one.

Erin go bragh, Eire go brath [*Ir*] Ireland forever!

ersatz [*Ger*] a poor imitation; an inferior substitute.

erwtensoep [*Dut*] favourite Dutch dish of thick pea soup with smoked sausage, pork fat and pig's knuckle.

escándalo [*Sp*] a scandal; a fuss.

escargots [*Fr*] (*es-kar-goh*) edible snails.

es fällt keine Eiche von einem Streiche [*Ger*] you can't fell an oak with a single stroke.

es ist nicht alles Gold, was glänzt [*Ger*] all is not gold that glitters.

es una trampa [*Sp*] it's a fix! Often shouted at sporting events.

espadrille [*Fr*] (*es-pah-dreel*) casual rope-soled canvas shoe.

esprit de corps [*Fr*] pride in belonging to a group; a shared sense of fellowship, loyalty and purpose.

esprit de l'escalier [*Fr*] (*es-pree duh les-kahl-yay*) the brilliant remark that one thinks of too late.

esprit fort [*Fr*] (*es-pree for*) an independent thinker.

es regnet in Strömen [*Ger*] it's pouring with rain.

es stirbt als Knabe, wen die Götter lieben [*Ger*] those whom the gods love die young.

estaminet [*Fr*] (*es-ta-mee-nay*) a small bar especially in the context of World War I.

est deus in nobis [*Lat*] there is a god within us (Ovid).

estiatorion [*Gk*] in Greece, an ordinary restaurant.

étagère [*Fr*] hanging set of shelves or bookshelves.

et alii (abbreviation *et al*) [*Lat*] and others; and other things.

état d'âme [*Fr*] the state of the soul; how a person feels deep down.

étoile [*Fr*] (*ay-twahl*) star; star-shaped.

être cousu d'argent [*Fr*] to be rolling in money.

et sequentia (abbreviation *et seq*) [*Lat*] and the following.

et tu, Brute! [*Lat*] (*et too, broo-tay*) 'and you, Brutus!' Allegedly Caesar's last words when he saw Brutus among his assassins. Used ever since to reproach a friend who betrays.

étude [*Fr*] (*eh-tood*) a short musical composition to highlight the technical virtuosity of a soloist.

eureka [*Gk*] 'I have found it!' said Archimedes upon discovering the principle of specific gravity. Now used as an expression of delight in finding the answer to a problem.

Europäische Wirtschafts Gemeinschaft [*Ger*] European Economic Community.

Europäische Union [*Ger*] European Union.

événement [*Fr*] event, occurrence, result; climax.

Ewigkeit [*Ger*] thin air; eternity; the unknown.

ex cathedra [*Lat*] with unquestioned authority; infallible.

exceptis excipiendis [*Lat*] when the appropriate exceptions have been made.

exempli gratia (abbreviation **e.g.**) [*Lat*] for example.

exeunt [*Lat*] a stage direction meaning 'they go out'.

ex granis fit acervus [*Lat*] many grains make a heap; every little helps.

ex gratia [*Lat*] (*eks gray-shuh*) a payment made as a favour, not by legal right.

ex libris [*Lat*] from the library of. Usually seen on bookplates.

ex nihilo nihil fit [*Lat*] nothing produces nothing.

ex officio [*Lat*] by virtue of one's office.

ex ore parvulorum veritas [*Lat*] out of the mouths of babes comes truth.

ex parte [*Lat*] (*eks part-ay*) in law, in the interests of one party only; a temporary injunction granted to one party in the absence of the other.

ex post facto [*Lat*] after the deed; becoming effective retrospectively.

extrait [*Fr*] a copy of a certificate; an extract: *extrait de naissance* – birth certificate; *extrait mortuaire* – death certificate.

extraordinaire [*Fr*] extraordinary; exceptional.

ex voto [*Lat*] something done in accordance with a vow; a votive object.

F

fabbrica [*It*] a factory.

faber est quisque fortunae suae [*Lat*] we are all architects of our fortunes.

façade d'honneur [*Fr*] the main frontage of a building.

facile largire de alieno [*Lat*] It is easy to be generous with what is another's.

facile princeps [*Lat*] (*fa-see-lay PRIN-seps*) easily the best; the acknowledged leader.

façon de parler [*Fr*] way of speaking; mere words, all effect and no sincerity.

facta non verba [*Lat*] deeds, not words.

factotum [*Lat*] a jack-of-all-trades.

fac ut gaudeam [*Lat*] make my day.

fadastikos! [*Gk*] Fantastic!

fahrt [*Ger*] ubiquitous word important to car drivers: *Durchfahrt verboten* – No entry; *Ausfahrt* – Exit; *Einfahrt frei halten* – Do not block entrance, etc.

faire la sourde oreille [*Fr*] to turn a deaf ear.

faire ses choux gras [*Fr*] to fatten your cabbages; to feather your nest.

fait accompli [*Fr*] an accomplished fact; something already done.

faits divers [*Fr*] short news items; news in brief.

faites vos jeux [*Fr*] (*fet voh zhur*) place your bets.

falafel [*Arab*] fried chickpeas sometimes served in pitta bread.

False Friends

They're called *Faux Amis*, dangerous duos, treacherous twins, *Mots-Pièges*, false friends. And with good reason: they are words of a foreign language that so closely resemble English words that we assume they share the same meaning. On the contrary: many have completely different meanings, and howlers inevitably result when the user is unaware of the difference. Here is just a small selection:

French false friends

Agenda: notebook, diary. *Commodité*: comfort, convenience. *Délayer*: to dilute, water down. *Demander*: sometimes to demand but also a mild request. *Éventuel*: possible. *Lunatique*: capricious, fickle. *Pet*: fart. *Prétendre*: to assert, to claim. *Supplier*: to beseech. *User*: to wear out.

German false friends

Bald: soon. *Chef*: boss, manager. *Fast*: almost, nearly. *Fatal*: annoying. *Fix*: quick, smart. *Genial*: brilliant, gifted, brainy. *Kaution*: guarantee, deposit. *Gift*: poison. *Slip*: knickers. *Spenden*: to give, to donate.

Italian false friends

Accidenti: damn! *Camera*: room. *Confetti*: sugar-coated almonds. *Lunatico*: moody. *Magazzino*: storehouse. *Parente*: a relative. *Promiscuo*: mixed. *Rumore*: noise. *Sofisticato*: adulterated. *Suggestivo*: striking, picturesque. *Superbo*: arrogant.

Spanish false friends

Advertir: to give warning. *Carpeta*: office file. *Constipado*: suffering from a cold. *Extenuar*: to weaken. *Injuria*: insult. *Intoxicado*: not drunk but poisoned. *Particular*: private, personal. *Suceso*: an event, happening. *Tormenta*: storm. *Voluble*: changeable.

Intoxicado: Not drunk but poisoned

farce est jouée [Fr] 'the comedy is over' – see *tirez le rideau*.
farceur [Fr] (*far-sur*) a wag or practical joker; a writer of stage farce.
fasullo [It] false, fake.
fata morgana [It] (*far-tuh mor-GA-nuh*) originally a mirage seen in the Straits of Messina; now any mirage or similar illusion.
faubourg [Fr] (*foh-boorg*) an inner suburb, usually a working-class

neighbourhood.

fausse dévote [*Fr*] pious hypocrite.

faute de mieux [*Fr*] (*foht duh myur*) for want of something better.

fauteuil [*Fr*] (*foh-tie*) An armchair with sides that are not upholstered.

faux bonhomme [*Fr*] (*foh bon-om*) seemingly friendly and generous, but in fact not.

faux frais [*Fr*] incidentals, details.

faux ménage [*Fr*] an ill-matched married couple.

faux naif [*Fr*] (*foh nah-eef*) pretending to be sincere and honest.

faux pas [*Fr*] (*foh pah*) an indiscretion; a mistake; a social slip one regrets.

favela [*Port*] a shantytown in Brazil.

fecit [*Lat*] (*FEH-kit*) he / she made it, seen on older paintings, sculpture, medals, coins, etc.

fee sehatak [*Arab*] cheers!

fellah [*Arab*] in Arabic countries, a peasant.

felo de se [*Lat*] literally, 'felon of yourself'; someone who commits suicide.

femme de chambre [*Fr*] (*fam duh sharm-bruh*) chambermaid.

femme fatale [*Fr*] (*fam fat-ahl*) a seductress who brings woe and ruination to her lovers.

femme savante [*Fr*] bluestocking.

fermatevi [*It*] stop!

fermeture annuelle [*Fr*] ('annual closing') the French summer holiday period in August when a good part of Paris shuts down and huge numbers of Parisians leave the city.

Ferragosto [*It*] the Italian bank holiday on 15 August.

festina lente [*Lat*] hasten slowly; more haste, less speed.

fête champêtre [*Fr*] an outdoor or country festival.

fête nationale [*Fr*] a country's national day, such as 14 July, Bastille Day.

feu de joie [*Fr*] (*fur duh zhwar*) a sustained salute by rifle fire at public ceremonies.

feuilleton [*Fr*] a serialised novel; that part of a newspaper devoted to fiction or light reading.

fianchetto [*It*] in chess, the flank development of a bishop to control a key diagonal.

fiat Dei voluntas [*Lat*] God's will be done.

fiat lux [*Lat*] let there be light.

Fidei Defensor (abbreviation *Fid Def*, *FD*) [*Lat*] (*fee-day-ee def-EN-sor*) Defender of the Faith. The abbreviation can be seen on certain British coins.

fidus Achates [*Lat*] a faithful friend; an intimate companion.

filer à l'anglaise [*Fr*] surreptitiously to slip away; to take 'French leave'.

fille de joie [*Fr*] a courtesan; prostitute.

fille du regiment [*Fr*] an army prostitute.

fils [*Fr*] son, used after the surname to distinguish the son from the father, e.g. 'Jones fils'.

fin de siècle [*Fr*] (*fa(n) duh syek-luh*) end of the century, specifically the end of the 19th century, with the suggestion of decadence and aestheticism.

fines herbes [*Fr*] (*feen zerb*) mixed chopped herbs.

finis coronat opus [*Lat*] the end crowns the work.

finita la commedia [*It*] the comedy is over; the farce has ended.

fin sourire [*Fr*] a knowing smile.

flambé [*Fr*] set alight. In cooking, to soak with brandy and ignite just before serving.

flâneur [*Fr*] (*fla-nur*) a loafer; idle man-about-town.

flecti, non frangi [*Lat*] to be bent, not broken.

fleur-de-lis [*Fr*] (*fluhr-duh-lees*) heraldic flower in the royal arms of France.

flic [*Fr*] cop; slang term for a police officer.

floreat [*Lat*] (*FLOH-ree-at*) may (it) flourish. The motto of Eton College: *floreat Etona*.

floruit (abbreviation *fl.*) [*Lat*] he/she flourished, used to state the period in which someone in history was most active when the actual birth/death dates are not known.

folâtre [*Fr*] playful.

folie [*Fr*] (*fol-ee*) madness; delusions.

folie à deux [*Fr*] madness or delusions simultaneously affecting two people who are close.

folie de grandeur [*Fr*] (*fol-ee duh grah(n)-dur*) delusions of grandeur; illusions of greatness.

fondre en larmes [*Fr*] to burst into tears; literally, 'to melt into tears'.

force de frappe [*Fr*] a strike force; now used to mean a nuclear deterrent.

force majeure [*Fr*] (*fors ma-zhur*) a superior, irresistible force; a compelling circumstance that will release a party (e.g. an insurance company) from fulfilling a contract.

foulard [*Fr*] headscarf or neckerchief.

fou qui se tait passe pour sage [*Fr*] a fool who holds his tongue passes for a wise man.

fous-moi le camp/foutez-moi le camp [*Fr*] bugger off! (A French stickler for propriety would insist on the latter form being used for someone one doesn't know well.)

fraise [*Fr*] Strawberry; *fraises des bois* – wild strawberries.

framboise [*Fr*] raspberry.

frappé [*Fr*] (*frah-pay*) chilled and iced; liqueur poured over crushed ice.

frapper [*Fr*] To strike; to knock. *Entrez sans frapper* – enter without knocking.

Frau [*Ger*] (*frow*) married woman; equivalent to Mrs.

Fräulein [*Ger*] (*FROY-leyn*) formerly unmarried woman; now equivalent to Ms.

fraus est celare fraudem [*Lat*] it is fraud to conceal a fraud.

frère [*Fr*] (*frair*) brother.

fresser [*Yidd*] glutton.

freundlich [*Ger*] kind, friendly, genial.

fricassée [*Fr*] stewed meat and vegetables served with a sauce.

fricatrice [*Fr*] lesbian; female homosexual.

frijoles [*Sp*] (*frih-HOLE-ays*) widely cultivated Mexican beans.

frisch auf! [*Ger*] cheer up!

fritto misto [*It*] (*free-toh mees-toh*) dish of mixed fried seafood.

Fröhliche Weihnachten! [*Ger*] Merry Christmas!

froideur [*Fr*] (*frwar-dur*) cooling; a romantic relationship that is cooling off.

froides mains, chaud amour [*Fr*] cold hands, warm love (heart).

fronti nulla fides [*Lat*] there's no trusting to appearances.

frou-frou [*Fr*] (*froo-froo*) originally the rustle of a woman's skirts; now over-frilly, fussy ornamentation.

frühe Hochzeit, lange Liebe [*Ger*] early marriage, long love.

fruits de mer [*Fr*] (*frwee duh mair*) seafood.

frustra laborat qui omnibus placere studet [*Lat*] he labours in vain who attempts to please everyone.

Fulano, Mengano y Zutano [*Sp*] the Spanish equivalent of 'Tom, Dick and Harry'. *Fulano* is used for 'So-and-so' when referring to someone whose name you can't remember.

Funkstreife [*Ger*] police radio patrol.

furor scribendi [*Lat*] a passion for writing.

Fürst der Schatten [*Ger*] the Prince of Shades: death.

fustanella [*It from Gk*] the stiff white cotton dress worn by Greek soldiers during ceremonial occasions.

futsch [*Ger*] done for; had it: *der Wagen ist futsch* – the car has had it.

G

gaieté de cœur [*Fr*] light-heartedness.

galette [*Fr*] the round, flat cake made to celebrate Twelfth Night on 6 January. *Galette* is also slang for money.

ganar [*Sp*] (*gah-NAR*) to make or win money.

gant de toilette [*Fr*] wash cloth, the equivalent of the English flannel, although often a towelling glove.

garce [*Fr*] slang for 'bitch'.

garçon [*Fr*] (*gar-sor(n)*) waiter; boy.

Garda [*Ir*] a police officer, or the Irish police force, in full *Garda Síochána* (Guard of the Peace).

gardez bien [*Fr*] take good care.

gare [*Fr*] railway station; platform; *Chef de gare* – station master; *Gare du Nord* – Northern Paris terminal.

gare! [*Fr*] look out!

Gastarbeiter [*Ger*] (*GAST-ar-byter*) literally, 'guest worker'; an immigrant worker.

Gasthaus [*Ger*] a small inn or restaurant.

Gasthof [*Fr*] hotel or inn.

gaudeamus igitur [*Lat*] (*gow-day-AHM-us IG-ee-tur*) let us therefore rejoice! First line of the well-known students' drinking song.

gavroche [*Fr*] street arab, from the gamin Gavroche in Hugo's *Les Misérables*.

gazpacho [*Sp*] cold tomato and cucumber soup, a speciality of Andalusia.

gefilte (fish) [*Yidd*] balls of seasoned minced fish cooked in broth.

gemütlich [*Ger*] (*guh-moot-likh*) good-natured, kindly.

genius loci [*Lat*] literally, 'spirit of the place', the characteristic atmosphere of a particular place.

gens de bien [*Fr*] respectable folk.

gens de couleur [*Fr*] people of colour.

German

German is spoken by more than 100 million people and is the official language of Germany and Austria and a principal language of Switzerland. Of the two main varieties *Plattdeutsch* (Low German) and *Hochdeutsch* (High German), the Low variety has a strong affinity with English. If you visit Schleswig-Holstein or anywhere along the north German coast, you will hear people saying they were born in 'neinteyn-hunder-fife-und-dirtig' (1935), talking about the 'veather' being 'colt' and asking 'what ist duh klok?' You are, of course, in that part of Germany from which in the 5th century the Angles decided to move to what is now England, along with the Saxons and the Jutes. That is perhaps why, apart from the difficult grammar and the propensity for word-building (something as simple as a matchbox is called a *Steichholzschachtelchen*), the English have little difficulty with German pronunciation. Almost automatically we sense that

au is pronounced as *ow* as in *Frau*
ei is pronounced as *eye* as in *Heine*
ie is pronounced as *ee* as in *diesel*
ee is pronounced as *ay* as in *Beethoven*
ch is pronounced as *kh* as in *Bach*
j is pronounced as *y* as in *Jaeger*
w is pronounced as *v* as in *Wagner*
z is pronounced as *ts* as in *Mozart*

The Germans are not so protective as the French about their language (although the *Deutscher Sprachverein*, the German Language Society, sniffs out transgressions and, to quote one example, insists that the wrestling hold called the hammerlock should be called *Ellenbogengelenkschlüssel*) and unsurprisingly it is becoming littered with anglicisms: *Pressekonferenzen, no komment, off die rekord, der Teenager, das Walkout, ein Steadyseller, der Cashflow* are some random (and horrible) examples.

gesacht, getan [*Ger*] no sooner said than done.

Gesämtkunstwerk [*Ger*] a total work of art; a combination of different forms of art in one work, such as music, drama and poetry combining to make up an opera.

Gesellschaft [*Ger*] Company; association; society.

Gesellschafterin [*Ger*] call-girl; hired female escort.

Gesetz ist mächtig, mächtiger ist die Not [*Ger*] the law is mighty but necessity is mightier (Goethe).

Gesundheit! [*Ger*] (*guh-ZOOND-hyt*) good health! Said to someone who sneezes; also used as a toast. *Gesundheit is besser als Reichtum* – health is better than riches.

geteilte Freude ist doppelte Freude [*Ger*] a joy shared is a joy doubled.

gettane le margherite ai porci [*It*] to throw pearls before swine.

Gewerkschaft [*Ger*] trade union.

gigot [*Fr*] (*zhee-goh*) leg of mutton.

gillie, ghillie [*Gael*] a helper or guide in the Scottish Highlands hunting regions.

giri [*Jap*] to observe one's moral duty in society.

gitano [*Sp*] gypsy.

gîte [*Fr*] (*zheet*) a furnished holiday cottage or small house for let in rural France.

glacé [*Fr*] (*glahs-say*) glazed; iced with sugar.

glasnost [*Rus*] (*glas-nuhst*) literally, 'publicity'. Openness; receptiveness to criticism.

gloire [*Fr*] (*glwahr*) French patriotic sense of honour and glory.

gloria in excelsis Deo [*Lat*] 'glory be to God on high', the prayer that follows the Kyrie of the Mass.

Glück auf! Glück zu! [*Ger*] good luck! *Glück auf den Weg* – have a pleasant journey.

Gluhwein [*Ger*] mulled wine, often indulged in *après-ski*.

gnocchi [*It*] (*NYOK-ee*) dumplings, served with soup or sauce.

gombeen-man [*Ir*] money-lender.

Gongchandang [*Ch*] Communist Party. *Gongchandangyuan* – Party member.

gospodart [*Rus*] gentleman.

Gospodin [*Rus*] Master, the equivalent of Mr or Sir.

Götterdämmerung [*Ger*] (*gur-tuh-DEM-uh-rung*) the twilight of the Gods; the end of the world.

Gott mit uns [*Ger*] God with us, motto of the Prussian kings.

Gott sei dank [*Ger*] God be thanked.

gouine [*Fr*] crude term for a lesbian; female homosexual.

goûter [*Fr*] literally, 'to taste'; a kind of French afternoon tea or snack, indulged in at about 4 pm.

gracias a Dios [*Sp*] thanks to God.

gradatum vincimus [*Lat*] we conquer step by step.

graffito [*It*] a slogan, often indecent, painted or scratched on walls. The form most used is the plural, *graffiti*.

grande amoureuse [*Fr*] (*grah(n)d am-uh-rurz*) a woman who gives her life to love affairs.

grande dame [*Fr*] (*grah(n)d dam*) great lady; aristocratic.

grande école [*Fr*] (*grah(n)d ay-kol*) one of a number of prestigious French Colleges of higher education of which the military *École Polytechnique* is the best

Graffito

known.

grande passion [*Fr*] a passionate and serious love affair.

grande vedette [*Fr*] a famous film or stage star.

Grand Guignol [*Fr*] (*grah(n) gee-nyol*) a short, macabre play intended to horrify.

grand siècle [*Fr*] the 17th century; the age of Louis XIV.

gran turismo [*It*] high-performance touring car.

grappa [*It*] Italian brandy made from grape pressings.

gratia gratiam parit [*Lat*] kindness produces kindness.

gravadlax, gravlax [*Swed*] dry-cured spiced salmon. ***Gravad strömming*** – dry-cured spiced herring.

graviora manent [*Lat*] the worst is yet to come.

grisette [*Fr*] literally, 'grey dress fabric'; a young working-class woman.

Groschenroman [*Ger*] the equivalent of English 'penny dreadful' novels, bodice-rippers and wild west pulp novels.

gros mot [*Fr*] colloquial for swear word.

guasto [*It*] out of order.

gueule de bois [*Fr*] literally, 'wooden face' (or 'jaws'), a colloquial term for a hangover.

guerre à outrance [*Fr*] total warfare; duel to the death.

Gum [*Rus*] (*goom*) State Universal Shop: the large Moscow department store.

gute Besserung [*Ger*] a wish for a speedy recovery.

Gymnasium [*Ger*] grammar school. Pupils are 11–16 years but most stay for a further three years.

H

habeas corpus [*Lat*] literally, 'you may have the body'; a writ ordering a person to appear before the court to establish whether or not detention is lawful.

habitué [*Fr*] a regular customer.

habrit ha khadasha [*Heb*] the New Testament.

hachimaki [*Jap*] the ubiquitous headbands worn by males to encourage concentration and effort.

haciendado [*Sp*] a person owning property; proprietor of a *hacienda*.

hadj, hajj [*Arab*] the Muslim pilgrimage to Mecca.

hadji, hajji [*Arab*] a Muslim who has made the pilgrimage to Mecca.

haec olim meminisse juvabit [*Lat*] in time it will be pleasing to remember (these events).

Hakenkreuz [*Ger*] literally, 'hooked cross'. The swastika.

hakuna matata [*Swa*] no worries!

halászlé [*Hun*] thick paprika-flavoured fish soup.

Halbstarker [*Ger*] a teenage hooligan; a delinquent.

hare Krishna [*Sans*] hail to Krishna.

hashi [*Jap*] chopsticks.

hasta la muerte todo es vida [*Sp*] until death, all is life; while there's life there's hope.

hasta la vista [*Sp*] goodbye; until we meet again.

haud fiet, et clavo fixum est [*Lat*] nothing doing, and that's final!

Haus und Hof [*Ger*] house and home.

Hausfrau [*Ger*] (*hows-frow*) housewife – not generally complimentary.

haute bourgeoisie [*Fr*] (*oht boor-zhwah-zee*) the upper-middle or professional class.

haute couture [*Fr*] (*oht kuh-tuur*) high-fashion dress design.

haute cuisine [*Fr*] (*oht kwih-zeen*) top-class cooking.

haute école [*Fr*] (*oht ay-kol*) classical art of horse-riding.

haut monde [*Fr*] (*oh mond*) high society.

heb' dich weg von mir, Satan [*Ger*] get thee behind me, Satan.

Heimat [*Ger*] home; one's birthplace.

Heimweh [*Ger*] homesickness.

Herrenvolk [*Ger*] master race: Nazi term for the German people.

Herzchen [*Ger*] darling.

heute mir, morgen dir [*Ger*] my turn today, yours tomorrow.

hic et ubique [*Lat*] here and everywhere.

hic jacet [*Lat*] (*heek YAK-et*) here lies (followed by name of deceased).

Himmel [*Ger*] heavens!

hinc illae lacrymae [*Lat*] literally, 'hence those tears'. That's the cause.

hin ist hin [*Ger*] gone is gone; forget it.

Hinz und Kunz [*Ger*] the equivalent of 'Tom, Dick and Harry'; sometimes *Krethi und Plethi*.

hiraeth [*Welsh*] (*HEER-ayth*) a mingled feeling of sadness, somewhere between homesickness and nostalgia.

hoch soll er leben [*Ger*] long may he live.

¡hola! [*Sp*] greeting to friends, roughly equivalent to 'hullo'.

homard [*Fr*] (*om-mahr*) lobster.

homme d'affaires [*Fr*] (*om dah-fare*) a businessman.

homme de lettres [*Fr*] (*om duh let-ruh*) man of letters.

homme du monde [*Fr*] (*om doo mo(n)d*) a man of the world.

Homo sapiens [*Lat*] literally, 'wise man'; the name given to modern human beings as a species.

homo trium literatum [*Lat*] a thief. The phrase translates as 'three letter man', meaning *fur*, Latin for thief.

honi soit qui mal y pense [*Fr*] shame on him who thinks ill of it, motto of the Order of the Garter.

hora fugit [*Lat*] the hour flies.

horresco referens [*Lat*] I shudder to tell.

horribile dictu [*Lat*] (*ho-REEB-ee-lay dik-too*) horrible to tell. The opposite is *mirabile dictu* – wonderful to tell.

hors concours [*Fr*] (*or koh(n)-koor*) superior, therefore not in competition; not competing for any prize.

hors de combat [*Fr*] (*or duh koh(n)-bah*) out of the fight; disabled.

hors d'oeuvre [*Fr*] (*or durv*) appetiser before main course.

hortus siccus [*Lat*] literally, 'dry garden'; a herbarium; collection of dried plants.

hôtel des postes [*Fr*] general post office.

hôtel de ville [*Fr*] town hall.

hoteru [*Jap*] hotel.

hubris [*Gk*] excessive pride or arrogance, especially of the kind that leads to someone's downfall.

huîtres [*Fr*] (*weet-ruh*) oysters.

huzur [*Arab*] your presence; polite form of address, as in 'Your Honour'.

hwyl [*Welsh*] (*HOO-eel*) religious or emotional fervour, as experienced with preaching, poetry reading, sporting events, etc.

I

ibidem (abbreviation *ibid*) [*Lat*] (*IB-id-em*) in the same place; used when referring

Ibid

to a quote previously cited.

ich danke Ihnen [*Ger*] I thank you.

ich dien [*Ger*] (*ik DEEN*) I serve, motto of the Prince of Wales.

ich kann nicht anders [*Ger*] I can do no other, from a speech by Martin Luther;

now used in the sense of standing by one's principles in the face of hostility.

ich liebe dich [*Ger*] (*eek leeb-uh deek*) I love you.

ici on parle français [*Fr*] French spoken here.

idée reçue [*Fr*] (*eed-ay rih-soo*) received idea; something that is generally accepted.

idem (abbreviation *id.*) [*Lat*] (*id-dem*) the same; to avoid repetition used in footnotes to refer to an author already named.

id est (abbreviation *i.e.*) [*Lat*] that is; used to say something in other words or explain what has been said.

iechyd da! [*Welsh*] good health!

Iesus Nazarenus Rex Iudaeorum [*Lat*] Jesus of Nazareth, King of the Jews. The initials, *INRI*, are often seen on paintings of the Crucifixion.

i frutti proibiti sono I piu dolci [*It*] forbidden fruits are the sweetest.

ignis fatuus [*Lat*] will-o'-the-wisp, a phosphorescence seen in swamps and marshes. Used now to mean a delusion or a foolish idea.

Igiriss [*Jap*] Great Britain.

ikebana [*Jap*] the art of Japanese flower arranging.

ik hou van je [*Dut*] (*eek how fan yuh*) I love you.

il faut cultiver son jardin [*Fr*] we must cultivate our own garden – Voltaire. We should attend to our own affairs.

il faut souffrir pour être belle [*Fr*] we (women) must suffer to be beautiful.

ils n'ont rien appris ni rien oublié [*Fr*] they have learned nothing and forgotten nothing. Said of the court of Louis XVIII.

immer schlimmer [*Ger*] from bad to worse.

immobiliste [*Fr*] someone who opposes change and progress.

imperméable [*Fr*] raincoat.

imposta sul valore aggiunto (*IVA*) [*It*] the equivalent of Value Added Tax (VAT).

in absentia [*Lat*] in the absence (of the party concerned).

in alio loco [*Lat*] in another place.

inamorato [*It*] lover. The feminine is *inamorata*.

in bona partem [*Lat*] (to be judged) favourably or sympathetically.

in camera [*Lat*] conducted in private, rather than in an open court.

inconnu [*Fr*] unknown; someone whose identity is not known.

Index Librorum Prohibitorum [*Lat*] for four centuries (1564–1966) the list of books prohibited or censored by the Roman Catholic Church.

in esse [*Lat*] in existence.

in extenso [*Lat*] at full length; entire.

in extremis [*Lat*] at the point of death.

in flagrante delicto [*Lat*] in the very act.

infra dignitatem, infra dig [*Lat*] beneath one's dignity.

ingénue [*Fr*] an innocent, naive or unsophisticated young woman.

in hoc signo vinces [*Lat*] by this sign thou shall conquer.

in loco parentis [*Lat*] in the place of a parent; with the responsibilities and authority of parents.

in memoriam [*Lat*] in memory of (followed by name of deceased).

in nomine Patris et Filii et Spiritus Sancti [*Lat*] in the name of the Father, and of the Son, and of the Holy Spirit.

in perpetuum [*Lat*] for ever.

in puris naturalibus [*Lat*] (*in pyoo-ris nat-yoo-RAHL-ih-bus*) starkers; naked.

in re [*Lat*] in the matter of; concerning.

in saecula saeculorum [*Lat*] for ever and ever; always.

insalutato hospite [*Lat*] leaving without saying farewell to your host.

in situ [*Lat*] (*in SIT-yoo*) in its original place; undisturbed.

inter alia [*Lat*] among other things.

interregnum [*Lat*] the period between reigns or rulers when the state is governed by a temporary authority.

in toto [*Lat*] completely; entirely.

intoxicado [*Sp*] *está intoxicado* means 'he is poisoned', not 'he is drunk'.

intoxication [*Fr*] poisoning. *Intoxication alimentaire* – food poisoning. A notorious faux ami (see article on False Friends, pages 614–5).

intra vires [*Lat*] (*in-truh VEE-reez*) within the power and authority of a person or institution.

in utero [*Lat*] in the womb.

in vino veritas [*Lat*] in wine there is truth; a drunk always speaks the truth.

in vitro [*Lat*] (*in VEET-roh*) in an artificial environment; in the laboratory.

in vivo [*Lat*] in the living organism; in the body.

ipse dixit [*Lat*] literally, 'he himself said it'. An unsupported assertion.

ipso facto [*Lat*] by that very fact.

is iyian [*Gk*] cheers!

Italian

Most of us know enough about Italian to be aware that **c** before **e** or **i** is pronounced **ch** as in **church** and *ciao*; that **ch** is pronounced **k**, as in *Chianti*; that the **g** of **gli** is silent, as in *intaglio*; and that **z** and **zz** are pronounced **ts**, as in *scherzo* and *intermezzo*. We know this because of the large number of Italian words that have been absorbed into English – especially in the fields of music, opera, food and drink – and because we continue to pronounce them the way the Italians do.

The Italians at home, however, find the going more complicated. Regional accents and dialects remain deep-rooted and millions of Italians have great difficulty in communicating with their fellow citizens. This is where the verbal gesture fills the gap, making the language one of the most expressive at football matches and in traffic arguments: *Bastardo! Stronzo! Maladetto fottuto!*

See also *polizia*.

Italia para nacer, Francia para vivir, España para morir [*Sp*] Italy to be born in,

France to live in, Spain to die in.

Ivrit [*Heb*] Hebrew.

izvestia, izvestiya [*Rus*] information; news. Also the title of one of Russia's national newspapers.

J

j'accuse [*Fr*] Emile Zola's famous public letter in *L'Aurore* to the government of France in 1898, for which he risked all to tell all and which was headlined *J'Accuse!* has lent its name to any published accusation of injustice or intolerance.

jacta alea est [*Lat*] the die is cast; there is no turning back. Said to have been spoken by Julius Caesar when crossing the Rubicon.

j'adoube [*Fr*] literally, 'I adjust'. To be said during a chess game before touching a piece to adjust it rather than make a move.

jai alai [*Basque*] (*hy uh-ly*) ball game played with a small basket attached to a hand.

jalousie [*Fr*] (*zhah-luh-zee*) slatted window shutters.

jamais de ma vie [*Fr*] never in my life; emphatically never.

jamal [*Arab*] Camel.

jambon [*Fr*] ham.

jardin des plantes [*Fr*] botanical garden.

jawohl [*Ger*] (*yah-vohl*) yes, certainly.

Jehad, Jihad [*Arab*] a crusade inspired by strongly held beliefs; specifically a Muslim holy war against unbelievers and enemies of Islam.

jellaba, djellabah [*Arab*] the loose-hooded cloak worn by males in some Arab countries.

je m'en fous [*Fr*] I don't give a damn.

je ne regrette rien [*Fr*] I regret nothing.

je ne sais quoi [*Fr*] I don't know what. Something that one can't specify or define.

jenever [*Dut*] Dutch gin.

je t'aime [*Fr*] (*zh tem*) I love you.

jeu de mots [*Fr*] (*zhur duh moh*) a play on words; for example, a pun.

jeu d'esprit [*Fr*] (*zhur de-spree*) a light-hearted witticism or display of cleverness.

jeune fille [*Fr*] (*zhurn fee-yuh*) young girl.

jeunesse dorée [*Fr*] (*zhurn-ess dor-ray*) gilded youth; the wealthy and fashionable young.

jiàngyóu [*Ch*] soy sauce.

joie de vivre [*Fr*] (*zhwah duh veev-ruh*) joy of life; high spirits.

jolie laide [*Fr*] a woman whose lack of beauty or irregular features are in themselves attractive or charming. Also called: *belle laide*.

jour de fête [*Fr*] (*zhoor duh fet*) a feast day.

Judenhetze [*Ger*] anti-Semitism.

julienne [*Fr*] shredded vegetables, often made into soup by adding to meat broth.

junta [*Sp*] (*JUHN-tuh* in UK; *HOON-tah* in Spanish) an unelected group, usually military officers, holding power.

jure divino [*Lat*] by divine right.

jus [*Fr*] (zhoo) a sauce in which a dish is served.

juste milieu [*Fr*] (*zhoost meel-yur*) the happy medium; the golden mean; a middle course.

justification du tirage [*Fr*] proof of the number of copies printed of limited edition books and prints.

j'y suis, j'y reste [*Fr*] (*zhee swee, zhee rest*) here I am, here I stay.

K

kabuki [*Jap*] popular drama in Japan.

kafenio [*Gk*] coffee-house.

Kaffeeklatsch [*Ger*] (*KAF-ay-klatsh*) the gossip of a group (usually women) having coffee. Often mistakenly used to mean a 'coffee morning'.

kakemono [*Jap*] Japanese hanging scroll picture on rollers.

kalamarakia [*Gk*] fried squid.

Kamerad [*Ger*] comrade. Its use dates from World War I and was the cry of surrendering German soldiers.

Kampf der Anschauen [*Ger*] a conflict of opinions.

kan pei! [*Ch*] bottoms up! cheers!

Kapellmeister [*Ger*] (*kah-PEL-meye-stuh*) orchestral or choir conductor.

kaput, kaputt [*Ger*] done for; finished; had it.

kashrut, kasher [*Heb*] kosher.

Katzenjammer [*Ger*] literally, 'the racket of mating cats'; a monumental

Katzenjammer

hangover.

Kaufhaus [*Ger*] large department store.

kávé [*Hun*] coffee.

Kazak [*Rus*] Cossack.

keiner kann über sich sehn [*Ger*] no man can see beyond himself. By this, the German philosopher Schopenhauer meant that nobody can appreciate the virtues of others without having some measure of those virtues within themselves.

keiretsu [*Jap*] a corporate structure of interlinked businesses.

Kellner [*Ger*] waiter; inn porter.

kermesse [*Fr*] a village fair or carnival. The Dutch version is *kermis*.

khabar, khubber [*Hind*] information; a news report.

khidmatgar [*Hind*] waiter or table servant.

khushi, khosh [*Hind, Pers*] happiness; pleasure; comfort; to take one's pleasure. Via the Raj the English word **cushy** derives from it.

kibitzer [*Yidd*] someone who interferes with unwanted advice. *Kibitz* is the verb – to interfere.

kiblah [*Arab*] the direction (of Mecca) in which Muslims pray.

kiquette, la, quéquette, la [*Fr*] vulgar slang for penis.

Kinder, Kirche, Küche [*Ger*] children, church, cooking – a woman's lot in life.

kitsch [*Ger*] anything vulgar or over-sentimental.

Kladderadatsch [*Ger*] a muddle; a mess.

Klappe [*Ger*] mouth. *Halt die Klappe!* – shut up!

kleiner Mensch [*Ger*] Literally, 'small man'. Narrow-minded.

klutz [*Yidd*] someone clumsy and stupid, often used in self-deprecation: 'I'm such a klutz!'

knäckebröd [*Swed*] crispbread.

Knesset [*Heb*] the Israeli parliament.

Köchel [*Ger*] usually abbreviated to *K*, the letter preceding the catalogue number of Mozart's compositions; thus K525 is his *Eine Kleine Nachtmusik*. From Ludwig von Köchel (1800–1877) who first classified the musician's works.

kotzen [*Ger*] Colloquial for vomiting; *es ist zum kotzen* – it's enough to make you sick.

krasi [*Gk*] wine; *krasi aspro* – white wine; *krasi kokino* – red wine.

Krasnaya Armeeya [*Rus*] Red Army.

Kriminalroman (abbreviation *Krimi*) [*Ger*] thriller novel.

Kripo [*Ger*] colloquial shortening of *Kriminalpolizei*, the detective branch of the German police.

Kümmel [*Ger*] liqueur flavoured with caraway.

Kunst ist die rechte Hand der Natur [*Ger*] art is the right hand of nature (Schiller).

kwela [*Xhosa, Zulu*] popular black music in South Africa, often featuring a penny whistle.

kvass [*Rus*] Russian beer made from grain and stale bread.

Kyrie, Kyrie eleison [*Gk*] Lord (have mercy), an invocation used in some Christian liturgies.

kyuji [*Jap*] waiter.

L

la belle dame sans merci [*Fr*] literally, 'the beautiful woman without mercy'.

labore est orare [*Lat*] work is prayer.

labore et honore [*Lat*] by labour and honour.

la critique est aisée et l'art est difficile [*Fr*] criticism is easy and art is difficult.

lacrymae rerum [*Fr*] the tears of things; the sadness or tragedy of life.

ladna [*Rus*] okay.

la donna è mobile [*It*] woman is a fickle thing. The title of a song from Verdi's Rigoletto.

La Gioconda [*It*] the smiling lady. Another name for the Mona Lisa.

laissez-aller, laisser-aller [*Fr*] (*less-ay ah-lay*) lack of constraint; letting things go; total freedom.

laissez-faire, laisser-faire [*Fr*] (*less-ay fair*) the policy of non-intervention, of not interfering, especially by a government.

lait [*Fr*] (*lay*) milk; *au lait* – with milk.

La Manche [*Fr*] (*lah mah(n)sh*) the English Channel.

lambris d'appui [*Fr*] wall panelling that rises to about a metre from the floor; *lambris de hauteur* – floor-to-ceiling wall panelling.

Land [*Ger*] country. *Länder* – German states. *Landtag* – legislature of a German state.

Landstrassenschreck [*Ger*] colloquial: roadhog; rotten driver.

Langlauf [*Ger*] cross-country or long-distance skiing.

langouste [*Fr*] small spiny rock lobster.

langoustine [*Fr*] small crayfish; large prawns.

lapin [*Fr*] rabbit.

la propriété c'est le vol [*Fr*] property is theft – Proudhon.

lapsus calami [*Lat*] (*lap-sus KAL-uh-mee*) a slip of the pen.

lapsus linguae [*Lat*] (*lap-sus LING-way*) slip of the tongue.

lapsus memoriae [*Lat*] (*lap-sus mem-OR-ee-ay*) slip of the memory.

larmes dans la voix [*Fr*] literally, 'tears in the voice'. The quaver in the voice that precedes tears.

l'art pour l'art [*Fr*] art for art's sake, free of practical, social and moral restrictions.

lasciate ogni speranza voi ch'entrate [*It*] all hope abandon, ye who enter here: inscription over the gates of Hell from Dante's *Inferno*.

lass das Vergang'ne vergangen sein [*Ger*] let bygones be bygones: from Goethe's *Faust*.

latet anguis in herba [*Lat*] there's a snake in the grass; something is concealed.

Latin

Latin is a dead tongue, as dead as dead can be,
First it killed the Romans; now it's killing me.
All are dead who wrote it,
All are dead who spoke it,
All are dead who learned it.
Lucky dead – they've earned it.

For a dead language, though, Latin is surprisingly persistent: many of the English words we use in English **video**, **propaganda** and **referendum** are derived from it, or still survive intact – *post mortem*, *per annum*, *ad infinitum*. The language arrived in Britain with the Romans, and had a great revival in the Renaissance with the rediscovery of classical texts. It was taken up by the church and the medical and legal professions, by scholars and scientists of all sorts, but is understood today only by a privileged few.

Latin has declined dramatically. It was abandoned as the medium of Catholic worship in the 1960s under the terms of the Second Vatican Council.

In the thirty years to 1992, the Queen's *annus horribilis*, the number of students taking O-level Latin shrank from 60,000 to under 14,000 – fewer than two per cent of children sitting GCSEs. Another ominous move was the abandonment of Latin – for centuries used by doctors and chemists to preserve their secrets – by the British Medical Journal.

And yet, if you've browsed through some of the hundreds of Latin entries in this book, you'll agree that it possesses the economical and elegant knack of turning a thought into an indelibly memorable phrase. Why, even 'Waltzing Matilda' has its Latin rendering:

Veni Matilda, veni Matilda,
Veni saltemus Matilda veni,
Et cantabat homo dum aestuaret cortina
Veni saltemus Matilda veni.

lato sensu [*Lat*] In the broad sense.

latte [*It*] milk; *latte condensato* – condensed milk; *latte detergente* – cleansing milk; *latte scremato* – skimmed milk. *Latte* is also used to mean *caffè e latte* – coffee made with hot milk.

lauda la moglie e tiente donzello [*It*] praise a wife and married life but stay single.

lavabo [*Lat*] (*lah-VAH-boh*) literally, 'I shall wash'; the ritual washing of hands after offertory at Mass. In Italian and French, a washbasin or bathroom sink. In French a fairly common euphemism for the lavatory.

Lebensabend [*Ger*] the twilight of life.

leben Sie wohl! [*Ger*] goodbye!

Lebensmut [*Ger*] zest for life.

Lebensraum [*Ger*] literally, 'living space'; territory claimed by a country for its expanding population. Especially applicable to Nazi Germany's annexation of border territory.

leben und leben lassen [*Ger*] live and let live.

Leberwurst [*Ger*] liver sausage.

le coût en ôte le goût [*Fr*] the cost spoils the taste.

leche [*Sp*] milk, but *mala leche* is 'bad blood'.

la douceur de vivre [*Fr*] a gentle way of life.

le fin mot [*Fr*] the key point; the gist.

Légion d'honneur [*Fr*] (*lay-zhor(n) doh-nur*) Legion of Honour, a civil or military order of merit introduced by Napoleon in 1802.

le meilleur vin a sa lie [*Fr*] even the finest wine has dregs.

le monde [*Fr*] the world; humankind; society.

le mot de l'énigme [*Fr*] the key to the mystery.

le mot juste [*Fr*] the exact word; the perfect word for the purpose.

le petit caporal [*Fr*] the little corporal: Napoleon.

le roi est mort; vive le roi [*Fr*] the king is dead; long live the king.

le Roi Soleil [*Fr*] the Sun King: Louis XIV.

les cinq lettres [*Fr*] four-letter words.

les États-Unis [*Fr*] (*layz aytahz-oo-nee*) the United States (of America).

les petites gens [*Fr*] humble people.

l'état, c'est moi [*Fr*] (*lay-tah, say mwar*) I am the state. Attributed to Louis XIV.

le tout ensemble [*Fr*] overall effect.

le vice anglais [*Fr*] (*luh vees ah(n)-glay*) male homosexuality.

lex non scripta [*Lat*] unwritten or common law.

lex talionis [*Lat*] law of revenge; of retaliation.

liberté, égalité, fraternité [*Fr*] liberty, equality, fraternity, motto of France.

libro cerrado no saca letrado [*Sp*] an unopened book never made a scholar.

licenciado [*Sp*] licenciate; a university graduate.

licencié [*Fr*] a university graduate, but *licencier* means to give someone the sack.

Licht, Liebe, Leben [*Ger*] light, love and life.

Liebchen [*Ger*] darling! beloved!

Liebeserklärung [*Ger*] a declaration of love.

Liebe wintert nicht [*Ger*] love knows no winter.

Lieb und Leid [*Ger*] joy and sorrow.

lied (plural *lieder*) [*Ger*] (*leed-uh*) German song, usually a solo with piano.

limbus fatuorum [*Lat*] a fool's paradise.

Literae Humaniores [*Lat*] Oxford degree subject concerned with Greek and Latin; the Classics.

litera scripta manet [*Lat*] the written word remains; it is always wise to put it in writing.

littérateur [*Fr*] (*lih-teh-ruh-tur*) a writer; man of letters.

livre de chevet [*Fr*] a favourite book; a companion book.

locum tenens [*Lat*] someone who replaces a professional colleague during an absence, especially doctors or dentists.

locus classicus [*Lat*] the authoritative statement on a subject.

loden [*Ger*] green-grey woollen material used to make traditional Bavarian peasant clothing; now fashionable for all kinds of clothing.

l'oeil du maître [*Fr*] the expert eye of the master.

logiciel [*Fr*] computer software. It has been partly displaced by *le software*.

longueur [*Fr*] (*lo(n)-ger*) a long and tedious passage in a book, play, musical concert or speech.

lotteria [*It*] lottery.

Lottoannahme [*Ger*] state lottery office.

louange perfide [*Fr*] literally, 'treacherous praise'. False praise intended to subvert and bring someone down.

lucri cause [*Lat*] for the sake of gain.

l'union fait la force [*Fr*] unity makes strength, motto of Belgium.

l'uomo propone, Dio dispone [*It*] man proposes, God disposes.

lupus in fabula [*Lat*] literally, 'the wolf in the fable'. The unexpected appearance of someone just as he or she is being talked about.

lusus naturae [*Lat*] a freak of nature; one of nature's jokes.

lux et veritas [*Lat*] light and truth.

lux mundi [*Lat*] light of the world.

lycée [*Fr*] (*lee-say*) one type of French secondary school.

M

maa as-salaamah [*Arab*] goodbye.

ma biche [*Fr*] literally, 'my doe'. My darling.

macchabée [*Fr*] corpse. Also colloquially *un macab*.

machismo, macho [*Sp*] pride in masculinity.

Macht ist recht [*Ger*] might is right.

Machtpolitik [*Ger*] power politics.

ma chère [*Fr*] (*ma-shair*) my dear (address only to women).

machin [*Fr*] equivalent to English 'thingummy' or 'wotsit'.

Mädchen [*Ger*] girl; maiden.

madeleine [*Fr*] Small sweet cake.

magari [*It*] If only it were so!

maggiore fretta, minore alto [*It*] more haste, less speed.

magister ceremoniarum (abbreviation *MC*) [*Lat*] master of ceremonies

magna cum laude [*Lat*] (*mag-nah kum LOW-dih*) with great distinction.

magna est veritas et praevalebit [*Lat*] truth is great and shall prevail.

Magnificat [*Lat*] (*mag-NIF-ih-kat*) hymn of the Virgin Mary: 'My soul doth magnify the Lord'; any hymn of praise.

Magyarország [*Hun*] Hungary. A Hungarian is a *Magyar férfi* (man) or a *Magyar nö* (woman).

maharani [*Hind*] a maharajah's wife or widow.

maharishi [*Hind*] Hindu seer or wise man.

mahatma [*Sans*] Exponent of Buddhism; a sage.

maidan [*Urdu*] In India and Pakistan, a space for meetings or a sportsground.

maillot jaune [*Fr*] the yellow jersey worn by the points leader in the Tour de France cycing race.

mains froides, coeur chaud [*Fr*] cold hands, warm heart.

mairie, maire [*Fr*] French town hall and mayor respectively.

maison de passe [*Fr*] a disreputable hotel, most likely a brothel. Such an establishment is also called a *maison de société* and a *maison de tolérance*, the latter being licensed.

maison de santé [*Fr*] private hospital; nursing home.

maître d' [*Fr*] hotel head-waiter.

maître de ballet, maîtresse de ballet [*Fr*] person who trains and rehearses a ballet company.

maîtresse en titre [*Fr*] a man's recognised mistress.

makimono [*Jap*] Japanese scroll painting that unrolls horizontally.

maladresse [*Fr*] clumsiness; lack of tact.

mal à propos [*Fr*] literally, 'not to the purpose'. Inappropriate. The term supplied Sheridan with the inspiration for Mrs Malaprop in his play *The Rivals*, hence **malapropism**: the unintentional misuse of words with similar sounds.

mal d'amour [*Fr*] Lovesickness.

mal de mer [*Fr*] (*mal duh mair*) seasickness. Other *maux* include *mal du coeur* – nausea; *mal au ventre* – stomach ache; *mal de tête* – headache; *mal de dents* – toothache.

mal du siècle [*Fr*] world-weariness; weariness of life.

male parte, male dilabuntur [*Lat*] easy come, easy go.

malgré lui [*Fr*] (*mal-gray lwee*) in spite of himself; against his will; contrary to his intentions.

malgré tout [*Fr*] (*mal-gray too*) in spite of everything.

malheur ne vient jamais seul [*Fr*] troubles never come singly.

mal mariée [*Fr*] an unhappily married woman.

mamma mia! [*It*] my mother! An expression of surprise etc.

mammismo [*It*] maternal control and interference by a mother that continues even when the family is fully grown.

mañana [*Sp*] tomorrow. Sometime.

mancia [*It*] a tip or gratuity.

manga [*Jap*] Japanese style of comic books, often violent or graphically sexual in content

mano a mano [*Sp*] hand-to-hand; one against one.

manqué [*Fr*] unfulfilled; failed; would-be: 'Like most of his crowd he was just a writer *manqué*.'

manque de goût [*Fr*] lack of good taste.

man spricht Deutsch [*Ger*] German spoken here.

maquerelle [*Fr*] the madam of a brothel.

maquillage [*Fr*] cosmetics; make-up.

marché [*Fr*] market; *un marché decouvert* – an open-air market; *le Marché Commun* – (European) Common Market.

mare nostrum [*Lat*] 'our sea': the Mediterranean.

mariage de convenance [*Fr*] (*mar-ih-azh duh koh(n)-veh-nah(n)s*) marriage of convenience, usually with financial motive.

Marianne [*Fr*] symbol of republican France and much prettier than John Bull or Uncle Sam.

marinare [*It*] to pickle; to marinate.

marmite [*Fr*] (*mahr-meet*) pot or saucepan.

marron glacé [*Fr*] crystallised chestnut.

mashallah [*Arab*] God has willed it.

masjid, musjid [*Arab*] an Islamic mosque.

más vale tarde que nunca [*Sp*] better late than never.

materfamilias [*Lat*] the mother or female head of the family.

matryoshka [*Rus*] traditional Russian decorative dolls.

Matryoshka dolls

mauvais coucheur [*Fr*] (*moh-vay koo-shur*) argumentative, cantankerous person.

mauvaise foi [*Fr*] (*moh-vay fwah*) bad faith.

mauvais goût [*Fr*] (*moh-vay goo*) bad taste.

mauvais moment [*Fr*] an unpleasant and embarrassing moment.

mauvais sang [*Fr*] bad feeling; bad blood.

mauvais sujet [*Fr*] (*moh-vay soo-zhay*) a 'black sheep'.

maxima cum laude [*Lat*] with the highest praise and distinction.

maxima debetur puero reverentia [*Lat*] the greatest reverence is due to a child (Juvenal); a child should be protected from vulgarity and indecency.

maxime fabulosum [*Lat*] absolutely fabulous!

mea culpa [*Lat*] the fault is mine; it's my fault.

médecine expectante [*Fr*] nature's cure; medical treatment left to nature.

medice, cure te ipsum [*Lat*] physician, heal thyself.

meditatio fugae [*Lat*] contemplating flight from justice.

Megali Vretania [*Gk*] Great Britain.

megillah [*Yidd*] an unnecessarily long and tiresome story or letter. From the Hebrew *Megillah*, the scroll of the Book of Esther.

mehr Licht! [*Ger*] more light! Goethe's last words, 1832.

Mehrwertsteuer [*Ger*] value-added tax.

mein Gott! [*Ger*] My God!

Mein Kampf [*Ger*] My Struggle: Adolf Hitler's 1924 autobiography.

mélange [*Fr*] (*may-lah(n)zh*) a mixture; a confusion.

melioribus annis [*Lat*] in happier times.

membrum virile [*Lat*] ('virile member') penis.

memento mori [*Lat*] a reminder of death; a symbolic reminder of death (e.g. a skull).

ménage [*Fr*] (*may-nahzh*) a household; housekeeping.

ménage à trois [*Fr*] (*may-nahzh ah trwah*) a domestic arrangement of husband and wife and a lover of one or both of them.

menefreghista [*It*] like Rhett Butler, someone who doesn't give a damn.

mensch [*Yidd*] an admirable, honourable person.

mens rea [*Lat*] (*mens ray-ah*) with criminal intent; with the knowledge that an action is a criminal offence.

mens sana in corpore sano [*Lat*] a healthy mind in a healthy body.

menus plaisirs [*Fr*] for life's little pleasures; pocket money.

méprisable [*Fr*] contemptible.

merci [*Fr*] (*mair-see*) thank you.

merde [*Fr*] (*maird*) excrement; shit. *Le merdier* – a mess.

meret qui laborat [*Lat*] he is deserving who is industrious.

mésalliance [*Fr*] (*may-zal-ih-ah(n)s*) a marriage with a partner who is socially inferior.

meschugge, meshugah [*Yidd*] mad; silly; daft; crazy.

Messaggero [*It*] Messenger. The title of one of Italy's big national newspapers.

métèque [*Fr*] an alien; a foreigner.

métier [*Fr*] (*may-tyay*) a profession; something that someone is particularly good at doing.

métis [*Fr*] (*may-tee*) someone of mixed blood (a term regarded as offensive by many). In Canada, of mixed American Indian and French-Canadian blood; in the USA known as an octoroon.

metteur au point [*Fr*] someone who provides the solution to a problem.

meum et tuum [*Lat*] (*may-um et too-um*) mine and thine: the principle of the rights of property.

mezé [*Turk*] (*mez-eh*) Greek and near-Eastern appetisers served with drinks.

mi casa es su casa [*Sp*] my house is your house; make yourself at home.

miches [*Fr*] vulgar slang in French for breasts.

Midi [*Fr*] the coastal plain contained by the Massif Central, Pyrenees and Alps in southern France.

midinette [*Fr*] Parisian shop assistant, usually in a dressmaker's or milliner's.

mierda [*Sp*] Spanish equivalent of *merde*.

mieux vaut tard que jamais [*Fr*] better late than never.

mignon [*Fr*] (*meen-yoh(n)*) small and dainty.

mijnheer [*Dut*] Dutch equivalent of Sir.

Milchmädchenrechnung [*Ger*] literally, 'milkmaid's reckoning'; a conclusion or speculation based on faulty reasoning.

mille-feuilles [*Fr*] (*meel-fur-yih*) iced puff pastry cakes filled with jam and cream.

millefiori [*It*] (*mee-leh-FYOR-ih*) ornamental glassware that features flower patterns.

mille verisimili non fanno un vero [*It*] a thousand probabilities make not a single truth.

mirabile dictu [*Lat*] (*mih-RARB-ih-lay DIK-too*) wonderful to relate.

mise-en-scène [*Fr*] the stage setting for a play.

miserere [*Lat*] (*mih-zer-AIR-ay*) have mercy. *Miserere mei, Deus* – Have mercy on me, Lord: the 51st Psalm.

missa solemnis [*Lat*] (*mis-suh soh-LEM-nis*) Roman Catholic High Mass.

Mist [*Ger*] colloquially, 'manure' rather than 'shit'. Its English equivalent would be 'rubbish'.

mistral [*Fr*] the notorious wind that blows from the Massif Central across the south of France.

mit Gewalt [*Ger*] by force; by compulsion.

mit gleicher Münze zahlen [*Ger*] to repay tit for tat.

Mitteleuropa [*Ger*] Central Europe.

modus operandi (abbreviation *MO*) [*Lat*] the way it works; method of operation.

modus vivendi [*Lat*] agreement to differ; a compromise arrangement between two parties in dispute.

moeurs [*Fr*] manners; customs.

moi non plus [*Fr*] me neither.

moment de vérité [*Fr*] moment of truth.

momzer [*Yidd*] literally, 'bastard'; a contemptible person.

mon ami [*Fr*] my friend. Feminine form is *mon amie*.

mon cher [*Fr*] my dear. Feminine form is *ma chère*.

mon chéri [*Fr*] my darling. Feminine form is *ma chérie*.

mon Dieu! [*Fr*] (*mor(n) dyur*) my God!

mont-de-piété [*Fr*] Licensed pawnshop, now known as *Crédit Municipal*. The equivalent in Spain is *monte de piedad*, and in Italy, *monte di pietà*.

Mord mit Messer und Gabel [*Ger*] literally, 'death with knive and fork, a colloquial term meaning death from overeating.

Morgenstunde hat Gold im Munde [*Ger*] literally, 'The morning has gold in its mouth'. As the English version has it: 'Early to bed, early to rise, makes a man healthy, wealthy and wise.

morgue anglaise [*Fr*] English condescension.

morituri te salutant [*Lat*] we who are about to die salute you. This was the gladiatorial salute to the Roman emperors.

morta la bestia, morto il veneno [*It*] when the beast is dead he cannot bite.

mot juste see *le mot juste*.

motu proprio [*Lat*] of one's free will.

moules [*Fr*] mussels; *moules marinières* – mussels served with a wine sauce.

mucho en el suelo, poco en el cielo [*Sp*] rich on earth, poor in the hereafter.

mudéjar [*Sp*] Moorish-influenced architectural style in Spain.

muezzin [*Arab*] in Muslim countries, the crier who calls the faithful to prayer.

muito falar, pouco saber [*Port*] many words, little knowledge.

multa cadunt inter calicem supremaque labra [*Lat*] there's many a slip 'twixt cup and lip.

multi sunt vocati, pauci sunt electi [*Lat*] many are called, few are chosen.

multis terribilis, caveto multos [*Lat*] if many fear you, beware of many.

multum in parvo [*Lat*] much in a small space.

Mumienschänder [*Ger*] 'mummy decorator'; a 'toy boy'; a young gigolo.

muor giovane colui ch'al cielo è caro [*It*] whom the gods love dies young.

mutatis mutandis [*Lat*] the necessary or appropriate changes having been made.

mutilé de guerre [*Fr*] a disabled ex-serviceman.

Mütterchen [*Ger*] grandma; old woman.

muu-muu [*Haw*] light, loose, and often colourful dress.

muzhik, moujik, mujik [*Rus*] Russian peasant.

N

nach und nach [*Ger*] little by little.

Nacktkultur (also *Freikörperkultur*) [*Ger*] naturism; the cult of nudism.

Nagy-Britannia [*Hun*] Great Britain.

naif [*Fr*] artless; ingenuous.

naschen [*Ger*] to eat sweets when one shouldn't. The Yiddish term *nosh* (food) derives from this.

nasi goreng [*Indonesian*] spiced rice dish topped with egg.

natura abhorret a vacuo [*Lat*] Nature abhors a vacuum.

natura il fece, e poi roppe la stampa [*It*] Nature made him, then broke the mould.

n'avoir pas le sou [*Fr*] to be without a sou; broke.

nazionale [*It*] *La Nazionale* – Italy's national football team. *Un nazionale* – an international player. For more on *il calcio* – Italy's national game – see *scudetto*.

nebech, nebbish [*Yidd*] a weak, ineffectual individual.

nec habeo, nec careo, nec curo [*Lat*] I have not, I want not, I care not.

ne choisitpas qui emprunte [*Fr*] He who borrows has no choice.

née [*Fr*] literally, 'born'. 'Her maiden name being'. Follows a woman's married name and indicates her original surname: *Lucinda Black, née White*.

nemine contradicente (abbreviation *nem. con.*) [*Lat*] with nobody dissenting; unanimously.

nemine dissentiente [*Lat*] nobody dissents, nobody opposes.

nemo dat quod non habet [*Lat*] no one can give what he does not possess.

nemo me impune lacessit [*Lat*] no one injures me with impunity, the motto of Scotland).

nemo mortalium omnibus horis sapit [*Lat*] no one is wise at all times.

ne plus ultra [*Lat*] literally, 'no more beyond'. The pinnacle; the ultimate in perfection.

nessun dorma [*It*] none shall sleep. Title and opening line of the famous aria from Puccini's opera *Turandot*.

n'est-ce pas? [*Fr*] isn't it?; isn't that so?

Neujahr [*Ger*] New Year.

Nicht alles, was glänzt ist Gold [*Ger*] all is not gold that glitters.

nihil ad rem [*Lat*] irrelevant; not to the point.

Nihon [*Jap*] Japan. ***Nihon-jin*** – Japanese person. ***Nihongo*** – Japanese language. Another more widely known transliteration is ***Nippon***.

nil carborundum illigitimi [Liar's Latin] don't let the bastards grind you down.

nil desperandum [*Lat*] never despair.

nil mortalibus arduum est [*Lat*] nothing is beyond the accomplishment of mortals.

noblesse oblige [*Fr*] (*noh-bless oh-bleezh*) originally the obligation of the nobility and aristocracy to act honourably; rank imposes obligations.

nochniye babochki [*Rus*] literally, 'night butterflies'. Prostitutes on the streets of Moscow.

Noh, No [*Jap*] elaborate stylised traditional Japanese drama.

noisette [*Fr*] (*nwah-zet*) small, round boneless cut of lamb; hazelnut.

nolens volens [*Lat*] whether willing or unwilling; having no alternative; willy-nilly.

noli irritare leones [*Lat*] don't annoy the lions.

Noli irritare leones

noli me tangere [*Lat*] do not touch me; a painting of Jesus appearing to Mary Magdalene after his resurrection.

nolle prosequi [*Lat*] official abandonment of a legal action or a prosecution.

nom de guerre [*Fr*] (*nom duh gair*) an assumed name or pseudonym. The French equivalent of the anglicised **nom de plume**.

non compos mentis [*Lat*] of unsound mind.

non generant aquilae columbas [*Lat*] eagles do not bear doves.

non mi ricordo [*It*] I don't remember.

non possumus [*Lat*] (*non pos-SOOM-us*) literally, 'we cannot'. In law, inability to act in a matter.

non ragioniamo di loro, ma guarda e passa [*It*] from Dante: 'Speak not of them, but look and pass them by'.

non sapere l'abbicci [*It*] literally, 'not to know the alphabet'. To be abysmally ignorant.

non so [*It*] I don't know – a phrase that infiltrates all everyday Italian speech as a 'sentence filler', equivalent to the English 'um y'know'.

nos da [*Welsh*] goodnight.

nostalgie de la boue [*Fr*] literally 'nostaligia for the mud', the perverse yearning of civilised people for sordid and degrading experiences.

nota bene (abbreviation *NB*) [*Lat*] note well; take notice.

Not bricht Eisen [*Ger*] necessity breaks iron; equivalent to 'necessity is the mother of invention'.

nous verrons ce que nous verrons [*Fr*] we shall see what we shall see.

nouveau riche [*Fr*] (*noo-voh reesh*) someone who has recently become wealthy but is regarded as socially inferior.

novus homo [*Lat*] a new man; an arriviste; an upstart.

nuda veritas [*Lat*] naked truth.

nudis verbis [*Lat*] in plain words.

nudnik [*Yidd*] a bore.

nul bien sans peine [*Fr*] no pain, no gain.

nulla mensa sine impensa [*Lat*] there's no free lunch.

nulla nulla [*Abor*] club used as a weapon by Australian aborigines.

nulla nuova, buona nuova [*It*] no news is good news.

nulli desperandum, quamdiu spirat [*Lat*] while there's life, there's hope.

nulli secundus [*Lat*] second to none.

nullo modo [*Lat*] no way!

nunc aut nunquam [*Lat*] now or never.

nunc dimittis [*Lat*] from the first line of the Latin version of Simeon's Canticle: 'Lord, now lettest thou thy servant depart in peace'.

nunc est bibendum [*Lat*] now is the time for drinking.

nunquam dormio [*Lat*] I never sleep; I am always on my guard, motto of *The Observer* newspaper.

nyet [*Rus*] no.

O

obi [*Jap*] the wide sash with a bow at the back, worn as part of their national costume by Japanese women.

obiter dictum [*Lat*] (*OB-ih-tur DIK-tum*) an incidental comment or observation. In law, a relevant observation on a point of law by a judge, but not binding.

objet d'art [*Fr*] (*ob-zhay dar*) a work of art.

objets d'occasion [*Fr*] second-hand goods.

obscurum per obscurius [*Lat*] trying to explain some obscure point by referring to something even more obscure.

ocha [*Jap*] Japanese tea. *Kocha* – Indian tea

oderint dum metuant [*Lat*] let them hate, so long as they fear.

odi et amo [*Lat*] I hate and love; the 'love-hate' syndrome.

o Dio! [*It*] common Italian expression meaning, roughly, Good Lord! Good heavens! Blimey!

odium scholasticum [*Lat*] the bitter disagreements among scholars. *Odium theologicum* – acrimonious debate between theologians. Similar for *odium medicum* (doctors) and *odium aestheticum* (aesthetics).

oeil-de-boeuf [*Fr*] (*uh-ee duh-buhf*) small round window in 17th- and 18th-century (French) buildings.

oeuf [*Fr*] (*uhf*) egg; *oeufs brouillés* – scrambled eggs; *oeuf dur* – hard-boiled egg; *oeuf poché* – poached egg; *oeuf sur le plat* – fried egg; *une omelette* – omelette.

oeuvre [*Fr*] (*urv-ruh*) the output of work, usually by a writer or artist.

ogni medaglia ha il suo rovescio [*It*] there are two sides to every medal (or coin).

ohne Wissen, ohne Sünde [*Ger*] without knowledge, without sin.

oleum addere camino [*Lat*] adding fuel to the fire.

olio [*Sp*] meat and vegetable stew. In Italian, *olio* – oil; *olio d'oliva* – olive oil.

omadhaun [*Ir*] a fool; an idiot.

omertà [*It*] code of silence among members of a criminal fraternity, especially the Mafia.

omnem movere lapidem [*Lat*] leave no stone unturned.

omnia ad Dei gloriam [*Lat*] all things to the glory of God.

omnia mors aequat [*Lat*] death levels all.

omnia vincit amor [*Lat*] (*om-nih-uh vin-kit ah-mor*) love conquers everything; *omnia vincit labor* – labour conquers everything.

on dit [*Fr*] (*o(n) dee*) literally, 'it is said'. Gossip; rumour.

onus probandi [*Lat*] the burden of proof; it is up to the accuser to prove the allegation.

opéra bouffe [*Fr*] (*op-ay-ruh boof*) comic opera.

opera buffa [*It*] (*op-er-ruh boof-uh*) comic opera.

opere citato [*Lat*] in the work quoted already; often seen in footnotes as the abbreviation *op cit*.

opéra comique [*Fr*] (*op-ay-ruh com-eek*) light opera, often comic, with spoken dialogue.

opus Dei [*Lat*] (*oh-pus day-ih*) the work of God.

ora et labora [*Lat*] pray and work.

ora pro nobis [*Lat*] pray for us.

orbis terrarum [*Lat*] the earth.

ordre du jour [*Fr*] order of the day; the agenda.

oshibori [*Jap*] the moist cloth for wiping hands before a meal.

osteria [*It*] an inn.

O tempora! O mores! [*Lat*] Oh, what times! Oh, what manners! A traditional lament at falling standards of behaviour.

oui [*Fr*] (*wee*) yes. The correct or authentically French pronunciation of *oui* is one of the most difficult of all to master.

outré [*Fr*] (*oo-tray*) exaggerated; excessive; eccentric; extravagant.

ouvrage de longue haleine [*Fr*] literally, 'a work of long breath'. A long, sustained achievement.

ouzeri [*Gk*] Greek bar that serves ouzo and beer with *mezés*, or snacks.

P

pace [*Lat*] (*pah-chay* also *pah-say* or *pay-see*) preceding a person's name, it expresses polite disagreement about some point, but with apologies.

pain [*Fr*] bread, in various shapes and sizes: *baguette, ficelle, bâtard, saucisson*, etc. *Le pain grillé* – toast.

palazzo [*It*] (*pa-LAT-zoh*) originally 'palace' but now any large mansion or building. *Palazzo municipale* – town hall.

palmam qui meruit ferat [*Lat*] let him bear the palm who has deserved it.

panem et circenses [*Lat*] bread and circuses (for the masses).

pannekoekhuisje [*Dut*] pancake house, serving up to 50 different kinds of these Dutch specialities.

paparazzo (plural *paparazzi*) [*It*] the ugly side of photography; 'sneak' news photographer.

papier [*Fr*] (*pap-yay*) paper; *papier hygiénique* – toilet paper; *papier de soie* – tissue paper; *papier machine (à écrire)* – typing paper.

papillon [*Fr*] literally, butterfly. Colloquially, a parking ticket.

papillote [*Fr*] buttered paper used to wrap meat or fish that is then baked.

par avion [*Fr*] by airmail.

para todo hay remedio sino para la muerte [*Sp*] there is a remedy for everything but death.

parbleu [*Fr*] my God! Euphemism for *par Dieu*.

par excellence [*Fr*] pre-eminently; above all.

par exemple [*Fr*] for instance.

pari passu [*Lat*] with equal speed; simultaneously.

paroles en l'air [*Fr*] idle words; pointless discussion.

partager le gâteau [*Fr*] to share the cake; split the takings.

partie carrée [*Fr*] (*par-tee kar-ray*) a group of four people, customarily two couples.

parti pris [*Fr*] (*par-tee pree*) a preconceived opinion; prejudiced.

parvenu [*Fr*] someone who, becoming wealthy and having risen socially, is considered to be an unsuitable member of his or her new class. Feminine: *parvenue*.

pas de chat [*Fr*] a ballet dancer's catlike leap.

pas de deux [Fr] a ballet dance for two dancers.

pas devant les enfants [Fr] (*pah duh-vah(n) layz ah(n)-fah(n)*) not in front of the children.

pas glissé [Fr] dance term; Gliding, sliding step.

passer une nuit blanche [Fr] literally, 'to pass a white night'. To have a sleepless night.

passim [Lat] here and there; in many places; usually a footnote to show that a reference occurs throughout a book.

pasto [It] meal; *antipasto* – hors d'oeuvre.

pastrami [Yidd] smoked, seasoned beef.

paterfamilias [Lat] the father; head of the household.

pâtisserie [Fr] French cake shop.

pavé [Fr] literally, 'a paving stone'. Colloquially, a large thick steak.

pax Britannica [Lat] peace imposed by the British during the empire period.

pax vobiscum [Lat] peace be with you.

paysage [Fr] (*pay-zahzh*) landscape; landscape painting.

peccavi [Lat] (*peh-KAH-vee*) I have sinned. It is used light-heartedly as an apology. And as a pun; when British Army general Sir Charles Napier captured the Indian province of Sind he sent HQ a telegram that simply said *Peccavi*.

pedir peras al olmo [Sp] don't try to find pears on an elm; don't expect the impossible.

peignoir [Fr] (*pen-wahr*) a woman's loose dressing-gown.

peintre de dimanche [Fr] a 'Sunday painter'; an amateur artist.

pelota [Sp] game played by two players with small baskets strapped to their wrists to hurl a ball at a marked wall. *See jai alai*, a similar game.

pendejo [Sp] literally, a pubic hair, but used colloquially to mean a fool; an idiot.

pensa molto, parla poco, e scrivi meno [It] think much, talk little, and write less.

pensée [Fr] (*pah(n)-say*) a thought expressed in elegant writing.

pentimento [It] revealing an addition or alteration made by an artist to a painting; revealing something previously hidden.

per capita [Lat] literally, 'by heads'. For or by each person.

per diem [Lat] each day.

père [Fr] father.

perestroika [Rus] (*peh-rih-STROY-kuh*) the reform and restructuring of the political and economic system of the former Soviet Union in the 1980s.

perfide Albion [Fr] treacherous England. A traditional view held by the French.

per incuriam [Lat] by negligence; by oversight.

per procurationem (abbreviations *per pro, pp*) [Lat] by proxy; by delegation to. The abbreviation *pp* is used by someone signing a letter or document on behalf of another.

per se [Lat] (*pur say*) in itself; by itself; essentially.

persona non grata [Lat] a person who is unacceptable or unwelcome.

pesca [It] peach; but also fishing; *pesce* – fish.

pesto [It] a paste or sauce based on basil, often served with pasta.

pétanque [*Fr*] another name for the game of boules.

pet-de-nonne [*Fr*] literally, 'nun's fart'. A light cake made with choux pastry.

péter [*Fr*] to fart; *péter le feu* – to fart fire; to be full of energy.

pétillant [*Fr*] describes wine that is slightly effervescent.

petit ami [*Fr*] boyfriend; *petite amie* – girlfriend.

petite bourgeoisie [*Fr*] (*puh-teet boor-zhwah-zee*) the lower middle classes; *petit bourgeois* – a member of this class, usually used in a derogatory sense.

petit maître [*Fr*] a dandy or toff.

petits fours [*Fr*] (*peh-tih foor*) fancily iced small cakes.

petits pois [*Fr*] (*peh-tih pwah*) small, fresh green peas.

phrase toute faite [*Fr*] a cliché; a common phrase.

piac [*Hun*] (*py-ut*) Hungarian open market. The biggest and best-known is the *Bosnyák téri piac* in Budapest.

pibroch [*Gael*] a theme with variations for the Scottish bagpipe.

picante [*Sp*] hot; highly peppered and spiced; *picantería* – restaurant specialising in hot food.

piccola morte [*It*] literally, 'little death'. An orgasm; a state of drug-induced oblivion.

Pidgin

Pidgin is a language formed from the vocabularies and grammars of other languages in order to facilitate communication between speakers of many different languages.

One of the most interesting pidgins today is Melanesian pidgin, the lingua franca of Papua New Guinea (which has some 600 mother tongues), Solomon Islands, Vanuatu and other islands of Melanesia. It is also the official language of the Papua New Guinea parliament and has a full grammatical structure. The number of people who use only pidgin, and who regard it as their mother tongue, is growing.

To speakers of English, the vocabulary of pidgin can seem strangely, even comically, familiar. The structure of the language leads to some vivid, seemingly incongruous juxtapositions. You may experience the shock of recognition in the following phrases:

ashes	*shit bilong faia*
moustache	*gras bilong maus* (mouth)
broken, ruined	*bagarup* (buggered-up)
house foundations	*ars bilong haus* (arse – bottom)
sexual intercourse	*push pushim*
of no consequence	*samting nating* (something nothing)
hurricane lamp	*lam wokabout*

Just as graphic but more economical are these instructions for using western toilets (*Hao Yu Usim Kloset*):

1. *Putim daon sit bilong kloset*
2. *Sidaon long maos bilong kloset*
3. *Taem yu finis flusim kloset*
4. *Wasem han bilong yu*

pièce de résistance [*Fr*] the principal or special creation of an artist, performer or chef.

pied-à-terre [*Fr*] (*pyay-dah-tair*) not a main residence, but usually a convenient town or city flat.

Pietà [*It*] the image of the Virgin Mary holding the dead body of Christ.

pijiu [*Ch*] beer.

pila in area tua est [*Lat*] the ball is in your court.

piña colada [*Sp*] a long drink made with rum, pineapple juice and coconut.

pinxit [*Lat*] he/she painted it.

pipi de chat [*Fr*] (*pee-pee duh shah*) cat's pee; used by wine experts to describe the pungent aroma of wine made from the Sauvignon Blanc grape. Also used colloquially to mean an unpleasantly rancid drink.

pique [*Fr*] (*peek*) a display of resentment or irritation.

piqué [*Fr*] (*pee-kay*) ribbed fabric of cotton and silk.

piropos [*Sp*] the 'compliments' shouted to women by Hispanic males: the articulated and often explicit equivalent to the admiring whistle that a woman is supposed to ignore.

pis aller [*Fr*] (*pee zah-lay*) a last resort, in the absence of anything better.

piscem natare docere [*Lat*] teaching a fish how to swim.

piscine [*Fr*] swimming pool.

pissoir [*Fr*] (*pee-swahr*) a public urinal.

piste [*Fr*] a ski-run, slope or course.

pisto [*Sp*] traditional Spanish dish of vegetables fried in olive oil. Do not confuse with *pito*, which is slang for penis.

place au soleil, une [*Fr*] a place in the sun.

plage [*Fr*] (plazh) a bathing beach.

plat du jour [*Fr*] (*plah doo zhoor*) a restaurant's dish of the day.

plein air [*Fr*] in the open air; a school of landscape painting.

plus ça change, plus c'est la même chose [*Fr*] (*ploo sah shah(n)zh, ploo say lah mehm shohz*) the more things change, the more they stay the same, often shortened to *plus ça change*.

poi [*Haw*] a dish made from fermented taro root.

pointillisme [*Fr*] style of painting, made famous by Seurat, which uses multi-coloured dots to achieve an impressionistic effect.

polenta [*It*] thick maize porridge.

polizia [*It*] Italian police. *Metropolitani* – Municipal police; *Corpo della Pubblica Sicurezza* – Public police; *Pubblica Siccurezza* and *Carabinieri* – Military police; *Guardia di Finanza* – Customs police; *Polizia Giudiziaria* – Criminal Investigation Department; *polizia stradale* – traffic police; *vigili notturni* – private security guards.

pommes frites [*Fr*] (*pom freet*) French fries; chips.

portière [*Fr*] the anti-draught curtain behind a door.

posada [*Sp*] Spanish inn.

poste restante [*Fr*] (*post res-tah(n)t*) section of a post office that keeps mail for collection, e.g. by people on holiday.

post meridiem (abbreviation *pm*) [*Lat*] after noon; afternoon.

post nubila, Phoebus [*Lat*] after clouds, the sun.

post obitum [*Lat*] after death.

postpartum [*Lat*] after childbirth.

post scriptum (*PS*) [*Lat*] an addition or note added below the signature.

potage [*Fr*] soup.

pot-au-feu [*Fr*] boiled beef in broth.

pot-pourri [*Fr*] (*poh-poo-ree*) a miscellany; a medley; a mixed collection; specifically a mixture of dried, fragrant rose and other flower petals.

pourboire [*Fr*] (*poor-bwahr*) a tip; gratuity.

pour encourager les autres [*Fr*] to encourage the rest. People often use this ironically, as did its originator, Voltaire, in commenting on the execution by the Royal Navy of Admiral Byng for negligence in 1757.

pour épater les bourgeois [*Fr*] to shock the middle classes.

pourquoi? [*Fr*] Why?

pour rire [*Fr*] In fun; not to be taken seriously.

pousse-café [*Fr*] literally, 'push-coffee'; a liqueur drunk after dinner, with or just after coffee.

précieuse [*Fr*] (*pray-syurz*) precious; affected.

préciosité [*Fr*] (*pray-sios-ih-tay*) extreme affectation.

prego [*It*] (*pray-goh*) the equivalent of 'don't mention it', said to someone who thanks you.

prêt-à-porter [*Fr*] ready to wear.

prima donna [*It*] literally, 'first lady'; a female opera star; also someone who is temperamental and difficult to deal with.

prima facie [*Lat*] (*pree-mah fay-sih*) at first sight; in law, using available but not necessarily complete or tested evidence to arrive at a conclusion.

primus inter pares [*Lat*] first among equals; having precedence but only equal authority.

pris sur le fait [*Fr*] caught in the act.

prix d'ami [*Fr*] a 'special price' for a friend.

prix fixe [*Fr*] an inclusive fixed price, usually for a meal.

pro bono (publico) [*Lat*] for the public good, not for a fee.

profanum vulgus [*Lat*] the herd; the common multitude.

pro forma [*Lat*] according to procedure; as a matter of form. A *pro forma* invoice is one issued before purchase and delivery of the goods.

pro rata [*Lat*] in proportion; proportionally.

pro rege et patria [*Lat*] for king and country.

prosit! [*Lat*] good health! German and other languages have it as *prost!*; the Dutch is *proost!*

pro tempore (abbreviation *pro tem*) [*Lat*] for the time being; temporarily.

prudens futuri [*Lat*] thinking of the future.

psaria [*Gk*] fish; *psarotaverna* – fish restaurant.

psistaria [*Gk*] restaurant specialising in charcoal grills.

puîné [*Fr*] younger. *Puisné* – Old French, meaning 'born later' from which is derived the class of judges known as puisne judges, i.e. of lower rank.

pukka [*Hind*] properly done; genuine.

puta [*Sp*] whore, and a common vulgarism; *hijo de puta* is one of the top ten Hispanic insults (*hijo* – son).

putsch [*Ger*] (*pootch*) a violent overthrow of authority.

Q

qarwah [*Arab*] coffee.

Quai d'Orsay [*Fr*] (*kay-dor-say*) the French Foreign Ministry.

qualche volta è virtù facere il vero [*It*] sometimes it is a virtue to conceal the truth.

qualis vita, finis ita [*Lat*] as in life, so is the end.

Quartier Latin [*Fr*] the Paris bohemian south bank area.

quattrocento [*It*] the period from 1400 to 1500 (*see cinquecento*); art of that period.

que besa sus pies [*Sp*] literally, 'who kisses your feet'. Shortened to *QBSP* it is a writer's fond sign-off in a letter to a woman.

quenelle [*Fr*] seasoned, fried meat or fish ball.

¿qué pasó? [*Sp*] colloquial greeting equivalent to 'how's it going?' or 'what's happening?'

quequette, quiquette [*Fr*] vulgar slang for penis.

que sais-je? [*Fr*] what do I know?

que será será [*Sp*] (*kay suh-RAR suh-RAR*) what will be will be.

que ta casquette ne sache ta guise [*Fr*] don't let even your cap know what thoughts it covers.

quid pro quo [*Lat*] something for something; an equitable exchange.

quieta non movere [*Lat*] let sleeping dogs lie.

qui m'aime aime mon chien [*Fr*] who loves me loves my dog; love me, love my dog.

quincaillerie [*Fr*] an ironmonger's shop, or the hardware and utensils sold there.

quinta [*Sp*] in Spain, originally a country house, but now usually a suburban villa.

quis custodiet ipsos custodes? [*Lat*] who will guard the guards?

qui s'excuse s'accuse [*Fr*] he who makes excuses for himself accuses himself.

Quittung [*Ger*] receipt.

qui vive [*Fr*] (*kee veev*) the alert.

quod erat demonstrandum (*QED*) [*Lat*] that which was to be demonstrated or proved.

quod vide (*q.v.*) [*Lat*] which see. The abbreviation *q.v.* is used to advise readers to consult other references on the subject in the same work.

quo vadis? [*Lat*] whither goest thou?

R

Rache trägt keine Frucht [*Ger*] revenge brings no fruit.

radschlagen [*Ger*] to perform a gymnastic cartwheel; *die Düsseldorfer Radschläger* – the cartwheel performances on the Königstrasse, well known to tourists.

raffreddore [*It*] the common cold in Italy; colloquially known as catching a *freddo*.

ragoût [*Fr*] (*rah-goo*) highly seasoned stew.

raison d'état [*Fr*] reason(s) of state; for the state's security.

raison d'être [*Fr*] (*ray-zoh(n) det-ruh*) reason for existing.

râle de la mort [*Fr*] death rattle, the rough breathing of a dying person.

Ramadan [*Arab*] the religious thirty-day sunrise-to-sunset fast in the ninth month of the Muslim year.

rapporteur [*Fr*] someone directed to investigate and to submit a report on the findings.

rapprochement [*Fr*] (*rah-prosh-mah(n)*) a coming together; establishing or re-establishing friendly relations.

rara avis [*Lat*] (*rah-ruh AY-vis*) literally, 'rare bird'; something or someone most unusual and rarely encountered.

Rara avis

Rasthaus [*Ger*] small motel by main roads and the *Autobahnen* in which travellers can rest for a few hours.

ratatouille [*Fr*] (*raht-ah-twee*) fried and stewed vegetable casserole.

Rathaus [*Ger*] (*RAH-tows*) German town hall.

Ratskeller [*Ger*] upmarket restaurant, as distinct from the *Gastkeller* where drinkers are likely to outnumber diners.

rav [*Heb*] rabbi.

Realpolitik [*Ger*] politics based on practicalities and opportunism rather than ideals and morals.

rebozo [*Sp*] shawl worn by Hispanic women over the head and shoulders.

réchauffé [*Fr*] (*ray-shoh-fay*) warmed up leftovers; anything rehashed from old, stale materials.

recherché [*Fr*] (*ruh-shair-shay*) refined and rare; obscure.

réclame [*Fr*] (*ray-klahm*) self-advertisement; publicity-seeking; a talent for notoriety.

reculer pour mieux sauter [*Fr*] a strategic retreat in order to make a more effective advance.

rédacteur [*Fr*] publishing editor; *rédaction* – editing.

Reden ist Silber, Schweigen ist Gold [*Ger*] speech is silver, silence is gold.

reductio ad absurdum [*Lat*] to prove the falsity of a proposition by demonstrating that its logical conclusion is absurd.

règlement [*Fr*] the rule or regulation; *il faut agir selon les règlements* – you must conform to the rules.

Reich [*Ger*] (*rykh*) German empire or state. Specifically, the **First Reich** (962–1806 or Bismarck's empire of 1871–1919); **Second Reich** (Weimar Republic, 1919–33); **Third Reich** (Nazi Germany, 1933–45).

relais routier [*Fr*] (*reh-lay root-yay*) roadside restaurant and rest-place used by travellers and lorry drivers.

relata refero [*Lat*] I tell it as it was told to me.

religieuse [*Fr*] nun; *religieux* – monk or brother.

reliquiae [*Lat*] remains, especially fossils of animals or plants.

remonte-pente [*Fr*] ski-lift.

rémoulade [*Fr*] herb mayonnaise sauce for salads.

renaissance [*Fr*] rebirth; revival; *Renaissance* – classical revival in the 15th-16th centuries.

renkött [*Swed*] reindeer.

renommé [*Fr*] celebrated; famous.

rentier [*Fr*] (*rah(n)t-yay*) someone who lives off investments or has independent means.

repas maigre [*Fr*] vegetarian (meatless) meal.

repêchage [*Fr*] (*reh-peh-sharzh*) a heat in a contest in which runners-up in previous heats compete for a place in the final.

répondez, s'il vous plaît (*RSVP*) [*Fr*] (*ray-poh(n)-day seel voo play*) reply if you please.

requiescat in pace (**RIP**) [*Lat*] (*rek-wih-ES-kat in pah-chay*) may he/she rest in peace.

retroussé [*Fr*] (*ruh-troo-say*) turned-up nose.

revanche [*Fr*] (*ruh-vansh*) literally, 'revenge'; *revanchisme* – policy of retaliation to regain something lost.

réveillon [*Fr*] French Christmas and New Year's celebrations usually involving meals and drinks after midnight.

revenons à nos moutons [*Fr*] literally, 'let's return to our sheep'. Let's return to the subject; let's get back to the point.

rex non potest peccare [*Lat*] the king can do no wrong.

ride bene chi ride l'ultimo [*It*] he laughs best who laughs last.

ridere in stomacho [*Lat*] to laugh up your sleeve.

rien ne va plus [*Fr*] no more bets. The roulette croupier's announcement before spinning the wheel.

rijstafel [*Dut*] (*rays-tah-fel*) Indonesian banquet based on rice with a variety of vegetables and meats.

rincer les yeux [*Fr*] 'eyewash'; colloquial for an admiring gaze at an attractive object, usually a woman.

ripopée [*Fr*] dregs; slops; what's left.

rira bien qui rira le dernier [*Fr*] he laughs best who laughs last.

rive gauche [*Fr*] (*reev gohsh*) the left bank of the Seine in Paris; the Latin Quarter.

rivière [*Fr*] multi-stringed necklace of precious stones.

robe de chambre [*Fr*] (*rohb duh shah(n)-bruh*) dressing-gown.

roman à clef [*Fr*] (*roh-mah(n) ah clay*) a novel that describes real events and has real people as characters.

romanesco, romano [*It*] the dialect of Rome.

roman-fleuve [*Fr*] series of novels about one group or family.

romanista [*It*] a Rome Football Club supporter. The other Roman team is the Lazio FC or the *biancoazzurri*, whose supporters are called *laziale*.

rompiscatole [*It*] literally, 'ball-breaker'; vulgar for a bore, pest or nuisance.

rondelet, rondelette [*Fr*] plump; chubby; a well-rounded person.

rondine [*It*] a swallow; *una rondine non fa primavera* – one swallow doesn't make a spring.

Rosh Hashanah [*Heb*] (*rohsh hah-SHAH-nuh*) Jewish New Year.

rôti [*Fr*] (*roh-tee*) in cooking, to roast; roasted food.

roublard [*Fr*] cunning; a sharp character.

roué [*Fr*] (*roo-ay*) a lecherous, debauched male.

roux [*Fr*] (*roo*) blend of butter or other fat and flour, used as the basis for sauces.

rusé [*Fr*] (*roo-zay*) wily; tricky; cunning.

rus in urbe [*Lat*] (*roos in UR-bay*) bringing the country to the city; the creation of rural atmosphere in a town.

ryokan [*Jap*] traditional Japanese inns in which guests can experience local food and customs.

S

sacré bleu! [*Fr*] curse it! Confound it!

sain et sauf [*Fr*] safe and sound.

salaam [*Arab*] (*sah-LAHM*) peace. A Muslim salutation.

salaud [*Fr*] (*sah-LOH*) bastard; swine; sod, etc; *petit salaud* – little bastard.

salata horiatiki [*Gk*] Greek salad.

salière [*Fr*] salt-cellar.

salle à manger [*Fr*] (*sal ah mah(n)-zhay*) dining room.

salle d'attente [*Fr*] (*sal dah-tah(n)t*) waiting room.

salope [*Fr*] a bitch.

salsa [*Sp*] spicy Latin American sauce. Also a kind of dance music.

saltimbanque [*Fr*] a quack; crook.

saltimbocca [*It*] herbed dish of folded veal and prosciutto.

salvete [*Lat*] welcome! Greetings!

salvo pudore [*Lat*] without offence to modesty.

salwar kameez [*Urdu*] the outfit of tunic and loose trousers worn by many Indian and Pakistani women.

samadhi [*Hind*] an ultimate trance-like state in yoga.

samizdat [*Rus*] self-published; published clandestinely.

san [*Jap*] the word you add to all Japanese surnames (which in Japan are written first: with Harawa Keiko, Harawa is the surname; Keiko is the given name) which is the all-purpose equivalent of Mr, Mrs and Ms.

sanctum sanctorum [*Lat*] the holy of holies; a private sanctum.

sang-froid [*Fr*] (*sah(n)-frwah*) composure; calmness; self-possession.

sans [*Fr*] (English pronunciation: *sanz*, not *so(n)*) without.

sans blague [*Fr*] (*sah(n) blahg*) without joking; seriously.

sans-culotte [*Fr*] (*sah(n)-koo-lot*) originally a poor revolutionary; any republican extremist.

Sashimi

sans doute [*Fr*] without doubt.

sans façon [*Fr*] (*sah(n) fah-soh(n)*) unceremoniously; brusquely.

sans gêne [*Fr*] (*sah(n) zhehn*) disregard for politeness; when someone is offending without realising it.

sans peur et sans reproche [*Fr*] without fear and above reproach.

sans prétensions [*Fr*] unpretentious; unaffected.

santé [*Fr*] (*sah(n)-tay*) good health.

Sartor Resartus [*Lat*] the tailor mended (from Thomas Carlyle's book of 1834).

sashimi [*Jap*] varieties of raw fish served as a meal.

Sassenach [*Scot*] an English person or Scottish Lowlander.

satis eloquentiae, sapientae parum [*Lat*] abounding eloquence, scant wisdom.

A Saucière of Sauces

The great French cook Alexis Soyer once wrote that 'Sauces are to cookery what grammar is to language'. This was about the time that England was reviled as a 'nation with one sauce' but since then things – and sauces – have moved on a bit and the average British diner today is familiar with at least a few of them. Are you?

sauce à la menthe	mint
sauce allemande	butter, flour, lemon juice, nutmeg
sauce au beurre	butter
sauce aux câpres	capers
sauce aux cornichons	brown sauce with gherkins
sauce béarnaise	egg yolks, butter, vinegar and tarragon
sauce béchamel	white roux with seasoning – the foundation of many other sauces
sauce bordelaise	with claret, shallots, seasoning
sauce bretonne	simple egg and butter sauce
sauce espagnole	thick basic brown sauce
sauce financière	with madeira or sherry
sauce génoise	fish stock, anchovy butter, claret
sauce hollandaise	warmed egg yolks, butter, lemon
sauce meunière	butter, parsley, lemon juice
sauce mousseline	*sauce hollandaise* with whipped cream
sauce régence	fish stock and Marsala wine
sauce tartare	for fish and seafood
sauce tournée	with onions and mushrooms
sauce valois	egg yolks, vinegar, shallots
sauce velouté	a variation of béchamel
sauce zwetschen	prunes, port, lemon juice, cinnamon

saucisse, saucisson [*Fr*] the former is an uncooked sausage; the latter is a cooked sausage for eating cold.

säufer [*Ger*] drunkard; alcoholic; *er säuft wie ein Loch* – someone who 'drinks like a fish'.

Sauregurkenzeit [*Ger*] literally, 'pickled gherkin time' – a period when nothing is happening in business or politics. Known elsewhere as the 'silly season'.

sauve-qui-peut [*Fr*] literally, 'save himself who can'. A situation of panic and disorder in which it is every man for himself.

savoir-faire [*Fr*] (*sav-wahr-fair*) polish; tact; the ability to do the right thing when required.

savoir-vivre [*Fr*] (*sav-wahr-veev-ruh*) ease; composure; the quality of being at ease in society.

sayonara [*Jap*] goodbye.

sbirro [*It*] colloquial for Italian policeman.

scappatella [*It*] flirtation; brief extra-marital relationship.

schadenfreude [*Ger*] (*SHAH-den-froy-duh*) a fashionable word of the 1990s meaning taking malicious pleasure from another's misfortune. Until relatively recently, as a non-anglicised word it would have carried a capital *S*.

schemozzle [*Yidd*] (*shih-MOZZ-ul*) a mix-up; mess; argument.

Schickse [*Ger*] Tart; trollop.

schifo [*It*] disgust; *mi far schifo* – it makes me sick! A widely used colloquial word for complaining.

schlafen Sie wohl! [*Ger*] sleep well!

Schlager [*Ger*] pop song; a musical hit.

schlemiel [*Yidd*] (*shluh-MEEL*) a simple person, usually a man, who has the best intentions but no luck; unlucky but uncomplaining.

schlep, shlep [*Yidd*] to drag or carry with effort.

Schlimmbesserung [*Ger*] an improvement that makes things worse.

schlock [*Yidd*] cheap; inferior; rubbish; in bad taste.

Schloss [*Ger*] a German castle; a country estate.

shmaltz [*Yidd*] sugary sentimentality.

shmuck [*Yidd*] someone who always does the wrong thing.

shnorrer [*Yidd*] (*shnor-ruh*) beggar.

schön [*Ger*] beautiful; nice; *Schönheitsfarm* – health farm.

Schrecklichkeit [*Ger*] the deliberate perpetration of atrocities to subjugate a population.

schtroumpfe [*Flemish*] equivalent to English 'thingummy'. *Schtroumpfes* was the name given by their Belgian creator to the little blue creatures we know as Smurfs.

Schuss [*Ger*] (*shooss*) in skiing, a straight fast downhill run.

schwarz [*Ger*] black, but like the English term 'black market' it can also mean 'illegal': *schwarzarbeiten* – earning extra untaxed income; *schwarzsehen* – to have a TV receiver without a licence.

scientiae causa [*Lat*] to carry out difficult or painful experiments in the cause of science.

scippo [*It*] bag-snatching – unfortunately a common occurrence in Italian cities; *scippatore* – bag-snatcher.

scudetto [*It*] *Lo Scudetto* – Italian First Division Soccer Championship for the tricolour shield. One of the top *Serie A* teams is AC Milan whose *tifosi* (supporters) fill Milan's San Siro stadium.

sculpsit [*Lat*] he/she sculpted it.

séance d'essais [*Fr*] a preliminary run by racing cars before a race to familiarise drivers with the course.

se battre contre des moulins [*Fr*] to tilt at windmills.

secrétaire [*Fr*] an enclosed writing desk with a drop writing table, drawers and pigeon-holes.

securus judicat orbis terrarum [*Lat*] the judgement of the whole world cannot be wrong.

s'emmerder [*Fr*] colloquial: to be bored.

semper fidelis [*Lat*] (*sem-per fih-DAY-lis*) always faithful, the motto of the United States Marine Corps.

semper in excretia sumus, solim profundum variat [*Lat*] we are always in the shit, only the depth varies.

Senhor, Senhora, Senhorita [*Port*] Portuguese form of address for a man, married woman and unmarried woman respectively.

Señor, Señora, Señorita [*Sp*] the Spanish addresses for a man, married woman and unmarried woman respectively.

sensu abscaeno [*Lat*] to take the obscene meaning of a word or statement.

Serenissima, La [*It*] colloquial for the Republic of Venice.

sérieux [*Fr*] serious; sincere; earnest.

se soûler la gueule [*Fr*] vulgar for 'to get drunk'.

sesquipedalia verba [*Lat*] Horace's pun 'words of a foot and a half'; extremely long words.

seul [*Fr*] alone; single; *tout seul* – by oneself; *un homme seul* – a lonely man; *seul à seul* – tête-à-tête.

sgian-dhu [*Gael*] (*skee-uhn doo*) the dirk or knife carried in a Scottish Highlander's sock.

shaay [*Arab*] Tea.

shabash! [*Hind*] well done! excellent!

shabat [*Heb*] the Sabbath.

shadchan [*Yidd*] a Jewish matchmaker or marriage broker.

shalom [*Heb*] (*shah-LOM*) peace; hello. A common Jewish salutation.

shekel [*Heb*] main Israeli unit of currency, divided into 100 *agorot* (singular *agora*).

shikker [*Yidd*] a drunk; *shikkered* – to be drunk.

shiksa, shikseh [*Yidd*] an insulting term for a non-Jewish girl; a girl who is Jewish by birth but is non-practising.

shinkansen [*Jap*] bullet train. The *hikari* is the express; the *kodama* is the high-speed stopping train.

shtik [*Yidd*] a routine unique to a performer; a special act.

shuk, suq [*Arab*] open market-place. Usually spelt *souk*.

shul, schul [*Yidd*] a synagogue.

sic [*Lat*] thus written; thus said. Used in brackets [*sic*] to indicate that a word, possibly misspelt, or a statement, possibly inaccurate, is being reproduced or quoted exactly.

sic semper tyrannis [*Lat*] thus be the fate of tyrants, uttered by Abraham Lincoln's assassin in 1865.

sic transit gloria mundi [*Lat*] thus passes the glory of the world; worldly attainments are soon forgotten.

Sieg heil! [*Ger*] (zeek HYLE) 'hail to victory: the infamous Nazi salute, accompanied by the raised arm.

si fractum non sit, noli id reficere [*Lat*] if it isn't broken, don't fix it.

Signor, Signora, Signorina [*It*] Italian forms of address for a man, married woman and unmarried woman respectively.

si jeunesse savait, si vieillesse pouvait [*Fr*] if youth but knew, if age but could.

s'il vous plaît [*Fr*] (*seel voo play*) If you please.

simpatico [*It*] pleasant; likeable; nice; *antipatico* – unpleasant; *simpaticone* – likeable person.

simplicissimus [*Lat*] a simple-minded man who, despite being exploited by others, is philosophical about his situation.

simpliste [*Fr*] simplistic; too simple to be credible.

sine die [*Lat*] (*see-nay dee-ay*) without a day or date being fixed.

sine qua non [*Lat*] (*see-nay kwah non*) an essential requirement or condition.

Sinn Féin [*Ir*] (*shin fayn*) literally, 'we ourselves'; Irish republican movement founded in 1905, the political arm of the Irish Republican Army (IRA).

si parla italiano [*It*] Italian spoken here.

sirocco [*It*] (*sih-ROH-koh*) the wind that blows from the Sahara, north to Italy: warm, oppressive and sandy.

sit venia verbis [*Lat*] pardon my words.

si vis pacem, para bellum [*Lat*] if you desire peace, prepare for war.

skal, skoal [*Swed*] cheers! good health!

sláinte [*Gael*] good health!

smorgasbord [*Swed*] traditional spread of food, from salt fish, meats and salads through to hot dishes and cheese, from which diners help themselves.

snobisme [*Fr*] snobbery.

Sociedad Anónima (SA) [*Sp*] equivalent of the English Limited Company.

Société Anonyme (SA) [*Fr*] equivalent of the English Limited Company.

Société Nationale des Chemins de Fer (SNCF) [*Fr*] the French nationalised railway system.

soi-disant [*Fr*] so-called; self-styled.

soigné [*Fr*] (*swahn-yay*) elegantly groomed.

soirée [*Fr*] (*swah-ray*) an evening gathering where guests talk and listen or dance to music.

soldi [*It*] money; *senza un soldo* – broke.

son et lumière [*Fr*] (*sohn ay loom-yair*) literally, 'sound and light'. An evening entertainment staged outside a historic building, with words, music and lighting effects to illustrate its history.

sortes Biblicae [*Lat*] (*sor-tez BIB-lee-kye*) 'Biblical lots'; prophesying by opening the Bible at any page and selecting the passage the eye first sees; this passage is prophetic. The same is done with the works of Virgil and Homer.

sotto voce [*It*] (*sot-toh VOH-chay*) in an undertone.

sottogoverno [*It*] Italian political patronage whereby the relatives of successful candidates and supporters of victorious parties share government posts, jobs, contracts and cash.

souk [*Arab*] *see* shuk.

soutane [*Fr*] (*soo-tahn*) Roman Catholic priest's cassock.

souteneur [*Fr*] a pimp or procurer.

spalpeen [*Ir*] itinerant worker; layabout; rascal.

Spätzündung [*Ger*] literally, 'retarded ignition'; *er hat Spätzündung* – he's slow on the uptake.

spécialité de la maison [*Fr*] the chef's special dish at a restaurant.

sperat infestis, metuit secundis [*Lat*] he hopes in adversity, fears in prosperity.

splendide mendax [*Lat*] telling a lie for a good cause.

splitterfasernackt [*Ger*] absolutely naked; starkers.

sprezzatura [*It*] the bravura or effortless technique of a great artist.

spurlos versunken [*Ger*] sunk or vanished without trace.

Stabat Mater [*Lat*] literally, 'the mother was standing'; a Latin devotional poem that begins with these words.

Stammplatz [*Ger*] a favourite place.

stamppot [*Dut*] traditional potato and vegetable hash, usually served with bacon and sausages.

Stasi [*Ger*] abbreviation of *Staatssicherheitspolitzei*, East German Secret Police.

status quo [*Lat*] existing or prevailing state of affairs.

stet [*Lat*] let it stand; used to say that an alteration marked on a printed proof should be ignored.

stet fortuna domus [*Lat*] may the fortunes of the house endure.

Stiefel [*Ger*] the peculiar large boot- or foot-shaped glass tankard filled with beer and passed from drinker to drinker at parties. The idea is to drink without the beer gurgling or surging out over the drinker.

stoep [*Dut*] (*stoohp*) the front verandah of a house.

Storbritannien [*Swed*] Great Britain.

Stundenhotel [*Ger*] at first sight a hostel for students but in fact a disorderly house or brothel.

Sturm und Drang [*Ger*] (*shtoorm oont drahng*) literally, 'storm and stress'. Originally an overheated German literary style, now an expression for tumult and extravagant passion.

style champêtre [*Fr*] in painting, idyllic pastoral scenes.

sua cuique sunt vitia [*Lat*] every man has his vices.

sub judice [*Lat*] (*sub DZHOO-dih-say*) under judicial consideration; as yet undecided by a court.

sub rosa [*Lat*] in secret; in strict confidence.

suburbio [*Sp*] in Latin American countries, the run-down shanty areas on the outskirts of cities.

succès de scandale [*Fr*] (*sook-say duh skah(n)-dahl*) success of a play or book because of its scandalous nature.

succès d'estime [*Fr*] (*sook-say deh-steem*) success of a play or book because of critical, rather than public, acclaim.

succès fou [*Fr*] (*sook-say foo*) a mad, wild, brilliant success.

suggestio falsi [*Lat*] misrepresentation without actually lying.

sui generis [*Lat*] of its own kind; unique.

summa cum laude [*Lat*] (*sum-uh kum LOW-day*) with the highest distinction; with the utmost praise.

summum bonum [*Lat*] the greatest good.

sumo [*Jap*] Japanese style of wrestling in which heavyweight opponents try to shove each other out of a ring.

Sunna [*Arab*] the body of Islamic law that orthodox Muslims accept as based on the words and acts of Mohammed.

supercherie [*Fr*] a hoax or fraud.

supermarché [*Fr*] supermarket. A really large supermarket is called *un hypermarché*.

suppressio veri [*Lat*] suppression of the truth; concealment of the facts.

supra vires [*Lat*] beyond a person's powers.

Sûreté [*Fr*] (*syoor-tay*) French police criminal investigation department. *Sûreté Générale* – French equivalent of Britain's Scotland Yard.

sushi [*Jap*] raw fish dishes; often small parcels of boiled rice wrapped in seaweed and topped with raw fish or vegetables.

suum cuique [*Lat*] to each his own.

Sverige [*Swed*] Sweden. *Svensk* – Swedish; *Svenska* – Swedish language.

Systemzwang [*Ger*] a compulsion for system and order.

szálloda [*Hun*] hotel. Smaller establishments, similar to bed-and-breakfasts, are *panzió* and *fogadó*. Chalet-type hotels for group accommodation are called *túristaszálló*.

T

tableau vivant [*Fr*] (*tab-loh vih-vah(n)*) a scene or painting represented by a posed group of still, silent people.

table d'hôte [*Fr*] (*tab-luh doht*) fixed price restaurant menu with minimal choice.

tabula rasa [*Lat*] literally, 'scraped tablet'. A fresh surface ready to receive a new impression; a fresh mind open to receive information; an opportunity for a fresh start.

taedium vitae [*Lat*] weariness of life.

Tageblätter [*Ger*] newspapers.

taille [*Fr*] clothes size. For shoes, socks, tights and gloves, size is expressed by *la pointure*.

tamal, tamales [*Sp*] hash of maize and meat wrapped in a leaf.

Tannenbaum [*Ger*] Christmas tree; pine tree.

tant mieux [*Fr*] (*tah(n) myur*) so much the better.

tant pis [*Fr*] (*tah(n) pee*) so much the worse.

Taoiseach [*Ir*] (*tee-sh uhle*) Prime Minister of the Irish Republic.

tapas [*Sp*] snacks served with drinks; also called *aperitivos*.

tapis [*Fr*] (*tah-pee*) a rug; *un tapis de bain* – bathmat.

taramasalata [*Gk*] pâté of cod's roe.

Tartufferie [*Fr*] hypocrisy, of which Molière's insincerely pious character **Tartuffe** was guilty.

tashinamu [*Jap*] devotion to a cause with little likelihood of recognition or success.

taverna [*Gk*] a Greek restaurant where wine is served.

Taxe à Valeur Ajoutée (*TVA*) [*Fr*] VAT or Value Added Tax.

tchin tchin [*Fr*] cheers!

tchotchke [*Yidd*] a trinket or knicknack.

Te Deum [*Lat*] Thee, God, we praise; hymn of praise and for giving thanks.

teishok [*Jap*] a fairly standard set meal of rice, soup, pickles and a selected dish; *tonkats teishok* – set meal with pork as the main dish.

tel père, tel fils [*Fr*] like father, like son.

témoignage [*Fr*] factual, unprejudiced testimony.

tempora mutantur et nos mutamur in illis [*Lat*] times change and we change with them.

tempura [*Jap*] crispy deep-fried seafood and vegetables.

tempus fugit [*Lat*] time flies.

tendresse [*Fr*] affection; fondness; tenderness.

tenue de ville [*Fr*] literally, 'town clothes'; a man's lounge suit; *tenue de soirée* is formal or evening dress.

tep-panyaki [*Jap*] beef and vegetables grilled at the table.

terminus vitae [*Lat*] death; end of life.

terra firma [*Lat*] firm ground; solid earth; a land mass.

terra incognita [*Lat*] (*teh-ruh in-KOG-nih-tuh*) unknown or unexplored regions.

tête-à-tête [*Fr*] (*teht-ah-teht*) a private conversation between two people.

tibi seris, tibi metis [*Lat*] as ye sow, so shall ye reap.

tic douloureux [*Fr*] a neuralgic affliction characterised by twitching facial muscles.

tiens! [*Fr*] really! you don't say! well, well!

timbres-poste [*Fr*] postage stamps.

timeo Danaos et dona ferentes [*Lat*] I fear the Greeks even when they bear gifts.

timor addidit alas [*Lat*] fear gave him wings (Virgil).

tirez le rideau, la farce est jouée [*Fr*] bring down the curtain, the farce is over, last words of Rabelais.

todo cae en el dedo malo [*Sp*] everything falls on the injured finger.

tokaji [*Hun*] (*toh-KAY*) Hungarian wine made from the furmint grape. The famous sweet wines are *Aszu* and *Aszu Eszencia*.

tonto [*Sp*] stupid; silly; *una tontería* – a stupid thing.

topi, topee [*Hind*] sun hat; pith helmet.

Torah [*Heb*] the scroll on which Jewish law is written.

tortilla [*Sp*] (*tor-TEE-yuh*) maize-flour pancake or omelette. Beware: *una tortillera* – vulgar in Spanish for lesbian.

Toto [*Ger*] *Länder* or state-controlled football pools in Germany.

totocalcio [*It*] Italian football pools. *La schedina* – pools coupon on which punters have to enter their predictions. *Fare un tredici* – a win: all thirteen predictions correct.

toujours [*Fr*] (*too-zhoor*) always; for ever.

toujours la politesse [*Fr*] it's always wise to be polite.

tour de force [*Fr*] (*toor duh fors*) a brilliant accomplishment.

Toussaint, La [*Fr*] All Saints' Day, 1 November, which is followed on 2 November by *Le Jour des Morts* – All Souls' Day, when wreaths are placed on graves.

tout à vous [*Fr*] yours truly.

tout comprendre c'est tout pardonner [*Fr*] to understand everything is to forgive everything.

tout court [*Fr*] briefly; with nothing added; simply.

tout de suite [*Fr*] at once; immediately.

tout ensemble [*Fr*] (*toot ah(n)-SAH(N)-buhl*) all things considered; the total impression; general effect.

tout le monde [*Fr*] everybody; the whole world.

tout ou rien [*Fr*] all or nothing.

tout passe, tout casse [*Fr*] nothing lasts for ever.

traducteur [*Fr*] translator; *traduction* – translation.

traduttori traditori [*It*] translators are traitors; true translation is impossible.

tranche de vie [*Fr*] slice of life.

trappistenbier [*Dut*] beer originally brewed by Trappist monks.

trattoria [*It*] restaurant or *ristorante*.

travailler [*Fr*] to work; *un travailleur* – labourer; worker.

tredicesima [*It*] thirteenth; *tredicesima mensilità* or *la tredicesima* – the thirteenth or extra month's pay received prior to Christmas.

Treppenwitz [*Ger*] the clever riposte you think of – too late! *See also* **espirit de l'escalier**.

tricolore [*Fr*] (*tree-KOL-ohr*) three-coloured; *le drapeau tricolore* – the French flag, of *bleu, blanc* et *rouge*.

tricoteuse [*Fr*] one of the three women who knitted while watching the executions during the French Revolution.

Trinkgeld [*Ger*] in Germany, a tip; gratuity.

tristesse [*Fr*] sadness; melancholy; gloom; depression.

troika [*Rus*] (*troy-kuh*) a carriage or sledge pulled by three horses; a controlling body consisting of three people or groups sharing power.

trompe-l'oeil [*Fr*] (*tro(m)p luh-yuh*) a painting that conveys the illusion of reality.

trop de cuisiniers gâtent la sauce [*Fr*] too many cooks spoil the sauce.

trouvaille [*Fr*] (*troo-vayuh*) a lucky find; a windfall; *trouver l'oiseau* – to find the rare bird; *trouver la perle* – to find a pearl.

truite [*Fr*] (*trweet*) trout; *truite saumonée* – salmon trout.

tsunami [*Jap*] huge destructive wave caused by submarine earthquakes or volcanic eruptions.

tuan [*Malay*] sir. Polite form of address by Malays.

tulp, tulpen [*Dut*] tulips.

tu quoque [*Lat*] tou too, used by someone being accused of something to accuse the accuser in turn.

turista [*Sp*] a not altogether sympathetic name for travellers' diarrhoea in Central America.

tutte le strade conducono a Roma [*It*] all roads lead to Rome.

Tutte le strade conducono a Roma

tutti-frutti [*It*] (*too-tih froo-tih*) fruit ice cream.

tzatziki [*Gk*] dip made from cucumber, yoghurt, garlic and oil.

Tziyonut [*Heb*] Zionism; *Tziyoni* – a Zionist.

U

Übermensch [*Ger*] superior man; a superman. From Nietzsche's *Also Sprach Zarathustra*.

ubi jus, ibi remedium [*Lat*] where there is a right there is a remedy.

ubi lapsus? quid feci? [*Lat*] where did I go wrong? what have I done?

ubi sunt qui ante nos fuerunt? [*Lat*] where are those who have gone before us?

Übung macht den Meister [*Ger*] practice makes the master.

ultima Thule [*Lat*] (*UHL-tih-muh TOO-lih*) the farthest limit; some faraway, unknown region.

ultra vires [*Lat*] (*uhl-truh VEE-rays*) beyond the legal powers of a person or organisation.

Um ein Haar [*Ger*] a close shave.

Umschwung [*Ger*] a sudden change of opinion or direction.

unberufen toi toi toi [*Ger*] an expression equivalent to the English 'touch wood' or 'knock on wood'.

uno ictu [*Lat*] at one blow.

uno saltu [*Lat*] with one bound; in a single leap.

un propos sale [*Fr*] a coarse remark.

Unterhosen [*Ger*] underpants; *Schlüpfer* – undershorts; *Slip* – men's briefs and ladies' knickers; *die Unaussprechenlichen* – the unmentionables.

unter vier Augen [*Ger*] literally, 'under four eyes'. Between two people only; between us; in confidence.

uovo [*It*] egg; *un uovo sodo* – a hard-boiled egg; *uova strapazzate* – scrambled eggs.

urbi et orbi [*Lat*] to the city and the world: the formal introduction for papal proclamations and blessings.

usus est tyrannus [*Lat*] fashion or custom is a tyrant.

uyezd [*Rus*] in Russia, a district or county.

V

vade mecum [*Lat*] literally, 'go with me'. A guidebook or handbook to carry around.

vade retro, Satana! [*Lat*] get thee behind me, Satan!

va fan culo [*It*] extremely vulgar but all too common Italian expression meaning, roughly, 'up your arse'.

vanitas vanitatum, omnia vanitas [*Lat*] vanity of vanities, all is vanity.

vase de nuit [*Fr*] chamberpot. *See bourdalou.*

vashe zdarov'ye [*Rus*] cheers! used as a toast.

vero? [*Lat*] really? you think so?

velatorio [*Sp*] Spanish wake – the twenty-four hours preceding a funeral during which the corpse is on view in its coffin.

velouté [*Fr*] a white sauce made with roux and stock.

vendeuse [*Fr*] (*vah(n)-derz*) female sales assistant.

veniente occurrite morbo [*Lat*] meet an approaching sickness; prevention is better than cure.

veni, vidi, vici [*Lat*] I came, I saw, I conquered. Julius Caesar's remark after his victory over Pharnaces.

ventre à terre [*Fr*] (*vah(n)-truh ah-tair*) literally, 'belly to the earth'. At full gallop; at full speed.

verbatim et literatim [*Lat*] word for word, and letter for letter.

verboten [*Ger*] forbidden; not allowed.

verbum sapienti sat est (abbreviation *verb. sap.*) [*Lat*] a word is enough for the wise. The abbreviation is used as a notice to the reader to take the preceding matter seriously.

veritas nunquam perit [*Lat*] truth never dies.

veritas omnia vincit [*Lat*] truth conquers everything. Often written *vincit omnia veritas*.

Verlag [*Ger*] publisher; publishing house.

vers de société [*Fr*] witty, topical verse.

vers libre [*Fr*] unrhymed free verse.

vexata quaestio [*Lat*] a disputed point; a vexed question.

Via Crucis [*Lat*] the Stations of the Cross; the 14 episodes in the Passion of Christ.

via dolorosa [*Lat*] literally, 'sorrowful road'. A series of distressing experiences.
    Via Dolorosa – Christ's route to Calvary and his crucifixion.

via media [*Lat*] a middle course; midway between extremes.

vice anglais [*Fr*] see *le vice anglais*.

victor ludorum [*Lat*] winner of the games; a sports champion.

vide [*Lat*] (*vee-day*) refer to; see. Used to direct a reader elsewhere in a book or to
    another reference.

videlicet (abbreviation *viz*) [*Lat*] namely; in other words. The abbreviation is
    used to introduce an example or explanation.

vie amoureuse [*Fr*] an account of someone's love affairs.

vie manquée [*Fr*] an ill-spent, wasted or misdirected life.

vieux jeu [*Fr*] (*vyu zhu*) old-fashioned; out of date.

vieux marcheur [*Fr*] a man, well past it, who still pursues women.

vingt-et-un [*Fr*] (*va(n)-tay-ur(n)*) twenty-one; blackjack; pontoon.

vin ordinaire [*Fr*] cheap table wine.

virgo intacta [*Lat*] a woman who is still a virgin.

visagisme [*Fr*] beauty care and make-up; *visagiste* – a beauty expert;
    cosmetician.

via medicatrix naturae [*Lat*] nature's cure; natural recovery from ailments
    without medicine.

vis-à-vis [*Fr*] (*veez-ah-vee*) In relation to; regarding; face to face with.

vita brevis, ars longa [*Lat*] life is short, art is long.

viva voce [*Lat*] (*vy-vuh voh-cheh*) by word of mouth; orally; an oral examination
    'viva'.

vive la différence! [*Fr*] (*veev lah dee-feh-rah(n)s*) long live the difference!: usually
    applied to the difference between the sexes.

vivir y vivamos [*Sp*] live and let live.

voilà! [*Fr*] (*vwah-lah*) there! see! presto!

volte-face [*Fr*] a reversal of a previous policy or opinion.

vox populi, vox Dei [*Lat*] the voice of the people is the voice of God; public
    opinion rules.

voyez! [*Fr*] look! see!

W

Wahlverwandtschaft [*Ger*] an intuitive or natural affinity between two people.

wàiguoren [*Ch*] foreigner.

Walpurgisnacht [*Ger*] Walpurgis Night, the eve of the feast day of St Walpurga (1 May); in German folklore the night of the witches' sabbath.

Weihnachten [*Ger*] Christmas. *Heiligabend* – Christmas Eve.

Weinstube [*Ger*] German inn, serving wine and beer.

Weltanschauung [*Ger*] a philosophy of life; a person's philosophical outlook.

Weltschmerz [*Ger*] sadness at the ills of the world; sentimentally pessimistic view of the world.

Wénhuà Dàgéming [*Ch*] the Cultural Revolution.

Wenn die Katze fort ist, tanzen die Mäuse [*Ger*] when the cat's away, the mice will play.

Wer den Sieg behält, der hat Recht [*Ger*] the victor is always in the right.

Wer ein Kalb stiehlt, stiehlt eine Kuh [*Ger*] he who steals a calf, steals a cow.

Wider den Strom schwimmen ist schwer [*Ger*] it's harder to swim against the current; don't kick against the pricks.

Winespeak

Every week, it seems, a few thousand more people become regular wine drinkers. And why not? The choice of wine today is breathtaking; hundreds of varieties pour in from dozens of countries and thousands of regions and makers. But with the wine comes a culture of wine terminology, most of it expressed in various foreign languages. A full list of all the names and terms you'll find on wine labels would require an encyclopaedia, but here, meanwhile, are some of the more common among them.

Appellation d'Origine Contrôlée (abbreviation *AOC*) [*Fr*] (*a-pe-la-syo(n) do-ree-zheen- ko(n)-tro-lay*) French legal designation guaranteeing the wine's geographical origin and quality.

blanc de blancs [*Fr*] (*bla(n) duh bla(n)*) white wine made only from white grapes.

brut [*Fr*] (*broot*) dry, when applied to sparkling wine.

cave [*Fr*] (*kahv*) cellar.

cépage [*Fr*] the wine grape variety.

cru [*Fr*] growth; applied to a vineyard and the wine it makes.

Denominación de Origen [*Sp*] Spanish equivalent of the French *AOC* (*see above*).

Denominazione di Origine Controllata [*It*] the Italian equivalent of the
  French *AOC* (*see above*).
en primeur [*Fr*] buying future wine, still in the cask.
flor [*Sp*] literally, 'flower'; a flavour-imparting yeast that grows on casked
  wine, usually sherry.
garrafeira [*Port*] Portuguese selected, aged wine.
négociant [*Fr*] merchant who buys wine from growers for blending,
  ageing, bottling and resale.
mis en bouteille au château [*Fr*] bottled at the château.
Qualitätswein [*Ger*] German wine classification for quality wines.
récoltant [*Fr*] wine grower.
Spätlese [*Ger*] (*shpayt-lay-zuh*) wine from sweet late-harvested grapes.
Tafelwein [*Ger*] table wine.
vinho verde [*Port*] green or young wine.
vinho maduro [*Port*] wine that has aged.
Vins Délimités de Qualité Supérieure (*VDQS*) [*Fr*] controlled French wine
  category not quite up to the *AOC* standard.

wunderbar [*Ger*] (*voon-duh-bar*) wonderful.
Wunderkind [*Ger*] (*voon-duh-kint*) a child prodigy.
Wurst [*Ger*] sausage. *Blutwurst* – black pudding; *Bockwurst* – pink sausage;
  Schinkenwurst – ham sausage; *Bratwurst* – fried *Bockwurst*.

XYZ

Xianggang [*Ch*] Hong Kong.
Xizang [*Ch*] Tibet.
yad rochetset yad [*Heb*] you help me, I help you.
Yahadut [*Heb*] Judaism.
yakitori [*Jap*] skewered chicken cooked on a grill.
yarmulke, yarmulka [*Yidd*] skull-cap worn by Orthodox Jewish males.
yashmak [*Arab*] face-concealing veil worn by Muslim women.
yeftah allah [*Arab*] the words that accompany an offer – usually well under the
  vendor's price – that a buyer is willing to pay, without giving offence.
yehudi [*Heb*] Jewish.
yenta [*Yidd*] a crude, loud, female gossip.
Yerushalayim [*Heb*] Jerusalem.

Yiddish

Yiddish, a blend of mostly German and some Hebrew, migrated during the last century to America where, even today, it continues to colour American English. *Fancy-schmancy* is fifth generation *Yidglish* but true Yiddishisms still surface. If you're called a *schmendrik*, start worrying; it means you think you're fantastic and cool but actually you've got a big hole in your trousers and you haven't noticed. Even so, it is better than being a *bupkiss* – a nothing.

Apart from its colour, Yiddish has a questioning quality: the propensity to answer a question with a question. – Why do Yiddish speakers do this? – Why shouldn't they? The answer lies in Genesis 4:9: '. . . the Lord said unto Cain, where is Abel thy brother?' And what does Cain say? 'Am I my brother's keeper?' A true Yiddisher.

Yinggélán [*Ch*] England. *Yingguó* – Britain.

Yom Kippur [*Heb*] annual Jewish Day of Atonement religious holiday.

yoni [*Sans*] in Hinduism, the venerated female genitalia.

zabaglione [*It*] (*zab-ah-lee-OH-nee*) whipped dessert of egg yolks, sugar and Marsala wine.

zapateado [*Sp*] the fast footwork and stamping feet of Spanish dancing.

Zeitgeist [*Ger*] (*tzeyt-guyst*) the attitude of a period; the spirit of the time.

Zeitung [*Ger*] newspaper; journal.

zhela yoo oodachee! [*Rus*] good luck!

Zhongguo [*Ch*] China. *Zhongguo rénmín* – the Chinese people.

Zijincheng [*Ch*] the Forbidden City.

zinc [*Fr*] colloquial for the counter in a bar or café; *manger sur le zinc* – eating at the bar.

Zivilcourage [*Ger*] to have the courage of one's convictions and to express them without fear.

zizi [*Fr*] childish slang for male genitalia, especially of young child.

zuppa [*It*] soup; *zuppa di verdura* – vegetable soup; *zuppa di pesce* – fish soup.

Zwieback [*Ger*] (*zwee-bahk*) baked bread rusk.

8

ABBREVIATIONS AND ACRONYMS

A-Z LISTING WITH FULL EXPLANATIONS

A

A absolute (temperature); ace (cards); adult; advanced; ammeter (electric circuits); ampere; anode; area; atomic; (as in **A-bomb**); Argentine austral (currency); blood type A; excellence in exam marking; American; annual; answer; April; August; Australia

a about; accepted; acceleration; acre; acreage; actual; address; adjective; afternoon; age; alto; *annus* = year; anonymous; answer; *ante* = before; area; arrive; arrived; arriving

A0-A10, etc paper sizes, from the largest (A0 = 841 x 1189 mm; A1 = 594 x 841 mm) to the smallest (A10 = 26 x 37 mm). The standard writing sheet is A4 = 210 x 297 mm

A1 first-class ships in Lloyd's Register; non-motorway arterial roads (e.g. **A2** from London to Dover)

AA Alcoholics Anonymous; advertising agency; age allowance; Air Attaché; American Airlines; Anglers' Association; anti-aircraft; Associate in Accounting; Associate in Agriculture; Automobile Association

aa absolute alcohol; after arrival; attendance allowance; author's alteration (proofreading)

AA1 superior credit rating (finance)

AAA Amateur Athletic Association (in England and Wales); Allied Artists of America; American Automobile Association; Australian Association of Accountants; Australian Automobile Association; highest credit rating (finance)

AAAA American Association of Advertising Agencies (*also* **4As**); Amateur Athletic Association of America; Australian Association of Advertising Agencies

AAAS American Academy of Arts and Sciences; American Association for the Advancement of Science

AAB Aircraft Accident Board

AAC Agicultural Advisory Council; Amateur Athletic Club

AAEC Australian Atomic Energy Commission

AAF Army Air Force (USA); Allied Air Forces

AAMI age-associated memory impairment

AANA Australian Association of National Advertisers

A&A, **a&a** additions and amendments

A&E Accident and Emergency (in hospitals)

a&h accident and health (insurance); **a&i** = accident and indemnity

A&N Army and Navy (Stores; Club)

a&s accident and sickness (insurance)

AAP Australian Associated Press; Association of American Publishers

A&R, **a&r** artists and repertoire (entertainment industry)

aar against all risks; average annual rainfall; aircraft accident report

AAS Association of Architects and Surveyors

AAT achievement anxiety test; Anglo-Australian Telescope (NSW)

AATA Anglo-American Tourist Association

AAU Amateur Athletic Union (USA); Association of American Universities

AB human blood type (along with A, B and O); able-bodied seaman

ABA Amateur Boxing Association (UK); American Bankers' Association; American Bar Association; Antiquarian Booksellers' Association; Association of British Archaeologists

ABBA Swedish pop group (Agnetha, Benny, Bjorn, Annifrid); Amateur Basketball Association

abbr abbreviation

ABC the English alphabet; American Broadcasting Company; Audit Bureau of Circulations; Associated British Cinemas; Australian Broadcasting Commission

ABC1s, C2s, etc social grading of the National Readership Survey of Britain (*see* **JICNARS**). A = upper middle class; B = middle class; C1 = lower middle class; C2 = skilled working class; D = working class; E = state pensioners, widows, casual and lowest grade workers

ABDP Association of British Directory Publishers

ABF Actors' Benevolent Fund; Associated British Foods

ABLS Association of British Library Schools

ABM Associate in Business Management; antiballistic missile

Abo Australian aborigine

A-bomb Atomic bomb (originally deployed over Hiroshima, Japan, in 1945)

ABPI Association of the British Pharmaceutical Industry

ABRACADABRA ABbreviations and Related ACronyms Associated with Defense, Astronautics, Business and RAdio-electronics. Name of original listing of space terms (USA, 1960s)

ABRS Association of British Riding Schools

ABS *anti-blockier* system = anti-lock brakes

ABSA Association of Business Sponsorship of the Arts

ABT Association of Building Technicians

ABTA Allied Brewery Traders' Association; Association of British Travel Agents

ABV alcohol by volume

a/c account, or account current (bookkeeping term)

AC alternating current; *appellation controlée* (quality control of French wines); Arts Council

ACA Agricultural Cooperative Association; Associate of the Institute of Chartered Accountants (England and Wales)

ACAS Advisory, Conciliation and Arbitration Service

ACC Army Catering Corps; Association of County Councils

ACCA Associate of the Chartered Association of Certified Accountants; Association of Certified and Corporate Accountants

ACGB Arts Council of Great Britain

ACGBI Automobile Club of Great Britain and Ireland

ACK Acknowledgement

ACORN A Classification Of Residential Neighbourhoods. A sampling system which divides the country into 38 neighbourhood types, from agricultural villages through inter-war semis to private flats

---

Acronyms

An abbreviation or an initial becomes an acronym when the letters are pronounceable and the resulting creation is accepted into the language. Typical examples include **RADAR**, **QANTAS**, **WASP** and **NIMBY**. Some acronyms are however derived from compressed words, such as **OXFAM** (Oxford Committee for Famine Relief). Others, like **scuba** (Self-Contained Underwater Breathing Apparatus) assume a life of their own as words for which the meaning of the initial letters are forgotten.

ACSN Association of Collegiate Schools of Nursing

ACT Australian Capital Territory; Advisory Council on Technology

ACTC Art Class Teacher's Certificate

ACTT Association of Cinematograph, Television and Allied Technicians

ACTU Australian Council of Trade Unions

ACU Auto-Cycle Union

ACV actual cash value; air cushion vehicle

ACW aircraft(s)woman

ACWS aircraft control and warning system

AD *anno Domini*: In the year of our Lord, i.e. any time after the beginning of the first century (*see* **BC**)

ADAS Agricultural Development and Advisory Service

ADC aide-de-camp; analogue-digital converter

ADD attention deficit disorder

ADHD attention deficit hyperactivity disorder

Adidas From the name of the German founder, Adolf Dassler

ADRA Animal Diseases Research Association

Adv adverb; advent

Advt advertisement

AEA Atomic Energy Authority (UK); Actors' Equity Association (USA)

AEC Atomic Energy Commission (USA)

AEROFLOT Soviet Air Lines

AEU Amalgamated Engineering Union

AEWHA All England Women's Hockey Association

AEWLA All England Women's Lacrosse Association

af, a/f as found; refers to the condition (usually poor) of an item in an auction catalogue

AFA Amateur Fencing Association; Amateur Football Association; automatic fire alarm

AFAM Ancient Free and Accepted Masons

AFASIC Association For All Speech Impaired Children. A play on the term *aphasia*, the total or partial loss of ability to communicate

AFBS American and Foreign Bible Society

AFIA Apparel and Fashion Industry Association

AFL American Football League

AFL-CIO American Federation of Labor and Congress of Industrial Organizations

AFP Agence France Presse

AFRAeS Associate Fellow of the Royal Aeronautical Society

AFTRA American Federation of Television and Radio Arts

Aga *Aktiebolaget Gas Accumulator*, Swedish oven manufacturers

AGA Amateur Gymnastics Association

AGB Audits of Great Britain

AGBI Artists' General Benevolent Institution

Agfa *Aktieengesellschaft fur Anilinfabrikation* (limited company for dye manufacturing)

Agitprop A former Soviet Communist Party bureau for the dissemination of propaganda and agitation. *Also* **agitpop**, the use of pop music for political purposes

AGM annual general meeting; air-to-ground missile

AGS American Geographical Society

AH *anno Hegirae*. After 622 AD, the Muslim dating system

ah ha! American Holistic Health Association's newsletter

AHQ Army Headquarters

AI artificial insemination; artificial intelligence

AIA Association of International Accountants

AIAA Association of International Advertising Agencies

AICC All India Congress Committee

AIDAS Agricultural Industry Development Advisory Service

AID artificial insemination by donor; acute infectious disease

AIDA advertising basics: Attention, Interest, Desire, Action

AIDS acquired immune deficiency syndrome; aircraft integrated data system

AIH artificial insemination by husband

AILAS automatic instrument landing approach system

AIME American Institute of Mining, Metallurgical and Petroleum Engineers

AIR All India Radio

AIS androgen insensitivity syndrome

AITC Association of Investment Trust Companies

AJA Anglo-Jewish Association; Australian Journalists' Association

AJC Australian Jockey Club

aka also known as

AL American Legion

ALA American Library Association

ALCM air-launched cruise missile

ALCS Authors' Licensing and Collecting Society

A level advanced level of education

ALF Animal Liberation Front; automatic letter facer

Algol algorithmic computer programming language

ALL acute lymphoblastic leukaemia

Ally Pally Alexandra Palace, London

ALPA Airline Pilots' Association

ALPO Association of Land and Property Owners

ALS, **als** autograph letter, signed

aM on the River Main (for certain German cities and towns)

AM, **am** amplitude modulation; *ante meridiem*, or before noon; Albert Medal; Member of the Order of Australia

AMA American Medical Association; Australian Medical Association; American Motors Corporation; Association of Management Consultants

---

American States and Territories

The following are the two-letter abbreviations used by the US Postal Service:

Alabama	AL	Guam	GU	Michigan	MI
Alaska	AK	Hawaii	HI	Minnesota	MN
Arizona	AZ	Idaho	ID	Mississippi	MS
Arkansas	AR	Illinois	IL	Missouri	MO
California	CA	Indiana	IN	Montana	MT
Colorado	CO	Iowa	IA	Nebraska	NE
Connecticut	CT	Kansas	KS	Nevada	NV
Delaware	DE	Kentucky	KY	New Hampshire	NH
District of		Louisiana	LA	New Jersey	NJ
Colombia	DC	Maine	ME	New Mexico	NM
Florida	FL	Maryland	MD	New York	NY
Georgia	GA	Massachusetts	MA	North Carolina	NC

Ohio	OH	South Carolina	SC	Virgin Islands	VI
Oklahoma	OK	South Dakota	SD	Virginia	VA
Oregon	OR	Tennessee	TN	Washington	WA
Pennsylvania	PA	Texas	TX	West Virginia	WV
Puerto Rico	PR	Utah	UT	Wisconsin	WI
Rhode Island	RI	Vermont	VT	Wyoming	WY

AMEX American Express; American Stock Exchange

AMF Australian Military Forces

AMIAE Associate Member of the Institute of Automobile Engineers

AMIEE Associate Member of the Institute of Electrical Engineers

AMIMechE Associate Member of the Institution of Mechanical Engineers

AML acute myeloid leukaemia

AMP Australian Mutual Provident Society

AMSAM anti-missile surface-to-air missile

AMSTRAD Alan Michael Sugar Trading (Company)

ANA Article Number Association (issues bar code numbers)

ANC African National Congress

anon anonymous (usually refers to an author, unknown)

ANZAAS Australian and New Zealand Association for the Advancement of Science

Anzac Australian and New Zealand Army Corps (WWI)

ANZUS Australia, New Zealand and USA defence pact

AOB, **aob** any other business

AOC *appellation d'origine controlée*

AOH Ancient Order of Hibernians

AONB Area of Outstanding Natural Beauty

AOP Association of Optical Practitioners

AOR album-oriented rock; album-oriented radio

AP Associated Press (USA)

APC acetylsalycylic acid, phenacetin and caffeine in combination as a popular headache remedy

APEX advance purchase excursion (a railway or airline reduced fare); Association of Professional, Executive, Clerical and Computer Staff

aph aphorism

APHI Association of Public Health Inspectors

APLE Association of Public Lighting Engineers

APR annual percentage rate

APT Advanced Passenger Train; automatic picture transmission

APTIS All Purpose Ticket Issuing System

APU Assessment Performance Unit (educational research unit)

ar, **arr** arrives; arrived

AR *anno regni* (in the year of the reign of)

ARC Aids-related complex

arch archaism; archaic; architect; architecture

ARCS Associate of the Royal College of Science

ARSR air route surveillance radar

artic articulated vehicle

AS air speed

ASA Advertising Standards Authority; Amateur Swimming Association; American Standards Association (photographic speed rating)

ASCII American Standard Code for Information Interchange

asap as soon as possible

ASEAN Association of South-East Asian Nations (Indonesia, Malaysia, Thailand, Singapore, Philippines)

ASH Action on Smoking and Health

ASIO Australian Security Intelligence Organisation

ASLEF Associated Society of Locomotive Engineers and Firemen

ASM assistant sergeant-major; assistant sales manager; assistant scout master; assistant stage manager; air-to-surface missile

ASN average sample number

ASO American Symphony Orchestra

ASPCA American Society for the Prevention of Cruelty to Animals

ASPEP Association of Scientists and Professional Engineering Personnel

ASPF Association of Superannuation and Pension Funds

ASR airport surveillance radar

AST Atlantic Standard Time

AT&T American Telephone & Telegraph Company

ATC air traffic control; Air Training Corps

ATD Art Teacher's Diploma; actual time of departure

ATHE Association of Teachers in Higher Education

ATM automatic teller machine

ATO assisted take-off

ATOL Air Travel Organisers' Licence

ATS Auxiliary Territorial Service, precursor of the present-day women's army, the WRACs

ATV Associated Television

AUBTW Amalgamated Union of Building Trade Workers

AUEW Amalgamated Union of Engineering Workers

AUO African Unity Organisation

AUT Association of University Teachers

Auth Ver Authorized Version of the Bible (*also* **AV**, **av**)

Aux, **aux** auxiliary

AV audio-visual; Authorized Version of the Bible

Av, **Ave**, **ave** avenue

Av, **Avg**, **avg** average

AVR Army Volunteer Reserve

AVS ANTI-VIVISECTION SOCIETY

AVS Anti-Vivisection Society
AWA Amalgamated Wireless (Australasia) Ltd
AWACS airborne warning and control system
AWBA American World's Boxing Association
AWGIE award presented by the Australian Writers' Guild
AWOL absent without leave
AWRE Atomic Weapons Research Establishment
AZT azidothymidine (Zidorudine), a drug used to supress HIV, the cause of
   Aids

B

B Thai baht (currency); Baumé (temperature); human blood type (of the ABO
   group); grade of softness in pencils (e.g. **2B**, **3B**, etc); American bomber series
   (e.g. **B-52**); battle; bishop (chess); breathalyser; bold; bachelor; Baptist; billion;
   British; occupational group (of ACB1, C2, etc); building; Venezuelan bolivar
   (currency)
b ball, batsman, bowled, bye (cricket); base; bass; bath; bedroom; before; billion;
   book; born; bound (bookbinding); bowels; breadth; by; euphemism for
   bloody, bugger
B0, B5, etc series of paper sizes (qv **A0-A10**, etc)
B4216, etc secondary roads (qv A1, M1)
BA Bachelor of Arts; British Airways; British Academy; able-bodied seaman;
   Booksellers' Association; British Association for the Adancement of Science
   (*also* **BAAS**); bronchial asthma; Buenos Aires; bank acceptance; British
   Association screw thread

BAA British Airports Authority; Bachelor of Applied Arts; Booking Agents' Association of Great Britain; British Archaelogical Association; British Astronomical Association

BAA&A British Association of Accountants and Auditors

BAAB British Amateur Athletic Board

BA(Admin) Bachelor of Arts in Administration (*also* **BAdmin**)

BAAF British Agencies for Adoption and Fostering

BA(Art) Bachelor of Arts in Art

BAAS British Association for the Advancement of Science (*also* **BA**)

BABS Blind Approach Beacon System (airports)

Bac, **bac** *baccalaureat* = study programme similar to British A levels, a prerequisite for university entrance

BAC British Aircraft Corporation; blood-alcohol concentration; British Association of Chemists

BACO British Aluminium Company

BACS Bankers' Automated Clearing Service

bact bacteria; bacteriology

BADA British Antique Dealers' Association

BAe British Aerospace

BAEA British Actors' Equity Association

BAEC British Agricultural Export Council

BA(Econ) Bachelor of Arts in Economics

BA(Ed) Bachelor of Arts in Education

BAFO British Army Forces Overseas

BAFTA British Academy of Film and Television Arts

BAGA British Amateur Gymnastics Association

BAgr Bachelor of Agriculture; **BAgEc** = Bachelor of Agricultural Economics; **BAgrSc** = Bachelor of Agricultural Science)

Bah Bahamas

BAHOH British Association for the Hard of Hearing

BAI Bachelor of Engineering

BAIE British Association of Industrial Editors

Ball, **Bal** Balliol College (Oxford); Ballarat (Victoria)

BALPA British Airline Pilots' Association

b&b bread and breakfast

BARC British Automobile Racing Club

Bart's St Bartholomew's Hospital, London

BASIC Beginners' All-purpose Symbolic Instruction Code, a computer programming language

BAT British-American Tobacco Company

Bat, **bat** battalion; battery

BAWA British Amateur Wrestling Association

BB Brigitte Bardot; very soft black lead pencil; pseudonym of prolific English country book author and illustrator Denys Watkins-Pitchford (1905–90).

BBBC British Boxing Board of Control

BBC British Broadcasting Corporation

BBFC British Board of Film Classification

bbl barrel; **bbls/d** = barrels per day (usually of oil production)

BBQ barbecue

BC before Christ; British Council; British Colombia, Canada

bcc blind carbon copy, i.e. one that the recipient of the original message is unaware of

BCCI Bank of Credit and Commerce International

BCF British Chess Federation

BCNZ Broadcasting Corporation of New Zealand

BCom Bachelor of Commerce

BD Bachelor of Divinity

BDA British Dental Association; British Dyslexia Association

BDD body dismorphic disorder – a preoccupation with a perceived defect in appearance, causing distress and impairment in functioning.

BDS Bachelor of Dental Surgery

BE British Empire

BEA British European Airways

BEd Bachelor of Education

Beds Bedfordshire

BEEB British Broadcasting Corporation (*also* **BBC**)

BEF British Expeditionary Force

BEM British Empire Medal

Benelux customs union between Belgium, the Netherlands and Luxembourg

BEng Bachelor of Engineering

Berks Berkshire

BeV unit of one billion electron volts

b/f brought forward

BFG big friendly giant

BFI British Film Institute

BFPA British Film Producers' Association

BFPO British Forces Post Office

BHS British Home Stores; British Horse Society

Bib Bible; Biblical

bibl bibliography; bibliographical

BIET British Institute of Engineering Technology

BIM British Institute of Management

BIOS Basin Input/Output System

BISF British Iron and Steel Federation

Bit, **bit** binary digit (BInary digiT)

BL Bachelor of Law

B/L, **b/l** bill of lading

BLE Bachelor of Land Economy

BLitt Bachelor of Letters

BLL Bachelor of Laws

BLT, **blt** bacon, lettuce and tomato (sandwich); built

blvd boulevard

BMJ *British Medical Journal*

B-movie low-cost supporting movie (originally Hollywood productions)

BMT British Mean Time; bone marrow transplant

BMTA British Motor Trade Association

BMus Bachelor of Music

BMW *Bayerische Motoren Werke*, Bavaria: car manufacturer

BMX bicycle motocross; a bicycle designed for rough or stunt riding

bn billion

BNA British Nursing Association

BNFL British Nuclear Fuels Limited

BNSc Bachelor of Nursing Science

BO, **bo** body odour; box office

BOAC British Overseas Airways Corporation

Bod Bodleian Library, Oxford

BOLTOP better on lips than on paper (usually placed below a 'paper kiss' – X – on the back of a lover's envelope)

BOOK box of organised knowledge (Anthony Burgess's definition of a book)

BOP *Boys' Own Paper* (boys' weekly, 1879–1967)

BOSS Bureau of State Security (South Africa)

BOT Board of Trade

bot botany; botanical; bottle; bottom

BOTB British Overseas Trade Board

BP British Petroleum

B-P Lord Baden-Powell, founder of the Scout movement

BPA British Philatelic Association

BPC British Pharmaceutical Codex; British Printing Corporation

bpm beats per minute (heart rate)

BPS British Pharmacological Society; bits per second

B&Q DIY chain store established by a Mr Block and a Mr Quayle in Southampton in 1968

br branch; bridge; brown

BR British Rail

bra brassiere

BRCS British Red Cross Society

Brig Brigadier; **Brig Gen** = Brigadier General

BRM British Racing Motors

Bro, **bro** Brother; brother

B-road secondary road

BS bullshit

BSC British Safety Council; British Steel Corporation; British Sugar Corporation; British Standards Council

BSc Bachelor of Science

BSCP British Standard Code of Practice

BSE bovine spongiform encephalopathy ('mad cow' disease)

BSG British Standard Gauge (railways)

BSI British Standards Institution

B-side the 'flip' or less important side of a vinyl record

BSkyB British Sky Broadcasting (an amalgamation of **Sky TV** and **BSB**, British Satellite Broadcasting)

BSRA British Sound Recording Association

BSSc Bachelor of Social Science (sometimes **BSocSc**)

BST British Summer Time

Bt, **Bart** Baronet

BTC British Transport Commission

btl bottle

BTU British Thermal Unit

BTW by the way

Bucks Buckinghamshire

BUPA British United Provident Association

BURMA be undressed, ready, my angel (on lover's envelope)

BV *Besloten Vennootschap* (private company in Holland)

BVDs men's one-piece underwear originally made by the US firm Bradley, Voorhees & Day

BVI British Virgin Islands

b/w black and white; monochrome

BWA British West Africa

BWIA British West Indies Airways

BWM, **bwm** burst water main

BWV *Bach Werke-Verzeichnis* (numbered catalogue of the works of J. S. Bach, first published in 1950)

BYO, **byo** bring your own; **BYOB** = bring your own bottle/beer

Byz Byzantine

C

C degree of heat in Celsius or centigrade; Carboniferous (geology); capacitance (physics); Cape; American series of cargo aircraft, (e.g. **C-10**); Catholic; Celtic; century; Roman numeral for 100; euphemism for cancer; cocaine; *calle* = street (Spanish); canon; canto; Captain; Cardinal; chief; Christian; circuit; club (cards); Conservative; copyright; coulomb; Commodore; Corps; council; Count; County; cold

c carat; capacity; carbon; catcher (baseball); caught (cricket); cent; centavo; centime; centre; century; chapter; child; church; circuit; *circa* = about (e.g. c1850); city; cloudy; cold; colt; commended; contralto; copy; copyright; council; county; coupon; court; cousin; crowned; cubic; curate; curacy; currency; cycle

C1 supervisory or clerical occupational category (ABC 1C2, etc)

C2 skilled or responsible manual worker occupational category

C3 low grade physical fitness category

C4 Channel Four Television

c/- care of (*also* **c/o**)

CA Consumers' Association; capital allowances; Caterers' Association; Central America; Certificate of Airworthiness; *chargé d'affaires*; Chartered Accountant; chronological age; civil aviation; Companies Act; *Corps d'Armée* = Army Corps; Chief Accountant; Court of Appeal; Croquet Association; Crown Agent; current assets

C/A capital account; credit account; current account

Ca Canada; Canadian; *compagnia* = company (Italy)

Ca *circa* = about (*see* **c**); close annealed

CAA Civil Aviation Authority; Capital Allowances Act; Clean Air Act; Civil Aeronautics Administration (USA); County Agricultural Advisor

CAB Citizens' Advice Bureau; Canadian Association of Broadcasters

cab taxi (from *cabriolet*); cabin; cabinet; cable

CAC Central Advisory Committee; Consumer Advisory Council (USA)

CAD Crown Agents Department; computer-aided design

CAE computer-aided education; computer-aided engineering; College of Advanced Education (Australian)

Caern Caernarvonshire

CAF Central African Federation; cost and freight (*also* **caf**, **cf**, **c&f**)

CAFE corporate average fuel economy (US fuel consumption standard)

CAG Concept Artists' Guild; Composers'-Authors' Guild

CAH chronic active hepatitis

CAI computer-aided instruction; *Club Alpino Italiano*; Canadian Aeronautical institute

CAL computer-aided (or -assisted) learning; Cornell Aeronautical Laboratory (USA)

Cal Calcutta; Caledonia

cal calibre; calendar; calorie

CALPA Canadian Air Line Pilots' Association

CALTEX California Texas Petroleum Corporation

CAM computer-aided manufacturing

Camb Cambrian, Cambridge

Cambs Cambridgeshire

CAMRA Campaign for Real Ale

Canadian Provinces and Territories

These are the two-letter abbreviations used by the Canadian Postal Service for its provinces and territories:

AB	Alberta	NT	Northwest Territories
BC	British Colombia	ON	Ontario
LB	Labrador	PE	Prince Edward Island
MB	Manitoba	PQ	Quebec
NB	New Brunswick	SK	Saskatchewan
NF	Newfoundland	UT	Yukon Territory
NS	Nova Scotia		

canc cancelled; cancellation

C&A chain stores named after Dutch brothers Clemens and Auguste Breeninkmeyer

C&M care and maintenance

Cant Canterbury

Cantab Cambridge (from the Latin *Cantabrigiensis*)

CAP Common Agricultural Policy (EU)

Cap, cap capital city; capacity; capital letter; captain (*also* **Capt**)

Card Cardinal

CARE Cooperative for American Relief to Europe (after WWII)

carr carriage

CARICOM Caribbean Community and Common Market

CARIFTA Caribbean Free Trading Area

cat catalogue

Cath Catholic; cathedral

CATNYP Catalogue of the New York Public Library

CATS students' Credit Accumulation Transfer Scheme

CATscan computerised axial tomography (body scan)

C&W country and western (music)

CATV cable/community antenna

CAVU Ceiling and Visibility Unlimited (aviation)

CB citizens' band (radio frequency); Companion of the Order of the Bath

CBC Canadian Broadcasting Corporation

CBE Commander of the Order of the British Empire

CBI Confederation of British Industries

cbk chequebook

CBS Columbia Broadcasting System

CBSO City of Birmingham Symphony Orchestra

CC Cricket/Croquet/Cruising/Cycling Club; City Council; County Council

cc carbon copy; cubic centimetre

c&c curtains and carpets

CCC Central Criminal Court, London (Old Bailey)

CCCP Union of Soviet Socialist Republics

CCITT *Comité Consultatif International Télégraphique et Téléphonique* (UN telecommunications committee in Geneva)

CCP Chinese Communist Party

CCTV closed circuit television

CD compact disc; Corps Diplomatique

cd fwd carried forward

CD-R compact disc that can be recorded on once

CD-ROM compact disc – read-only memory

CD-RW compact disc that can be recorded on over and over

CDT Central Daylight Time (North America)

CDV compact video disc

CE Church of England; chief engineer; civil engineer; Common Entrance (exam)

CET Central European Time

cf *confer* = compare; calf (bookbinding); centre foward (football); centre fielder (baseball)

c/f carried forward

CFC chlorofluorocarbon gases

cfi cost, freight and insurance

CFS chronic fatigue syndrome (*see* **ME**)

cg centigram; centre of gravity

CGA Country Gentlemen's Association

cgt capital gains tax

ch chain; chapter; chairman or chair

The Chemical Elements

actinium	Ac	europium	Eu	molybdenum	Mo
aluminium	Al	fermium	Fm	neodymium	Nd
americium	Am	fluorine	F	neon	Ne
antimony	Sb	francium	Fr	neptunium	Np
argon	Ar	gadolinium	Gd	nickel	Ni
arsenic	As	gallium	Ga	niobium	Nb
astatine	At	germanium	Ge	nitrogen	N
barium	Ba	gold	Au	nobelium	No
berkelium	Bk	iron	Fe	osmium	Os
beryllium	Be	hafnium	Hf	oxygen	O
bismuth	Bi	hassium	Hs	palladium	Pd
boron	B	helium	He	phosphorus	P
bromine	Br	holmium	Ho	platinum	Pt
cadmium	Cd	hydrogen	H	plutonium	Pu
caesium	Cs	indium	In	polonium	Po
calcium	Ca	iodine	I	potassium	K
californium	Cf	iridium	Ir	praseodymium	Pr
carbon	C	iron	Fe	promethium	Pm

cerium	Ce	krypton	Kr	protoactinium	Pa
chlorine	Cl	lanthanum	La	radium	Ra
chromium	Cr	lawrencium	Lr	radon	Rn
cobalt	Co	lead	Pb	rhenium	Re
columbium	Cb	lithium	Li	rhodium	Rh
copper	Cu	lutetium	Lu	rubidium	Rb
curium	Cm	magnesium	Mg	ruthenium	Ru
dubnium	Db	manganese	Mn	rutherfordium	Rf
dysprosium	Dy	meitnerium	Mt	samarium	Sm
einsteinium	Es	mendelevium	Md	scandium	Sc
erbium	Er	mercury	Hg	seaborgium	Sg
selenium	Se	tellurium	Te	uranium	U
silicon	Si	terbium	Tb	vanadium	V
silver	Ag	thallium	Tl	xenon	Xe
sodium	Na	thorium	Th	ytterbium	Yb
strontium	Sr	thulium	Tm	yttrium	Y
sulphur	S	tin	Sn	zirconium	Zr
tantalum	Ta	titanium	Ti	zinc	Zn
technetium	Tc	tungtsen	W	zirconium	Zr

Ches Cheshire
chq cheque
Chi Chicago
chron chronological
CI Channel Islands
CIA Central Intelligence Agency (USA)
CIB Criminal Investigation Branch
CICB Criminal Injuries Compensation Board
CID Criminal Investigation Department
Cie *Compagnie*: French company (as in *Bracquart et Cie*)
C-in-C Commander-in-Chief
CIP Common Industrial Policy; cataloguing in publication data
circ circulation (of publications); circular
cit citation; cited
CIVB *Conseil Interprofessionnel du Vins de Bordeaux*
CJD Creutzfeldt-Jakob disease
CKD completely knocked down (of disassembled cars, products, etc)
cl centilitre; class; cloth (bookbinding)
Cllr Councillor
clr clear
cm centimetre; cm^2 = square centimetre; cm^3 = cubic centimetre
Cmdr Commander
Cmdre Commodore

CMG Companion of St Michael and St George
CND Campaign for Nuclear Disarmament
CNN Cable News Network
CNR Canadian National Railway
CO Commanding Officer; Central Office
Co, co company; county
c/o in the care of; cash order
cob close of business
COBOL Computer Business Oriented Language
COD cash/collect on delivery
CODOT Classification of Occupations and Directory of Occupational Titles
COED computer-operated electronic display; Concise Oxford English Dictionary
co-ed co-educational
CofA Certificate of Airworthiness
CofE Church of England
COI Central Office of Information
Col Colonel
coll collection; college; colloquialism
Comdr Commander
Comdt Commandant
COMECON Council for Mutual Economic Assistance (EU)
COMPAC Commonwealth Trans-Pacific Telephone Cable
compo plastering composition; compensation
conc concentrated
cond condition; conduct
condo condominium
confed confederation; confederate
Cons, cons Conservative; Consul; constitution
consols consolidated annuities (Government securities)
cont continued
Co-Op co-operative society or union
COPAT Council for the Prevention of Art Theft
COPS Cognitive Profiling System
CORE Congress of Racial Equality (USA)
Corp, corp Corporation
corr correction; correspondent
COSLA Convention of Scottish Local Authorities
COTS Childlessness Overcome Through Surrogacy
CO^2 carbon dioxide gas
CP Common Prayer; Communist Party; Country Party (Australia); Court of Probate
cp compare
CPA Canadian Pacific Airlines; certified public accountant (USA)
CPI consumer price index

cpi characters per inch

Cpl Corporal

CPLP Community of Portuguese-speaking Countries

CPR cardiopulmonary resuscitation

CPRE Council for the Protection of Rural England

CPRW Council for the Protection of Rural Wales

CPU central processing unit (computers)

CRE Commission for Racial Equality

Cres, cres crescent

CRO Criminal Records Office

CRS Chinese restaurant syndrome (allegedly due to overuse of the flavour enhancer monosodium glutamate)

CSA Child Support Agency

CSC Civil Service Commission

CSE Certificate of Secondary Education

CS gas ortho-chlorobenzal malononitrile; named after the originators, Ben Carson and Roger Staughton

CSI Chartered Surveyors' Institution

CSIRO Commonwealth Scientific and Industrial Research Organisation

CSM Company Sergeant-Major

CSO Central Statistical Office

CSR Colonial Sugar Refining Company (Australia)

CST Central Standard Time

Ct Carat (unit of weight for precious stones, pearls, gold alloys, etc). *See also* **Kt** (karat) in the USA

CTC carbon tetrachloride (fire retardant)

CTN confectioner, tobacconist and newsagent's shop

CTO cancelled to order (philately)

CTR Control Traffic Zone (airports)

Ctrl the modifier key on a computer

CTT capital transfer tax

CTV Canadian Television Network

cu cm cubic centimetre (*also* **cu m** = cubic metre; **cu in** = cubic inch; **cu ft** = cubic foot; **cu yd** = cubic yard)

CUNY City University of New York

CUP Cambridge University Press

CURE Care, Understanding, Research organisation for the welfarE of drug addicts

CV, cv *curriculum vitae*: a summary of a person's career and attainments

CW common wisdom

CWA Civil Works Administration (USA); Country Women's Association

CWL Catholic Women's League

cwo cash with order

cwt hundredweight (112 lbs)

cyl cylinder

Cz Czech Republic

D

D Roman numeral for 500; Gambian dalasi (currency); December; Democrat, Democratic (USA); demy (paper size); *Deus* = God; *Deutschland* = Germany; Devonian (geology); diameter; dinar; Vietnamese dong (currency); occupational category; *Dominus* = Lord; Dom; Don; *douane* = French customs; Duchess; Duke; Dutch

d day; date; dam (animal pedigrees); daughter; dead; deceased; decree; degree; delete; deliver; delivery; density; *denarius* = old British pence (1d, 2d, 9d, etc); depart; departure; depth; desert; diameter; died; dinar; discharged; distance; dividend; dose; drachma

DA District Attorney (USA); Department of Agriculture (USA); deputy assistant; Algerian dinar (currency); Diploma in Anaesthetics; Diploma in Art; dopamine

D/A deposit account; days after acceptance; delivery on acceptance; digital to analogue (*also* **D-A**)

DAB digital audio broadcasting; Dictionary of American Biography

DAD deputy assistant director

DAF, daf *Doorn Automobielfabriek* = Dutch car manufacturer

daffs daffodils

DAGrSc Doctor of Agricultural Science

DAI, dai death from accidental injuries

Dan Danish

D&B Dun and Bradstreet (US financial reports); discipline and bondage

D&C, d&c dilation and curettage; dean and chapter

d&d drunk and disorderly; death and dying

D&V diarrhoea and vomiting

dap documents against payment; do anything possible

DAR Daughters of the American Republic (USA)

DARE demand and resource evaluation

DAS Dramatic Authors' Society

DASc Doctor of Agricultural Science

DAT digital audio tape; digital analogue technology; dementia of the Alzheimer type

DATA Draughtsmen's and Allied Technicians' Association

DATV digitally assisted television

DAX *Deutsche Aktien-index* = German price share index

dB, db decibel

DB Bachelor of Divinity; delayed broadcast; *Deutsche Bundesbank*; *Deutsche Bundesbahn* (German railways); double-barrelled

DBH diameter at breast height (forestry)

Dbn Durban, South Africa

DBS direct broadcast by satellite

DC Distict of Columbia (as in Washington, DC); death certificate; Deputy Commissioner; Detective Constable; direct current; District Commissioner; Douglas Commercial (US aircraft series, e.g. **DC3**, **DC10**, etc); documents against cash

dc dead centre; double column (printing); direct current; drift correction

DCA Department of Civil Aviation (Australia)

DCM Distinguished Conduct Medal

d col double column (publishing)

DD Doctor of Divinity

DDA Disabled Drivers' Association

D-day start of Allied invasion of mainland Europe, WWII

DDG deputy director general

DDR *Deutsche Demokratische Republik* (formerly East Germany)

DDS Dewey Decimal System (library classification); Doctor of Dental Surgery

DDT dichloro-diphenyl-trichloroethane (insecticide)

Dec December

dec deceased; decimal; decrease

def definition; definitive; defect; deficit

del *delineavit* = drawn by (on engravings); delegate

deli delicatessen

demo demonstration

Den Denmark

dep depart; departure; depot; deposit

Dept, dept department

der derivative; derivation

derv diesel-engined road vehicle

DES Department of Education and Science

DET diethyltryptamine (hallucinogenic drug)

Det, det Detective; detached

DEWLINE distant early warning viewing line (US defence)

DF Defender of the Faith

DFC Distinguished Flying Cross

DFM Distinguished Flying Medal

DG, D-G director-general

DHA District Health Authority

DHSS former Department of Health and Social Security (now split into **DoH** and **DSS**)

DI Detective Inspector; donor insemination

diag diagonal; diagram

diam diameter

dib, dib, dib *see* **dyb**

DIC drunk in charge (police term)

dil dilute

DIN *Deutsche Industrie fur Normen* (measurement of speed of photographic film)

DINKY double income, no kids yet

Dip, **dip** diploma (*also* **dipl**)

DipAD Diploma in Art and Design

DipCom Diploma of Commerce

DipEd Diploma of Education

Dir, **dir** director

dis district; distinguished; distance

div division

DIY, **diy** do it yourself

DJ, **dj** dinner jacket; disc jockey

d/j = dust jacket (books); *also* **d/w** dust wrapper

DLitt Doctor of Letters; Doctor of Literature

DLO Dead Letter Office

DLP former Democratic Labor Party (Australia)

dlr dealer

DM *Deutschmark*

DMS data management system; Diploma of Management Studies

DMT dimethyltryptamine (hallucinogenic drug)

DMus Doctor of Music

DMZ demilitarised zone

DNA deoxyribonucleic acid, the main constituent of chromosomes

DNB Dictionary of National Biography

D-notice Government restriction warning prohibiting publication of information considered vital to national security

DNS Department for National Savings

DOA dead on arrival

DOCG *Denominazione di Origine Controllata Garantita*: Italian guarantee that wine is from the district named on the label

---

Doctors' Abbreviations

In Britain patients are legally entitled to see their medical casenotes. But if you did peek at your doctor's scrawl, peppered with arcane slang and medical abbreviations, would you understand it even it if was legible? You would have cause for alarm if you spotted **Review SOS**, but in fact SOS here is short for the Latin *sid opus sit*: if symptoms persist. On the other hand, the letters **DNR** effectively disguise a truly grim reality: do not resuscitate. Other common abbreviations include **VMI** (very much improved) and **NAD** (nothing abnormal detected).

More common are the 'gallows humour' acronyms known to all medical students and young doctors, like **GORK** (God only really knows!) and **ADT** on a prescription (any damn thing!). Then there are **LOL in NAD** (little old lady in no apparent distress); **CC** (chief complaint); **YoYo**, the sign-off for discharged patients (you're on your own!) and the ghoulish **GPO** (good for parts only); **MFC** (measure for coffin) and **ECU** (eternal care unit, i.e. morgue). **FLK** on a child's notes means 'funny looking kid', while **GRINED** means '*Guardian* reader in ethnic dress'.

DOD Department of Defense (USA)

DOE Department of the Environment

DOM *Deo Optimo Maximo*: Latin for 'God is best and greatest', the motto of the Benedictine Order and seen on the labels of Benedictine liqueur; dirty old man

DORA Defence of the Realm Act, enacted during World War I to enforce security restrictions

dorm dormitory

DOS disc (or disk) operating system, as in **MS-DOS** and **PC-DOS**

doz dozen

DP displaced person; data processing

DPh Doctor of Philosophy

DPM Deputy Prime Minister; Diploma of Psychological Medicine

DPP Director of Public Prosecutions

DPW Department of Public Works

Dr doctor

dr debit; debtor; drachm; drachma; drawn; drive

D-RAM dynamic random access memory

DSC Distinguished Service Cross

DSc Doctor of Science

DSM Distinguished Service Medal

DSO Distinguished Service Order

DSS Department of Social Security

DST daylight saving time

dstn destination

DTI Department of Trade and Industry

DTP desktop publishing

DTs delirium tremens

dub dubious

dup duplicate

Dur Durham

DV Domestic Violence Division, Scotland Yard

DVD digital video disc; **DVD-Rom** = recordable DVD

DVM Doctor of Veterinary Medicine

d/w dust wrapper; *also* **d/j** = dust jacket (books)

D/W deadweight

DWD driving while disqualified

DWI Dutch West Indies

dwt pennyweight (one twentieth of an ounce)

DX telecom symbol for long distance; deep six (to 'deep-six' something is to bury it, literally or figuratively)

dyb Do Your Best (Scout's motto). Hence the traditional Cubs' call, 'dyb, dyb, dyb!'

Dylan Dynamic LANguage, an Apple computer programming language

E

East, West and Other Points of the Compass

Starting with *north* and moving clockwise: **N** (north); **NNE** (north-northeast); **NE** (northeast); **ENE** (east-northeast); **E** (east); **ESE** (east-southeast); **SE** (southeast); **SSE** (south-southeast); **S** (south); **SSW** (south-southwest); **SW** (southwest); **WSW** (west-southwest); **W** (west); **WNW** (west-northwest); **NW** (northwest) and **NNW** (north-northwest).

E Earl; earth (planet); earth (electric circuit); East; eastern; postcode for East London; Easter; ecstasy (drug); elliptical galaxy (astronomy); England; English; E-number *(see* detailed entry); energy; equator; lowest occupational category; equator; evening; evensong; electromotive force (physics); *España* = Spain; second-class merchant ship (Lloyd's Register)

e edition; eldest; electric; electricity; electromotive; electron; engineer; Erlang (telecommunications unit); error (baseball); evening; excellent; excellence; transcendental number (mathematics)

EA East Anglia; educational age; electrical artificer; *Ente Autonomo* = Autonomous Corporation (Italy); environmental assessment

ea each

EAA Edinburgh Architectural Association

EAAA European Association of Advertising Agencies

EAC East African Community; Educational Advisory Committee; Engineering Advisory Council

EACSO East African Common Services Organisation

E&OE errors and omissions excepted

EAON, **eaon** except as otherwise noted

EAP English for academic purposes; Edgar Allan Poe (US author)

EAR employee attitude research

EAS equivalent air speed

EAT earliest arrival time (*also* **eat**); Employment Appeal Tribunal

EAX electronic automated exchange (telecommunications)

EB *Encyclopedia Britannica*; electricity board; electronic beam

EBA English Bowling Association

EBC European Billiards Confederation; European Brewery Convention

EBL European Bridge League

EBM expressed breast milk

EBU European Boxing Union; European Badminton Union; European Broadcasting Union; English Bridge Union

EBV Epstein-Barr virus

EC European Community (*now* **EU**, European Union); postcode for East Central London; East Caribbean; Episcopal Church

ec earth closet; enamel coated; *exempli causa* = for example

ECA Electrical Contractors' Association

ecc *eccetera* = etc (Italy)

ECD early closing day; estimated completion date

ECG electrocardiogram; electrocardiograph; export credit guarantee

ECHO virus Enteric Cytopathic Human Orphan virus (*also* **echovirus**)

ECM European Common Market (*now* **EU**)

ECO English Chamber Orchestra

ECS European Communications Satellite

ECSC European Coal and Steel Community

ECU English Church Union; extra close-up (film and TV)

ecu European currency unit

ed editor; edition; edited

EDC European Defence Community

Edin Edinburgh

EDM electronic distance measurement (surveying)

EDP, **edp** electronic data processing

EDSAT Educational Television Satellite

EDT Eastern Daylight Time

EDTA ethylenediaminetetra-acetic acid (bleach stabiliser in detergents)

ee errors excepted

EEC European Economic Community (*now* **EU**)

EEG electroencephalogram; electroencephalograph

EENT eye, ear, nose and throat (medical specialism). *See* **ENT**

EET Eastern European Time

EETPU Electrical, Electronic, Telecommunications and Plumbing Union

EFL English as a foreign language

EFTA European Free Trade Association

EFTPOS electronic funds transfer at point of sale

EFTS electronic funds transfer system

e.g. *exempli gratia* = for example

EGM extraordinary general meeting

EGU English Golf Union

EHF European Hockey Federation; extremely high frequency

EHO environmental health officer

EIS Educational Institute of Scotland

EL easy listening (radio format)

el elevated railroad (USA); electrical

E-layer lower layer of ionised gases in the earth's ionosphere that reflects radio waves (*also* **Heaviside layer**)

elev elevation

ELF Eritrean Liberation Front; extremely low frequency

Eliz Elizabeth; Elizabethan

ELT English language teaching

ELU English Lacrosse Union

email, e-mail electronic mail

emer emergency; emeritus

EMI Electric and Musical Industries Limited

Emp Emperor; Empress; Empire

EMS European monetary system

EMU European monetary unit; economic and monetary union; electromagnetic unit (*also* **emu**)

EN enrolled nurse

encyc encyclopedia

ENEA European Nuclear Energy Agency

ENG electronic news gathering

Eng England; English

eng engine; engineer

engr engraver; engraved

ENO English National Opera

ENT ear, nose and throat (medical speciality) *see* **EENT**

env envelope

EOC Equal Opportunities Commission

EOKA Cypriot Campaign for Union with Greece

EPC Educational Publishers' Council

EPCOT experimental prototype community of tomorrow (at Disney World, Florida)

EPNS electroplated nickel silver

E Numbers

These are code numbers for natural and artificial additives to food and drink that have been accepted as safe throughout the European Union. Numbers without the E on product labels are additives approved by the UK but not yet by the EU. Some of the E numbers denote traditional natural additives such as E120 (red cochineal colouring), E140 (green chlorophyll), E406 (agar, used in icecream), E220 (sulphur dioxide, a preservative). Others are undoubtedly creations from the test tube, such as E233 (2-thiazol-4-yl benzimidazole thiabenzadole, used to treat bananas).

Here are some of the more common E numbers:

Colours
E100   curcumin – used in flour and margarine
E101   riboflavin
E102   the notorious tartrazine, used to heighten the orange colour of soft drinks and blamed by many for 'driving hyperactive kids barmy'.

E104   quinoline yellow – used to colour smoked fish
E150   caramel
E153   vegetable carbon – used in liquorice
E162   beetroot red (betanin) – used in ice cream
E171   titanium oxide – used in sweets
E174   silver (yes, the metal!) – used in cake decorations

Antioxidants

E300   L-ascorbic acid – used in fruit drinks and bread
E307   synthetic alpha-tocopherol – used in baby foods
E310   propyl gallate – chewing gum, vegetable oils
E320   butylated hydroxytoluene – soup mixes, cheese spreads

Preservatives

E200   sorbic acid – soft drinks, yogurt, cheese slices
E201   sodium sorbate
E202   potassium sorbate
E203   calcium sorbate – frozen pizzas, cakes, buns
E210   benzoic acid
E221   sodium sulphite
E227   calcium bisulphite – dried fruit and vegetables, fruit juices,
       sausages, dairy desserts, cider, beer and wine
E252   potassium nitrate – used for curing ham, bacon, corned beef, some
       cheese

Emulsifiers and stabilisers

E322   lecithins – chocolate and low fat spreads
E400   alginic acid – icecream, soft cheese
E407   carrageenan – milk shakes, jellies
E410   carob gum – salad cream
E412   guar gum – packet soups
E413   gum tragacanth – salad dressing, cheese
E414   gum arabic – confectionery
E440   pectin – jams and preserves
E465   ethylmethylcellulose – used in gateaux

Others

E420   sorbitol – diabetic jams and confectionery
E170   calcium carbonate
E260   acetic acid
E290   carbon dioxide – carbonates fizzy drinks
E330   citric acid
E334   tartaric acid
E338   orthophosphoric acid – flavourings

Be warned that non-E numbers on packaging include potentially harmful agents: 507 (hydrochloric acid), 513 (sulphuric acid), 536 (potassium ferrocyanide), 925 (chlorine). The frequently criticised flavour enhancer monosodium glutamate or MSG sometimes hides behind its code number, 621.

EPOCH End Physical Punishment of Children
EPOS electronic point of sale
EPP executive pension plan
eps earnings per share
equiv equivalent
ER *Elizabeth Regina* = Queen Elizabeth; *Eduardus Rex* = King Edward
ERA Education Reform Act
ERBM extended range ballistic missile
ERG electrical resistance gauge
ERGOM European Research Group on Management
ERM European Rate Mechanism
ERNIE electronic random number indicator equipment (selects prizewinners from Premium Bond numbers)
ERS earnings related supplement
ERU English Rugby Union
ERV English Revised Version of the Bible
E's the elements that can cause angina: exertion, emotion, eating, extremes and entercourse (doctors can't spell)
ESA Educational Supply Association; environmentally sensitive area
ESCAP Economic and Social Commission for Asia and the Pacific
ESCO Educational, Scientific and Cultural Organisation (UN)
ESG English standard gauge
ESL English as a second language
ESN educationally subnormal (60–80 IQ)
ESP English for special purposes; extra-sensory perception
esp especially
Esq, esq esquire
ESRO European Space Research Organisation
ESSO Standard Oil Company
est established; estate; estimated; estuary
EST Eastern Standard Time; electric shock treatment
ESU English Speaking Union; electrostatic unit
ETA estimated time of arrival
et al *et alii* = and others; *et alibi* = and elsewhere
etc *et cetera* = and so on
ETD estimated time of departure
ETF electronic transfer of funds
et seq *et sequens* = and the following; *et sequentia* = and those that follow
etym, etymol etymology; etymological
EU European Union; Evangelical Union
EVA extra vehicular activity (outside a spacecraft)
evg, evng evening
EWO educational welfare officer
ex, exc excellent; excess; excursion; exempt; excluding; former (as in ex-Army, ex-husband, etc)

Exc Excellency
exch exchange
excl exclusive; excluding
ex div ex dividend
exec executor; executive
exes expenses
exhib exhibit; exhibitor
ex int ex interest
Exon Bishop of Exeter
exp expense; expenses; experience; experiment; export; express
expo large-scale exposition or exhibition
expurg expurgate
ext extension; exterior; external; extra; extinct

F

F Fahrenheit; family; farad; father; fathom; February; Federation; Fellow; feminine; fiction; filly; fine (metallurgy, numismatics); fog; folio; foolscap (paper size); foul; franc; francs; *Frauen* = woman; France; French; *Frère* = Brother; Friday; US fighter aircraft series (**F-111**, etc); filial generation (genetic; **F1**, **F2**, etc)

f face value (numismatics, philately); fair; father; fathom; feet (*also* **ft**); female; feminine; filly; fine; f-number (photographic focal length/ aperture ratio, e.g. **F6**); following; *forte* = loudly; formula; folio; foul; fog; founded; franc; freehold; frequency; furlong; Dutch guilder

FA Football Association; fatty acid; filtered air; fire alarm; Finance Act; folic acid; furnace annealed; Fanny Adams (euphemism for *fuck all*)

FAA Federal Aviation Aministration (USA); Fellow Australian Academy of Science; Film Artists' Association; Fleet Air Arm; free amino acid

FAAAS Fellow of the American Academy of Arts and Sciences

fab fabric

fabbr *fabbrica* = factory

Fab Soc Fabian Society

FACS Fellow of the American College of Surgeons

fac facsimile (*see* **FAX, fax**)

FACT Federation Against Copyright Theft

fad free air delivered

Faer Faeroe Islands

FA Cup Football Association Cup, open to all teams of the Association

Fahr Fahrenheit (*also* **Fah, fahr**)

FAI *Fédération aeronautique internationale* = International Aeronautical Federation

FAIA Fellow of the Association of International Accountants

Falk I Falkland Islands

fam family; familiar

FANY First Aid Nursing Yeomanry
f&a fore and aft
f&d freight and demurrage
f&f fixtures and fittings
f&t fire and theft
FAO Food and Agriculture Organisation (UN)
fao for the attention of; finished all over
faq fair average quality; free alongside quay
FAR free for accident reported (no claim on insurance)
FASA Fellow of the Australian Society of Accountants
FAST factor analysis system
fath fathom
fav favourite
FAX, fax facsmile transmission; facsimile equipment
FB fire brigade; fisheries board; Forth Bridge; Free Baptist
F-B full-bore (guns)
fb fullback (football)
FBA Fellow of the British Academy
FC Forestry Commission
fcp foolscap (paper size)
FCC Federal Communications Commission (USA)
FCCA Fellow of the Chartered Association of Certified Accountants
FCI International Federation of Kennel Clubs
FCII Fellow of the Chartered Insurance Institute
FCO Foreign and Commonwealth Office
FD *Fidei Defensor* = Defender of the Faith
fd forward; found; founded
FDA Food and Drug Administration (USA)
FDC first day cover (philately)
FDR Franklin Delano Roosevelt, former US president
fdr founder
Feb February
fec *fecit* = made by (on antique prints and engravings)
Fed Federal; Federal Reserve Bank (USA)
fem female; feminine
FES foil, épée and sabre
Fest, fest festival
FF Fianna Fail (Irish polical party)
ff folios; fixed focus
FG Fine Gael (Irish political party)
F/H, f/h freehold (*also* **fhold** and **fhld**)
FHA Federal Housing Administration (USA)
FHB 'family hold back' (warning to children not to eat before the guests)
FIA Fellow of the Institute of Actuaries

FIAT *Fabbrica Italiana Automobili Torina*, Turin car makers

fict fiction (*also* **fic**)

FICA Federal Insurance Contributions Act (USA)

Fid Def *Fidei Defensor* (see FD)

FIDE *Fédération Internationale des Echecs* = International Chess Federation

FIDO Federation of Irate Dog Owners; dedicated to the reform of Britain's animal quarantine laws (*see* **PFP**)

FIFA *Fédération Internationale de Football Association* = International Association Football Federation; International Federation of Art Film Makers

FIFO first in, first out

15 cert British Board of Film Classification for films not suitable for children under 15

fig figure

FIH *Fédération Internationale de Hockey* = International Hockey Federation

FILO first in, last out

FIM *Fédération Internationale Motocycliste* = International Motorcyclists' Federation

fin *finis* = the end; final; financial

FINA *Fédération internationale de natation amateur* = International Amateur Swimming Federation

Findus Fruit INDUStries Limited

fix fixture

fl floor; fluid; guilder (in the Netherlands)

FLAK fondest love and kisses

Flak *Fliegerabwehrkanone* = anti-aircraft fire or artillery; now means a quantity of adverse criticism

fld filed

fldg folding

FLN *Front de Libération Nationale* = National Liberation Front of Algeria

fl oz fluid ounces

flrg flooring

FM frequency modulation

fm farm

FMCG fast-moving consumer goods

fmr former; farmer

FNMA Federal National Mortgage Association (USA), fondly known as 'Fannie Mae'

FMV full motion video

FO Foreign Office; Flying Officer (*also* **F/O**)

FOAF friend of a friend

FOB, fob free on board

FoC, foc father of the chapel (print unions)

fo'c's'le forecastle (on a ship)

FoE, FOE Friends of the Earth

FOH front of house (theatres)

fol folio; following

F-111 famous swing-wing US fighter-bomber launched in 1968

Footsie *see* **FT-SE 100**

FOR free on rail

FOREST Freedom Organisation for the Right to Enjoy Smoking Tobacco

FORTRAN FORmula TRANslation: computer programming language

48, The Bach's two books of preludes and fugues for clavier

4WD four-wheel drive

FP, fp fireplace; fresh paragraph; fully paid; freezing point

FPA Family Planning Association

FPO field post office (Army)

FPS Fellow of the Pharmaceutical/Philosophical/Physical Society

fps frames per second; feet per second

fr franc (sometimes **Ffr** for French franc, etc); front; from; frequent; fruit; father

FRAME Fund for the Replacement of Animals in Medical Experiments

FRCM Fellow of the Royal College of Music

FRCP Fellow of the Royal College of Physicians

FRCS Fellow of the Royal College of Surgeons

FRCVS Fellow of the Royal College of Veterinary Surgeons

FRED Fast Reactor Experiment, Dounreay, Scotland

FRGS Fellow of the Royal Geographical Society

Fri Friday

FRICS Fellow of the Institute of Chartered Surveyors

front frontispiece (*also* **frontis**)

FT *Financial Times*, London. *See* **FT Index**, **FT-SE 100**

ft foot; feet. **sq ft** = square foot/feet; **cu ft** = cubic foot/feet

FTC Federal Trade Commission (USA)

FT Index Financial Times Industrial Ordinary Share Index

FTP file transfer protocol

FT-SE 100 Financial Times Stock Exchange 100 Index (*also* **Footsie**)

FU Farmers' Union

fur furlong

FWA Federal Works Agency (USA)

FWD, fwd forward; front-wheel drive; four-wheel drive

fyi for your information

FZS Fellow of the Zoological Society

G

G General Exhibition (film classification category in some countries); German; Germany; Gibbs function (thermodynamics); good; Haitian gourde (currency); grand (slang for $1,000); grey; green; Guernsey; Gulf; Paraguayan guarani (currency)

g gallon; gale; garage; gas; gaseous; gauge; gelding; gender; general; gilt; goal; goalkeeper; gold; gram; gravity; great; green; grey; guardian; guilder; guilders; guinea; guineas

GA General Assembly (UN); General American (language); Geographical Association; Geologists' Association; general anaesthetic; graphic arts

G/A, **g/a** ground to air (missiles); general average (*also* **GA**, **ga**)

GAA Gaelic Athletic Association

GAC granular activated carbon

Gael Gaelic

GAFTA Grain and Free Trade Association

Gal Galway, Ireland

gal gallon (*also* **gall**)

GALAXY General Automatic Luminosity high-speed scanner at the Royal Observatory, Edinburgh

galv galvanised; galvanic; galvanometer

GAM guided aircraft missile

Gam The Gambia

G&AE general and administration expenses

G&O gas and oxygen (anaesthesia)

G&S Gilbert and Sullivan

G&T gin and tonic

GAP Great American Public

GAPAN Guild of Air Pilots and Air Navigators

GAPCE General Assembly of the Presbyterian Church of England

gar garage; garden (*also* **gard**); garrison

GAR guided aircraft rocket

GARP Global Atmospheric Research Programme

GATCO Guild of Air Traffic Control Officers

GATT General Agreement on Tariffs and Trade (*also* **Gatt**)

GAUFCC General Assembly of Unitarian and Free Christian Churches

GAV gross annual value

GAW gross annual wage

GAYE give as you earn (scheme to deduct charitable contributions from employees' pay packets)

gaz gazette; gazetted

GB Great Britain; gigabyte

GBE Grand Cross of the British Empire

GBH grievous bodily harm

GBS dramatist George Bernard Shaw

GC George Cross (gallantry award)

GCA ground control approach (airports)

GCB Grand Cross of the Most Honourable Order of the Bath

GCE General Certificate of Education

GCHQ Government Communications Headquarters

GCM Good Conduct Medal; General Court Martial

GCMG Grand Cross of the Order of St Michael and St George

GCSE General Certificate of Secondary Education

GCVO Grand Cross of the Royal Victorian Order

gd good

GDBA Guide Dogs for the Blind Association

gdn, gdns garden; gardens

GDR German Democratic Republic (former East Germany)

GE General Electric Co (USA)

ge gilt edge (books)

GEC General Electric Corporation

GEMS Global Environmental Monitoring System

Gen General

gen gender; general; generic; genuine

gent gentleman; **Gents** = men's lavatory

geog geography; geographical

GEOREF International Geographic Reference System

GESTAPO *GEheime STAats-POlizei*, former German secret police

G5 Group of Five (France, Japan, USA, Germany and UK as a currency stabilising group)

GF General Foods

GFR German Federal Republic (former West Germany)

GFS Girls' Friendly Society

GG Grenadier Guards

GGA former Girl Guides' Association

GHQ general headquarters

gi galvanised iron

GI Government Issue (term for US soldier, WWII)

Gib Gibraltar

GIFT gamete intra-fallopian transfer (fertilisation technique)

GIGO garbage in, garbage out (computer term)

GKN Guest, Keen & Nettlefold's (engineering)

Gk Greek

gl glass; gloss

glad, gladdie gladiolus; Gladys Moncrieff, former Australian soprano (d.1976) known as 'Our Glad'

Glam Glamorgan

GLASS Gay and Lesbian Assembly for Student Support (USA)

GLC Greater London Council

gld guilder

GLOMEX Global Oceanographic and Meteorological Experiment

Glos Gloucestershire

GM General Motors Corporation; George Medal; general manager; genetically modified

gm gram

G-man officer of the Federal Bureau of Investigation (Government man)

GMB Grand Master of the Order of the Bath; General, Municipal and Boilermakers' Union

GMBE Grand Master of the Order of the British Empire

GmbH *Gesellschaft mit beschrankter Haftung*, a limited liability company in Germany

GMC General Medical Council

GMDSS Global Maritime Distress and Safety System, which replaced Morse code in February 1999

GMT Greenwich Mean Time

GMWU National Union of General and Municipal Workers

gn, gns guinea; guineas

gnd ground

GNP gross national product

GOM Grand Old Man (originally Prime Minister Gladstone) but today used to describe a senior and respected person

GOP Grand Old Party (US Republican party); *Girls' Own Paper*

Gov Governor

Gov-Gen Governor-General

govt government

GP general practitioner (medical doctor); Grand Prix; general purpose

Gp Capt Group Captain

gph gallons per hour

GPI general paralysis of the insane

GPO general post office

GPS Great Public Schools (Australia)

GQ general quarters

Gr Greek; Grecian

gr gram; grain; gross; grand; group; grade

GRA Greyhound Racing Association

grad graduate; gradient

GRI *Georgius Rex Imperator* = George, King and Emperor

grm gram

gr wt gross weight

GS Geological Survey; gold standard; general secretary; general staff

G7 Group of Seven (economic policy coordinating committee of seven leading industrial nations, excluding the former USSR: Canada, France, Germany, Italy, Japan, UK and USA)

G77 Group of Seventy Seven (the world's developing countries)

GSM general sales manager; group sales manager

GSO General Staff Officer

GSOH good sense of humour

GT *gran turismo* = luxury high-performance sports saloon

GTC General Teaching Council (Scotland)

G10 Group of Ten: original 1961 committee of nations that established IMF drawing rights (Belgium, Canada, France, Italy, Japan, Netherlands, Sweden, UK, USA and West Germany)

gtd guaranteed

gte gilt top edge (books)

guar guarantee; guaranteed

GUI graphical user interface

Gulag *Glavnoye Upravleniye ispravitel'no-trudovykh LAGerei* = a group of Russian labour camps, the subject of Alexander Solzhenitsyn's 1973 novel, *The Gulag Archipelago*

GUM *Gosudarstvenni Universalni Magazin* = official Russian department store

GUS Great Universal Stores (UK)

GUT great unified theory

guv guv'nor; governor (Cockney term which recognises that 'you're the boss')

GV *Grande Vitesse* = fast French train

GVHD graft versus host disease

gvt government (*also* **govt**)

GWP Government white paper

GWR Great Western Railway

gym gymnasium; gymnastics

H

H degree of hardness in pencils, e.g. **2H**, **3H**, etc; Hamiltonian (physics); Harbour; hearts (cards); heroin; histamine receptor; horn (music); hospital; hour; hydrant

h harbour; hard; hardness; heat; height (*also* **ht**); high; hit (ball sports); heavy; horse; hot; hour; house; hundred; husband

HA hardy annual (horticulture); Hautes-Alps (French department); Health Authority; high altitude

ha hectare

Ha Hawaii, Hawaiian, Haiti

ha *hoc anno* = in this year; high angle

HAA hepatitis-associated antigen

HA&M *Hymns Ancient and Modern* (first published 1861)

hab habitat; habitation

hab corp *habeas corpus*

HAC high alumina cement; Honourable Artillery Company

had hereinafter described

haem haemoglobin; haemorrage

HAI hospital acquired infection

hal halogen

Ham Hamburg, Germany

Han Hanoverian

H&C, **h&c** hot and cold (water)

H&E heredity and environment; *Health & Efficiency* (naturist journal)

h&t hardened and tempered

H&W Harland & Wolff, Belfast shipbuilders

hanky handkerchief (*also* **hankie**)

HAS Health Advisory Service

haz hazard; hazardous

HB hard black pencil

Hb haemoglobin (*also* **hem**)

H-beam H-cross-section steel girder or joist

hbk hardback (book)

hbr harbour

HC Headmasters' Conference; High Commissioner; High Court; health certificate; highly commended; *hors de concours* = not for competition; Hague Convention; house of correction

Hcap, **hcp** handicap

HCB House of Commons Bill

HCE recurring abbreviation in James Joyce's *Finnegans Wake*, being the initials of the main character, H. C. Earwicker

HCSA Hospital Consultants' and Specialists' Association

hcw hot and cold water (*also* **hc**, **h&c**)

hdbk hardback; handbook

HDipEd Higher Diploma in Education

hdle hurdle

hdlg handling; **hdlg chg** = handling charge

hdqrs headquarters

HDV heavy duty vehicle

HE Her/His Excellency; His Eminence; high explosive

Heb Hebrew; Hebraic

HEC Health Education Council

HECTOR Heated Experimental Carbon Thermal Oscillator Reactor

hem haemoglobin (*also* **Hb**); haemorrhage

Her Herefordshire

HERALD Highly Enriched Reactor at Aldermaston, Berkshire

herb herbarium; herbaceous; herbalist

HERMES Heavy Element and Radioactive Material Electromagnetic Separator

HERO Hot Experimental Reactor O-power

Herts Hertfordshire

HET heavy equipment transporter

het heterosexual

hex hexagon; hexagonal

HF high frequency; hard firm pencil

hf half; **hf cf** = half calf binding (books)

hgr hangar

HG Home Guard

HGH human growth hormone
hgt height
HGV heavy goods vehicle
HH His Holiness; His/Her Honour; heavy hydrogen
hh hands (height measurement of horses)
hhd hogshead
Hib Hibernian
hi-fi high fidelity
HIM His/Her Imperial Majesty
Hind Hindi; Hindu; Hindustani
hist historic; historical; historian
histol histology; histologist
HIV human immunodeficiency virus
HIV-P human immunodeficiency virus – positive
HJ *hic jacet* = here lies; *hic jacet sepultus* = here lies buried
HK Hong Kong; House of Keys (Manx Parliament)
HKJ Hashemite Kingdom of Jordan
HL House of Lords
hl hectolitre
HLA system human leucocyte antigen system
HM Her/His Majesty; harbour master
hm headmaster; headmistress; hectometre
HMAS Her/His Majesty's Australian Ship
HMC Headmasters' Conference (*also* **HC**)
HMCS Her/His Majesty's Canadian Ship
HMG Her/His Majesty's Government
HMHS Her/His Majesty's Hospital Ship
HMIS Her/His Majesty's Inspector of Schools
HMIT Her/His Majesty's Inspector of Taxes
HMP Her/His Majesty's Prison
HMS Her/His Majesty's Ship; Her/His Majesty's Service
HMSO Her/His Majesty's Stationery Office
HMV His Master's Voice
HNC Higher National Certificate
HND Higher National Diploma
HO Home Office; head office
ho house
HOC, hoc held in charge
HoC House of Commons (*also* **HC, HofC, HOC**)
HoD head of department
HoL House of Lords (*also* **HofL**)
hol holiday; holidays
Holl Holland
HOLLAND hope our love lasts and never dies
homeo homoeopathic

homo homosexual

Hon Honorary (i.e. **Hon Sec** = honorary secretary); Honourable (i.e. the Hon Matilda Smythe)

hons honours

hon sec honorary secretary

HOPEFUL hard-up old person expecting full useful life

hor horizon; horizontal

horol horology; horologist

hort horticulture; horticulturalist

hosp hospital

HP Houses of Parliament; hot pressed (paper manufacture)

hp horsepower; hire purchase; high pressure

HP sauce Houses of Parliament sauce

HPTA Hire Purchase Trade Association

HQ, hq headquarters

HR House of Representatives (USA)

hr hour

HRE Holy Roman Empire

HRH Her/His Royal Highness

Hrn *Herren* = gentlemen (plural of *Herr*)

HRT hormone replacement therapy

HS Home Secretary; high school (*also* **HSch**)

HSE Health and Safety Executive

hse house

HSH His/Her Serene Highness

HST high speed train

HSV herpes simplex virus

ht height; heat; high tension; half time

h/t halftone (printing)

HTML hypertext markup language (World Wide Web)

htd heated

http hypertext transfer protocol

ht wkt hit wicket (cricket)

Hun, Hung Hungary

HURT Help Untwist Rape Trauma

HVA Health Visitors' Association

hvy heavy

h/w hot water; husband and wife

HWLB high water, London Bridge

HWS, hws hot-water system

hwy highway

hyb hybrid (botany)

hyd hydraulic; hydrate

hypo sodium thiosulphate, formerly sodium hyposulphate (photography)

Hz hertz (unit of frequency)

I

I *Iesus* = Jesus; roman numeral for one; instananeous current (physics); *Imperator* = Emperor; *Imperatrix* = Empress; Imperial; Peruvian inti (currency); Independence; Independent; India; Institute; International; Ireland; Irish; Island; Isle; Italian

i incisor (dentistry); intransitive; interest (banking)

IA Indian Army; infected area; initial allowance (tax); Institute of Actuaries; intra-arterial

ia immediately available; *in absentia* = while absent; indicated altitude

I/A Isle of Anglesey

IAA International Advertising Association

IAAA Irish Amateur Athletic Association; Irish Association of Advertising Agencies

IAAF International Amateur Athletic Federation

IAAS Incorporated Association of Architects and Surveyors

IAB Industrial Arbitration Board; Industrial Advisory Board

IACA Independent Air Carriers' Association

IACP International Association of Chiefs of Police; International Association of Computer Programmers

IAE Institute of Automotive Engineers; Institute of Atomic Energy (USA)

IAEA International Atomic Energy Agency

IAF Indian Air Force; International Astronautical Federation

IAM Institute of Administrative Management

IAS indicated air speed; Indian Administrative Service; instrument approach system (aeronautics); infrared absorbed spectroscopy

IASA International Air Safety Association

IAT, **iat** International Atomic Time; inside air temperature

IATA International Air Transport Association

IBA Independent Broadcasting Authority; Independent Bankers' Association; International Bar Association

IBID international bibliographical description

ibid *ibidem* = in the same place

Ibid, Idem, Inf and Other Footnotes

Here are the meanings of some of those italicised footnote abbreviations we suspect are put there simply to puzzle us:

abr = abridged; **app** = appendix; **ca** or **circa** = about; **cf** = compare; **esp** = especially; **et seq** = and the following; **f** = and the following page; **ff** = and the following pages; **ibid** = in the same place; **id** or **idem** = by the same (author); **inf** = below; **loc cit** = in the place cited; **ms** = manuscript; **mss** = manuscripts; **NB** = take note of; **nd** = no date; **op cit** = in the work cited; **passim** = throughout; **pl** = plate; **pp** = pages; **pub** = published; **qv** = which see; **ser** = series; **sup** = above; **suppl** = supplement; **trans** = translated or translation; **vide** = see; **viz** = namely

IBM International Business Machines; intercontinental ballistic missile
IBS irritable bowel syndrome
IC *Iesus Christus* = Jesus Christ; Imperial College of Science and Technology, London (*also* **ICS**); industrial court; information centre
ic internal combustion; integrated circuit; identity card
i/c in charge; **2i/c** = second in charge/command

i/c in charge

ICA Institute of Contemporary Arts, London; Institute of Chartered Accountants; ignition control additive; internal carotid artery
ICAA Invalid Children's Aid Association
ICAI Institute of Chartered Accountants in Ireland
ICAN International Commission for Air Navigation
ICAO International Civil Aviation Organisation
ICBM intercontinental ballistic missile
ICC Imperial Cricket Conference; International Chamber of Commerce; International Correspondence Colleges
ICCF International Corresponding Chess Federation
ICE Institute of Chartered Engineers; Institution of Civil Engineers; International Cultural Exchange
ICEF International Council for Educational Films

ICFTU International Confederation of Free Trade Unions
IChemE Institute of Chemical Engineers
ICI Imperial Chemical Industries
ICIANZ Imperial Chemical Industries, Australia and New Zealand
ICJ International Court of Justice
ICN International Council of Nurses
ICOM International Council of Museums
ICPO International Criminal Police Organisation (*also* **Interpol**)
ICS Imperial College of Science and Technology, London; Indian Civil Service;
    International Correspondence School
ICSU International Council of Scientific Unions
ICU intensive care unit
ID identification (card); Institute of Directors
IDA International Development Association; Industrial Diamond Association
IDB illicit diamond buyer
IDD iodine deficiency disorder
IDL international date line
IDP integrated data processing
IE Indo-European (languages)
i.e. *id est* = that is
IEA Institute of Economic Affairs; Institution of Engineers, Australia
IEE Institution of Electrical Engineers
IF intermediate frequency
IFA independent financial adviser
IFJ International Federation of Journalists
IFLA International Federation of Library Associations
IFR instrument flying regulations
IFTA International Federation of Travel Agencies; International Federation of
    Teachers' Associations
IG inspector general
IGF International Gymnastic Federation
IGM International Grandmaster (chess)
IGWF International Garment Workers' Federation
IGY International Geophysical Year (1957–58)
IHF International Hockey Federation
IHRB International Hockey Rules Board
II Roman numeral for two (2)
III Roman numeral for three (3); Investment in Industry organisation
IKEA initials of Ingrar Kamprad, founder of the retail furniture chain, and his
    home, 'Elmtaryd', in Agunnaryd, Sweden
ILC International Law Commission
ILEA Inner London Education Authority
ILGA Institute of Local Government Administration
ILGWU International Ladies' Garment Workers' Union
ill illustration; illustrated

ILO International Labour Organisation
ILR independent local radio
ILS instrument landing system
IM International Master (chess)
IMarE Institute of Marine Engineers
IMCO Intergovernmental Maritime Consultative Organisation
IMechE Institution of Mechanical Engineers
IMinE Institution of Mining Engineers
IMF International Monetary Fund; International Motorcycle Federation
imp impression (printing); imperial; imported
IMPACT implementation planning and control technique
imperf imperforate (philately)
in inch; in^2 = square inch; in^3 = cubic inch
IN Indian Navy
Inc, inc incorporated; income
INCB International Narcotics Control Board
incl include; included; including; inclusive; incline
IND *in nomine Dei* = in the name of God
Ind India; Indian
ind independent; index; indirect; industry; industrial
indef indefinite
indic indicator; indicative
indie independent recording or film production company
inf information (*also* **info**); infantry; inferior
infl influence; influenced
infra dig *infra dignitatem* = undignified; beneath one's dignity
init initial
INLA Irish National Liberation Army
INRI *Iesus Nazarenus Rex Iudaeorum* = Jesus of Nazareth, King of the Jews
INSET in-service education and training
Inst institute
inst instant; instrument
INTELSAT International Telecommunications Satellite Organisation
Interpol International Criminal Police Organisation (*also* **ICPO**)
intl internal; international
inv *invenit* = designed by; *inv et del* = designed and drawn by (on antique prints and engravings)
INTUC Indian National Trade Union Congress
IO intelligence officer
IOC International Olympic Committee
IOF Independent Order of Foresters (friendly society)
IOM, IoM Isle of Man
IOJ International Organisation of Journalists
IOOF Independent Order of Oddfellows (friendly society)
IOU I owe you

IOW, IoW Isle of Wight

IP Internet protocol

IPA International Phonetic Alphabet; Institute of Practitioners in Advertising; International Publishers' Association; India pale ale

IPAA International Prisoners' Aid Association

IPARS International Programmed Airline Reservation System

IPC International Publishing Corporation

IPR Institute of Public Relations

ips inches per second

IPTPA International Professional Tennis Players' Association

IPU Inter-Parliamentary Union

IQ intelligence quotient

iq *idem quod* = the same as

IR Inland Revenue; infrared

Ir, Ire Ireland

IRA Irish Republican Army

iran inspect and repair as necessary

IRBM intermediate-range ballistic missile

IRC International Red Cross

IRF International Rowing Federation

IRO International Refugee/Relief Organisation; Inland Revenue Office; industrial relations officer

irreg irregular

IRS Internal Revenue Service (USA)

ISA individual savings account; **ISAS** = individual savings accounts

ISAM Infants of Substance Abuse Mothers

ISBN International Standard Book Number

ISC Imperial Staff College; International Supreme Council (Freemasons)

ISD international subscriber dialling

ISDN Integrated Services Digital Network

ISF International Shipping Federation

ISIS Independent Schools Information Service

ISO International Standards Organisation; Imperial Service Order

ISP Internet Service Provider

ISPA International Society for the Protection of Animals

ISS Institute for Strategic Studies

ISSN International Standard Serial Number

ISU International Skating Union

IT information technology

It, Ital Italy; Italian

ITA Initial Teaching Alphabet; Independent Television Authority (now the **IBA**); Institute of Travel Agents

ital italic; italics

ITALY I trust and love you

IT&T International Telephone and Telegraph Corporation

ITC Imperial Tobacco Company; Independent Television Commission

ITCA Independent Television Contractors' Association

ITE Institute of Terrestrial Ecology

ITGWF International Textile and Garment Workers' Federation

ITMA 'It's that man again!'– title of 1940s radio show by comedian Tommy Handley

ITN Independent Television News

ITO International Trade Organisation

ITTF International Table Tennis Federation

ITU International Telecommunications Union; International Temperance Union; intensive therapy unit

ITV Independent Television

ITWF International Transport Workers' Federation

IU, **iu** international unit

IUD intrauterine device (*also* **IUCD** = intrauterine contraceptive device)

IUS International Union of Students

IV Roman numeral for four (4)

IVA interim voluntary arrangement (bankruptcy proceedings)

IVB invalidity benefit

IVBF International Volley-Ball Federation

IVF in vitro fertilisation

IVR International Vehicle Registration

IWTA Inland Water Transport Association

IWW Industrial Workers of the World

IYHF International Youth Hostels Federation

IYRU International Yacht Racing Union

J

J jack (cards); joule (unit of electrical energy); Jacobean; January; Jesus; Jew; Jewish; Journal; Judaic; July; June; Jurassic; Judge (**JJ** = Judges); Justice

JA Judge Advocate; joint account (*also* **J/A**); Justice Appeal

Ja January (*also* **Jan**)

JAA Jewish Athletic Association

JAC Junior Association of Commerce (USA)

JAG Judge Advocate General

Jag Jaguar (car make)

JAL Japan Air Lines; jet approach and landing chart (aeronautics)

Jam Jamaica

Jan January

J&B Justerini and Brooks (brand of Scotch whisky)

J&K Jammu and Kashmir

JANET joint academic network (computers)

JAP J. A. Prestwich & Co, auto and motorcycle engine maker; Jewish American princess

Jap Japan; Japanese

jap japanned

jar jargon

JATCRU joint traffic control radar unit

JATO jet-assisted take-off

jav javelin (athletics)

JAYCEE Junior Chamber of Commerce (*also* **JC**)

JB *Juris Baccalaureus* = Bachelor of Laws

jb, JB junction box (electric circuits)

JBC Japan Broadcasting Corporation

JBES Jodrell Bank Experimental Station

JBS John Birch Society (USA)

JC Jesus Christ; Jewish Chronicle; Jockey Club; Julius Caesar; Junior Chamber of Commerce (and member of same); junior college (USA); juvenile court

J-C *Jesus-Christ* = Jesus Christ (in French)

JCB initials of Joseph Cyril Bamford, inventor of the internationally used earth-moving machines; Bachelor of Canon Law

JCC Jesus College, Cambridge; Junior Chamber of Commerce

JCI Junior Chamber International

JCNAAF Joint Canadian Navy-Army-Air Force

JCL job control language (computers)

JCR junior common room

JCS Joint Chiefs of Staff; Joint Commonwealth Societies

jct junction

JD Justice Department (USA); Diploma in Journalism; juvenile delinquent

jd joined

JEC Joint Economic Committee (US Congress)

Jer Jersey; Jerusalem

JET Joint European Torus (nuclear fusion research machine)

JEEP straying acronym meant to express general all-purpose vehicle (**GP**). Thus Willy's GP became the famous Willy's Jeep

Jes Coll Jesus College, Oxford

JETRO Japan External Trade Organisation

JFK John Fitzgerald Kennedy, former US president; New York airport

JHS junior high school

JICNARS Joint Industry Committee for National Readership Surveys

jnr junior (*also* **jr**)

joc jocular

JOGLE John o'Groats to Land's End

journo journalist

JP Justice of the Peace

JUD Doctor of Canon and Civil Law

jur juror

JRC Junior Red Cross
jt joint
Jul July
Jun June
jurisp jurisprudence
juv juvenile
JW Jehovah's Witness (religious organisation)
JWB Jewish Welfare Board
jwlr jeweller
JWT J. Walter Thompson advertising agency
JWU Jewish War Veterans

K

K kelvin (unit of thermodynamic temperature); Cretaceous (geology); Russian kopek; Papua New Guinea kina, Laotian kip, Zambian kwacha, Burmese kyat (currency units); king (chess, cards); Kirkpatrick (catalogue of Scarlatti's works); Köchel (catalogue of Mozart's works – *see* **KV**); strikeout (baseball); one thousand
k karat (*also* **kt**); killed; kilo; king (*also* **K**)
k&b kitchen and bathroom
KANU Kenya African National Union
Kar Karachi
Kash Kashmir
kayo knockout (boxing); *also* **KO**
KB King's Bench; Knight Bachelor; king's bishop (chess); *Koninkrijk Belgie* = Kingdom of Belgium; kilobyte (computers)
kb kilobar (physics)
KBC King's Bench Court
kbd keyboard
KBD King's Bench Division
KBE Knight Commander of the Order of the British Empire
KBES knowledge-based expert system (computers); *also* **KBS**
Kbhvn *København* = Copenhagen
KBP king's bishop's pawn (chess)
KBW King's Bench Walk, London
kbyte kilobyte
KC King's Counsel; King's College; King's Cross, London; Knight Commander; Knights of Columbus; Kennel Club
kc kilocycle
KCB Knight Commander of the Most Honourable Order of the Bath
KCC King's College, Cambridge
K cell killer cell (immunology)
KCH King's College Hospital, London

KCL King's College, London

KCMG Knight Commander of the Order of St Michael and St George

Kcs Czech koruna (currency unit)

kcs kilocycles per second

KD knocked down (at auction; also unassembled furniture, equipment, etc); kiln dried; *Kongeriget Danmark* = Kingdom of Denmark; Kuwaiti dina (currency unit)

kd killed

KDG King's Dragoon Guards

KE kinetic energy

Ken Kensington, London; **S Ken** = South Kensington; Kenya

KEY keep extending yourself

kg kilogram (*also* **kilo**)

KG Knight of the Most Noble Order of the Garter

KGB *Komitet Gosudarstvennoye Bezopasnosti* = Russian State Security Committee police

KGCB Knight of the Grand Cross of the Bath

KhZ, khz kilohertz

kilo kilogram (*also* **kg**)

KISS keep it simple, stupid!

KKK Ku Klux Klan, US anti-black organisation

KL Kuala Lumpur, Malaysia

kl kilolitre

KLM *Koninklijke Luchtvaart Maatschappij* = Royal Dutch Air Lines

km kilometre; **km/h** = kilometres per hour

kn krona, krone; knot

Knt Knight

KO knockout (*also* **kayo**)

KofC Knight of Columbus (*also* **KC**)

kop kopek

kpr keeper (cricket); **wkt kpr** = wicket keeper

Kr krona; krone (*also* **Kn**)

K ration Army emergency rations, World War II, the initial of its creator, American physiologist Ancel Keys

KRL knowledge representation language (artificial intelligence)

KStJ Knight of the Order of St John

Kt Knight; karat

KV *Köchel Verseichnis* = catalogue of Mozart's music by Ludwig von Köchel, 1862 (*also* **K**). Thus K.492 is Mozart's opera *Le nozze di Figaro* (*The Marriage of Figaro*)

kV kilovolt

kW kilowatt; **KWH** or **kWH** = kilowatt-hour

KWIC key word in context

KWOC key word out of context

KYD keep your distance

L

L Roman numeral for fifty (50); learner driver / rider; Liberal; lire; lira; lek; large; low; pound sterling (*libra* = **L** = **£**)

l latitude; length; light; late; large; litre; left; low; lease / leasehold

LA Legislative Assembly

Lab Labour Party; Labour Party member / supporter; Labrador

lab laboratory; label; labourer

LAC leading aircraftman

LACW leading aircraftwoman

LADDER National Learning and Attention Deficit Disorders Association

lag lagoon

LAIA Latin American Integration Association

LAM London Academy of Music

lam laminate

LAMDA London Academy of Music and Dramatic Art

LAN local area network

Lancs Lancashire

LASER Light Amplification by Stimulated Emission of Radiation

Lat Latin (*also* **L**); Latvia

lat latitude

LATCC London Air Traffic Control Centre

lav lavatory

lb pound weight (16 ounces avoirdupois)

LB Bachelor of Letters

LBC London Broadcasting Company

LBCH London Bankers' Clearing House

lbd little black dress

LBJ Lyndon Baines Johnson, former US president

LBO leveraged buyout

LBS London Graduate School of Business Studies

LBV late bottled vintage (port wine)

lbw leg before wicket (cricket)

LC Library of Congress

L/C letter of credit

lc lower case (typography); left centre (theatre); little change (weather)

LCC Former London County Council

LCCI London Chamber of Commerce and Industry

LCD, lcd liquid crystal display; lowest common denominator

LCJ Lord Chief Justice

LCM London College of Music

lcm lowest common multiple

L/Cpl Lance Corporal

LD Doctor of Letters; lethal dose

Ldg Leading seaman

ldg landing; leading; lodging

ldmk landmark

Ldn London (*also* **Lon**)

L-dopa LevoDihydraOxyPhenylAlanine (used to treat Parkinson's disease)

LDP Liberal-Democratic Party (*also* **Lib-Dem**)

ldr leader; ledger

L-driver learner driver

LDS (Church of) Latter-day Saints

LE labour exchange

LEA Local Education Authority

LEB London Electricity Board

LED light-emitting diode

leg legal; legation; legion; legislature; legitimate

Lego *leg-godt* = play well (Danish)

Leics Leicestershire

LEM lunar excursion module

LEPRA Leprosy Relief Association

LETS local exchange trading system

LF low frequency

LFB London Fire Brigade

LGB Local Government Board

lge large (*also* **lg**); league

lgth length

LGU Ladies' Golf Union

LH, **lh** left hand; **lhs** = left-hand side; **LHD**, **lhd** = left-hand drive

LI Lincoln's Inn, London; Long Island (USA)

Lib Liberal; Liberal Party; Liberal Party member/supporter

lib library; librarian; libretto

Lib Cong Library of Congress, Washington (*also* **LC**)

Lib-Lab Parliamentary alliance during 1920s

lic licence; licensed; licentiate

Lieut Lieutenant

LIFFE London International Financial Futures Exchange

LIFO last in, first out

LIHG *Ligue Internationale de Hockey sur Glace* = International Ice Hockey Federation

LILO last in, last out

lim limit; limited

limo limousine

lin line; lineal; linear

Lincs Lincolnshire

lino linoleum

Lintas Lever's international advertising service

liq liquid; liquor

LISP list processing (computer language)

lit literally; literary; literature

litho lithography

LittB Bachelor of Letters/Literature

LittD Doctor of Letters/Literature

LJ Lord Justice

LL London Library; Lord Lieutenant

Llanfair-PG Llanfairpwllgwyngyllgogerychwyrndrobwllllantysiliogogogoch, a village in Anglesey, Wales

LLB *Legum Baccalaureus* = Bachelor of Laws

LLD *Legum Doctor* = Doctor of Laws

LLM *Legum Magister* = Master of Laws

lm lumen (unit of light)

LMD local medical doctor

LME London Metal Exchange

LMH Lady Margaret Hall, Oxford

LMR former London Midland Region of British Rail

LMS former London, Midland and Scottish Railway; local management of schools

LMus Licentiate of Music

LNB low noise block down converter (the gubbins mounted at the centre of a satellite dish)

LNER former London and North Eastern Railway

LNG liquefied natural gas

Lnrk Lanarkshire

LNWR former London and North Western Railway (*also* **L&NWR**)

LOA leave of absence; Local Overseas Allowance (Civil Service)

loc local; location; letter of credit

loco locomotive

Lond London

LOST Law of the Sea Treaty

LOX, lox liquid oxygen

LP long-playing (vinyl) record; Labour Party; life policy; Lord Provost; low pressure

L/P letterpress (printing)

LPE London Press Exchange

LPG liquefied petroleum gas

L-plate red-on-white L to indicate vehicle is driven or ridden by a learner-driver/rider

LPN Licensed Practical Nurse

LPO London Philharmonic Orchestra; local post office

L'pool Liverpool

LPS London Philharmonic Society; Lord Privy Seal

LRCA London Retail Credit Association

Lrs Lancers

LRSC Licentiate of the Royal Society of Chemistry

LRT London Regional Transport

LS Law Society; Linnean Society; Licentiate in Surgery; long shot (film making); licensed surveyor

ls signed letter; **als** = autograph signed letter

LSD lysergic acid diethylamide (hallucinogenic drug); League of Safe Drivers; pounds, shillings and pence (£sd)

LSE London School of Economics; London Stock Exchange

LS&GCM Long Service and Good Conduct Medal

LSO London Symphony Orchestra

LSSO London Schools Symphony Orchestra

LST local standard time

Lt Lieutenant

LTA Lawn Tennis Association

LTAA Lawn Tennis Association of Australia

LTB London Transport Board; London Tourist Board

Lt Cdr Lieutenant Commander

Ltd, ltd limited (liability company) in the UK

Lt Gen Lieutenant General

Lt Gov Lieutenant Governor

ltr litre
LU loudness unit
lub lubricate; lubricant; lubrication
lug luggage
LV luncheon voucher; licensed victualler
Lv lev; leva
lv low voltage; leave of absence
LVA Licensed Victuallers' Association
LW long wave (frequency); low water
LWB, lwb long wheel base
LWL length at waterline (shipping)
LWM low water mark
LWONT low water, ordinary neap tide
LWOST low water, ordinary spring tide
LWT London Weekend Television

M

M *Monsieur*; Monday; Mach number; medium; million; mark; male; mile; medieval; Roman numeral for one thousand (1,000); Messier catalogue of nebulae and star clusters (1784); the Secret Service chief in Ian Fleming's *James Bond* novels

m masculine; metre; member; meridian; mile; month; minute; mountain; maiden over (cricket scoring); *mille* (1,000); memorandum; middle

MA Master of Arts; Military Academy; mental age

MA&F former Ministry of Agriculture and Fishing (*see* **MAFF**)

ma'am madam; madame

MAC multiplexed analogue component

Mac MacIntosh computer

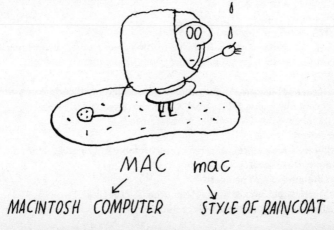

MAC mac
MACINTOSH COMPUTER   STYLE OF RAINCOAT

mac macintosh or mackintosh (style of raincoat)

Mach Mach number (ratio between speed and speed of sound; **Mach 1** is the speed of sound)

mach machinery

MAD mutual assured destruction; mean absolute deviation

MADD Mothers Against Drunk Driving (USA)

MAFF Ministry of Agriculture, Fisheries and Food

mag magazine; magnetic; magnitude

Magd Magdalen College, Oxford

maitre d' maitre d'hotel

Maj Gen Major General

MAN *Maschinen Augsburg-Nurnberg AG* (German firm)

m&b mild and bitter (ale)

M&B693 May and Baker 693, sulphapyridine, a pioneer sulpha drug

Man Dir managing director (*also* **man dir**, **MD**)

M&Ms button-size chocolate-coated sweets

M&S Marks & Spencer, department store chain

Man Ed managing editor (*also* **man ed**)

MANWEB former Merseyside and North Wales Electricity Board

Mar March

mar married; marine; maritime

marg margarine (*also* **marge**)

Marq Marquis

mart market

MARV manoeuvrable re-entry vehicle

masc masculine (*also* **mas**)

MASH Mobile Army Surgical Hospital (USA); also the TV series

mat matrix; matte; matinee; maternity; mature

maths mathematics (**math** in the USA)

Matric Matriculation (higher education entry examination)

MAW model, actress, whatever

max maximum

MAYDAY *m'aidez* = help me (distress call)

MB *Medicinae Baccalaureus* = Bachelor of Medicine; medical board; marketing board; maternity benefit; methyl bromide (fire retardant)

mb millibar

MBA Master of Business Administration (also 'Mind my Bloody Arse', aimed at over-cautious young MBAs unable to make decisions)

MBE Member of the Order of the British Empire

mbr member

MC Military Cross; master of ceremonies; Member of Congress (USA)

mc motorcycle (*also* **m/c**); megacycle

MCB miniature circuit breaker

MCC Marylebone Cricket Club; Melbourne Cricket Club

MCh *Magister Chirurgiae* = Master of Surgery

MCP male chauvinist pig

MCPS Mechanical Copyright Protection Society; Member of the College of Physicians and Surgeons

MCU medium close-up (cinemaphotography)

MD *Medicinae Doctor* = Doctor of Medicine; managing director; musical director; mentally deficient

MDA Muscular Dystrophy Association

Mddx Middlesex

MDF medium-density fibreboard

MDR, mdr minimum daily requirement

MDS Master of Dental Surgery

mdse merchandise

ME marine/mechanical/mining engineer; Middle East; myalgic encephalomyelitis

mech mechanical

MEd Master of Education

Med Mediterranean

med medical; medicine; medium; median; medieval

MEF Mediterranean Expeditionary Force

MEK methyl-ethyl-ketone (industrial solvent)

Melb Melbourne

mem member; memorial; memorandum

Mencap Royal Society for Mentally Handicapped Children and Adults

MEP Member of the European Parliament

Mer Merionethshire

mer meridian

Merc Mercedes (car)

MERLIN Medium Energy Reactor, Light water Industrial Neutron source

Messrs *Messieurs* = gentlemen

Met Metropolitan Opera House, New York; meteorological office

met metropolitan; meteorological

metall metallurgy; metallurgical

Meth Methodist

meths methylated spirit (*also* **meth, metho**)

Metro *Chemin de fer metropolitain* (Paris underground)

MeV one million electron volts

Mex Mexico; Mexican; **Tex-Mex** = Texan-Mexican food

MEZ *Mitteleuropaische Zeit* = Central European Time

MF medium frequency

MFB Metropolitan Fire Brigade

MFD minimum fatal dose

mfd manufactured

mfg manufacturing

mfr manufacturer; manufacture

Mg magnesium

MG Morris Garage (sports cars)

mg milligram; morning

MGB *Ministerstvo Gosudarstvennoye Bezopasnosti* = former Soviet Ministry of State Security (renamed **KGB** in 1954)

MGM Metro-Goldwyn-Mayer (Hollywood film studio)

MGN Mirror Group Newspapers

mgr manager

mgt management

MHA Member of the House of Assembly (Australia, Canada); Methodist Homes for the Aged

MHF medium high frequency

MHR Member of the House of Representatives (Australia, USA)

MHW mean high water

MHWNT mean high water, neap tide

MHWST mean high water, spring tide

MHz megahertz

MIA missing in action

MIAA Member Architect of the Incorporated Association of Architects and Surveyors

MIBE Member of the Institution of British Engineers

Mich Michaelmas; Michigan

MICR magnetic ink character recognition

MIDAS missile defence alarm system

Middx Middlesex (*also* **Mddx**)

MIF milk in first (before pouring tea, considered non-U)

MI5 Section 5, Military Intelligence (British Government counter-intelligence agency)

MiG, MIG Initials of Mikoyan and Gurevich, designers of Russian fighter aircraft of which the MiG-15 fighter, the supersonic MiG-19 and the MiG-21 fighter are the most notable

MIG metal inert gas welding technique

mike microphone

Mil Military

mill *millionen* = German million

MIMechE Member of the Institution of Mechanical Engineers

MIMinE Member of the Institute of Mining Engineers

MIMS Monthly Index of Medical Specialties

MIMT Member of the Institute of the Motor Trade

MIMunE Member of the Institution of Municipal Engineers

Min Minister; Ministry

min minimum; mineralogy; minute; minor

MInstT Member of the Institute of Technology

MIP maximum investment plan; monthly investment plan

MIPS million instructions per second (computers)

Miras mortgage interest relief at source

MIRTE Member of the Institute of Road Transport Engineers

MIRV multiple independently targeted re-entry vehicle

misc miscellaneous

MI6 Military Intelligence, Section 6 (British Government intelligence and espionage agency)

MIT Massachusetts Institute of Technology

MITI Ministry of International Trade and Industry (Japan)

MJQ Modern Jazz Quartet

Mk, **mk** mark (currency); marque or mark (type of car)

mkt market; **mktg** = marketing

ml millilitre; mile

MLA Member of the Legislative Assembly (especially Northern Ireland); Modern Language Association of America

MLC Member of the Legislative Council (Australia, India)

MLD minimum lethal dose

Mlle *Mademoiselle* = Miss (in France)

MLR minimum lending rate

MLS, **mls** medium long shot (cinematography)

MLWNT mean low water, neap tide

MLWST mean low water, spring tide

MM *Messieurs* = French equivalent of **Messrs** = plural of **Mr**; Military Medal; Mercantile Marine

mm millimetre; mm^2 = square millimetre; mm^3 = cubic millimetre

MMDS multipoint microwave distribution system (*also* **MDS**)

Mme, **Mmes** *Madame* = Mrs; *Mesdames* = Ladies (in France)

MMQ minimum manufacturing quantity

MMR measles/mumps/rubella (combination children's vaccine)

MMus Master of Music

MN Merchant Navy

mng managing; **Mng Dir** = managing director

mngr manager (*also* **mgr**); **mngmt** = management

M-number number of nebulae and star clusters in Messier catalogue

MO Medical Officer; Meteorological Office; mail order; money order

Mo Monday

mo month; also used to indicate the size of a book's page, as in **12mo**, **24mo**, **32mo** and **64mo**, where a sheet is folded and cut to form 12, 24, 32 and 64 pages respectively; moment (as in *half a mo'*)

MOC Mother of the Chapel (NUJ term)

MOD, **MoD** Ministry of Defence

mod moderate; modern

mod cons modern coveniences

Model-T Ford's first mass-produced car (15 million produced between 1908 and 1927)

modem modulator/demodulator; device for connecting a computer to a telephone

MOH Medical Officer of Health

Moho Mohorovicic discontinuity (the boundary between the earth's crust and mantle, after Croatian discoverer Andrija Mohorovicic)

MOMA Museum of Modern Art, New York

Mon Monmouthshire; Monday

M1, M2, B2065 designation of British roads; **M** = motorway; **A** = Class 1 road; **B** = Class 2 road

Mons, M *Monsieur* = Mr (in France)

Moped motorised pedal cycle

MOPS mail order protection scheme

MOR middle of the road (radio music)

Mor Morocco

mor morocco (bookbinding)

MORI Market and Opinion Research International (public poll)

MOS metal oxide semiconductor; Mail on Sunday

mos months

MOT motor vehicle test certificate (Ministry of Transport)

MOUSE Miniature Orbital Unmanned Satellite, Earth

MP Member of Parliament; Military Police; Mercator's projection (cartography); Mounted Police

mp melting point

MPA Music Publishers' Association

mpc maximum permissible concentration

MPG main professional grade (teachers' salary scale)

mpg miles per gallon

mph miles per hour

MPLA-PT *Movimento de Libertacao de Angola – Partido de Trabalho* = Popular Movement for the Liberation of Angola Workers' Party

MPO military post office

MPS Member of the Pharmaceutical/Philological/Physical Society

MPTA Municipal Passenger Transport Association

MR map reference; Master of the Rolls; motivational research

Mr Mister; Master

MRA Moral Rearmament

MRBM medium range ballistic missile

MRC Medical Research Council

MRE meals ready to eat

MRH Member of the Royal Household

MRI magnetic resonance imaging

MRIA Member of the Royal Irish Academy

MRP manufacturer's recommended price

Mrs Mistress (17th century) prefix for a married woman

MRSC Member of the Royal Society of Chemistry

MRT mass rapid transport

MS multiple sclerosis; medium shot (cinematography); Microsoft (computer software company); Master of Surgery; *memoriae sacrum* = sacred to the memory of (on gravestones)

Ms optional prefix for a woman, whether married or not

ms manuscript (plural **mss**)

m/s metres per second

MSc Master of Science

MS(Dent) Master of Surgery (Dental Surgery)

MS-DOS MicroSoft Disk Operating System (computers)

MSF Manufacturing, Science, Finance (trade union)

MSG monosodium glutamate (food flavour enhancer)

Msgr Monsignor

MSI medium scale integration

MSL mean sea level

MSP Member of the Scottish Parliament

MST Mountain Standard Time (North America)

mt mount; mountain

MTB motor torpedo boat

MTBE methyl-tertiary-butyl ether (anti-knock lead-free petrol additive)

MTech Master of Technology

mtg mortgage; meeting

MTV Music Television (24-hour music channel)

MU Musicians' Union; Manchester United Football Club; former Mothers Union

mum mother; chrysanthemum

mun municipal

mus museum; music; musical

MusB Bachelor of Music

MusD Doctor of Music

MV market value; motor vessel; muzzle velocity

MVD *Ministerstvo Vnutrenhikh Del* = former Soviet Ministry of Internal Affairs, succeeded by the **KVD** (Soviet Committee for Internal Affairs)

MVO Member of the Royal Victorian Order; male voice-over (TV and films)

MVS Master of Veterinary Surgery

MVSc Master of Veterinary Science

MW Master of Wine; megawatt; medium wave

mW milliwatt

MY motor yacht

MYOB mind your own business

mycol mycology; mycological

myth mythology; mythological

myxo myxomatosis (Australia)

N

N North; Northern; Norway; Norwegian

n name; near; negative; nephew; new; noon; north; northern; noun; number; neutral; neuter; normal

NA North America

n/a not applicable; not available

NAACP National Association for the Advancement of Colored People

Naafa North American Association for Fatness Acceptance

NAAFI Navy, Army and Air Force Institutes (*also* **Naafi, Naffy**)

NAB National Assistance Board; National Association of Broadcasters

NAC National Advisory/Anglers'/Archives Council

NACF National Art Collections Fund

NACRO National Association for the Care and Resettlement of Offenders

nad no appreciable difference; nothing abnormal detected

NAfr North Africa

NAFTA New Zealand and Australia Free Trade Agreement

NAGS National Allotments and Gardens Society

NAHA National Association of Health Authorities

NAI nonaccidental injury

NAI register national register of children considered to be at risk of abuse and injury from parents or guardians

NALGO National and Local Government Officers' Association

NAMH National Association for Mental Health

NAO National Audit Office

NAPF National Association of Pension Funds

NAPO National Association of Property Owners

nar narrow

NAS Noise Abatement Society

NASA National Aeronautics and Space Administration (USA)

NASEN National Association for Special Educational Needs

NAS/UWT National Association of Schoolmasters/Union of Women Teachers

nat native; natural; national; nationalist

NATCS National Air Traffic Control Service

NATE National Association for the Teaching of English

NATFHE National Association of Teachers in Further and Higher Education

NATO North Atlantic Treaty Organisation

NATSOPA Former National Society of Operative Printers and Assistants

NATTKE Former National Association of Theatrical, Television and Kine Employees

NatWest National Westminster Bank

NAV net asset value

nav naval; navigable; navigation (*also* **navig**)

Nazi *Nationalsozialisten* = German National Socialist Party member

NB, nb *nota bene* = note well; no ball (cricket)

NBA Net Book Agreement (former); National Boxing/Basketball Association (USA)

NBC National Broadcasting Company (USA)

NBG, nbg no bloody good

NC National Curriculum

nc, n/c no charge

NCA National Cricket Association

NCB former National Coal Board; no claim bonus

NCC Nature Conservancy Council

NCCL National Council for Civil Liberties

NCCVD National Council for Combating Venereal Diseases

NCO non-commissioned officer

NCP National Country Party (Australia)

NCR National Cash Register Company; no carbon/copy required

NCU National Cyclists' Union

NCVO National Coucil for Voluntary Organisations

nd no date (undated); not drawn; no decision

NDA National Dairymen's Association

NDE near-death experience

Ndl Netherlands (*also* **Neth**)

NDP net domestic product

NDT non-destructive testing

NEA North East Airlines (USA)

NEB National Enterprise Board; New English Bible

NEC Nippon Electrical Company (Japan)

NEDC National Economic Development Council (*also* **Neddy**, both now defunct)

nee *née* = French for born (i.e. Mrs Joan Smith, nee Jones, indicates that Mrs Smith's maiden name was Jones)

ne'er never

neg negative

Neg Negro

nem con *nemine contradicente* = no contradictions; unanimous

NERC Natural Environment Research Council

NESB non-English speaking background (applied to some foreign immigrants in Australia)

NESTOR NEutron Source Thermal reactOR

net after all deductions (*also* **nett**)

Neth Netherlands

neur neurological

neut neutral; neuter

NF National Front

N/f, n/f no funds

NFA National Federation of Anglers

NFL National Football League (USA and Canada)

NFS National Fire Service; not for sale

NFT National Film Theatre, London

NFU National Farmers' Union

NFUW National Farmers' Union of Wales

NFWI National Federation of Womens' Institutes

NFYFC National Federation of Young Farmers' Clubs

NG New Guinea; National Guard (USA)

ng no good; narrow gauge (railway)

NGA National Graphical Association

NGC New General Catalogue (of nebulae, galaxies and star clusters)

NGk New Greek

NGL natural gas liquids

NGO non-governmental organisation

NGS National Geographic Society

NHI National Health Insurance

NHK *Nippon Hoso Kyokai* = Japan Broadcasting Corporation

NHS National Health Service

NI National Insurance; Northern Ireland; News International

NIC newly industrialised country; national insurance contribution

NICAM near-instantaneous companding audio multiplex system (digital recording)

NIHE National Institute for Higher Education

NII nuclear installations inspectorate

Nimby not in my backyard!

NIRC National Industrial Relations Court

N Ire Northern Ireland (*also* **N Ir**)

NIREX Nuclear Industry Radioactive Waste Disposal Executive

NJ nose job; New Jersey

NKr krone (Norwegian currency unit)

NL New Latin; no liability (Australia); Netherlands

NLF National Liberation Front

NLS National Library of Scotland

nlt not less than; not later than (**nmt** = not more than)

NLW National Library of Wales

nm nanometre; nautical mile

NMGC National Marriage Guidance Council

NMHA National Mental Health Association

NMR nuclear magnetic resonance scanner

NMU National Maritime Union

NNP net national product

no. number (**nos** = numbers); north; northern; not out (cricket)

No. 1 No. 1, Apsley House, Piccadilly, London, former home of the Duke of Wellington

No. 10 10 Downing Street, London, the UK Prime Minister's residence

nol pros *nolle prosequi* = abandonment of court action by plaintiff in civil cases (*also* **nolle pros**)

nom nomenclature; nominated; nominal

non res non-resident

non seq *non sequitur* = it does not follow, i.e. a statement or conclusion that does not logically follow from what preceded

non-U not upper class

NOP National Opinion Poll

Nor Norway; Norwegian

Norm Norman

norm normal

Northants Northamptonshire

Northmb Northumberland

NORWEB former North Western Electricity Board

nos numbers

Notts Nottinghamshire

Nov November

NoW News of the World (Sunday newspaper)

NP Notary Public; neuropsychiatry; noun phrase

np new pence (Britain's decimal coinage introduced in 1971); new paragraph (printing); nickel plated

n/p net proceeds (*also* **np**)

NPA National Pigeon Association; Newspaper Publishers' Association

NPD new product development

NPFA National Playing Fields Association

NPK nitrogen, phosphorus and potassium fertiliser

NPL National Physical Laboratory

NPV net present value; no par value

NQU not quite us (social status observation)

nr near

NRA National Rifle Association

NRC Nuclear Research Council

NRCA National Retail Credit Association

NRF National Relief Fund

NRFL Northern Rugby Football League

NRS National Readership Survey

NRV net realisable value

NS Nova Scotia; nuclear ship; not satisfactory

NSA National Skating Association

NSAID non-steroidal anti-inflammatory drug

NSB National Savings Bank

NSC National Safety Council

nsf not sufficient funds (*also* **n/s**, **n/s/f**)

NSFGB National Ski Federation of Great Britain

NSG nonstatutory guidelines (education: National Curriculum)

NSPCC National Society for the Prevention of Cruelty to Children

NSU non-specific urethritis

NSW New South Wales

NT National Theatre, London; National Trust; Northern Territory (Australia); New Testament

Nth North; Northern

NTP normal temperature and pressure (meteorological)

NTS National Trust for Scotland

NTSC National Television System Committee (US body controlling colour television standards)

NTV Nippon Television

nt wt net weight

NUAAW National Union of Agricultural and Allied Workers

NUJ National Union of Journalists

num numerical; numeral; number

numis numismatics

NUM National Union of Mineworkers

NUPE National Union of Public Employees

NUR National Union of Railwaymen

NURA National Union of Ratepayers' Associations

NUS National Union of Students; National Union of Seamen

NUT National Union of Teachers

NVQ National Vocational Qualification

NWAWWASBE Never wash a window with a soft boiled egg (slogan from the 1940s' radio programme *It's That Man Again* (ITMA)

NY New York

NYC New York City

NYD not yet diagnosed

NYO National Youth Orchestra

NYPD New York Police Department

NYSE New York Stock Exchange

NYT National Youth Theatre

NYTO National Youth Jazz Orchestra

NZ New Zealand

NZBC New Zealand Broadcasting Commission

NZMA New Zealand Medical Association

NZRFU New Zealand Rugby Football Union

NZRN New Zealand Registered Nurse

O

O ocean; human blood type, ABO group

o octavo (paper size); old; owner; only; over (cricket)

OA older adult

O&E operations and engineering

O&M Ogilvie & Mather (advertising agency); organisation and method

OAP old age pensioner

OAPEC Organisation of Arab Petroleum Exporting Countries

OAS Organisation of American States; *Organisation de l'armée secrète* (former pro-French political organisation in Algeria)

OAU Organisation of African Unity

OB Old Bailey, London; outside broadcast; old bonded whisky; old boy

OBAFGKMRNS classification of stars by US astronomer Henry Draper according to temperature and luminosity (mnemonic: *Oh Be A Fine Girl, Kiss Me Right Now, Susan*)

OBE Order of the British Empire; one button exposed (shielded warning that a man's fly is open); other bugger's efforts

obit obituary

obj object; objective

obl oblique; oblong

OBM Ordnance Bench Mark

obs obsolete (*also* **obsol**); obscure; observer; obstetrics; obstetrician

OC Officer Commanding

oc ocean (*also* **o**); office copy; over the counter

o/c overcharge; overcharged

o'c of the clock = o'clock

occ occupation; occupational; occasional; occurrence

OCD obsessive compulsive disorder

OCR optical character recognition/reader

OCS Officer Candidate School

Oct October

oct octavo (printing)

OCUC Oxford and Cambridge Universities' Club

OD Officer of the Day; outside diameter; overdose (**OD'd** = overdosed)

O/D overdrawn; overdraft; on demand

ODA Overseas Development Administration of the Foreign and Commonwealth Office

ODETTE Organisation for Data Exchange Through Tele-Transmission in Europe

ODM Ministry of Overseas Development

ODP overall development planning

OE Old English (language)

oe omissions excepted

OECD Organisation for Economic Cooperation and Development

OED Oxford English Dictionary

OEDIPUS Oxford English Dictionary Interpretation, Proofing and Updating System

OEEC Organisation for European Economic Cooperation

OEM original equipment manufacturer (computers)

o'er over

OF Old French (language)

off official (*also* **offic**); office; officer

Ofgen Office of Power Supply (gas and electricity)

oflag *offizierslager* = German POW camp for captured Allied officers

Oflot Office of the National Lottery

OFS Orange Free State (South Africa)

Ofsted Office for Standards in Education

OFT Office of Fair Trading

oft often

Oftel Office of Telecommunications

Ofwat Office of Water Services

OG Officer of the Guard; original gum (philately)

og own goal (football)

OGM ordinary general meeting

oh overhead (*also* **o/h**); on hand

ohc overhead camshaft

OHG Old High German

OIT *Organisation internationale du travail* = International Labour Organisation

ojt on the job training

OK, ok all right; everything in order (*also* **okay, okeh**)

Okie migrant worker in 1930s' California (from Oklahoma)

OLC Oak Leaf Cluster (US military award); online computer

Old Test Old Testament

O-level Ordinary level examinations; now **GCSE**

OM Order of Merit; ordnance map

OMM *Officier de l'Ordre du Mérite Militaire* = French military decoration

OMS *Organisation Mondiale de la Santé* = World Health Organisation

on appro on approval

ONC Ordinary National Certificate

OND Ordinary National Diploma

ono or nearest offer

Ont Ontario, Canada

ont ordinary neap tide

OOD Officer of the Deck

OOG Officer of the Guard

ooo of obscure origin (dictionary term)

o/o/o out of order

007 British Secret Service codename for Ian Fleming's fictional spy James Bond

OOW Officer of the Watch

OP out of print; old people; other person

op operation (**ops** = operations); operator; operational; opposite (*also* **opp**); optical; opaque

Op art optical art (optically influenced designs, launched in 1960s)

op cit *opere citato* = in the work cited

OPC ordinary Portland cement

OPEC Organisation of Petroleum Exporting Countries

OPEX operational, executive and administrative personnel

ophth ophthalmic

opp opposite (*also* **op**); opposed

opr operator

opt optical; optician; optimum; optional

OR official receiver; orderly room; other ranks

or owner's risk; overhaul and repair (*also* **o/r**)

ORBIS orbiting radio beacon ionospheric satellite

ORBIT online retrieval of bibliographical information

orch orchestra

ord ordained; ordinary; ordnance

org organisation; organic; organ

orig original; origination

O-ring rubber oil seal ring used in machinery

orn ornithology (*also* **ornith**); ornamental

Orth, orth Orthodox (religion); orthopaedic; orthography

o/s, OS out of stock; out of service; outsize; ordinary seaman; operating system (computers)

OSA Order of Saint Augustine

OSB Order of Saint Benedict

OSD Order of Saint Dominic

o'seas overseas

OSF Order of Saint Francis

OSS Office of Strategic Services (USA)

OST Office of Science and Technology

OT overtime; occupational therapy; Old Testament (*also* **Old Test**)

OTB off-track betting (USA)

OTC Officer Training Corps

otc over the counter

OTE on-target earnings

OTL overturned lorry

OTT over the top

OU Oxford University; Open University

OUP Oxford University Press

ov over; overture

OWLS Oxford Word and Language Service

OXFAM, Oxfam Oxford Committee for Famine Relief

Oxon *Oxoniensis* = Oxford; Oxford University; Oxfordshire

Oxbridge Oxford-Cambridge; also used to describe the older, classical universities in the UK

Oz Australia

oz ounce (**ozs** = ounces)

P

P Post Office (on maps); park; parking; postage; pawn (chess); pedestrian; Protestant; public; port; positive

p page (**pp** = pages); paragraph; passed (exams); penny; pence; peso; peseta; piastre; pint; post; population; present

PA personal assistant; Patients' Association; personal allowance (tax); public address (system); press attache; prosecuting attorney; Publishers' Association; purchasing agent; press agent

pa per annum

P/A power of attorney; private account

PABX private automatic branch exchange telephone system

PAC Pacific Air Command (USA)

Pac Pacific

PACE Police and Criminal Evidence Act; precision analogue computing equipment; performance and cost evaluation

pad paddock

PAIS partial androgen insensitivity syndrome; **AIS** = androgen insensitivity syndrome

PAL phase alternation line (625-line British TV standard from 1967)

Pal Palestine; palace

pal palaeontology; palace

pamph pamphlet

Pan Panama

pan panchromatic (photographic film)

Pan-Am Pan-American Airways

P&G Procter and Gamble (manufacturers)

p&l, P&L profit and loss

P&O Peninsular and Oriental (steamship company)

p&p packing and postage

P&Q peace and quiet: prison term for solitary confinement

panto pantomime

Pap-NG Papua-New Guinea

Pap test Papanicolaou smear = cervical smear test for precancerous cells named after its inventor George Papanicolaou

PA Press Association

par paragraph; parallel; parish; parochial; parenthesis

para airborne parachute troop (paras = plural)

Parl Parliament; parliamentary

parl proc parliamentary proceedings

part participle; particular

PAs popular mountaineering boots, named after climber Pierre Allain

pass passenger; passenger train

PA system public address system

Pat, pat patent; patented (*also* **patd**); **pat pend** = patent pending

PATA Pacific Area Travel Association

pathol pathology; pathologist

Pat Off Patent Office

PATSY Performing Animal Top Star of the Year (Hollywood movie award)

PAU Pan American Union

PAWC Pan-African Workers' Congress

PAX private automatic telephone exchange

PAYE pay as you earn (income tax payment system)

PB prayer book; personal best

PBI poor bloody infantry

pbk paperback (book)

PBM permanent benchmark (surveying)

PBX private branch telephone exchange

PC Police Constable (*also* **Pc**); Privy Councillor; politically correct; personal computer; Progressive Conservative (Canada); parish council; parish councillor

pc per cent; percentage; piece; postcard

P/C, p/c petty cash; price current

PCB printed circuit board

PCC parochial church council

PCI potential criminal informant

pcl parcel

PCOS polycystic ovary syndrome

PCP phencyclidine, depressant drug (also called angel dust)

PCR polymerase chain reaction (DNA reproduction)

PD Police Department; production department

pd paid; passed; postage due; post dated (*also* **p/d**)

PDA public display of affection; personal digital assistant

pdq pretty damn quick!

PDR price-dividend ratio

PE physical education; probable error

P/E price-earnings ratio; port of embarkation; part-exchange

Pem Pembrokeshire

PEN Club International Association of Poets, Playwrights, Editors, Essayists and Novelists

Pen, pen Peninsula; penitentiary

PEP personal equity plan (tax advantage savings scheme); political and economic planning

PER Professional Employment Register

per *per procurationem* = on behalf of; every or each, e.g. three serves per person; person; period

P/E ratio price-earnings ratio

per cent *per centum* = of every hundred (i.e. six per cent or 6% = six hundredths of the whole)

perf perforated (philately); perfect; performance

perfin perforated with initials (philately)

PERK physical evidence recovery kit (forensics)

perk perquisite

perm permanent wave (hairstyle); permutation (pools)

perp perpendicular

pers person; personal

PERT programme evaluation and review technique

pet petroleum; petrology

Peta People for the Ethical Treatment of Animals

PET scan positron emission tomography

Pf, pf pfennig (*also* **pfg**); perfect; preferred

Pfc Private First-Class (US Army)

PFI Public Finance Initiative

PFP Passports For Pets. Changed from **FIDO** following complaints from cat lovers

PG parental guidance required (motion picture classification); postgraduate
pg page
PGA Professional Golfers' Association
PGR parental guidance recommended (Australia). *See* **PG**
pH potential of hydrogen = measurement scale of acidity and alkalinity
ph phase; philosophy (*also* phil, philos); phone
pharm pharmaceutical; pharmacy; pharmacist
PHC pharmaceutical chemist
PhD Doctor of Philosophy (*also* **DPhil**)
Phil Philharmonic; Philadelphia (*also* **Phila**, **Philly**); Philippines
phil philology (*also* **philol**)
philos philosophy; philosopher
phon phonetic; phonetics; phonetically
phot photography; photographic
phr phrase
phys physician; physicist; physics; physical
physio physiotherapy
physiol physiological
physog physiognomy
PI per inquiry; petrol injection; programmed instruction, Philippine Islands
PIA Personal Investment Authority
pic picture; pictorial
PID pelvic inflammation disease
PIE Paedophile Information Exchange (banned organisation)
PIN personal identification number
PinC Priest in charge
pix motion pictures
pixel picture element (computers)
pk park (*also* **P**); pack; peak
pkg package
pkt packet
PL Plimsoll line (safe loading line on ships)
Pl Place
pl place; plain; plate; plural
PLA Port of London Authority; People's Liberation Army (China)
plat platoon; plateau; platform
PLATO programmed logic for automated learning operation
PLC, **plc** public limited company
PLN Nationalist Party, Nicaragua
PLO Palestine Liberation Organisation
PLP Parliamentary Labour Party
PLR Public Lending Right
plur plural

Plum Pelham = nickname for two celebrities: the comic author P G (Pelham Grenville) Wodehouse and the English cricketer Sir Pelham Warner

PLUTO pipeline under the ocean (supplied Allied forces during the Normandy landing in World War II)

Ply Plymouth

PM Prime Minister; Police Magistrate; Provost Marshal; postmaster; paymaster

pm, PM post meridiem = after noon; post mortem

PMG Postmaster General; Paymaster General

pmh past medical history

pmk postmark

PMS premenstrual syndrome; Pantone matching system (colour printing)

PMT premenstrual tension; photomechanical transfer (graphics)

pmt payment

PN promissory note (*also* **P/N**, **pn**)

PND postnatal depression

PNdB perceived noise decibel

PNG, png *persona non grata* = unacceptable or inadmissible person

pntr painter

PO Post Office; postal order; Pilot Officer; Petty Officer; personnel officer; power operated

po chamberpot

POB post office box

POC port of call

POD pay on delivery

POE port of entry/embarkation

POETs day piss off early, tomorrow's Saturday (i.e. it's Friday)

POL petroleum, oil and lubricants

Pol Poland; Polish

pol police; political; politician; polarise

polio poliomyelitis

poly polytechnic (college)

POM prescription-only medicine

POP Post Office preferred (envelope size); Point of Presence (Internet 'phone exchange')

Pop *popina* = cookshop, Eton club that maintains school discipline

pop population; point of purchase; popular (music)

Pop art art with allusions to popular culture, launched in the 1950s

por portion; portrait (*also port*); porous

PORIS Post Office Radio Interference Station

porn pornography; pornographic

Port Portugal; Portuguese

port portable; portrait

Portmanteau Words

As they result from the blending of two or more words, portmanteau words are close relatives of acronyms. A selection:

agitprop	from AGITate and PROPaganda
avionics	from AVIation and electrONICS
brunch	from BReakfast and lUNCH
camcorder	from CAMera and reCORDER
chunnel	from CHannel and tUNNEL
cyborg	from CYBernetics and ORGanism
denim	from serge DE NIMes (in France, where it was developed)
moped	from MOtorbike and PEDal
motel	from MOTorcar and hotEL
napalm	from NAPhthalene and pALMitate
prissy	from PRIm and siSSY
simulcast	from SIMULtaneous and broadCAST
sitcom	from SITuation and COMedy
smog	from SMoke and fOG
squiggle	from SQUirm and wrIGGLE
Swatch	from SWiss and wATCH
Velcro	from VELour and CROche (French for 'hooked')

pos position (*also* **posn**); point of sale; positive

POSSLQ person of opposite sex sharing living quarters

poss possible; possibility; possession

posse *posse comitatus* = assembly of able-bodied men called by a town's sheriff to help maintain law and order

POST point of sale terminal

posthum posthumous

pot potential

POUNC Post Office Users' National Council

POV point of view (cinematography); privately owned vehicle; peak of operating voltage

POW prisoner of war

PP parliamentary papers; parish priest; past president; parcel post

pp pages; *per procurationem* = by proxy or by delegation to; post paid; pre-paid; parcel post; privately printed

PPA Periodical Publishers' Association; Pools Proprietors' Association

PPE philosophy, politics and economics (university course)

PPL private pilot's licence

ppm parts per million

PPP personal pension plan; Penelope's pony paddock (used by estate agents to describe a small field attached to a country cottage); Private Patient's Plan; purchasing power parity (banking)

PPS Parliamentary Private Secretary

pps *post postscriptum* = an additional postscript

PQ parliamentary question; Parti Quebecois (Canada)

pq previous question

PR proportional representation; public relations; postal regulations; progress report; Puerto Rico

pr pair (**prs** = plural); per; present; print; printer; painter; price

pram perambulator (baby carriage)

PRB Pre-Raphaelite Brotherhood (19th-century artists' group)

PRC People's Republic of China

preb prebendary

pref preface; preferable; prefect; preference; preferred; preferential

prefab prefabricated

prefs preference shares; preferred stock

prelim preliminary (**prelims** = introductory pages of a book)

prem premium; premature infant

premed premedical (usually preparing patient for an operation)

prep preparatory; **prep school** = preparatory school

Pres President; Presbyterian (*also* **Presb**)

pres present

prev previous; previously

pri private (*also* **pvt**, **priv**); priority

prim primary; primitive; primate

Prin Principal; Principality

prin principal; principle

PRO public relations officer; Public Records Office

pro professional

pro-am professional-amateur (sport)

prob probable; problem; probate

proc proceedings (e.g. **Proc Roy Soc** = *Proceedings of the Royal Society*); process

prod product; production; producer; (in Northern Ireland) Protestant

Prof Professor

prog programme; prognosis; progressive

prole proletarian

PROLOG programming logic, a mathematical logic-based computer language

PROM programmable read-only memory (computers)

promo promotion

Proms annual Albert Hall Promenade Concerts in which certain sections of the audience can walk about (or promenade) during performances

pron pronounced; pronunciation; pronoun

prop property (**props** = theatrical property); proposition; propeller; proprietor (*also* **propr**); proprietary; proper

Prot Protestant; Protectorate

pro tem *pro tempore* = for the time being

prov province; provincial; provisional; proverb

Provo Provisional = member of the Provisional Irish Republican Army

PRS Performing Right Society Ltd

PRT petroleum revenue tax

Pru Prudential Assurance Company

PS Police Sergeant; Philological Society; public school; private secretary: Parliamentary Secretary

ps, PS *post scriptum* = postscript

PSA Property Services Agency; Public Service Association (New Zealand); pleasant Sunday afternoon; prostate specific antigen

PSAB Public Schools Appointments Bureau

PSB Premium Savings Bond

PSBR public sector borrowing requirement

pseud pseudonym; a pretentious person (*also* **pseudo**)

psf pounds (lbs) per square foot

PSI Policy Studies Institute

psi pounds (lbs) per square inch

PSK phase shift keying (digital data modulation system)

PSL private sector liquidity

PST Pacific Standard Time (North America)

PSTN public switched telephone network

PSV public service vehicle

PT Public Trustee; pupil teacher; physical training

Pt Port; Point

pt part; pit; point; past tense; patient

PTA Parent-Teacher Association; Passenger Transport Authority

pta peseta

PT boat patrol torpedo boat

ptd printed; painted

PTE Passenger Transport Executive

ptg printing

PTI physical training instructor

PTO please turn over; power take-off

pt/pt point to point (horse racing)

PTS Philatelic Traders' Society

pts parts; payments; pints; points

Pty proprietary = private limited company (Australia, NZ, S Africa)

pub public house; published (*also* **publ**); publisher; **pub date** = date on which a book is to be published

pud pudding; pick up and deliver

pug pugilist

punc punctuation (*also* **punct**)

pur purchase; purchased; purple; purify

PVA polyvinyl acetate (plastic)

PVC polyvinyl chloride (plastic)

PVR premature voluntary retirement

pvte private

PWA Public Works Administration (USA); people with aids

PWD Public Works Department

PWR pressurised water reactor

PX physical examination; US version of NAAFI

pxt *pinxit* = he/she painted it (*also* **pinx**, **pnxt**)

PYO pick your own

Q

Q Queen (royalty; chess; cards); Quebec (*also* **Que**); Queensland (*also* **Qld**); quartermaster (*also* **QM**); quetzal; quality

q quarter; quarterly; quart; quarto; question; query; quire; quantity; quintal

Q&A question and answer

QANTAS, **Qantas** Queensland and Northern Territory Aerial Service (now the Australian international airline)

QB Queen's Bench; **QBD** = Queen's Bench Division (law)

Qbc Quebec

QC Queen's Counsel; Queen's College

qe *quod est* = which is

QE2 *Queen Elizabeth II*, Cunard Line cruise ship

QED *quod erat demonstrandum* = which was to be proved

QF quality factor

Q fever query fever (from its unknown cause until late 1930s when it was discovered to be a viral infection)

QGM Queen's Gallantry Medal

QHP Queen's Honorary Physician

QHS Queen's Honorary Surgeon

Qld Queensland (*also* **Q**)

QM Quartermaster; **QMG** = Quartermaster General

qnty quantity

QPM Queen's Police Medal

QPR Queens Park Rangers Football Club

qq quartos; questions

qqv *quae vide* = which see (refers to more than one cross-reference); *see* **qv**

qr quarter; quarterly; quire (measure of paper and newspaper bundles

QS quarantine station; quantity surveyor; Quarter Sessions (law)

QSGs quasi-stellar galaxies

Q-ship armed merchant ship used as decoys (WWI); *also* **Q-boat**

QSM Queen's Service Medal (New Zealand)

QSO Queen's Service Order (New Zealand)

Q-sort 'agree/disagree' psychological test
qt quart (**qts** = quarts); quiet (**on the qt** = clandestinely)
qty quantity
qu question; query
quad quadrangle; quadrant; quadruple
quake earthquake
qual qualification; quality
quango quasi-autonomous non-governmental organisation
Que Quebec (*also* **Q**, **Qbc**)
quot quotation
qv *quod vide* = which see (cross-reference to related item)
qy query

R

R rabbi; rand; railway; Réaumur (degree of heat); Republic; Republican; rector; registered (postal); river; Registered at the US Patent Office; Regiment; rupee; rook (chess); restricted; rouble; route
r radius; rare; right; red; road; rod; retired; railway; runs (cricket and baseball); rain; recipe; rouble
RA Royal Academy; Royal Academician; Ratepayers' Association; Referees' Association; Royal Artillery; Ramblers' Association; Rear Admiral
RAA Royal Academy of Arts
RAAF Royal Australian Air Force
Rab R A Butler, British Conservative politician
RAC Royal Automobile Club; Royal Aero Club; Royal Agricultural College, Cirencester
RACE rapid automatic checkout equipment
racon radar beacon
Rad Radnorshire
rad radius, radian; radar; radio; radiology; radical; unit of radiation absorbed dose
RADA Royal Academy of Dramatic Art
radar radio detection and ranging
RADAS random access discrete address system
R Adm Rear Admiral
RAE Royal Academy of Engineering; Royal Aircraft Establishment
RAEC Royal Army Education Corps
RAF Royal Air Force
RAFVR Royal Air Force Volunteer Reserve
RAH Royal Albert Hall, London
RAHS Royal Australian Historical Society
RAI *Radio Audisioni Italiane* = Italian Broadcasting Corporation
RAM random access memory (computers); Royal Academy of Music

RAMAC random access memory accounting (computers)
RAMC Royal Army Medical Corps
RAN Royal Australian Navy
R&A Royal and Ancient Golf Club, St Andrews, Scotland
R&B rhythm and blues (music)
R&CC riot and civil commotions
R&D research and development
r&r rest and recreation; rock and roll
RAOC Royal Army Ordnance Corps
RATO rocket-assisted takeoff
RAVC Royal Army Veterinary Corps
RBA Royal Society of British Artists
RBE relative biological effectiveness
rbl rouble (*also* **R, r**)
RBS Royal Society of British Sculptors
RC Red Cross; Roman Catholic; Reformed Church; Reserve Corps
rc reinforced concrete
RCA Royal College of Art; Royal Canadian Academy; Radio Corporation of America
RCAF Royal Canadian Air Force
RCD residual circuit device
rcd received
RCM Royal College of Music
RCMP Royal Canadian Mounted Police
RCN Royal College of Nursing; Royal Canadian Navy
RCO Royal College of Organists
RCP Royal College of Physicians
RCS Royal College of Surgeons; Royal College of Science; Royal Corps of Signals
RCSB Royal Commonwealth Society for the Blind
RCT Royal Corps of Transport
RCVS Royal College of Veterinary Surgeons
rd, RD road; rendered; round; rod; refer to drawer (*also* **RD, R/D**)
RDA recommended daily allowance
RDC Rural District Council
RDS radio data system (transmission of digital signals)
RDT&E research, development, test and evaluation
RDZ radiation danger zone
RE religious education; Royal Engineers; Reformed Episcopal
Re rupee (*also* **Rs, rs** = rupees)
rec received; receipt; recent; record; recorded; recreation; recipe
recce reconnaissance
recd received (*also* **rec**)
Rect Rector; Rectory
rect rectangular; rectify
red reduced

ref referee; refer; reference; refund (*also* **refd**)
Ref Ch Reformed Church
Reg Regina; Regent; registered (*also* **regd**)
reg registered; regular; regulation; regiment

European Car Registration Letters

The letters GB, IRL, F and NL on motor vehicles are commonly seen and most of us know that they identify the country of registration: Great Britain, Ireland, France and the Netherlands (Holland). But what of GBJ or SLO? Here's an identification list of European motor vehicle code letters now increasingly seen on British roads:

A	Austria	AL	Albania	AND	Andorra
B	Belgium	BG	Bulgaria	CH	Switzerland
CY	Cyprus	CZ	Czech Rep	D	Germany
DK	Denmark	E	Spain	F	France
FL	Liechtenstein	FR	Faroe Is	GB	Britain
GBA	Alderney	GBG	Guernsey	GBJ	Jersey
GBM	Isle of Man	GBZ	Gibraltar	GR	Greece
H	Hungary	I	Italy	IRL	Ireland
IS	Iceland	L	Luxembourg	M	Malta
MC	Monaco	N	Norway	NL	Holland
P	Portugal	PL	Poland	RO	Romania
RSM	San Marino	S	Sweden	SF	Finland
SK	Slovakia	SLO	Slovenia	V	Vatican
YU	Yugoslavia				

REGAL range and elevation guidance for approach and landing (airports)
Reg Prof Regius Professor
Reg TM Registered Trade Mark (*also* **RTM**)
RI8 cert British film classification (no under 18s admitted)
rej reject
rel relative; religion; relic; release
REM rapid eye movement; Roentgen Equivalent in Man = unit measuring radiation exposure
REME Royal Electrical and Mechanical Engineers
Renf Renfrewshire
Rep Republican (USA)
rep representative; repeat; repertory; reprint; repaired; report
repl replace; replacement
repo repossess; **repo man** = person hired to repossess goods

repr represented; representative; reprint; reprinted

repro reproduction

rept receipt; report

req request; requisition; required

res residence; resident; reserved; reservoir; research; reservation; resolution; resigned

resig resignation

resp respectively; respondent

rest restaurant (*also* **restr**)

ret, retd retired; return; returned; retained

retro retrorocket

Rev, Revd Reverend

rev reverse; revolution (**revs** = revolutions); revised; revision; review; revenue

Rev Ver Revised Version of the Bible

rew reward

RF radio frequency; Royal Fusiliers; rugby football

RFC Royal Flying Corps; Rugby Football Club

RFL Rugby Football League

RFS render, float and set (plastering)

RFSU Rugby Football Schools' Union

RFU Rugby Football Union

rgd registered

RGN Registered General Nurse

RGS Royal Geographical Society

Rgt Regiment

RH Royal Highness; relative humidity; right hand

Rh factor rhesus factor, inherited agglutinating agent in blood, first observed in rhesus monkeys

rh right hand

RHA Regional Health Authority; Royal Horse Artillery

rhd, RHD right-hand drive

rheo rheostat

rhet rhetorical

RHG Royal Horse Guards

rhino rhinoceros

R Hist S Royal Historical Society

rhp rated horsepower

RHS Royal Historical Society; Royal Horticultural Society; Royal Humane Society

RI Royal Institution, London; Royal Institute of Painters in Watercolours; *Regina et Imperatrix* = Queen and Empress; religious instruction

RIA Royal Irish Academy

RIAA curve international standard for microgroove disc reproduction

RIAC Royal Irish Automobile Club

RIAI Royal Institute of Architects in Ireland

RIAM Royal Irish Academy of Music

RIBA Royal Institute of British Architects

RIC Royal Institute of Chemistry

RICS Royal Institution of Chartered Surveyors

RIF reduction in force (US euphemism for retrenchment)

RIIA Royal Institute of International Affairs

RIP *requiescat in pace* = rest in peace

RIS Radio Interference Service

riv river

RKO Radio Corporation of America/Keith Orpheum Theatres; from 1931–53 one of the big Hollywood studios

RL Rugby League

RLF Royal Literary Fund

RLPAS Royal London Prisoners' Aid Society

RLPO Royal Liverpool Philharmonic Orchestra

RLS Robert Louis Stevenson, writer and poet

RLSS Royal Life Saving Society

rly railway (*also* **rlwy**); relay

RM Royal Marines; Royal Mail; registered midwife

rm room; rms = rooms

RMA Royal Military Academy, Sandhurst

RMC Royal Military College

R-methodology statistically based psychological test (*see* **Q-sort**)

rmm relative molecular mass

R months the eight months with 'r' in their names during which it is claimed that oysters may safely be eaten

RN Royal Navy

RNA ribonucleic acid

RNAS Royal Naval Air Service; renamed Naval Air Command

RNC Royal Naval College

RNIB Royal National Institute for the Blind

RNID Royal National Institute for the Deaf

RNLI Royal National Lifeboat Institution

RNR Royal Naval Reserve

RNVR Royal Naval Volunteer Reserve

RNZAF Royal New Zealand Air Force

RNZN Royal New Zealand Navy

ro run out (cricket); rowed over (rowing); run on (editing mark)

ROAM return on assets managed

ROARE reduction of attitudes and repressed emotions (sex offenders' treatment programme)

ROC Royal Observer Corps

ROI Royal Institute of Oil Painters; return on investment

Rolls Rolls-Royce cars and engines

ROM read-only memory (computers)

Rom Roman; Romania; Romanian; Romance (languages)

roo kangaroo

R101 British airship that crashed in 1930

rop run of paper (newspaper publishing)

RORC Royal Ocean Racing Club

RORC rating waterline length, sail area, beam and draught formula used to handicap racing yachts

RORO, roro roll on/roll off (car and truck ferries)

ROSPA Royal Society for the Prevention of Accidents

rot rotary

ROW, row right of way

Roy, roy Royal; royalty

RP received pronunciation; Royal Society of Portrait Painters; reply paid

Rp rupiah

RPE rate of perceived exertion (aerobics)

RPG report programme generator (business computer programming language)

rph revolutions per hour

RPI retail price index

rpm revolutions per minute; retail price maintenance (*also* **RPM**); reliability performance measure

RPO Royal Philharmonic Orchestra; railway post office

RPS Royal Photographic Society

rps revolutions per second

rpt repeat; reprint; report

RPV remotely piloted vehicle

RQ respiratory quotient

RR railroad (USA); Rolls-Royce; Right Reverend

RRB Race Relations Board

RRP, rrp recommended retail price

RS Royal Society

Rs rupees

RSA Royal Scottish Academy/Academician; Royal Society of Arts; Returned Services Association (NZ); Republic of South Africa

RSC Royal Shakespeare Company; Royal Chemical Society

RSE Royal Society of Edinburgh

RSG Regional Seat of Government; rate support grant

RSGB Radio Society of Great Britain

RSI Royal Sanitary Institute

RSJ, rsj rolled steel joint

RSL Royal Society of Literature; Returned Services League (Australia)

RSM regimental sergeant major; Royal Society of Medicine; Royal School of Mines; Royal School of Music; Royal Society of Musicians

RSNC Royal Society for Nature Conservation

RSNO Royal Scottish National Orchestra

RSNZ Royal Society of New Zealand

RSPB Royal Society for the Protection of Birds

RSPCA Royal Society for the Prevention of Cruelty to Animals

RSSPCC Royal Scottish Society for the Prevention of Cruelty to Children

RSV Revised Standard Version of the Bible

RSVP *Répondez s'il vous plaît* = reply if you please

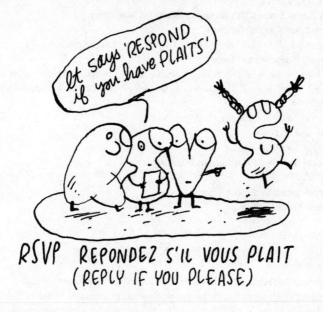

RSWS Royal Scottish Watercolour Society

rt right

RTA road traffic accident

RTB return to base

rtd returned; retired; **rtd ht** = retired hurt (cricket)

RTDS real time data system

RTE *Radio Telefís Eireann* = Irish Radio and Television

rte route

RTF Rich Text Format

rtg rating

Rt Hon Right Honourable

RTL resistor transistor logic (electronic circuits)

RTM registered trade mark

rtn retain; return

RTR Royal Tank Regiment

Rt Rev Right Reverend

RTT radioteletype

rtw ready to wear

RTZ Rio Tinto Zinc Corporation

RU Rugby Union; Readers' Union

RUA Royal Ulster Academy of Painting, Sculpture and Architecture

RUC Royal Ulster Constabulary

RUG restricted users group (computers)

RUI Royal University of Ireland

RUKBA Royal United Kingdom Beneficent Association

RUPP road used as public path

RUR *Rossum's Universal Robots*, Karel Capek's 1921 stage play

Rus Russia; Russian (*also* **Russ**)

RV Revised Version of the Bible; rateable value; research vessel; recreational vehicle; *Ryom Vivaldi Verzeichnis* = inventory of Vivaldi's compositions by Peter Ryom

RVCI Royal Veterinary College of Ireland

rwd rear-wheel drive

RVO Royal Victorian Order

RWS Royal Society of Painters in Water Colour

Rwy railway

RYA Royal Yachting Association

RYS Royal Yacht Squadron

S

S Saint; Scotland; September; Senate; schilling; South; southern; Socialist; school; summer; *Señor*; *Signor*; *Signora*; sucre; Svedburg unit; sea; Sweden; Sabbath

s section; sign; signed; southern; small; shilling; single; slow; spherical; stratus (cloud); sunny; *sur* = on (French place names)

SA South Africa; South Australia; *Société Anonyme* (French/Belgium/ Switzerland/Luxembourg limited liability company); *Sociedad Anonima* (Spanish and Portuguese limited liability company); South America; Society of Antiquaries/Arts/Authors; Salvation Army; *Sturmabteilung* = storm troopers; surface-to-air missile

sa semi-annual; sex appeal

S/A subject to approval/acceptance

SAA South Africal Airways; small arms ammunition

SAAA Scottish Amateur Athletic Association

SAAB *Svensk Aeroplan Aktiebolag* (Swedish car, aircraft and missile manufacturer)

SAAF South African Air Force

Sab Sabbath

SABA Scottish Amateur Boxing Association

SABC South African Broadcasting Corporation

SABENA *Société anonyme belge d'exploitation de la navigation aerienne* = Belgian airline

SAC Scientific Advisory Council; Scottish Autombile Club; State Athletics Commission (USA)

SAD Seasonal Affective Disorder

SADF South African Defence Force

SADIE scanning analogue-to-digital input equipment

SAE stamped addressed envelope; self-addressed envelope; Society of British Automotive Engineers; Society of Automotive Engineers oil viscosity scale (USA)

SAF Strategic Air Force (USA)

SAFE South African Friends of England

S Afr South Africa

SAG Screen Actors' Guild (USA)

SAGA Social Amenities for the Golden Aged (British help and leisure organisation); Society of American Graphic Artists

SAGB Spiritualist Association of Great Britain

SAH Supreme Allied Headquarters

SAID Sexual Allegations in Divorce

SAIDS simian acquired immune deficiency syndrome

sal salary

Salop Shropshire

SALP South African Labour Party

SALT Strategic Arms Limitation Talks (USA and former USSR)

Salv Salvador

SAM surface-to-air missile; sex appeal and magnetism

Sam Samoa

S Am South America

Samar Samaritans

SAMH Scottish Association for Mental Health

san sanatorium; sanitary

sand sandwich

s&d song and dance

S&F stock and fixtures; shopping and fucking – a so-called genre of popular fiction featuring explicit sex scenes

S&FA shipping and forwarding agents

S&H shipping and handling charges

S&L savings and loan association (USA)

S&M, **s&m** sadism and masochism, commonly sadomasochism; stock and machinery; sausages and mash

SANDS Stillborn and Neonatal Death Society

s&s sex and shopping (popular fiction style)

Sane Schizophrenia A National Emergency

SANR subject to approval, no risk

Sans Sanskrit

SAP South African Police

sap soon as possible (*see* **asap**)

sapl sailing as per (Lloyd's shipping) list

SAR search and rescue; South African Republic;

Sar Sarawak

SARs severe acute repiratory syndrome

SARAH search and rescue homing (radar)

sarge sergeant

sarl *Société à responsibilité limitée* = private limited company in France, Belgium, Switzerland and Luxembourg

SAS Special Air Service; Scandinavian Airlines System; small astronomical satellite

SAT scholastic aptitude test (USA)

Sat Saturday; Saturn

S At South Atlantic

sat satellite

SATB soprano, alto, tenor and bass (choral music)

SATCO signal automatic air traffic control system

sav stock at valuation; sale at valuation

SAW surface accoustic wave

sax saxophone

SAYE save as you earn

SB small business; savings bank; Special Branch (Police political security department); sub-branch; stillborn

sb single-breasted (suit style); stolen base (baseball)

SBA School of Business Administration; standard beam approach (airports); sick-bay attendant

SBAC Society of British Aerospace Companies

SBC Schools Broadcasting Council; single board computer

SBD silent but deadly (passing wind)

SBNO Senior British Naval Officer

SBO small bowel obstruction

SBS sick-building syndrome; Special Boat Service

SBU strategic business unit

SBV seabed vehicle

SC School Certificate (Aust and NZ); Signal Corps; Senior Counsel; Supreme Court; Special Constable; Star of Courage (Canada); Social Club; Staff Corps; Staff Captain; Schools Council

Sc Scandinavia; Scotland; science; sculptor

sc scale; sculptor; *sculpsit* = carved or engraved by; self-contained; small capitals (typesetting); science; scruple (weight)

SCA Special Conservation Area; sickle-cell anemia (*also* **SCD**)

Scan Scandinavia (*also Sc,* **Scand**)

s caps small capitals (typesetting)

SCAR Scientific (sometimes Special) Committee on Antarctic Research

Scarab Submerged Craft Assisting Repair and Burial

SCB Speedway Control Board; Solicitors Complaints Bureau

ScBC Bachelor of Science (Chemistry)

ScBE Bachelor of Science (Engineering)

SCBU special care baby unit

SCC Sea Cadet Corps

scc single column centimetre (print advertising)

SCCAPE Scottish Council for Commercial, Administrative and Professional Education

SCCL Scottish Council for Civil Liberties

SCE Scottish Certificate of Education

SCF Save the Children Fund; Senior Chaplain to the Forces

SCG Sydney Cricket Ground

SCGB Ski Club of Great Britain

sch school; scholar; scholarship; schedule; schooner

sched schedule (*also* **sch**)

schizo schizophrenic

SCI Scottish Central Institutions; Society of the Chemical Industry

sci single column inch (print advertising)

SCID severe combined immunodeficiency disease

sci-fi science fiction

SCL Scottish Central Library

SCLC small cell lung cancer (carcinoma)

SCM State Certified Midwife

SCOFF Society for the Conquest of Flight Fear

SCOOP Stop Crapping On Our Property (warning to dog owners)

SCOR Scientific Committee on Oceanic Research

Scot Scotland; Scottish; Scotsman

SCP single-cell protein; Social Credit Party (Canada)

SCPS Society of Civil and Public Servants

SCR senior common room (universities); selective catalytic reactor

scr script; scruple

Script Scripture

SCS space communications system; Soil Conservation Service (USA)

SCSI Small Computer System Interface ('scuzzy')

SCSS Scottish Council of Social Service

SCU Scottish Cycling Union; Scottish Cricket Union

scuba self contained underwater breathing apparatus

sculp sculptor; sculpture

SCUM Society for Cutting Up Men (a creation of Valeria Solanis who shot and wounded artist Andy Warhol in 1968)

SCV *Stato della Citta del Vaticano* = Vatican City State

SCWS Scottish Wholesale Cooperative Society

SD standard deviation; Secretary of Defense (USA); senile dementia; send direct; special delivery; special duty; State Department (USA)

sd same date; semi-detached; standard deviation (statistics); safe deposit; signed; said; sailed; sewed (bookbinding)

S/D sight draft (banking)

SDA Scottish Development Agency; Seventh Day Adventist

SDAT senile dementia (Alzheimer type)

SDG *Soli Deo Gloria* = Glory to God Alone

SDI Strategic Defense Initiative (US 'Star Wars' project)

SDLP Social Democratic and Labour Party (Northern Ireland)

SDMJ September/December/March/June: traditional months for quarterly repayments

SDO senior duty officer

SDP Social Democratic Party; social, domestic and pleasure (insurance)

SDRs special drawing rights (banking)

SDS scientific data system; strategic defense system (USA)

SE Stock Exchange (*also* **S/Ex, S/E**); South Eastern; Standard English

se standard error (statistics); single-engined; single entry

SEAC South East Asia Command; School Examination and Assessment Council

SEAF Stock Exchange automatic exchange facility

SEAL sea-air-land (US Military)

SEAQ Stock Exchange automated quotations

SEATO South East Asia Treaty Organisation

SEB Former Southern Electricity Board

SEC Securities and Exchange Commission (USA)

sec secretary; second; sector; seconded; section

SECAM *sequential couleur à memoire* = French standard television broadcasting system

SECC Scottish Exhibition and Conference Centre

Sec Gen Secretary-General

secy secretary

SED Scottish Education Department; shipper's export declaration

SEDAR submerged electrode detection and ranging

SEE Society of Environmental Engineers

SEEA *Société européenne d'énergie atomique* = European Atomic Energy Society

SEF Shipbuilding Employers' Federation

seg segment; segregate; segue

SEH St Edmund Hall, Oxford University

Sel Selwyn College, CambridgeUniversity

sel select; selected; selection

SELNEC South-East Lancashire and North-East Cheshire

SEM scanning electron microscopy

Sem Semitic

sem seminary; semester (USA); semicolon

semi semi-detached house

SEN special educational needs; State Enrolled Nurse

Sen Senate; Senator

sen senior (*also* **sr, snr**)

Sen M Senior Master; **Sen Mist** = Senior Mistress

senr senior (*also* **sen, sr, snr**)

SEO senior executive officer

sep separate; separation; sepal (botany)

Sept September (*also* **Sep**)

seq sequel; sequence; *sequens* = the following one; **seqq** = *sequentia* = the following ones

ser series; serial; sermon; service; servant; service

Serb Serbian

SERC Science and Engineering Research Council

SERPS State Earnings-Related Pension Scheme

SERT Society of Electronic and Radio Technicians

serv service; servant

SES Stock Exchange of Singapore; **SESI** = Stock Exchange of Singapore Index

SET former selective employment tax (abandoned 1973)

SETI search for extraterrestrial intelligence

sew sewer; sewage; sewerage

SF Sinn Fein; Society of Friends; science fiction; San Francisco; senior fellow; signal frequency; standard frequency; special forces

sf science fiction; *sub finem* = towards the end; signal frequency

SFA Scottish Football Association; sweet Fanny Adams = nothing

SFC specific fuel consumption

Sfc Sergeant first-class (USA)

SFI *Société Financière Internationale* = French International Finance Corporation

SFL Scottish Football League; sequenced flashing lights (airports)

SFO Serious Fraud Office; Superannuation Funds Office; Senior Flag Officer

SFOF space flight operations facility (Nasa)

SFr Swiss franc

SFU suitable for upgrade (airline ticketing)

SG Secretary General; Solicitor General; Scots Guards; senior grade; Stanley Gibbons (postage stamp identification number); Society of Genealogists; Surgeon General

sg specific gravity

sgd signed

SGF Scottish Grocers' Federation

SGHWR steam-generating heavy-water reactor

sgl single

SGM Sea Gallantry Medal

SGML Standard Generalised Markup Language

Sgt Sergeant; **Sgt Maj** = Sergeant Major

SGU Scottish Golf Union

SH schoolhouse; scrum half (rugby); showers; Southern Hemisphere; Schleswig-Holstein

sh second hand (*also* **s/h**); shilling; share (*also* **shr**); sheep; sheet; sacrifice hit (baseball)

SHA Scottish Hockey Association; sidereal hour angle

SHAC Shelter Housing Aid Centre

SHAEF Supreme Headquarters Allied Expeditionary Forces (under General Eisenhower, London, World War II)

Shak Shakespeare (*also* **Sh**, **Shake**)

shd should

Shef Sheffield (*also* **Sheff**)

SHF superhigh frequency

SHM Society of Housing Managers

SHMO Senior Hospital Medical Officer

SHO Senior House Officer

sho shutout (baseball)

shorts short-term bonds; short-dated securities (investing)

SHP single-flowered hardy perennial (horticulture)

shpg shipping

shpt shipment

shr share; shower

Shrops Shropshire

SHS *Societatis Historicae Socius* = Fellow of the Historical Society

SHT single-flower hybrid tea (rose growing)

'shun attention!

SHW safety, health and welfare

SI Most Exalted Order of the Star of India; Staten Island; seriously ill; sum insured; *see* **SI unit**

SIA Society of Investment Analysts; Spinal Injuries Association

SIB Special Investigation Branch (Police); Savings and Investment Bank; Securities and Investment Board; self-injurious behaviour

Sib Siberia

SIC Standard Industrial Classification

Sic Sicily; Sicilian

SICAV *Société d'investissement à capital variable* = unit trust

SID *Spiritus in Deo* = His/Her spirit is with God; Society for International Development

SIDA the AIDS acronym in French, Spanish and Italian

SIDS sudden infant death syndrome (cot death)

SIF stress intensity factor (engineering)

SIG special interest group

Sig *Signor* = Mr; *Signore* = Sir (Italian)

sig signature; signal; signifies

SII *Société internationale de la lèpre* = International Leprosy Association

SIM self-inflicted mutilation; survey information on microfilm; *Société internationale de musicologie* = International Musicological Society

SIMA Scientific Instrument Manufacturers' Association

SIMC *Société internationale pour la musique contemporaine* = International Society for Contemporary Music

SIMCA *Société industrielle de mécanique et carrosserie automobiles* = French car manufacturer

SIMD single instruction, multiple data (computers); *see* **SISD**

sing singular

SIO Senior Intelligence Officer

SIS Security Intelligence Service (MI6)

sis sister

SISD single instruction, single data (computers); *see* **SIMD**

SISTER Special Institutions for Scientific and Technological Education and Research

SIT Society of Industrial Technology

SITA Students' International Travel Association

sitcom situation comedy (type of television programme)

sit rep situation report

sit rm sitting room

sit vac situation vacant; **sits vac** = situations vacant

SI unit *Système International d'Unités* = system of international units (e.g. ampere, metre, kilogram, kelvin, second, etc)

SIV simian immunodeficiency virus

SIW self-inflicted wound; *see* **SIM**

$64,000 question the essential question

SJ Society of Jesus (Jesuits)

sj *sub judice* = under judicial consideration

SJAA St John Ambulance Association

SJAB St John Ambulance Brigade

SJC Supreme Judicial Court (USA)

sk sketch

SKC Scottish Kennel Club

S Ken South Kensington

SKF *Svenska Kullagerfabriken* = Swedish steelmaking organisation

SKr Swedish krona

SL sea level; Second Lieutenant; solicitor-at-law; scout leader; Squadron Leader; short lengths

sl sleep; sleet; *sine loco* = without place of publication (bibliography)

SLA Scottish Library Association; special landscape area

SLADE Society of Lithographic Artists, Designers, Engravers and Process Workers

SLAET Society of Licensed Aircraft Engineers and Technologists

SLAS Society for Latin American Studies

Slav Slavonic

SLBM submarine-launched ballistic missile

SLCM sea-launched cruise missile

SLD Social and Liberal Democrats; specific learning difficulty

sld sailed; sealed; sold; self-locking device

S Ldr Squadron Leader

SLI specific language impairment

SLLW solid low-level waste (radioactive material); *also* **SLW**

SLO Senior Liaison Officer

SLP Scottish Labour Party; Socialist Labor Party (USA)

SLR single lens reflex (camera)

SLS sodium lauryl sulphate (detergents)

SLSC surf life saving club

SLTA Scottish Licensed Trade Association

SLV standard (or space) launch vehicle

SM sales manager; stage manager; Sergeant Major; station master; silver medallist; Society of Miniaturists; stipendiary magistrate; Sons of Malta; Sisters of Mercy; strategic missile; sado-masochism

sm small

SMAC Standing Medical Advisory Committee

SMATV satellite master antenna television

SMAW shielded metal arc welding

SMBA Scottish Marine Biological Association

SMBG self-monitoring blood glucose (diabetes check)

SMC Scottish Mountaineering Club; Small Magellanic Cloud (astronomy); standard mean chord

sm caps small capitals (typesetting)

SMetO Senior Meteorological Officer

SMHD The Worshipful Company of Spectacle Makers' Higher Diploma in Ophthalmic Optics

SMIA Sheet Metal Industries Association

SMJ Sisters of Mary and Joseph

SMO Senior Medical Officer

SMP statutory maternity pay

SMPS Society of Master Printers in Scotland

SMPTE Society of Motion Picture and Television Engineers (USA)

SMR standard metabolic rate

SMTA Scottish Motor Trade Association

SMTP Simple Mail Transfer Protocol

SMW standard metal window

SN, sn serial number; service number; shipping note (*also* **S/N**); snow

Snafu situation normal, all fucked / fouled up

SNB sellers no buyers

SNCF *Société Nationale des Chemins de Fer* = French National Railways

S/N curve = stress number curve

snd sound

SNF strategic nuclear forces; spent nuclear fuel; solids, not fat

SNFU Scottish National Farmers' Union

SNG substitute natural gas

SNH Scottish National Heritage

SNIG sustainable non-inflationary growth

SNLR services no longer required

SNOBOL string oriented symbolic language (computers)

SNP Scottish National Party

SNPA Scottish Newspaper Proprietors' Association

SNR Society for Nautical Research; signal to noise ratio (*also* **S/N ratio**)

Snr, snr Senior (*also* **Sr**)

Snr *Señor* = Mr (in Spanish); *also* **Sr**

Snra *Senhora* = Mrs (in Portuguese)

Snra *Señora* = Mrs (in Spanish); *also* **Sra**

S/N ratio signal to noise ratio

Snrta *Senhorita* = Miss (in Portuguese)

Snrta *Señorita* = Miss (in Spanish)

SO Scottish Office; Senior Officer; Scientific Officer; Signal Officer; Staff Officer; Stationery Office; Symphony Orchestra

So Southern

so, SO selling order; shipping order; standing order; strike out

SOA state of the art

SOAP subjective, objective, analysis, planning (medical)

SOAS School of Oriental and African Studies, London

SOB silly old bastard; son of a bitch (North America)

SOC Scottish Ornithologists' Club

Soc Society; *società* = Italian company or partnership; Socrates

soc social; society; socialist; sociology

Soc Dem Social Democrat

sociol sociology; sociologist

SOCO scene-of-crime officer (police)

SOCONY Standard Oil Corporation of New York

sod sodium

SODOMEI Japanese Federation of Trade Unions

SOE Special Operations Executive (World War II)

SOED Shorter Oxford English Dictionary

SOF sound on film

SOFAA Society of Fine Art Auctioneers

SOGAT Society of Graphical and Allied Trades

SOHIO Standard Oil Company of Ohio

SoHo South of Houston Street (district in Manhattan); small office and home office (business description)

Sol, sol solicitor (*also* **Slr**); solution; soluble

SOLAS Safety Of Life At Sea

Sol Gen Solicitor General

solv solvent

SOM Society of Occupational Medicine

Som Somerset

sonar sound navigation and ranging

SOP standard operating procedure

sop soprano

Soph Sophocles (Greek poet and dramatist)

soph sophomore

SOR sale or return

SOS save our souls; the Morse code signal for distress

Sou Southern; Southampton

Sov Soviet; **Sov Un** = Soviet Union

sov shut off valve; sovereign

Soweto Southwestern Townships (Black African district in South Africa southwest of Johannesburg)

SP Socialist Party; starting price (race betting); stop payment; supply point; *Summus Pontifex* = Supreme Pontiff, i.e. the Pope

Sp Spain; Spanish; Spaniard; spring

sp single phase (electrical); space; special; species; speed; sport; special position (advertising); spelling; specimen; spirit

SpA *Società per Azioni* (Italian public limited company)

spag spaghetti

SpAm Spanish American

Span Spanish; Spaniard (*also* **Sp**)

SPANA Society for the Protection of Animals in North Africa

SPARS Women's Coast Guard Reserve (USA) from *semper paratus* = always ready (World War II)

SPACT South Pacific Air Transport Council

SPC Society for the Prevention of Crime

SPCA Society for the Prevention of Cruelty to Animals (USA)

SPCK Society for Promoting Christian Knowledge

SPD *Sozialdemokratische Partei Deutschlands* = German Social Democratic Party; Salisbury Plain District

SPDA single premium deferred annuity

SPE Society of Petroleum Engineers

SPEC South Pacific Bureau for Economic Cooperation

spec specification; special; specimen; speculation; **specs** = specifications; spectacles

SPECTRE Special Executive for Counter Intelligence, Revenge and Extortion, the fanciful terrorist organisation in Ian Fleming's *James Bond* novels

SPF sun protection factor (effectiveness of sun-screen products)

SPG Society for the Propagation of the Gospel

SPGA Scottish Professional Golfers' Association

SPGB Socialist Party of Great Britain

sp gr specific gravity (*also* **sg**)

sp ht specific heat

SpLD special learning difficulties (education)

SPNC Society for the Promotion of Nature Conservation

SPO senior press officer

SPOD Sexual Problems of the Disabled

SPOT *Satellite Pour l'Observation de la Terre* = series of French reconnaissance satellites; satellite positioning and tracking

SPQR *Senatus Populusque Romanus* = the Senate and People of Rome; small profits, quick return

SPR Society for Psychical Research

Spr Spring

SPRINT solid-propellant rocket-intercept missile

sprl *société de personnes à responsibilité limitée* = French private limited company

sptg sporting

SPUC Society for the Protection of the Unborn Child

SPVD Society for the Prevention of Venereal Disease

SQ sick quarters; survival quotient

sq square; sequence

SQA software quality assurance (computers)

Sqdn Ldr Squadron Leader (*also* **Sq Ldr**)

sq cm square centimetre; **sq ft** square feet/foot; **sq in** square inch; **sq km** square kilometre; **sq m** square metre; **sq mi** square mile (*also* **sq m**); **sq mm** square millimetre; **sq yd** square yard

sqq *sequentia* = the following ones (see **seq, seqq**)

SR Saudi riyal; Seychelles rupee; self-raising (flour); Southern Region (railway); sodium ricinoleate (in toothpaste); Society of Radiographers; standard rate (taxation); synthetic rubber

S/R sale or return (*also* **SOR**)

Sr *Senhor* = Mr/Sir (Portuguese); *Señor* = Mr/Sir (Spanish); Senior

sr short rate (finance); senior

SRA Squash Rackets Association

Sra *Senhora* = Mrs (Portuguese); *Señora* = Mrs (Spanish)

SRAM short range attack missile

SR&CC strikes, riot and civil commotion (insurance)

SRC Science Research Council; *sociedad regular colectiva* (Spanish partnership); Students' Representative Council; Swiss Red Cross

SRCN State Registered Children's Nurse

S-R connection stimulus-response connection (psychological unit of learning)

Srl *società a responsibilita limitata* = Italian private limited company

SRO sold right out; standing room only; single room occupancy; self-regulatory organisation; Statutory Rules and Orders

SRP State Registered Physiotherapist; suggested retail price

SRS *Societatis Regiae Sodalis* = Fellow of the Royal Society

Srta *Senhorita* = Miss (Portuguese); *Señorita* = Miss (Sp‾

SRU Scottish Rugby Union

SS *Schutzstaffel* = Nazi paramilitary organisation; Social Security; Secret Service; Secretary of State; steamship; Sunday school; stainless steel (*also* **ss**); standard size; Straits Settlements; surface to surface (missiles)

S/S same size; silk screen

ss short stop (baseball); stainless steel

SSA Scottish Schoolmasters' Association; Social Security Administration (USA); Society of Scottish Artists

SSAE stamped, self-addressed envelope

SSAFA Soldiers', Sailors' and Airmens' Families Association

SSAP Statement of Standard Accounting Practice

SSC *Societas Sanctae Crucis* = Society of the Holy Cross; Scottish Ski Club; Species Survival Commission

SSE soapsuds enema

SSFA Scottish Schools' Football Association

S/Sg Staff Sergeant (*also* **SSgt**)

SSHA Scottish Special Housing Association

SSI site of scientific interest (*see* **SSSI**)

SSM surface to surface missile

SSN severely subnormal; Standard Serial Number

SSP statutory sick pay

ssp sub-species

SSPCA Scottish Society for the Prevention of Cruelty to Animals

SSRI selective serotonin re-uptake inhibitor

SSS Secretary of State for Scotland; sick sinus syndrome; standard scratch score (golf)

SSSI site of special scientific interest (*see* **SSI**)

SST supersonic transport

SSTA Scottish Secondary Teachers' Association

SSU Sunday School Union

ST Standard Time; speech therapist; spring tide; Summer Time; *The Sunday Times*

St Saint; Strait; Street; Statute

st stanza; statement; street; strait; *stet* ('let it stand', in printing); stone (14lbs weight); stumped (in cricket); stitch (knitting)

STA Swimming Teachers' Association; Sail Training Association

sta station; stationery

stab stable; stabilise; stabiliser

Staffs Staffordshire

STAGS Sterling Transferable Accruing Government Securities

stand standard (*also* **std**); standardised

St And St Andrews, Scotland

START Strategic Arms Reduction Talks

stat statistic; **stats** = statistics; statue; stationery

Stationers' Hall, London

STC Samuel Taylor Coleridge (English poet); Satellite Test Centre (USA); State Trading Corporation (India); Sydney Turf Club; Standard Telephones and Cables Ltd

STD subscriber trunk dialling; sexually transmitted disease

STE Society of Telecom Executives

Ste *Sainte* = Saint (fem); *société* = Co = French company

STEL short-term exposure limit (radiation levels)

STEM scanning transmission electron microscope

Sten World War II sub-machine gun invented by Shepherd and Turner of Enfield, England

sten stenographer (*also* steno)

STEP Special Temporary Employment Programme

ster stereotype; sterling (*also* Stg, £Stg)

stg, Stg sterling (*also* **Stlg, £stg, ster**)

St Ex Stock Exchange

stge stage; storage

STGWU Scottish Transport and General Workers' Union

Sth, sth South; southern (*also* **sthn**)

STI *Straits Times* Index (Singapore Stock Exchange)

Stipe Stipendiary Magistrate (*also* **Stip**)

Stir Stirlingshire

stir, STIR surplus to immediate requirements (*see* **STR**)

stk stock

STL studio-to-transmitter link

STM short-term memory

stn station

STO senior technical officer; standing order (*also* **S/O**)

STOL short take-off and landing (aircraft)

STOP Students Tired Of Pollution

S to S ship to shore; station to station

STP scientifically treated petroleum; a mescaline type hallucinogenic drug

stp standard temperature and pressure

STR, str surplus to requirements (*see* **STIR**)

str straight; strait (*also* **Str**); structure; structural; strings (in music)

STRAC strategic air command; strategic army corps (USA)

STRAD signal transmitting, receiving and distribution

Strad Stradivarius (violin)

strep streptococcus virus

STTA Scottish Table Tennis Association

STUC Scottish Trades Union Congress

stud student

STV Scottish Television Ltd; subscription television; standard test vehicle

stwy stairway

SU Scripture Union; strontium unit

Su Sunday; Sudan

sub subject; subscription; submarine; subsidiary; substitute; suburb; sub-editor; subsidy; subway

subd subdivision

subj subject (*also* **sub**)

Sub Lt Sub-Lieutenant (*also* **Sub-Lt**)

subs subscriptions

Suff Suffolk

suff sufficient; suffix

Sult Sultan

sum summer; summary

Sun Sunday

SUNFED Special United Nations Fund for Economic Development

SUNY State University of New York

sup superior; superfine; supply; supplement; supplementary; supreme

sup ben supplementary benefit

superhet supersonic heterodyne

supp supplement; supplementary (*also* **sup, suppl**)

supr supervisor

supt superintendent

Sur Surrey (*also* **Surr**)

sur surface; surplus

surg surgeon; surgery; surgical

Surr Surrey

surr surrender; surrendered; surrounds; surrounded; surrogate

surv survey; surveyor; surveying; survived

Surv Gen Surveyor General

SUS Students' Union Society; Scottish Union of Students

susp suspend; suspended

Suss Sussex

SUT Society for Underwater Technology

SV safety valve (*also* **sv**); stroke volume (automotive); *Sancta Virgo* = Holy Virgin; *Sanctitas Vestra* = Your Holiness

sv safety valve; side valve; sailing vessel; save (baseball); surrender value (*also* **s/v**)

SVD swine vesicular disease

svg saving (**svgs** = savings)

SVO Scottish Variety Orchestra

svp *s'il vous plait* = if you please

SVS still camera video system

SW southwest; southwestern; southwesterly; senior warden; South Wales; small woman (clothing); short wave; southwest London postcode (e.g. **SW10**)

Sw Sweden; Swedish

sw saltwater; seawater; seaworthy (*also* **s/w**); short wave; switch

SWA South West Africa (now Namibia)
SWACS space warning and control system
SWAG scientific wild-assed guess
SWALK sealed with a loving kiss
SWAPO South West Africa People's Organisation
s/ware software (computers)
SWAT Special Weapons and Tactics (US police unit)
Swatch Swiss watch (brand name)
SWB, **swb** short wheel base
swbd switchboard
swd sewed (bookbinding)
SWEAT Student Work Experience and Training (US career programme)
SWEB South Wales Electricity Board (former)
Swed Sweden; Swedish
SWF single white female
SwF Swiss franc
SWG standard wire gauge
SWH solar water heating
SWIE South Wales Institute of Engineers
SWIFT Society for Worldwide Interbank Financial Transmission
SWIMS Study of Women in Men's Society (USA)
Swing sterling warrant into gilts (gilt-edged stock)
Switz Switzerland
SWL safe working load
SWLA Society of Wildlife Artists
SWMF South Wales Miners' Federation
SWOA Scottish Woodland Owners' Association
SWOPS single well oil production system
SWOT strengths, weaknesses, opportunities, threats (formula used in marketing
    analysis of new products)
SWP safe working pressure
SWRB Sadler's Wells Royal Ballet (former)
SWWJ Society for Women Writers and Journalists
Sx Sussex
Sy Sydney, New South Wales (*also* **Syd**)
S Yd Scotland Yard
SYHA Scottish Youth Hostels Association
syll syllabus (*also* **syl**)
sym symptom; symbol; symbolic; symmetrical; symphony; symphonic
symp symposium
syn synonym; synthetic
sync synchronous; synchronise; synchronisation
synd syndicate; syndicated
synop synopsis

synth synthetic; synthesiser

Syr Syria

syr syrup

syst system; systematic

T

T telephone; temperature; time; Tuesday; temporary; Territory; tenor; teacher; Trinity

t table; tabulated; tabulation; taken; teaspoon(ful); tense; terminal; temperature; tenor; time; ton; tonne; town; troy (weight); turn

TA telegraphic address; Territorial Army (former); table of allowances

T/A technical assistant; temporary assistant

TAA Territorial Army Association; Trans-Australia Airlines

TAB Totalizator Agency Board (Australia and New Zealand); standard typhoid vaccine

tab table; tabulate; tabulation; tablet

TAC Tactical Air Command (USA); Technical Assistance Committee (UN); Tobacco Advisory Committee; Trades Advisory Council

tach tachometer

TACS tactical air control system

TAI *Temps atomique international* = International Atomic Time

Tai Taiwan

TAL traffic and accident loss

Tal *Talmud Tora,* Jewish laws and traditions

TALISMAN Transfer Accounting Lodgement for Investors and Stock Management

tal *qual talis qualis* = average quality

TAM television audience measurement; tactical air missile

Tam Tamil

Tamba Twins and Multiple Births Association

tan tangent

T&A tits and ass (used to describe certain magazines and tabloid newspapers); tonsils and adenoids

t&b top and bottom

T&CPA Town and Country Planning Association

T&E, t&e test and evaluation; tired and emotional (i.e. drunk)

t&g tongued and grooved (timber)

t&o taken and offered (betting)

t&p theft and pilferage

t&s, T&S toilet and shower (real estate); transport and supply

T&T Trinidad and Tobago

TANS terminal area navigation system

TAO Technical Assistance Operations (UN)

TAP Transportes Aeros Portugueses = Portuguese Airlines

TAPS Trans-Alaska Pipeline System

TAR terrain-avoidance radar

Tarmac bituminous surfacing (tar + John McAdam, pioneering roadmaker)

tarp tarpaulin

TAS true air speed (aircraft)

Tas Tasmania

TASS *Telegrafmpye Agentsvo Sovetskovo Soyuza* = Russian Press Agency

TAT transatlantic telephone cable; thematic apperception test (psychology)

TATT tired all the time (*also* **TAT**). A vague but medically recognised stress disorder

Tatts Tattersall's (Australian lottery company)

TAURUS Transfer and Automated Registration of Uncertified Stock

t-a-v *tout-a-vous* = yours ever (correspondence)

TAVR Territorial and Army Volunteer Reserve (former)

tax taxation

TB torpedo boat; Treasury Bill; trial balance; tuberculosis

tb true bearing (navigation); total bases (baseball)

TBA, tba to be announced; tyres, batteries and accessories

tb&s top, bottom and sides

TBCEP tribetachlorethyl phosphate (fire retardant)

tbcf to be called for

tbd to be decided / determined

TBI total body irradiation

T-bill Treasury bill

TBL through bill of lading

TBM temporary benchmark; tactical ballistic missile; tunnel boring machine

TBO, tbo total blackout (theatres); time between overhauls (aircraft)

T-bond Treasury bond

TBS training battle simulation; tight building syndrome

tbs tablespoon; tablespoonsful (*also* tbsp)

TBT tributyle tin (ingredient in marine paint)

TC technical college; temporary clerk; town clerk; training centre; Trinity College; tennis club; temporary constable; Transport Command; tungsten carbide; twin carburettors

tc temperature control; terra cotta; traveller's cheque; till cancelled; true course

TCA tricyclic antidepressant (drug); trichloracetic acid (herbicide)

TCA cycle tricarboxylic acid cycle (series of biochemical reactions)

TCAS Threat Alert and Collision Avoidance System (aeronautics)

TCB Thames Conservancy Board; take care of business

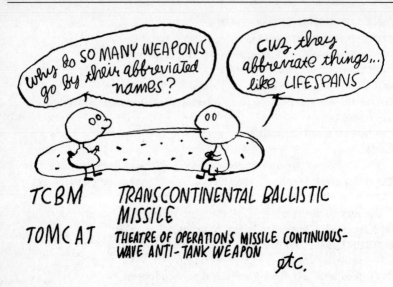

TCBM transcontinental ballistic missile

TCC Trinity College, Cambridge; Transport and Communications Commission (UN)

TCCB Test and County Cricket Board

TCD Trinity College, Dublin

T-cell T-lymphocyte

TCDD tetrachlorodibenzodioxin (environmental pollutant)

TCE trichlorethylene (solvent and anaesthetic)

TCF time correction factor; Touring Club of France

TCGF T-cell (lymphocyte) growth factor

tchr teacher

TCI Touring Club of Italy

TCM Trinity College of Music, London (*also* **TCL**)

TCO Trinity College, Oxford

TCP trichlorophenylmethyliodisalicyl (antiseptic)

TCPA Town and Country Planning Association

TD Teaching Diploma; technical drawing; *Teachta Dala* = member of the Irish *Dail*; Territorial Decoration; Tilbury Docks; Treasury Department; trust deed; Tunisian dinar

td technical data; test data; touchdown (American football)

TDB *temps dynamique barycentrique* = barycentric dynamic time

TDC Temporary Detective Constable

tdc top dead centre (engineering)

TDG twist drill gauge

T-DNA transferred deoxyribonucleic acid

TDO tornado (meteorology)

TDRS tracking and data relay satellite system

TDS tabular data stream (computers)

TE, **te** thermal efficiency; trace element; transverse electric; twin-engined (*also* **t/e**); trailing edge

TEA terminal education age (age at which individuals leave school, college or university)

TEAC Technical Education Advisory Council

TEC Training and Enterprise Council; thermal expansion coefficient

tec, **'tec** detective

tech technical; technology; technician; technique

TEF toxicity equivalence factor

TEFL teaching English as a foreign language

teg top edge gilt (bookbinding)

Teh Tehran

TEL tetraethyl lead (petrol additive)

tel telephone; telegram; telegraphic (*also* **tele**, **teleg**)

telex teleprinter exchange

telly television; television receiver

TELNET teletype network (computers)

TEM transmission electron microscopy; transverse electromagnet; Territorial Efficiency Medal

temp temperature; temporary; temporal; *tempore* = in the time of

Templar tactical expert mission planner

ten tenant; tenor

TENS transcutaneous electrical nerve stimulation

TEPP tetraethyl pyrophosphate (pesticide)

ter, **terr** terrace; territory; territorial

TERCOM terrain contour mapping

term terminal; terminate; termination; terminology

tert tertiary

TES *The Times Educational Supplement*; thermal energy storage

Tesco T E Stockwell and Sir John Cohen, supplier and founder of the supermarket chain

TESL teacher of English as a second language

Tessa Tax Exempt Special Savings Account

test testimony; testimonial; testament; testator; testatrix

T-et-G *Tarn-et-Garonne* = French department north of Haute Garonne

Tex-Mex Texan-Mexican (cuisine)

text textile

TEXT MESSAGES

Abbreviations are an integral part of computer culture, and have become very popular with both Internet and mobile phone users. Many 'text message' abbreviations have thus evolved to represent common phrases that people use while chatting to each other. Abbreviations can also be fun (and some are naughty) but the more offensive ones have been omitted in the following list.

^5	A cyber high five
1FTR	One for the road
2	To or Two
24/7	24 hours a day, 7 days aweek
2Day	Today
2Moro	Tomorrow
2U	To You
4	For or Four

A

A/S	Age/Sex?
A/S/L	Age/Sex/Location?
AAA	Any Advice Appreciated
AAMOF	As A Matter Of Fact
ADGR	All Donations Gratefully Received
ADN	Any Day Now
AFAIAA	As Far As I Am Aware
AFAIC	As Far As I'm Concerned
AFAICS	As Far As I Can See
AFAICT	As Far As I Can Tell
AFAIK	As Far As I Know
AFAIR	As Far As I Remember; As Far As I Recall
AFAIUI	As Far As I Understand It
AFK	Away From Keyboard
AIR	As I Remember; As I Recall
AISB	As I Said Before
AISI	As I See It
AIW	As It Were/Was
AMAP	As Much/Many As Possible
APAC	All Praise And Credit
ATB	All The Best

ATM	At the Moment
ATTN	Attention
ATTYOB	Anything That Turns You On Baby
AWCIGO	And Where Can I Get One
AWGTHTGTATA	Are We Going To Have To Go Through ALL This Again?
AWGTHTGTTA Again?	Are We Going To Have To Go Through This
AWHFY	Are We Having Fun Yet?
AY	Always Yours
AYT	Are You There?

B

B/C	BeCause (frequently just b/c)
B3	Blah, Blah, Blah
B4	Before
B4N	Bye for Now
BAC	By Any Chance
BAK	Back At Keyboard
BB	Be Back
BBFN	Bye Bye For Now
BBIAB	Be Back In A Bit
BBIAF	Be Back In A Few
BBIAM	Be Back In A Moment/Minute
BBIAS	Be Back In A Second
BBL	Be Back Later
BBS	Be Back Soon
BBW	Big Beautiful Women
BC	Basket Case
BCNU	Be seein' you! (saying goodbye)
BEG	Big Evil Grin
BF	Boyfriend
BFG	Big Friendly Giant
BFI	Brute Force and Ignorance
BFMI	Brute Force and Massive Ignorance
BFN	Bye For Now
BG	Big Grin (as in <bg>)
BIBO	Beer In, Beer Out
BIC	Best In Class
BICBW	But I Could Be Wrong
BIL	Brother In Law

BION	Believe It Or Not
BK	Because
BKA	Better Known As
BL	Belly Laugh
BOC	But Of Course
BOF	Birds Of a Feather
BOL	Best Of Luck
BOT	Back On Topic
BOTE	Back Of The Envelope
BOTEC	Back Of The Envelope Calculation
BRB	Be Right Back
BSG	Broad Sweeping Generalization; Big Smiling Grin
BTA	But Then Again (in response to IOW)
BTAICBW	But Then Again I could Be Wrong
BTAIM	Be That As It May
BTDT	Been There, Done That
BTDTGTTS	Been There, Done That, Got The T-Shirt
BTHOOM	Beats The Hell Out Of Me
BTOBD	Be There Or Be Dead
BTW	By The Way
BWL	Bursting With Laughter
BY	BusY
BYKT	But You Knew That
BYKTA	But You Knew That Already

C

C	See
C&G	Chuckle And Grin
C,S,G	Chuckle, Snigger, Grin
C/P/S	City or Country / Profession / Status (married/single)
CB	Call Back
CFD	Call For Discussion
CHOWUR	see (C) HOW yoU aRe
CHUR	see (C) How yoU aRe
CIC	Christ, I'm Confused
CICO	Coffee In, Coffee Out
CID	Crying In Disgrace
CIIYIMFL	Can I Include You In My Friends List?
CIO	Cut It Out

CLA	CAP LOCK ALERT
CLAB	Crying Like A Baby
CMIIW	Correct Me If I'm Wrong
CO	COnference
COB	Close Of Business
COTFLGOHAHA	Crawling On The Floor Laughing Guts Out And Having A Heart Attack
CP	Chat Post
CPF	Can Pigs Fly?
CRBT	Crying Really Big Tears
CRPG	Character (or computer) Role Playing Game
CU	see (C) yoU
CUL	see (C) yoU LateR
CUL	C (see) U (you) Later
CUL8R	see (C) yoU LateR (L8R)
CUL8TR	see (C) yoU LaTeR (L8TR)
CWYL	Chat With You Later
CYA	Cover Your Ass; see (C) YA
CYL	see (C) You Later or Catch You Later

D

D&C	Duck and Cover
D/L	Download, transmit to you
D2BU	Dressed To Be Undressed
DAY	Dreamed About You
DBA	Doing Business As
DBN	Doing Business, Not
DD	Darling Daughter
DEU	Dumb End User
DGT	Don't Go There!
DGUYDJ	Don't Give Up Your Day Job
DH	Dear Hubby; Dumb Hubby; Deaf Hubby; Darling Hubsand
DIIK	Damned If I Know
DIL	Daughter In Law
DK	Don't Know
DKU	Drop Kick Ugly
DL	Download, transmit to you
DLG	Devilish Little Grin
DLTBBB	Don't Let The Bed Bugs Bite
DNA	Did Not Answer

DNPM	Darn Near P---ed Myself
DOR	Day Of Rest
DOS	Dozing Off Soon
DQM	Don't Quote Me
DRA	Don't Recognize Acronyms
DS	Darling Son
DTA	Don't Trust Anybody
DTRT	Do The Right Thing
DUCWIC	Do You see (C) What I see (C)
DUK	Dead Upon Keyboard
DW	Darling Wife
DWB	Don't Write Back
DWIM	Do What I Mean
DWIMC	Do What I Mean, Correctly
DWIMNWIS	Do What I Mean, Not What I Say
DWISNWID	Do What I Say, Not What I Do
DWKOTA	Deep Wet Kiss On The Ass
DWKOTL	Deep Wet Kiss On The Lips
DYE	Damn Your Eyes!
DYHWIH	Do You Hear What I Hear
DYJHIW	Don't You Just Hate It When ...
DYSWIS	Do You See What I See
DYTIC	Do You Think I Care
DYTIGAD	Do You Think I Give A Damn
DYTIGAS	Do You Think I Give A Shit

E

E2EG	Ear to Ear Grin
ED	Emotionally Disturbed
EDP	Emotionally Disturbed Person
EG	Evil Grin
EIF	Exercise In Futility
EMSG	Email Message
EOB	End Of Business
EOD	End Of Discussion
EOF	End Of File
EOL	End Of Lecture
EOT	End Of Thread (i.e., don't reply to this message)
ESOSL	Endless Snorts of Stupid Laughter
ETE	Estimated Time En route

F

F2F	Face To Face
FAS	For A Second
FC	Fingers Crossed
FCFS	First Come, First Served
FCOL	For Crying Out Loud
FDROTFL	Falling Down Rolling On The Floor Laughing
FEIYD	Forever In Your Debt
FI	Forget It
FICCL	Frankly, I Couldn't Care Less
FIL	Father-in-Law
FIOFYF	Figure It Out For Yourself, F---er
FISH	First In, Still Here
FITB	Fill In The Blank
FMTEYEWTK	Far More Than Everything You've Ever Wanted To Know
FOAF	Friend Of A Friend
FOCLMAO	Fell Off Chair Laughing My Ass Off
FOR	For Obvious Reasons
FOT	Full Of Tripe
FOTCL	Falling Off The Chair Laughing
FotR	Fellowship of the Rings (a Tolkien work)
FTASB	Faster Than A Speeding Bullet
FTBOMH	From The Bottom Of My Heart
FTF	Face To Face
FTL	Faster Than Light
FUD	Fear, Uncertainty and Doubt
FWIW	For What It's Worth
FYA	For Your Amusement or For Your Attention
FYED	For Your Eyes Only
FYI	For Your Information

G

G	Grin (as in <g>)
G/F	Girlfriend
G2G	Got to Go
G2GN	Got To Go Now
G4AL	Game For A Laugh
GA	Go Ahead
GAC	Get A Clue

GAFIA	Get Away From It All
GAFM	Get Away From Me
GAG	Get A Grip
GAL	Get A Life
GBH&K	Great Big Hugs & Kisses
GBH&KB	Great Big Hugs & Kisses Back
GBTM	Get Back To Me
GBY	God Bless You
GD&H	Grinning, Ducking & Hiding
GD&R	Grinning, Ducking & Running
GD&RF	Grinning, Ducking & Running Fast!
GD&RVVF	Grinning, Ducking & Running Very Very Fast!
GD&W	Grinning, Ducking & Weaving
GF	Girlfriend
GG	Good Game
GGG	GiGGle (as in <ggg>)
GGL	Giggle
GGN	Gotta Go Now
GGP	Gotta Go Pee
GHY	God Help You
GIWIST	Gee, I Wish I'd Said That
GL	Good Luck
GLG	Goofy Little Grin
GLGH	Good Luck and Good Hunting
GMAB	Give Me A Break
GMAC	Give Me A Clue
GMBO	Giggling My Butt Off
GMTA	Great Minds Think Alike
GOK	God Only Knows
GOOML	Get Out Of My Life
GOTFIA	Groaning On The Floor In Agony
GOWI	Get On With It
GSHIWMP	Giggling So Hard I Wet My Pants
GSOVSS	Go Sit On A Very Sharp Stick
GTABO	Get That Ass Back On (in response to ROFLMAO)
GTBOS	Glad To Be Of Service
GTG	Got To Go
GTP	Gone To Pee
GTSY	Glad To See You

H

HA	Heart Attack
H&K	Hugs and Kisses
H2	How To
HAGN	Have A Good Night
HAK	Hugs And Kisses
HAND	Have A Nice Day
HHGTTG	HitchHiker's Guide To The Galaxy
HHIS	Hanging Head In Shame
HHO 1/2 K	Ha Ha Only Half Kidding
HHOJ	Ha Ha Only Joking
HHOK	Ha Ha Only Kidding
HHOS	Ha Ha Only Serious
HIAH	Help Is At Hand
HIB_	Have I Been _____?
HIG	How's It Going?
HIRTA	HereInafter Referred To As
HLV	Hasta La Vista
HLVB	Hasta La Vista, Baby
HRU	How Are You?
HSIK	How Should I Know
HSP	Highly Sensitive Person
HTB	Heavens To Betsy
HTH	Hope This Helps
HUA	Head Up Ass
HWISTKT	How Was I Supposed To Know That

I

IAC	In Any Case
IAE	In Any Event
IAH	In All Honesty
IBB	I'll Be Back
IBC	Inadequate, But Cute
IC	I see
ICB	I Care Because . . .
ICBW	I Could Be Wrong
ICIHICPCL	I Can't Imagine How I Could Possibly Care Less
ICQ	I Seek You

ICTYBTIHTKY	I Could Tell You But Then I'd Have To Kill You
ICUR	I see You Are
ICYDK	In Case You Didn't Know
IDD	InDeeD
IDGAD	I Don't Give A Damn
IDGAS	I Don't Give A S---
IDGI	I Don't Get It
IDK	I Don't Know
IDTS	I Don't Think So
IDTT	I'll Drink To That!
IHTBS	It Has To Be Shown
IHTFP	I Have Truly Found Paradise
IIABDFI	If It Ain't Broke, Don't Fix It
IIRC	If I Recall/Remember Correctly
IITYWIMIWHTKY	If I Tell You What It Means, I Will Have To Kill You
IIWY	If I Were You
IJLS	I Just Like Saying
IK	I Know
IKWYM	I Know What You Mean
ILI	I Like Ike
ILICISCOMK	I Laughed, I Cried, I Spat Coffee/Coke/Cadmium On My Keyboard
ILN	It's Looking Nice / It Looks Nice
ILSHIBAMF	I Laughed So Hard I Broke All My Furniture!
ILU	I Love yoU
ILY	I Love You
IM or Pm –	Instant or Private Message aka whisper
IMAO	In My Arrogant Opinion
IMBO	In My Biased Opinion
IMCDO	In My Conceited Dogmatic Opinion
IMCO	In My Considered Opinion
IME	In My Experience
IMHO	In My Humble Opinion
IMMOR	I Make My Own Rules
IMMSMC	If My Memory Serves Me Correctly
IMNSHO	In My Not So Humble Opinion
IMNSVHO	In My Not So Very Humble Opinion
IMO	In My Opinion
IMOBO	In My Own Biased Opinion
IMPOV	In My Point Of View
IMS	I Am Sorry or I Must Say

IMTI4U	I'm The One For You
IMU	I Miss yoU
IMVHO	In My Very Humble Opinion
INGSI	I'm Not Gonna Say It
INPO	In No Particular Order
INT	I'll Never Tell
IOW	In Other Words
IRL	In Real Life
IRMC	I Rest My Case
ISAGN	I See A Great Need
ISO	In Search Of
ISTM	It Seems To Me
ISTR	I Seem To Remember
ITAH?	Is There Anybody Here?
ITFA	In The Final Analysis
ITM	In The Meantime
ITYM	I Think You Mean
IUTKATS	I Used To Know All That Stuff
IWALU	I Will Always Love You
IWBNI	It Would Be Nice If
IWIK	I Wish I Knew
IWW or IWY	I Wonder Why
IYD	In Your Dreams
IYDMMA	If You Don't Mind Me Asking
IYKWIM	If You Know What I Mean
IYKWIMAITYD	If You Know What I Mean And I Think You Do
IYSWIM	If You See What I Mean
IYW	If You Wish

J

J/K	Just Kidding
J4G	Just For Grins
J4TR	Just For The Record
J4U	Just For You
JAM	Just A Moment; Just A Minute
JAS	Just A Second
JFF	Just For Fun
JFYI	Just For Your Information
JIC	Just In Case
JJ	Just Joking

JKU	Just Kidding You
JMO	Just My Opinion
JMOOC	Just My Opinion Of Course
JPW	Just Plain Weird
JTLYK	Just To Let You Know
JTYWTK	Just Thought You Wanted To Know

K

K	oKay
KIBO	Knowledge In, Bulls --- Out
KIC	Kiss On Cheek
KIL	Kiss on Lips
KIS	Keep It Simple
KISS	Keep It Simple Stupid
KITA	Kick In The Ass (type of therapy)
KIU	Keep It Up
KMYF	Kiss Me You Fool
KOTC	Kiss On The Cheek
KOTL	Kiss On The Lips
KUTGW	Keep Up The Good Work
KWIM	Know What I Mean?
KYHOOYA	Keep Your Head Out Of Your Ass

L

L	Laugh
L.Off	Log Off
L.On	Log On
L8R	Later
L8RG8R	Later 'Gater
LAB&TYD	Life's A Bitch & Then You Die
LHM	Lord Help Me
LHO	Laughing Head Off
LHU	Lord Help Us
LHY	Lord Help You
LJBF	Let's Just Be Friends
LLTA	Lots and Lots of Thunderous/Thundering Applause
LMA	Leave Me Alone
LMAO	Laughing My Ass Off

LMAOROTF	Laughing My Ass Off Rolling On The Floor
LMC	Lost My Connection
LMCOA	Lost My Connection Once Again
LMK	Let Me Know
LMSO	Laughing My Socks Off
LOBL -	Lots of Belly Laughs
LOI	Lack Of Interest
LOL	Laughing Out Loud; Little Old Lady
LotR	Lord of the Rings (a Tolkien work)
LSFIAB	Like Shooting Fish In A Barrel
LSHIPMP	Laughing So Hard I Peed My Pants
LSHMBB	Laughing So Hard My Belly's Bouncing
LSHMBH	Laughing So Hard My Belly Hurts
LSP	Less Sensitive Person
LTBF	Learn To Be Funny
LTIP	Laughing Til I Puke
LTMSH	Laughing Til My Sides Hurt
LTNS	Long Time, No See
LTS	Laughing To Self
LTUAE	Life, The Universe, And Everything (3rd part of THHGTTG)
LUSER	Loser USER
LUWAMH	Love You With All My Heart
LY	Love Ya!
LY4E	Love Ya Forever
LZ	Loser!

M

m/f	male or female
MAY	Mad About You
MAYB	Mad About You, Baby
MH	Mostly Harmless (5th part of THHGTTG)
MHB	My Heart Bleeds
MHB4U	My Heart Bleeds For You
MHOTY	My Hat's Off To You
MIL	Mother In Law
ML	More Later
MMIF	My Mouth Is Full
MOF	Matter Of Fact
MORF	Male Or Female
MOS	Member of the Opposite Sex

MOTAS	Member Of The Appropriate Sex
MOTD	Message Of The Day
MOTM	Member Of The Month
MOTOS	Member Of The Opposite Sex
MOTSS	Member Of The Same Sex
MS	More of the Same; (Masters Degree)
MSG	Message
MSS	Member of the Same Sex
MTF	More To Follow
MTFBWY	May The Force Be With You
MYOB	Mind Your Own Business

N

NADT	Not A Damn Thing
NAGI	Not A Good Idea
NAHM	Not A Happy Man
NAHW	Not A Happy Woman
NAVY	Never Again Volunteer Yourself
NBD	No Big Deal
NBL	Not Bloody Likely
NBTD	Nothing Better To Do
NC	No Comment
NEI	Anyone
NG	News Group
NHOH	Never Heard Of Him/Her
NIAA	No Idea At All
NIDWTC	No I Don't Want To Chat
NIH	Not Invented Here
NIMFYE	Not In My Front Yard Either
NIMTO	Not In My Term of Office
NINO	Nothing In, Nothing Out
NIT	Not In Therapy
NM	Never Mind
NN	Night Night
NOOT	Nine Out Of Ten
NOPE	Not On Planet Earth
NOYB	None Of Your Business
NP	No Problem
NPF	No Problem Found
NPLU	Not People Like Us
NQA	No Questions Asked

NQOS	Not Quite Our Sort
NTG	Not Too Good
NTH	No Therapy Helpful
NTIBOA	Not That I'm Bitter Or Anything
NTIM	Not That It Matters
NTIMM	Not That It Matters Much
NTL	NeverTheLess / NoneTheLess
NW	No Way
NWIH	No Way In Hell
NYM	New York Minute
NYP	Not Your Problem

O

O	Over (to you)
OAO	Over And Out
OATUS	On A Totally Unrelated Subject
OAUS	On An Unrelated Subject
OB	Obligatory (frequently Ob)
OBTW	Oh, By the Way
OD	Oh Dear
OIC	Oh, I see (C)
OJ	Only Joking
OK	Only Kidding
OMG	Oh My God!
ONNA	Oh No, Not Again
ONNTA	Oh No, Not This Again
OO	Over and Out
OOSOOM	Out Of Sight, Out Of Mind
OOTB	Out Of The Blue
OOTB	Out Of The Box
OPM	Other People's Money
OPP	Other People's Problems
OSIF	Oh Sugar, I Forgot!
OSIM	Oh Shoot, It's Monday
OT	Off Topic
OT1H	On The One Hand
OTBE	Over Taken By Events
OTD	Out The Door
OTF	On The Floor
OTL	Out To Lunch
OTOH	On The Other Hand; On The One Hand

OTOOH	On The Other Other Hand
OTTH	On The Third Hand
OTTOMH	Off The Top Of My Head
OTW	On The Whole
OW	Oh Well
OWTTE	Or Words To That Effect

P

PBM	Play By Mail (games)
PCB	Please Call Back
PCO	Please Carry On
PD	Public Domain
PDN	Public Data Network
PDS	Please Don't Shoot
PEBCAK	Problem Exists Between Chair And Keyboard
PF&HOMW	Printed, Framed & Hanging On My Wall
PHB	Pointy Haired Boss (from Dilbert, i.e., doesn't have a clue)
PhD	Piled Higher and Deeper
PIMP	Pee In My Pants (often in combination)
PITA	Pain In The Ass
PITBY	Put It in Their Back Yard
PKB	Pot, Kettle, Black!
PLBKAC	Problem Lies Between Keyboard And Chair
PLMOK?	Please Let Me Know, Ok?
PMBI	Pardon My Butting In
PMETC	Pardon Me ETC.
PMFBI	Pardon Me For Butting In
PMFJI	Pardon Me For Jumping In
PMFJIH	Pardon Me For Jumping In Here
PMJI	Pardon My Jumping In
PMP	Pee'd My Pants
PMYMHMMFSWGAD	Pardon Me, You Must Have Mistaken Me For Someone Who Gives a Damn
POAHF	Put On a Happy Face
POC	Prisoner Of Chat; Peeping Other Chatters
POETS	Piss Off Early/Piss On Everything, Tomorrow's Saturday
POITS	Piss On It Tomorrow's Saturday
POM	Phase Of the Moon
POP	Point Of Presence; Post Office Protocol

POSSLQ	Person of Opposite Sex Sharing Living Quarters
POV	Point Of View
POYHF	Put On Your Happy Face
PPL	PeoPLe
PPP	Petty Pet Peeve; Point to Point Protocol
PPPP	Previous Paragraph was Polemical Position
PTB	Powers That Be
PTM	Please Tell Me

Q

QED	Quite Easily Done
QOTM	Quick Off The Mark
QSL	Quite Stupid Looking
QT	Cutie
QT	QuieT
QTP	Cutie Pie

R

R	Are
RA	Research Assistant; Resident Assistant
RAK	Random Act of Kindness
RFC	Request For Comments
RFD	Request For Discussion
RFT	Request For Thinking
RIP	Rest In Peace
RL	Real Life
RLCO	Real Life COnference
RNA	Ring, No Answer
ROFFNAR	Rolling On the Floor For No Apparent Reason
ROFL	Rolling On the Floor Laughing
ROFLAHMSL	Rolling On the Floor Laughing And Holding My Sides Laughing
ROFLAPMP	Rolling On Floor Laughing And Peeing My Pants
ROFLAPMPWTIME	Rolling On Floor Laughing And Peeing My Pants With Tears In My Eyes
ROFLASC	Rolling On the Floor Laughing And Scaring the Cat

ROFLASTC	Rolling On the Floor Laughing And Scaring The Cat
ROFLGO	Rolling On Floor Laughing Guts Out!
ROFLOL	Rolling On the Floor Laughing Out Loud
ROFLOLVH	Rolling On the Floor Laughing Out Loud Very Hard
ROFLUTS	Rolling On the Floor, Unable To Speak
ROFTTPOF	Rolling On the Floor Trying To Put Out Flames
ROTF	Rolling On The Floor
ROTFL	Rolling On The Floor Laughing
ROTFLAHMS	Rolling On The Floor Laughing And Holding My Side
ROTFLMAAOBPO	Rolling On The Floor Laughing My Ass And Other Body Parts Off
RotK	Return of the King (a Tolkien work)
ROTM	Right On The Money
RPG	Role Playing Games
RSN	Real Soon Now
RT	Real Time
RTI	Real Time Interruption
RTS	Read The Screen
RUMF	aRe yoU Male or Female?
RUOK?	Are You Ok?

S

S	Smile
S/O	SomeOne (frequently just s/o)
S/TH	SomeTHing (frequently just s/th)
S^	S'Up (What's Up)
S2BX	Soon To Be eX
SAYOR	Speak At Your Own Risk
SBB	Stupid Beyond Belief
SCNR	Sorry, Could Not Resist
SDI	So Do I
SDIHTT	SomeDay I'll Have The Time
SEP	Somebody Else's Problem
SETE	Smiling Ear to Ear
SFT	Sorry For That
SHLH	Sitting Here Laughing Hysterically
SHTSI	Somebody Had To Say It

SICS	Sitting In Chair Snickering
SIG	Special Interest Group
SIIN	Stuffed If I Know!
SIL	Son In Law
SITD	Still In The Dark
SLATFATF	So Long, And Thanks For All The Fish (4th part of THHGTTG)
SMO	Serious Mode On
SMOFF	Serious Mode OFF
SNERT	Snot-Nosed Egotistical Rude Teenager
SO	Significant Other
SOH	Sense Of Humour
SOHF	Sense Of Humour Failure
SorG	Straight Or Gay
SOSO	Same Old, Same-Old
SOT	Short Of Time
SOTMG	Short of Time Must Go
SOVS	SomeOne Very Special
SPK2M	Speak To Me
SSIA	Subject Says It All
ST	Star Trek; Such That (frequently just s.t.)
STB	Simply The Best
STBY	Sucks To Be You
STS	So To Speak
SUFID	Screwing Up Face In Disgust
SUNOILTY	Shut Up, No One Is Listening To You
SUP?	What's Up?
SUYP	Shut Up You Pervert
SW	SoftWare; So What?; Says Who?; StarWars
SWL	Screaming With Laughter
SWMBO	She Who Must Be Obeyed
SWYP	So What's Your Problem?
SYS	See You Soon
SYT	Sweet Young Thing

T

T	Tea
T/Y	Thank You
T2YL	Talk To You Later
TA	Thanks Again
TAF	That's All, Folks!

TAFN	That's All For Now
TAL	Thanks A Lot
TANJ	There Ain't No Justice
TANSTAAFL	There Ain't No Such Thing As A Free Lunch
TAT	Turn Around Time
TBC	To Be Continued
TBE	To Be Expected
TBH	To Be Honest
TBYB	Try Before You Buy
TC	Telephone Call; Take Care
TCB	Taking Care of Business
TCBY	Taking Care of Business, Ya'll
TCOY	Take Care Of Yourself
TDM	Too Damn Many
TEOTWAWKI	The End Of The World As We Know It
TFTT	Thanks For The Thought
TGAL	Think Globally, Act Locally
TGAWE	Totally Gorgeous And Well Educated
TGTF	Thank God Tomorrow's Friday
THHGTTG	The HitchHiker's Guide To The Galaxy
THNQ	Thank You
TIA	Thanks In Advance
TIATLG	Truly, I Am The Living God
TIC	Tongue In Cheek
TIE	Take It Easy
TILII	Tell It Like It Is
TIME	Tears In My Eyes (often in combination)
TIMTOWTDI	There Is More Than One Way To Do It
TINALO	This Is Not A Legal Opinion
TINAR	This Is Not A Recommendation
TINSTAAFL	There Is No Such Thing As A Free Lunch
TINWIS	That Is Not What I Said
TIP	To Insure Promptness
TLG	The Living God
TMI	Too Much Information
TMIKTLIU	The More I Know, The Less I Understand
TMTT	Too Much To Type
TNOTVS	There's Nothing On Television, So ...
TNT	Till Next Time
TNTL	Trying Not To Laugh
TNX	Thanks (as in ThaNX)
TOY	Thinking Of You
TPAE	The Possibilities Are Endless

TPTB	The Powers That Be
TRDMC	Tears Running Down My Cheeks
TSOHF	Total Sense Of Humour Failure
TT4S	Try This For Size
TTBE	That's To Be Expected
TTBOMK	To The Best Of My Knowledge
TTL4N	That's The Lot For Now
TTUL	Talk (or Type) To you Later
TTYL	Talk To You Later
TTYRS	Talk To You Real Soon
TTYS	Talk To You Soon
TWIMC	To Whom It May Concern
TWYAS	That's What You All Say
TWYT	That's What You Think
TYLE	Took You Long Enough
TYVL, YWEL	Thank You Very Little, You're Welcome Even Less
TYVM	Thank You Very Much

U

U	You
U/L	Upload, send to the BBS
u/l	upload, send to the BBS
UBD	User Brain Damage
UDS	Ugly Domestic Scene
UL	Upload, send to the BBS
ULC	You'll See
UNA	Use No Acronyms
UOK	yoU OK?
URLCM	yoU aRe weLCoMe
UTC	Under The Counter; Coordinated Universal Time
UTT	Under The Table

V

VBG	Very Big Grin (as in <vbg>)
VC	Virtual Community
VGI	Very Good Idea
VH	Virtual Hug

VM	Very Much
VR	Virtual Reality
VT	Virtual Time

W

W	Wink
W/	With (frequently just w/)
W/O	WithOut (frequently just w/o)
w/o	without
W8	Wait
W8ING	WaitING
WAB?	What, Another Bill?
WABOL	What A Bunch Of Losers
WADR	With All Due Respect
WAEF	When All Else Fails
WAIDW	What Am I Doing Wrong
WAY?	Who Are You?
WB	Welcome Back
WBS	Write Back Soon
WCAGA	What Comes Around, Goes Around
WDYMBT	What Do (or Did) You Mean By That?
WDYTARAJ	Why Don't You Take A Run And Jump
WDYTYA	Who Do You Think You Are!
WFHIT	What Fresh Hell Is This? (from the writings of Dorothy Parker)
WFM	Works For Me
WHYD	What Have You Done
WIBAMU	Well I'll Be A Monkey's Uncle
WIBNIF	Wouldn't If Be Nice IF...
WMMOWS	Wash My Mouth Out With Soap
WOA	Work Of Art
WOFTAM	Waste Of Flaming Time And Money
WOM	Word Of Mouth
WOMBAT	Waste Of Money, Brains, And Time
WRT	With Regard To; With Respect To
WSD	Willing Suspension of Disbelief
WTG	Way To Go
WTGD	Way To Go Dude!
WTH	What The Hell (or Heck)
WUASTC	Wake Up And Smell The Coffee

WYBMADIITY	Will You Buy Me A Double If I Tell You?
WYGIWYG	What You Got Is What You Get
WYGIWYPF	What You Get Is What You Pay For
WYLABOCTGWTR	Would You Like A Bowl Of Cream To Go With That Remark?
WYLASOMWTC	Would You Like A Saucer Of Milk With That Comment?
WYMM?	Will You Marry Me?
WYP	What's Your Point?
WYSBANRTWYG	What You See Bears Absolutely No Relation To What You Get
WYSBYGI	What You See Before You Get It
WYSOH	Where's Your Sense Of Humor?
WYTYSYDG	What You Thought You Saw, You Didn't Get

X

X	Extra
XH	Extra Hot
XHNS	Extra Hot N Spicy
XLNT	Excellent

Y

Y	Why
Y3	Yadda Yadda Yadda
YAC	are You Available to Chat?
YAFIYGI	You Asked For It, You Got It
YANETUT	You Are Not Expected To Understand This
YAP	Yet Another Ploy
YBS	You'll Be Sorry
YCLIU	You Can Look It Up
YG	Young Gentleman
YGM	You've Got Mail
YGP	You've Got Post
YGTBK	You've Got To Be Kidding
YGWYPF	You'll Get What You Pay For
YHB_	You Have Been _____
YHBW	You Have Been Warned
YHL	You Have Lost
YHTBT	You Had To Be There

YKIYEI	You Killed It, You Eat It
YKWIM	You Know What I Mean
YKYB	You Know You've Been
YKYB_TLW	You Know You've Been _____ing Too Long When . . .
YL	Young Lady
YM	Young Man
YM	You Mean
YOYO	You're On Your Own
YR	Yeah Right
YSS	You Suck Severely
YW	You're Welcome
YWHOL	Yelling WooHoo Out Loud
YWSYLS	You Win Some, You Lose Some

Z

ZIAO	Zoning In and Out
ZZZ	Sleeping

TF, tf tax free; thin film (**TFR** = thin film transistor); *travaux forces* = hard labour (prison sentence)

TFA Tenant Farmers' Association; total fatty acids

tfr transfer

TG Tate Gallery, London; thank God!; transformational grammar; Translators' Guild

tg type genus

TGAT Task Group on Assessment and Testing (Education)

TGB *Très Grande Bibliothèque* = planned new French National Library

TGI Target Group Index

TGIF Thank God it's Friday

TGT turbine gas temperature

tgt target

TGV *train à grande vitesse* = French high-speed passenger train

TGWU Transport and General Workers' Union

TH Trinity House, London (**TLWM** = Trinity House Low Water Mark; **THWM** = Trinity House High Water Mark); town hall; *Technische Hochschule* = German technical college

Th Thursday; Theatre

th hyperbolic tangent; thermal

ThB Bachelor of Theology

THC tetrahydrocannabinol (active agent in cannabis)

THD total harmonic distortion
ThD Doctor of Theology
theol theology; theological
theor theory; theorem
therm thermometer
THES *The Times Higher Education Supplement*
THF Trust-house Forte
THI temperature-humidity index
tho, tho' though
thoro thoroughfare
thou thousand
THR total hip replacement
3i Investors In Industry
3M Minnesota Mining and Manufacturing Company (USA)
3Rs readin', 'ritin' and 'rithmetic
thro, thro' through (*also* **thru** in the USA)
Thur Thursday
TI Texas Instruments Corporation (USA); thermal imaging; technical inspection
T/I target indicator/identification
TIA Tax Institute of America; transient ischemic attack (stroke)
Tib Tibet; Tibetan
TIBOR Tokyo Inter-bank Offered Rate
TIC taken into consideration; total inorganic carbon; tourist information centre
TIF *Transports Internationaux par Chemin de Fer* = International Railway Transport; telephone interference
TIFF tagged image file format
TIGR Treasury Investment Growth Receipts (bonds)
TIG welding tungsten inert gas welding
TILS Technical Information and Library Service
TIM time is money; transient intermodulation distortion
timp timpani
TIMS The Institute of Management Sciences
TIN taxpayer identification number
tinct tincture
TIO Technical Information Officer
TIR *Transports Internationaux Routiers* = International Road Transport
TIRC Tobacco Industry Research Committee
TIROS television and infrared observation satellite
TIS technical information service
'tis it is
tit title; titular
TJ triple jump (athletics)
Tk Bangladeshi taka (monetary unit)
TKO, tko technical knockout (boxing)

tks thanks (*also* thnks)

tkt ticket

TL thermoluminescence; transmission line; Turkish lira

T/L total loss; time loan; trade list

TLC tender loving care (but also 'total lack of concern'!); total lung capacity; Trades and Labour Council (Australia)

tld tooled (bookbinding)

TLO Technical Liaison Officer

TLR twin lens reflex (camera)

tlr tailor; teller; trailer

TLS *The Times Literary Supplement*

TLs typed letter, signed

TM trademark; transcendental meditation; Their Majesties; technical memorandum; tone modulation; transverse magnetic; tropical medicine; true mean (*also* **tm**)

TMA Theatrical Management Association; Trans-Mediterranean Airways

T-men US Treasury law enforcement agents

tmbr timber

TMJ temporomandibular joint dysfunction

TML three-mile limit (shipping); tetramethyl lead

TMS temporomandibular syndrome

TMV tobacco mosaic virus; true mean value

TN true north

tn telephone number; ton; tonne; town; train; transportation

T-note Treasury note (in USA)

TNP *Théâtre National Populaire* = French national theatre

TNT 2-4-6 trinitrotoluene (explosive)

T-number total light transmission number (cameras)

TO take-off; turnover (*also* **t/o**); telegraphic order; technical officer; transport officer

T/O turnover (*also* **t/o**)

TOB temporary office building

ToB Tour of Britain (cycling race)

tob tobacco

TocH Christian help organisation founded in 1915 by the Rev 'Tubby' Clayton. **Toc** = old Army signal for the letter **T**, for Talbot House, the movement's headquarters in London

TOD time of delivery; The Open Door (organisation for phobia sufferers)

TOE theory of everything

TOET test of elementary training

Tok Tokyo

TOL Tower of London

TOM *territoire d'outre mer* = French overseas territory

tom tomato

TOMCAT Theatre of Operations Missile Continuous-wave Anti-tank Weapon

TOMS Total Ozone Mapping Spectrometer

TON total organic nitrogen

tonn tonnage

TOP temporarily out of print

TOPIC Teletext Output Price Information Computer

topog topography

TOPS Training Opportunities Scheme

Tor Toronto

torn tornado

torp torpedo

TOS temporarily out of service / stock

Toshiba Tokyo Shibaura Electrics Corporation

tot total

tote totalisator

TOTP Top of the Pops (TV programme)

tour tourist; tourism

tourn tournament (*also* tourney)

tox toxicology; toxicologist (*also* toxicol)

TP, tp taxpayer; to pay; test panel; town planner; title page; true position; third party; treaty port; *tout payé* = all expenses paid; *tempo primo* = at the original tempo; *tempore Paschale* = at Easter

TPC Trade Practices Commission (Australia); The Peace Corps (USA)

TPI tax and price index; threads per inch; totally and permanently incapacitated

TPO Tree Preservation Order; travelling post office

TPR temperature, pulse and respiration

Tpr Trooper

TPS toughened polystyrene

tpt trumpet

TQM total quality management

TR Territorial Reserve; *tempore regis / reginae* = in the time of the king / queen; test run; tracking radar; Theodore Roosevelt (US president); trust receipt

T/R transmitter / receiver (*also* **TR** = transmit-receive)

tr trace; track; tragedy; train; trainee; transaction; transfer; translate; translation; translator; transport; transpose; treasurer; truck; trust; trustee

trad traditional (**trad jazz** = traditional jazz); *traduttore* = translator; *traduzione* = translation

TRADA Timber Research and Development Association (*also* **TRDA**)

trag tragedy

trannie transistor radio

Trans Transvaal

trans transaction; transfer; transferred; transit; transitive; translated; translation; translator; transparent; transport; transpose (*also* **tr**); transverse

trav travel; traveller

TRC Thames Rowing Club; Tobacco Research Council

tr co trust company

Trd Trinidad (*also* **Trin**)

Treas Treasury; Treasurer

TRF tuned radio frequency (*also* **trf**)

trf tariff

trg training

TRH Their Royal Highnesses

trib tribal; tributary

Tribeca Triangle Below Canal Street (New York City neighbourhood)

TRIC trachoma inclusion conjunctivitis

trig trigonometry; trigonometric

Trin Trinidad; Trinity College (Oxford); Trinity Hall (Cambridge)

trip tripos (final examination for Cambridge University honours degree)

TRM trademark

TRNC Turkish Republic of Northern Cyprus

TRO temporary restraining order

trom trombone (*also* **tromb**)

trop tropical (**trop med** = tropical medicine)

trs transfer; transpose

TRSB time reference scanning beam

TRSR taxi and runway surveillance radar

TS Television Society; Theosophical Society; Tourette's syndrome; training ship; Treasury Solicitor; test summary; tough shit

ts, TS tensile strength; till sale; twin screw; typescript; temperature switch

TSA time series analysis; total surface area

TSB Trustee Savings Bank

TSE Tokyo Stock Exchange; Toronto Stock Exchange; transmissible spongiform encephalopathy

TSgt Technical Sergeant

TSH thyroid stimulating hormone (thyrotropin)

TSO Trading Standards Officer

tsp teaspoon; teaspoonful

TSR tactical strike reconnaissance; Trans-Siberian Railway

TSS toxic shock syndrome; time-sharing system; twin screw steamship

TSSA Transport Salaried Staff's Association

TSU, tsu this side up

tsvp *tournez s'il vous plaît* = please turn over

TT Tourist Trophy (Isle of Man TT motorcycle races); technical training; teetotaller; telegraphic transfer; tetanus toxoid; Trust Territories; tuberculin-tested (milk)

TTA Travel Trade Association

TTC teachers' training course; Technical Training Command

TTF Timber Trade Federation

TTFN Ta-ta for now (catchphrase of 1940s' radio star Tommy Handley, and later of American TV comedy character Sergeant Bilko)

TTL, ttl through-the-lens (cameras); transistor-transistor logic

TTT Tyne Tees Television, Newcastle upon Tyne; team time trial

TTTC Technical Teachers' Training College

TU trade union; thermal unit; transmission unit; Tupolev (range of Russian aircraft, e.g. supersonic TU-144)

Tu Tuesday (*also* **Tue**)

TUAC Trade Union Advisory Committee

tub tubular

TUC Trades Union Congress

TUCC Transport Users' Consultative Committee

TUCGC Trades Union Congress General Council

turb turbine; turboprop

Turk Turkey; Turkish

TURP Transurethral resection of the prostate

turps turpentine

TV, tv television; television receiver; test vehicle; terminal velocity

TVA Tennessee Valley Authority (USA); *taxe à la valeur ajoutée* = French value-added tax

TVP textured vegetable protein

TVR television rating (audience measurement)

TVRO television receive only (antennae)

TW, tw tail wind; travelling wave (TV antennae)

T/W three-wheel (vehicle)

TWA Thames Water Authority; Trans-World Airlines

TWN teleprinter weather network

2,4,5-T 2,4,5-trichlorophenoxyacetic acid (herbicide)

TWOC taking without owner's consent (police term for car theft); also **TAWOC** = taken away without owner's consent

TW3 That Was The Week That Was (1960s' BBC satire programme)

TWU Transport Workers' Union (USA)

TYC Thames Yacht Club; two-year-old course (racing)

TYO, tyo two-year-old (racing)

typ typical; typing; typist; typography; typographer

typh typhoon

typo typographical error; typography

typw typewriter; typewritten

U

U Universal Certificate (movies that may be seen by children unaccompanied by adults); university; united; unionist; upper class (as in **U** and **non-U** for acceptability); Burmese equivalent of Mr; you (as in **IOU** = I owe you); unit; unsatisfactory; urinal

u unit; unsatisfactory; *und* = and (German)

UA United Artists Corporation (Hollywood); under age

U/a underwriting account

UAA United Arab Airlines

UAB Universities Appointments Board

UAC Ulster Automobile Club

UAE United Arab Emirates

UAL United Airlines

UAM underwater-to-air missile

u&lc upper and lower case (printing)

u&o use and occupancy

UAOD United Ancient Order of Druids (friendly society)

UAP United Australia Party

UAR United Arab Republic

UARS upper atmosphere research satellite

UART universal asynchronous receiver-transmitter

uas upper airspace

UAU Universities Athletic Union

UAW United Automobile Workers (USA)

UB United Brethren

UBA ultrasonic bone analysis

UBC University of British Columbia

UBF Union of British Fascists

UB-40 registration card issued to the unemployed

U-boat *Unterseeboot* = submarine

UBR Uniform Business Rate (tax); University Boat Race (annually between Cambridge and Oxford)

UBS United Bible Societies

UC University College; urban council; under construction; under cover; uterine contraction

Uc film and video classification suitable for and of interest to children

uc upper case (printing)

u/c undercharged

UCA United Chemists' Association

UCAE Universities' Council for Adult Education

UCAS Universities and Colleges Admissions Service

UCATT Union of Construction, Allied Trades and Technicians

UCBSA United Cricket Board of South Africa

UCC Universal Copyright Convention; Union Carbide Corporation

UCD University College, Dublin

UCH University College Hospital, London

UCHD usual childhood diseases (*also* **UCD**)

UCI *Union cycliste internationale* = International Cyclists' Union; University of California at Irvine

UCL University College, London

ucl, UCL upper cylinder lubricant

UCLA University of California at Los Angeles

UCM University Christian Movement

UCMSM University College and Middlesex School of Medicine

UCNW University College of North Wales

UCR unconditioned response (psychology)

UCS University College School, London; unconditioned stimulus (psychology)

UCSB University of California at Santa Barbara

UCSD University of California at San Diego

UCSW University College of South Wales

UCTA United Commercial Travellers' Association (former)

UCW Union of Communication Workers; University College of Wales

UD United Dairies

UDA Ulster Defence Association

UDC Urban District Council; universal decimal classification; Urban Development Corporation; United Daughters of the Confederacy (USA)

udc upper dead centre (engineering)

UDCA Urban District Councils' Association

UDF Ulster Defence Force; United Democratic Front (South Africa)

UDI Unilateral Declaration of Independence

UDM Union of Democratic Mineworkers

UDP United Democratic Party

UDR Ulster Defence Regiment

UEA University of East Anglia; Universal Esperanto Association

UED University Education Diploma

UEFA Union of European Football Associations

UER university entrance requirements; *Union Européenne de Radio-diffusion* = European Broadcasting Union; unsatisfactory equipment report

UF United Free Church of Scotland (*also* **UFC**); urea formaldehyde

UFA unsaturated fatty acid

UFC University Funding Council

UFCW United Food and Commercial Workers International (USA)

UFF Ulster Freedom Fighters

UFI University for Industry

UFFI urea formaldehyde foam insulation

UFO unidentified flying object

UFTAA Universal Federation of Travel Agents' Associations

UFU Ulster Farmers' Union

u/g underground
UGWA United Garment Workers of America
UHF, **uhf** ultra-high frequency
UHT, **uht** ultra-high temperature; ultra-heat-treated (as for milk)
UHV, **uhv** ultra-high voltage; ultra-high vacuum
U/I, **u/i** under instruction
UJ universal joint; union jack (**UJC** = Union Jack Club, London)
UK United Kingdom
UKAEA United Kingdom Atomic Energy Authority
UKAPE United Kingdom Association of Professional Engineers
UKBG United Kingdom Bartenders' Guild
UKCOSA United Kingdom Council for Overseas Students' Affairs
UKDA United Kingdom Dairy Association
UKLF United Kingdom Land Forces
UKOTS United Kingdom Overseas Territories (formerly the unfortunately abbreviated **BOTS** = British Overseas Territories)
UKPA United Kingdom Pilots' Association

UK Postcodes

Aberdeen	AB	Harrow	HA
Bath	BA	Harrowgate	HG
Belfast	BT	Hemel Hempstead	HP
Birmingham	B	Hereford	HR
Blackburn	BB	Huddersfield	HD
Blackpool	FY	Hull	HU
Bolton	BL	Ilford	IG
Bournemouth	BH	Inverness	IV
Bradford	BD	Ipswich	IP
Brighton	BN	Kilmarnock	KA
Bristol	BS	Kingston-upon-Thames	KT
Bromley	BR	Kirkcaldy	KY
Cambridge	CB	Kirkwall	KW
Canterbury	CT	Lancaster	LA
Cardiff	CF	Leeds	LS
Carlisle	CA	Leicester	LE
Chelmsford	CM	Lerwick	ZE
Chester	CH	Lincoln	LN
Cleveland	TS	Liverpool	L
Colchester	CO	Llandrindod Wells	LD
Coventry	CV	Llandudno	LL
Crewe	CW	London, East Central	EC

Croydon	CR	London, East	E
Darlington	DL	London, North	N
Dartford	DA	London, Northwest	NW
Derby	DE	London, Southeast	SE
Doncaster	DN	London, Southwest	SW
Dorchester	DT	London, West Central	WC
Dudley	DY	London, West	W
Dumfries	DG	Luton	LU
Dundee	DD	Manchester	M
Durham	DH	Medway	ME
Edinburgh	EH	Milton Keynes	MK
Enfield	EN	Motherwell	ML
Exeter	EX	Newcastle upon Tyne	NE
Falkirk	FK	Newport	NP
Galashiels	TD	Northampton	NN
Glasgow	G	Norwich	NR
Gloucester	GL	Nottingham	NG
Halifax	HX	Oldham	OL
Oxford	OX	Stoke-on-Trent	ST
Paisley	PA	Sunderland	SR
Perth	PH	Sutton	SM
Peterborough	PE	Swansea	SA
Plymouth	PL	Swindon	SN
Portsmouth	PO	Taunton	TA
Preston	PR	Telford	TF
Reading	RG	Tonbridge	TN
Redhill	RH	Torquay	TQ
Romford	RM	Truro	TR
Salisbury	SP	Twickenham	TW
Sheffield	S	Wakefield	WF
Shrewsbury	SY	Walsall	WS
Slough	SL	Warrington	WA
Southall	UB	Watford	WD
Southampton	SO	Wigan	WN
Southend-on-Sea	SS	Wolverhampton	WV
Stevenage	SG	Worcester	WR
Stockport	SK	York	YO

Ukr Ukraine
UL university library; upper limb; upper limit
ULCC ultralarge crude carrier (bulk oil)
ULF, ulf ultra low frequency
ULM ultrasonic light modulator; universal logic module

ULS, **uls** unsecured loan stock

ULSEB University of London School Examinations Board

ult ultimate; ultimately; *ultimo* = during the previous month

um, **u/m** unmarried

UMF Umbrella Makers' Federation

UMFC United Methodist Free Churches

UMi Ursa Minor (**UMa** = Ursa Major)

UMIST University of Manchester Institute of Science and Technology

ump umpire

UMTS Universal Mobile Telephone System

UN United Nations

un united; unified; union; unsatisfactory

unauth unauthorised

UNB universal navigation beacon

unclas unclassified (*also* **unclass**)

UNCLE United Network Command for Law Enforcement (from the fictional TV programme, *The Man from U.N.C.L.E*)

uncir uncirculated (numismatics)

uncond unconditional

uncor uncorrected

undergrad undergraduate

undtkr undertaker

unexpl unexplained; unexplored; unexploded

uni university (*also* **univ**)

unif uniform

Unit Unitarian

UNITA *Uniao Nacionale para a Independencia Total de Angola* = National Union for the Total Independence of Angola

UNIVAC universal automatic computer

unkn unknown

unm unmarried

unop unopened

UNP United National Party (Sri Lanka)

unpd unpaid

unpub unpublished

unsat unsaturated; unsatisfactory

uoc ultimate operating capacity/capability

UOD ultimate oxygen demand

UP United Press; United Presbyterian; Union Pacific; University Press; Uttar Pradesh (India); Ulster Parliament; unsaturated polyester/polymer

up, **u/p** underproof (alcoholic content)

UPA United Productions of America (film studio)

UPC universal product code (bar code); Universal Postal Convention

upd unpaid

UPF untreated polyurethane foam
UPGC University and Polytechnic Grants Committee
uphol upholstery
UPI United Press International
UPNI Unionist Party of Northern Ireland
UPOA Ulster Public Officers' Association
UPR unearned premiums reserve; Union Pacific Railroad (USA)
UPS United Parcel Service; uninterruptible power supply (computers)
UPU Universal Postal Union
UPUP Ulster Popular Unionist Party
UR unconditoned reflex/response (psychology)
Ur Uruguay; Urdu (*also* **Urd**)
URBM ultimate range ballistic missile
URC United Reformed Church
urg urgent; urgently
URI upper respiratory infection (**URTI** = upper respiratory tract infection)
URL Unilever Research Laboratory; uniform resource locator
urol urology; urologist
US United States (**US66** = United States Highway Route 66); ultrasonic; ultrasound; Undersecretary; unconditioned stimulus
u/s, U/S unserviceable; unsaleable
USA United States of America
USA/ABF United States of America Amateur Boxing Federation
USAC United States Air Corps; United States Auto Club
USAEC United States Atomic Energy Commission
USAF United States Air Force
USAFE United States Air Forces in Europe
USAID United States Agency for International Development
USB universal serial bus
USC Ulster Special Constabulary; United Services Club; United States Congress; University of Southern California
USCG United States Coast Guard
USDA United States Department of Agriculture
USDAW Union of Shop, Distributive and Allied Workers
usf *und so fort* = and so on, etc (**usw** = *und so weiter* = and so forth)
USFL United States Football League
USG United States Government; United States Standard Gauge (railroads)
USGA United States Golf Association
US gall United States gallon
USGS United States Geological Survey
USh Uganda shilling
USIS United States Information Service
USLTA United States Lawn Tennis Association
USM unlisted securities market; underwater-to-surface missile; United States Mail; United States Marines; United States Mint

USMA United States Military Academy

USMC United States Marine Corps

USN United States Navy

USNA United States Naval Academy

USNR United States Naval Reserve

USO United Service Organisation (USA)

USP unique selling proposition (advertising); United States patent (also **USPat**); United States Pharmacopeia

USPC Ulster Society for the Preservation of the Countryside

USPG United Society for the Propagation of the Gospel

USPO United States Post Office (**USPS** = United States Postal Service)

USS United States Ship/Steamship; Undersecretary of State; United States Senate; Universties Superannuation Scheme

USSR Union of Soviet Socialist Republics

USTA United States Tennis Association

usu usual, usually

USVI United States Virgin Islands

USW, usw ultrashort wave

UT unit trust; universal time; urinary tract; Union Territory (India)

ut utility; user test

UTA *Union de Transports Aeriens* (French airline); Ulster Transport Authority; Unit Trust Association

UTC universal time coordinated

Utd United

UTDA Ulster Tourist Development Association

ute utility (Australian pick-up truck)

U3A University of the Third Age

UTI urinary tract infection

UTS ultimate tensile strength

UTWA United Textile Workers of America

UU Ulster Unionist

UUUC United Ulster Unionist Council

UUUP United Ulster Unionist Party

uuV *unter ublichen Vorbehelt* = errors and omissions excepted

UV ultraviolet (**UV-A** = radiation with wavelength of 320–380nm; **UV-B** = radiation with wavelength of 280–320nm)

UVAS ultraviolet astronomical satellite

UVF Ulster Volunteer Force

UVL ultraviolet light

UW, uw underwater; unladen weight

UWA University of Western Australia

UWC Ulster Workers' Council

UWIST, Uwist University of Wales Institute of Science and Technology

UXB unexploded bomb

Uz Uzbekistan

V

V Venerable, Vice, Very (in titles); Viscount; the Roman numeral 5; *Via* = Italian street; Vicar; verb; volume; volt; voltmeter; Volunteer

v vacuum; valley; vale; valve; vein; ventral; verb; verse; velocity; version; verso (printing and numismatics); versus; vertical; very; via; vide; vicarage; vice (in titles); village; violin; virus; visibility; vocative (grammar); voice; volcano; volume; *von* = of in German name; vowel

VA Royal Order of Victoria and Albert; value-added; Veterans' Administration (USA); Voice of America (radio); value analysis

va value analysis; verb active; viola

VABF Variety Artists' Benevolent Fund

vac vacant; vacancy; vacation; vacuum

vacc vaccine; vaccination

VAD Voluntary Aid Detachment (to the Red Cross)

VADAS voice-activated domestic appliance system

V-Adm Vice-Admiral

vag vagrant; vagrancy; vagina

val valuation; valued; valley

valid validation

Valpo Valparaiso

van advantage (tennis); vanguard; vanilla

Vanc Vancouver

V&A Victoria and Albert Museum, London

v&t vodka and tonic

V&V, v&v verification and validation (computers)

VAPI visual approach path indicator (aeronautics)

vap prf vapour proof

var variable; variation; variant; variety; various; visual aural range (also **VAR**)

Varig *Empresa de Viacao Aerea Rio Grandense* = Brazilian national airline (*also* **VARIG**)

varn varnish

varsity university

vas vasectomy

VASARI Visual Art System for Archiving and Retrieval of Images (computers)

vasc vascular

VASI visual approach slope indicator (aeronautics)

VAT value-added tax

Vat Vatican

VATE versatile automatic test equipment

vaud vaudeville

VAV variable air volume

VAWT vertical axis wind turbine

vb verb (**vbl** = verbal)

VBI vertebronasilar insufficiency

VC Victoria Cross; Vatican City; Vice-Chairman; Vice-Chancellor; Vice Consul; Vickers Commercial aircraft (e.g. **VC10**, etc); Viet Cong; venture capital; vinyl chloride; vapour compression

vc violoncello; cello; visual communication

VCA vinyl carbonate

VCC Veteran Car Club of Great Britain

VCCS voltage controlled current source

VCE variable-cycle engine

Vce Venice

VCG Vice Consul-General; vertical centre of gravity

VCM vinyl chloride monomer (plastic)

VCO voltage-controlled oscillator

VCR video casette recorder / recording; visual control room (airports)

Vcr Vancouver

VD venereal disease; vascular dementia

vd void

V-Day Victory Day (*see* **VE Day**, **VJ Day**)

VDC Volunteer Defence Corps

VDH valvular disease of the heart

VDI virtual device interface (computers)

VDP *vin de pays* = quality French local wine (*see* **VDQS**, **AOC**)

VDQS *vins délimités de qualité supérieure* = high-quality French wine classification (*see* **AOC**, **VDP**)

VDT visual display terminal

VDU visual display unit

VE Day Victory in Europe Day (8 May 1945)

veg vegetables (*also* **veggies**), vegetarian; vegetation

veh vehicle; vehicular

V8 auto engine with eight cylinders arranged in V-formation (*also* **V2**, **V4**, **V6**, **V12** and **V16**)

vel vellum; velocity; velvet

Velcro *velours* + *croche* = hooked velvet (Swiss-invented fastener)

Ven Venerable; Venice; Venetian; Venus; Venezuela

ven veneer; venereal; venison; ventral; ventricle; *vendredi* = Friday; venomous

vent ventilation; ventriloquist

Ver *Verein* = German company or association)

ver version; verify; verification; verse; vermilion (*also* **verm**); vertical

VERA versatile reactor assembly
verb et lit *verbum et literatim* = word for word, letter for letter
verb sap *verbum sapienti sat est* = a word is enough for the wise (also **verb sat**)
Verl *Verlag* = publisher
verm vermiculite; vermilion
vern vernacular
vers version (*also* **ver**)
vert vertebra; vertical
Very Rev Very Reverend
vet veterinary surgeon; veteran
Vet Admin Veterans' Administration (USA)
VetMB Bachelor of Veterinary Medicine
vet sci veterinary science
VF video frequency; voice frequency
vf very fair (weather); very fine (numismatics)
VFA volatile fatty acid
VFM value for money
VFR visual flight rules (aeronautics)
VG Vicar General; very good
vg very good; *verbi gratia* = for example
VGA video graphics array
vgc very good condition
VH, vh vertical height
VHC very highly commended
VHD video high density
VHF very high frequency; very high fidelity
VHS Video Home System (videotape standard)
VHT very high temperature
VI Virgin Islands; Vancouver Island; vertical interval; viscosity index; volume
    indicator
vi *vide infra* = see below (*also* **vid**)
VIA Visually Impaired Association
viad viaduct
vib vibration; vibraphone
Vic Victoria, Australian State
vic vicar; vicarage; vicinity; victory
Vice-Adm Vice-Admiral
vid *vide* = see, refer to; video
vign vignette
vil village
VIN vehicle identification number (USA)
vini viniculture

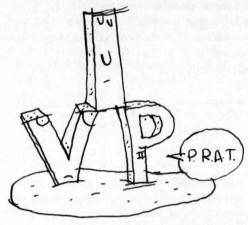

VIP   VERY IMPORTANT PERSON

VIP very important person
VIR *Victoria Imperatrix Regina* = Victoria, Empress and Queen
Vis Viscount; Viscountess
vis visible; visibility; visual
visc viscosity
vit vitreous
vit stat vital statistics
viz *videlicet* = namely
VJ Day Victory over Japan Day (end of WWII, 15 August 1945)
VL Vulgar Latin
vl violin
vla viola
Vlad Vladivostok
VLB vertical lift bridge
VLBC very large bulk carrier
VLBW very low birth weight
VLCC very large crude carrier
VLF very low frequency
VLLW very low level waste (radioactivity)
vln violin
VLR very long range (aircraft)
VLS vapour-liquid-solid
VLSI very large scale integration (computers)
VM Victory Medal; Virgin Mary; velocity modulation; virtual machine; volatile matter

VMC visual meteorological conditions

VMD Doctor of Veterinary Medicine

VMH Victoria Medal of Honour (Royal Horticultural Society)

VMS Voluntary Medical Services; virtual machine system (computers)

VO voice over (in film-making, TV); Royal Victorian Order; valuation officer; very old (brandy, spirits); veterinary officer

vo verso

VOA Voice of America; Volunteers of America

VOC volatile organic compound

voc vocalist; vocation

vocab vocabulary

vol volume (**vols** = volumes); volatile; volcanic; voluntary; volunteer

V1, V-1 *Vergeltungswaffe* = World War II German pulsejet robot bomb

VOP Very Old Port; very oldest procurable (port, brandy, etc)

VP Vice President; vanishing point; variable pitch; verb phrase; vent pipe; Vice-Principal

vp vanishing point; variable pitch

VPC *vente par correspondence* = French mail order

vpd vehicles per day (**vph** = vehicles per hour; **vpm** = vehicles per mile)

VPL visible panty line

VPO Vienna Philharmonic Orchestra

Vpo Valparaiso

V Pres Vice-President

vps vibrations per second

VR *Victoria Regina* = Queen Victoria; Volunteer Reserve; velocity ratio; virtual reality; voltage regulator; vulcanised rubber

VRAM video random access memory (computers)

VRB, vrb variable (meteorology)

VRC Victoria Racing Club, Melbourne; Volunteer Rifle Corps

V Rev Very Reverend

vrg veering (meteorology)

VRI *Victoria Regina et Imperatrix* = Victoria, Queen and Empress

VRO vehicle registration office

VS, vs veterinary surgeon; variable speed; *vide supra* = see above; volatile solid; *volti subito* = turn over quickly

vs versus = against (e.g. England vs West Indies)

VSAM virtual storage access method (computers)

VSB, vsb vestigial sideband (telecommunications); *see* **VSM**

VSCC Vintage Sports Car Club

VSD ventricular septal defect; vendor's shipping document

VSI vertical speed indicator

VSL venture scout leader

VSM vestigial sideband modulation (qv VSB)

VSO very superior old (port, brandy, etc); Vienna State Opera; Voluntary Service Overseas

VSOP very superior old pale (port, brandy, etc)

VSR very special reserve (wine); very short range

VST Virtual Studio Technology (computer composing)

VT, vt variable time; variable transmission; ventricular tachycardia

VTC Volunteer Training Corps

vtg voting

VTL variable threshold logic (computers)

VTOL vertical take-off and landing (aircraft)

VTR videotape recorder / recording

V2, V-2 *Vergeltungswaffe* = World War II German rocket-powered ballistic missile used to bombard London

VU volume unit (acoustics)

Vul Vulgate (*also* **Vulg**)

vv vice versa; viva voce

VVL visible vest line (*see* **VPL**)

VVO very, very old (port, brandy, etc)

VW Very Worshipful; *Volkswagen* = literally, people's car (German car make)

VWF vibration white finger (debilitating miner's disease caused by prolonged exposure to drill vibration)

VX Lethal nerve gas (USA)

W

W Wales; Welsh; watt (*also* **w**); Wednesday; West; Western; white; widow; widowed; wide; women's size (clothing); warden; Wesleyan

w waist; war; warm; water; watt; weather; west; wet; week; weight; white; wicket (cricket); wide (cricket); width; wife; wind; wire; with; widow; widower; win; won; woman; work

WA West Africa; Western Australia; Westminster Abbey

WAAA Women's Amateur Athletic Association

WAAAF Women's Auxiliary Australian Air Force

WAAC Women's Army Auxiliary Corps

WAAF Women's Auxiliary Air Force

WAAS Women's Auxiliary Army Force

WAC Women's Army Corps (USA)

WACB World Association for Christian Broadcasting

WACCC Worldwide Air Cargo Commodity Classification

WADF Western Air Defense (USA)

WAE, wae when actually employed

WAF, waf with all faults

WAFFLE wide angle fixed field locating equipment

W Afr West Africa

WAGGGS World Association of Girl Guides and Girl Scouts

WAIS Wechsler Adult Intelligence Scale; **WAIS-R** = Wechsler Adult Intelligence Scale – Revised (*see* **WISC**)

Wal Walloon

wam wife and mother

w&i weighing and inspection

W&M William and Mary (architectural style, early 18th century)

w&s whisky and soda

w&t wear and tear

WAR Women Against Rape

War Warwickshire (*also* **Warks**); Warsaw

war warrant; **warr** = warranty

WARC World Alliance of Reformed Churches

warn warning

WASA Welsh Amateur Swimming Association

Wash Washington

WASP White Anglo-Saxon Protestant (*also* **Wasp**)

WAST Western Australia Standard Time

Wat Waterford

WATA World Association of Travel Agencies

WAT curve weight-altitude-temperature curve (aeronautics)

WATS wide area telephone service

W Aus Western Australia

WAVES Women Accepted for Volunteer Emergency Service (US Navy)

WAYC Welsh Association of Youth Clubs

WB Warner Brothers (Hollywood film studio); Water Board; World Bank for Reconstruction and Development

wb, **WB** water ballast; waste ballast; waveband; waybill; weekly benefits; westbound; wheelbase

WBA World Boxing Association; West Bromwich Albion Football Club

WBC World Boxing Council; white blood count/cell

WBF World Bridge Federation

WBI whole body irradiation

wbi will be issued

WBS whole body scan

WBT wet-bulb temperature

WC War Cabinet; water closet; West-Central postal district of London; working capital; workmens' compensation

wc water closet; water cock; without charge; wheelchair

W/C Wing Commander (*also* **W Cdr**)

WCA Women's Christian Association; Wildlife and Countryside Act

WCAT Welsh College of Advanced Technology

WCC War Crimes Commission; World Council of Churches

WCEU World Christian Endeavour Union

WCF World Congress of Faiths

WCL World Confederation of Labour

WCP World Council for Peace

WCT World Championship Tennis

WCTU Women's Christian Temperence Union (North America)

WCWB World Coucil for the Welfare of the Blind

WD War Department; well developed (*also* **w/d**); Works Department

wd warranted (*also* **w/d**); wood; word; would

W/D withdrawal

WDA Welsh Development Agency; write-down analysis (tax)

WDC War Damage Commission; Woman Detective Constable; World Data Centre

wdf wood door and frame

WDM wavelength division multiplex (telecommunications system)

WDS Woman Detective Sergeant

WDV, **wdv** written down value (tax)

w/e weekend; week ending

WEA Workers' Educational Association

wea weather; weapon

WEC World Energy Conference; wind energy converter

Wed Wednesday (*also* **Weds**)

wef with effect from

WEFC West European Fisheries Conference

WEFT wings, engine, fuselage, tail (aeronautics)

weld welding

Well Wellington, New Zealand

WES World Economic Survey; Women's Engineering Society
west western
Westm Westminster
WET Western European Time
Wex Wexford
WF white female; wave function; Wells Fargo
wf wrong font (printing)
WFA Women's Football Association; White Fish Authority
WFC World Food Council
WFD World Federation of the Deaf
WFEO World Federation of Engineering Organisations
WFMH World Federation for Mental Health
WFP World Food Programme (UN)
WFPA World Federation for the Protection of Animals
WFTU World Federation of Trade Unions
WG Welsh Guards; W G Grace (English cricketer, 1848–1915)
WGA Writers' Guild of America
WGC Welwyn Garden City, Hertfordshire
Wg/Cdr Wing Commander
W Glam West Glamorgan
WGU Welsh Golfing Union
WH White House (USA); water heater; withholding (*also* **w/h**)
Wh watt hour (*also* **Whr**)
wh wharf (*also* **whf**); which; white
WHA World Hockey Association; World Health Assembly (UN)
whb wash hand-basin
whf wharf (*also* **wh**)
whfg wharfage
WHO World Health Organisation; White House Office (USA)
WHOI Woods Hole Oceanographic Institute
WH question a question beginning with *who*, *which*, *what*, *where*, *when* or *how*, designed to elicit information rather than 'yes' or 'no' answers
WHRA World Health Research Centre
whsle wholesale
WHT William Herschel Telescope at La Palma
WI Women's Institute; West Indies; West Indian; Windward Islands
wi wrought iron; when issued (finance)
WIA wounded in action
Wick Wicklow
wid widow; widower
WIF West Indies Federation
Wig Wigtown, Scotland
wigig when it's gone, it's gone (retailing term)
WILCO will comply (radio signal)
Wilts Wiltshire

WIMP windows, icons, menus, pointers (computer screen display system)

WIN Windows, Microsoft's operating system

Winch Winchester

W Ind West Indies; West Indian

Wing Cdr Wing Commander

WINGS, **Wings** warrants in negotiable government securities

Winn Winnipeg, Canada

wint winter

WIP work in progress; waste incineration plant

WIPO World Intellectual Property Organisation

WIRDS weather information reporting and display system

WISC Wechsler Intelligence Scale for Children; **WISC-R** = Wechsler Intelligence Scale for Children – Revised

WISP wide-range imaging spectrometer

wit witness

WITA Women's International Tennis Association

Wits Witwatersrand, South Africa

WJC World Jewish Congress

WJEC Welsh Joint Education Committee

wk week; weak; well known; work; wreck

wkg working

wkly weekly

wkr worker

wks weeks; works

wkt wicket (cricket); **wkt kpr** = wicketkeeper

WL waiting list; water line; West Lothian; *wagon-lit* = railway sleeping car; Women's Liberation; wavelength (*also* **w/l**)

WLA Women's Land Army

wld would

wldr welder

WLHB Women's League of Health and Beauty

WLM Women's Liberation Movement

WLPSA Wild Life Preservation Society of Australia

WLR Weekly Law Reports

WLTM Would Love To Meet (used in personal classified ads)

WLUS World Land Use Survey

WM white male; war memorial; watt-meter; wire mesh

WMA World Medical Association

WMAA Whitney Museum of American Art, New York

WMC Ways and Means Committee; working men's club; World Meteorological Centre; World Methodist Council

wmk watermark (papermaking, philately)

WMO World Meteorological Organisation

wmp with much pleasure

WMS World Magnetic Survey

wndp with no down payment

WNE Welsh National Eisteddfod

WNL, **wnl** within normal limits

WNO Welsh National Opera

WNP Welsh Nationalist Party

WO War Office; Warrant Officer; welfare officer; wireless operator; walkover; written order

w/o without; written off

WOAR Women Organised Against Rape

wob white on black (graphics); washed overboard

WOC waiting on cement (**WOCS** = waiting on cement to set)

woc without compensation

woe without equipment

WOG Wrath of God Syndrome (AIDS)

wog water, oil or gas; with other goods

wogs workers on government service

Wolfs Wolfson College, Oxford

Wolves Wolverhampton Wanderers Football Club

WOMAN World Organisation for Mothers of All Nations

WOO World Oceanographic Organisation

wop with other property

WOR without our responsibility

Wor Worshipful (*also* **Wp**)

Worc Worcester College, Oxford

Worcs Worcestershire

WORM write once, read many times (computers)

WOW Women Against Ordination of Women; waiting on weather

wowser reputedly, *We Only Want Social Evils Removed* – Australian term for someone devoted to the abolition of alcohol and the reform of alcoholics and drinkers

WP Western Province (South Africa); West Point (USA); White Paper; without prejudice; word processor; working party

wp waste paper; waste pipe; weather permitting; wild pitch (baseball); will proceed; word processor

WPA Water Polo Association; Works Projects Administration (USA, 1935–43); World Pool-Billiards Association; World Presbyterian Alliance

wpb waste-paper basket

WPBSA World Professional Billiards and Snooker Association

WPC Woman Police Constable

wpe white porcelain enamel

wpg waterproofing

WPGA Women's Professional Golfers' Association

WPI World Press Institute; wholesale price index

wpm words per minute (keyboard typing speed)

WPRL Water Pollution Research Laboratory

wps with prior service

WR West Riding, Yorkshire; Western Region; *Willelmus Rex* = King William; Wassermann reaction (VD test)

wr water repellent; war risk (insurance); warehouse receipt

WRA Water Research Association; Wisley Rose Award (Royal Horticultural Society)

WRAAC Women's Royal Australian Army Corps

WRAAF Women's Royal Australian Air Force

WRAC Women's Royal Army Corps

WRAF Women's Royal Air Force

WRANS Women's Royal Australian Naval Service

WRC Water Research Council

WRE Weapons Research Establishment (Australia)

w ref with reference

WRI war risks insurance

WRNR Women's Royal Naval Reserve

WRNS Women's Royal Naval Service (Wrens)

wro war risks only (insurance)

WRP Worker's Revolutionary Party

WRU Welsh Rugby Union

WRVS Women's Royal Voluntary Service

WS water-soluble; wind speed; weapon system

W Sam Western Samoa

WSC World Series Cricket

WSCF World Student Christian Federation

WSJ *Wall Street Journal* (USA)

WSM Women's Suffrage Movement

wsp water supply point

WSSA Welsh Secondary Schools Association

W star Wolf-Rayet star (*also* **WR star**)

WSTN World Service Television News

WT withholding tax; wireless telegraphy (*also* **W/T**)

wt weight; warrant; watertight

WTA Women's Tennis Association; World Transport Agency; winner takes all

WTAA World Trade Alliance Association

wtd warranted

WTG wind turbine generator

wthr weather

WTN Worldwide Television News

WTO Warsaw Treaty Organisation; World Tourism Organisation

wtr winter; writer

WTT World Team Tennis

WTTA Wholesale Tobacco Trade Association (of GB and N Ireland)

WTUC World Trade Union Conference

WU Western Union

WUJS World Union of Jewish Students
WUPJ World Union for Progressive Judaism
WUS World University Service
w/v weight to volume ratio; water valve (*also* **wv**)
WVA World Veterinary Association
WVF World Veterans' Federation
WW worldwide
w/w weight for weight; wall-to-wall (carpets); white wall (tyres)
WWI World War One (1914–18); *also* **WW1**
WWII World War Two (1939-45); *also* **WW2**
WWF World Wildlife Fund (now Worldwide Fund for Nature)
WWMCCS World Wide Military Command and Control System
WWO Wing Warrant Officer
WWSSN worldwide standard seismograph network
WWSU World Water Ski Union
WWW World Weather Watch; Who Was Who (yearbook); World Wide Web
WX women's extra-large (clothing size)
WYR West Yorkshire Regiment
wysiwyg what you see is what you get (computer to printer)
Wz *Warenzeichen* = German trade mark
WZO World Zionist Organisation

X

X Roman numeral for 10; 'Adults Only' motion picture certificate (now '18' symbol); symbol for a location on maps ('X marks the spot'); ballot paper choice; a kiss; a cross (e.g. King's X = King's Cross); an error; a variable; an unknown factor; an illiterate signature; an extension (e.g. X123 for a phone line)

x symbol for multiplication (maths); variable (algebra); extra; coordinate; hoar-frost (meteorology)

xan xanthene; xanthic (chemistry)

XAS X-ray absorption spectroscopy

xb ex-bonus

xc ex-capitalisation; ex-coupon (*also* **xcp**)

xcl excess current liabilities

XCT X-ray computed tomography

xd ex-dividend (*also* **xdiv**)

x'd deleted, crossed-out (*also* **x'd out**)

Xer Xerox copier or reproduction

XES X-ray emission spectroscopy

XFA X-ray fluorescence analysis (*also* **XRFA**)

XI X-ray imaging

xi ex-interest (*also* **x in**)

XJ Range of Jaguar cars (introduced 1968)

XL extra large (clothing size)

X, les ex-students of the *Ecole Polytechnique*

xlwb extra-long wheel base

XM experimental missile

XMS extended memory specification (computers)

Xn Christian (**Xnty** = Christianity)

XO executive officer; fine cognac (brandy)

XP first two Greek letters (*khi, rho*) of *Khristos* = Christ; express paid

xpl explosive; explosion

X-position position in sexual intercourse (described in Dr Alex Comfort's *The Joy of Sex* but ultimately impossible to illustrate adequately)

XPS X-ray photoelectron spectroscopy

Xr examiner

X-rated unofficial classification for adult movies and videos

X-ray short wavelength electromagnetic radiation (*also* **x-ray**)

XRD X-ray diffraction

x rd crossroad (**x rds** = crossroads)

XRE X-ray emission

XRM X-ray mammography

XRMA X-ray microphobe analysis

XRT X-ray topography

xs, ex's expenses

Xt Christ

x-unit unit of length of wavelengths of gamma – and X-rays

XX double strength ale (**XXX** = triple strength; **XXXX** = quadruple strength, or 3.9 per cent alcohol by weight)

XXXX euphemism for four-letter words

xyl xylophone

XYZ examine your zipper

Y

Y Japanese yen, Chinese yuan (currencies); Yugoslavia; short for **YMCA**, **YWCA**.

y yard; yacht; year; yellow; young; youngest; variable (algebra); dry air (meteorology); symbol for any unknown factor (as in xy)

YA young adult

YAG yttrium-aluminium garnet (artificial diamond)

YAL Young Australia League

Y&LR York and Lancaster Regiment

Y&R Young and Rubicam (advertising agency)

YAR York-Antwerp Rules (marine insurance)

Yard, The Scotland Yard

YAS Yorkshire Agricultural Society

YAVIS young, attractive, verbal, intelligent, successful (ideal profile)

YB, yb yearbook

YC Young Conservative; yacht club; Yale College (USA); youth club

YCA Youth Camping Association

Y2K Second millennium; year 2000

YCL Young Communist League

YCW Young Christian Workers; you can't win

yd yard (**yds** = yards)

YE Your Excellency

yel yellow

Yem Yemen; Yemeni

YEO Youth Employment Officer

yer yearly effective rate of interest

YES Youth Employment Service; Youth Enterprise Scheme

YFC Young Farmers' Club

YFG yttrium-ferrite garnet (*see* **YAG, YIG**)

YH youth hostel

YHA Youth Hostels Association

YHANI Youth Hostels Association of Northern Ireland

YHWH consonant letters of the Hebrew name for God (Yahweh or Jehovah), regarded as too sacred to be pronounced (*also* **YHVH, JHVH, JHWH**)

YIG yttrium-iron garnet (*see* **YFG, YAG**)

YMBA Yacht and Motor Boat Association

YMCA Young Men's Christian Association

YMCU Young Men's Christian Union

YMFS Young Men's Friendly Society

YMHA Young Men's Hebrew Association

YMV yellow mosaic virus

yo year-old (e.g. a 2-yo stallion)

YOB, yob year of birth

YOC Young Ornithologists' Club (RSPB)

YOD, yod year of death

YOM, yom year of marriage

YOP Youth Opportunities Programme

Yorks Yorkshire

YP young person; young prisoner

yr year; your; younger

YRA Yacht Racing Association

yrbk yearbook

yrly yearly

yrs years; yours (*also* **Yrs**)

YS Young Socialists
Ys Yugoslavia; Yugoslavian (*also* **Yugo**)
YT Yukon Territory
YTD, ytd year to date
YTS Youth Training Scheme
YTYTK 'You're too young to know!' (catchphrase from ITMA radio show)
Yugo Yugoslavia; Yugoslavian car brand
Yuk Yukon
yuppie young upwardly mobile professional (profile)
YWCA Young Women's Christian Association
YWCTU Young Women's Christian Temperence Union
YWHA Young Women's Hebrew Association
YWS Young Wales Society

Z

Z zaire (Dem Rep of Congo currency); zero; Zionist; *Zoll* = German Customs
z zero; zenith; zone; symbol for haze (meteorology); variable (algebra)
Zag Zagreb, Croatia
Zam Zambia
Zan Zanzibar
ZANU Zimbabwe African National Union
ZAPU Zimbabwe African People's Union
ZB Zen Buddhist
zB *zum Beispiel* = for example, e.g.
Z car police patrol car ('zulu' = radio call sign for Z)
Z chart business chart accumulating daily, weekly and monthly totals
ZD zenith distance (astronomy)
ZEBRA zero-energy breeder reactor assembly
Zeep zero-energy experimental pile
ZEG zero economic growth
zen zenith
ZENITH zero-energy nitrogen-heated thermal reactor
zero-g zero gravity
ZETA zero-energy thermonuclear assembly
ZETR zero-energy thermonuclear reactor
ZF, zf zero frequency
ZG zoological gardens
ZH zero hour
zH *zu Handen* = care of, **c/o**
ZIF zero insertion force (electronics)
ZIFT zygote intrafallopian transfer (infertility treatment)
ZIP, zip zone improvement plan; **zip code** = US postcode

Zl Polish zloty

zod zodiac

zoo zoological gardens

zool zoology; zoological; zoologist

ZPG zero population growth

ZSI Zoological Society of Ireland

ZST Zone Standard Time (**ZT** = zone time)

Ztg *Zeitung* = German newspaper (**Zs** = *Zeitschrift* = magazine)

Zur Zurich, Switzerland

ZZ UK vehicle registration letters for temporarily imported cars

zzzz sleep; snoozing

INDEX

Abbreviations 96, 590, 664–819
abbreviations and full stops 98
active and passive voice 24–25, 28, 503–4, 509
adjectival clause 39
adjectival economy 81
adjective phrase 28, 39, 76, 123, 490
adjectives 32, 33, 35–36, 37, 68, 71, 74–82, 86, 89, 91, 131, 172, 173, 379, 433
  absolute 80
  arranging 76
  central and peripheral 79
  commas with 102
  pronouns as 53
  proper 80
  recognising 77
adverbial phrase 39, 91–92, 104
adverbs 33, 34, 35, 68, 70, 71, 74–76, 81–85, 172, 433, 490, 498
  commas with 102, 106
  positioning 83–84, 498
  misplaced 84
  squinting 84
ages, punctuating 135
Allen, Dave 469
alliteration 504, 505, 506
Amis, Kingsley 170
Amis, Martin 104, 507
and, starting sentences with 30
announcements 527
apology, letter of 520
apostrophes 45, 49, 54, 57
  contraction 122
  possessive 122
applying for jobs 554–59
around and round 94
asterisk 129
Austen, Jane 73, 96, 131
auxiliary verbs 35, 64–65, 66–67

Bad debt, letter chasing 526

bad financial advice, complaining about 539
bank service, complaining about 540, 545
begging letter 518
between and among 93
Bible 31
biblical colon 108
Blake, William 31
bold type 130
brackets 108–110
  square 113
brevity 502–503, 509
building work, complaining about 541, 542
bullets 130
Bush, President George 19, 451, 460–61
but, starting sentences with 30

Cancelling a contract, letter 546
capitalisation 131–34
Carey, G. V. 111
Churchill, Winston 31, 94, 458
circumlocution 64–68
Citizens' Advice Bureau 530, 543
classes, word, open and closed 33
clauses 31, 38–41
  misplaced 41
  types of 39–41
clichés 472–488
Coleridge, Samuel Taylor 458
collective nouns see nouns
colloquialism 506
colons 96, 104, 107–8, 110
  biblical 108
  in stageplays 108
commas 99–104
  as parenthesis 103
  Oxford or final 103
  placement 99
  reduction 101

commiseration, letter of 525
complaint, letters of 530–53
condolence, letters of 522, 523, 524
congratulations, letters of 515, 519
conjunctions 28, 37–38, 88–92
    coordinating 38, 89
    correlative 38, 90
    subordinating 38, 89
Consumer Credit Act 530, 569, 570, 571
Consumer Protection Act 530
copywriting 572–581
Council, letter to 533
credit rating, letters reinstating 569–72
Crystal, David 83
curriculum vitae or CV 564–568
Daily Express 31
Daily Mail 47
Daily Mirror Style Book 306
Daily Telegraph 47, 48, 237, 272, 290, 322, 449, 492, 496
danglers and floaters 499–500
dangling participle *see* participles
dash 110
Data Protection Act 583
dates, punctuating 135–36
definite article 37
Defoe, Daniel 17–18
determiners 37, 43, 53, 57
    exclamative 55
dictionaries 34, 35, 431–35
dimensions and measurements, punctuating 136
direct debits and standing orders 547
direct speech 126–27
Donald, David 507
double negatives 24, 458

Effluxion 446–47
elegant variation 507
Elements of Style, The 500–504
ellipsis 26–27
    three-dot 129
e-mail 581–84

euphemism 469–72
Ewart, Gavin 458
exclamation mark 120
exclamations *see* interjections

Facsimile or fax 582
faulty goods, letters complaining about 536–538
foreign-derived words 45–46
forms of address 584–588
Fowler, H. W. 17, 107, 121, 287, 302, 313, 321, 507
fractions, punctuating 136
full stop 98–99

Gender 44, 59
gerunds 69, 72–74
Gettysburg Address 490
get well letter 519
Gilbert and Sullivan 163, 164, 506
gobbledegook 458–461
good and *well* 84
Gombrich, Richard 489
Gowers, Sir Ernest 92, 112, 224
grammar, role of 15–16
'grammatical glue' 85–94

Harding, President 19
harmony in sentences 27–30, 53
Hawkespeak 459
hire-purchase agreement, letter terminating 544
hire-purchase payments, letters regarding difficulties with 547
holiday problem letters 534, 535
hopefully 85
Human Rights Act 583
hyperbole 505
hyphens 111–18
    as wordbreaks and linebreaks 112

Idiom 506
indefinite article 37
Independent, The 496

infinitives 70–71
    split 71–72
insurance claim disputes, letters
    regarding 548, 549
interjections 38
Internet 580
inverted commas *see* quotation marks
invitations 527–529
it as a pronoun 53
italics 130

Jargon 461–65
job application letters 556–59
Johnson, Dr Samuel 128, 501, 509
Joyce, James 98, 701

Kipling, Rudyard 31

Larkin, Philip 513
late or non-delivery, letter
    complaining about 536
Lawrence, T. E. 104
Lawson, Nigel 461
legal action, letter avoiding 552
legal action, letter threatening 551
like, use of 498
Lincoln, Abraham 490, 507, 654
litotes 24
logorrhoea 460
love, jargon definition of 461
love letters 514
Lymington Chronicle 450
Macaulay, Thomas 31
Maugham, Somerset 96, 501
Maverick, Maury 460
may and *might* 67, 499
measurements, punctuating 136
Member of Parliament, writing to 553
metaphor 504–5
money amounts, punctuating 136
mood, of a sentence 25
    imperative 25
    indicative 25
    subjunctive 25
muddle in writing 495–500

Names 42
    apostrophising 122–25
National Times, The 459
neologisms 33
noise, letter complaining about 532
non sequitur 494–95
non-sexist language 59–60, 471
noun phrase 39, 48
nouns 34, 42–49
    abstract and concrete 34, 43–44
    collective 34, 46–49
    common and proper 34, 43
    compound 44, 46
    concrete *see* nouns, abstract and
    concrete
    countable and uncountable 34,
    44–45
    gender 44
    mass 45
    possessive 49
    singular and plural 43, 44, 45–46,
    49
number pronouns 37, 57
numbers, punctuating 134–36

Object, direct and indirect 21–22, 52–3
Observer, The 48, 296, 500, 639
off of 93
one, as pronoun 53
onto and *on to* 93
Orwell, George 96, 104, 504
overloaded sentences 491–95
Oxford comma 103

Paragraph 18, 19, 31
parenthesis 108–109
Parris, Matthew 499
parsing 32
participles 63–64, 69
    dangling or misplaced 69–70
Partridge, Eric 26, 93, 292, 472
parts of speech 31–41
passive voice 24–25, 28, 503–04, 509
period (full stop) 97–99

personal letters 513–29
phrasal verbs 68
phrases 31, 38–39
plagiarism 508–09
pleonasm 454
pluralising nouns 45–46
point of view, of sentences 28
political correctness 469
Pope, Alexander 472, 502
Post Office 509
predicate 20–22, 52
prepositional phrase 39
prepositions 38
Pride and Prejudice 73
pronouns 36–37, 42, 49–60
    as adjectives 53
    demonstrative 37, 50, 54
    indefinite 37, 50, 56–57
    intensifying 54
    interrogative 37, 50, 55
    number 57
    perplexing 57–60
    personal 37, 50, 51–53
    possessive 37, 50, 53–54
    reciprocal 37, 50, 57
    reflexive 37, 50, 54
    relative 37, 50, 55
    types of 50
    uni-gender third person 59–60
proper nouns 34, 43–44
psychobabble 466
punctuation 95–136
    British and American 128
pun 507–08

Question mark 119–120
quotation marks 125–28
    closing 127–28
quoting direct speech 126

Redundancy in writing 445, 454
reference, letter asking for a 562
reference, writing a 563
Regulation of Investigatory Powers
    Act 583

resignation letter 561
Rime of the Ancient Mariner, The 458
round and *around* 94

Salary increase, letter asking for 560
Sale and Supply of Goods Act 530
Sale of Goods Act 536, 537
sales letters 572–581
Salinger, J. D. 60
semicolons 104–106
    Society for the Preservation of 104
'semi'-question 120
sentences 17–31, 39, 52
    incomplete 18, 20
    long-winded 18–19
    regular types of 23–24
    simple, compound, complex
    22–23, 39
Shakespeare, William 27, 30, 52, 94,
    470, 472, 489
shall and *will* 66–67
Shaw, George Bernard 73, 104
simile 505
singular nouns 44–49
Small Claims Court 531
Solicitors Act 550
solicitor's bill, letter disputing 550
split infinitives 71–72
square brackets 109–110
stock modifiers 472
stop *see* full stop
stroke 130
style 500–502
subject, of sentence 20–22, 52–53
Sunday Times, The 47, 218, 245, 300,
    331, 761
Supply of Goods (Implied Terms) Act
    544
Supply of Goods and Services Act
    538
syllabification 112
sympathy, letter of 522, 523, 524
synecdoche 506
synonym 435

Tautology 454–58
Tennyson, Alfred, Lord 30
tenses 61, 64–65
thanks, letters of 516, 517
that 50, 54, 58, 59
that and *which* 58
that and *who* 58
thesaurus 435
third person pronoun 59–60
Thomson, Richard 500
Thoreau, Henry 106
time, punctuating 135
Times, The 30, 41, 47, 48, 59, 73, 84, 97,
    101, 103, 110, 124, 129, 191, 195,
    225, 229, 247, 251, 256, 265, 267,
    268, 270, 275, 279, 290, 296, 304,
    305, 339, 418, 499, 509, 768
Trade Descriptions Act 530
Truman, President Harry S 467

Unattached participles 499
underlining 130
Unfair Contract Terms Act 530

Verbal diarrhoea 460

verbals 68
verb phrase 39, 64
verbs 35, 60–74
    action 61–62
    auxiliary 35, 64, 66–67
    finite and infinite 35
    main 35
    phrasal 68
    regular and irregular 35, 62–64
    transitive and intransitive 67–68
voice, active and passive 24–25, 28

Waffle 458–61
Waterhouse, Keith 490, 501
well and *good* 84
Wells, H. G. 129
which and *that* 58
who or *whom* 55
who and *that* 58
will and *shall* 66–67
witter 458–61
Wood, Mrs Henry 129
word (definition) 31
    · class 33
word processing 581